Human Development in Adulthood

The Plenum Series in Adult Development and Aging

SERIES EDITOR:
Jack Demick, *Suffolk University, Boston, Massachusetts*

Human Development in Adulthood

Lewis R. Aiken

Pepperdine University, Retired
Malibu, California

Plenum Press • New York and London

Library of Congress Cataloging-in-Publication Data

Aiken, Lewis R., 1931–
    Human development in adulthood / Lewis R. Aiken.
        p.   cm. –– (Plenum series in adult development and aging)
    Includes bibliographical references and index.
    ISBN 0-306-45734-2
    1. Adulthood. 2. Life cycle, Human. 3. Adulthood––Psychological
aspects. 4. Aging––Psychological aspects.   I. Title. II. Series.
HQ799.95.A49   1998
305.24––dc21   97-51716
                                                                    CIP

ISBN 0-306-45734-2

© 1998 Plenum Press, New York
A Division of Plenum Publishing Corporation
233 Spring Street, New York, N.Y. 10013

http://www.plenum.com

10 9 8 7 6 5 4 3 2 1

Printed in the United States of America

Preface

Human Development in Adulthood is designed as a comprehensive overview of adult development for students of psychology, sociology, and social work, as well as those planning to enter nursing and other health-related or human-service professions. It is written so anyone who is interested in the topic can learn and benefit from reading the material. Concepts, theories, research findings, and practical implications of the information are all presented thoroughly and understandably. In addition to physical, cognitive, personality, social, and sexual development in adulthood, the book deals with gender and ethnic group differences and issues, love and marital relations, living conditions and economic problems, crime and war, and aging and death.

This book is interdisciplinary, including concepts, theories, and research findings from biology, psychology, sociology, anthropology, economics, political science, and other disciplines. Emphasis is placed on the fact that human beings are similar in many ways, but that everyone is a unique entity with his or her own perceptions, attitudes, and behaviors. Each person of a particular age, sex, race, culture, and socioeconomic status is shaped somewhat differently by the interaction between biological, psychological, and social structures and events.

A guiding theme of the book is that, rather than ending with childhood and adolescence, development and change continue across the life span. People do not abruptly cease being children and become adolescents overnight, nor do they stop being adolescents at age 18 and suddenly become adults. Human development is much more gradual than that, and we may scarcely notice when boys and girls turn into adults. Adulthood is both a transition between the beginning and end of life and a continuing journey from youth to old age. It is often convenient to divide that journey into a series of stages, but the stages are rarely abrupt breaks with the past. Like other journeys, adulthood is one in which later circumstances are affected by earlier experiences and choices. Not only are adults similar to and different from each other but also they are similar to and different from what they were at earlier stages of development.

The organizational plan of the book reflects the fact that, although individual development is punctuated occasionally by sudden leaps, there is a great deal of continuity in the experiences and behaviors of the individual over a lifetime: The child is father to the man (or woman) and the past is prologue to the future. Some of us, and all of us in some ways, never grow up; we remain children or adolescents in certain respects even into later life. Although we may behave "maturely" most of the time, certain features of our personality and behavior can remain at an earlier "stage" of development, or when under great pressure we may respond as we did years before.

Adulthood is a time for decisions concerning marriage, career, parenting, and, in general, the style of life we want to live. The continuity of adult development is reflected in the fact that what we decide and do today affects what we become tomorrow. The choices and decisions that we make now may have both short- and long-term implications for what we attain or achieve next week and next year. Those choices are not always easy to make, because their consequences are never completely predictable. Still, we must choose, live with those choices if we can, and try to correct them if the outcomes are unbearable.

The world of today is a pluralistic, multicultural, technologically based, and—at least in Western nations—individualistically oriented macrocosm replete with environmental, social, and political problems. The rules for peaceful coexistence have changed since yesteryear and the need to understand people of different cultures and in different economic, social, and political circumstances has become even more critical. The population of the world continues to expand, and its demographics are forever changing. People of various nationalities and ethnic groups have become physically and functionally closer and are competing for the same space and resources. Consequently, a comprehensive discussion of adult development should consider the important issues of today, including those centered in cultural, racial, gender, social class, economic, religious, and political differences. This I have tried to do.

Many people have contributed to this book, including Eliot Werner, Herman Makler, and Jacquelyn Coggin. In the end, however, the responsibility for whatever shortcomings it may have is mine.

Lewis R. Aiken

Contents

CHAPTER 1

The Study of Adult Development

Which of the following persons would you consider to be *adults*?

A. A 35-year-old male who is severely mentally retarded.
B. An 85-year-old victim of Alzheimer's disease who has a profound memory loss and requires complete nursing care.
C. A 40-year-old female who is socially withdrawn and has no friends.
D. A 30-year-old male who is financially dependent on his parents.
E. A 10-year-old female victim of progeria who looks like a little old woman.
F. A mentally gifted 14-year-old who has just been awarded a college degree in mathematics.
G. A 13-year-old female who is married and has a one-year-old child.

CONCEPTS AND FOUNDATIONS

If we define an *adult* as a person who has reached 20 years of age, it is clear that A, B, C, and D are adults and E, F, and G have not yet attained that status. In addition to being defined in terms of chronological age, however, the concept of *adulthood* can be viewed from a biological, legal, psychological, economic, and even a social or cultural perspective. From a biological or physical perspective, an adult is a person who is fully grown. This definition takes into account the fact that different people grow at different rates, and that physical maturity may be attained at age 15 by one person, age 20 by another person, or even age 25 or later by another. At a more refined level, biology recognizes that physical growth also varies with the particular organ or organ system. The reproductive system, for example, usually ages and matures more rapidly than the nervous system.

Adulthood Defined and Undefined

The legal definition of adulthood, which has varied with place and time, is related to the notion of responsibility. An adult is a person who is capable of assuming responsibility for his or her own affairs, an age that has been, somewhat arbitrarily, set at somewhere between 18 and 21 years. The law also recognizes, however, that individual responsibility and the related concept of *competency*—the ability to handle one's life and property—vary not only with chronological age but also with the physical, cognitive, and emotional state of the person. In fact, at one time, mentally retarded persons, and certain mentally disordered persons as well, were referred to by both the legal and medical profession as "children" or, by the compromise term "adult-children." In popular parlance, an adult can also have "the mind of a child" or behave "like a child."

In addition to the mentally retarded and mentally disordered, there has always been a sizable group of people who, though old enough and mentally capable of exercising the responsibility of adulthood, continued to be dependent on some other person or group for their very survival. This was particularly true of women living during previous centuries: In many ways, they were treated as if they were children who could not take care of themselves and did not know what was best for them. Husbands and boyfriends of today often treat mature women as children, referring to them as "baby," "baby doll," "my little girl," or similar diminutive terms of the sort that are more appropriate for small children.

Economic and social changes during our own time have extended the period of dependency on parents and the age at which most young people are able to assume the responsibilities of "adulthood." A modern man or woman may not have a full-time job until after age 30 and wait until after age 35, or even age 40, to marry and have children. In fact, Keniston (1970) proposed that a new developmental stage between adolescence and young adulthood, which he referred to as *youth*, came into being during the 1950s and 1960s. This *youth stage* consists of individuals who spend many years as undergraduate and graduate students in colleges and universities before entering the adult world of work. A reluctance or inability to assume the role of an adult may keep young people in school long after they are scheduled to graduate.

In addition to adults who act like children, many individuals who do not chronologically qualify as adults look and behave as if they were. Though legally classified as children, early maturing boys and girls may seem older than they are. This is especially true of physically or mentally precocious teenagers who engage in purposeful, productive work, and who have children and assume the responsibilities of caring for dependents and contributing to the community. Early maturation is, however, not invariably associated with good adjustment, particularly in the case of girls. Finally, a small percentage of children are afflicted with physical disorders such as *progeria*, which make them look much older than their chronological ages would indicate.

The Status and Welfare of Children

The distinction between adulthood and childhood and the associated notions of maturity and immaturity are obviously not fixed but vary with the particular cultural or social group. Many pictures of children who lived during previous centuries depict them as dressed in the same sort of clothing as adults. Prior to the seventeenth century in Europe, and to some extent even later, children were viewed as miniature adults, frequently "full of the devil" and not to be spared beatings when necessary ("Spare the rod and spoil the child.") (Aries, 1962). Children were expected to be dutiful, obedient, and hardworking and were sternly disciplined when they failed to live up to familial or social expectations. Most received little formal schooling, and the lessons were usually accompanied by heavy doses of moral and virtuous pronouncements. Depending on the social class into which they were born, children might be expected to work and assume many of the other responsibilities of adulthood by age 10 at the latest.

Due to scientific, technological, and economic progress during the industrial revolution of the eighteenth and nineteenth centuries, the demand for uneducated physical laborers declined. Workers with at least enough education to run "assembly line" machines and to manage the production and marketing activities of an industrially developing economy were needed. Consequently, children were now expected to spend more time doing schoolwork and less time in physical labor. Those who continued to slave at menial tasks in sweatshops came increasingly to the attention of social reformers and elected officials who were concerned with the exploitation and welfare of children. These social and political concerns were stimulated and disseminated by writings and researches on all aspects of childhood.

In response to increasing public interest in child welfare, the child study movement, designed to gather information about age differences in physical and psychological characteristics and to study children in their own right, was launched toward the end of the last century. The early years of this movement witnessed the establishment of numerous social programs— children's aid societies, juvenile courts, orphanages, child health programs, societies for the prevention of child abuse—designed to improve the treatment and living conditions of children (Siegel & White, 1982). Concern for the welfare of children led to scientific studies of the physical, mental, emotional, and social characteristics of children by educators, physicians, psychologists, and social workers. Professional associations focusing on the rights and welfare of children were established, and legislation designed to protect those rights was also passed.

The societal and scientific interest in children that was associated with the technological and economic changes occurring in Europe and North America was not immediately shared by the less developed nations. However, during this century, most of the underdeveloped nations of Africa, Asia, and South America have become more westernized in their attitudes and practices with regard to the health and education of the younger members of their societies. Yet, thousands of children are still found throughout the world who are illiterate, labor physically for long hours, become addicted to drugs, work as female or male prostitutes, commit crimes that are more characteristic of adults, and, because of poor nutrition and unhealthful living conditions, have little to look forward to other than chronic poor health and an early death.

Adolescence and Later Life

Consideration of the teenage years as a separate stage of life did not occur until many decades after childhood became recognized and treated as a distinct period of human development. As the demand for technically and professionally trained individuals grew and children began remaining in school for many more years than formerly, a kind of subculture began to form. Individuals in these groups, who were between 12 and 20 years of age, had their own interests, attitudes, values, and behaviors, which often led to consternation on the part of the dominant adult community and the characterization of adolescence as a period of "storm and stress!" The publication in 1904 of G. Stanley Hall's two-volume treatise on *Adolescence* is generally viewed as the beginning of the field of adolescent psychology. Hall was also a pioneer in another developmental field, that of *gerontology*—the study of all aspects of aging and later life. Hall's *Senescence: The Last Half of Life* was the first published book on this topic in the United States and one of the first in the world.

Life expectancy—the number of years that a group of people born in a given year can be expected to live—and the median age of the population have increased markedly during this century. These increases, in addition to declines in infant mortality, have been associated with medical advances in the treatment of infectious disease and in improvements in sanitation, nutrition, and overall health care. One consequence of the "greying of America," reflected in the greater number of older adults, has been increased political and economic power of this segment of the population.

Epigenesis and Maturation

A time-honored maxim of scientists who study the physical and behavioral changes in people over time is that *development*, the sequence in which these changes occur, is the result of the inborn, genetically programmed makeup of the individual interacting with the environment. Biologists applied the term *epigenesis* to the progressive sequence by which the genetic substrate of an organism is expressed in physical structure and function. Epigenesis does not stop at birth, but, coupled with the experiences of the individual in a sociocultural context, continues to affect development throughout the individual's lifetime.

An enduring question concerns the extent to which genetically based structures and functions simply "unfold" without external influence as opposed to being subject to modification by the environment. Environment, of course, is not limited to intrauterine or even physicochemical events but includes all internal and external, physical and experiential stimuli. The assumption that human characteristics and behaviors result from the complex interaction of heredity and environment applies to height, color blindness, intelligence, and, in fact, everything that a person is or does. Precisely how the heredity × environment interaction takes place, and the relative contributions that genes and environment make to it, is the subject of continuing debate. Still, at least with respect to cognitive abilities, personality characteristics, and behavior, it is a foregone conclusion that both sets of factors are essential.

Related to the concept of epigenesis is that of *maturation*, the process of development that results in orderly changes in behaviors characteristic of a species. Earlier studies of human development seemed to demonstrate that motor skills such as walking are not significantly affected by restriction of movement or special training (Dennis, 1940). However, later research showed that severe restriction of practice and stimulation distinctly retards the development of sitting and locomotion (Dennis, 1960). Developmental psychologists now believe that experience can affect the rate of maturation of all physical abilities, but the magnitude of the effect varies with the individual and the particular ability. Both maturation and training are important in the development of psychomotor skills; special training is more efficient and effective when the readiness of the individual is at an optimum level to profit from it.

Ages and Stages

Western societies have typically viewed the human life span as consisting of a series of periods or stages, beginning with conception and ending in death. The *prenatal stage*, from conception until birth, is divided into the *germinal period* (first 2 weeks), the *embryonic period* (2–8 weeks), and the *fetal period*. The time from birth to the end of the second year is *infancy*, and *early childhood* is the preschool period from 2 to 5 or 6 years. *Middle childhood* is from age 6 to puberty, and *adolescence* is from the start of puberty to age 20 (or adulthood). The third and fourth decades of life (ages 20–40) are known as *early adulthood*, age 40 to 65 is *middle adulthood*, and age 65 until death is known as *later adulthood*, or old age. Each stage is characterized by certain milestones in the development of physical and psychosocial characteristics. As indicated earlier in the chapter, today, many physically mature individuals remain dependent on their parents or other caretakers and do not assume the economic and social roles of adulthood until well past their twentieth birthday. Consequently, at least from a socioeconomic and a psychosocial perspective, these individuals are not yet adults.

The stage- or age-grading of development and its association with social status also occurs in non-Western societies and cultures, though the designations are not the same as those in Western cultures. For example, the St. Lawrence Eskimos have only a two-stage system consisting of boys and men or girls and women. The Arusha people of East Africa, on the other hand, group males into six social strata according to age—youth, junior warriors, senior warriors, junior elders, senior elders, and retired elders. The Arusha also place adolescent boys who have been circumcised in the coming-of-age ceremony in a separate group. Other societies employ other methods of grouping according to age (Keith, 1990).

The Adult Population

Whether adulthood begins at age 20, 25, or even later, as illustrated in Figure 1–1 adults are far and away the largest portion of the general population. Over 74% of the entire U.S. population consists of adults over 18 years of age. These percentages vary with gender and ethnicity. In 1997, approximately 48% of those 18 years and over were male; 52% female; 84% white; 11.7% black; .8% Native American, Eskimo, and Aleut; 3.6% Asian/Pacific Islander; and 9.5% of Hispanic[1] origin (unpublished data, U.S. Bureau of the Census). The percentages of older adolescents and adults in the populations of Canada, Europe, and East Asia are similar to those of the United States, but they are substantially lower in the countries of Africa, Southeast and Western Asia, and South and Central America (Population Reference Bureau, 1997).

The poorer nutrition and higher incidence of infectious diseases in many of these countries severely limits the number of individuals surviving into adulthood and particularly old age. Consequently, only 56% of Africans, 67% of South Americans, 64% of Southeast Asians, and 68% of West Asians are estimated as being over 14 years old (Population Reference Bureau, 1997).

The Formative Years

Biological and behavioral scientists who study the development of the human organism have emphasized the early years, because this is the time

[1]Individuals of Hispanic origin may be of any race.

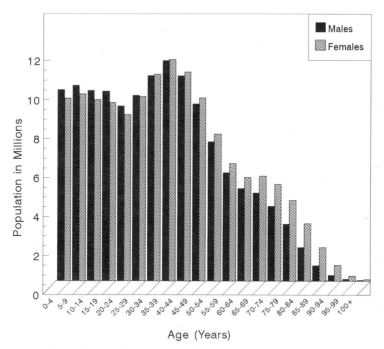

Figure 1–1   Estimated United States Population in April 1997 by Chronological Age. (Based on unpublished data from the U.S. Bureau of the Census, April 1, 1997.)

when the individual develops most rapidly. The so-called "law of primacy" that first events and experiences are the most important has been applied to human development in all its forms—physical, cognitive, emotional, social, and so on. The emphasis on the first few years of life did not, however, originate in science. Philosophers, theologians, poets, novelists, and teachers of many stripes have underscored the formative significance for later development of the first 5 or 6 years after birth. Sigmund Freud, the founder of psychoanalysis, and Ignatius Loyola, the founder of the Society of Jesus (the Jesuits), may not have agreed on many things, but one thing on which they did concur is the importance for psychological development of the preschool period. Loyola's statement, "Give us the child for the first six years of life and you may have him after then, for he will forever remain a good Jesuit" and Freud's assertion that "the child is father to the man" are both recognitions of the lasting effects of early childhood experiences. Freud, in particular, emphasized that the roots of adult personality and psychoneuroses are to be found in early childhood.

So if the formation of the personality and character of the individual is essentially complete by early or even late childhood, what is the purpose of psychological investigations of adulthood? To begin, not everything of importance to the psychological well-being of the individual occurs during childhood and adolescence. Among the significant events or tasks of adulthood that require decisions and adjustments on the part of the individual and have serious consequences for his or her survival and happiness are

1. Training or becoming educated for a vocation or career.
2. Entering the career and adapting to the conditions associated with it.
3. Establishing a relatively permanent sexual/love relationship with a partner.
4. Having and rearing children.
5. Maintaining and reinforcing ties with family and friends.
6. Keeping up with events in the community and the world.
7. Establishing a secure financial base, making judicious purchases, and planning financially for the future.
8. Caring for and educating one's children and making plans for their future.
9. Engaging in satisfying leisure activities.
10. Attending to one's spiritual development, ethical code, and philosophy of life.
11. Adjusting to age-related physical changes, illnesses, and injuries.
12. Adjusting to the deaths of friends and relations, and preparing for one's own death.

These are not the only tasks of adulthood, but this list should suffice to demonstrate why this period of life is worthy of study in its own right. The question is, what are the processes by which people meet these challenges successfully while continuing to grow as human beings and attain personal happiness?

A few years ago, I found a student assistant of mine crying on her twentieth birthday. Somewhat uncertain as to whether they were tears of joy or sadness, I asked her why she was crying on what should be a happy day—a milestone and a cause for celebration. She confessed that she was not crying for joy but because of a feeling of sadness at no longer being a happy-go-lucky teenager. I hope that by now she has discovered that adulthood is a new beginning rather than an end, and is continuing to have experienced many exciting and rewarding things. If she is like the rest of us, not everything that has happened to her has been delightful, but I trust that by having met and mastered the bad experiences and remembering and being grateful for the good ones, she has become a more secure, self-satisfied person.

RESEARCH METHODS

Research on human development is a cross-disciplinary enterprise, involving contributions from biology, psychology, sociology, and other natural and social sciences. The major goal of such research is to describe the structural and dynamic continuities and changes in people over time, to determine the correlates and causes of those continuities and changes, and to discover ways of controlling (accelerating or retarding) them if need be.

Mendel and Darwin

The study of biological factors in development was founded in the researches of two nineteenth-century pioneers—Charles Darwin and Gregor Mendel. Every schoolchild should know that Mendel was the father of genetics and that his studies of inheritance in plants precipitated a line of thought that has advanced to the present-day interest in DNA and the genome. Also well known is the name of Charles Darwin, whose monumental volumes on the *Origin of Species* in 1859 ushered in a new way of thinking about the sources of differences in species through natural selection and the survival of the fittest. Two cornerstones of Darwin's theory of evolution are that complex forms of life are descendants of simpler forms and that the biological features originally appearing as the result of chance mutations or other factors became relatively permanent features of a species because of their survival value.

Another Darwinian notion is that *ontogeny recapitulates phylogeny,* that the development of the individual organism parallels the development of the species of which the organism is a member. This concept was also a guiding principle of much early research on animal and human development. Thus, the development of the fetus *in utero* was thought to proceed through a series of steps that tracked the ascent of man from organisms lower on the phylogenetic scale. The extension of Darwin's ideas to individual and even social development, unfortunately, got a bit out of hand during the early years of this century. The concept of social Darwinism and its "survival of the fittest" corollary, that the strong were meant to survive and the weak to die out, was found to be more palatable in totalitarian societies than in democracies. This misapplication of the *principle of natural selection* was, in any case a gross overgeneralization.

Demography

Another foundation stone in the study of human development was *demography*, the science that is concerned with the examination of both the structural factors (distributions by age, sex, marital status, etc.) and dynamic factors (births, deaths, migratory patterns, etc.) in human populations. The work of pioneer demographers such as John Graunt, Edmund Halley, Adolphe Quetelet, and Benjamin Gompertz led to the establishment of civil registries of births, deaths, marriages, and other demographic events in countries throughout the world. Such information was particularly important to the growth of life insurance companies during the nineteenth century. Most countries now have a bureau of demography or a health statistics center for maintaining records of vital statistics on the country's population. In the United States, the National Center for Health Statistics of the U.S. Department of Health and Human Services collects nationwide data concerning births, marriages, divorces, and deaths by age, sex, race/ethnicity, geographical region, and month, and makes this information available in publications such as the *Monthly Vital Statistics Report.* Statistical information on various countries throughout the world is available from the United Nations and certain other organizations. Particularly noteworthy is the Population Reference Bureau, which annually publishes a *World Population Data Sheet* including statistics by country, continent, and regions within continents on population (overall and by age), projected population, births, deaths, infant mortality rate, fertility rate, life expectancy, contraceptive usage by women, secondary-school enrollment, per capital gross national product (GNP), and certain other derived statistics.

Observation

The most basic of all procedures employed by scientists, including demographers, is *observation*—taking note of events or occurrences and making a record of what is seen, heard, or otherwise observed. Most of the information that behavioral scientists have about people has been obtained from careful observations made in clinics, classrooms, and naturally occurring situations. These observations are usually uncontrolled, in the sense of being uncontrived and representing behavior "on the wing," with no attempt to influence or control the situation. Uncontrolled observation is also referred to as *naturalistic* when it takes place in the field or in a "natural" situation. Standing on a street corner and watching people pass by or watching children play in a park are examples of naturalistic observation.

In many investigations, a better understanding of the factors that are responsible for a particular characteristic or behavior can be obtained by setting up a situation and making planned observations and measurements of what occurs. Thus, we might observe the reactions of a group of students to teachers who conduct a class in different, preplanned ways. To make certain that our observations are unobtrusive—that the students do not behave unnaturally because they know they are being watched, we may observe them by means of a closed-circuit television monitor.

Much available information concerning the personality characteristics of adults comes from observations made in clinical situations. A counselor or psychotherapist observes the verbal and nonverbal behavior of a client or patient in response to certain questions, assessment materials, tasks, and other purposefully or accidentally presented stimuli. *Clinical observations* also provide information that contributes to the making of psychiatric and medical diagnoses.

Observations made in naturalistic or field situations are typically uncontrolled, but the observers usually attempt to remain as unobtrusive as possible. On the other hand, social anthropologists, who spend months and even years observing people in other societies or cultures, have argued that valid information on the typical behaviors, norms, roles, and customs of a society can be obtained by *participant observation*, becoming a participant in the activities of the group they are observing. This technique only works, however, when the observer is successful in being accepted as an unobtrusive member of the group.

Case Study

More detailed information about a person can be obtained through a *case study*, consisting of a biographical description of the person's behavior and circumstances during a part or all of his or her lifetime. Case studies are conducted in clinical and educational contexts both for research purposes and for determining the causes(s) of a specific problem. Details on background and behavior are obtained from the individual and other significant persons. Information on the family, culture, medical history, developmental history, educational history, economic history, and the person's daily activities may all be collected in preparing a case study or case history. If the purpose of the case study is to discover the cause(s) of a specific problem, then hypotheses concerning those causes may be formulated and suggestions for intervention (treatment, training, etc.) made on the basis of the obtained information.

Diaries and Autobiographies

In addition to observing other people, a person may serve as an observer, or at least a commentator, of himself. Many people keep diaries,[2] write long letters, prepare autobiographies, make drawings, and keep other personal documents. Such materials can provide a wealth of information on the thoughts, behavior, personality, and development of the writer. The content analysis of written documents is, however, a complex, laborious process (Wrightsman, 1994a). Report 1–1 includes an abstract of a research study with diaries and a second study with autobiographies.

Interviewing

At least as popular as observation as a method for research on adult development is interviewing. The straightforwardness and simplicity of the

[2]Probably the most famous of all diarists was the Englishman Samuel Pepys (1633–1703), but the diaries kept by Charles Darwin and Jean Piaget on the development of their own children are better known to developmentalists.

REPORT 1–1

Abstracts of Research Using Diaries and Autobiographies

Kemper, S. (1990). Adults' diaries: Changes made to written narratives across the life span. *Discourse Processes, 13*(2), 207–223.

Analyzed life-span changes in adults' narratives based on a longitudinal sample of language from the diaries of 8 adults born between 1856 and 1876. The analysis focuses on the complexity of the narrative structure and the cohesion of the text. Across the life span, the Ss' narratives became structurally more complex, although they became less cohesive as ambiguous anaphors increased. The topic and time-frame shifts are consistent with those noted in adults' reconstructive or retrospective accounts of the significance of life events. Concerns during adulthood and midlife, as conceptualized by B. Neugarten (1973, 1977) and E. Erikson (1959), were reflected in Ss' frequent recountings of the past, focus on people and relationships, and peak entries about death during their 50s and 60s. (Reprinted with permission of the American Psychological Association, publisher of Psychological Abstracts and the PsycLIT database. All rights reserved.)

Mackavey, W. B., Malley, J. E., & Stewart, A. J. (1991). Remembering autobiographically consequential experiences: Content analysis of psychologists' accounts of their lives. *Psychology and Aging, 6*(1), 50–59.

The autobiographies of 49 eminent psychologists were content analyzed in terms of autobiographically consequential experiences (ACEs). Most memories for ACE were not single episodes. Episodic ACEs did, however, share many characteristics of "flashbulb" and vivid memories elicited in studies using more traditional experimental procedures. Memories were concentrated during the college and early adult years. Thus, as in other autobiographical memory studies that have used older Ss, there was a pronounced reminiscence effect. Results are considered in light of Erikson's theory (E. Erikson et al., 1986) of adult personality development. (Reprinted with permission of the American Psychological Association, publisher of Psychological Abstracts and the PsychLIT database. All rights reserved.)

---

interviewing technique may be deceptive, but in the hands of a skillful questioner, a personal interview can yield a great deal of useful information. Sometimes, and particularly when dealing with sensitive topics, interviewing is the only approach available to the researcher. *Structured interviewing*, in which the interviewer asks a set of preplanned questions and records the answers, requires the least amount of training and provides the most objective data. Most developmental studies involving interviewing use structured interviews because of their efficiency and relatively greater reliability. On the other hand, *unstructured interviewing*, in which there is a general plan for the topics to be covered but the exact questions to be asked are left up to the interviewer, can yield richer and more comprehensive information. By being sensitive to the interviewee and making subsequent questions dependent on the answers given to previous ones and other reactions to them, more detailed, informative data can be obtained.

Despite its popularity, interviewing is not renowned for its reliability or validity. *Reliable* data are consistent and relatively free from errors of measurement. *Valid* data reveal what they are supposed to or meant to rather than something else. Thus, the information obtained from an interview designed to assess fitness for a particular position should be consistent (reliable) and correct (valid). However, the appearance, attitudes, and behavior of the interviewer can affect the responses given by the interviewee, and the latter's appearance, biases, and behavior can affect the manner in which the interviewer presents the questions and what questions are asked. If the influence of the interviewer's appearance and style is strong enough, then the result is unreliable and invalid information. Thorough training of interviewers and electronic recording of interview data can improve the reliability and validity of interviewing as a research method. Nevertheless, supplementing an interview with more objective data from other sources is generally recommended in research on adult development (see Report 1–2).

REPORT 1–2

Abstract of a Study Combining Interviewing with Questionnaires

Vaillant, G. E., & Vaillant, C. O. (1990). Determinants and consequences of creativity in a cohort of gifted women. *Psychology of Women Quarterly, 14*(4), 607–616

Forty women who had been selected by L. Terman (1925) in 1921 for a study of intellectually gifted California schoolchildren were reinterviewed in 1987 when their mean age was 77 yrs. These Ss had been prospectively followed by questionnaire over the intervening 65 yrs. Their capacity for creativity (putting something in the world that was not there before) was assessed by review of their prospectively gathered questionnaires and by retrospective interview. The 20 Ss viewed as most creative (usually for literary publication, art, music, or starting an organization) were more likely in the past to have manifested generativity, and at the present to have adjusted well to old age. Although the ego defenses of sublimation, humor, and altruism were more frequent among creative Ss, no differences were noted in the happiness of their childhoods or their health prior to the present. (Reprinted with permission of the American Psychological Association, publisher of Psychological Abstracts and the PsycLIT database. All rights reserved.)

Surveys, Correlations, and Experiments

Observations and interviews can provide a great deal of descriptive data, but they fall short in the task of explanation. The same is true of information obtained from tests, questionnaires, inventories, rating scales, and other psychometric devices administered in person-to-person or mailed surveys. With proper care, a survey questionnaire consisting of many different demographic and personal-opinion items can be administered in person, by mail, or over the telephone to a sample of persons representative of the population of interest. The obtained responses to the various questions and scores computed from them can also be correlated with measures on other variables or criteria, and appropriate conclusions can be drawn from the results. But because possible extraneous variables that may affect the responses have not been controlled for, it is not appropriate to draw cause–effect conclusions. If the correlation between two of the variables, say A and B, is significant, we can predict the occurrence or score on one variable from the other variable, but we are not justified in saying that variable A causes variable B or vice versa. The latter conclusion requires conducting an experiment in which A is the independent variable, B is the dependent variable (or vice versa), and, by means of random assignment or matching, other (extraneous, confounded, concomitant) variables are controlled. It is possible to conduct experiments in certain kinds of developmental studies, say, in a study of the effects of a drug or special training on memory in four different chronological age groups, but experimentation is definitely limited as a method for studying human development. For this reason, special developmental research methods and quasi-experimental procedures have been devised.

Longitudinal and Cross-Sectional Studies

The most straightforward approach to assessing physical and behavioral changes in people over time is to conduct a *longitudinal study* in which the same group of individuals are followed up over a long period of time and periodically reevaluated. Unfortunately, due to carryover effects and mortality, this approach does not always yield valid information. Carryover effects result in measurements taken at time B being affected by the same measurements taken previously at time A. Mortality refers to the loss of subjects due to moving, dying, or refusing to participate further in the study. The result may be that the persons who are assessed at later periods is different in significant ways from those with whom the study began. Finally, the fact that a longitudinal study may continue for many years can result in the study not being completed by the same researchers who began it.

An alternative to the longitudinal approach to developmental research is a *cross-sectional study*, in which groups of people of different chronological ages are measured at the same point in time. For example, a cross-sectional study of changes in cognitive abilities during adulthood might involve administering appropriate measures of these abilities to groups of individuals of different ages from 20 to 80. The cross-sectional approach, which was first used by Adolphe Quetelet in 1838, is less expensive and more efficient than the longitudinal approach but has its own drawbacks. One drawback is that the different age groups must be matched initially on variables that might confound the relationship between age and the variable of interest (the *criterion variable*). For example, in a study of changes in cognitive abilities over the life span, the investigator should match various age groups on education before comparing them on measures of cognitive abilities. This matching process is not always easy to do, and even so, it may still not be clear whether differences among selected age groups on the criterion variable are a result of the developmental process, cohort (generational, cultural, etc.) differences, or other variables associated with chronological age. Thus, the researchers may not be able to tell whether the observed differences among the age groups on the criterion variable are caused by the aging process itself, by generational or cultural differences (*cohort differences*), or by time-related changes in the attitudes and values of society. In short, whereas the longitudinal approach confounds chronological age with the times at which the physical and behavioral characteristics are assessed, the cross-sectional approach confounds chronological age with cohort (generational) differences.

To obtain a clearer picture of the effects of age, apart from cohort and time-of-measurement effects, investigators have employed research designs consisting of a combination of the longitudinal and cross-sectional procedures. One approach, proposed by Warner Schaie (1967) is the three-component model in Figure 1–2. As depicted in the figure, a simple cross-sectional study might involve comparing the characteristics of behaviors of representative samples of 25-, 35-, 45-, and 55-year-olds (A, E, H, and J in the figure). On the other hand, a simple longitudinal design might involve comparing the characteristics or behaviors of the same group of individuals at ages 25, 35, 45, and 55 (A, B, C, and D in the figure). A third type of age-related comparison is a *time-lag design*, in which several cohorts are examined, each at a different time period. As depicted by the letters M, J, G, and D in the figure, the subjects in this design are all of the same chronological age (55) when they are assessed, but they were born in different years and are assessed in different years. Unfortunately, like the cross-sectional and longitudinal designs, the time-lag design does not enable the investigator to evaluate the true effects of aging, free from the confounding effects of cohort differences and the time at which the assessments are made.

Other proposals for separating differences in characteristics or behaviors due to age from those due to cohort and time-of-measurement differences were made by Baltes (1968) and Schaie (1977). One of these proposals, Schaie's (1977) *most efficient design*, involves a combination of three different research strategies. To begin, a cross-sectional study is conducted, in which two or more age groups are measured at the same point in time.

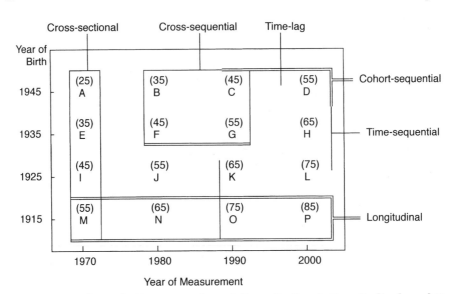

Figure 1–2 Schematic Representation of Cross-Sectional, Longitudinal, and Sequential Designs for Developmental Research. Ages in years are above letters in table. See text for further explanation.

Longitudinal data on several cohorts are provided by retesting these groups after several years. In addition, two or more new age groups are tested to form a second cross-sectional study. The longitudinal data can be added to by retesting previously tested age groups every 5–10 years, and the cross-sectional data can be added to by testing new age groups.

There are three ways of analyzing the results of a study employing a most-efficient design—cohort-sequential, cross-sequential, and time-sequential. The interactive effect of cohort and age on the dependent variable is of concern in a *cohort-sequential analysis*. For example, changes in cognitive abilities from age 45 to 55 in a group of people born in 1945 may be compared with such changes from age 45 to 55 in a group born in 1935. Referring to Figure 1–2, the difference between C and D is compared with the difference between F and G. In the second or *cross-sequential analysis*, the interaction between cohort and time of measurement is of concern. For example, changes in cognitive abilities from 1980 to 1990 in a group born in 1945 are compared with the changes in abilities during the same period in a group born in 1935. Referring to Figure 1–2, the difference between B and C is compared with the difference between F and G. Finally, the interaction between age and time of measurement is of concern in a *time-sequential analysis*. For example, the cognitive abilities of 65-year-olds are compared with those of 75-year-olds, both in 1990 and 2000. Referring to Figure 1–2, the difference between K and O is compared with the difference between H and L. An abstract of a study

REPORT 1–3

Abstract of a Study with Cross-Sectional, Longitudinal, and Sequential Research Designs

Whitbourne, S. K., Zuschlag, M. K., Elliot, L. B., & Waterman, A. S. (1992). Psychosocial development in adulthood: A 22-year sequential study. *Journal of Personality and Social Psychology, 63*(2), 260–271.

Data supporting the notion of adult personality stability are challenged by the present findings, in which developmental change was demonstrated using the Eriksonian-stage-based Inventory of Psychosocial Development (A. Constantinople, 1969). A sequential design over the ages 20–42 was used on 2 cohorts of college students and alumni originally tested in 1966 and 1976–1977 (*ns* in 1988 = 99 and 83, respectively), and a 3rd cohort of college students in 1988–1989 (*n* = 292). Results of longitudinal, cross-sectional, and sequential analyses challenged ideas about personality stability, with evidence of increasingly favorable resolutions of the early Eriksonian psychosocial stages up through the oldest age studied. There was evidence of a trend over the past decade toward less favorable resolution of ego integrity vs. despair. The findings were interpreted in terms of developmental change processes during the adult years interacting with culturally based environmental effects on psychosocial development (Reprinted with permission of the American Psychological Association, publisher of Psychological Abstracts and the PsycLIT database. All rights reserved.)

that employed several types of developmental research designs—cross-sectional, longitudinal, and sequential—is given in Report 1–3.

Retrospective and Prospective Investigations

Longitudinal investigations designed to determine the *risk factors* associated with a particular disease are frequently conducted by medical researchers. These *epidemiological studies* may be either prospective or retrospective. *Prospective studies* follow up individuals who are initially free of the disease over a period of time to determine what characteristics and behaviors differentiate between people who eventually develop the disease from people who remain free of it. In contrast to prospective studies, which involve looking forward in time, *retrospective studies* look backward in that they examine the life histories of people who currently have the disease (*index cases*) to identify correlates and causes of it. These index cases may also be compared on selected variables with people who are currently free of the disease. Like the longitudinal, cross-sectional, and other developmental research designs described earlier, prospective and retrospective studies may

---

My Life 1–1

The Past Recaptured

Forgive me, dear reader, for reminiscing occasionally in this book. It is not that my own life has been more extraordinary than the lives of others, though it has been intriguing and always challenging. Rather, I do not believe in letting "the dead past bury its dead," because I agree with the historian that one who does not study the past and learn from it is doomed to repeat it. Reflecting on the events and decisions that played a role in making me what and where I am today has certainly helped me to cope with the present and plan more effectively for whatever tomorrows I may yet enjoy. Furthermore, I hope that my "life review" will inspire you, "Dear Reader," to get in touch with yourself by engaging in a similar process.

With today's emphasis on the "here and now," introspection is not as fashionable as it was BTV (before television). Objective observation and experimentation have become the sine qua non of science and even self-understanding. But the personal past is no longer with us in an objective sense, only memories of it and a few reminders in the form of a familiar face or place. To understand why certain things occurred and how they shaped the persons whom we are requires a trip down memory lane and an effort to recall as clearly as possible what happened then and the circumstances surrounding it.

According to what I somewhat crudely call the "garbage pail" nature of memory, the mind is not particularly selective in what is remembered: It does not recall just a single event or person, but a hodgepodge of things that were there when the event occurred or the person was present. Thus, when I remember the first time I dated a particular girl, I also remember what she was wearing, the movie we saw, and the old car I drove. So now, the memory of her face can be triggered by seeing that same movie on television or a similar car. The writer Marcel Proust knew this, but he was

---

be conducted to determine changes and stability in physical and psychological characteristics over time. It should be emphasized, however, that all of these designs yield only descriptive and correlational results, not causal explanations. The results can be interpreted as one chooses, and they may provide ideas for the generation of interesting causal hypotheses. However, it still requires an experiment, and usually a series of experiments, to produce data interpretable in causal terms.

Statistical Methods

A variety of statistical methods are employed in analyzing data collected in research on adult development—chi-squares, correlation coefficients,

much more proficient at it than I. An odor, a sound, or a familiar object could resurrect a whole host of detailed memories of things that occurred in his childhood and youth. He also found that recall could be facilitate by isolating himself from other people and things, so the only voices he was aware of were internal ones. As it was with Proust, most of our memories are still available to us if, in solitude, we simply relax and focus on some object or person associated with a particular experience. In this way we can recapture, or shall I say "reconstruct," the past.

Once we have remembered, we can reexamine particular events and even experiment with them: What might have been the result if this had happened instead of that, if I had responded in this way rather than that? Granted, these are only hypothetical experiments, or "thought experiments" as Einstein labeled them, and the outcomes may not actually have been as we imagine. Still, like Einstein, we can exercise our critical faculties in testing the hypothetical outcomes for plausibility and obtain the opinions of other people. In any case, by speculating on other possible outcomes we become free of the fatalism of "whatever will be will be" and that nothing we could have done would have prevented what actually happened.

Life is full of mystery and uncertainty, but this is just what makes it so incredibly interesting. Obtaining insight into the mystery of what we are and why we turned out this way requires attending not only to how other people react to us but also to what our memories and inner voices tell us about ourselves. "Know thyself," advised the Oracle at Delphi; the road to self-knowledge lies within you. We need not bewail with the poet that "For all sad words of tongue or pen, the saddest are these 'It might have been.'" True, preoccupation with the past and things we cannot change may be depressing. However, recollection and self-examination can be beneficial if they teach us how to make our personal present and future better and motivate us to help others become aware of alternative ways of looking at things and the multiple options in their own lives.

analyses of variance, multiple regression analyses, and so on. Both chi-square and correlation coefficients are measures of relationship between variables, whereas analysis of variance is used to determine the significance of differences between mean scores on a dependent variable obtained at various levels of one or more independent variables. Analysis of variance actually consists of a family of designs and procedures by which a series of F ratios can be computed to determine (1) between-subject and within-subject effects, (2) main effects and interactions, (3) univariate (one dependent variable) or multivariate (two or more dependent variables) effects of treatment (independent variable) conditions, as well as controlling for one or more concomitant variables (covariates).

Because most developmental studies involve several variables, multivariate procedures such as multivariate analysis of variance, multiple regression

---

REPORT 1–4

Abstracts of Illustrative Studies Using Correlational and Multiple Regression Analyses

Wilbur, J., Dan, A., Hedricks, C., & Holm, K. (1990). The relationship among menopausal status, menopausal symptoms, and physical activity in midlife women. *Family and Community Health*, *13*(3), 67–78.

375 women (aged 34–62 yrs.) completed questionnaires on demographics, health, dietary calcium intake, and physical activity. Ss represented 4 menopausal status groups: premenopausal, perimenopausal, postmenopausal, and hysterectomy. Vasomotor and general symptoms were significantly related to menopausal status. Significant negative correlations were found between leisure activity and nervous and general symptoms, and between aerobic fitness and nervous and general symptoms. There was a significant positive correlation between occupational activity and general health symptoms. (Reprinted with permission of the American Psychological Association, publisher of Psychological Abstracts and the PsycLIT database. All rights reserved.)

Julian, T., McKenry, P. C., & McKelvey, M. W. (1992). Components of men's well-being at mid-life. *Issues in Mental Health Nursing*, *13*(4), 285–299.

Examined correlates of psychological well-being for 75 middle-aged professional men. Three sets of predictor variables (interpersonal family factors, role adjustment, and extrafamilial interpersonal factors) were hierarchically entered into a multiple regression equation. Well-being was influenced by interpersonal family factors. Role adjustment and extrafamilial interpersonal factors did not account for a significant increase in variance. The best univariate predictors of men's well-being at midlife were perceived closeness to child, perceived closeness to wife, adjustment to the husband role, and number of close friends. (Reprinted with permission of the American Psychological Association, publisher of Psychological Abstracts and the PsycLIT database. All rights reserved.)

---

analysis, discriminant analysis, and canonical correlation are often applied. The first abstract in Report 1–4 summarizes a study employing correlational analysis, and the second abstract is of a study using multiple regression analysis. A multiple regression analysis assigns different numerical weights to several independent variables in predicting a single dependent variable. In the multiple regression analysis described in Report 1–4, psychological well-being is the dependent variable predicted by the independent variables of interpersonal family factors, role adjustment, and extrafamilial interpersonal factors. Discriminant analysis is similar to multiple regression except that, rather that predicting scores on a dependent variable from scores on several independent variables, discriminant analysis differentiates between various

Birren, J. E., Kenyon, G. M., Ruth, J., Schroots, J. J. F., & Svensson, T. (Eds.). (1996). *Aging and biography: Explorations in adult development.* New York: Springer.

Birren, J. E., & Schroots, J. J. F. (1996). History, concepts, and theory in the psychology of aging. In J. E. Birren, K. W. Schaie, R. P. Abeles, M. Gatz, & T. A. Salthouse (Eds.), *Handbook of the psychology of aging* (4th ed., pp. 3–23). San Diego, CA: Academic Press.

Fitzgerald, J. M. (1981). Research methods and research questions for the study of person perception in adult development. *Human Development, 24*(2), 138–144.

Keith, J. (1990). Age in social and cultural context: Anthropological perspectives. In R. H. Binstock & L. K. George (Eds.), *Handbook of aging and the social sciences* (3rd ed., pp. 91–111). San Diego, CA: Academic Press.

Kimmel, D. C., & Moody, H. R. (1990). Ethical issues in gerontological research and services. In J. E. Birren & K. W. Schaie (Eds.), *Handbook of the psychology of aging* (pp. 489–501). San Diego: Academic Press.

Miller, S. A. (1987). *Developmental research methods.* Englewood Cliffs, NJ: Prentice-Hall.

Nahemow, L. (1991). Teaching adulthood and aging through research with older people. *Gerontology and Geriatrics Education, 12*(2), 79–91.

Siegel, A., & White, S. H. (1982). The child study movement: Early growth and development of the symbolized child. In H. W. Reese (Ed.), *Advances in child development and behavior* (Vol. 17). (pp. 234–285). New York: Academic Press.

CHAPTER 2

The Aging Human Body

"Youth is the most wonderful time of life; it's too bad it is wasted on the young." This has probably been the unexpressed sentiment of many older adults who wake up one morning to find grey hair, wrinkles, sagging cheeks, and a double chin in the mirror, hair in the wash basin, and aches, pains, and stiffness in places where they did not even know they had places. The physical changes that accompany aging appear gradually, not without warning, but nevertheless disturbing the eternal summer of young adulthood, when it seems as if one might very well live forever. In our more rational, reflective moments, we realize that we cannot remain perpetually young, but the mind rarely entertains the thought of personal mortality, and denial keeps us going during the endless round of days.

Whether we like it or not, all of us age—some more rapidly than others and not all organs and systems at the same rate. Most people reach a physical peak, "the prime of life," during their early twenties. This is when they are stronger, quicker, healthier, sexier, and their bodies are generally at a higher performance level than at any other age. The digestive, respiratory, neurological, genitourinary, and, in fact, almost all organs and systems are functioning optimally at this time. The heart and circulatory system, however, have reached their peak somewhat earlier—in late adolescence.

By the late twenties, most body functions have reached a plateau. As shown in Figure 2–1, many physical functions change significantly after early adulthood, some more slowly than others. Because of these changes, at the beginning of middle adulthood, the physical functioning of a typical person is 20% less efficient than it was at its peak.

Proper exercise and nutrition, and a lifestyle keyed to moderation and happiness, can slow down the rate of age-related decline. But regardless of how much we might wish it were otherwise, changes associated with genetically based *primary aging* or *senescence* are inevitable. More under one's personal control is the *secondary aging* produced by living conditions, trauma, disease, and other events not directly related to heredity. Still, it is important to emphasize that, even after middle adulthood, the age-related changes in body structure and functioning are gradual and less severe than one might expect.

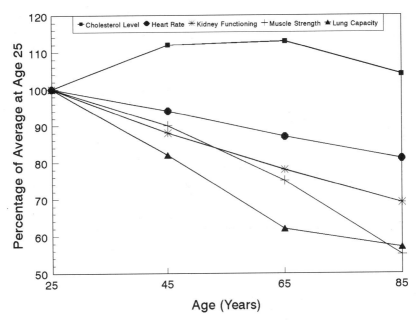

Figure 2–1   Age changes in five physical functions. (Based on data reported in *Newsweek*, March 5, 1990, pp. 44–47.)

PHYSICAL APPEARANCE

Throughout life, appearance is an important part of the self-concept. Physical attractiveness is a highly valued social asset. This is particularly true for women, for whom the sociocultural link between youthful beauty and sexual attractiveness is stronger. The "looking-glass theory," according to which people's view of themselves is the result of their perception of how other people view them, emphasizes the importance for social acceptability of looking good and behaving appropriately.

Physical attractiveness is, of course, not a simple matter of body symmetry, cuteness, curvaceousness, or muscularity. Many people possess excellent physical attributes but are not perceived as beautiful or handsome because they do not feel or act that way. Thus, beauty is not merely "skin deep." As seen in the fact that the perception of it varies from culture to culture, beauty is "in the eye of the beholder." Traditionally, our own culture has emphasized a more Anglo–Saxon concept of female beauty—blond, blue-eyed, and busty, but this has changed to some extent during the past three or so decades. Dark, emaciated women are now viewed by a large percentage of Americans as paragons of female attractiveness.

Whatever the beauty ideal may be, relatively few people can live up to it—at least, not for very long. Beginning at around age 30, greying hair and facial wrinkles—the two physical features that are most highly correlated with chronological age—appear. Actually, the hairlines of men with *male-pattern baldness* begin to recede in the early twenties. And after age 40, the beginning of middle adulthood, numerous age-related physical changes become visible.

Many of the changes listed in Table 2–1 occur gradually and not at the same age in everyone. For example, men of Asian ancestry do not show greying hair as early as men of European ancestry. Age-related differences in physical appearance also occur between the sexes: Women tend to lose more height and show more facial wrinkling than men.

Not all physical changes associated with aging are caused by the aging process alone. For example, squinting, smiling, frowning, and other repeated facial expressions can increase furrowing and wrinkling of the face; continued exposure to the sun's ultraviolet rays causes the skin to become dry and less flexible, and to develop spots and growths; lack of exercise can cause muscles to atrophy; and scalp disease can cause hair loss. Be that as it may, many of the physical changes listed in Table 2–1 are inevitable. Moisturizing

TABLE 2–1 **Common Age-Related Changes in Physical Appearance**

Skin

Wrinkles
Rougher
Drier
Less elastic
Paler
Sags into folds and jowls
Bruises and blisters more easily
Slower to heal
Small growths or spots
Dilated blood vessels
Varicose veins
More likely to itch

Hair

Grayer, whiter
Less lustrous
Sparser, balding
Hairs in nostrils, ears, and eyebrows dark, coarse, and long
Patches of facial hair in women
Less hair in armpits and pubic area

Nose and mouth

Nose gets wider and longer
Lines from nostrils to sides of mouth
Loss of teeth
Gums shrink
Wrinkles around mouth
Double chin

Eyes

Eyelids thicken and droop
"Crow's feet" around eyes
Eye sockets develop hollow appearance
Cloudy or opaque areas in the lens (cataracts)
Cornea often loses its sparkle

Other parts of face and head

Jaw recedes
Cheeks sag
Forehead lines
Ears longer
Earlobes fatter
Head circumference greater

Body shape

Height reduced
Musculature reduced
Middle-age spread
Hips broaden
Waist broadens
Shoulders narrow
Curved or stooped posture
Height shrinks
Widow's "hump"
Sagging breasts

MY LIFE 2–1

My Athletic Aspirations

As far back as I can remember, I wanted to be big and strong. Unlike my sister, who always desired to be pretty, I didn't care how ugly I was as long as I could be tough enough to compete in athletics and defend myself. Because I weighed 11 pounds when I was born, I had a good start on the "big" part. Unfortunately, I was so fat as a baby that my mother called me "Jiggs" after the comic strip character. My paternal grandmother was somewhat kinder in labeling me "Junior," but that name carried the implication of smallness or inferiority.

Somehow I made it through elementary school, being referred to as "Jiggs" in Florida and "Junior" in Georgia. My size was unremarkable and my athletic prowess average or below. Desperate to grow, I measured my height and weight frequently, even when my mother assured me that I was normal and that a "watched pot never boils." On occasion she confessed that she wished I would stop growing so the clothes and shoes she bought for me could wear out before she had to purchase new ones.

In any event, to compensate for my physical mediocrity, I studied hard and became a "scholar." Several of my teachers liked me and gave me all sorts of good things to eat and wear, so the consequences of being a "greasy grind" weren't all bad. By the beginning of junior high, I decided that the only way to improve my physique and athletic fortune was to take a Charles Atlas course. The possibility of a 90-pound weakling turning into a muscle man who could kick sand in bullies' faces inspired me. Though I worked hard with "dynamic tension," I ended up looking more like a rectangle with bulges than like the guy in the ad. In any event, the Atlas course improved my self-esteem enough to make me venture to ask a female classmate for a date.

In high school I went out for football and became a first-string benchwarmer and wood collector. I managed to catch a forward pass in one game, but was almost flattened by a goal post while doing so. The resulting laughter

---

creams, cosmetic surgery, exercise, special diets, or even laughter and a positive attitude cannot ward off the "ravages of time" forever.

Whether they like it or not, middle-aged adults look different from young adults, and older adults look different from middle-aged and young adults. Older adults may not feel any older in a psychological sense and are often taken aback when they catch a glimpse of themselves in the mirror. As one 80-year-old man expressed it, "I don't feel like an old man. I feel like a young man who has something the matter with him" (Cowley, 1989, p. 4). And some older people react quite negatively to their changed appearance:

> I loathe my appearance now; the eyebrows slipped down toward the eyes, the bags underneath, and the air of sadness around the mouth that wrin-

caused me to conclude that I would be more successful in show business than sports, so I acted in a couple of plays and even wrote one. One musical play, sponsored by the Latin Club, brought the house down when I, playing the role of Caesar, rose up after being stabbed by Brutus and his co-assassins, and burst into singing. Before the play was presented, the class prodigy recited the Lord's Prayer in Latin. However, he had to keep his eyes open while doing so because he couldn't remember anything with them closed.

By the time I was 18 I weighed 175 pounds and was an inch over six feet. That should have been sufficient for almost any athlete in those days, but, as one coach revealed to me, I was deficient in muscular coordination. I did learn to skate, ride a bicycle, and play a passable game of tennis, but I frequently hit bloopers in baseball. My adolescent habit seems to have carried over into adulthood, for I now do the same thing in golf. This aberration may be another example of my always attempting to get to the bottom of things.

Despite my lack of athletic prowess, I managed to survive a few pugilis-tic encounters in both military and civilian life. Usually, I could bluff my way out of a fight by acting tough or crazy, but my adeptness with the choke hold saved me from a thrashing on one or two occasions. When I wasn't fighting, I flexed my biceps, squeezed balls, and was never mugged—even in Chicago.

In my twenties I stopped growing vertically, but a couple of decades later I started expanding horizontally. Although I never exceeded 210 pounds, adding weight (and hair) in undesirable places was disconcerting. In later years I detected that I was beginning to collapse physically, and jokes about "settling down" and turning into the "incredible shrinking man" did nothing to ease the pain.

It is now pretty late in my life, but I still haven't resigned myself to being average in size, strength, and sports. In my dreams, I imagine that I'm growing taller and stronger than an NBA center. Furthermore, I am absolutely convinced that there is a sport out there in which I can be a champion, and I'll find it or die trying!

kles always bring. Perhaps the people I pass in the street see merely a woman … who simply looks her age, no more no less. But when I look I see my face as it was, attacked by the pox of time for which there is no cure. (de Beauvoir, 1972)

This rejection of one's body image in middle- and late life is probably more common in people who have been preoccupied in youth with how they look and for whom looking good had commercial as well as social and romantic value. Unfortunately for them, unlike the protagonist in Oscar Wilde's *The Picture of Dorian Grey*, it is the person whose appearance changes rather than just the portrait. Time marches on, and the years will have their due regardless of our piety, our wit, or the care with which we live our lives.

INTERNAL ORGANS AND SYSTEMS

The *vital signs* of a person consist of pulse rate, body temperature, blood pressure, and respiration rate. Of all bodily systems, functioning of the cardiovascular and respiratory systems is considered most indicative of the general condition of a person. As long as the heart is pumping blood at the correct pressure and breathing is regular, the person is viewed as being in no immediate mortal danger.

In this section I discuss some of the details of age-related changes in physical functioning. To some extent, the majority of these changes are the inevitable consequences of aging. Rather than occurring suddenly at age 30, 40, 50, 60, or later, most of them are quite gradual. In fact, rather than beginning in middle- or late life, aging actually begins before early adulthood. For example, *vital capacity*—the amount of air that can be moved in and out of the lungs in a deep breath—peaks at around age 18 to 20. Furthermore, the range of individual differences in the structure and functioning of the human body is greater among older adults than among younger ones. Most people begin taking it easier in their sixties, but others continue to exercise vigorously well into their seventies, and still others engage in gainful employment during their eighties and nineties.

It has sometimes been said that if you wish to live a long life, you should choose your own grandparents. Certainly, the rate of aging is influenced by heredity, but the severity of age-related changes in the body is also affected by disease, injury, exercise, nutrition, smoking, environmental pollution, and other lifestyle factors. Even in old age, changes in heart rate, blood pressure, and respiration can be moderated by regular physical exercise. And though their bodies may not function as efficiently as they did in earlier years, people can learn to compensate for disabilities by exercising good judgment with regard to their health and capabilities, and pace themselves accordingly. Like the person who bounces back and recuperates quickly after a serious illness or accident, one can learn to cope with the physical changes that accompany the aging process and make the most of what he or she has. This does not mean that concerns about age-related changes in abilities and feelings are necessarily counterproductive or abnormal. Such concerns are quite reasonable, and if they do not lead to obsessive preoccupation with appearance and physical well-being, they can contribute to the reduction of pain and disability, and the enhancement of daily living.

Cardiovascular System

Aging is associated with decrements in body structure and function in many different organs and systems. For example, heart rate, breathing rate, bone density, brain size, and kidney functioning all decrease, and blood cholesterol level increases. The organ that is perhaps most reflective of the

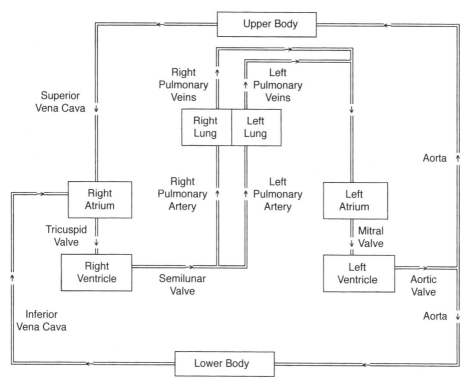

Figure 2–2 Schematic diagram of the cardiovascular system, showing direction of blood flow.

overall vitality of a person and the failure of which is the number one cause of death is the heart.

As schematized in Figure 2–2, the human heart consists of four chambers (left atrium, right atrium, left ventricle, right ventricle), a series of valves, and a complex of arteries and veins. The carbon dioxide–filled blood returns to the heart from various parts of the body and flows into the *right atrium* by way of two large veins, the *superior* and *inferior vena cava*. The right atrium fills, contracts, and the blood is pushed through the interconnecting tricuspid valve into the *right ventricle*. When it is full the right ventricle contracts, the *tricuspid valve* closes, the *semilunar valve* between the right ventricle and the *pulmonary arteries* opens, and blood is pumped through the left and right pulmonary arteries into the corresponding lungs. After being oxygenated in the lungs, blood flows through the pulmonary veins into the *left atrium*; when full, the left atrium contracts and squeezes the blood through the mitral valve into the *left ventricle*. The filled left ventricle then contracts, forcing the blood through the *aortic valve* into the *aorta*. The many branches of the aorta carry blood to all parts of the body except the lungs.

The relaxation/filling (*diastolic*) phase of heart action takes place on both sides of the heart simultaneously, as does the contraction/emptying (*systolic*) phase. Arterial blood pressure is expressed as systolic over diastolic pressure in pounds per square inch. The regular, periodic beating or rhythm of the normal heart, which occurs roughly 3 billion times during a life span of 75 years, is produced by the alternative diastolic and systolic phases. The number of heartbeats per minute, which varies with the individual and the need for oxygen, is approximately 70 in the normal adult resting heart. Maximum heart rate, however, may increase to 200 beats per minute in a young adult. Resting heart rate does not show much age variation, but maximum heart rate ranges from 200 beats per minute in young adults to as low as 150–160 in older adults.

Among the structural changes in the cardiovascular system that occur with aging are atrophying of heart tissue, decreases in the size of cardiac muscle cells, and increases in connective tissue and in fat and calcium deposits in the heart. The result is that the heart muscle and valves thicken and stiffen. The coronary arteries, which supply nourishment and oxygen to heart muscles, become narrower, less flexible, and clogged. Due to cross-linkages in collagen molecules, the aorta and cardiac vessels also harden, shrink, and become less elastic. The blood cholesterol level increases and hemoglobin and red blood cell count decrease after age 65. Because the muscles of the heart become less efficient with advancing age, the maximum heart rate and stroke volume decrease, heartbeats are fewer and more irregular, blood volume output is less, blood pressure increases, and the volume of blood supplied to the body and to the heart itself is reduced. Consequently, both the rate at which oxygen and nutrients are transported to the cells and the rate at which waste products are carried away decline. The effects on behavior are seen in the fact that older people tire more quickly and take longer to return to a resting state after exerting themselves.

Respiratory System

One of the most characteristic symptoms of aging is shortness of breath, a sign of the reduced ability of the respiratory system to collect oxygen and deliver it to the bloodstream. Among the structural changes that lead to shortness of breath and other respiratory problems with aging are the decrease and weakening of chest wall muscles, modifications in collagen in lung tissue and blood vessel walls, increase in the size of alveoli (air cells in lungs) and bronchioles, calcification of the cartilage in the trachea and bronchial tubes, cross-linkages in the collagen contained in the walls of the alveoli, and thickening and stiffening of blood vessels that bring carbon dioxide to the lungs and take oxygen out. The result is reduced expansion of the lungs, rigidity of the trachea and bronchial tubes, and reduced elasticity of the alveoli walls. Measures such as *vital capacity* (maximum one-breath capacity), maximal oxygen uptake, oxygen content of the blood, basal oxygen consumption, and pulmonary tissue compliance (nonrelaxation after inspiration) decrease, whereas residual lung volume and time to return to normal breathing after exertion increase. The heart and lungs make up an interactive system, with decrements in the functioning of one organ leading to decrements in functioning of the other. Thus, carbon dioxide in blood entering the lungs from the heart by way of the pulmonary arteries is removed, and oxygen needed by the heart and other body structures is supplied by the lungs. In turn, the rate and volume with which blood reaches the lungs are controlled by the heart.

As is true of the cardiovascular system as well, the functioning of the respiratory system is affected not only by the rate of primary aging but also by lifestyle and environment. Cigarette smoking and living in a polluted, chemically hazardous environment, in particular, have debilitating effects on the efficiency with which the lungs function in getting carbon dioxide out of the body and oxygen into it.

Musculoskeletal System

Just as the cardiovascular and respiratory systems work together, the musculoskeletal, nervous, and sensory systems cooperate in the performance of psychomotor skills. The musculoskeletal system consists of the striped muscles and bones whose purpose is to move the arms, legs, and other mobile organs of the body. The efficiency with which such movement takes place depends on the condition of the muscle cells, the bones, and the joints at which the bones are connected with each other.

Age-related structural changes in the musculoskeletal system include a decrease in the total amount of muscle in body tissue after age 40 and its replacement by fat tissue, an increase in deposits of mineral salts in the bones, a decrease in cartilage around joints, and a decrease in the quantity of synovial fluid in the joints. Muscular tone, strength, flexibility, speed, and stamina decline; the relaxation/contraction time of muscles increases and injured muscles heal more slowly.

Aging is also associated with greater sponginess and fragility of the dense part of the bones, a significant increase in stiffness and pain in the joints of the lower spine, hips, and knees, and fractures of the vertebrae, ribs, and hips. Decreased density and greater porosity of bones, and a consequent tendency to fracture more easily are associated with *osteoporosis*. In this disorder, which is more common during later life and particularly in older women, there is a gradual long-term loss of bone mass.

Combined with changes in the nervous and sensory systems, age-related decrements in the functioning of the musculoskeletal system lead to one of the most characteristic things about being older—being slower. Figure 2–3 shows that simple reaction time to an auditory stimulus increases appre-

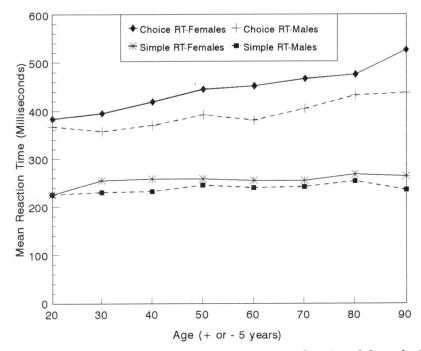

Figure 2–3   Mean reaction time and movement time as a function of chronological age. (Based on data reported in Fozard, Vercruyssen, Reynolds, Hancock, & Quilter, 1994.)

ciably with aging in both males and females and that disjunctive (choice) reaction time increases even more. Likewise, muscle strength follows muscle mass in being greatest at around age 25, decreasing to 90% of the maximum by age 45, 75% by age 65, and 55% by age 85. To some extent, these decrements can be compensated for by regular exercise.

Gastrointestinal System

There is some truth to the old saying that "you are what you eat," but individual differences in metabolism certainly play a role in determining how a person is affected by what he or she ingests. Old age is sometimes caricatured as a time of digestive and eliminative disturbances, and, like many other caricatures, this one has some degree of accuracy. As a person grows older, there is a decline in esophageal and intestinal peristalsis and fewer stomach contractions. Food moves more slowly down the digestive tract and metabolism is slower. Appetite is usually not as keen, and almost all foods are less appealing. Constipation, which is exacerbated by low fluid intake, lack of fiber in the diet, and lack of exercise, is more common, leading to increased use of laxatives. Periodontal disease, hemorrhoids, and diverticulosis (inflammation of the walls of the colon) may compound the digestive problems of older adults. Contributing to these functional changes are declines in stomach acid and intestinal secretions, an increase in body fat, changes in the liver and gall bladder, loss of teeth, and a 50% decline in taste buds.

Genitourinary System

Considering the frequency of urinary disorders in older men, it is not surprising that the majority of urology patients are in their fifties or older. Shrinkage of the kidneys, loss of elasticity and capacity by the bladder, and enlargement of the prostate gland combine to increase the frequency of urination, cause urination to be less complete and bladder control to be lost, as well as other urological disorders. Reductions in the number of functioning excretory units (*glomeruli*) and, consequently, lower renal blood flow and a lower filtration rate of the kidney's result in body toxins and wastes being excreted less efficiently. Not only is less urine excreted and excreted less efficiently with aging, but it also contains more creatine. Like older men, older women sometimes experience problems with bladder control and incontinence. Urinary problems are not as common in older women as in older men, but cancer of the genitourinary tract is no respecter of gender. Prostate cancer occurs frequently in older men and ovarian or uterine cancer in older women.

Secretions of both male and female sex hormones decline with age, and sexual activity is reduced. The testes shrink somewhat, the cervix and uterus are reduced in size, and the vaginal mucosa atrophies. The incidence of impotence is higher in old age, but many people continue to enjoy a full sex life well into their seventies and eighties (see Chapter 6).

Nervous System

Our intelligence, our planning ability, our humaneness—things which make us different from other animals—are more a matter of the superior human nervous system than any other body structure. Perception, consciousness, language, learning, memory, thinking, and the social, creative behaviors produced by them are all functions of the nervous system. Consequently, we begin to worry when we are no longer as alert as we once were, cannot remember things that we did, or experience difficulties with abstractions. Decrements in these functions may not be inevitable consequences of aging, but comparing our mental abilities with how they used to be, or with the abilities of younger adults, older adults often find themselves coming up short.

The basic building blocks of the nervous system are *neurons*. Neurons increase in size and complexity as the individual matures, but their number and size decrease gradually after then. Age-related changes occur in both the central (brain and spinal cord) and the peripheral nervous system, and particularly in the former. The volume and weight of the brain decline, the gyri or ridges in the brain become smaller, and the fissures become larger. Cerebral blood flow and oxygen and glucose consumption by the brain decline, while the volume of ventricular fluid increases. The number of granules of *lipofuscin*, a pigmented material containing lipids, carbohydrates, and protein, increases with aging. Fatty tissue and calcified material referred to as *plaque* accumulate in the cerebral blood vessels, and bundles of paired, helical filaments known as *neurofibrillary tangles* are found in small numbers in normal aged brains and in large numbers in diseased brains.

With respect to behavior regulated by the nervous system, many central nervous system reflexes and responses controlled by the autonomic nervous system become slower or weaker as a person ages. Sleep, which is neither as deep nor as refreshing as it was during the early adult years, decreases in amount. Signs of aging can also be found in the brain waves and in cognitive functions such as short-term memory. Such changes occur at different rates and to different degrees in different people. Age-related decrements in intellectual functioning can be arrested to some degree by intellectual exercise and, in any case, compensated for by careful planning, use of memory aids, and other procedures.

Immune System

The immune system, which has the job of making the body immune to infection and disease, consists of the bone marrow, thymus gland, spleen, lymph nodes, and tonsils. *Lymphocytes*, or white blood cells, are produced in the bone marrow. Some of these cells travel to the thymus, mature into *T cells*, and are then sent into the bloodstream to become "killer" or "helper" T cells. *Killer T cells* reject foreign tissue and destroy viruses, fungi, and parasites, whereas *helper T cells* assist another group of white cells known as B cells. *B cells* are lymphocytes that have traveled from the bone marrow to mature in the spleen or lymph nodes. At maturity, B cells enter the bloodstream, where they produce antibodies to resist bacteria. In addition to the two types of lymphocytes, two other types of cells that contribute to immunity are monocytes and leukocytes.

The effectiveness of white blood cells, and hence the efficiency with which the body is able to eliminate foreign substances, decreases with aging. Even after an immunization injection, the immune systems of older adults take longer to erect defenses against specific diseases. The number of T and B cells is not affected by the aging process, but the number of cells failing to mature increases and their functioning becomes less efficient. The lessened effectiveness of B cells is seen in the production of fewer antibodies and an impairment of their ability to differentiate between foreign invaders and the body's own cells. Consequently, the antibodies may attack the cells of the body itself, a so-called *autoimmune disorder.*

SENSATION AND PERCEPTION

Neural impulses containing sensory information are conveyed from specialized receptors by way of efferent (sensory) nerves to the central nervous system (spinal cord and brain). Then, neural impulses are conveyed from the central nervous system by way of efferent (motor) nerves to the muscles and glands. Combined with the secretions of certain glands, the two types of peripheral nerves—afferent and efferent—make up the information highway of the body. The efficiency with which sensory information is received, conducted, processed, and acted upon determines how effectively the individual is able to sustain and enhance his or her existence. Conducting information from the external world to the spinal cord and brain is, of course, not only a matter of the intactness of neural transmission pathways but also the specialized receptors connected to those pathways.

At least since Aristotle's time, over 2000 years ago, it has been commonly asserted that there are five senses—vision, hearing, taste, smell, and touch. Any educated person of today realizes, however, that there are many more senses than the traditional five. There are at least four skin senses alone—pressure, pain, warmth, and cold—in addition to senses of balance, position, gravity, rotary motion, and linear motion. Similar to the internal organs and systems discussed in the last section, the sensory receptors and connecting peripheral nerves are functioning at peak efficiency in early adulthood. The corresponding sensory thresholds are lowest and the ability to distinguish between sensations of different magnitude, quality, and complexity is greatest during the twenties. Consequently, a typical 20-year-old is more alert and perceptive of changes in the environment than a typical 60- or 70-year old. Beginning in the thirties and forties and increasing in severity during the sixties and seventies, however, sensations become duller and are responded to more slowly. One effect of declining sensory acuity is the perception of older adults as inattentive, distractible, and dull rather than merely less perceptive.

Though the decline in sensory abilities is to some extent inevitable with aging, the range of individual differences in this regard is extensive. Some older adults take pride in the fact that they can see or hear "as well as when I was young." In addition, older adults can learn to compensate for normal sensory losses by using good judgment and relying on their past experiences. They can wear appropriate sensory aids, avoid situations that demand acute sensory receptivity, and "fill in the gaps" created by undetected sensory information.

Vision

Although later life is noted for the occurrence of visual defects, the average 45- or 50-year-old does not simply wake up one morning and discover that the dials on the television set or the stove are not clear, or that the newspaper must be held at arm's length to be read. Young children have relatively poor visual acuity, but it improves until about age 20 and then remains fairly steady until the early forties. During the forties or early fifties, and 3–5 years earlier in women than in men, *presbyopia* ("old-sightedness") gradually manifests itself. The result is that reading glasses or bifocals must be worn for close work and brighter lighting becomes necessary.

The loss of visual acuity during middle- and later adulthood is due in part to the decreasing diameter of the pupils of the eyes and to the obstruction of vision caused by sagging eyelids. The major cause of the problem, however, is the thickening and hardening of the lenses and the consequent decrease in their flexibility. The lenses are unable to accommodate, or change their focal length, as quickly and as effectively as before, making it difficult to see things close up.

In addition to reduced acuity and presbyopia (*senile miosis*), "normal" age-related changes in vision include the following:

1. Decreased ability to differentiate among colors. The yellowing lenses of the eyes filter out greens, blues, and violets, making these colors more difficult to distinguish than yellows, oranges, and reds.
2. Glare produced by increased scattering of light within the eyes due to reduced transparency of the lenses.
3. Poorer peripheral vision due to glare and reduced sensitivity to light.
4. Slower adaptation to changes in ambient illumination—from light to dark (*dark adaptation*) or dark to light (*light adaptation*).

Other common eye complaints in later adulthood include tiny spots or specks that float across the visual field (*floaters*), light flashes, and too much or too little tearing.

Aging is accompanied not only by changes in visual sensations but also in the perception (sensation plus meaning) of visual stimuli. For example, there is a deterioration in the ability to perceive objects in depth. In addition, the *critical fusion frequency* (*CFF*)—the highest frequency of a flickering light at which they flashes appear to fuse into a continuous beam—becomes lower. Rather than being caused by changes in the eyes, the lower CFF for older adults appears to be due to the dynamics of the central nervous system. According to *stimulus persistence theory*, the lower CFF and the general tendency of older adults to react more slowly than younger adults to a series of stimuli presented in rapid succession is due to the longer time required for an older nervous system to recover from stimulation (Axelrod, Thompson, & Cohen, 1968). This theory may also explain why older adults find it more difficult to detect contrasting patterns involving small differences between light and dark. In any event, the greater cautiousness of older adults may also contribute to their slower responsiveness to visual stimuli.

Senile miosis (presbyopia) is certainly a visual defect but not a visual disorder or disease in the same sense as cataracts, glaucoma, or retinal degeneration or detachment. Cataracts are a condition in which the opacity of the lens of the eye obstructs the passage of light to the retina. Cataracts increase with age, but the affected lens can be surgically removed and a special lens inserted in its place.

Also increasing with age and even more serious than cataracts is glaucoma. This disorder, which is caused by improper drainage of the intraocular fluid and hence increased intraocular pressure, leads to a reduction in the size of the visual field and eventually damage to the optic nerve and blindness if not treated. The pressure screening test for glaucoma is a part of a routine eye examination. When glaucoma is diagnosed, it is treated by means of prescription eyedrops, oral medications, laser treatments, and surgery.

Three other eye diseases that increase in frequency with aging are macular degeneration, diabetic retinopathy, and retinal detachment. In macular degeneration, the macula, a yellowish area in the center of the retina, stops functioning efficiently and central vision is affected. In diabetic retinopathy, the blood vessels to the retina fail to supply it properly with blood. In retinal detachment, the outer retinal layer becomes separated from the inner layer and must be treated with laser surgery.

Hearing

For convenience, the ear may be divided into three parts: the outer ear for collecting sound, the middle ear for transforming sounds to mechanical vibrations, and the inner ear for transforming the mechanical vibrations to electrical neural impulses. Wax buildup in the middle ear and sluggishness of operation of the three small bones in the middle ear (malleus, incus, and stapes) can produce a condition known as conduction deafness. Conduction deafness can occur at any age, but a decline in the number and strength of the muscle fibers that support the eardrum makes it more likely in older adults.

More serious than conduction deafness and more characteristic of older adulthood is inner-ear deafness (nerve deafness). Degeneration of the cochlear hair cells, the primary auditory receptors in the inner ear, begins as early as age 20 but does not have a noticeable effect on auditory acuity until the forties and fifties. At that time, a decline in sensitivity to high-pitched sounds, referred to as presbycusis, becomes apparent. Hearing sounds over 3,500 hertz, such as the sibilants s, sh, and ch, is particularly affected by presbycusis. Presbycusis may result from atrophy and degeneration of the cochlear hair cells, a reduction in nutrients to the hair cells, or a loss of neurons in the auditory pathway from the ear to the brain. Damage to the auditory area in the temporal lobes of the brain, as in a cerebral injury or tumor, causes a condition known as *central deafness*.

Presbycusis is more common in men than in women and progressively increases after age 50. At first, the affected person may not even realize that anything is wrong with his or her hearing. It only seems as if people do not speak as clearly as they once did, that their speech is slurred or mumbled. In addition, certain sounds appear too loud and are annoying, and shows, concerts, or parties are not as enjoyable as they once were.

After the late forties, the number of people with some hearing loss increases every year, reaching about 75% by age 75. Although only 15% of individuals aged 65 and over are legally deaf, the majority suffer from presbycusis. Years of noise bombardment, and especially living and working in a noisy environment, produce further destruction to the inner ear and further hearing loss. The deafening effects of noise or loud sounds are even greater during exercise, because increased blood flow to the ears as a result of exercising increases the vulnerability of auditory receptors to injury. Consequently, wearing earphones while jogging or otherwise listening to loud music while exercising can be destructive to your hearing.

Because contextual cues can compensate for some degree of hearing loss, everyday speech is easier for a person with some hearing loss to understand than less familiar or complex material. Even when listening to music consisting of many high-frequency overtones, familiarity with the musical composition may assist the individual in filling in tonal gaps and "hearing" frequencies to which he or she is insensitive. Background noise, and particularly the persistent hissing or ringing sound in the ears known as *tinnitus*, is distracting and can affect auditory perception.

Hearing, of course, interacts with the other senses, and hearing loss can be compensated for to some extent by facing the speaker and familiarity with what he or she is talking about. Speaking slowly, but not especially loudly, and lowering the pitch of the voice can facilitate communication with a person who has presbycusis.[1] Movements and gestures are also helpful, as, of course, are hearing aids and the ability to read lips. Because differential sensitivity in the two ears can affect the ability to tell from which direction a sound in coming, it may be necessary to have a different hearing aid in each

---

[1]In addition to raising the volume instead of lowering the pitch of the voice when speaking to an elderly person, there is a tendency on the part of some younger and middle-aged adults to be patronizing or infantilizing. This is especially true of nurses and other helpers who have stereotyped perceptions of older patients or clients. *Patronizing speech* consists of speaking slower and in a higher pitch, exaggerating one's intonation, repeating statements, asking tag and closed-ended questions, and simplifying one's vocabulary and grammar. Secondary baby talk, or *infantilization*, consists of addressing an older person by his or her first name when it is unwarranted, and employing terms of endearment (sweetheart, baby, dearie, etc.), simplified expressions, and short imperatives, in addition to cajoling to obtain compliance and acting as if the older person has little or no memory. These behaviors indicate a lack of respect and are demeaning to the elderly listener (Whitbourne, Culgin, & Cassidy, 1995).

ear. Unfortunately, many older people are reluctant to wear hearing aids, perhaps because of vanity, perhaps because of the association of hearing problems with the "deaf and dumb" label.

In addition to loss of communication and information, a severe hearing disorder can have untoward psychological and social effects. The affected individual may experience isolation, loneliness, and emotional distress. Because of the frustration and embarrassment of not being able to hear or of saying something inappropriate, social interactions may be avoided. In extreme cases, a hard-of-hearing person may become so chronically suspicious of what other people are saying that she or he becomes paranoid.

Taste and Smell

Animals in the wild depend more than humans on the chemical senses of gustation (taste) and olfaction (smell), and have more acute tasting and smelling abilities. Vision and hearing are the major human senses, but taste and smell also provide important information on the environment and make our lives safer and more enjoyable.

The receptors for taste are located in the taste buds, which are concentrated on the tip, sides, and back of the tongue. Of the four taste modalities— sweet, bitter, sour, and salty—the front of the tongue is more sensitive to sweet, the back to bitter, the sides to sour, and the front and sides to salty. The receptors for smell are located in the olfactory epithelium at the top of the nasal passageway near the base of the brain. Substances must be in solution to be tasted, and can be tasted more effectively when they are swished around in the mouth. In order to be smelled, however, a substance must follow an air route; the olfactory experience can be hastened and enhanced by sniffing the aromatic substance.

Everyday observations and folklore point to declines in the acuity of taste and smell with age. For example, the saying "too old to cut the mustard" originated in a time when mustard was ground at home and "cut" by adding vinegar to it. Because older adults had a tendency to put too much vinegar into the mixture, an older person who performed any task ineffectively came to be referred to as "too old to cut the mustard." Another source of reported age decrements in taste sensitivity are complaints from older adults that "everything tastes flat" or is "boring." To compensate for the flat taste, they tend to use greater amounts of salt, pepper, and other seasonings in their foods. Food complaints among older adults may also be the results of attitude, personal problems, and feelings of isolation or abandonment.

With respect to changes in the sense of smell, the observation that older people have a greater tolerance for foul odors has caused them to be the objects of numerous jokes and labels. Less humorous is the research finding that they are less adept at identifying the odor of mercaptan, a substance placed in natural gas to make it more detectable. The fact that older adults can sense the odor of roses as well as younger adults has prompted the suggestion that it might be better to replace the mercaptan in natural gas with rose extract.

What can be concluded from research on age-related declines in taste and smell sensitivity? Because taste and smell interact, it is difficult to separate the effects of one sense from the other. In addition, both senses are affected by experience, disease, psychological factors, and sociocultural factors, which must be controlled to determine whether they decline with age. In general, the number of taste buds and smell receptors is somewhat less in older than in younger adults (Miller, 1988; Spitzer, 1988). However, the loss of receptors is not closely correlated with sensitivity. Although there is some age-related decrement in taste sensitivity, compared with sensitivity to odors it remains fairly stable (Bartoshuk & Weiffenbach, 1990; Weiffenbach, Cowart, & Baum, 1986). Sensitivity to sweetness and saltiness is fairly stable across age groups, but there is some decline in sensitivity to bitterness (Bartoshuk & Weiffenbach, 1990; Spitzer, 1988).

Aging appears to have a greater effect on smell than on taste, although at least some of the decline appears to be caused by a lifetime of living in a particular odor environment. In any event, the finding that the ability to detect various odors is poorer in older than in younger adults has received wide research support (Murphy, 1986; Stevens & Cain, 1985, 1986, 1987). Differences between children and adults in odor preferences have also been found; children prefer fruity odors such as strawberry, and adults prefer flowery smells such as lavender (Engen, 1977).

Even when age-related changes in sensitivity to flavors and odors are observed, it is possible that they are due to disease or other variables associated with aging. For example, the ability to identify odors declines in Alzheimer's disease, and the ability to both detect and identify odors declines in Parkinson's disease (Doty, Deems, & Stellar, 1988; Koss, Weiffenbach, Haxby, & Friedland, 1988). The sense of smell can also be damaged by viral and bacterial infections and head trauma (Bartoshuk & Weiffenbach, 1990).

The Somesthetic Senses

The somesthetic senses consist of the cutaneous (skin) senses (pressure, pain, warmth, cold), the kinesthetic sense, and the vestibular senses. Receptors for the *kinesthetic senses*, which provide information on the position of the limbs, are located in the muscles and joints. Receptors for the vestibular senses, which provide information on the position and movement of the head, are located in the inner ear. The receptors for the vestibular senses consist of hair cells in the semicircular canals and the vestibular sacs. The hair-cell receptors in the semicircular canals are sensitive to movement of the head in three dimensions—the so-called rotational sense; the hair-cell receptors in the vestibular sacs, from which crystals of calcium carbonate, or *otoliths*, are suspended, provide information on the position of the head and linear movement.

Even after many decades of research, the receptors for the cutaneous and kinesthetic senses have still not been clearly differentiated. Examination of cross-sections of the skin reveals various structures that have been proposed as receptors for the respective sensations: Meissner corpuscles—touch, Pacinian corpuscles—deep pressure, Ruffini cylinders—warmth, Krause end bulbs—cold, and free nerve endings—touch and pain. In addition, structures designated as annulospiral endings and flower-spray endings, which are found in muscles and joints, have been proposed as the receptors for kinesthetic sensitivity. Unfortunately, the validity of these matchings has not been completely confirmed.

Concerning changes in the various somesthetic senses with aging, touch sensitivity has been found to remain relatively unchanged until the early fifties, after which the absolute threshold for touch increases. The increase in touch thresholds with age is greater in the smooth (nonhairy) portions of the skin than in the hair-covered parts (Axelrod & Cohen, 1961; Kenshalo, 1977). Furthermore, Corso (1977) demonstrated that touch sensitivity on the ankles, knees, and other lower areas in the lower extremities is more impaired with aging than touch sensitivity to the wrists, shoulders, and other areas in the upper extremities of the body.

Sensitivity to vibratory stimuli of the sort used in a massage or neurological exam also declines with aging, particularly when the vibrations are of high frequency (Verrillo, 1980). The effects of aging per se should be distinguished from those of disorders such as thiamin deficiency and diseases such as anemia and diabetes, which are also associated with reduced vibratory sensitivity.

The results of research on age-related changes in temperature sensitivity are mixed, but, in general, there appear to be slight increases in the absolute thresholds for both warmth and cold (Schieber, 1992; Whitbourne, 1985). Furthermore, the ability of the body to regulate extremes of temperature declines with aging. After age 65, there is a significant decrease is the temperature of the skin and body core (Verrillo & Verrillo, 1985).

Impairments in sensitivity of both the kinesthetic and vestibular senses have been observed in later life. In summarizing findings on active and passive movement of the muscles and joints, Ochs, Newberry, Lenhardt, and Harkins (1985) concluded that with increasing age, there is greater deterioration in the perception of movement for the great toe, several joints, the knees, and the hips, whereas judgments of tension with active movement of these structures are relatively unaffected. Decrements in the sense of balance occurring with aging are associated with feelings of dizziness and sensations of spinning (*vertigo*). Such decrements, which are accompanied by increased body sway, can result in the loss of balance and severe falls. However, vision can help compensate for decrements in vestibular sensations and enable the person to keep from falling.

Of all the somesthetic senses, the greatest amount of research on age-related changes has been conducted on the sense of pain. The results of earlier investigations suggested that older adults are less sensitive than younger adults to pain (Kenshalo, 1977; Whitbourne, 1985). This conclusion continues to enjoy fairly wide support. Recent studies, however, have pointed to a confounding variable, namely, the tendency on the part of older adults to underreport lower levels and overrate higher levels of pain (Harkins, Price, & Martinelli, 1986). Older adults tend to be more cautious in their reports than younger adults, reporting that they feel pain only when they are certain that it is present. Changes in pain sensitivity with age also vary with the area of the body stimulated, the type of stimulation, and various personal and social factors. Attention, attitudes, beliefs, emotions, ethnic background, motivation, personality traits, prior experience, socioeconomic status, and suggestion are also related to the perception of pain.

THEORIES OF BIOLOGICAL AGING

As witnessed by the search for the "fountain of youth" and the time-honored popularity of tales and treatments concerned with the aging process, prolongevity has been a continuing quest since the dawn of human history. Although the commercial and health literature abounds with suggestions for staying healthy, looking good, and living as long as one can, the inevitability of corporeal existence is universally recognized. Acceptance of personal mortality does not mean, however, that the human life span cannot be prolonged. But in order to achieve prolongevity, if not immortality, we first need to know what makes us age.

Hippocrates was the first medical researcher to study the aging process, which he attributed to a loss of body heat. Erasmus Darwin, a nineteenth-century British physician, considered aging to be due to a loss of irritability in the neural and muscular tissue, whereas Eli Metchnikoff viewed it as being caused by a state of *autointoxication*, or poisoning by a toxic substance produced by the body. More recent explanations for the aging process may be classified, for convenience, into breakdown theories, substance theories, and genetic theories. These proposed explanations, which are more appropriately designated as "hypotheses" rather than theories, are not mutually exclusive. In fact, a combination of several theories will probably be necessary to obtain a reasonable explanation of why we age.

Breakdown, or *wear-and-tear theories*, propose that aging is the result of wear and tear, stress, or exhaustion of organs and cells. Body organs certainly seem to wear out with usage and exposure to certain environmental stimuli, but the fact that active exercise enhances the functioning of many organs—at least up to a point—would seem to contradict a simple wear-and-tear explanation. Another "breakdown" explanation is based on the observation that readjusting after physical exertion or exercise becomes progressively more difficult with aging. For this reason, Comfort (1964) considered aging to be the consequence of accumulating homeostatic faults or errors and the resulting failure to maintain a steady internal balance.

Two additional examples of breakdown theories are *immunological theory* and *autoimmune theory*. The former views aging as a result of the gradual deterioration of the immune system, leading to a decline in the ability of the body to defend itself against disease, injury, and foreign or abnormal cells. Disorders such as adult-onset diabetes, senile dementia, and certain vascular diseases are consistent with this explanation. So is the diminished production with aging of hormones secreted by the thymus gland that regulate the production of T cells (Zatz & Goldstein, 1985). However, the fact that animals without immune systems still age would suggest that, rather than being a cause of aging, the observed decline in the functioning of the immune system may merely be the result of changes in the endocrine system.

The *autoimmunity theory* is based on the notion that the aging body becomes progressively less adept at differentiating between normal and abnormal cells, and consequently produces antibodies to attach both kinds of cells. This rejection of the body's own tissues is seen, for example, in rheumatoid arthritis, a disease found more often in older than younger adults. Like changes in the immune system, however, autoimmunity is probably a correlate or consequence of aging rather than a cause of the process.

Substance theories view aging as resulting from changes in collagen and the proliferation of mutant cells, cross-linkage of molecules, the accumulation of free radicals at the cellular level, or the secretion of certain hormones. At the tissue level, strands of *collagen*, a protein material found in connective tissue, increase with aging, causing reduced elasticity of the visceral organs, slower healing, and other changes in the body. Abnormal and mutant cells also proliferate with aging, increasing the chances of developing cancer. In fact, one theory of aging—*error accumulation theory*—holds that the accumulation of random errors in the mechanism by which new proteins are synthesized causes dysfunctioning and ultimately the death of cells.

Cross-linkage, the inadvertent coupling of large intracellular and extracellular molecules that cause connective tissue to stiffen, also increases with aging. When such cross-linkages occur between strands of DNA molecules, the cells may be unable to read genetic information properly and thereby fail to produce enzymes that maintain body functions. Like changes in the immune system, however, cross-linkage is thought to be a result rather than a cause of aging.

Also directed toward the cellular levels is the theory that aging is due to the accumulation of *free radicals* and other chemical garbage within cells. Free radicals are highly reactive molecules or parts of molecules produced by adverse reactions of body cells to radiation, air pollution, and oxygen. The popularity of antioxidants such as vitamins A, C, and E is based to some extent on the finding that the production of new free radicals is inhibited by them. Although free radicals are important to the functioning of the immune and digestive systems, they contribute to many degenerative conditions (e.g., sagging skin, cancer, heart disease) and may damage other cells or their DNA (Harman, 1987). The damage, however, is usually repaired too promptly to be a primary cause of biological aging.

Other kinds of "garbage" or waste products that can affect cell functioning do increase with aging. For example, *mitochondria*, the small "energy machines" within the cytoplasm that are composed of highly unsaturated fats, sugar, and protein molecules, have been suggested as a possible factor. This theory holds that aging is caused by oxidation of the fat molecules in the mitochondria, a process that interferes with their energy-releasing function. Another cellular-garbage theory points to the accumulation of inert substances such as the *lipofuscins*, pigmented granules containing lipids, carbohydrates, and protein, as interfering with the functioning of cells.

Hormonal theories have been stimulated by observations of the massive amounts of hormones released by Pacific red salmon before they die. Denckla (1974) proposed that aging is due to "blocking hormones" such as antithyroid hormones released by the hypothalamus or DECO (decreased oxygen consumption) hormones secreted by the pituitary that keep cells from using thyroid hormones. It has also been suggested that an "aging clock" in the hypothalamus alters the level of hormones and brain chemicals in older adults, thereby deregulating body functioning and hastening death.

As indicated previously, the existence of an "aging clock," or a prewired, genetically based aging program in the hypothalamus or elsewhere in the body has been proposed by a number of researchers. Supporting this notion is the finding that the cells of a particular species can subdivide only a certain number of times before they die (approximately 50 in humans), a limit that is lower for older than younger members of a species (Hayflick, 1977, 1980). This *Hayflick limit* has been determined only *in vitro*, however, and, in any case, is not reached during the course of a normal human life span.

As mentioned at the beginning of this section, no single theory is adequate by itself to explain the aging process. Heredity certainly affects the rate of aging, but so does the way in which you live—what you eat and drink, whether you smoke, what kinds of physical, chemical, and social environments you live in, whether you exercise and rest properly, how much psychological stress you experience.[2] Thus, the rate of aging varies not only from species to species but also from individual to individual within the same species, and within the same tribe or primary group. Furthermore, the evidence points to multiple sites of aging—tissue, cellular, and nuclear—and at least two kinds of aging processes—accidental damage to molecules, membranes, or body parts, and aging due to a genetic program. Particularly fas-

[2]The longest-living person in recent years was Jeanne Calment, a Frenchwoman who died in 1997 at the ripe old age of 122. Madame Calment, who recalled meeting Vincent Van Gogh in 1888, attributed her long life to an occasional glass of port and a diet rich in olive oil (*Los Angeles Times*, August 5, 1997, p. A18).

cinating is research, stimulated by the genetic program or "aging-clock" hypothesis, on the DNA and RNA molecules that are responsible for cell replication and what turns them on and off. The possible locus of such a clock in the hypothalamus, pituitary gland, and thymus gland and its functioning are also under continuing investigation.

SUMMARY

Age changes in appearance and physical functioning in adulthood are inevitable, but they occur at different rates in different individuals and species. The effects of these changes on the self-concept also vary from person to person. Greying hair, wrinkles, and other signs of old age are obviously of greater concern to individuals for whom a youthful appearance is more important for occupational success and social prestige. Physical appearance, of course, is not the exclusive concern of aging women, though the cosmetics industry and purveyors of other "treatments" for aging skin and bodies focus principally on the female sex.

Aging is accompanied by alterations in physical appearance and by declines in the structure and functioning of the cardivascular, respiratory, musculoskeletal, gastrointestinal, genitourinary, and nervous systems, as well as the sense organs. The efficiency with which the heart pumps blood is affected by the thickening and stiffening of heart muscle and valves and the narrowing of coronary arteries. The result is a decline in the rate at which oxygen and nutrients are conveyed to the body cells and waste products are carried away.

The respiratory system interacts with the heart in supplying clean, oxygenated blood to the body. Shortness of breath and other respiratory problems associated with aging are caused by structural changes in the lungs and the supporting muscles. Functioning of both the heart and lungs is affected not only by primary aging but also by secondary factors in the environment and the person's lifestyle.

A decrease in muscle tissue, cartilage, and synovial fluid, and an increase in fat tissue and bone mineral salts during middle adulthood affect the tone, strength, flexibility, speed, and stamina of the muscles. The bones and joints are also affected, increasing the stiffness and painfulness of movement. Consequently, the movements of older adults are characteristically slower than those of younger adults.

Declines in the efficiency of digestion and elimination during later life are caused by changes in the stomach, intestines, liver, gall bladder, and teeth. Shrinkage of the kidneys, decreased bladder elasticity and capacity, and enlargement of the prostate gland combine to produce urinary malfunctions. Changes in the sex glands and organs also contribute to a decline in sexual activity during middle- and late life.

Age-related changes in the nervous system include decreases in the number and size of neurons and increases in plaque and neurofibrillary tangles in the brain. The effects are slower and weaker responses and declines in certain cognitive functions. The ability of the body to ward off infection and disease is affected by decreased functioning of the immune system.

With respect to sensation and perception, presbyopia ("old-sightedness"), cataracts, and presbycusis (inner-ear deafness) are common accompaniers of aging. More severe but also less common disorders of vision, such as glaucoma, macular degeneration, and retinal detachment, also increase with aging. The senses of touch, vibration, temperature, pain, kinesthetic, and balance decline with aging. Although inevitable, age-related changes in the internal organs and sense receptors vary greatly from person to person. Heredity is certainly a factor in determining structural and functional changes with aging, but injury, disease, nutrition, exercise, smoking, environmental pollution, and other lifestyle factors exert considerable influences on the rate and severity of these changes.

Theories of aging include (1) wear-and-tear explanations that the body's tissues, organs, or cells gradually wear out as a result of overuse or accidents; (2) substance explanations that aging is caused by the accumulation of errors or chemical garbage such as free radicals and lipofuscins; (c) hormonal theories that implicate the activities of the hypothalamus, pituitary, and thyroid glands; (d) genetic theories of a programmed limit (an "aging clock") to the life span. No single theory is adequate in itself to explain the aging process. Rather it appears that a combination of theories or hypotheses, confirmed by research, will be needed to explain why we age.

SUGGESTED READINGS

Cart, C. S., Metress, E. K., & Metress, S. P. (1992). *Biological bases of human aging and disease.* Boston: Jones & Bartlett.

Fozard, J. L. (1990). Vision and hearing in aging. In J. E. Birren & K. W. Schaie (Eds.), *Handbook of the psychology of aging* (3rd ed., pp. 150–170). San Diego: Academic Press.

Hayflick, L. (1994). *How and why we age.* New York: Ballantine Books.

Rose, M. R. (1991). *Evolutionary biology of aging.* New York: Oxford University Press.

Spence, A. P. (1995). *Biology of human aging* (2nd ed.). Englewood Cliffs, NJ: Prentice-Hall.

Spirduso, W. W., & MacRae, P. G. (1990). Motor performance and aging. In J. E. Birren & K. W. Schaie (Eds.), *Handbook of the psychology of aging* (3rd ed., pp. 184–200). San Diego: Academic Press.

Weindruch, R. (1996, January). Caloric restriction and aging. *Scientific American,* pp. 46–52.

Whitbourne, K. (1996). *The aging individual.* New York: Springer.

Why we get old. (1997). In *Annual editions: Aging* (11th ed., pp. 19–22). Sluice Dock, CT: Dushkin Publishing Group/Brown & Benchmark.

CHAPTER 3

Health and Illness

Changes in sensory abilities are a part of normal aging, but so, unfortunately, is susceptibility to certain kinds of diseases and injuries. The percentage of people with health problems rises steadily with advancing age. All four indicators of health status—*mortality* (death rate), *morbidity* (disease frequency), *disability* (inability to perform normal activities), and *vitality* (energetic feelings)—are affected by aging. In addition to the increased likelihood of developing physical disorders, recuperating from the effects of such conditions becomes more difficult as one grows older. Although they may not be fatal or even incapacitating, many disorders are *chronic*, or of long duration, persisting at a certain level despite sustained efforts to treat and cope with them.

Young adults are, of course, not totally free of illness; in particular, they may suffer from various *acute* conditions (e.g., infective and parasitic illness, respiratory ailments, accidental injuries). However, people in their twenties and thirties typically rebound fairly quickly from an illness or injury and spend little time worrying about their health. This is true of young adults in general, and particularly so for those who take good care of themselves. Young adulthood is the time when vigor, vitality, strength, fitness, and stamina—all synonyms of "health"—are taken for granted.

Nine out of 10 adults between the ages of 17 and 44 describe their health as "good or excellent," and when they are hospitalized, it is usually due to an accident or childbirth (National Center for Health Statistics, 1992). By middle age, however, declines in physical functioning and health become increasingly more apparent, serving as a reminder of personal mortality and that we are not what we used to be. Both middle-aged and older adults are more vulnerable than younger adults to disease and hence more likely to require hospitalization and incur physical disability. Influenza and similar illnesses, which may be perceived as only uncomfortable nuisances by young adults, can lead to pneumonia and death in older adults. In fact, at one time, pneumonia caused the deaths of so many older people who were afflicted with other chronic illnesses that it was referred to as "the old man's friend." Final relief from the nonfatal chronic illnesses was provided by death from pneumonia.

Most middle-aged and older adults maintain that they are in good health, but, beginning in their forties and fifties, illness typically begins to take its toll in terms of energy, ability, productivity, and enjoyment of life. The number of people suffering from some chronic ailment, as well as the number of chronic illnesses that a typical person has, increase significantly after age 50. The debilitating effects of disease begin ever so slightly to affect the enjoyment of living, the sense of well-being, participation in most social roles, and treatment by other people, as well as one's interests, cognitive abilities, and overall attitude toward life. Then, the meanings of the terms "dis-ease" and "dis-order," in terms of their effects on personal feelings and the ability to get things done, become ever more apparent.

Although the probability of disease increases with age, it is unfair to characterize later adulthood as synonymous with "sickness." Only about 5% of all adults over age 65 reside in nursing homes or other institutions designed for long-term health care. Also incorrect is the popular notion that older people are hypochondriacs who needlessly complain without end about how sick they are. It was a middle-aged hypochondriac who arranged to have "Now do you believe me?" inscribed on his tombstone.

Sensible lifestyles and improved medical care have resulted in today's older adults being healthier than those of previous generations (Lentzner, Pamuk, Rhodenhiser, Rothberg, & Powell-Griner, 1992; Manton, Corder, & Stallard, 1993). In particular, individuals who have suffered heart attacks, cancer, and stroke—the three principal causes of death in middle- and late adulthood—are surviving longer than ever before.

This chapter and the next one deal with two of the three folk requirements for a happy life—health and wisdom. The third ingredient of the time-honored recipe for happiness—wealth—is considered in Chapter 11. Health, wealth, and wisdom are, of course, not independent states: Each ingredient is related to and interacts with the others in attaining the goal of a good, long life. Nevertheless, it would seem that "health" is more crucial than the other two parts of the mixture. No matter how wise or affluent one is, happiness is difficult to attain when one's health is poor.

DEMOGRAPHIC DIFFERENCES

Among the findings of the National Health Interview Study conducted in 1990 were that 92% of adults aged 25–44, 84% of adults aged 45–64, but only 72% of adults aged 65 and over evaluated their health as "Good to Excellent" (American Association of Retired Persons, 1996b; National Center for Health Statistics, 1991). To what extent is this age-related decline in ratings of personal health confirmed by patient information obtained by hospitals and physicians? Concerning the relationships of age to frequency and duration of treatment, data summarized by the American Association of Retired Persons (1996b) show that, in 1994, older adults accounted for 37% of all hospital stays and 47% of all days of care in hospitals. The average length of a hospital stay for older adults was 7.4 days, compared to only 4.8 days for those under 65. Older adults also averaged more contacts (11) with doctors compared with the average number of contacts (5) for those under 65. The average length of hospital stays and the number of physician contacts were greater for women than for men, for whites than for blacks, and for people with higher than lower incomes (National Center for Health Statistics, 1995).

Information on the relationship of age to disorders in general, as well as the 12 most frequent disorders, is provided by the 1994 national hospital discharge data summarized in Figure 3–1 (Graves & Gillum, 1996). For all except two of the categories listed—injury and poisoning and mental conditions—the numbers of individuals in the 65+ age groups are higher than those in the two younger age groups.

Chronological age is, of course, not the only demographic variable related to health and disease. Health status also varies with sex, race, socioeconomic status, nationality, and lifestyle. Arthritis, diabetes, and other less lethal conditions are more common in women, whereas more lethal conditions such as heart disease and cancer are more common in men. Type of health care received also varies with sex: Men with chronic disorders are more likely to be cared for at home by their wives, whereas older women with

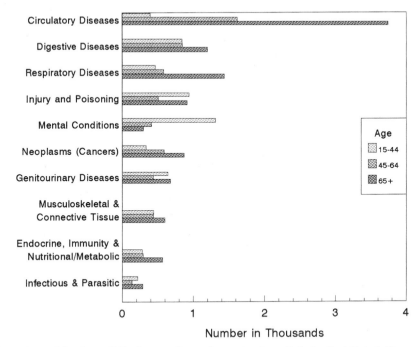

Figure 3–1   Number of discharges from short-stay hospitals by first-listed diagnosis, sex, and age: United States, 1994. (Based on data from Graves & Gillum, 1996.)

chronic disorders are more likely to be widows and thus cared for in nursing homes. Perhaps not surprising is the fact that being unmarried increases the chances of being restricted for both older men and women suffering from long-term illnesses (Lentzner et al., 1992).

With respect to ethnicity, whites (and Asians) are typically healthier than blacks and are more likely to view their health as good. In the 1990 National Health Interview Study, for example, older blacks were much more likely to rate their health as fair or poor (44%) than were older whites (27%) (National Center for Health Statistics, 1991). Older blacks also average significantly more days in bed in which their usual activities are restricted because of illness or injury (American Association of Retired Persons, 1996b). Throughout adulthood, the death rates for blacks are significantly higher than those for whites, and the two ethnic groups have different death rates for specific conditions. For example, among the disorders with the highest death rates, blacks have higher rates than whites for cancer, HIV infection, and diabetes mellitus, whereas whites have higher rates than blacks for heart disease and respiratory diseases (Singh, Kochanek, & MacDorman, 1996).

The fact that socioeconomic status is associated with ethnicity should be taken into account in evaluating the relationships of race to health and disease. Not surprisingly, people of higher socioeconomic status tend to enjoy better health and to rate themselves as healthier than those of lower socioeconomic status. Self-assessments of health status in Americans over 65 become increasingly more positive as family income, one of the principal factors in determining socioeconomic status, increases. Not only are poorer health and physical disabilities more common in older adults of lower socioeconomic status, but they are also evident at an earlier age than in those of higher socioeconomic status.

Health status and the prevalence of specific diseases vary with both nationality and area of residence within a particular nation. Diet, climate, sanitation, and other variables that affect health also vary with geography and undoubtedly affect the relationships between health, nationality, and area of residence. The rate of heart disease, for example, tends to be greater in areas where the typical diet is high in fats, and the incidence of hypertension is higher in areas where there is a great deal of salt in the diet. One study found that death rates for alcohol-caused cirrhosis of the liver and venereal disease were higher in California and other Western states than in most Eastern states, but that the rate of deaths due to diabetes and heart disease were significantly higher in the eastern United States than elsewhere in the country. These results were attributed to regional differences in diet and lifestyle (Nelson, 1982).

Genetic differences may, of course, play a role in determining the relationships of health and disease to sex, race, socioeconomic status, nationality, and other demographic variables. Perhaps of even greater importance are pollution, diet, poor sanitation, and other environmental factors. A factor that presumably contributes to the poorer health of men than women is that men are more likely to be employed in industrial areas where a great deal of environmental pollution exists. The relationship between health and socio-economic status may be attributable, at least to some extent, to the fact that people of meager economic resources tend to eat less nutritious food and enjoy less adequate health care than their more affluent contemporaries. Also associated with poorer health and higher death rates are smoking, alcohol and drug abuse, inadequate exercise, stress, and lack of social support (Brannon & Feist, 1992).

Advances in medicine and living conditions during this century have led to a healthier population than ever before. Improvements in sanitation, nutrition, mass immunization, and antibiotics have contributed to the control of many diseases. For example, measles, diphtheria, influenza, pneumonia, and tuberculosis are no longer as threatening as they once were. However, heart disease, cancer, cerebrovascular disorders—the three more frequent killers of Americans, and many other diseases are still common. In addition to acute and chronic diseases, accidents, murder, and suicide continue to take their toll in causing distress, disability, and death.

ACUTE AND NONLETHAL CHRONIC DISORDERS

Acute conditions are of relatively short duration and range in seriousness from a cut or bruised hand or foot to influenza and pneumonia. Infections, parasitic disorders, and respiratory illnesses of an acute nature decline from the twenties through the sixties and seventies. Because of their greater exposure to cigarette smoke and air pollutants, older men are particularly susceptible to acute respiratory disorders such as bronchitis, emphysema, and fibrosis. The frequencies of acute digestive disorders and accidental injuries decline from age 20 to 65 but show an upswing in old age. Prior to middle age, acute disorders are more common in women and lead to a longer period of restricted activity than in men, but after age 45, there is less difference between the sexes in this respect (National Center for Health Statistics, 1991).

In contrast to acute conditions, chronic disorders are of longer duration and more common among older adults. Chronic disorders can be potentially fatal, as is the case with heart disease, or nonfatal but nevertheless disabling and painful. Nonfatal chronic disorders such as arthritis, rheumatism, auditory and visual impairments, cataracts, osteoporosis and other orthopedic conditions, and varicose veins increase fairly steadily in frequency from middle- and late adulthood (see Figure 3–2). Arthritis and visual impairments are more common among older women, whereas older men are more likely to have hearing problems. Certain chronic conditions, such as hernias and hemorrhoids, are less serious, whereas others, such as prostate disorders, chronic respiratory illness, diabetes mellitus, and hypertension are of greater concern. Less serious chronic conditions usually impose few limitations on

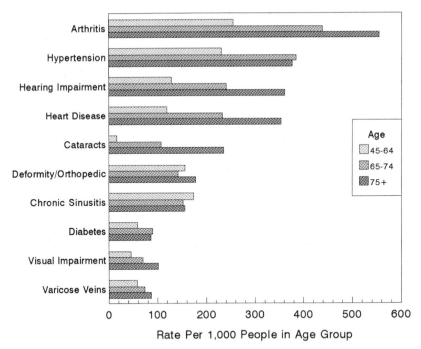

Figure 3–2 The top 10 chronic disease conditions. (Based on data from National Center for Health Statistics, "Current Estimates from the National Health Interview Survey." *Vital and Health Statistics Series* 10, No. 176, October 1990.)

activities, but the limitations on activity imposed by more serious disorders can be quite restrictive. In addition, even when it is not life threatening, a persistent illness and associated disability can have a debilitating effect on a person's sense of life-satisfaction and well-being.

Arthritis

As shown in Figure 3–2, approximately half of the age 65 and over segment of the population suffers from arthritis and 40% suffer from hypertension. Chronic *arthritis* consists of inflamed joints and associated pain, stiffness, movement difficulties, and possible structural changes. Arthritis increases in frequency after middle adulthood and is more common in women than men. The hips, knees, and other large joints are most commonly affected, but the disorder can also attack the smaller joints of the ankles, fingers, and vertebrae. Because of the pain and movement problems associated with arthritis, affected individuals experience difficulties in getting around and engaging in routine activities.

There are various "types" of arthritis, including osteoarthritis, rheumatoid arthritis, gout, and collagen disease. *Osteoarthritis*, which is the most common type and appears to have a hereditary component, is associated with pain in the joints, degeneration and loss of cartilage at the ends of bones, and the formation of sharp "spurs" in the joints. Most likely to be affected are the large, weight-bearing joints of the knees, ankles, hips. *Rheumatoid arthritis*, characterized by swelling and stiffness in the hands, wrists, and feet, is also potentially deforming and quite disabling. Thought to be due to a breakdown in the immune system, rheumatoid arthritis is more common in women than in men. In contrast, *gout*, which is associated with swelling and pain in the ankles, knees, elbows, wrists, hands, and toes (especially the great toe) is more common in men than in women. A diagnostic sign of gout is an excess of uric acid in the blood.

Osteoporosis

The loss of minerals in the bones that accompanies aging reduces bone mass and increases the porosity and brittleness of bones. The result may be chronic pain in the joints of the lower spine and hips, a height reduction of several inches, other skeletal deformities (e.g., dowager's hump), and an increased danger of fractures to the vertebrae, hips, ribs, and wrists. These are the symptoms of *osteoporosis*, a disorder that is four times more common among postmenopausal women than men in the same age range (45–50 years). Osteoporosis affects almost half of all women over 50, and as many as 90% of women over 70. It is more common among whites and Asians than among blacks and is also associated with chronic hyperthyroidism, long-term steroid therapy, and heredity.

Foods rich in calcium and vitamin D, or daily supplements of these and other substances (e.g., estrogens, fluoride, vitamin K, magnesium, growth hormones) are prescribed treatments for osteoporosis. Preventive treatments include hormone replacement therapy and progesterone, and a program of exercises that place stress on the long bones (walking, jogging, dancing, bicycle riding). Also recommended is that the intake of alcohol and certain drugs, as well cigarette smoking, be controlled.

LIFE-THREATENING DISORDERS

The 10 leading causes of death in the United States in 1995 were, in order, diseases of heart, malignant neoplasms, cerebrovascular diseases, chronic obstructive pulmonary diseases, accidents and adverse effects, pneumonia and influenza, diabetes mellitus, HIV infection, suicide, and chronic liver disease and cirrhosis (Rosenberg, Ventura, Maurer, Heuser, & Freedman,

MY LIFE 3–1

Back Pain

Sometimes I think of my back pain as a familiar companion. He may not be overly friendly, but he certainly has remained with me for a long time.

I can remember when we first met. I was sitting on a stool at a punch card machine, and all of a sudden he was there. Although I have often wished it were otherwise, I knew then that he was determined to stay with me—if not forever, at least until I gave up the ghost.

One thing he did do was provide me with the opportunity to learn about doctors and what they can and cannot do. In my eagerness to be rid of him, I consulted internists, orthopedists, neurologists, neurosurgeons, osteopaths, chiropractors, acupuncturists, naturopaths, and even psychiatrists. I was prodded, punctured, massaged, radiated, needled, vibrated, and electrically stimulated. I had X rays, myelograms, CAT scans, MRI scans, PET scans, muscle examinations, and many other kinds of tests. I took aspirin, Indocin, Tofranil, acetaminophen, ibuprofen, Prozac, cortisone, and myriad other pain killers, stimulants, and relaxants. I did exercises, wore a Taylor back brace, had hot packs, took steam baths and whirlpool baths, and had my neck and back twisted and cracked. Some of the treatments had what I now realize was a placebo effect, but I began to suspect that it was more than balanced out by an iatrogenic effect. Any improvement I experienced was temporary and not worth the cost and discomfort of the treatment.

Eventually, I resigned myself to the notion that my back pain was like the man who came to dinner and decided to stay. But a funny thing happened on the road to despair. When I simply decided to quit worrying about the pain, when I learned to avoid situations in which the pain was intense and to stop immediately and relax when it came calling, it abated and was more tolerable. I gave up looking for a dramatic cure and learned, if not to love, at least to feel at home with a certain amount of pain.

Today, my old companion is still with me, but he is not as irksome as he once was. Somehow, we have worked out a kind of modus vivendi in which I don't concern myself so much about him and he reciprocates by not bothering me as much. Perhaps this is the way it is with all lasting companionships. We only learn to live together when we stop trying to change each other, take each others' moods and idiosyncracies into account, and thank our lucky stars that we are able to get along as well as we do. It also helps to know that everything ends sometime.

1996). With the exception of HIV infection, and chronic liver disease and cirrhosis, the death rates for all of these disorders increase steadily with age.[1]

Circulatory-System Diseases

The elevation of blood pressure, and diastolic pressure in particular, known as *hypertension*, is fairly common in middle- and late life and especially among older women. The average blood pressure for adults is 120/80, but between 110/70 and 140/90 is not considered a problem. When a person's blood pressure goes over 140/90, however, some form of treatment—losing weight and keeping it off, eating less salt, cutting down on alcohol, getting more exercise, and/or prescribed drugs—is required.

High blood pressure can be a serious problem, but it is usually viewed as potentially fatal only by virtue of its association with heart (*hypertensive heart disease*), kidney, (*hypertensive renal disease*), or cerebrovascular disease. The designation *essential hypertension* is used when no other signs of disease are present, or *malignant hypertension* when the disease has progressed rapidly. Hypertension is significantly more common among blacks than among whites, the difference between the percentage of black and white women with hypertension (39% vs. 25%) being especially pronounced (American Heart Association, 1995). Treatment for hypertension includes dieting, reduced salt intake, relaxation, and various prescription drugs. Considering the American penchant for eating, and salty foods in particular, complying with the first part of this treatment is often difficult.

Heart disease, by far the most common cause of death in the United States, may be caused by blood clots, holes in the chamber walls of the heart, or defective heart valves. Both stationary (*thrombus*) and moving (*embolus*) blood clots are due principally to *arteriosclerosis*, an abnormal hardening and thickening of the arteries caused by fatty (*atherosclerosis*) and calcium deposits known as *plaque* on arterial walls. The result is a narrowing of the coronary arteries, which carry blood to the heart muscle. Thus, the heart must work harder, increasing the blood pressure and the likelihood of clotting. Inadequate supply of blood and oxygen to the muscles of the heart can produce chest pains or *angina*. In advanced cases of arteriosclerosis, the inadequate blood flow causes heart muscle to die and precipitates a heart attack or *myocardial infarction*. The symptoms of a heart attack include a sudden dull pain and a feeling of heaviness in the chest that moves down the arms, unrelieved indigestion, pain in the jaw or shoulders, and shortness of breath. These symptoms vary with the age of the individual, severe chest pains being less common in older adults.

Heart failure can also result in the third most common cause of death in

[1]The death rate for HIV infection peaks between ages 35 and 44, whereas the death rate for chronic liver disease and cirrhosis peaks between the ages of 65 and 74 (Singh, et al., 1996).

the United States—*cerebrovascular accident* (CVA), or stroke. A stroke, which may be even more disabling than a heart attack, is caused by an embolism (clot) or hemorrhage in a small ("small stroke") or large ("major stroke") blood vessel of the brain. Strokes come on suddenly, leading to dizziness or unconsciousness, temporary dimness or loss of vision, sudden falling, temporary loss of speech or difficulty speaking or understanding speech, and sudden weakness or numbness in an arm, a leg, the face, or on one side of the body (American Heart Association, 1995).

As shown in Figure 3–3, circulatory diseases of all kinds increase in frequency with age. On the whole, circulatory diseases are also more common among men than women and among blacks than whites (Singh, et al., 1996). Rates of death due to heart disease are, however, substantially lower for Asian/Pacific Islander, Hispanic, and Native Americans than for whites in the older adult range (National Center for Health Statistics, 1991). The lower rates of heart disease among Asians has been attributed, at least in part, to the higher amounts of vegetables and lower amounts of animal fat in their diets than in those of North Americans and Western Europeans. The heavy vegetarian diet of the Japanese, for example, enables them to maintain a low blood-cholesterol level. The high salt intake of the typical Japanese diet, however, increases blood pressure and thereby the likelihood of developing hypertension. The typical diet of the French is also instructive: large meals

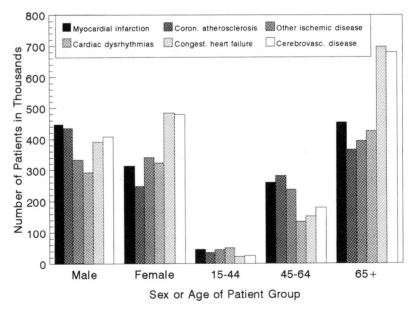

Figure 3–3   **Number of discharges with first-listed diagnosis of diseases of the circulatory system from short-stay hospitals by first-listed diagnosis, sex, and age: United States, 1994.** (Based on data from Graves & Gillum, 1996.)

accompanied by wine but few between-meal snacks. This diet presumably contributes to the lower rate of cardiovascular disease found among the French than among North Americans.

In addition to varying with sex, race, and nationality, the incidence of cardiovascular diseases is related to heredity and lifestyle. Among the lifestyle factors of importance are lack of physical inactivity, heavy smoking, obesity, and psychological stress. Increased attention to these and other lifestyle factors has undoubtedly contributed to the reduction in heart disease in the United States since 1960. For example, it is now generally accepted that by increasing cardiac output, blood flow, and oxygen consumption, and lowering blood pressure, regular and moderate physical exercise reduces the incidence of cardiovascular disease (Blair et al., 1989; Hill, Storandt, & Malley, 1993; Paffenbarger, Hyde, Wing, & Hsieh, 1986). Another controllable factor in heart disease and several other disorders is cigarette smoking. Heavy cigarette smoking causes reduced cardiac output, increased heart rate and blood pressure, and constriction of the peripheral blood vessels. Recent increases in smoking by women, and older women in particular, have contributed to the rise in smoking-related illness.

Obesity, which is associated with hypertension and digestive disorders, is also a factor in heart disease. A standard way of describing obesity is in terms of the *body mass index* (BMI), computed as 697.5 times the weight (in pounds) divided by the square of the height (in inches). The World Health Organization's international standard for measuring obesity is a BMI above 25, but the U.S. government has defined obesity as a BMI of 27.8 or over for men and 27.3 or over for women (Willman & Colker, 1996). To maintain the BMI at an acceptable level, it is recommended that a prudent diet, in which 30% or less of the calories are obtained from fats, be followed.

The incidence of heart disease has also been found to be greater among single, widowed, and divorced people than among married people (Lynch, 1977) and higher among people with so-called *Type A personality*. This is a personality pattern characterized by a combination of behaviors, including aggressiveness, competitiveness, hostility, quick actions, and constant striving. Reviews of research on Type A and related, disease-prone personalities have concluded that a personality characterized by depression, anger/hostility, and anxiety is an important contributor to coronary heart disease (Friedman, 1990; Friedman & Booth-Kewley, 1987). Finally, perhaps related to stress is the finding that the risk of a heart attack in the working population is significantly greater on Monday than on any other day of the week (Willich et al., 1992).

Cancer

Malignant neoplasms, or cancers, are second only to heart disease as a cause of death in American adults. Cancer may attack the skin, the oral

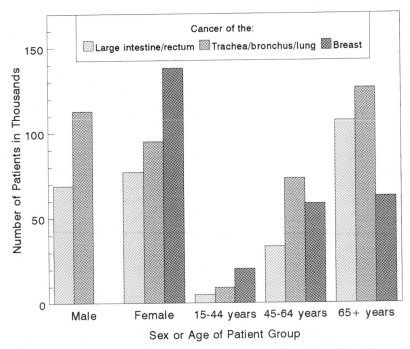

Figure 3–4 Number of discharges with first-listed diagnosis of malignant neoplasms from short-stay hospitals by first-listed diagnosis, sex, and age: United States, 1994. (Based on data from Graves & Gillum, 1996.)

cavity, the digestive organs, the respiratory organs, the breasts, the genital organs, the urinary organs, the blood, and other body sites. Death rates are highest for cancer of the respiratory and digestive organs, but cancer of the breast, which is more treatable, also occurs at a higher frequency. As shown in Figure 3–4, the incidence of these three types of cancer increases during adulthood. In general, the death rates for all types of cancer are greater during later adulthood than during young and middle adulthood. However, cancer also occurs among young adults and children: Leukemia and brain tumors are more common in childhood, whereas cervical, lung, and stomach cancer increase during the middle thirties. Finally, the frequency of cancer of the breast, uterus, colon, stomach, and liver is highest in older adulthood (Krakoff, 1993). Middle-aged and older women, in particular, are at high risk for breast cancer, and older men are at high risk for lung cancer and prostate cancer.

The incidence and death rates of different types of cancer vary with ethnicity and sex. In the United States, for all ages combined, the highest rate of death due to malignant neoplasms and respiratory cancer occurs among black males, followed by white males, black females, and white females. The death rate for breast cancer is also higher among black women than white women (National Center for Health Statistics, 1995). The cancer death rate for men surpasses that for women in all age ranges except ages 25–44, when the rate is slightly higher for both white and black women than for men (Singh et al., 1996). Note that these are the childbearing years for women.

Because cancer often goes undetected until it is well advanced, it is sometimes referred to as the "silent killer." Emphasis should be placed on early detection and diagnosis, however, because treatment is usually more effective in the early stages of the disease. It is recommended that persons having one or more of the following "seven warning signs" of cancer should consult a physician: (1) a sore that doesn't heal; (2) change in a wart or mole; (3) a lump or thickening in the breast or elsewhere on the body; (4) persisting hoarseness or cough; (5) chronic indigestion or difficulty swallowing; (6) unusual bleeding or discharge; (7) change in bowel or bladder habits.

As is the case with heart disease, an ounce of prevention is probably worth a pound of cure when it comes to cancer; early diagnosis is critical to surviving cancer at any age. A number of potential carcinogenic (cancer-producing) agents, ranging from alcohol to sunlight, have been studied. Polluting physical and chemical substances in the environment, nutritional deficiencies, and excessive intake of fats, hormones, and radiation have all been examined as possible contributing causes to cancers of the liver, skin, bladder, lungs, larynx, esophagus, liver, breast, uterus, vagina, and prostate. Many of these agents have marginal, if any, significant effects on the development of cancers and, in any case, may not be under direct control. One of the most preventable lifestyle factors implicated in cancer, however, is cigarette smoking. It has been linked to over 80% of all cases of lung cancer and 30% of all deaths due to cancer (American Cancer Society, 1987).

Standard treatments for cancer include radiation therapy (external administration of X rays, internal administration of radioactive materials), chemotherapy (antimetabolites, antibiotics, metallic salts, hormones), surgery, and supportive treatments. Although a great deal of media attention has been devoted to the role of psychological factors such as depression, coping style, and internal locus of control in the etiology and treatment of cancer, related research findings have not been impressive (Jamison, Burish, & Wallston, 1987; Richardson, Zarnegar, Bisno, & Levine, 1990).

Respiratory Disorders

Chronic obstructive pulmonary diseases, including bronchitis, emphysema, asthma, and allied conditions, ranked fourth as causes of death in the United States in 1994, while pneumonia and influenza ranked sixth (Rosenberg et al., 1996). Over 100,000 people in this country died of obstructive pulmonary diseases, and over 80,000 died of pneumonia and influenza in that year.

With the exception of deaths caused by asthma, which increase steadily until age 75 and then decline, deaths due to most respiratory disorders decline during childhood and then increase in frequency throughout adulthood. The death rate for chronic obstructive pulmonary diseases is slightly higher for males than females, but the reverse is true for deaths caused by pneumonia and influenza. Furthermore, the death rates for almost all respiratory diseases are higher for whites—male and female—than for blacks.

Cigarette smoking, air pollution, stress, and sedentary habits are among the risk factors for respiratory illnesses. Because of the ready availability of pneumococcal and influenza vaccines, influenza and pneumonia are much less common than they once were. Despite advances in the prevention and treatment of these two acute disorders, many patients whose bodies have been ravaged by heart disease, arthritis, rheumatism, and other diseases may eventually die from pneumonia. Older adults, in particular, are highly susceptible to influenza, pneumonia, and tuberculosis.

HIV Infection

HIV infection, or AIDS, was the eighth leading cause of death in the United States in 1995. During that year, an estimated 42,506 people in this country died from complications caused by this disorder, a rate of 16.2 per 100,000 population (Rosenberg et al., 1996). The human immunodeficiency virus (HIV) attacks the body's immune system and makes the infected person more vulnerable to a host of viral, bacterial, and malignant disease. The virus can be transmitted by hypodermic needles or drug paraphernalia, by transfusions of infected blood, and from an infected mother to her child during delivery. The principal method of transmission of the virus is from men having sex with men, followed by drug injections, heterosexual contact, blood transfusion, and use of HIV-infected blood coagulants by hemophiliacs.

Death due to HIV infection is more common during young and middle adulthood (ages 25–44), in men than in women, and higher in blacks—male and female—than in whites. However, the disorder is no respecter of age. For example, the HIV death rate for men between the ages of 45 and 64 was 26.4 for whites and 127.1 for blacks in 1994 (Singh et al., 1996).

HIV is a progressive disorder, in that infected individuals do not seem to be sick at first but often develop serious infections or cancers after several years. The symptoms of HIV infection—feelings of tiredness, confusion, loss of appetite, and swollen glands—are not unlike those accompanying many other illnesses and are therefore easy to confuse with them. Additional symptoms are problems of balance and coordination, in addition to declines in memory, concentration, decision-making ability, and self-control. The presence of such symptoms, combined with a positive blood test for HIV, leads to a diagnosis of *AIDS* (acquired immunodeficiency syndrome). Death may not come for several years in an infected individual, but when it does, the typical immediate cause is pneumocystis carinii pneumonia (PCP) or a rare type of skin cancer known as Kaposi's sarcoma.

Neither a vaccine to prevent HIV infection nor a cure for AIDS is presently available, but certain drugs can inhibit the spread of the virus. Efforts to control the AIDS epidemic have involved health education programs designed to increase public knowledge of the disorder and how it spreads. Such programs emphasize condom usage, decreasing the number of sex partners, other safe-sex practices (including abstinence), and an avoidance of needle sharing among intravenous drug users.

Organic Brain Disorders

Even when it does not precipitate a stroke, chronic hardening and thickening of the arteries in the brain in old age—*cerebral arteriosclerosis*—can lead to confusion, disorientation, incoherence, restlessness, and occasional hallucinations. The patient may complain of headaches, dizziness, and fatigue, and sometimes paralysis on one side of the body and/or seizures. Other psychological symptoms, such as anxiety and depression, may also occur as a result of the stress precipitated by the disorder. Organic brain damage in later life also produces symptoms of mental disorders, as in multi-infarct dementia and Alzheimer's disease. Both of these disorders are associated with the degeneration of cerebral neurons, leading to atrophy and related destruction of brain tissue. Becoming more apparent after age 65 and peaking around age 70, approximately one-third of the over-80 population and half of the nursing home population suffer from these disorders.

The symptoms of *multi-infarct dementia*, which is associated with hypertension and vascular damage, are related to localized areas of dying or dead cerebral tissue known as *infarcts*. These symptoms include memory defect, periods of confusion, and lowered work efficiency; abstract thinking, judgment, and impulse control can also be affected. The patient may complain of dizziness, weakness, confusion, and fatigue, and may experience episodes of sham emotion, difficulty swallowing, disorientation, and problems in assimilating new experience. As time passes, memory becomes worse, speech and the performance of routine tasks are affected, personal habits deteriorate, little interest is shown in external events, and the patient becomes preoccupied with eating, eliminating, and other body functions.

Less common than multi-infarct dementia but still a serious disorder in the older adult population is *Alzheimer's disease*. This disease is characterized by a gradual deterioration of memory and other cognitive abilities, disorientation, and disintegration of personality and behavior. Mental alertness, adaptability, sociability, and tolerance for new things or changes in routine all decline gradually. The individual becomes more self-centered in his or her thoughts and activities, untidy, agitated, and preoccupied with natural functions. Although Alzheimer's disease has stimulated a great deal of research and attention by the media, its exact cause is still unknown.

Other Disorders

Many other diseases affect adults and take their toll in discontented and lost lives in the United States each year. Among these are viral hepatitis, meningococcal infection, syphilis, and tuberculosis; diseases of internal organs such as the liver (hepatitis), the gallbladder, the kidneys, the pancreas (diabetes), and the prostate gland; and blood diseases such as the anemias. Some disorders are more common in one sex than the other.

Improvements in prenatal care and delivery during this century have dramatically reduced the incidence of maternal mortality in the United States. The maternal mortality rate was 8.3 per 100,000 live births in 1994, but the rate was three times as high for black women as for white women. Furthermore, the group of 328 women in this country reported as dying of maternal causes in 1994 consisted only of those who died of complications of pregnancy, childbirth, and the puerperium, and not of all deaths in pregnant women. Of the 328 deaths, 41 were attributed to "pregnancy with abortive outcome" and 267 to "direct obstetrical causes." The most common cause of maternal mortality during pregnancy was ectopic pregnancy, in which the fetus is in an abnormal position. The most common direct obstetrical causes were hemorrhage of pregnancy and childbirth and toxemia of pregnancy (Singh et al., 1996).

ACCIDENTS

An *accident* is an unplanned event that results in bodily injury and/or property damage. Accidents claimed 89,703 lives in the United States in 1995, 41,786 of which were motor-vehicle accidents. The death rate for unintentional injuries due to accidents is higher for males than for females in all age groups and higher for blacks than for whites after age 24 (Rosenberg et al., 1996). The death rate for firearm injuries is higher for males than females and higher for blacks than whites. The highest death rate due to motor-vehicle crashes occurs among Native American males, followed by black males, Hispanic males, and white males, in that order. The lowest death rate for motor-vehicle crashes in the United States is for Asians—male and female (National Center for Health Statistics, 1995).

The National Safety Council classifies accidents according to type and class. The *type* of accident indicates where it occurred or what caused it. Motor-vehicle accidents are the most common type, followed by falls, poisoning, drowning, fires and burns, suffocation (ingested), firearms, and gas/vapor poisoning. As shown in Figure 3–5, the death rate due to motor vehicles

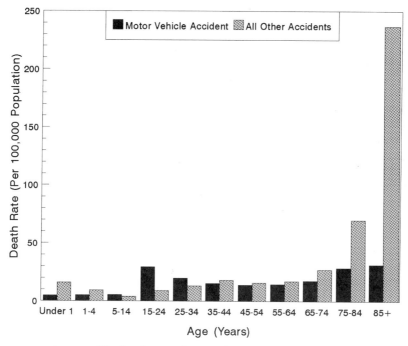

Figure 3–5   Age-specific death rates for accidents and adverse effects, 1994. [Based on data from Anderson, Kochanek, & Murphy, 1997.]

increases only slightly with age, but the frequency of deaths caused by other types of accidents as a group rises dramatically in later life. The rise in accidental deaths in old age is attributable in large measure to an increase in deaths due to falls, the second most common cause of death after age 55. Poisoning by solids and liquids is the second most common cause of accidental death for adults aged 25 through 54. With the exception of deaths due to falls, fires and burns, and the ingestion of food or other objects, deaths caused by accidents are more than twice as numerous for males as for females (National Safety Council, 1996).

The *class* of an accident is determined by where (in what location) it occurred. As shown in Table 3–1, the frequency of accidental injuries in 1995 varied with both the class or place of the accident and the age of the victim. Falls are the most frequent type of accidents in the home, followed by poisoning, fires, suffocation, firearms, and drowning, in that order. Regarding places in the home where accidents are most likely to occur, they are most common in bedrooms, kitchens, and the yard. Next to motor-vehicle accidents, falls are the most common class of accidents occurring in public. Falls are also the second-ranked cause of death and the third-ranked cause of injury from work-related accidents. However, careful attention to safety rules and practices in

TABLE 3–1 Number of Episodes of Accidental Injuries to Adults
in United States in 1994, by Age and Class or Place of Accident

Class or place	Age			
	18–24	25–44	45–64	65+
Moving motor vehicle	622,000	1,628,000	609,000	197,000
Traffic	565,000	1,522,000	554,000	139,000
Work	1,810,000	6,003,000	916,000	48,000
Place of accident				
Home	1,057,000	5,205,000	3,554,000	3,266,000
Street, highway	775,000	2,713,000	762,000	625,000
Industrial place	1,334,00	4,324,000	862,000	48,000
Other	3,337,000	4,134,000	1,059,000	680,000
All episodes	7,827,000	20,322,000	8,411,000	5,973,000

Source: Data from National Safety Council, 1996.

job and other organizational settings has lowered the accident rates in those
places (National Safety Council, 1996).

Accidents are more likely to occur at night than during the day, on
weekends, during holidays, during the summer and fall months, and during
times of economic expansion. Unsafe conditions or situations do not typically cause accidents by themselves; they must be combined with unsafe acts.
Consumption of alcohol and drugs is a particularly important unsafe act that
is closely related to motor-vehicle accidents and fatalities. Speeding, failing
to yield the right of way, and driving on the wrong side of the road are other
unsafe driving practices.

Unsafe acts vary with chronological age, health, fatigue, intelligence,
personality, and other "person" variables. For example, motor-vehicle accidents are the primary cause of accidental death in the late teens and twenties
(see Figure 3–5). Male drivers around age 20 are more likely than those in
other age groups to be involved in and killed in automobile crashes or to kill
pedestrians. Unlike the slower response times, greater cautiousness, and
physical disabilities in adults over age 65, which contribute to the somewhat
higher accident rate in this age group than in middle-aged adults, the higher
accidental death rate in teenagers and young adults reflects inexperience,
excessive risk taking, alcohol or drug abuse, and desire for peer approval.
Other causes of accidents and accidental death also vary with age. For example, drownings are the second cause of accidental death prior to the forties,
and falls are second from ages 45 to 74.

Death rates for non-motor-vehicle accidents are particularly high after
age 65, when sensorimotor abilities decline and people spend more time in
the home. Older adults are less likely than younger ones to see a small object
on the floor or counter, an open door or other projecting object, or to smell
something that is burning. And even when a potentially dangerous condition

or situation is perceived, an older adult may not respond quickly or precisely enough.

The frequency of injuries of various types sustained in accidents also varies with the sex of the victim. The fact that the number of individuals in the 18–44 year age range is greater than the number in the 45 and over range who are involved in accidents accounts, at least in part, for the greater number of injuries in the lower adult age bracket. However, sex interacts with age: The number of injuries sustained by women between 18 and 44 years of age is less than the number sustained by men in that age range, but the number of injuries for women who are 45 years and older is greater than that for men of the same age. This difference may be attributable in part to the fact that there are more older women than older men, and that older women who sustain falls are more likely than older men to be seriously injured (U.S. Bureau of the Census, 1990a).

Although the notion of an *accident-prone personality* has not stood the test of time, research evidence indicates that personality has some relationship to accidents. It has been found, for example, that, as a group, accident repeaters are less emotionally stable, more hostile toward authority, and higher in anxiety (Shaw & Sichel, 1971). In another study, accident repeaters had more problems getting along with other people, and their work histories were less stable than those of nonrepeaters (Niemcryk, Jenkins, Rose, & Hurst, 1987). From these and other studies (e.g., Hansen, 1989), it can be concluded that personality variables are related to all kinds of accidents in all sorts of populations.

HEALTH MAINTENANCE
AND DISEASE PREVENTION

As noted previously in this chapter, the occurrence and severity of many kinds of diseases are associated with the habits and lifestyle of the person. Lifestyle is, of course, not the only causative factor in promoting disease, but it is an important one and one about which the individual himself can do something. In young adulthood, the ability of the body to ward off disease and to cope with the effects of accidents and stress is at a maximum, but as one grows older, the body's ability to deal with these problems declines. Unfortunately, the health and energy of young adults may obscure their perception of the negative consequences of a poor diet, smoking, alcohol abuse, and other insults to the body that will have carryover effects on their health in middle- and late life.

Even in old age, there are many things that can be done to maintain a reasonably healthy state and consequently continue to enjoy life. Among the recommendations for adding both years to life and life to years are to maintain physical fitness and positive wellness by proper exercise, nutritional awareness, effective stress management, and refraining from or reducing cigarette smoking and consumption of alcoholic beverages. But despite the efforts of schools, the government, and other organizational spokespersons to convince people to get a good night's rest, eat breakfast, stop smoking, drink alcohol in moderation (if at all), and exercise, a substantial portion of the population continues to resist those recommendations (see Figure 3–6). The consequence of such an unhealthy lifestyle is pain, disease, and a shortening of the life span.

Exercise

It is a well-known fact that regular exercise can reduce the severity of system disorders (Hill, Storandt, & Malley, 1993). Oxygen consumption, ventilation capacity, cardiac output, blood flow, muscle tonus, muscle strength, and the flexibility of the joints can all be increased by exercises such as walking, swimming, calisthenics, jogging, and other moderate aerobic exercises (Blumentahl et al., 1991). Exercise also results in reduced body fats, poisons, blood pressure, the response times of body cells and organs, and nervous tension. Regular physical exercise also enhances one's sense of well-being, feelings of self-efficacy and control, the ability to cope with psychologically stressful situations, and general psychological health (King, Taylor, Haskell, & DeBusk, 1989). It can also have beneficial effects on depression,

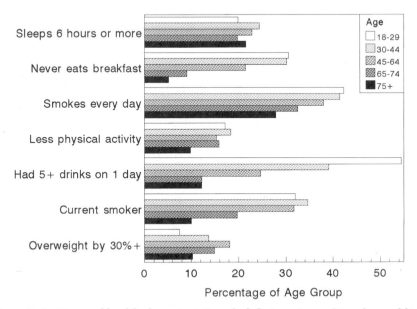

Figure 3–6   Personal health characteristics of adult Americans. (Based on published data from National Health Interview Survey.)

anxiety, and other symptoms of psychological disorder (McNeil, LeBlanc, & Joyner, 1991; Petruzello, Landers, Hatfield, Kubitz, & Salazar, 1991).

Older adults do not exercise as much as younger adults, particularly strenuous aerobic exercise such as jogging or running. The difference between older and younger adults in the amount of moderate exercise is small, but even moderate exercise drops off significantly after age 75 (see Figure 3–6).

Nutrition

Advances in technology, agriculture, and product distribution in the developed nations of the world during the twentieth century have resulted in increased eating and decreased physical activity. For example, the advent of remote controls for television and other electronic gadgets has even eliminated the need to engage in the minor exercise of getting up to turn on, turn off, or adjust the television set. In the United States, the number of overweight people is now greater than the number of normal-size people ("Overweight People Now a Majority," 1996).

Although our culture does not view being underweight as a particularly serious problem, many young women with anorexia nervosa suffer from malnutrition and thereby become more susceptible to disease. Interestingly, research has demonstrated that sharply reducing caloric intake while keeping the intake of proteins, vitamins, and minerals at recommended levels can assist in the avoidance of many diseases and slow the aging of various body systems (Weindruch & Walford, 1988).

Malnutrition in two age groups—schoolchildren and older adults—has presumably declined as a result of the efforts of various organizations, but the problem has not been solved. The high cost of food and the lack of available transportation contributes to poor nutrition among older Americans. Social isolation, which is more common among the elderly than other age groups, also affects the judicious selection and enjoyment of foods, encouraging unplanned snacks and unbalanced diets. Be that as it may, most older Americans have better eating habits than their younger contemporaries. Most older adults eat breakfast every day, are less likely to eat between meals, and are not as likely to be overweight. The fattest Americans are people in their fifties: According to one survey, 73% of men and 64% of women in this age group are overweight ("Overweight People Now a Majority," 1996).

Good eating habits among senior citizens are encouraged by the low-cost "Meals on Wheels" provided by the Nutrition Program for Older Americans. Even more extensive is the Food Stamp Program, which involves all age groups and is directed toward low-income families. The stamps may be exchanged for foodstuffs, or for meals delivered to the homes of persons over 60. Several other federally sponsored programs also make emergency food supplies and services available to older adults with low incomes.

Unlike both active and passive smoking, which are extremely important causative factors in cancer, heart disease, and certain other disorders, alcohol is not always bad for a person. Alcohol abuse, which is most common in middle age, certainly contributes to diabetes, neurological problems, and many other disorders. However, by increasing the supply of high-density lipoprotein (HDL), which reduces the level of cholesterol in the blood, a moderate intake of alcohol can help to reduce the probability of developing blood clots and prevent clogged arteries (Cahalan, 1991).

Long-Term Health Care

Most Americans are not physically handicapped, but the percentage of adults who experience difficulties in performing daily activities increases with age. These *activities of daily living* (ADLs), which reflect the person's capacity for self-care, refer to the following sociobiological functions: eating, bathing, dressing, transferring in and out of a bed or chair, walking, getting outside, and using the toilet. More complex behaviors that enable the person to live independently in the community are referred to as *instrumental activities of daily living* (IADL). IADLs include doing light housework, managing money, shopping for groceries or clothes, using the telephone, preparing meals, and taking medications.

Impairments in ADLs and IADLs vary not only with age but with sex, ethnicity, and other demographic and personal variables. For example, the percentage of Americans over age 65 who, because of physical disabilities or functional limitations, require assistance with everyday activities is higher for women than for men, higher for blacks and Hispanics than for whites, and higher for people with smaller than those with larger incomes (U.S. Bureau of the Census, 1990b).

Despite some functional impairments, the majority of Americans with physical disabilities do their best to compensate by managing their lives and activities in ways that take their limitations into account. They experience problems but are not, do not need to be, and do not want to reside in a nursing home or other institution. They are usually able to obtain sufficient long-term help from their spouses, other relatives, friends, home health care services, and community service organizations to enable them to remain in the community (see Dey, 1996).

A small minority (approximately 5%) of older adults are in institutions at any one time, and most remain for only a few months. Most are older white female patients in nursing homes, whose numbers have increased since the enactment of Medicare and Medicaid. They usually suffer from several chronic disorders, the primary ones being cardiovascular diseases, cancer, and chronic brain disorders. In all likelihood, attempts were made initially to care for them at home, but, when they became disoriented and confused, wandered away from home, were incontinent, and otherwise revealed a need for more extensive care, they were placed in a nursing home. The transfer was seldom a pleasant one: Moving to new surroundings that lack privacy, have different rules and regulations, patients and staff from other social and cultural backgrounds, and separation from relatives and friends is often traumatic.

Like most institutions, nursing homes vary widely in the quality of care they provide. Skilled nursing facilities are usually best—but also the most expensive, followed by intermediate care facilities and nonskilled institutional or private home facilities. Government-run homes tend to be better than private homes, but this depends to some extent on cost. For people who qualify, a substantial percentage of nursing home care is paid for by Medicaid (see Figure 3–7). The result has been a profit bonanza for some entrepreneurs, and the quality of care has not always kept pace with the profits.

Because of extensive abuses and inadequate care, many nursing homes have not been able to meet federal standards for care. Passage of the Nursing Home Quality Reform Act (1987) established stricter standards for nursing homes, penalties for violating them, and a patients' "bill of rights" (e.g., right to privacy, right to voice grievances and have them responded to promptly). A combination of poor nursing home care and increased cost has led to a

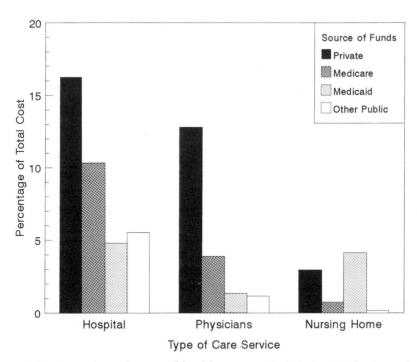

Figure 3–7   Percentage of personal health care cost in U.S. in 1993 by type of care and source of funds. (Based on data from National Center for Health Statistics, 1993.)

movement away from hospital-based and nursing home treatment to home health care, day-care centers, and preventive medicine clinics in recent years. However, institution-based treatment is an entrenched part of the medical model of personal health care in the United States; alternative treatment models have been widely discussed but not readily put in place. Additional material on nursing homes is presented in Chapter 9.

Financing the American Health Care System

The burgeoning cost of health care in the United States is a source of great concern to the federal government, private citizens, and health practitioners. Expenditures for health care are the second largest item in the federal budget, even larger than defense appropriations. These costs have increased at an alarming rate during the past three decades, accounting for a larger share of the gross domestic product than that of any other major industrialized country in the world. National health care expenditures are now almost $1 trillion annually, over one-third of which goes for hospital care and another 20% for physicians' services (National Center for Health Statistics, 1995).

As seen in Figure 3–7, a major portion of the cost of health care is paid from private funds, including private insurance, out-of-pocket expenses, and other private sources. In addition, 13% of the population is covered by Medicare, 12% by Medicaid, and 4% by military health care. Be that as it may, over 40 million Americans, or 15% of the total U.S. population and 29% of the poorer segment, had no type of health insurance at all in 1994. Not surprisingly, the uninsured included over twice as many unemployed persons and part-time workers as full-time workers (U.S. Bureau of the Census, 1996).

Due in large measure to its complex, multifaceted nature and the vested interests of physicians, pharmaceutical supply houses, and insurance providers, reforming the American health care system has proved to be extremely difficult. Certain piecemeal reforms, such as the portability of health insurance from one place of employment to another, have been accomplished, but the system as a whole remains mired in dispute and paperwork.

The greater expense of fee-for-service as contrasted with managed care has led to the rapid growth of health maintenance organizations (HMOs) in recent years. Unfortunately, the adequacy of the services provided by many HMOs has become another source of contention. A related problem is that, unlike other sectors of the economy in which an increase in supply relative to demand lowers cost, in the health sector, an increase in the supply of physicians, hospitals, and other services has been accompanied by ever-increasing cost of treatment. It seems that, rather than settling for merely adequate supplies and services, when it comes to their personal health, people opt for the most successful doctor, the best-equipped hospital, and whatever other superior supplies and services they can obtain.

Another matter of continuing debate in the U.S. Congress and a cause for worry among older Americans in particular is the status of Medicare and Medicaid. In 1993, the Medicare program cost $150 billion and the Medicaid program, $102 billion (National Center for Health Statistics, 1995). Part A of Medicare is financed by a portion of the Social Security tax, and Part B (Supplemental Medical Insurance) is paid for by a monthly deduction from the applicant's Social Security check. However, a number of different services and supplies (custodial care, dentures, and routine dental care, eyeglasses, hearing aids, examinations to prescribe and fit them, nursing home care, prescription drugs, routine physical checkups and related tests) are not paid for by Medicare. In addition, a deductible amount and a percentage of the remaining cost of treatment must be paid by private insurance or from other private sources. Because Medicare pays less than half of the medical bills of older Americans, patients who cannot pay the remaining amount must look to either charity or Medicaid.

Medicaid is administered by local welfare departments using federal and state funds. The program is designed for poor people, who are required to pass a financial "means test" in order to qualify. Medicaid covers the same services and supplies as Medicare, in addition to prescription drugs, eyeglasses, long-term care in licensed nursing homes, and certain other items.

So far, federal entitlement programs such as Medicare, Medicaid, and Social Security have resisted the contemporary zeal for large cuts in governmental services. However, concerns continue to be voiced by older Americans and their advocates that these programs will not remain immune to the federal budget axe. Although seniors tend to be fairly independent, when it comes to federal programs that benefit them, bloc voting is much more likely to occur. For this reason, politicians who wish to be reelected must often walk a tightrope between exercising fiscal responsibility and attentiveness to the social and political realities of taking accustomed benefits away from a large and powerful group of constituents.

SUMMARY

Physical illnesses may be brief and severe (acute) or of long duration (chronic). Acute disorders such as infections, parasitic illnesses, and accidental injuries are more common in children and young adults; chronic disorders such as arthritis, hypertension, and heart disease occur more often in older adults. Middle-aged and older adults are generally more vulnerable to disease and take longer to recuperate than younger persons. Not only are chronic illnesses physically debilitating, but also they may have pronounced effects upon attitudes, abilities, and the general enjoyment of living. Despite the fact that sickness occurs more often in later life, older Americans of today are healthier than ever before and consider themselves to be so.

Less lethal conditions such as arthritis and diabetes are found more frequently in women, whereas more lethal disorders such as heart disease and cancer occur more often in men. As a group, whites and Asians are healthier than blacks, and more affluent people are healthier than less affluent ones. Ratings of personal health by individuals in different groups are positively related to their actual health.

Susceptibility to disease varies with sex, race, nationality, culture, socioeconomic status, and other demographic variables, as well as with heredity, diet, environmental pollution, and sanitation. Smoking, alcohol and drug abuse, lack of exercise, stress, and lack of social support can also contribute to poor health.

The four principal types of arthritis are osteoarthritis, rheumatoid arthritis, gout, and collagen disease. Rheumatoid arthritis is more common in women, and gout in men. Another chronic disorder is osteoporosis, in which the bones become more porous and brittle, hence more susceptible to fracture; it is much more prevalent in older women than in older men.

The three leading causes of death in the United States are heart disease, cancer, and stroke. Other potentially deadly diseases include chronic obstructive pulmonary disorders, pneumonia and influenza, diabetes, AIDS, and cirrhosis. With the exception of AIDS, the death rates for these disorders are higher in older than in middle- and young adulthood.

Both heart disease and stroke are precipitated by blood clots, the former in the coronary arteries, and the latter in the cerebral arteries. Heart disease and stroke, and, in fact, circulatory diseases of all kinds, increase with aging. These diseases are more common in men than women, in blacks than whites, and in whites than Asians, Hispanics, and Native Americans. Heredity and lifestyle factors (physical inactivity, heavy smoking, obesity, psychological stress, etc.) are important contributors to cardiovascular diseases.

The incidence of cancer and deaths caused by it also increase with age during adulthood. Middle-aged and older women are at higher risk for breast cancer, whereas older men are more likely to develop cancer of the lungs or prostate. The death rate for cancer is greater for men than for women and higher for blacks than for whites.

Chronic obstructive pulmonary diseases, which are the four leading cause of death in the United States, are slightly more common in men than in women. Pneumonia and influenza, the sixth leading cause of death, are more common in women than in men. The death rates for nearly all respiratory disorders are higher for blacks than for whites.

The death rate for HIV infection is higher from age 25 to 44 than at other ages, higher in men than in women, and higher in blacks than in whites. A combination of behavioral and neurological symptoms, together with a positive test for HIV infection, is used in the diagnosis of AIDS. By ravaging the immune system, AIDS makes death due to pneumonia (pneumocystis carinii) and cancer (Kaposi's sarcoma) more likely.

Hardening of the arteries of the brain (cerebral arteriosclerosis) in old age increases the likelihood of organic brain damage and attendant psychological symptoms. Multi-infarct dementia is the most common organic mental disorder in old age, but Alzheimer's disease has received more attention from researchers and the media.

Accidents claim approximately 90,000 lives in the United States every year, half of them involving motor vehicles. Accident statistics are recorded by class and type of accident. Motor-vehicle accidents are the most common type, and falls are second. Death rates for motor-vehicle accidents are higher from age 15 to 34 and after age 65 than at other ages; the death rate for non-motor-vehicle accidents increases dramatically after age 65. Accidents are caused by a combination of unsafe conditions and unsafe acts.

Years can be added to life and life to years by maintaining physical fitness and positive wellness by means of proper exercise, rest, nutrition, and stress management, and by refraining from cigarette smoking and alcohol or drug abuse.

Impairments in activities of daily live (ADLs) and instrumental activities of daily living (IADLs) increase with aging. However, the great majority of adults with physical disabilities are able to compensate and manage their lives with some assistance, without requiring full-time care or institutionalization.

Only about 5% of older Americans reside in nursing homes or other treatment institutions. Nursing homes vary widely in the quality of care they provide, but federal standards have helped to ensure better care for residents.

The cost of the health care system in the United States—from both public and private sources of funds—is enormous and increases every year. Despite continuing efforts by the federal government and other organizations to reform the health care system, the costs of hospital care, physicians' fees, and other health services and supplies continue to rise. Popular federal programs such as Medicare are rapidly becoming insolvent, but there is no general agreement on what to do about the program.

SUGGESTED READINGS

Bond, L. A., Cutler, S. J., & Grams, A. (1995). *Promoting successful and productive aging.* Thousand Oaks, CA: Sage Publications.

Elias, M. F., Elias, J. W., & Elias, P. K. (1990). Biological and health influences on behavior. In J. E. Birren & K. W. Schaie (Eds.), *Handbook of the psychology of aging* (3rd ed., pp. 79–102). San Diego: Academic Press.

Exercise isn't just for fun. (1991). In H. Cox (Ed.), *Aging* (11th ed., pp. 15–18). Sluice Dock, Guilford, CT: Dushkin Publishing Group/Brown & Benchmark.

Kirkland, R. I. (1994, February 21). Why we will live longer … and what it will mean. *Fortune,* pp. 66–68, 70, 74–75, 78.

Krause, N. (1990). Illness behavior in later life. In R. H. Binstock and L. K. George (Eds.), *Handbook of aging and the social sciences* (3rd ed., pp. 227–244. San Diego: Academic Press.

Lieberman, F., & Collen, M. F. (1993). *Aging in good health: A quality lifestyle for the later years.* New York: Plenum Press.

Ory, M. G., Abeles, R. P., & Lipman, P. D. (Eds.) (1992). *Aging, health, and behavior.* Newbury Park, CA: Sage.

CHAPTER 4

Cognitive Development and Change

The term *cognition* is derived from the Latin word for "knowing." The association between human awareness or consciousness and cognition was perhaps expressed most succinctly by René Descartes in his famous assertion, "Cogito ergo sum" (I know, therefore I am). However, *epistemology*, the branch of philosophy concerned with the acquisition and elaboration of knowledge, goes back at least to Plato's time. Both Plato and Descartes were believers in "innate ideas," the notion that the contents of the mind are, at least to some extent, inborn. The ensuing philosophical debate over nativism versus empiricism attracted many of the most famous philosophers of the eighteenth and nineteenth centuries. Nativists emphasized the inborn nature of human knowledge and mental activity, whereas empiricists maintained that the mind is a *tabula rasa*—a blank state—at birth, a slate on which experience writes the contents of the mind. Both positions helped shape scientific psychology, but the empiricistic camp had the greatest influence on behaviorism and, through it, on American psychology in the twentieth century.

A great deal of the psychological research during this century has been concerned with human and animal learning. Much of this research was conducted by American psychologists of a behavioristic persuasion and based primarily on an objective, empiricistic tradition. In recent decades, however, there has been a revival of interest in consciousness, thinking, creativity, and other mentalistic concepts. Advances in the measurement and understanding of brain functions and in the treatment of psychological disorders have contributed to this interest.

Among the thousands of research studies on cognition conducted during this century, hundreds have been concerned with individual differences in intelligence, memory, problem solving, and creative thinking. The construction of intelligence tests and other psychological assessment instruments has provided methods for measuring these differences and speculating about their meanings and origins. Behavioral, physiological, and subjective report data obtained from correlational and experimental investigations have been evaluated by various statistical procedures. Among the many correlational studies are those dealing with demographic differences in learning, memory, intelligence, problem solving, and creativity.

While not neglecting other factors that affect or are related to cognitive variables, this chapter focuses on the demographic variable of chronological age. The general question posed by the research studies reviewed here concerns the extent to which the various cognitive measures vary with age during adulthood.

INTELLIGENCE

Scientific interest in the concept of *intelligence* began with the research and writings of the Englishman Francis Galton in the latter half of the nineteenth century. Stimulated by his belief in the hereditary basis of individual differences in mental giftedness, Galton devised a number of simple sensorimotor tests (movement speed, muscular strength, touch and pain sensitivity, weight discrimination, reaction time, etc.) that, collectively, he believed would measure human intelligence. This approach to the measurement of intelligence was consistent with the doctrine of mental associationism espoused by many philosophers of the time. Associationism held that the contents of the mind are the results of combinations and elaborations of elementary sense impressions ("Nothing is in the mind which was not first in the senses"). Unfortunately for Galton, his tests did not prove useful in predicting performance in schoolwork or on other tasks that presumably involve intelligence.

Galton's efforts to measure the concept of intelligence were soon superseded by the work of two Frenchmen—Alfred Binet and Théodore Simon. Binet and Simon were commissioned by the Paris school system to devise a method for distinguishing between children who could benefit from formal educational instruction and those who could not. Applying themselves to the problem, Binet and Simon constructed the first practical intelligence test. Unlike the simple sensorimotor tests administered by Galton and his associates, the tests on the Binet–Simon Intelligence Scale consisted of school-type tasks that increasing numbers of children could perform at successive age levels. Examples are memory for digits and sentences, and identifying objects and body parts.

Early intelligence tests such as the Binet–Simon scale and an American adaptation and extension, the Stanford–Binet Intelligence Scale, were designed primarily for the assessment of intelligence in children. Numerous definitions of the *intelligence* measured by these tests were offered, including Binet's "the ability to judge well, to comprehend well, to reason well" and Terman's "the ability to carry on abstract thinking." Whatever definition may have been preferred, the tests were used primarily to determine the ability of children to learn school-type tasks and for grade-placement purposes. The

Stanford–Binet Intelligence Scale was an age scale on which a child's perfor-mance was converted to a mental age and then to an intelligence quotient, by dividing the mental age by the chronological age and multiplying by 100.

Some of the tests on the Stanford–Binet were appropriate for adults, but it was not considered to be an adequate measure of intelligence in adults. During World War I, tests were devised specifically for measuring the intel-ligence of adults. In contrast to individual tests such as the Stanford–Binet, which was administered to one examinee at the time, these group tests—the Army Examinations Alpha and Beta—could be administered simultaneously to a large group of individuals. Group testing subsequently became even more extensive than individual testing. Between the end of World War I and the beginning of World War II, many educational and psychological tests—both group and individual—were constructed and administered. The most fa-mous of the new individual tests of intelligence was the Wechsler–Bellevue Intelligence Scale.

Wechsler–Bellevue Intelligence Scale

This test, published initially in 1939 by David Wechsler, a clinical psy-chologist at Bellevue Hospital in New York, was designed exclusively for adults. As seen in his later definition of intelligence as "the aggregate or global capacity of the individual to act purposefully, think rationally and to deal effectively with his environment" (Wechsler, 1958, p. 7), Wechsler, like Galton, Binet, and Terman, believed in the existence of a general mental ability.

It was Wechsler's hope that his test would prove to be not only a valid measure of adult intellectual functioning but would also contribute to making clinical diagnoses. Unlike the age-scale format of the Stanford–Binet, the Wechsler–Bellevue was a point scale on which points were earned for pass-ing subtests and were then converted to scaled scores and IQs. The test as a whole was divided into two sections, Verbal and Performance, consisting of five to six subtests each. On the verbal subtests, the examinee provided verbal answers to a series of questions; on the performance subtests, the examinee performed a task requiring perceptual/motor responses. Each of the subtests was scored separately, the raw scores being converted to standard scores having a mean of 10 and a standard deviation of 3. Three IQs—Verbal, Performance, and Full Scale—were determined on a standard score (devia-tion IQ) scale having a mean of 100 and a standard deviation of 15. The difference between the Verbal and Performance IQs, the pattern or scatter of standard scores on the various subtests, and the qualitative nature of the responses made by the examinee were analyzed in arriving at a clinical diagnosis. In addition to being one of the principal psychometric instruments designed for use for clinical and counseling situations, the Wechsler–Bellevue Form I and its successors have been used extensively in research.

MY LIFE 4–1

Intelligence Testing

My first encounter with intelligence tests was when, as a high school senior, I was required to take the California Test of Mental Maturity. Our English teacher had previously warned us that administration of this group test was imminent and had drilled us on items she recorded from the previous year's test. The drill was apparently beneficial, because the class performed fairly well. Observing, however, that some students did better than others, and being trained in the old school of pedagogy, she posted our IQ scores in rank order by name on the hall bulletin board. The highest score was obtained by a 13-year-old intellectual prodigy who knew four foreign languages, could work a slide rule faster than most of us could think, and was exempt from physical education because he screamed too loudly when injured.

Some years later I took another intelligence test—the Army General Classification Test— on a cold gymnasium floor early in the morning at the beginning of my Marine Corps career. The examiner assured us that the less-than-optimal testing conditions would have no effect on the scores of "real marines," so we set to work and did our best. After the tests had been scored,

our drill instructor showed even greater creativity than our high school English teacher in reporting the scores. While we were marching in ranks, he rhythmically intoned each recruit's score by name, such as, "Smith's GCT is 123, but he doesn't know his right from his left!" This may have been amusing to him, but it was traumatic to one low-scorer who tried to escape from the shame by swimming across the Savannah River; he was bitten by an alligator but survived. Another recruit with an exceptionally low score was made to march 40 paces behind the platoon for the rest of his boot camp experience.

When I became a graduate student in psychology, I was able to make a few extra dollars by administering the Stanford–Binet Intelligence Scale in schools, churches, courthouses, or wherever living, breathing human beings could be found. I tested them on dining tables, on lawns, in broom closets, on dirty floors, and even in cobweb-covered corners. Despite the informal testing conditions, most examinees were cooperative, and even if they weren't, I doggedly persevered until an IQ estimate was obtained on every single one of them. The test scores were used for grade-placement purposes after consulting with the parents

---

Following its initial publication in 1939, the Wechsler–Bellevue Intelligence Scale was revised in 1946, 1955, 1981, and 1997. The 1981 edition, called the Wechsler Adult Intelligence Scale—Revised (WAIS-R), is appropriate for individuals aged 16 years and over. The WAIS-R consists of the following six Verbal (V) and five Performance (P) subtests administered in alternating order, as follows:

and teachers. Sometimes it was difficult to get parents and teachers to be flexible in interpreting the scores. For example, one parent wanted to know if her boy's score of 72 meant that he was mentally retarded. She was told that a child had to score below 70 before he or she was placed in a special class for retarded children. The obviously relieved mother exclaimed, "I knew he was just lazy, and I'm gonna beat hell out of him until he does better in his school work!"

During several of my testing outings, I discovered numerous mistakes that had been made by other examiners in scoring intelligence tests. In some cases, the scores were based on incorrect or unknown birth dates that resulted in children being placed in the wrong category and hence the wrong grade or section. Such mistakes were not limited to graduate-student examiners, but were made by professional psychologists as well.

One might think that sophisticated college and university professors would be immune to reification of the IQ concept, but such has not always been the case. For example, I overheard an argument between two famous psychologists concerning some abstruse matter pertaining to learning theory. One of the gentlemen became so vexed that he blurted out that his IQ was higher than his opponent's and therefore his opinion was more likely to be correct.

Perhaps it was overhearing interchanges like this one that encouraged a group of students to suggest listing professors' IQs by their names in the campus newspaper to help students select courses. In any event, on a bet from a friend of mine that I couldn't pass the intelligence test for Mensa—an organization for superintellects, I signed up and reported at the designated place and time. Imagine my delight when the examination turned out to be my old friend, the California Test of Mental Maturity!

During the heyday of IQ testing, some young men were known to ask their dates' IQs before taking them out a second time, and certainly before becoming engaged. In fact, the provisions in the will of one famous pioneer in the mental testing movement made the amount of money bequeathed to each of his two sons contingent on the tested abilities of the women they married. Reportedly, only one of the sons, a eugenics enthusiast, went along with the provision. Even I was swept up in the enthusiasm over the role of intelligence testing in mate selection when I administered the Wechsler Adult Intelligence Scale to a young woman I was dating some years ago. However, she took it in her stride and agreed to marry me on the condition that she could verify my own IQ first. Fortunately, we settled the matter out of court.

Information (V)　　　Arithmetic (V)
Picture Completion (P)　　Object Assembly (P)
Digit Span (V)　　　Comprehension (V)
Picture Arrangement (P)　Digit Symbol (P)
Vocabulary (V)　　　Similarities (V)
Block Design (P)

The WAIS-R was standardized on nine age groups of "normal" American adults: 16–17, 18–19, 20–24, 25–34, 35–44, 45–54, 55–64, 65–69, and 70–74 years. The sample selected in each age category was stratified by sex, geographical region, ethnicity (white vs. nonwhite), education, and occupation. Care was taken in selecting the older age samples so that, unlike the older adult sample of the preceding edition of the test, they were representative of the population of Americans in those categories.[1]

Testing Adults

Administering an intelligence test, or any other psychometric instrument, is not simply a matter of reading a set of printed directions to the examinees. Even when administering a group test to many people simultaneously, the examiner should study the test format and directions carefully beforehand, making certain that the test is scheduled at a convenient, appropriate time, ensuring that the testing environment is conducive to the examinees' doing their best without cheating, and obtaining the required *informed consent* of the examinees or persons legally responsible for them. During the test, the directions should be followed carefully, and the examiner should remain alert and prepared for special problems and emergencies. Although the establishment of *rapport*, a cordial, friendly relationship between the examiner and the examinees, is less crucial in group than in individual administration, in either case, the examiner should remain interested, patient, and tactful.

The preceding recommendations are applicable to the administration of tests to all persons, regardless of age, sex, ethnicity, or social class. In addition, the examiner should be sensitive to physical or cultural differences among examinees and take them into consideration in selecting and administering the tests. Some flexibility may be appropriate even on standardized tests, but deviations from the standard directions for administration should be noted when reporting the test results. This is particularly true when testing physically handicapped or emotionally disturbed individuals, very young children, or persons who express strong negative attitudes toward the testing procedure.

Because of a lack of time, perception of the test tasks as meaningless, fear of doing badly, or other factors, older adults are often more reluctant to be tested than other age groups. Laboratory-type tasks such as memorizing a set of numerical digits or nonsense syllables or solving math problems and puzzles may strike an older adult as silly and irrelevant to real life. In addition, older adults tend to be slower, more cautious, more distractible, and

---

[1]In addition to revised forms of the 11 subtests on the WAIS-R, the WAIS-III, which was published in 1997, contains three new subtests: Matrix Reasoning, Symbol Search, and Letter-Number Sequencing. The sample on which WAIS-III was standardized consisted of 2450 Amerian adults aged 16–89 years, stratified by race/ethnicity, sex, educational level, and geographical region within each age group.

more easily fatigued by the test materials. And when the examiner is much younger than the examinee, establishing rapport with the examinee and motivating him or her to do well on the test may be especially difficult. This is more likely when the examiner has had little or no training or experience in testing older adults.

Even when older adult examinees are motivated to do their best, sensory defects, other physical disabilities, and the tendency to respond more slowly and tire more easily can interfere with test performance. For these reasons, special procedures may be needed for older examinees to demonstrate their capabilities. Among these procedures are the following:

1. Provide ample time for the examinee to respond to the test material.
2. Allow sufficient practice on sample items.
3. Use shorter testing periods than with younger adults.
4. Watch out for fatigue and take it into consideration.
5. Be sensitive to, and make provisions for, visual, auditory, and other sensory defects.
6. Arrange for the examination room to be as free as possible from distractions.
7. Employ a generous amount of encouragement and positive reinforcement.
8. Do not try to force examinees to respond to test items when they repeatedly refuse to do so.

Of course, most of these recommendations are appropriate for examinees of all ages.

Demographic Variables

Scores on intelligence tests such as the WAIS-R have been correlated with a host of demographic variables—age, sex, education, ethnicity, occupation, socioeconomic status, culture, nationality, urban–rural residence, family size, birth order, and others. Intelligence test scores have also been related to diet, drugs, hormones, exposure to other chemical substances, genetic disorders, neural anatomy and physiology, climate, season of birth, and many other biological, environmental, behavioral, and personality variables. For example, comparisons of the correlation between the IQs of identical twins with the correlations between the IQs of individuals with other familial relationships provide support for a strong genetic basis for whatever is measured by intelligence tests (Bouchard, Lykken, McGue, Segal, & Tellengen, 1990; Bouchard & McGue, 1981; Plomin, 1988, 1989). Another important research finding, the significant relationship between lead exposure and intelligence test scores, indicates that exposure to high levels of lead during early childhood can have adverse effects on intellectual development (Fulton et al., 1987; McMichael et al., 1988; Needleman, Schell, Bellinger, Leviton, & Allred, 1990). In addition, research has documented the effects of fetal and infant malnutrition on low intelligence and the persistence of such effects throughout childhood and adolescence (Stoch & Smythe, 1963; Zeskind & Ramey, 1981).

Sex Differences.   Sex differences in overall scores on the Wechsler tests and other measures of general mental ability are usually nonsignificant, but the differences in specific cognitive and psychomotor abilities are noteworthy. Females usually score higher than males on measures of verbal fluency, reading comprehension, finger dexterity, and clerical skills, whereas males typically score higher than females on tests of mathematical reasoning, visuo-spatial ability, and speed and coordination of large bodily movements (Minton & Schneider, 1980). The superiority of women to men in verbal ability and the superiority of men to women in performance abilities tend to persist over the life span. It has also been found that, as a group, women's verbal abilities increase more than those of men during adulthood, but the reverse is true for performance abilities (Eichorn, Hunt, & Honzik, 1981). Whether these sex differences are due mainly to biological differences between the sexes or to differences in social expectations and experiences has been the subject of debate. Admittedly, social expectations are greater for girls to become more adept in linguistic and social skills and for boys to perform better in mathe-matical, mechanical, and spatial reasoning. Still, findings concerning the role of hormones and other biological variables in promoting sex differences in abilities are provocative (Christiansen & Knussman, 1987; Hier & Crowley, 1982; Kimura & Hampson, 1993).

Ethnicity.   Even more controversial than the results of research on sex differences in mental abilities are those obtained from studies of racial differ-ences in intelligence and specific cognitive abilities. For example, whites outscore blacks by approximately one standard deviation on both the WAIS-R (Reynolds, Chastain, Kaufman, & McLean, 1987) and the Stanford–Binet: Fourth Edition (Thorndike, Hagen, & Sattler, 1986). These findings have been interpreted in various ways. Jensen (1980) maintained that blacks have lower mean scores than whites on measures of abstract reasoning and problem solving but equivalent mean scores on measures of rote learning ability because the frequency of genes carrying higher intelligence is lower in the black population than in the white. Supporters of an experiential explanation for black–white differences in intelligence test scores have taken issue with Jensen's conclusion. They interpret racial differences in scores on tests of mental abilities as the consequence of variations in educational and cultural experiences rather than genetics. However, an environmental explanation must also account for the fact that Native Americans, Hispanics, and Asians living under poor socioeconomic conditions score higher than blacks. In fact, Asians score higher than whites on tests of quantitative ability and, at least in the case of Japanese tested in their own country, in many instances on measures of general intelligence (Lynn, 1982, 1987).

Education, Socioeconomic Status, and Occupational Status. The fact that groups of people with less education and of lower socioeconomic status tend to make lower intelligence test scores than people of higher educational and socioeconomic levels is not surprising. Both educational attainment and socioeconomic status are negatively correlated with scores on intelligence tests. Educational attainment, socioeconomic status, and IQ scores are also related to occupational status. Individuals with more education, higher socioeconomic status, and higher IQs tend to enter higher-status occupations. Although the reasons for these relationships are not entirely clear, Cronin, Daniels, Hurley, Kroch, and Webber (1975) concluded that intelligence is related to occupational status because both variables are associated with socioeconomic status. According to these investigators, parents of middle- or upper-class backgrounds are more likely than those of lower-class backgrounds to prepare their children for entry into higher-status occupations by encouraging them to do well in schoolwork and on tests.

Education and socioeconomic status are also related to ethnicity, so it is possible that ethnic-group differences in measured intelligence stem from educational and/or social-class differences rather than ethnicity per se. The results of one research study suggest, however, that intelligence rather than education or social class is the pivotal variable (Thomas, Alexander, & Eckland, 1979). These investigators found that the positive correlation between IQ and educational attainment remained significant even when socioeconomic status was statistically controlled. On the other hand, when IQ was statistically controlled, the correlation between socioeconomic status and educational attainment was slightly negative. These findings were interpreted as demonstrating that intellectual ability affects both socioeconomic status and educational level.

Place of Residence and Family Structure. Three other demographic variables that are related to intelligence test scores, as well as to education and socioeconomic status, are urban versus rural residence, family size, and birth order. Studies conducted earlier in this century found significantly lower IQs in individuals living in rural than in urban areas (McNemar, 1942). Advances in information transmission and transportation during the past several decades, however, have broadened the educational and social experiences of children and improved the living conditions of Americans in all geographical areas. Television, better schools, and other sources of intellectual stimulation have undoubtedly contributed to the improved intelligence test scores of persons living in rural areas of the United States and other countries as well (Cronbach & Drenth, 1972; Scribner & Cole, 1973).

It has been noted by scientists for over a century that mentally duller individuals tend to come from larger families than mentally brighter individuals. Studies supporting this observation are plentiful (e.g., Belmont & Marolla, 1973; Kellaghan & MacNamara, 1972; Zajonc, 1976). The negative correlation between family size and IQ scores is not entirely due to socioeconomic status, because the correlation remains significant when differences between the socioeconomic status of large and small families are statistically controlled.

Not only do children from larger families tend to have lower IQs than those from smaller families, but IQ also varies with the birth order of children within families. Firstborn children, on the whole, make higher intelligence test scores than subsequently born children. Whether this is due to the greater attention, encouragement, and assistance provided by parents to firstborn than to later-born children or to some other factor is debatable (Kilbride, Johnson, & Streissguth, 1977; MacPhee, Ramey, & Yeats, 1984). Whatever the cause, firstborn children are, as a group, more serious, responsible, studious, and competitive than later-borns, whereas later-born children are more outgoing, relaxed, imaginative, and athletic than firstborns. These are characteristics that would seem to be shaped to a large extent by differential treatment of children within families rather than by biological variables.

Chronological Age Differences

A person's score on an intelligence test is not a fixed number that remains invariant from year to year and test to test. The fact that test scores are not perfectly reliable means that a person's score will change somewhat with time, test, and conditions of administration. For example, IQ scores on the Stanford–Binet Intelligence Scale vary on the average about 5 points from testing to testing, though variations as large as 20 points can occur with dramatic changes in physical health, emotional adjustment, or living circumstances.

Of particular interest to developmental psychologists have been age-related changes in intelligence test scores. The results of earlier cross-sectional studies (e.g., Jones & Conrad, 1933; Yerkes, 1921) suggested that, on the average, test scores decline steadily after late adolescence. For example, Yerkes found that mean scores on the Army Examination Alpha administered to large groups of American soldiers during and shortly after World War I declined from the late teens through the sixth decade of life. The general form of the curve drawn from data obtained from Jones and Conrad's classic study of 1,200 New Englanders between 10 and 60 years of age was an increase in mean scores on the Army Alpha from age 10 to 16 and a gradual decline to the age-14 level by age 55. These findings of a decline in intelligence test scores during middle and later adulthood were supported by Wechsler's (1958) analysis of scores on the Wechsler–Bellevue Form I and, more recently, by standardization data from the WAIS-R. As shown in Figure 4–1, the mean sum of scaled scores on the Verbal, Performance, and Full Scales of the WAIS-R reach a peak at a somewhat later age than that found in earlier studies; the

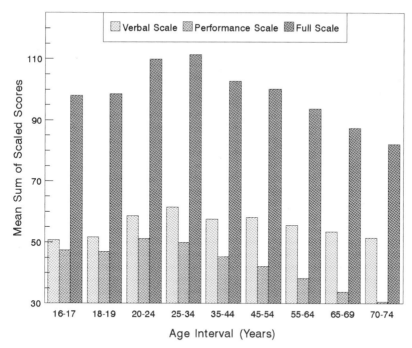

Figure 4–1   **Mean sum of scaled scores on the Verbal, Performance, and Full Scales of the WAIS-R at various age levels.** (Based on data in the *Manual for the Wechsler Adult Intelligence Scale-Revised.* Copyright © 1981 by The Psychological Corporation. Reproduced by permission. All rights reserved.)

scores increase from the late teens to the late twenties or early thirties and then gradually decline throughout middle and late adulthood.

Figure 4–1 shows the *classic aging pattern* of a steeper decline on the Performance Scale than on the Verbal Scale. Figure 4–2, which is also based on the 1981 WAIS-R standardization data, shows the rate of decline of standard scale scores on three Verbal subtests (Information, Vocabulary, Arithmetic) and three Performance subtests (Picture Completion, Picture Arrangement, Digit Symbol). The age-related decline in subtest-scaled scores after ages 25–34 is clearly greater for all three of these Performance subtests than for any of the three Verbal subtests. Similar patterns of decline in mental abilities have been found on the Primary Mental Abilities Test (Schaie, 1983), the Stanford–Binet IV (Thorndike, et al., 1986), and other individual and group intelligence tests.

The difficulties experienced in interpreting the results of cross-sectional investigations such as those described here are discussed in Chapter 1. These types of studies compare the scores of different age cohorts, people of differ-

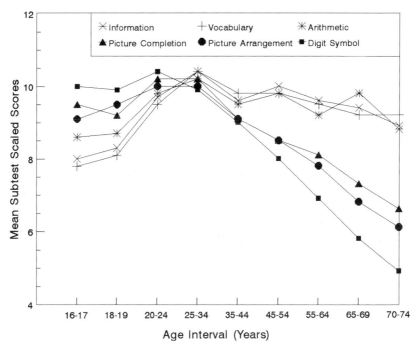

Figure 4–2   Mean scaled scores on six WAIS-R subtests by age. (Based on data in the *Manual for the Wechsler Adult Intelligence Scale-Revised.* Copyright © 1981 by The Psychological Corporation. Reproduced by permission. All rights reserved.)

ent ages who have been brought up in different social and cultural conditions. An important variable that cannot be controlled when comparing different age cohorts is education, which is significantly related to scores on intelligence tests. Because comparisons of the intelligence test scores of different age cohorts confound the effects of education and age, it is impossible to conclude from the results of a cross-sectional study how much of the observed decline is due to age per se and how much is due to differences in education or other cohort-related variables. Because intelligence test scores are positively correlated with both educational level and socioeconomic status, it is possible that the lower test scores obtained by older adults are caused by the fact that they had less formal education and grew up during less intellectually stimulating times. In addition to educational experiences, people of different ages may vary in motivation, susceptibility to fatigue, response times, test anxiety, social isolation, depression, attentiveness, sensory acuity, nutrition, physical health, and other factors that can effect test scores (Reese & Rodeheaver, 1985).

It is more difficult to conduct longitudinal studies than cross-sectional studies of changes in ability test scores with age. Assuming that the selected

sample is representative of the population to which the results will be generalized, the problem of differential mortality or *selective attrition*, in which individuals of lower intelligence are less likely to be available for repeated testings, still remains. In addition, the practice effect of having taken a particular test on one or more previous occasions can inflate scores in longitudinal studies. Another methodological shortcoming of longitudinal studies is the *regression effect*, in which individuals who score very high or very low on an initial administration of a test tend to obtain scores closer to the mean on a subsequent administration of the same test. Such methodological and individual factors can interfere with an accurate estimate of the effects of chronological age per se on intelligence test scores. In any case, the results of several longitudinal investigations indicate that intelligence test scores tend to remain fairly stable or to decrease only slightly after early adulthood (Bayley & Oden, 1955; Campbell, 1965; Nisbet, 1957; Owens, 1953, 1966). Most of these studies, however, were conducted on college graduates, so the results are not necessarily representative of the general population. Other longitudinal studies conducted with people of average intelligence (Charles & James, 1964; Eisdorfer, 1963; Tuddenham, Blumenkrantz, & Wilkin, 1968) and noninstitutionalized mentally retarded adults (Baller, Charles, & Miller, 1967; Bell & Zubek, 1960) have, however, yielded similar findings. The findings have been interpreted as indicating that intelligence continues to increase somewhat during early adulthood and reaches a plateau in the late twenties. After that, a slow decline is observed in individuals of below-average intelligence, particularly if they fail to use their abilities. On the other hand, people of above-average intelligence may show no decline at all or may even improve until their early fifties.

In general, the results of longitudinal studies reveal a slower decline in cognitive abilities in later adulthood than those obtained from cross-sectional studies. Warner Schaie and his coworkers (Schaie, 1979, 1983, 1990, 1994) have found, however, that whether and how much cognitive abilities decline in later life depends on the specific ability and the individual. They maintain that, except perhaps for individuals with cardiovascular disorders or other serious illnesses, declines in cognitive abilities during later life are by no means inevitable.

The conclusion that the magnitude of age-related declines in abilities varies with the specific ability and the individual is supported by the results of both cross-sectional and longitudinal data. In the Seattle Longitudinal Studies, Schaie (1990, 1994) examined the relationships of age to scores on the SRA Mental Abilities Tests of Verbal Meaning, Spatial Orientation, Inductive Reasoning, Number, and Word Fluency. Figure 4–3 shows that the percentage of individuals who declined in these abilities increased with age. During middle adulthood, the rate of decline was greatest for spatial orientation and inductive reasoning and less for word fluency, verbal meaning, and number. However, scores on verbal meaning, which is a somewhat speeded test, showed the greatest drop in old age. Though the number of individuals

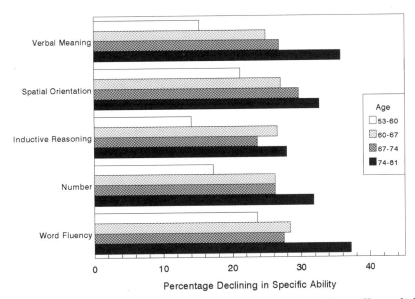

Figure 4–3 **Percentage of individuals showing decline in specific intellectual abilities during four age periods.** (Based on data from Schaie, 1990.) Cambridge, UK: Cambridge University Press.

who showed a decline in one or more of these five abilities increased with age, only a small percentage declined in all five.

A lively debate concerning age decrements in cognitive abilities has been waged by Warner Schaie and John Horn over the years. Horn maintains that intelligence may begin to decline as early as the twenties and thirties and that it becomes particularly noticeable during middle age. Following his mentor, R. B. Cattell, Horn makes a distinction between fluid and crystallized ability. *Crystallized ability* is Cattell's term for cognitive ability (knowledge, skills) acquired through experience and education; it is specific to certain fields, such as school learning, and applied in tasks where habits have become fixed. In contrast, *fluid ability* is inherent, genetically determined mental ability, as manifested in problem-solving or novel responses. The items in Figure 4–4, which are samples from the Culture Fair Intelligence Test, are illustrative of the kinds of tasks involving fluid intelligence. Horn states that the decline in abilities during middle age is seen particularly in scores on measures of fluid intelligence that deal with the flexibility of thinking and problem solving (Horn, 1985; Horn & Donaldson, 1976, 1980; Horn & Hofer, 1992). A number of other investigations (e.g., Christensen et al., 1994) have also found greater age-related declines in fluid ability than in crystallized ability.

While recognizing that cognitive abilities decline with age, Schaie (1983) believes that the decrement is much less than Horn asserts and is caused in

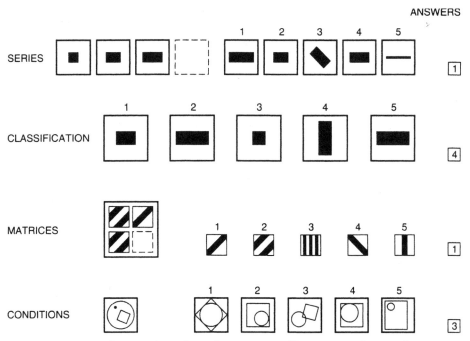

Figure 4–4   Sample items from the Culture Fair Intelligence Test. (Copyright © 1949, 1960, by the Institute for Personality and Ability Testing, Inc. All rights reserved. Reproduced by permission.)

large measure by differences in the experiences of younger and older adults during their formative years. The wide range of individual variations in intelligence, in addition to its multidimensionality and modifiability, led Schaie to conclude that it is a very plastic variable. Environments in which there are varied opportunities for intellectual stimulation and a flexible life-style can, according to Schaie, contribute to the maintenance of an optimal level of intellectual functioning in adulthood. Rather than simply accepting the conclusion that a decline in intelligence during later adulthood is inevitable, Schaie feels that psychologists should explore ways of improving memory, abstract reasoning, concentration, and other aspects of intellectual functioning in older adults. In this regard, Schaie and his coworkers (Baltes & Willis, 1982; Schaie & Willis, 1986; Willis, 1990) have had some success in training older adults to improve their performance on intelligence tests. In many instances, however, it is not clear whether the training procedures truly arrest and reverse declines in cognitive abilities or whether the subjects simply learn new test-taking skills. Furthermore, both older and younger adults show improvements in test scores as a result of the training.

Improvements in cognitive skills can be obtained not only by instruction in specific skills but also by anxiety-reduction training (Yeasavage & Rose, 1984). In addition, older adults can continue to perform effectively by limiting their involvement in areas where deficits are more obvious and by emphasizing activities in which ability losses are less noticeable. They can also compensate for losses in abilities by employing reminders, being more careful, and finding other ways of accomplishing certain tasks. Even when there are significant losses in cognitive abilities, most people have enough reserve capacity to continue functioning at an acceptable level. Adaptation to the environment and daily life seldom requires all of one's capacities, and older adults usually have untapped abilities that can be called upon when needed. Furthermore, older adults often possess highly specialized knowledge and abilities that are not tapped by conventional tests of intelligence. These "practical abilities" enable many older adults to be more competent than younger adults in dealing with everyday problems that are not always covered in school.

Terminal Drop

The fact that cognitive abilities may show a general decline with aging is seen in the phenomenon known as the *terminal drop*. Research on this phenomenon, which is signaled not only by decrements in IQ, memory, and cognitive organization, but also in reaction time, assertiveness, and other sensorimotor abilities and personality characteristics during the last few months of life, was prompted by the observations made by a nurse in a home for the aged. She claimed that she was able to predict which patients were going to die soon, because they just "seem to act differently" (Lieberman, 1965, p. 181). Research studies initiated in response to the nurse's observations found that patients who died within an year after psychological assessments showed declines on various measures of cognitive and sensorimotor abilities and adaptation to the environment (Granick & Patterson, 1972; Lieberman & Coplan, 1969; Reimanis & Green, 1971; Riegel & Riegel, 1972).

Riegel and Riegel (1972) maintained that the terminal drop becomes evident up to 5 years before death, but more recent research indicates that it does not begin until about 2 years before death and even then is apparent only in certain abilities (White & Cunningham, 1988). Studies conducted at Duke University (Palmore, 1982; Palmore & Cleveland, 1976; Siegler, McCarty, & Logue, 1982) found that the decline in abilities is more pronounced on nonspeeded tests such as vocabulary than on speeded tests of perceptual or problem-solving skills. Patients who showed no declines in these abilities died after a significantly longer period following testing.

It is noteworthy that the imminence of death may be signaled by a drop in a crystallized ability such as vocabulary. Declines in vocabulary and other crystallized abilities are not typical of normal aging (Cooney, Schaie, & Willis,

1988), and it can be argued that a drop in crystallized abilities late in life is indicative of a disease process or impending death.

To the extent that the terminal drop is a genuine phenomenon and not a methodological artifact, it is probably due to changes in the functioning of the cerebrovascular system and other vital systems during later life. Changes in personality may also contribute to these declines in cognitive functioning. Dying people tend to become more preoccupied with themselves, which, according to Lieberman (1965), represents a desperate attempt to keep from falling apart psychologically. Because they are unable to organize and integrate complex sensory input efficiently and cope with the demands of the environment, they experience feelings of chaos and impending doom, and consequently are less willing and able to perform well on psychological tests.

Neurophysiological Factors

The effects of heredity, sensorimotor abilities, health and disease, nutrition, substance abuse, and other biological factors on intellectual functioning may be even more important than specific experiences and education. For example, Lindenberger and Baltes (1994) found that visual and auditory acuity, which decline with age, were among the best predictors of scores on measures of knowledge, reasoning, memory, word fluency, and response speed in older adults. Differences in auditory acuity, in particular, accounted for a large portion of the age-related variability in scores on cognitive tests.

Related to differences in sensory abilities is response speed. The fact that older adults tend to respond more slowly than their younger contemporaries has prompted the hypothesis that age differences in the speed with which cognitive processes take place contribute to differences in intellectual functioning between young and old adults. Evidence supporting this hypothesis comes from various sources (e.g., Lindenberger, Mayr, & Kliegl, 1993; Miller, 1994; Nettelbeck & Rabbitt, 1992). In a summary of research on reaction time and information processing, Miller (1994) concluded that more intelligent people have faster and less variable reaction times, that reaction time becomes longer with age, and that it increases more rapidly with increased task complexity in older than in younger adults. Furthermore, Miller concludes that people with large brains (relative to their body sizes) are more intelligent, that more intelligent brains use less energy, and that age differences in intelligence reflect differences in myelination of neural axons.

Many supporters of a neurological explanation of age-related declines in intelligence view it as the result of small changes in the brain produced by high blood pressure, alcoholism, and other pathological conditions (Rinn, 1988). It is certainly true that intellectual functioning is affected by health status and that people with higher intellectual abilities are healthier and live longer than those with lower abilities. Self-reports of physical and mental health confirm the results of medical diagnoses in this regard (Perlmutter &

Nyquist, 1990). It is arguable whether good health produces better cognitive abilities, or vice versa, but it is clear that poor health can lead to a loss of energy, depression, and less motivation to express oneself intellectually and socially (Perlmutter et al., 1987).

As discussed in Chapter 3, organic brain disorders can have a pronounced effect on behavior and abilities. This is particularly evident in Alzheimer's disease, a disorder that afflicts approximately 20% of individuals in the 75- to 84-year age range and about 47% of those over 85 (Evans et al., 1989). An even greater percentage of older Americans suffer from hypertension, another disorder that is associated with reduced intellectual functioning (Hertzog, Schaie, & Gribbin, 1978; Sands & Meredith, 1992) and which can lead to cardiovascular disease and stroke. By interfering with the oxygen flow to the brain, a major stroke can affect not only intellectual abilities but also speaking, walking, and other skills. The brain's blood supply can also be temporarily reduced by emphysema, acute infection, poor nutrition, injuries, and surgery. The loss of neuronal tissue, changes in metabolic rate, and a decline in blood circulation also have depressing effects on cognitive functioning. Although aging is accompanied by the death of many brain neurons, the remaining neurons continue to grow even in people's seventies and eighties (Coleman, 1986).

Cognitive Development

The psychometric approach to assessing cognitive abilities by means of specific tests has, for the most part, not adhered to any specific theory. Rather, it has been guided by the empirical results of correlational and factor-analytic studies designed to isolate the basic dimensions of intellectual functioning. Recently, more attention has been devoted to establishing certain theoretical foundations, based on research in child development, brain physiology, information-processing, and computer-oriented concepts. For example, construction of the Kaufman Adolescent and Adult Intelligence Test (KAIT) was guided by Cattell's theoretical distinction between fluid and crystallized intelligence. Certain intelligence tests are also based on neuropsychological theories such as Aleksandr Luria's conception of different brain areas as being responsible for simultaneous and successive processing of information (see Das, Naglieri, & Kirby, 1994). Of all conceptions of intelligence, however, the most influential in guiding research and practice has been Jean Piaget's theory of cognitive development.

Piaget conceptualized human cognition as developing in a sequence of four successive stages: sensorimotor (from birth to 2 years), preoperational (from 2 to 6 years), concrete operations (from 7 to 11 years), and formal operations (from 11 to 15 years). Cognitive development begins with the assimilation of environmental experiences and accommodating (adapting) one's behavior and mental representations of those experiences (*schemas*).

The reversible mental actions (*operations*) by which a child accommodates his or her perceptions and thoughts to reality become increasingly more complex as the child matures, initially involving only concrete dimensions but proceeding to more abstract, formal dimensions.

By age 15, according to Piaget, the average child has reached cognitive maturity and can solve problems involving formal operations. Adolescents can employ logic and verbal reasoning and perform higher level, more abstract cognitive tasks. After age 15, knowledge continues to accumulate but intelligence, which Piaget defined as the ability to solve new problems, increases no further and may, in fact, decline. Note that this is also the age at which Cattell and Horn maintain that fluid intelligence has reached maturity.

Certain psychologists have quarreled with Piaget's conclusion that cognition stops developing at age 15 and have maintained that it continues to develop throughout early and middle adulthood. These critics assert that the thought processes of adults are qualitatively different from the more formal thought processes of logical reasoning and problem-solving characteristic of Piaget's older adolescents. For example, Riegel (1973, 1976) argued that mature adult thinking does not involve the search for a single "correct" solution. Rather, it is characterized by an understanding that, paradoxically, something may be both true and false. Following Riegel, Pascual-Leone (1983) and Basseches (1984) maintained that there is an additional reasoning stage in adulthood: *dialectical thought*. It involves movement or change and is made up of a continuous chain of thesis, antithesis, and synthesis.

> Dialectical thinking is an organized approach to analyzing and making sense of the world one experiences that differs fundamentally from formal analysis. Whereas the latter involves the effort to find fundamental fixed realities—basic elements and immutable laws—the former attempts to describe the fundamental process of change and the dynamic relationships through which this change occurs. (Basseches, 1984, p. 24).

An example of dialectical thinking is the realization that a quarrel may be nobody's "fault" and must be resolved by both opponents changing and adapting their demands to the situation. Compared to absolutist or even relativistic thinking, this type of thinking consists of understanding the merits of different viewpoints and the possibility of integrating them into a workable situation. Designated as *postformal thought* by Commons, Richards, and Kuhn (1982), dialectical thinking recognizes that the solution to a problem varies with the situation, must be realistic, and may also involve ambiguity and contradiction, as well as emotion and other subjective factors.

Although they accept the view that dialectical or postformal thinking is more characteristic of middle and later adulthood, Rybash, Hoyer, and Roodin (1986) question the assumption that it represents a separate stage of cognitive development. Rather than requiring a reorganization of thought, they see it as simply a style of thinking that emerges in some adults but lacks the characteristics of a unique, separate developmental stage.

Schaie and his associates (Labouvie-Vief, 1985; Schaie, 1977–1978) have also maintained that mature adult thinking, which requires the integration of emotion and logic, is different from the thought processes of childhood, adolescence, and young adulthood. Schaie proposed a four-stage model that is markedly different from Piaget's conception. The four stages in Schaie's model of cognitive development are the Acquisitive Stage (during childhood and adolescence), the Achieving Stage (during young adulthood), the Responsible and Executive Stage (during middle age), and the Reintegrative Stage (during old age). The child's question, "What should I know?" gives way to the young adult's question, "How should I use what I know?", which itself is replaced in older adulthood by the question, "What should I know?" During the achieving stage of young adulthood, not only the problem but also the context in which it is to be solved is taken into account. Young adults focus more on long-term goals, such as those involving decisions about careers and marriage, and the possible consequences of their decisions. At the responsible/executive stage of midlife, the adult applies his or her cognitive skills in situations involving social responsibility, such as establishing a family and meeting the needs of one's spouse and children. During the last, or reintegrative, stage, the acquisition and application of information is guided more by one's interests, attitudes, and values than in young or middle adulthood. An older adult is less willing to expend great effort on a problem unless it is one that he or she faces in everyday life.

MEMORY AND LEARNING

Of all cognitive processes that are involved in everyday living, memory has been the most extensively researched (Poon & Siegler, 1991). Many famous psychologists and physiologists have studied the nature of memory and its physiological basis during the past several decades. Despite these efforts, precisely how memories are stored and retained is not completely understood, and our models of memory are mostly descriptive rather than explanatory.

Rather than being a single process that takes place in a particular area of the brain, there are several kinds of memory and they appear to involve various neural structures and functions. Not only the cerebral cortex but also subcortical structures such as the hippocampus are involved in memory storage and retention.

Learning and memory have been of particular interest to psychological researchers, especially those of a behavioristic persuasion. The two topics are, of course, inseparable: Evidence for learning is based on memory, and memories are formed through learning. Psychological research has focused on three processes or stages in learning and remembering: acquisition or learning, encoding or storage, and recall or retrieval. *Acquisition* is concerned with acquiring skills and information by means of the senses. Learning and memory may be conscious or unconscious, explicit or implicit, but acquisition is more likely to occur when the learner is motivated and attentive.

Memory Storage

Table 4–1 is a glossary of memory terms. As indicated by the terms *sensory memory* or sensory register, the first stage of memory is a sensory impression of the material to be recalled. This stage lasts only a few seconds, until the impression is registered in short-term memory (STM or *primary memory*). A familiar example of primary memory, which lasts no longer than half a minute, is remembering a specific telephone number only until it has been dialed. To be remembered for a longer period of time, that is, to be

TABLE 4–1 A Glossary of Memory Terms

Declarative memory: Knowledge about the world; includes *episodic* and *semantic* memories. [*Frontal* ... *temporal* ... *parietal*]

Echoic memory: Auditory sensory memory.

Episodic memory: E. Tulving's term for memory of the place and time of specific personal events.

Expert memory: Memory shown by chess masters and other experts that is based on extensive experience in a particular area of expertise; intuitive or less bound by formal rules.

Explicit memory: Intentional, conscious memory.

Iconic memory: Visual, sensory memory.

Implicit memory: Memory occurring without conscious intention to remember.

Incidental memory: Unintentional memory; not based on conscious experience, attention, or planned action.

Long-term memory (LTM): Secondary or tertiary memory. Memory that lasts at least 10–20 minutes and involves more permanent storage in the brain.

Metamemory: Understanding how one's memory works.

Primary memory: Retention in memory of 5 to 7 bits of information in temporary storage.

Procedural memory: E. Tulving's term for stored knowledge of skilled, automatic actions or procedures. [How to do — never really loose this]

Prospective memory: Memory of plans for reaching a designated goal, to be carried out at some future date; remembering to remember.

Secondary memory: Fairly short-term memory having a capacity of more than 5 to 7 bits of information, based on active rehearsal of material in primary memory; repository of newly acquired information.

Semantic memory: Memory of organized factual knowledge and rules for manipulating knowledge about the world.

Sensory memory: Temporary impression of one-fourth to several seconds duration, requiring no conscious effort at attention.

Short-term memory (STM): Primary memory.

Tertiary memory: Long-term, relatively permanent memory of overlearned, meaningful material.

Working memory: Primary memory. Used to manipulate information for the next stage of memory processing.

transferred to long-term memory (LTM), the material in primary memory must be encoded or processed in some way. Two long-term stages have been designated: *secondary memory*, which has a duration of a few minutes to several hours; and *tertiary memory*, which may last from a few hours to many years.

Many intelligence tests contain subtests designed to measure primary memory. It was assumed by the test designers that the number of digits, words, or other stimuli that an individual can remember is important in overall intellectual functioning. However, there are numerous examples of individuals ("idiot savants") who could not learn the skills and information acquired by most people and yet were able to perform remarkable feats of memory. Also of interest in research on individual differences has been the effects of aging on primary memory. On almost every kind of memory task, older adults do not perform as well as younger adults. If the assumption that older adults are more distractible or less attentive than younger adults is correct, then we could expect some deficits in both sensory and primary memory. Certainly the sensory/perceptual and motor systems are affected by aging, but central processing speed and sensory memory appear to be relatively unaffected (Strayer, Wickens, & Braune, 1987). The results of research on primary memory and aging have been mixed (Poon, 1985). Some studies have found that older adults do not do as well as younger adults when the information to be repeated or the actions to be performed are very long and complex (e.g., Inglis, Ankus, & Sykes, 1968). On the other hand, the results of other studies indicate that primary memory remains fairly stable and efficient with aging. In a review of studies of STM, Poon (1985) concluded that aging does not affect primary memory as such, but rather affects the encoding or transfer of information from STM to LTM.

In order to be stored more permanently, information in primary memory must be rehearsed and encoded by means of a mnemonic (memory-facilitating) operation. The most common mnemonic is to associate the material to be learned with something familiar or already known (Kausler, 1985). This is the basis of traditional "mnemonic schemes" such as the peg-word method and the method of loci.[2]

---

[2]If a list of, say, 20 words is to be memorized, in the *peg-word method*, the person begins by learning and rehearsing a list of peg words that rhyme with the numbers 1 to 20 ("One is a gun," "Two is a shoe," "Three is a tree," etc.). Then, the list of 20 words to be memorized is presented, and each word is imagined to be interacting with the same-numbered peg word. For example, if the first word is *cantaloupe*, then an image of a gun blasting a cantaloupe could be formed. If the second word is *potato*, one could imagine a potato being kicked by a shoe, and so on. In the *method of loci*, the person selects a series of distinct locations along a familiar route from one place to another and imagines each object to be remembered as being placed at a particular location along the route. For example, if the route is one that leads from home to the grocery store, then the cantaloupe could be imagined perched on the first location, say a mailbox, the potato could be imagined placed in the arch of a tree, the next location, and so on. Then, on arriving at the grocery store, one has only to take a mental trip along the route and pick up the (imaginary) objects placed at each location.

With respect to the effects of aging on secondary memory, in general, older adults are less adept at organizing, associating, and integrating material so that it gets into permanent storage (Hoyer & Plude, 1980). Age deficits in secondary memory have been found to occur across a wide age range (30–80 years) (Arenberg & Robertson-Tchabo, 1977). The deficits are greater in semantic than in procedural memory, and greater in explicit than in implicit memory (see Table 4–1 for definitions) (Hultsch & Dixon, 1990). Compared to younger adults, older adults have greater difficulty in forming associations and using visual images to encode and retrieve information. The retrieval problems are due in part to the fact that the material was not encoded or processed adequately or deeply into long-term storage. Consequently, the gist of a text or other verbal and perceptual materials may be recalled, but details are not remembered as well as they are by younger adults. The age-related deficit in LTM is greater when testing the recall rather than the recognition of learned material (Craik & McDowd, 1987; Poon, 1985; Schonfield & Robertson, 1966).

Being engrossed with one's tertiary memories is characteristic of people who are said to "live in the past." For example, Kastenbaum (1966) found that many of the 276 centenarians whom he studied were much more concerned with their memories of the distant past than with more recent events and had clearer memories of the former than the latter. Although it is almost impossible to obtain valid data on the storage and retrieval of tertiary memories, the existing data indicate that there is no age decrement (Perlmutter & Mitchell, 1982).

As a group, older adults experience more problems than younger adults in both storing and retrieving LTMs, and especially the latter. Sensory defects, inattentiveness, distractibility, slowness, overcautiousness, and neurological defects have all been suggested as possible causes for deficits of older adults with secondary memories. Note that this conclusion applies to older adults in general and not to any specific person. Despite the common concern of middle-aged and older adults that they will lose or are losing their memory, old age is not the "mother of forgetfulness" for everyone. The memories of many adults in their seventies and eighties are just as good as those of adults in their twenties and thirties. In a study conducted by Cutler and Grams (1988) on a national sample of adults aged 55 and over, 25% reported no memory problems at all, and only 15% said they experienced frequent memory problems.

The degree of memory deficit in old age varies not only with the health and intelligence of the individual but also with the kind and level of difficulty of the material to be remembered and whether it is relevant to the person's life. Memory training can help, even in the case of people in their eighties and nineties (Willis & Nesselroade, 1990). With proper motivation, older adults can improve their memories with practice and by using memory aids, cues, or reminders. Trainers who provide clear instructions on how to sort and organize the material or procedure to be learned and try to make it as meaningful and relevant as possible can help older adults to improve the acquisition, retention, and retrieval of information and skills.

Learning in Adulthood

As was emphasized earlier in the chapter, maintaining an interest in the physical and social environment and continuing to use one's problem-solving skills can help arrest declines in intellectual functioning with age. Whatever their age may be, adults who keep up with current events and continue to explore their world through reading, conversations, course work, and hobbies experience less decline in cognitive abilities (Jarvik & Bank, 1983; Schaie, 1983; Siegler, 1983). Furthermore, the effects of heredity on cognition abilities persist into late life. Environment and heredity are equally influential in the ability to think and remember even after age 80 (McClearn et al., 1977).

The popular belief that old people have trouble learning new things because they are "set in their ways," and because old memories and experiences get in the way of the new, may have some merit. But even though learning performance may decline in older adulthood, in most cases, the decline is not marked until after age 70 or so (Arenberg & Robertson-Tchabo, 1980). However, the behavior of most people is fairly modifiable or plastic even in later life. With appropriate motivation, sufficient time, and expert instruction, and an environment that is conducive to learning, older adults can continue to expand their capabilities, interests, and attitudes. Even individuals in poor health or those who, for other reasons, are handicapped and limited in their abilities can benefit from patient, flexible, and insightful instruction. Some of the general characteristics of older learners that should be taken into account are that (1) they prefer a slower instructional pace, (2) they are more cautious and hence inclined to make more errors of omission, (3) they are more disrupted by emotional arousal, (4) they are less attentive, (5) they are less likely to use imagery and other mnemonic schemes or mediators spontaneously, and (6) they are less willing to learn material or procedures that they view as irrelevant to their lives (Aiken, 1995). Note that these are *general* characteristics of the population of older learners and may not apply to a specific person.

PROBLEM SOLVING AND CREATIVITY

Rote learning and memory are important cognitive functions at all periods of human development, and especially during the school days of childhood and adolescence. Schooling provides us with the knowledge and skills that have been acquired throughout human history and relieves us of the task of rediscovering an answer to every question or a solution to every problem that we encounter. On occasion, however, we are confronted with a problem for which we have no ready-made solution and which may demand a new approach—something outside the range of our immediate experience.

Problem Solving and Reasoning

The abilities of human beings and other animals to solve problems and the ways in which they go about it have been of interest to psychologists for many decades. Some of the earliest studies of problem solving were conducted by the Gestalt psychologists, but the topic was also of concern to behaviorists. Experiments on the interference effects of *mental sets*, such as the inability to perceive an object as having anything other than its customary function (*functional fixedness*), is one of the topics on which a great deal of research has been conducted. The technique of *brainstorming*, which consists of a "green light" stage in which many possible solutions are suggested, and a "red light" stage in which each solution is evaluated, was proposed as a procedure for breaking up mental sets in group problem solving (Osborn, 1953). Also of interest to researchers and practitioners were stage or step theories of problem solving, one popular example being the four-stage sequence of preparation, incubation, illumination, and verification (Wallas, 1926).

The traditional approach to solving problems follows a scientific reasoning procedure: (1) The problem arises, (2) relevant known information is collected, (3) a hypothesis (potential solution) is proposed, (4) the hypothesis is tested, (5) the hypothesis is affirmed or disconfirmed. This sequence of steps is, of course, not a one-way street. In actual practice, there is a great deal of back-and-forth movement between steps.

Scientific reasoning is an example of logical reasoning, which may be either deductive or inductive. In *deductive reasoning*, or syllogistic reasoning, we begin with a generalization and deduce a particularity (e.g., all men are mortal; John is a man; therefore, John is mortal). *Inductive reasoning*, on the other hand, begins with a particular instance or example and infers a general conclusions from it. A favorite, though perhaps fictitious, example of inductive reasoning is Isaac Newton's induction of the principle of gravity from the experience of being hit on the head by a falling apple. Hundreds of studies have been conducted on the abilities of children and adults to reason deductively and inductively, frequently with disappointing results. The atmosphere or context of the problem about which the person is asked to reason can have a strong interfering effect on the accuracy of the reasoning process.

As on intelligence tests, performance on problem-solving or reasoning tasks declines with age (Giambra & Arenberg, 1980; Rabbitt, 1977). Older adults are slower in solving complex problems, require more assistance to find a solution, and are less flexible in using the information provided. Age decrements in problem-solving ability are more apparent when a great deal of information must be kept in mind in order to discover a solution.

Creativity

Also of interest to psychologists who study problem solving is J. P. Guilford's (1967) distinction between convergent and divergent thinking. *Convergent thinking* consists of applying logical reasoning to arrive at a single, correct answer or solution to a problem. *Divergent thinking*, on the other hand, is more open-ended in that multiple solutions are possible. Divergent thinking is applied to the questions on measures of creativity such as the Torrance Tests of Creative Thinking and Guilford's Measures of Creativity. Responses to items on creativity tests are typically scored in terms of fluency (the number of ideas presented) and novelty (newness, originality).

Creativity actually goes beyond the realm of problem solving and into problem generation. A highly creative person not only solves problems in a new and different way, but also recognizes the existence of problems that other people fail to see. For example, Johannes Gutenberg's contemporaries may not have seen the need for a printing press. However, Gutenberg saw the need and was also able to combine two objects that were not obviously associated (lettered dies and an olive press), a process referred to as the "bifurcation of associates." Not only does creativity demand a great deal of expertise in the area of interest but also imagination, a venturesome personality, a high level of motivation, and a supportive environment (Sternberg & Lubart, 1991, 1992).

The history of science and art reveals that many of the most original ideas were developed when the individuals concerned were still young adults. For this reason, it is commonly believed that creativity declines in middle- and later adulthood. Although research findings (e.g., Cole, 1979; Dennis, 1966; Lehman, 1953; McCrae, Arenberg, & Costa, 1987) support the conclusion that the peak period of creative productivity occurs in early or middle adulthood, the shape of the productivity x age curve varies with the discipline and the individual (see Figure 4–5).

A list of general conclusions based on research concerning the relationship of creative productivity to chronological age is given in Table 4–2. In general, creativity tends to persists throughout the individual's life, reaching a peak in the middle or late years. Furthermore, the decline in creativity in later life may be caused by a number of factors, including the demands of other activities, illness, personal problems, increased stress, and loss of interest or motivation in the field of creative endeavor. And even though creative productivity declines in most older people, the lives of Michelangelo, Verdi, Goethe, Picasso, Sophocles, Monet, and other creative geniuses illustrate that highly original work is possible in a person's seventies, eighties, and even nineties.

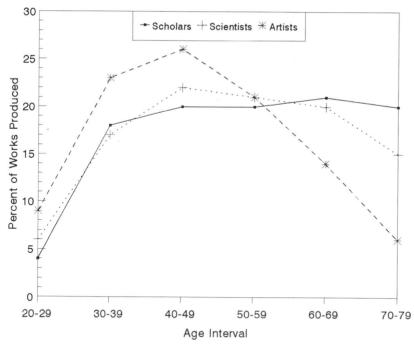

Figure 4–5   Age changes in creative productivity in three fields of endeavor. (Based on data from Dennis, 1966.)

TABLE 4–2 A Dozen Conclusions Concerning Creativity across the Life Span

1. Creative productivity peaks in early adulthood.
2. The peak of creative productivity occurs at different ages for different fields of endeavor.
3. The ratio of the quality to the quantity of creative productions remains fairly constant across the life span.
4. Creative productivity across the life span varies significantly from person to person.
5. Creativity at all age levels can be encouraged or discouraged by social and cultural groups.
6. People who begin their careers early and maintain a high level of output will tend to continue being productive in late life.
7. Age decrements in ability are seldom great enough for people to become devoid of creativity in later life.
8. The magnitude and rate of age declines in creativity vary with the particular field or domain of endeavor.
9. A resurgence of creativity may be experienced in later adulthood.
10. Many, if not all, older adults can renew themselves both creatively and personally.
11. The focus or style of creativity may change in later life.
12. The level of creative productivity in later years depends on a person's creative potential at the beginning of his or her career.

Sources: Extracted from Kastenbaum (1993) and Simonton (1990).

SUMMARY

Intelligence testing during this century has had wide practical applications in educational, clinical, employment, and forensic contexts. Intelligence tests, such as the Wechsler Adult Intelligence Scale, have also been used extensively in research concerned with individual and group differences on a host of demographic and biological variables. The correlations of IQ scores with ethnicity, socioeconomic status, occupation, and certain other demographic variables are associated with level of education and cultural factors.

Declines in scores on intelligence tests after middle adulthood have been found in both cross-sectional and longitudinal studies, but the decline is steeper in the former than the latter type of study. The rate of age-related declines on intelligence tests varies significantly with the particular cognitive abilities measured by different subtests. The classic aging pattern is that of a greater age-related decline on performance tests than on verbal tests. Measures of fluid abilities also reveal greater age-related declines than measures of crystallized abilities. A rapid decline in scores on intelligence tests just prior to death—the so-called terminal drop—has also been found in a number of studies.

Piaget's four-stage theory of cognitive growth, culminating in the stage of formal operations at around 15 years of age, has had an important influence on developmental psychology. However, certain psychologists have maintained that cognitive abilities expand into dialectical thinking or postformal thought during adulthood.

Although some researchers view memory as consisting of a unitary process, most research on memory has been based on a three- or four-stage model: sensory memory (iconic or echoic); primary (short-term) memory, or STM; secondary (long-term) memory, or LTM; and tertiary (very long-term) memory, or VLTM. The rate of age-related declines in sensory, primary, and tertiary memory appears to be minimal, but the decline is quite pronounced on measures of secondary memory. The degree of age decrement in secondary memory, which has been documented by various methodologies, is affected by illness, persistence in scholarly activities, and psychological factors such as stress and motivation. The scores of many older adults on tests of memory and other cognitive abilities can be improved by special training, but it is not clear whether inherent abilities or merely test-taking skills are improved by such training. Educational attainment is inversely related to chronological age, a circumstance that may account, at least in part, for age declines on tests of cognitive abilities.

Like intelligence and memory, problem-solving ability and creativity vary with age. The efficiency of problem solving in old age is influenced by memory, motivation, cautiousness, rigidity, and other personality variables. The peak of creative productivity occurs at different ages for different fields of endeavor, ranging from early adulthood through late middle age. Research on creativity has been hampered by the difficulty of defining criteria of creative performance and of differentiating between originality, utility, and productivity.

SUGGESTED READINGS

Baltes, P. B. (1993). The aging mind: Potential and limitations. *Gerontologist, 33,* 580–594.

Baltes, P. B., Smith, J., & Staudinger, U. M. (1991). Wisdom and successful aging. In M. T. Sonderegger (Ed.), *The Nebraska Symposium on Motivation: Volume 39. Psychology and aging* (pp. 123–167). Lincoln: University of Nebraska Press.

Hultsch, D. F., & Dixon, R. A. (1990). Learning and memory in aging. In J. E. Birren & K. W. Schaie (Eds.), *Handbook of the psychology of aging* (3rd ed., pp. 258–274). San Diego: Academic Press.

Light, L. L. (1990). Interactions between memory and language in old age. In J. E. Birren & K. W. Schaie (Eds.), *Handbook of the psychology of aging* (3rd ed., pp. 275–290). San Diego: Academic Press.

Schaie, K. W. (1996). Intellectual development in adulthood. In J. E. Birren, K. W. Schaie, R. P. Abeles, M. Gatz, & T. A. Salthouse (Eds.), *Handbook of the psychology of aging* (4th ed., pp. 266–285). San Diego: Academic Press.

Simonton, D. K. (1990). Creativity and wisdom in aging. In J. E. Birren & K. W. Schaie (Eds.), *Handbook of the psychology of aging* (3rd ed., pp. 320–329). San Diego: Academic Press.

Sternberg, R. J. (1997). The concept of intelligence and its role in lifelong learning and success. *American Psychologist, 52,* 1030–1037.

Wagner, R. K. (1997). Intelligence training and employment. *American Psychologist, 52,* 1059–1069.

CHAPTER 5

Personality Development and Disorders

Personality is the sum total of all the qualities, traits, and behaviors that characterize a person's individuality and by which, together with his or her physical attributes, the person is recognized as unique. As witnessed by the persistence of temperament or psychological reaction patterns from birth to adulthood, heredity plays an important role in shaping personality: Active, outgoing children and passive, inhibited children tend to retain those same characteristics in adulthood. This does not mean that the roles of environment and experience are not as important as heredity in shaping personality. The society and culture into which a child is born interact with his or her genetic predispositions in determining the kind of person the child becomes, that is, how those predispositions are molded and expressed. Like the cognitive abilities discussed in Chapter 4 and, in fact, all human characteristics, personality is the product of the dynamic interaction between genetic make-up and the physical and psychosocial environments to which the individual is exposed in growing up.

The number and variety of a person's experiences increase with age. For most children, the journey of life begins in a family setting and expands to the community, the school, and the world of work. Depending on the appearance and behavior of the individual, as well as the nature of the social situation and the people comprising it, social encounters may be friendly or unfriendly, successful or unsuccessful. Relatives, peers, fellow students, and coworkers can be competitive or cooperative, accepting or rejecting. In general, the more socially active a person is, the more friendly and unfriendly contacts he or she has. More frequent social interaction produces sympathetic, helping behavior as well as quarrelsomeness and aggression. Throughout it all, most individuals learn that social and psychological survival depends on being able to give and take, and that happiness requires attention to the needs of others as well as oneself. Most people learn this lesson in childhood, whereas some never seem to do so.

THEORIES OF PERSONALITY DEVELOPMENT

The idea that the experiences of childhood are important determiners of adult personality is a part of folklore as old as humanity itself. However, Sigmund Freud proposed the first systematic theory of how childhood experiences leave an imprint on the individual that persists into adulthood. To Freud, adult personality and character are end products of the frustrations and conflicts experienced by the child during the oral, anal, phallic, latency, and genital stages of psychosexual development. At each of these stages, sexual energies are concentrated on a particular region of the body and conflicts develop with regard to their expression. Failure to progress from one psychosexual stage to another, referred to as *fixation*, results in the sexual energies of the person becoming permanently attached to that stage. In addition, traumatic events or extreme stress can result in *regression*, a reenactment of behaviors typical of an earlier psychosexual stage. For example, nail-biting, overeating, overtalkativeness, smoking, and thumbsucking, combined with an excessively dependent, greedy, and passive personality in an older child or adult, were viewed as symptoms of fixation at or regression to the oral stage. Fixation at the anal stage, on the other hand, was seen as reflected in a compulsive, orderly, excessively conforming, stingy, and stubborn adult personality.

Erikson's Psychosocial Stages

Unlike classical psychoanalysis, which viewed personality as essentially complete by adolescence, Erik Erikson (1963) maintained that personality continues developing throughout an individual's lifetime. Also unlike Freudian theory, Erikson's stages are "psychosocial" rather than "psychosexual." Erikson emphasized the importance of social interactions in the resolution of the crisis or conflict at each stage. The first five stages in his model of development are temporally parallel to Freud's five psychosexual stages. However, Erikson extended the range of personality development to include three additional stages in adulthood. These stages are similar in certain respects to Robert Havighurst's (1953) description of the developmental tasks of early adulthood, middle age, and later maturity.

To Havighurst, mating, establishing a home, beginning an occupation, and rearing children are the major tasks of young adulthood. Helping younger people, developing leisure-time activities, fulfilling civic and social responsibilities, and adjusting to physiological changes are the major tasks of middle age. Adjusting to decreasing strength, retiring, adjusting to the death of a spouse, and affiliating with one's age group are the major tasks of later maturity.

Though similar, Erikson's developmental stages are more "psychological" and less "social" in their orientation than Havighurst's. As shown in Table 5–1,

TABLE 5–1 Erikson's Eight Stages of Psychosocial Development

Infancy. The major crisis or conflict in this stage is between trust and mistrust. The goal or resolution of this crisis is to acquire a basic sense of trust. Consistency, continuity, and sameness of experience lead to trust. Inadequate, inconsistent, or negative care may arouse mistrust.

Early Childhood. The major crisis or conflict in this stage is between autonomy and shame and doubt. The goal or resolution of this crisis is to attain a sense of autonomy. Opportunities to try out skills at one's own pace and in one's own way lead to autonomy. Overprotection or lack of support may lead to doubt about one's ability to control oneself or the environment.

Play Age. The major crisis or conflict in this stage is between initiative and guilt. The goal or resolution of this crisis is to develop a sense of initiative. Freedom to engage in activities and parents' patient answering of questions lead to initiative. Restriction of activities and treating questions as a nuisance lead to guilt.

School Age. The major crisis or conflict in this stage is between industry and inferiority. The goal or resolution of this crisis is to become industrious and competent. Being permitted to make and do things and being praised for accomplishments lead to industry. Limitations on activities and criticism of what is done lead to inferiority.

Adolescence. The major crisis or conflict in this stage is between identity and role confusion. The goal or resolution of this crisis is to achieve a personal identity. Recognition of continuity and sameness in one's personality, even when in different situations and when reacted to by different individuals, leads to identity. Inability to establish stability, particularly regarding sex roles and occupational choice, leads to role confusion.

Young Adulthood. The major crisis or conflict in this stage is between intimacy and isolation. The goal or resolution of this crisis is to become intimate with someone. Fusing one's identity with another leads to intimacy. Competitive and combative relations with others may lead to isolation.

Middle Age. The major crisis or conflict of this stage is between generativity and self-absorption. The goal or resolution of this crisis is to develop an interest in future generations. Establishing and guiding the next generation produces a sense of generativity. Being concerned primarily with oneself leads to self-absorption.

Old Age. The major crisis or conflict in this stage is between integrity and despair. The goal or resolution of this crisis is to become an integrated and self-accepting person. Acceptance of one's life leads to a sense of integrity. Feeling that it is too late to make up for missed opportunities leads to despair.

Source: Adapted from Erikson (1963).

at each of Erikson's eight stages there is a different crisis or conflict to be solved. The manner in which that crisis is resolved produces certain feelings and behaviors on the part of the individual that may persist throughout life. Five of these stages, or crises, occur during childhood and adolescence, and three occur in adulthood.

Resolution of the major crisis of young adulthood, *intimacy versus isolation*, determines whether the individual develops a lasting intimate relationship with another person or remains isolated from a persisting, close relationship. Failure to resolve this crisis by achieving the virtue of *love* and the self-definition of "I am what I love" can retard emotional development and lead to persisting unhappiness.

The major crisis of the second adult stage (middle age) in Erikson's model is *generativity versus stagnation*. Generativity involves the development of a concern for the next generation and those who will follow. Failure to develop this concern leads to stagnation, boredom, emotional impoverishment, and a pessimistic feeling that this is where it all ends. Erikson maintained that middle age is the time when the virtue of *care* and the self-definition of "I am what I create" develops, as witnessed by parenting, teaching, supervising, and otherwise assisting the next generation.

The major crisis of the last stage (old age) in Erikson's model of personality development is *integrity versus despair*. The principal goal of this stage is to become an integrated and self-accepting person. The way in which the individual handles this crisis is affected by personality characteristics developed over the years, the individual's physical health and economic situation, and the meaningfulness of the roles to be played. Emerging from successful resolution of the crisis of integrity versus despair age are the virtue of *wisdom* and the self-definition of "I am what survives me." Wisdom consists of the ability to accept one's life and what has been accomplished. If the crises in all preceding stages have been resolved, old age becomes a time when one can live each day with hope, will, purpose, competence, fidelity, love, care, and wisdom.

Erikson's theory has been quite popular with developmental psychologists, but like all stage theories, it has been difficult to evaluate empirically. The theory has also been criticized for being too optimistic about human nature, too moralistic in its tone, and too supportive of the status quo. The overemphasis on ego attributes and conscious impulses to the neglect of sexual, aggressive, and unconscious drives has also been perceived as a shortcoming by psychodynamic theorists. Still, Erikson's ideas did contribute to a shift in the emphasis of psychoanalysts from instinctive urges that are beyond conscious control toward social and cultural influences on personality development.

Loevinger's Stages of Ego Development

Jane Loevinger's (1976) stage theory of ego development is based on Erikson's theory of psychosocial stages in addition to Lawrence Kohlberg's (1969, 1976) conception of six stages of moral development. According to Loevinger, the ego is the principal organizing process of the personality, the integrator of morals, values, goals, and cognition. Shaped by the dynamic interaction of the person and the environment, the ego develops and its integrating functions change in a sequence of eight stages, beginning in infancy and progressively building on previous stages. Loevinger describes six stages of ego development in adulthood:

1. *Conformist*: Obedience (absolute conformity) to external social rules.
2. *Conscientious–Conformist*: Separation of norms and goals; realization that acts affect others.

3. *Conscientious*: Beginning of self-evaluated standards; understanding of the true complexity of the world.
4. *Individualistic*: Respect for individuality and recognition that the process of acting is more important than the outcome.
5. *Autonomous*: Respect for each person's individuality; high tolerance for ambiguity with conflicting needs within oneself and others.
6. *Integrated*: Resolution of inner conflicts.

No specific age range is associated with a particular stage; it may occur at any time during adulthood. At each stage, four areas are important to developmental progress:

- *Character development*: The standards and goals of the person.
- *Interpersonal styles*: The person's pattern of relations with others.
- *Conscious preoccupations*: The most important things on the person's mind.
- *Cognitive style*: The characteristic way in which the person thinks.

In part because of its empirical foundation based on the Sentence Completion Test, which Loevinger designed to assess ego development, the theory has had a marked impact on research in adult development. For example, it has been applied in research on the relationships between ego development and cognitive development (King, Kitchener, Wood, & Davison, 1989) and between ego development and the coping strategies employed at different ages (Labouvie-Vief, Hakim-Larson, & Hobart, 1987).

Loevinger's theory is only one of several extensions and modifications of Erikson's model of psychological development. Another extension, proposed by Robert Peck (1968), is based on the results of clinical observations, case studies, and interviews of older adults. Specifically, Peck divided the "integrity versus despair" crisis of Erikson's old-age stage into three subcrises or conflicts. The first of these subcrises—*ego differentiation versus role preoccupation*—centers on whether the individual views him- or herself as a flexible, complex person who can perform several roles or is restricted to a single role activity. The second subcrisis of old age—*body transcendence versus body preoccupation*—is concerned with whether the individual is able to transcend the infirmities and unattractiveness of his or her own body and to value physical, mental, and social activities despite declining health. The third subcrisis—*ego transcendence versus ego preoccupation*—centers on whether the individual goes beyond his or her own ego or is constantly preoccupied with the self and cannot accept the reality of death.

Levinson's Stages of Man

According to *transition theorists*, psychological needs such as control over one's life, enthusiasm for activities, commitments to other people and values, and the belief that one matters to others cannot be satisfied for all time but must be continuously renegotiated. Because the demands and expectations of society change as one passes through the age-graded social structure, the individual must acquire new attitudes, roles, and beliefs in order to fulfill his or her needs. The nature of the new social contract negotiated by the maturing individual, that is, the particular psychological changes that are deemed necessary in order to meet one's needs, vary with the person and thereby define his or her personality (Reedy, 1983).

Daniel Levinson's conception of psychological development in adulthood is a mixture of discrete stages and transitions between adjacent stages. Based on in-depth interviews of 10 men in each of four occupational groups, Levinson's (1978) theory defines the goal of adult development as the construction of a life structure consisting of both an external, sociocultural side and an internal, personal side. A person's life structure develops in a series of stages ranging from 6 to 8 years in length and separated by transition periods of 4–5 years each. The four stages and five transitions of adulthood are described in Table 5–2. Each of the transition periods is spent in a reconsideration of one's life in preparation for the next stage. The most widely discussed of these transitions, the *midlife transition*, and the associated notion of the *midlife crisis*, was popularized by Gail Sheehy's books *Passages* (1976) and *Pathfinders* (1981). The midlife crisis is supposedly precipitated by a review and reevaluation of one's past during the midlife transition or the age-50 transition periods. However, research has found the midlife crisis to be far from a universal phenomenon (Reinke, Holmes, & Harris, 1985; Roberts & Newton, 1987; Valliant, 1977).

Although Levinson's initial research was limited to middle-class American men, he maintains that the theory also applies to women, different social

TABLE 5–2 Levinson's Stages and Transitions in Adult Development

---

Early Adult Transition (17–22). Goal is to terminate adolescent life structure and form a basis for living in the adult world.

Entering the Adult World (22–28). Form and test out preliminary life structures and provide a link between oneself and adult society.

Age 30 Transition (30–33). Revise life structure of previous period and form a basis for a more satisfactory life structure to be created in the settling-down stage.

Settling-Down Stage (33–40). Establish one's niche in society ("early settling down"), work at advancement, and strive for further success ("become one's own man").

Midlife Transition (40–45). Evaluate success in attaining goals of settling-down stage, take steps toward initiating midlife, and deal with relationship between oneself and the external world (*individuation*).

Entering Middle Adulthood (50–55)

Age 50 Transition (50–55)

Culmination of Middle Adulthood (55–60). Analogous to settling-down stage of young adulthood.

Late-Adult Transition (60–65). Changing mental and physical capacities intensify one's own aging and sense of mortality.

Source: Adapted from Levinson (1978).

classes, different cultures, and different periods of history (Levinson & Levinson, 1996). Roberts and Newton (1987) found that Levinson's model was applicable to young and middle-aged women, but there were differences between the sexes. One of these differences concerned the nature of early adulthood "dreams." Levinson defines a "dream" as a set of aspirations that serves as a goal for the person's adult life. According to Roberts and Newton, women's dreams are more complex than men's. The "dreams" of men tended to center on occupational accomplishments, whereas the "dreams" of many women are split, involving both interpersonal relationships and occupational accomplishments. These findings are consistent with the idea that men are more likely than women to retain their identities by breaking away from their families and pursuing their interests and goals in individual achievements. The identities of women, however, are more likely to stem from the attachments and responsibilities associated with interpersonal relationships (Baruch, Barnett & Rivers, 1983; Gilligan, 1982).

Scripts and Life Stories

The fact that people are attracted to environments that appear to "fit" their personalities presumably accounts for some of the stability of personality traits (Ahammer, 1973). Slow-paced, gentle people tend to prefer small towns, athletic people tend to migrate to the Sunbelt states, and shy people avoid public encounters. The choices of specific living environments and lifestyles result in greater stability of personality, a stability created more by the individual than the environment (Lerner & Busch-Rossnagel, 1981).

In addition to selecting their living environments, people create environments to suit their own needs and goals. According to *script theory*, people attempt to maintain a sense of continuity or order in the important features (*scenes*) of their lives. A *life script* enables the individual to anticipate, respond to, control, and create meaningful events. Following this script, personality develops by means of a two-way process—past to future and future to past. The way in which the past has been constructed changes as a consequence of later experience. Anticipations of what the future will bring both color the present and revise the past, and past experiences return to alter the individual's perceptions of the present (Carlson, 1981).

Somewhat similar in conception to script theory is McAdams' (1993, 1994) *life-story model* of identity formation. According to this model, adults derive a sense of identity by creating and modifying their life stories in response to changes in both themselves and their environments. A *life story* is an internalized narrative with a beginning, a middle, and an anticipated ending. The emotional feel of the story, which can range from bleak pessimism to blithe optimism, is referred to as the *narrative tone* of the person's identity. The imagery, themes, ideological setting, nuclear episodes, characters, and ending of the story are all important descriptors of the person's identity. These elements change as identity develops over time, a process that may be conscious or unconscious. A successful life story is one that possesses coherence, credibility, and openness to new possibilities; it is richly differentiated, reconciles the opposing aspects of the self, and integrates the self into the sociocultural context (McAdams, 1993, 1994).

PERSONALITY TRAITS

A variety of methods and instruments have been applied to the measurement of personality development and change. Systematic and unsystematic observations, structured and unstructured interviews, checklists, rating scales, questionnaires, personality inventories, and projective techniques represent the major approaches to personality assessment in research and applied contexts. The designs of certain instruments or procedures have been guided by concepts and propositions from a particular theory of personality, whereas other instruments are based primarily on the results of empirical, statistical analyses of responses to a variety of words, statements, or other stimuli.

The Self and Self-Esteem

The psychodynamic theories of Sigmund Freud, Carl Jung, Alfred Adler, and Erik Erikson, the phenomenological (self) theories of Carl Rogers and Abraham Maslow, and the social learning theories of Julian Rotter and Albert Bandura have all provided suggestions and guidelines for the construction of a number of personality assessment instruments. The psychoanalytic concepts of the *ego*, Erikson's concept of *identity*, the phenomenological concept of the *self*, and associated concepts in social learning theory (e.g., Rotter's *locus of control* and Bandura's *self-efficacy*) have stimulated the development of many psychometric procedures and research on how the perception of the central core of the personality—the "I" or "me"—of the individual develops and changes over time. Research with such measures has shown, for example, that self-esteem changes with age but that the manner in which the change occurs varies with the sex of the person. Kermis (1986) found that, for men, the peak in self-esteem is typically reached during middle age and declines somewhat after then. For women, however, self-esteem tends to peak during the childbearing and child-rearing years, after which it declines until around age 65 and then rises again. Rather than being the result of aging per se, however, the decline in self-esteem of many older adults is due to events occurring at that time. Such events include accidents, war, economic depression, and other upheavals in the physical and social environments, as well as failures, serious health problems, and other personal setbacks.

Traits and Types

Although many theories and research findings have contributed to the development of personality assessment instruments, the most influential of all conceptualizations have been those that view human personality as a conglomeration of traits. Broadly defined, a *trait* is a cognitive, affective, or psychomotor characteristic that is possessed in different amounts by different people. A *type*, on the other hand, is a larger dimension of personality, consisting of a particular complex of traits. For example, Reichard, Livson, and Petersen's (1962) five clusters of personality in older men (mature, rocking chair, armored, angry, and self-hating) are personality types. A related example of types is found in the results of Neugarten, Havighurst, and Tobin's (1968) study of the relationships of long-standing personality characteristics and social activity to happiness in a sample of people aged 70 to 79. This study was concerned with four major personality types: integrated, armored–defended, passive–dependent, and unintegrated. The *integrated* personalities, who functioned well and had complex inner lives as well as intact cognitive abilities and egos, were divided into three patterns of role activity: reorganized, focused, and disengaged. The *armored–defended* personalities, consisting of achievement-oriented individuals who pushed themselves, were designated as either holding-on or constricted people. The *passive-dependent* personalities were designated as either succor-seeking or apathetic people, and the *unintegrated* or disorganized personalities were those with serious psychological problems.

Though they represent smaller dimensions of personality than types, traits may still be quite broad. For example, traits such as "authoritarianism," "humanitarianism," "narcissism," and "Machiavellianism" (power-striving) may be so dominant or pervasive in a person's life that they are expressed in almost all of his or her activities.

Cattell and Eysenck

Of the many psychologists who have viewed personality from a trait–factor perspective, three of the most influential are Gordon Allport, Raymond Cattell, and Hans Eysenck. Cattell's multifactor theory is perhaps the most comprehensive model of personality in terms of traits or factors, but Eyenck's model is the most parsimonious. Both conceptions are based on the results of *factor analysis*, a set of statistical procedures for determining what factors (psychological constructs) are sufficient to explain the correlations among a large group of scores on psychometric instruments. Whereas Cattell describes personality in terms of 16 or more source traits, Eysenck maintains that three "supertraits"—introversion–extraversion, emotional stability–instability, and psychoticism—are adequate to describe human personality.

The Five-Factor Model and the NEO

Somewhere between Cattell and Eysenck in the number of proposed traits is the *five-factor model* (Costa & McCrae, 1986; Goldberg, 1980). The five factors or traits in this model are:

Neuroticism. High scorers on measures of this factor are described as anxious, insecure, self-conscious, self-pitying, worrying, and vulnerable; low scorers are described as calm, comfortable, even-tempered, secure, self-satisfied, and unemotional.

Extraversion. High scorers on measures of this factor are described as active, affectionate, fun-loving, sociable, passionate, and talkative; low scorers are described as passive, quiet, reserved, retiring, sober, and unfeeling.

Openness to Experience. High scorers on measures of this factor are described as creative, curious, imaginative, independent, liberal, and original; low scorers are described as conforming, conservative, conventional, down-to-earth, uncreative, and uncurious.

Agreeableness. High scorers on measures of this factor are described as acquiescent, generous, good-natured, helpful, softhearted, and trusting; low scorers are described as antagonistic, critical, ruthless, stingy, suspicious, and uncooperative.

Conscientiousness. High scorers on measures of this factor are described as careful, conscientious, hardworking, persevering, punctual, and well organized; low scorers are described as careless, disorganized, late, lazy, negligent, and weak-willed. Report 5–1 is a profile and computer-based report of scores on the NEO Personality Inventory–Revised, a paper-and-pencil instrument designed to assess a person's standing on these five factors.

A great deal of research has been conducted on the five-factor, or "Big Five," model of personality. Though the results of some studies point to a great deal of consistency in the factors across different nationalities and cultures (Angleitner & Ostendorf, 1994; Goldberg, 1994; McCrae & Costa, 1987), the validities of the model (Block, 1995) and the NEO Personality Inventory (Ben-Porath & Waller, 1992; Butcher & Rouse, 1996) have been questioned.

Trait Stability

The assertion of both stage and transition theorists that personality changes during adulthood is only partially supported by research. Many investigators (e.g., Costa & McCrae, 1980; Neugarten, 1977; Schaie & Parham, 1976) have found that personality can change during adulthood, but the overall picture is one of stability and continuity rather than reorganization and extensive changes (McCrae & Costa, 1990). A longitudinal study conducted some years ago in Kansas City (Neugarten, 1964, 1973, 1977) found. for example, that the coping styles, ways of attaining life satisfaction, strength of

goal-directed behavior, and other socially adaptive behaviors of the participants did not change extensively from middle- to old age. Compared to the
40-year-olds, the 60-year-olds in the study tended to have a more passive
view of the self and to be more concerned about their inner lives. In addition
to these shifts from *active to passive mastery* and toward greater *interiority*,
the older men were characterized as more nurturant in their impulses and the
older women as more aggressive than their middle-aged counterparts (Neugarten, 1973).

In another investigation of age-related changes in personality, Schaie and
Parham (1976) followed up eight different age cohorts over a period of 7 years.
They found that, though stability was the rule rather than the exception, the
degree of stability in personality varied with the individual participant and
the specific trait. In addition, many of the age-related differences obtained in
cross-sectional analyses of the data obtained in these studies were attributable to cohort (generational) effects. This was true for traits such as introversion, behavioral rigidity, attitudinal flexibility, and social responsibility.
Other studies have found differences between older and younger adults in
cautiousness, conformity, passivity, self-confidence, flexibility, and temporal
orientation (Bortner & Hultsch, 1972; Cooper & Gutmann, 1987; Gutmann,
1974, 1977; Klein, 1972; Riley & Foner, 1968; Ullmann, 1976), but the differences are typically not great and may be attributable in some measure to
cohort effects. Certainly, the self-concept shows a great deal of consistency
from early adulthood through old age (Eisenhandler, 1989).

One of the longest-running of all longitudinal studies, the Berkeley Older
Generation Study, involved the testing of young, middle-aged, and older
adults over a 55-year period. The traits of intellect, extraversion, agreeableness, satisfaction, and energetic were assessed by means of open-ended interviews. With the exception of "energetic," these traits were similar to those in
the five-factor model. Field and Millsap's (1991) analysis of these data showed
that the traits of "satisfaction" and " agreeableness" remained quite stable
over the lifetimes of the participants, but the traits of "intellect," "energetic,"
and "extraversion," showed moderate declines with aging.

Taken as a whole, the results of research concerned with the stability of
personality indicate that any age-related changes are likely to be quantitative
rather than qualitative. The pattern of one's personality traits, which is established fairly early in life, becomes more pronounced with aging and its
attendant stresses, but the pattern does not change appreciably. Thus, a
young, extroverted male is likely to remain outgoing in middle and later life,
even though there is a general tendency for men to become more introverted
and introspective in old age. It should be emphasized, however, that these
conclusions regarding the continuity of personality over time do not necessarily apply to the personality of a particular individual. Different lives
follow different courses; some show great consistency in personality over
time, whereas others continue to develop and change during adulthood. A
traumatic experience, severe brain damage, successful psychotherapy, a pro-

---

REPORT 5–1

Sample Report of Scores on the NEO Personality Inventory–Revised

Client name: jim ffi   NEO-FFI
Test date: 04/01/94   INTERPRETIVE REPORT

NEO-FFI Data Table

Scale	Raw score	T score	Range
(N) Neuroticism	25	60	High
(E) Extraversion	25	46	Average
(O) Openness	28	52	Average
(A) Agreeableness	21	28	Very low
(C) Conscientiousness	16	20	Very low

Validity Indices

Validity indices are within normal limits and the obtained test data appear to be valid.

Basis of Interpretation

This report compares the respondent to other adult men. It is based on self-reports of the respondent.

This report is based on a short version of the Revised NEO Personality Inventory. It provides information on the five basic personality factors. More precise estimation of standing on the factors and more detailed information about specific traits that define them can be obtained by administering the NEO PI-R.

Global Description of Personality: The Five Factors

The most distinctive feature of this individual's personality is his standing on the factor of Conscientiousness. Men who score in this range have little need for achievement, putting personal interests or pleasure before business. They prefer not to make schedules, are often late for meetings and appointments, and have difficulty in finishing tasks. Their work is typically accomplished in a haphaz-

---

found religious experience or conversion, and even constant daily hassles can affect one's perceptions and responses to the environment. Depending on the personal (intelligence, physical health, temperament, etc.) and socio-cultural (economic status, family supports, etc.) factors, severe personal losses or frustrations and other major life events may be viewed by one individual as challenges to be mastered and by another as extremely stressful and discouraging (see Brim & Ryff, 1980; Dohrenwend, Krasnoff, Askensay, &

ard and disorganized fashion. They lack self-discipline, prefer play to work, and may seem aimless in setting goals for their lives. They have a relaxed attitude toward duties and obligations, and typically prefer not to make commitments. Raters describe such people as careless, neglectful, unreliable, and negligent.

This person is very low an Agreeableness. People who score in this range are antagonistic and tend to be brusque or even rude in dealing with others. They are generally suspicious of other people and skeptical of others' ideas and opinions. They can be callous in their feelings. Their attitudes are tough-minded in most situations. They prefer competition to cooperation, and express hostile feelings directly with little hesitation. People might describe them as relatively stubborn, critical, manipulative, or selfish. (Although antagonistic people are generally not well-liked by others, they are often respected for their critical independence, and their emotional toughness and competitiveness can be assets in many social and business roles.)

Next, consider the individual's level of Neuroticism. Individuals scoring in this range are likely to experience a moderately high level of negative emotion and occasional episodes of psychological distress. They are somewhat sensitive and moody, and are probably dissatisfied with several aspects of their lives. They are rather low in self-esteem and somewhat insecure. Friends and neighbors of such individuals might characterize them as worriers or overly emotional in comparison with the average person. (It is important to recall that Neuroticism is a dimension of normal personality, and high Neuroticism scores in themselves do not imply that the individual is suffering from any psychological disorder.)

This person is average in Extraversion. Such people enjoy other people but also have periods when they prefer to be alone. They are average in level of energy and activity, and experience a normal amount of pleasant and cheerful feelings.

Finally, the individual scores in the average range in Openness. Average scorers like him value both the new and the familiar, and have an average degree of sensitivity to inner feelings. They are willing to consider new ideas on occasion, but they do not seek out novelty for its own sake.

Dohrenwend, 1978; Hultsch & Plemons, 1979). Certain life events, such as the cessation of menstruation, are associated with a particular chronological age range, whereas others may occur at any time during adulthood. In any case, depending on how the individual perceives and copes with them, such events can have either negative or positive effects on personality. Furthermore, people are not mere automatons, cast and tossed this way and that by the external environment. Rather, to some extent, they create their own environments and their own personalities. People are thinking, planning, future-oriented creatures with aspirations and dreams concerning what they want to become and the "prizes" they expect to win.

STRESS AND COPING

Almost every day, people encounter events or have experiences that they did not expect or for which they are unprepared. The result is the physical, mental, and emotional strain known as *stress*. Stimuli that produce stress are referred to as *stressors*. One of the most common types of stressor is everyday *hassles*, which are annoying or irritating but typically fairly easy to deal with. Major life events such as the death of a relative, a serious illness or injury, being fired or suspended, or a personal failure usually cause more intense and enduring reactions than hassles. Disasters and catastrophes such as an airplane crash, an earthquake, a bombing, or a flood cause many people to be under stress at the same time.

Among the symptoms of prolonged stress are persisting anxiety, depression, irritability, fatigue, loss of appetite, headache, and backache. Continuing stress can affect the course and severity of physical disorders such as peptic ulcers, migraine headaches, skin conditions, chronic backache, and bronchial asthma.

Most people learn in the course of growing up that a certain amount of stress is a normal part of life and, like all experiences, must be dealt with in some way. The various ways in which people deal or cope with stress are known as *coping strategies*. Coping strategies range all the way from direct aggression through denial and withdrawal, but all have the function of reducing the level of stress so one can get on with the business of living.

Stress Syndromes

Three of the most publicized states associated with prolonged stress are burnout, bereavement, and posttraumatic stress disorder. The symptoms of *burnout*, a condition precipitated by the stress of overwork, include emotional exhaustion, reduced productivity, and feelings of depersonalization. The emotional exhaustion in burnout may be accompanied by physical symptoms such as headaches and backaches, in addition to social withdrawal. Compulsive, insecure workaholics whose jobs have ceased to provide them with self-fulfillment are particularly prone to burnout. Such individuals attempt to compensate for low self-esteem from off-the-job activities by dedicating themselves to their jobs and becoming workaholics.

Another job-related event that is potentially stressful is retirement. As noted by Butler and Lewis (1982, pp. 128, 130),

> In retirement, otherwise perfectly healthy men and women may develop headaches, depression, gastrointestinal symptoms, and oversleeping.... Irritability, loss of interest, lack of energy, increased alcoholic intake, and reduced efficiency are all familiar and common reactions.

Though these symptoms are certainly not the norm, retirement is often accompanied by a sense of diminished usefulness, insignificance, loss of independence, and sometimes feelings that life is essentially over.

Bereavement, like retirement, is more likely to occur in later adulthood. Depression, sleep disturbances, loss of appetite and weight, chronic fatigue, lack of interest in external things, and difficulties in concentrating are among the symptoms of bereavement. In some cases, reactions to the death of a spouse or other close relative are so intense that severe physical illness, a serious accident, or even death may result (Parkes, 1972).

One of the most dramatic and widely discussed disorders stemming from the Vietnam War is *posttraumatic stress disorder* (PTSD). Similar conditions were called "shell shock" in World War I and "combat fatigue insomnia" or "combat neurosis" in World War II and the Korean War. PTSD is, of course, not limited to the casualties of war: Earthquakes, fires, airplane crashes, and other disasters produce their share of victims. PTSD involves feelings of anxiety, insomnia, nightmares, problems with social relationships, and other emotional responses. In many cases, "flashbacks" associated with the stressful experience may occur months or even years after the stressful experience (Roberts, 1988).

Stress and Personality

Reactions to stressful situations are a function not only of the severity of the event but also of the physical and psychological makeup of the affected individual. In a longitudinal study of men who had been psychologically examined as college students, those who were diagnosed as "poorly adjusted" were much more likely to become seriously ill and die in middle adulthood than those who had been diagnosed as "well adjusted" (Valliant, 1979). These findings led Valliant to conclude that personality adjustment in young adulthood influences a person's physical health in midlife. Good adjustment and positive mental health appear to slow the physical decline that begins in midlife, whereas poor adjustment hastens it.

Vulnerability to pathogenic agents may be increased by *identity disruption*, an erosion in a person's identity or sense of self, produced by events that are inconsistent with that identity (Brown & McGill, 1989). Investigations of the connections between personality and physical health have also focused on variables such as hardiness, repression–sensitization, locus of control, and learned helplessness. According to Kobasa (1979), *hardiness*, the ability to withstand stress and remain healthy in the face of it, consists of three characteristics: commitment, control, and challenge. *Commitment* consists of a clear sense of purpose, involvement with other people, and the ability to recognize one's goals, priorities, and values. *Control* is concerned with the ability to select a course of action, to incorporate external events into a dynamic life plan, and to be motivated to achieve. *Challenge* is a feeling that change is positive and that one has an opportunity to integrate his or her life goals into new situations. Kobasa, Maddi, and Kahn (1982) found that, compared with those having a high incidence of physical illness, individuals with a low incidence of physical illness scored higher on measures of all three components of hardiness.

Several cognitive models of adaptation and coping with stress have been proposed. These models postulate different cognitive strategies that may be preferred by people with different personalities. An earlier model of this sort is Byrne's (1961) *repression–sensitization* conception of a continuum representing different responses to stress. Information-avoidance behaviors are at the repression end of the continuum, and information-seeking behaviors at the sensitization end.

Another cognitive model of coping is Folkman and Lazarus's (1980) distinction between problem-focused and emotion-focused strategies. A *problem-focused strategy* consists of obtaining additional information to actively change a stressful situation, whereas an *emotion-focused strategy* is concerned with employing behavioral or cognitive techniques to manage the emotional tension produced by stressful situations. Rather than focusing on one strategy, most people employ a combination of the two. Although Folkman, Lazarus, Pimley, and Novacek (1987) found no sex differences in the use of the two strategies, there were some age differences. Younger adults preferred more problem-focused forms of coping (confrontation, planning, seeking social support), whereas older adults preferred more emotion-focused forms (e.g., distancing, accepting responsibility, positive reappraisal).

Lazarus and Folkman (1984) maintained that the perception of potentially stressful events involves both primary and secondary appraisal processes. *Primary appraisal* is the process of determining whether an event is stressful, and *secondary appraisal* involves adapting to the stressful event by identifying one's coping resources and determining the costs of using them. Secondary appraisal is presumably influenced by a personality characteristic that Rotter (1966) labeled locus of control. *Locus of control* is a cognitive-perceptual style characterized by the typical direction from which people perceive themselves as being controlled—"internal" (from within oneself, by oneself) or "external" (outside oneself, by other people). A person with an internal locus of control believes that he or she can control his or her own life, whereas a person with an external locus of control believes that his or her life is controlled by fate, luck, or other external forces.

Whether a person feels in control and believes that his or her actions are effective is influenced by experiences in which the person's continuing efforts were successful or unsuccessful. Unsuccessful attempts to cope with stress can lead to an acquired perception that one has no influence or control over external events, a phenomenon referred to as *learned helplessness* and characterized by defeatism, apathy, and depression (Seligman, 1992).

Age Differences in Coping Strategies

In their study of coping strategies in young, middle-aged, and older adults, Folkman et al. (1987) found that older adults were less likely than young and middle-aged adults to employ confrontation and aggression. Rather than becoming highly emotional when faced with stressful circumstances, older adults tended to cope by using denial, repression, and other passive strategies (Felton & Revenson, 1987; Folkman et al., 1987). As they become older, most adults relinquish coping strategies that, though presumably appropriate in young adulthood, have now outlived their usefulness. Confronting stress with detachment and humor is more characteristic of older than younger adults (Valliant, 1977).

Lazarus and his colleagues (DeLongis, Coynce, Dakof, Folkman, & Lazarus, 1982; Lazarus & Folkman, 1984) also found that the reported number of stressful life events declined from middle to older adulthood. However, this does not necessarily mean that older adults experience less stress than younger adults. Older adults may simply appraise the same event as less stressful. They may be more realistic than younger adults, adapting their coping strategies to fit the situations they can control. Older adults also seem to better understand when environmental resources can assist them in coping with a stressful situation. Compared with older adults, young adults and adolescents employ denial and other defense mechanisms more often (Blanchard-Fields & Irion, 1988; Blanchard-Fields & Robinson, 1987).

Age differences in stress and coping have also been found in the kinds and number of daily hassles experienced (Folkman, Lazarus, Dunkel-Schetter, DeLongis, & Gruen, 1986; Folkman, Lazarus, Gruen, & DeLongis, 1986). Younger adults reported more hassles than older adults regarding economic (finances) and work-related matters. College students also reported hassles with wasting time, meeting high standards, and being lonely. Environmental and social problems, home upkeep, and health were found to be more common concerns in older adulthood.

At all ages, social support from caring, interested people can lower the level of stress that must be endured. Interacting with others—confiding in them and engaging in mutually satisfying activities—makes "outrageous fortune" easier to bear. Not only does social interaction provide emotional support in times of stress, but it also provides information about the sources of stress, what can be expected, and what actions might be taken to deal with them. Much of the social support received by adults comes from marital relationships, but close friends can also provide catharsis and a boost to one's confidence. Finally, because of the physical debilitation resulting from long-term stress, attention to adequate nutrition, exercise, rest, and care is also important.

MENTAL DISORDERS

Severe, unremitting stress does not invariably lead to a mental disorder, but when combined with a particular biological and experiential predisposition, it is quite possible for stress to precipitate a disorder. As with all personality and behavioral patterns, most mental disorders are the results of interactions between the hereditary makeup of the individual and the physical and psychological environment. Among the biological factors that contribute to mental disorders are cerebral trauma, neurochemical imbalances, and maturational differences. Other significant predisposing factors include psychosocial and socioeconomic variables such as child-rearing practices, family stability, poverty, and discrimination.

Definitions of normal and abnormal behavior are by no means absolute; they vary to some extent with culture and the times. The attitudes, expectations, and needs of a society or culture affect its tolerance for unusual behavior. In most Western cultures, people who have poor interpersonal relations, who display socially inappropriate behavior, who have no acceptable goals, and who repeatedly violate social norms are considered abnormal. Depending on society's interpretations of an individual's behavior and whether it, as well as the person who manifests it, is valued or disdained, such behavior may be praised, punished, ignored, endured, or subjected to medical and humanitarian treatment.

Mental health professionals are rarely satisfied with a statistical (frequency of occurrence) or sociocultural definition of abnormality and mental disorder. Rather, they try to delve more deeply into the subjective feelings of the person—the level of satisfaction, anxiety, depression, isolation, and disruptive thoughts and perceptions experienced—and the person's efforts to cope.

Incidence and Diagnosis

It is often said that the stress of modern living is responsible for the large number of mentally disordered people seen in families, clinics, institutions, and in the streets. Because of poor record keeping in previous times, growth of the general population, and changes in diagnostic criteria, it is difficult to determine if and by how much the incidence of mental disorders has risen over the years. Available statistics do indicate that mental disorders associated with old age have increased during this century, but most of these conditions are organic disorders due to an increase in the population of older adults. Concerning the percentage of mentally disordered persons in the population as a whole, Adelson (1985) estimated that approximately 20% of the population manifest at least moderately severe symptoms of mental disorders.

Breakdowns in the Family

I don't recall that any member of my extended family was ever judged insane, but there were a few nervous breakdowns. That's what we called mental disorders in those days. People also got "hysterical," were occasionally "beside themselves," had "spells," and even "went off the deep end," but they weren't insane. The term *insanity* conjured up fears of hereditary taints and violence that kept a family from holding up their collective heads in public.

Some of the incidents in which members of my family lost control of themselves were exciting to a young boy. I remember the time when an inebriated aunt cavorted on our front lawn in the nude during the wee hours of the morning. On another occasion, a great aunt was sitting in a rocking chair by a burning fireplace and disposed of herself by rocking into the fire. For the most part, however, when a family member started behaving irrationally, it was due either to old demon Rum, frustration and anger, or a combination of these. In such a state the person would yell, break things, run around the house, and eventually doze off. I knew enough to stay out of the way when someone was in such a fix, and things soon returned to normal.

To my knowledge, no one in our family was ever carted off to an insane asylum (mental hospital), but that isn't to say that a brief stay wouldn't have done several of them some good. Years later, when I worked in a mental hospital in North Carolina, I met a patient who voluntarily admitted himself for a 2-week sequestration every summer when his problems became insurmountable. According to this patient, the mental hospital was the best hotel he had ever been in and was also priced quite reasonably. Sometimes I think that is exactly what a certain uncle of mine should have done. One time, suffering from depression due to the departure of his wife, he was drinking and driving at 90 miles per hour. Actually, the car was mine, which made it even more frightening to me. Both an open bottle of liquor and a loaded gun were on the seat beside him when he was stopped by a highway patrolman. The patrolman, who apparently had some knowledge of psychology, asked my uncle what his problem was and if he could help. My uncle responded that the patrolman didn't want to hear about it, but the latter assured my uncle that he did. On being told that the problem was "family trouble," the patrolman admitted that my uncle was right: He didn't want to hear about it. Because the patrolman apparently did not see the open liquor bottle or the loaded gun, my uncle avoided a stay in jail on that occasion. However, he made up for the oversight in later years.

Though not strictly insanity, there was a case of apparent fugue—amnesia accompanied by actual physical flight—in our family. Another one of my uncles walked off one fine day and disappeared without a trace. My grandmother hired detectives to search for him, but the trail ran cold in San Francisco. It was widely believed in our family that he had either been shanghaied or voluntarily signed on to a ship going to the Far East. Whether he fell, jumped, or was pushed off the ship, or whether he converted to Orientalism, remains a mystery. Frankly, I've always believed that he found a better life somewhere else, a place where people were less exhibitionistic in responding to their troubles than some of the members of our family.

Determining the nature and extent of a mental disorder, that is, arriving at a diagnosis, involves careful observation of the patient, interviewing the patient and those close to him or her, and conducting medical and psychological examinations. The patient's symptoms are then compared with standard descriptions of various diagnostic categories, such as those listed in the *Diagnostic and Statistical Manual of Mental Disorders* (DSM-IV) of the American Psychiatric Association (1994). The major diagnostic categories in DSM-IV are given in Table 5–3. These categories are purely descriptive, in that they are not based on any particular theory of personality or abnormal behavior. Mental disorders are grouped according to similar symptoms, with no specification of causation or recommended treatment.

The DSM-IV diagnostic system is multiaxial, classifying each patient on five axes referring to different kinds of patient information:

- Axis I: Clinical Disorders
- Axis II: Personality Disorders
- Mental Retardation
- Axis III: General Medical Conditions
- Axis IV: Psychosocial and Environmental Problems
- Axis V: Global Assessment of Functioning

Each disorder is labeled and numbered with a five-digit code on Axes I and II, and its severity is specified as "mild, moderate, or severe." Accompanying physical disorders and conditions are classified on Axis III, the severity of psychosocial stressors is classified on Axis IV, and a global assessment of the patient's functioning (GAF) is indicated on Axis V.

Patients admitted to state and country mental hospitals, private psychi-

---

TABLE 5–3 Major Diagnostic Categories in DSM-IV

Delirium, Dementia, and Amnesic and Other Cognitive Disorders
Mental Disorders Due to a General Medical Condition
Substance-Related Disorders
Schizophrenia and Other Psychotic Disorders
Mood Disorders
Anxiety Disorders
Somatoform Disorders
Factitious Disorders
Dissociative Disorders
Sexual and Gender Identity Disorders
Eating Disorders
Sleep Disorders
Impulse–Control Disorders Not Elsewhere Classified
Adjustment Disorders
Personality Disorders
Other Conditions That May Be a Focus of Clinical Attention

Source: American Psychiatric Association (1994).

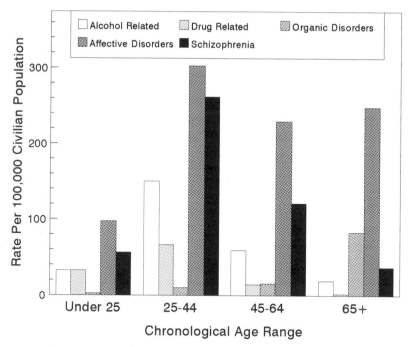

Figure 5–1   Average rates for inpatient psychiatric diagnoses in state and county mental hospitals and private psychiatric hospitals during 1986. (Based on data from National Center for Health Statistics, 1995.)

atric hospitals, nonfederal general hospitals, and other inpatient psychiatric organizations are diagnosed on admission. Figure 5–1 provides an indication of the frequency of five diagnostic categories by age group. Note that the most common diagnoses are "affective disorders" and "schizophrenia," but that the frequency of a particular disorder varies with chronological age. Organic disorders are, as expected, more common in patients over age 65, whereas schizophrenia is more common in patients in their late twenties to early forties.

Organic Disorders

Organic brain disorders are either acute or chronic. Acute brain dysfunctions can result from myriad conditions: alcohol intoxication, anemia, brain tumors, cardiovascular disorders, emphysema, fever, infections, infectious diseases, lead poisoning, liver disease, medication, mercury poisoning, multiple sclerosis, stroke, thyroid disorders, and vitamin deficiencies. The two most common chronic brain disorders—Alzheimer's disease and multi-infarct dementia—are discussed in Chapter 3. Other, less common, chronic brain disorders include Parkinsonism, Korsakoff's syndrome, Creutzfeldt–Jakob disease, and AIDS dementia complex. Of all adults over age 75 admitted to psychiatric treatment institutions, an estimated 85% are diagnosed as having organic brain disorders (LaRue, Dessonville, & Jarvik, 1985).

The symptoms of organic brain disorders, also known as *dementias*, include mental confusion, memory loss, incoherent speech, poor orientation to the environment, and, in some cases, motor incoordination, agitation, depression, and delirium. Agitated patients may scream, pace, and have violent outbursts in which they verbally and physically abuse the nursing staff (Raskind & Peskind, 1992).

Schizophrenia

The three major psychotic disorders for which no biological (i.e., organic) basis has been scientifically established are schizophrenia, delusional disorders, and affective (mood) disorders. One of the largest categories of institutionalized mental patients consists of schizophrenics, individuals with severe disturbances of thinking and often perception. Symptomatic of schizophrenics are withdrawal from contact with reality, loss of empathy with other people, disturbances of concept formation, regressivity, and bizarre behavior; hallucinations (false perceptions) and delusions (false beliefs) may also be present.

Schizophrenia typically begins in adolescence or early adulthood and, if untreated, may persist for the patient's lifetime. Men typically become schizophrenic at an earlier age than women, and the two sexes display different symptom pictures. So-called *negative symptoms*—mutism, blunted affect, social withdrawal, apathetic behavior, inattentiveness—are more characteristic of men than of women. Female schizophrenics are more likely to manifest *positive symptoms* such as hallucinations, delusions, bizarre behavior, and disordered thought processes (Lewine, 1981).

Although the symptoms of schizophrenia usually appear before age 40, initial onset in old age is not common. Schizophrenia that has its onset in old age is called *paraphrenia* and is typically a milder form of the disorder. Late-onset schizophrenics tend to have marked and vivid delusions of persecution or other false beliefs, less disturbed thought processes, and manifest more emotion than other schizophrenics. Hallucinations, when present, are likely to be sensory in nature.

Most chronic schizophrenics are meek and mild individuals who are not dangerous to other people. If permitted, many would spend much of their lives in mental hospitals. However, due to the fact that nondangerous mental patients cannot be legally required to remain institutionalized forever, many schizophrenics are released and end up wandering and living in the streets.

Delusional Disorders

The term *delusional* or *paranoid* encompasses a wide range of mental disorders characterized by suspiciousness, projection, excessive feelings of self-importance, and delusions. The delusional patient's cognitive abilities are usually intact, but thinking, affect, and behavior are all affected by delusions of grandeur (or persecution).

Delusions sometimes form part of the symptom picture in schizophrenia, particularly in younger patients, but delusions without schizophrenia are more common. The frequency of delusional disorders tends to increase with age, being exceeded only by dementia and depression in older adults. The delusions of older patients are often accompanied by a chronic hearing loss, which makes it difficult for them to understand what other people are saying and invites suspiciousness, and by cognitive disturbances, as in Alzheimer's disease. Older loners who have lived most of their lives in relative isolation from other people are more likely to be delusional than individuals with normal social interactions (Berger & Zarit, 1978).

Affective Disorders

As shown in Figure 5–1, one of the most common classes of mental disorders at all ages involve extremes of affect or mood. Either extreme elation (*mania*), profound depression, or periodic swings between the two extreme states can occur. In *affective psychoses*, not only disturbances of mood but also a loss of contact with reality takes place.

Bipolar disorder, in which the patient's mood fluctuates fairly regularly between mania and depression, is a classic pattern. During the manic phase of the illness, the patient is elated, overtalkative, and irritable; motor activity increases and thoughts appear to be strange. In the depressive phase of the cycle, the patient is deeply despondent, sometimes stuporous, expresses feelings of guilt and self-deprecation, and complains of aches and pains. These same symptoms are present in *psychotic depression*, but without the bipolar mood swings.

Feelings of intense sadness, hopelessness, pessimism, low self-esteem, loss of appetite and interest, insomnia, fatigue, aches and pains, and memory problems that are symptomatic of depression can also occur as a reaction to the loss of a loved one, physical disorders, financial insecurity, social isolation, or any other serious problem. Unlike psychotic depression, in which guilt, self-deprecation, and bodily complaints are extreme and grossly unrealistic, the apathy, inertia, and withdrawal seen in neurotic or reactive depression are less bizarre and more closely associated with external circumstances.

Depressive disorders appear to peak in frequency in the early twenties, decline through age 60 or so, and then rise again (Burke, Burke, Regier, & Rae, 1990; Mirowsky & Ross, 1992). A variety of losses (marital, employment, financial, health, etc.) contribute to the increase in depression during older adulthood (Weiner, 1992). In addition, antihypertensive drugs and other prescribed and over-the-counter medications can produce symptoms of depression and add to diagnostic confusion. Depression in younger adults is associated more with guilt, shame, and self-hatred, whereas in older adults it occurs more frequently as a reaction to the decline in self-esteem occasioned by physical, economic, and social-role losses (LaRue et al., 1985; Phifer & Murrell, 1986). Until age 80, depressive disorders are more common in women than in men, after which the gender difference is reversed (LaRue et al., 1985). Depression also reportedly occurs more often in Hispanics than in whites or blacks (Santos, Hubbard, & McIntosh, 1983).

Suicide

Severe depression is usually accompanied by the danger of attempted suicide. Over 30,000 Americans commit suicide each year, and many thou-

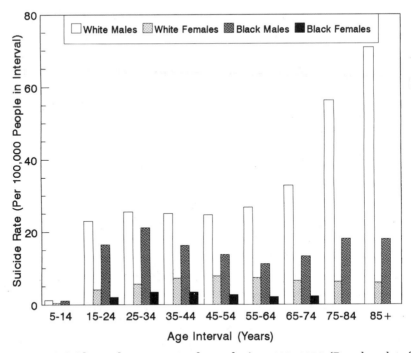

Figure 5–2   Suicide rate by age, sex, and race during 1990–1992. (Based on data from the National Vital Statistics System)

sands more attempt it (Rosenberg et al., 1996). As shown in Figure 5–2, white men have a higher suicide rate than other sex/ethnic groups, a rate that remains fairly constant until older adulthood and then accelerates. Among younger adults, attempted suicide is more often a "plea for help" or a "ploy for sympathy," but older men who attempt suicide are more serious and also more likely to be successful in their attempts.

Regardless of age, depression is the most common factor in suicide (Carson & Butcher, 1992). However, it is not the only factor. Despite the fact that depression is significantly more prevalent among females than males, the suicide rate is substantially lower for females than males—white or black. Contributing to the higher rate for males is the fact that males who attempt suicide employ more lethal methods, such as firearms. Another factor contributing to the sex difference in suicide rate is that the more assertive, achievement-oriented, middle-aged man has greater difficulty than the more passive, nurturant, middle-aged woman adapting to role changes in later life. Women also tend to have more extensive social supports, which can act as a buffer against despair. Many older men, especially the less affluent, are unable to attain satisfaction in their new roles while retaining the "macho" myth that they can only maintain their dignity or manliness by keeping quiet about their problems and dealing with them by themselves. Consequently, at some point they may "throw in the towel" and abandon the game entirely.

Nonpsychotic Disorders

The highest frequency of occurrence among nonpsychotic mental disorders is found in substance abuse and alcoholism, which affect over 16% of the general U.S. population (Regier & Burke, 1989). Although alcoholism is at its peak in middle age, many older adults turn to alcohol as a means of coping with grief, loneliness, and pain. Alcoholism in early and middle adulthood occurs more often in men than in women, but, because of loneliness and depression, many women also start drinking in later life (LaRue et al., 1985). Older alcoholics are more likely to manifest impairments in memory and thinking.

Because alcohol is rich in carbohydrates but low in proteins and vitamins, long-term users can develop cirrhosis of the liver due to protein deficiency or Korsakoff's syndrome due to vitamin B deficiency. The symptoms of Korsakoff's syndrome, a chronic brain disorder occurring most often in chronic alcoholics in their fifties and sixties, include disorientation, impulsiveness, memory loss, confabulation,[1] and inflammation of the peripheral nerves of the body.

Less common than alcoholics and other substance abusers are *antisocial*

---

[1]*Confabulation* is filling in a memory gap with details or a falsification that the individual believes to be true.

personalities, individuals who possess little conscience or regard for other people. Antisocial personalities become less numerous with age, seeming to "burn out" by the fifth decade of life.

Other serious, nonpsychotic mental health problems include generalized anxiety, phobias, panic disorders, obsessive–compulsive behavior, and hypochondriasis. If untreated, these conditions can persist throughout life, often becoming more intense as the individual is confronted with the physical and psychological stresses of aging.

Phobias are irrational, persisting fears of some object, person, or situation. One of the most common phobias is *agoraphobia*, an abnormal fear of being alone or in open, public places, where escape might be difficult in case of a panic attack. Recurring panic attacks triggered by specific stimuli or situations are usually diagnosed as *panic disorder*. The role of generalized anxiety in neurotic conditions is particularly apparent in phobias and panic attacks, but it is also important in *obsessive–compulsive behavior*. In this disorder, *obsessions*—recurring thoughts or ideas—and *compulsions*—specific behaviors performed in a rigid, repetitive manner—serve the function of controlling anxiety.

Another nonpsychotic disorder that presumably helps to control anxiety is *hypochondriasis*, an excessive preoccupation with health in the absence of significant physical pathology. Hypochondriacs are preoccupied with their bodily processes and irrationally afraid of disease. Hypochondriasis may occur at any age, but older adulthood, in particular, is often accompanied by an increase in hypochondriacal behavior. This disorder ranks third among nonorganic disorders in older adults, depression being first and delusional disorders second (LaRue et al., 1985). Hypochondriacs tend to shift from system to system within the body, complaining one week of kidney problems, the next week of stomach problems, and the week after of a respiratory disorder. Hypochondriasis has sometimes been associated with "dependency neurosis," in that it provides a way of escaping from stress by assuming the role of an invalid.

Treatment

A wide range of physical and psychological methods are applied to the treatment of mental disorders. Drugs, diet, electroshock, and surgery are the major classes of medical treatment, but exercise, massage and manipulation, and other physical procedures may also be appropriate. Psychological and psychosocial methods of treatment include individual and group counseling and psychotherapy, behavior modification, environmental intervention, occupational therapy, and recreational therapy. The particular treatment methods that are applied depend, of course, on the nature of the disorder, but the availability of the treatment, the patient's age, mental abilities, personality characteristics, and economic situation also play a role.

Antidepressant and antipsychotic drugs are the most common treatments for psychotic depression and schizophrenia, but electroshock therapy is still employed in some cases. Antianxiety drugs are quite popular for treating anxiety disorders, and short- and long-term psychotherapies are also used. Individual psychotherapy, behavioral and cognitive therapies, group therapy, and family therapy have all been found to be effective in treating a variety of patients—young and old, nonpsychotic and psychotic, mildly and severely disturbed (Gatz, Popkin, Pino, & VandenBos, 1985). The goals of psychotherapy vary with the presenting symptoms and with other characteristics of the patient. In addition to the relief of symptoms, the goals of psychotherapy may include delaying physical and psychological deterioration; enabling the patient to adapt to his or her current situation; improving the patient's self-help skills and interpersonal relationships; helping the patient become more self-reliant, self-accepting, and active; and providing relief for the patient's family (Wellman & McCormack, 1984).

A combination of physical and psychological methods is often used in treating a particular disorder. The treatment process can, in any case, be quite long and provides no guarantee of success. A typical patient is not "cured" in the sense that the disorder is gone forever. Rather, the patient is helped by the medications and counseling to attain greater control over his or her life and to maintain some semblance of normality. When therapy is successful, the patient has a more positive self-attitude, a more accurate perception of reality, a greater mastery over the environment, and a growth toward self-actualization (Jahoda, 1958).

The community in which people live can also contribute to the therapeutic process. Social supports from one's family, peers, and other people in the community are critical to the healthy psychological functioning of the individual. A therapeutic community provides not only social supports but also readily accessible medical, legal, social, religious, and economic services to outpatients and other residents who have had or are experiencing problems with living.

SUMMARY

The psychodynamic theories of Freud and Erikson depict personality as developing in a series of psychosexual or psychosocial stages. According to these theories, failure to progress successfully from one stage to the next places an indelible stamp on the individual's character that persists into adulthood. In contrast to Freud, who saw personality as essentially completed by the end of childhood, Erikson maintained that, in addition to five preadult stages, there are three adult stages (crises) of development: intimacy versus isolation in young adulthood, generativity versus stagnation in middle adulthood, and integrity versus despair in later adulthood. Three other stage theories related to Erikson's are Havighurst's developmental tasks, Loevinger's theory of ego development, and Peck's division of Erikson's old-age crisis of "integrity versus despair" into three subdivisions.

Levinson's conception of psychological development in adult men is a mixture of stages and transitions between the stages. According to Levinson, the goal of adult development is to form a life structure having both socio-cultural and personal sides. This structure is formed during a progressive series of four stages and five transitions, beginning with the early-adult transition and ending with the late-adult transition. Levinson argues that, with some modifications, his stage–transition model can also be applied to women.

Both script theory and the life-story model of personality development emphasize cognitive activities of the individual in creating a continuing but modifiable drama of his or her life in order to achieve control, meaning, and a sense of self or identity in that life.

Although many other theories have served as a basis for constructing personality assessment instruments and procedures, the greatest influence has been exerted by trait–factor theories. One of the most popular trait–factor theories is the five-factor ("The Big Five") model. The five factors, which may be assessed by the NEO Personality Inventory and other instruments, are neuroticism, extraversion, openness to experience, agreeableness, and conscientiousness.

Research findings indicate that, although personality can change during adulthood, the overall picture is one of stability and continuity rather than reorganization and change. The degree of consistency in personality traits across the adult years varies to some extent with the particular trait. However, when changes in trait measures occur, they are usually quantitative rather than qualitative in nature.

The symptoms of psychological stress include persisting anxiety, depression, irritability, loss of appetite, headaches, and backaches. Psychophysiological ("psychosomatic") disorders can also be precipitated or exacerbated by prolonged stress. Daily hassles are a normal part of life, but they can be quite stressful. Even greater stress is evident in burnout, bereavement, and PTSD.

Studies have shown that older adults are less likely than young and middle-aged adults to use confrontation and aggression, and more likely to use denial, repression, and other passive methods in coping with stress. Sources of stress also vary with age: Stress caused by economic and work-related matters is more common in young adults, whereas health, social, and domestic problems cause greater stress in older adults. Whatever the person's age may be, social support makes it easier to deal with stress.

The diagnosis of mental disorders in the United States usually follows the classification system of the *Diagnostic and Statistical Manual of Mental Disorders*. Common intake diagnoses in inpatient psychiatric organizations are affective disorders, schizophrenia, and alcohol-related, drug-related, and organic disorders. However, the incidence of these disorders varies with chronological age. Affective disorders, and depression in particular, are most common in all age groups. Schizophrenia is second in frequency of occurrence in young adulthood, and organic disorders are second in old age.

Organic brain disorders may be either acute (sudden onset) or chronic (long term). The two most common organic disorders in old age are multi-infarct dementia and Alzheimer's disease. The three major psychotic disorders for which no organic basis has been found are schizophrenia, delusional disorder, and affective disorders. The symptom picture of schizophrenia is one of withdrawal from reality and disturbed thought process and perceptions; blunted affect, hallucinations, delusions, and other bizarre behaviors may also be present. Schizophrenia usually has its onset in early adulthood and tends to occur in men at a younger age than in women. The symptoms vary somewhat with the sex of the patient, men tending to manifest "negative" symptoms and women "positive" symptoms of the disorder.

Patients suffering from delusional disorders are suspicious, self-centered, and paranoid; the delusions are usually those of grandeur. Delusional disorders increase with aging and are fairly common among older adults with severe hearing problem or cognitive impairments caused by organic brain disease.

Affective psychoses may be bipolar (manic–depressive) or unipolar (mania or depression). Psychotic depression is the most common affective psychosis. Feelings of guilt, self-deprecation, and bodily complaints are more common in psychotic than in neurotic (reactive) depression. Suicide is an ever-present danger in cases of deep depression. More men, especially older men, than women and more whites than blacks commit suicide.

Substance abuse and alcoholism are highest in frequency among nonpsychotic mental disorders. Alcoholism is more common in men than in women and in young and middle adulthood than late adulthood. Antisocial personality is also more common in youth than in old age. Conditions marked by anxiety, such as phobias, panic disorder, and obsessive–compulsive disorder are present among people of all ages. Hypochondriasis can also occur at any age but is particularly common in later life.

Typical treatments for psychotic disorders are antipsychotic and antidepressant drugs and other medications; electroshock and psychosurgery are also used in certain cases. Nonpsychotic disorders are treated with antianxiety drugs, other medications, and counseling or psychotherapy. A combination of physical and psychological methods is usually most effective in treating mental disorders. In addition, general medical care, occupational and recreational therapy, other intervention procedures, and a supportive, therapeutic environment can help patients function more effectively.

SUGGESTED READINGS

Berenger, M., Haseqawa, K., Finkel, S. T., & Nishimua, T. (1992). *Aging and mental disorders: International perspectives.* New York: Springer.
Caspi, A., & Bem, D. J. (1990). Personality continuity and change across the life course. In L. A.

Pervin (Ed.), *Handbook of personality theory and research* (pp. 549–575). New York: Guilford.

Cohen, G. D. (1990). Psychopathology and mental health in the mature and elderly adult. In J. E. Birren & K. W. Schaie (Eds.), *Handbook of the psychology of aging* (3rd ed., pp. 359–371). San Diego: Academic Press.

Kogan, N. (1990). Personality and aging. In J. E. Birren & K. W. Schaie (Eds.), *Handbook of the psychology of aging* (3rd ed., pp. 330–346). San Diego: Academic Press.

McCrae, R. R., & Costa, P. T., Jr. (1990). *Personality in adulthood.* New York: Guilford.

Sadavoy, J., & Fogel, B. (1992). Personality disorders in old age. In J. E. Birren, R. B. Sloane, & G. D. Cohen (Eds.), *Handbook of mental health and aging* (2nd ed., pp. 433–462). San Diego: Academic Press.

Sheikh, J. L. (1992). Anxiety and disorders in old age. In J. E. Birren, R. B. Sloane, & G. D. Cohen (Eds.), *Handbook of mental health and aging* (2nd ed., pp. 410–432). San Diego: Academic Press.

Wrightsman, L. S. (1994). *Adult personality development* (Vols. 1 & 2). Thousand Oaks, CA: Sage.

CHAPTER 6

Sex, Love, and Marriage

The traditional order of the three topics discussed in this chapter is "love, marriage, sex," but a more contemporary sequence is reflected in the title. Other arrangements of the three topics are also possible, and, in many cases, one or two of them may be omitted altogether. Thus, sex frequently occurs without being preceded or succeeded by love or marriage.

It can be argued, at least from a biological perspective, that the purpose of life is reproduction. From this viewpoint, people who have already reproduced have fulfilled the purpose of their lives and hence have no other biological reason for continuing to live. Historically, most people who were going to have children had done so by age 30, and after then, nature had no further use for them.

It is doubtful that many people would be satisfied with a life that involved only physical maturation, procreation, and deterioration. For most of us, life has to be more than growing up, "getting it on," and growing old. Life is about relationships—with the environment, the past, the future, and especially with other people. We are gregarious, mutually dependent creatures who feel secure when we are close to our own kind. We desire to be touched, caressed, and cuddled, as well as wanted, valued, and respected. Our need to be in contact with other people—physically, mentally, emotionally, and spiritually—is manifested in all sorts of ways, but particularly in sex and loving. We never outgrow these desires and needs, even in old age. Furthermore, sex is a lifelong habit pattern: Men and women who are more sexually active in their youth and experience more coital orgasms tend to retain their sexual interest and activity well into old age (Pfeiffer, Verwoerdt, & Davis, 1974; Shock et al., 1984; Walters, 1987).

SEX IN ADULTHOOD

Freud was right: Preschool children have sexual desires. So do 80- and 90-year-old adults. For most people, sex is a lifelong interest and activity. It does not stop with aging, and it does not kill you. Unfortunately, it does not make you live longer, either, but it may make you wish that you could.

MY LIFE 6–1

Sex Then and Now

I don't know exactly how old I was when I first became aware of sex differences. I must have been fairly young, because I had a mother, a sister, and two grandmothers, and there were several aunts and female cousins around. My first memories of girls were that, unlike boys, they had long hair, wore dresses instead of trousers (pants), played with dolls a lot, were poorer at sports but better at talking than boys, tended to cry when they were hurt or fussed at, and were generally cleaner than boys. (Much of that changed after "women's liberation," but I can still tell the difference about 90% of the time.)

Unlike the sentiments expressed by many other boys my age, I really didn't dislike girls when I was growing up. They were just different. A girl kissed me once in a game of post office, and we subsequently exchanged autographs, but that was pretty much as far as it went. I also helped girls with their homework on occasion, and one of them shared her lunch with me. I suppose it was in junior high that I first became aware of girls in a romantic or sexual sense, but girls my age were so tall that I thought of them as Amazons rather than sex objects.

Having spent quite a bit of time on a farm, as a boy I knew something about the "birds and the bees," or rather the dogs, cats, cows, horses, and pigs. Although much of their information concerning reproduction was grossly inaccurate, my friends talked quite a bit about "doing it," "making out," and assorted sexual aberrations. A few boys also told dirty stories or jokes and used bathroom vocabulary. Because my slightly puritanical parents and grandparents had warned me about the dangers of precocious sexual thoughts and behavior, I mostly limited myself to merely ogling rather than indulging. The girls my age were even more sexually naive than I. The daughter of our elementary school principal brought a package of condoms to class for "Show and Tell," explaining that she had found "these cute little white balloons" in her father's desk drawer, and proceeded to inflate them.

Our junior and senior high schools offered no sex education classes or even marital/premarital advice, and

---

Sex is more than intercourse. Closeness, touching, hugging, kissing, and petting are an important part of it. Sexual attraction brings people together so they can give and receive affection. "It's not so much how powerful the orgasm is or how many orgasms you have. It's just touching and being together and loving" (Kotre & Hall, 1990, p. 331).

Sex is not just a way of achieving closeness and expressing love and affection. It may also be used to dominate or to exert power over another person, to increase one's self-esteem, to enhance one's feelings of masculinity or femininity, to combat boredom, or to make up after an argument (Neubeck,

occasionally a female student became pregnant. If there was any uncertainty concerning the identity of the father, a list of suspects was drawn up and a shotgun wedding of sorts was held in due course. One case provided an occasion for barely suppressed hilarity when the culprit was suspected for a time of being one of the history teachers. Because continued attendance at school would presumably have been embarrassing to both the victim and the institution (as well as playing havoc with the morals of the other students), in such cases the unhappy, expectant mother was banished from school and none of us ever saw her again. Some of the more wayward and adventurous boys expressed a desire to visit her, but I doubt if it ever happened. I don't remember what social sanctions were applied to the father other than having to marry the expectant mother, but he was certainly not ostracized in the same fashion as she. The double standard was in full force in those days.

Things have certainly changed since these events took place. Not long ago I revisited several members of my high school class. Although time had shrunk the class (but not my classmates), enough of us remained to engage in some serious reminiscing. After spending a few minutes getting reacquainted, we began talking about the "good old days." Almost everyone agreed that adolescents today have more freedom than we did at their age and that sex has really "come out of the closet." We attributed this change in large measure to Kinsey, Hefner, X-rated movies, and the decade of the sixties. We also agreed that greater freedom has not necessarily been accompanied by greater happiness. Certainly the gender gap is narrower than it was a half-century ago, and for the most part we felt that to be an improvement. However, we also viewed women's liberation and the increased opportunities for both sexes as having come at something of a price. We felt, for example, that for many young people the mystery and romance of sex and sex differences is no longer a part of their lives. It may be that failing memory and a rose-colored reconstruction of the past gave us oldsters a distorted view of how things once were, and that the "good old days" were not nearly as good as they seem in retrospect. As the song goes, perhaps something has been lost but something has also been gained. In any event, despite the depletion of our hormones, most of my surviving classmates were still interested in talking (and dreaming) about sex.

1972). Sex can serve as a means of expressing both the good and the bad, the affectionate and the angry side of human nature. But whatever its underlying motivation may be, sex is a necessary and an extremely interesting part of life.

Hormones and Sex

In both males and females, sexual behavior is influenced by biology and experience. The biological part includes the secretions of hormones by the ovaries, the testes, and certain other glands. The production of hormones in the testes is controlled by two hormones—follicle-stimulating hormone (FSH) and luteinizing hormone (LH)—secreted by the pituitary gland. In males, the maturation of sperm depends on FSH, and the production of testosterone by the testes depends on LH. In females, the growth of the ovarian follicles, in which ova mature, depends on FSH, whereas ovulation and the production of estrogen and progesterone depend on LH. The pituitary gland continues secreting FSH and LH even after menopause, when the production of estrogen declines. The ovaries and the adrenal glands of females also produce androgens, some of which are converted to estrogen.

The pituitary gland and the testes form a closed feedback loop in which a decline in testosterone by the testes causes the pituitary to increase its secretion of LH, and an increase in testosterone level causes the pituitary to decrease its secretion of LH. The testosterone level usually declines somewhat in old age, and older men do not show the morning peak in testosterone level that is characteristic of young men. Furthermore, increased sexual activity appears to increase the testosterone level in the blood, whereas decreased sexual activity produces the opposite effect. Among older men, in particular, low testosterone levels usually accompany reduced sexual activity (Harman & Talbert, 1985). There is truth in the saying that if you don't use it, you'll lose it.

Regarding changes in the number and motility (activity level) of sperm with aging, the number of sperm is not affected as much as their motility. Unlike the continued production of sperm by males, females are born with all the ova (albeit in immature form) they will ever have. In addition, with each passing decade of later life, an increasing number of men stop producing sperm altogether. As described later in this chapter, other structural and functional changes in the sex organs also occur in older men.

Though surgery and hormonal treatments can affect sexual behavior, the effects are not always predictable. Castration of prepubertal boys inhibits the appearance of sexual behavior, but postpubertal castration does not always result in a decline in sexual activity. Following a hysterectomy or mastectomy, women, like men who have undergone prostate surgery, may lose interest in sexual intercourse. This result is, however, by no means invariable. The effects of removing the ovaries (ovariectomy) on the sex drive of women are highly variable, often increasing it. It should also be emphasized that the sexual behavior of humans depends not only on biology but also on sensory stimulation, learning, and psychological factors.

The Sexual Response Cycle

There are four phases in the sexual response cycle: I. excitation, II. plateau, III. orgasm, and IV. resolution (Masters, Johnson, & Kolodny, 1994). In men, phase I (*excitation*) is characterized by erection of the penis. Phase I takes place more slowly in women and is characterized by the production of lubricating fluid in the vagina, an increase in the diameter of the clitoris, and increased congestion of the labia with blood. For both sexes, phase II (*plateau*) is marked by a rise in the blood congestion of the pelvis and a strong feeling of sexual tension. A "sex flush" colors the forehead, neck, and chest, sometimes extending to the abdominal area. Phase III (*orgasm*) occurs in two stages in men: a preejaculatory contraction of the muscles involved in ejaculation, and actual ejaculation. The same muscles are involved in the orgasms of women as those of men. During phase IV (*resolution*), which is usually completed more quickly in men than in women, the congestion of the blood vessels that occurred during the previous phases of the sexual response cycle decreases. After a time, the cycle can be repeated. The duration of this recovery, or *refractory period*, is generally longer for men than for women; some women are capable of having several orgasms in fairly rapid succession.

With aging, both sexes experience a decline in all four phases of the sexual response cycle. Be that as it may, most older adults continue to appreciate and enjoy sexual intercourse. The degree of enjoyment is not dictated by biological factors alone, but depends to a large extent on the closeness and compatibility of the relationship between the sexual partners and how often they have sexual intercourse.

Age Changes in Sexual Behavior

Today, sex appears to be more popular than ever. Both the frequency of sexual intercourse and the variety of techniques used are appreciably greater than they were prior to the 1960s (Rosen & Hall, 1984). In one study, it was found that three-fourths of all 19-year-olds reported having sexual intercourse. Apparently, a sizable number of this group was quite busy in college. An estimated 28% of males and 29% of females in their freshman year of college reported having had premarital intercourse, but these figures had risen to 82% and 86%, respectively, by their senior year (Centers for Disease Control, 1992). Statistics such as these provide support for the description of late adolescence and early adulthood as a time of "raging hormones," a characterization that seems truer for males than for females. In males, the sexual urge reaches a peak during the late teens or early twenties, but not until a decade or so later has it reached its peak in females. This observation provides support for the suggestion that young men should seek mates 10 years older rather than 5 years younger than they.

Masters, Johnson, and Kolodny (1991) describe the sexual behavior of young adults in terms of a number of patterns—experimenters, seekers, and traditionalists. *Experimenters* employ proficiency and variety in their sexual behavior, *seekers* view sex as a way of finding an ideal marriage partner, while *traditionalists* limit sexual intercourse to more serious relationships. With regard to their interest in marriage, cohabitation—at least, for a time—has become quite popular among today's youth. During the 1980s and 1990s, however, the fear of contracting AIDS began to put a damper on casual sex.[1]

It is estimated that the average young-adult American couple has sexual intercourse two to three times per week (Masters et al., 1991). As indicated by Figure 6–1, the frequency of sexual intercourse declines every decade after people reach their thirties. The modest decline in the frequency of intercourse during the fifth decade is attributable in some degree to career interests, family concerns, other obligations, and a decline in the energy level of the partners. The *Coolidge effect*, manifested in extramarital sex, also suggests that boredom with the same partner may play a role in the decline.[2] The need for variety appears to be more characteristic of men than of women who engage in extramarital affairs.[3] Married women who become involved with other men usually do so for emotional reasons rather than for sex or variety. These extramarital affairs may be intense and enduring, but most seem to be "one-night stands" (Masters et al., 1991). Chronological age is, of course, not the only demographic factor that is related to sexual activity: Ethnicity, culture, socioeconomic status, religion, educational level, and marital status are others. Attitude toward sex and the warmth of the relationship between partners also affect sexual behavior (Crooks & Bauer, 1980; Geer, O'Donohue, & Schorman, 1986).

Despite the decline in the frequency of sexual intercourse in middle- and late adulthood, sexual interest does not usually drop dramatically until people reach their seventies. Even so, many "sexy senior citizens" in their seventies and eighties continue to enjoy sexual intercourse (Pfeiffer et al., 1974; Schover, 1986). The decline in sexual activity, but not in sexual capacity, is more marked for women than for men. In addition to biological changes with age, fatigue, boredom, poor physical health, and fear of failure may contribute to the decline in sexual interest and activity seen in older adult men. Older women also experience these problems, which, along with other distractions, may leave them little time to be interested in sex. For the typical married woman or widow, however, it is her husband's behavior and physical condition that are the principal cause of the decline in her sexual functioning. Because of her unwillingness or inability to find another sexual partner, the

---

[1]In the United States, during 1995, an estimated 643 people aged 15–24, 30,465 people aged 25–44, and 10,202 people aged 45–64 died of AIDS (Rosenberg et al., 1996).

[2]The *Coolidge effect* refers to the observation that males who find themselves unable to copulate with one partner can often perform vigorously with a new partner. This "effect" was named after President Calvin Coolidge. The story goes that, while touring a poultry farm, Mrs. Coolidge asked the farmer how so many eggs could be produced when he had such a small number of roosters. The farmer explained that each of the roosters did his duty several times a day. "Perhaps you could point that out to Mr. Coolidge," exclaimed Mrs. Coolidge in a loud voice. On overhearing the remark, President Coolidge inquired as to whether each rooster serviced the same hen each time. The farmer answered, "No, there are many hens for each rooster." "Perhaps you could point that out to Mrs. Coolidge," responded the President.

[3]The record for most marriages was held by Glynn "Scotty" Wolfe until his death in 1997. During his 89 years, Mr. Wolfe tied the knot 29 times! (Moehringer, 1997)

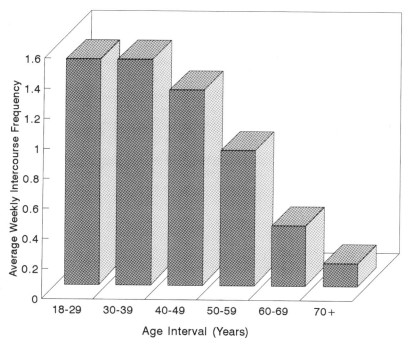

Figure 6–1 Weekly sexual intercourse frequency by American adults. (Based on data from Smith, 1990.)

older woman is relegated by her husband's decision to a state of sexual abstinence. Although being a widower or otherwise unmarried does not necessarily reduce the sexual activity of older men, most sexual activity for older women takes place within a marital relationship. Ninety percent of the older women who were interviewed in a study conducted at Duke University (Pfeiffer et al., 1974) reported that they stopped having sexual intercourse at a median age of 60, compared with 68 for males, when their husbands died or became ill or impotent. Even when both partners were healthy, the husband was almost always the one who made the decision to terminate sexual intercourse.

Menopause

The climacteric or *menopause*, the cessation of menstruation, occurs by age 50 in most women and marks the end of the childbearing years. Some women manage to give birth during their fifties and even sixties, but for most, the period of fertility ends sometime during the fifth decade.

Associated with menopause is a sharp drop in the production of estrogen and consequent changes in the structure and functioning of certain body tissues and organs. Among the structural changes are a decrease in the size of the cervix and uterus; cells in the vaginal walls also atrophy, causing the walls to become thinner. The reduction in estrogen contributes to the difficulty of uptaking calcium to strengthen the bones and a consequent thinning of the bones (*osteoporosis*).

The degree of vasocongestion of the breasts, clitoris, and vagina is also affected, and vaginal lubrication is reduced with menopause. The decreased acidity of vaginal secretions also increases the likelihood of infection. These changes in the vagina may result in pain and discomfort during sexual intercourse and an aching, burning sensation afterward. A minority of menopausal women experience these symptoms to any great degree, and they can, of course, be treated (Corby & Solnick, 1980). For example, vaginal irritation can be treated with a water-based lubricant such as K-Y, and by enhancing lubrication by means of estrogen creams and estrogen replacement therapy (ERT). However, because of the increased risk of uterine and breast cancer associated with ERT, this treatment is usually reserved for severe cases and consists of a minimum dosage for the shortest possible time to be effective. The risk of cancer is also reduced by combining ERT with the administration of progestin.

Another unpleasant experience associated with menopause are sensations of extreme heat, particularly in the upper part of the body. These so-called "hot flashes," which are often accompanied by a drenching sweat, diminish gradually and usually disappear altogether within a year or two following their onset.

Along with a drop in testosterone in approximately half of all menopausal women, the aforementioned changes presumably contribute to a decline in the sex drive reported by 30% or so women after menopause (Sheehy, 1993). Perhaps an even more important factor in the reduced sexual activity of widows, however, are social mores that view sex as something that older women should not be interested in. Despite the decline in sexual activity for most older women, the increased independence and assertiveness experienced by many postmenopausal women are often accompanied by a renewed interest in sex.

The term "male menopause" is sometimes applied to the structural and functional changes that occur with age-related reductions in the production of testosterone during later life, but there is no scientific justification for this term (Kolodny, Masters, & Johnson, 1979). Changes in the structure and functioning of the sex organs are also typical of older males, but the notion that all men eventually experience a "male menopause" akin to that in women is inaccurate. Among the changes that occur in older men are a slight shrinkage of the testes, the production of fewer sperm, and an increase in the size of the prostate gland. Older men require longer to achieve an erection, have a softer erection, and lose it more quickly after ejaculation. They experience fewer genital spasms, the force and volume of the ejaculate are less, and the refractory period is longer (Burt & Meeks, 1985; Masters et al., 1991; Spence, 1989). Secondary sex changes, such as a loss of hair, increased flabbiness, and an elevated voice pitch, also occur in later life.

Sexual Dysfunctions

Sexual dysfunction can occur at any age but is more common after age 50. In males, sexual dysfunction includes the inability to have or maintain an erection (*erectile dysfunction*), *premature ejaculation*, and an inability to ejaculate into the vagina (*retarded ejaculation*). In females, sexual dysfunction includes an inability to experience orgasm (*orgasmic dysfunction*) and painful intercourse caused by spasms of the muscles surrounding the vaginal opening (*vaginismus*). Inflammation of the vagina (*vaginitis*) and fungal infection of the vagina (*vaginomycosis*) can also contribute to the loss of sexual desire in women.

Erectile dysfunction, or *impotence*, is fairly common in older males. It may be a temporary condition brought about by overeating, excessive alcohol consumption, fatigue, boredom with the sexual partner, marital conflict, and other sources of emotional stress. Impotence is also a chronic condition associated with a variety of diseases (cancer, diabetes, endocrine or vascular disorders, neurological lesions, prostate disorders and surgery). Another health-related problem that may unnecessarily lead to impotence is the fear among heart patients that sexual intercourse will bring on another attack. This fear is usually unwarranted. Following a heart attack or open-heart surgery, most men can safely resume intercourse within 8–12 weeks and are encouraged by physicians to do so. Medications such as antihypertensive and psychotropic drugs and steroids, as well as chronic substance abuse, can also produce impotence. There is also the so-called *widower's syndrome*, a label for impotence in men who have lost a spouse and have not had sexual intercourse for a long time.

A *hysterectomy* performed to treat slippage or improper positioning of the uterus, to eliminate fibroid tumors, or as a treatment for uterine cancer may contribute to a woman's loss of interest in sex. A hysterectomy is referred to as "simple" when the uterus and cervix are removed, and as "total" when the ovaries and fallopian tubes are also removed. Though removal of the ovaries causes menopause in a woman who has not yet reached that stage, hysterectomy does not interfere with the ability to have sexual intercourse and experience orgasm. However, women who have undergone a hysterectomy or a mastectomy may lose interest in sex and avoid intercourse.

Certain diseases and medications affect the sexual desires of women and men. The pain and stiffness of osteoarthritis and rheumatoid arthritis can interfere with the enjoyment of sex; cancer can affect the sex organs as well as the blood and nerve supplies to them; drugs for controlling high blood pressure (thiazide diuretics, beta blockers) can impair vaginal lubrication.

Difficulty in performing heterosexual intercourse is, of course, not the only sexual disorder that occurs during adulthood. Voyeurism (peeping), exhibitionism (displaying one's genitals), pedophilia (sexual relations with children, child molestation), and more bizarre sexual behaviors occur. In addition, not all sexual activity is directed at a person of the opposite biological gender. Masturbation is fairly common among adults, declining only slightly with age. Homosexuality has also "come out of the closet" and is openly practiced by a sizable minority of the adult population. An estimated 4% of adult males and 2% of adult females are exclusively homosexual (Hyde, 1986). Although homosexuality was once labeled a mental disorder, in 1973, the American Psychiatric Association removed it from its list of officially recognized disorders. In addition to heterosexuals, homosexuals, and autosexuals, there are many bisexual adults who switch from same to opposite-sex partners at will.

Sex Therapy

Like homosexuality, sex problems and their treatment are no longer taboo topics. They are widely discussed in the media, the movies, and by medical experts throughout the world. The importance of good health care, proper nutrition, and appropriate medications to the maintenance of an active sex life are generally recognized. Moderation in the intake of food, coffee, alcohol, and tobacco; proper exercise; protection against sexually transmitted diseases (STDs); and an awareness that if you do not use it, you will lose it are recommended ("Sexuality and Aging," 1997). Perhaps most important of all are love and respect for one's sexual partner and acceptance of sex as normal and desirable at all ages.

Good physical health and a cooperative, understanding partner are necessary but sometimes insufficient in dealing with a sexual problem that has strong emotional components. In such cases, some form of reeducation or psychotherapy may be required.

The rapid but effective treatment of sexual inadequacy was pioneered by Masters and Johnson (1970). Many of the patients seen by them and their students were older adults who had stopped having sexual intercourse because of a misunderstanding about the normal biological changes that accompany aging. An illustrative case is described in Report 6–1. After 1 week of therapy, this couple had regained confidence and sexual functioning. The therapy helped them to realize that the increased time to attain an erection and the reduction in seminal fluid by the man, in addition to the decreased vaginal lubrication by the woman, were normal problems of aging with which they could deal. The couple became convinced that, despite these problems, they could continue to enjoy sexual intercourse.

Additional procedures for treating sexual dysfunctions are described by Masters et al. (1994). In treating impotence and other problems in older adults, sex therapists may advocate a variety of techniques ranging from the

---

REPORT 6–1

Treatment of Sexual Inadequacy

Mr. and Mrs. A. were 66 and 62 years of age, respectively, when referred to the foundation for sexual inadequacy. They had been married 39 years.

They had maintained reasonably effective sexual interchange during their marraige. Mr. A. had no difficulty with erection, reasonable ejaculatory control, and ... had been fully committed to the marriage. Mrs. A., occasionally orgasmic during intercourse and regularly orgasmic during her occasional masturbatory experiences, had continued regularity of coital exposure with her husband until 5 years prior to referral for therapy.

At age 61,... Mr. A. noted for the first time slowed erective attainment. Regardless of his level of sexual interest or the depth of his wife's commitment to the specific sexual experience, it took him progressively longer to attain full erection. With each sexual exposure, his concern for the delay in erective security increased until finally ... he failed for the first time to achieve an erection quality sufficient for vaginal penetration.

When coital opportunity (next) developed,... erection was attained, but again it was quite slow in development. The next two opportunities were only partially successful from an erective point of view, and thereafter, he was secondarily impotent.

After several months, they consulted their physician and were assured that this loss of erective power comes to all men as they age and that there was nothing to be done. Loath to accept the verdict, they tried on several occasions to force an erection with no success. Mr. A. was seriously depressed for several months but recovered without apparent incident.

Although initially the marital unit and their physician had fallen into the sociocultural trap of accepting the concept of sexual inadequacy as an aging phenomenon, the more Mr. and Mrs. A. considered their dysfunction, the less willing they were to accept the blanket concept that lack of erective security was purely the result of the aging process. They reasoned that they were in good health, had no basic concerns as a marital unit, and took good care of themselves physically.... Each partner underwent a thorough medical checkup and sought several authoritative opinions (none of them encouraging), refusing to accept the concept of the irreversibility of their sexual distress. Finally, approximately 5 years after the onset of a full degree of secondary impotence, they were referred for treatment.

Source: Masters and Johnson, 1970, pp. 326–328. Used with permission.

---

viewing of pornographic movies and live strippers to self-stimulation and sex education programs (Butler & Lewis, 1993). Many therapists also recommend masturbation and fantasy for adults who do not have sexual partners and want to reduce their sexual tensions.

Because there are many misunderstandings pertaining to sex in later life, gerontologists and sex therapists have emphasized the reeducation and reassurance of both older adults and the general public concerning sex after age 60 (Butler & Lewis, 1993). Adults of all ages need to realize that sexual activity in the later years is desired by and satisfying to older adults and important to their physical and mental well-being. The nature and extent of these activities, which may include not only sexual intercourse but oral sex, masturbation, and other practices as well, are generally consistent with those engaged in during the earlier adult years. Some readjustment is usually necessary to maintain satisfying sexual relationships in later life, but people with available partners can usually manage the changes necessitated by physiological decline (Starr, 1993).

LOVE AND LOVING

Freud was wrong. Love is not merely the diversion or sublimation of the sex drive into more socially acceptable feelings of tenderness and affection. Rather than being a substitute for sex, feelings of love between two people are often kindled and intensified by sexual stimulation and intercourse (Dermer & Pyszczynski, 1978).

Considering how much has been written, said, and sung about the topic of love, it may seem strange that so little scientific effort has been directed toward understanding it. For years, psychological researchers avoided the topic, feeling perhaps that Freud had the last word or that "love" was only romantic nonsense, fit for entertainment and youthful fantasizing but not worthy of serious scientific study. During the past few decades, however, motivated to some extent by investigations of human sexual behavior, research on love has become more acceptable and progress has been made in understanding it.

Varieties of Love

Some observers see love as a unidimensional state ranging in intensity from simple liking to profound, passionate affection for another person. Other philosophers and psychologists have viewed love as multidimensional, varying not only in depth but also in kind. One ancient classification system, which differentiates between the *eros* of Plato, the *philia* of Aristotle, and the *agape* of St. Paul, was adopted by Rollo May (1969) in his theory of love and is described in Table 6–1.

Perhaps more familiar to nonclassicists is the distinction between passionate and companionate love (Hatfield & Walster, 1981; Rubin, 1973; Walster & Walster, 1978). *Passionate love* is an intense, emotional state in which the partners are deeply absorbed with each other. The ardent sexual passion of passionate love typically has a relatively short life span, but it may be transformed into companionate love. As depicted in romantic novels, plays, and

TABLE 6–1 The Many Faces of Love

ELAINE HATFIELD

Passionate love: an intense emotional state of ardent sexual passion and positive absorption in another person.

Companionate love: an affectionate, tranquil, stable state in which two people depend on each other and enjoy being together.

ABRAHAM MASLOW

D-love ("deficiency love"): the need to receive love from other people.

B-love ("being love"): nonpossessive, giving, honest, and richer and more enjoyable than D-love.

ROLLO MAY

Eros: the desire to form a psychological union with or feel as one with a love partner.

Philia: the feeling of companionship or friendship that a person has with a loved one, even in the absence of sex and eros.

Agape: unselfishly giving oneself in a love relationship, with no expectation of receiving anything in return.

JOHN LEE

Eros: a need to know the loved one completely and experience everything about him or her.

Mania: obsessive, demanding love, accompanied by pain and anxiety because of the insatiable need for attention from the loved one.

Ludis: self-centered, playful love, in which love is treated as a game to be won.

Storge: companionate, solid, peaceful love between close friends.

Agape: saintly, "thou"-centered love that is patient, forgiving, and kind.

Pragma: logical, practical love, given only when the partner is considered to be a "good catch."

ROBERT STERNBERG

Infatuated love: love that is high on passion but low on intimacy and decision/commitment.

Romantic love: love that is high on passion and intimacy but low on decision/commitment.

Fatuous love: love that is high on passion and decision/commitment but low on intimacy.

Empty love: love that is low on passion and intimacy but high on decision/commitment.

Consummate love: love that is high on passion, intimacy, and decision/commitment.

Companionate love: love that is low on passion but high on intimacy and decision/commitment.

---

poetry, passionate love can range from the extreme high of ecstasy to the extreme low of loss and depression.

Companionate love consists of a strong but tranquil feeling of affection between two people. Companionate love partners depend on and trust each other, and they enjoy spending a lot of time together. Their feelings for each other are less intense but more stable than those of passionate lovers and are based on mutual self-disclosure and understanding. As companionate love grows, the partners reveal more and more about themselves. Companionate love is obviously different from passionate love, but the two states are not mutually exclusive. Romance and passion remain an important part of many enduring relationships (Murstein, 1985; Skolnick, 1981; Traupmann, Eckels, & Hatfield, 1982).

Many other ways of classifying love have been proposed. The humanistic

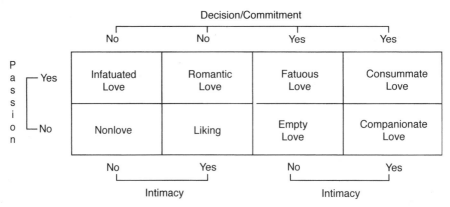

Figure 6–2 Sternberg's triangular model of love. (Based on Sternberg, 1986.)

psychologist Abraham Maslow distinguished between *D-love* ("deficiency love") and *B-love* ("being love"). D-love, expressed as a need to receive love, often involves selfish efforts to obtain affection from others. B-love is more honest, nonpossessive, generous, and enjoyable (Maslow, 1970).

More research-based than the conceptions of Maslow and May is Robert Sternberg's (1986) three-factor theory of love. As illustrated in Figure 6–2, the theory describes love in terms of three dimensions: *passion* (intense physiological desire for someone), *intimacy* (sharing thoughts and emotions with someone), and *decision/commitment* (willingness to remain with someone). The various combinations of these three components yield different types of love: infatuated love, romantic love, fatuous love, empty love, companionate love, and consummate love (see Figure 6–2). *Infatuation,* or "love at first sight," is based on strong physical attraction. *Romantic love* is an intimate, passionate relationship without commitment. *Fatuous love,* in which the partners are "swept off their feet" but do not develop intimacy, leads to rapid courtship and marriage. In *empty love,* there is no passion or intimacy but the couple remains committed to the relationship because of children or other obligations. Long-term friendships or marriages in which passion has diminished are *companionate love* relationships. And the ideal type of love, in which passion, intimacy, and commitment are all present, is *consummate love.* Two other states in Sternberg's classification system involve either no passion, no intimacy, and no decision/commitment (*nonlove*) or intimacy but no passion and no decision/commitment (*liking*).

Sternberg (1986) stresses that all three components—passion, intimacy, and commitment—of his theory of love are dynamic and change in particular ways in both successful and unsuccessful relationships. Passion consists of a quickly developing positive force and a more slowly developing but longer lasting negative force. Following a "breakup," the negative force can lead to heartache but eventually disappears. The intimacy component of love grows steadily at first and then levels off in enduring relationships. When intimacy fades, the relationship usually fails. Commitment grows gradually at first, more rapidly as the relationship progresses, and then either levels off (in long-term relationships) or declines (in failed relationships).

Falling in Love

As indicated in the preceding paragraph, different aspects of love develop at different rates. The initial "blindness" of love, which is based on physical attractiveness and other superficial characteristics, gives way to deeper, more enduring feelings of attachment as lovers confide in each other and recognize their similar attitudes, beliefs, and interests (Adams, 1979; Levinger, 1978). For love to develop and last, passion must be complemented by sharing, caring, and loyalty. Each partner comes to value the other and is as much concerned about the other's welfare as about his or her own.

Unless, like Narcissus, we settle for being in love with ourselves, falling in love requires a partner. But how does one find a partner and become attracted to him or her? According to Byrne (1971), there are three determinants of attraction: proximity, physical attractiveness, and similarity. Unlike the way that it was in the days of slow transportation and communication, the supply of potential partners is no longer limited to our neighbors, schoolmates, and coworkers. Nevertheless, it is still true that one is more likely to become familiar with people in the immediate vicinity. We can meet potential lovers through the newspaper, a dating service, or even the Internet, but, like our predecessors in previous times, we are more likely to meet them in places that we frequent or through introductions provided by friends, family, and associates. In addition to proximity, physical attractiveness is an obvious determinant of attraction for both men and women, and particularly the former. Attractiveness is, of course, more than simply a matter of physical characteristics. Beauty is in the eye of the beholder and, to some extent, depends on the seeker's own physical characteristics. Similarities in educational and social background, values, interests, attitudes, and other characteristics are also important determinants of love interest—particularly in long-lasting relationships. In general, research has failed to confirm the *complementarity hypothesis* that "opposites attract." In most cases, people are attracted to those who are like themselves in physical, cognitive, and personality characteristics.

Both initial and more enduring attraction between individuals is also stimulated by various body signs or nonverbal behaviors. For example, both men and women "flirt," signaling their interest and availability by various gestures (Table 6–2). Lovers pay special attention to their physical appearance (preen, groom), spend a lot of time just looking into each other eyes, stand close, touch, hug, kiss, and in other ways indicate their preoccupation and affection. They spend as much time as possible with each other, often neglecting their friends, families, and other responsibilities (Johnson & Leslie, 1982).

TABLE 6–2 Fifty-Two Ways That Women Flirt

Monica Moore and teams of graduate students spent hundreds of hours in bars and student centers covertly watching women and men court. The following is a list of 52 gestures they found that women use to signal their interest in men (Moore, M. M., 1995):

Facial/Head Patterns

Coy smiles	Laugh
Eyebrow flash	Lip lick
Face to face	Lipstick application
Fixed gaze	Neck presentation
Giggle	Pout
Hair flip	Room-encompassing glance
Head toss	Short, darting glance
Head nod	Smile
Kiss	Whisper

Posture Patterns

Aid solicitation	Lateral body contact
Approach	Lean
Breast touch	Parade
Brush	Placement
Dance (acceptance)	Play
Foot to foot	Point
Frontal body contact	Request dance
Hang	Shoulder hug
Hug	Solitary dance
Knee touch	Thigh touch

Gestures

Arm flexion	Caress (torso)
Buttock pat	Gesticulation
Caress (arm)	Hand hold
Caress (back)	Hike skirt
Caress (face/hair)	Palm
Caress (leg)	Primp
Caress (object)	Tap

Traditionally, love and hate have been viewed as opposites, but they also possess similarities, and one can easily turn into the other. Both love and hate involve high levels of arousal—one component of emotion. Once aroused, and depending on the particular stimulus situation, the person may become passionately loving or passionately angry and hateful. Depending on who is present and what he or she says or does to the highly aroused person, either love or hate may be the expressed outcome (see Dutton & Aron, 1974).

Age Differences

The human need for love is not limited to a particular chronological age or gender, but its features vary with age and sex. The desire for emotional closeness appears to be stronger in younger than in older women, and greater in older than in younger men. Passion and sexual intimacy are generally of greater importance to younger adults, whereas affection and faithfulness are more important to older adults (Huyck, 1982). It seems that the passions of youth either burn out or become transformed into more serene and tender feelings in old age. There are, however, both similarities and differences in the way adults of different ages perceive love. For example, in a study of factors important in love at different chronological ages, Reedy, Birren, and Schaie (1981) found that, at all ages, emotional security was ranked first, followed by respect, communication, help and play behaviors, sexual intimacy, and loyalty. Although the relative rankings of these factors remained constant across age groups, the exact scores on each variable varied somewhat with age. Thus, the communication score was higher for younger adults than for middle-aged and older adults, sexual intimacy was higher for younger and middle-aged adults than for older adults, and emotional security and loyalty were higher for older adults than for younger and middle-aged adults. However, because most such studies are cross-sectional, it is possible that the results reflect cohort differences rather than aging per se. Thus, when today's young adults reach middle- and older adulthood, it may be that their judgments of factors important in love will be more similar to what they are now than to those of today's older adults.

Gender Differences

The socialization of girls in our society places more emphasis on relationships with other people, whereas in the socialization of boys relationships are subordinated to achievement or accomplishment (Gilligan, 1982). One consequence of this difference in treatment is that women are more interested in social relations and usually have more friends than men. In addition, perhaps because they sense a greater interest and sympathy on the part of women, people are more willing to confide in women than in men (Derlega, Winstead, Wong, & Hunter, 1985).

Women also fall in love in different ways than men. Men tend to fall in love faster, to fall out of love more slowly, and, because they have no one in whom to confide, suffer more from a breakup (Hill, Rubin, & Peplau, 1976; Rubin, Hill, Peplau, & Dunkel-Schetter, 1980). Men also tend to be more romantic than women, believing in love at first sight, that there is one true love for them, and that love is magical and incomprehensible. In contrast, women tend to be more cautious and pragmatic about love relationships, emphasizing financial security as much as passion, that there are many people with whom they could be equally happy, and that love cannot conquer all differences or problems (Peplau & Gordon, 1985). Women are more likely than men to experience both the agony and the ecstasy of love and to disclose both their positive and negative feelings about a relationship (Jourard, 1971). When men share their views, they are more likely to discuss their strengths and politics, whereas women are more likely to discuss their fears and feelings about other people (Rubin et al., 1980).

The extent to which dissatisfaction with a relationship is predictive of its demise also varies with gender. Because the desire to make a relationship work is a more important feature of love for women than for men, women are more apt to "stick it out" when they become dissatisfied with a relationship (Cowan & Cowan, 1992).

Culture

It is said that the largely Western concept of romantic love was introduced into Europe by Eleanor of Aquitaine, who was a Queen of England during the twelfth century. Queen Eleanor loved stories, poems, and songs about love and presumably employed them to calm her volatile husband, King Henry the Second. Wherever and whenever romantic love may have begun, it was not a common reason for marrying until fairly modern times. Even today, in more "traditional" cultures (e.g., China, India, Iran, and Nigeria), marriage occurs for more pragmatic and familial reasons than merely because two people have fallen in love. Many marriages in these countries are still "arranged," and the bride and groom have little to say about the matter. In more "modern" countries such as England, the Netherlands, Finland, and Sweden, not only is romantic love a popular concept but also marriage without benefit of clergy is widely practiced (Buss et al., 1990)

Though countries throughout the world have become extensively westernized during the twentieth century, it is still possible to rate cultures on a continuum from traditional to modern in terms of their courtship and marriage practices. For example, Mediterranean countries tend to be more traditional and Scandinavian countries more modern in their dating and mating practices. Not only marital customs but also the qualities that one looks for in a mate vary with the culture. In a cross-cultural study conducted by Buss et al. (1990) of the characteristics valued in a potential mate, chastity showed the greatest variability. Some countries and cultures placed a high value on chastity, whereas others valued it very little. Other characteristics that varied appreciably from country to country in their perceived importance in a mate were intelligence, education, and refinement. There were, however, some cross-cultural similarities as well. For example, women throughout the world tended to place high value on a man's earning potential, whereas men placed greater value on a woman's physical attractiveness.

MARRIED AND UNMARRIED ADULTS

Most, but not all, Americans get married at least once during their lifetimes. The percentage of married women in the United States peaks in the midforties and declines rather abruptly thereafter as the number of widows increases. The percentage of married men, however, does not peak until the midfifties. The percentages of divorced women and men also peak in the midforties, and the percentage of "never marrieds" declines fairly steadily into older adulthood.

Singles

Between 5% and 10% of American women never marry, but the percentage is higher for black than for white women (Saluter, 1996). Among middle-aged and older adults who never marry are priests, nuns, and others who have chosen lifestyles that preclude marriage. Most never-marrieds do not consciously intend to make their single status permanent, but for one reason or another, they have never "tied the knot." Many prefer the single life, whereas others have real or imagined handicaps that contribute to an inability to attract a mate (Corby & Zarit, 1983).

In former times, the traditional role of woman as wife and homemaker led to a great deal of social pressure on unmarried women in their late twenties. Friends and family were preoccupied with the single status of a woman and constantly concerned themselves with finding a suitable mate for her. However, social attitudes have changed markedly during this century, and now many men and women feel comfortable waiting until their thirties to marry, or they decide not to marry at all. These individuals are much less likely to experience the social censure and alienation to which their nonmarried predecessors were subjected in previous times.

Certain psychologists and psychiatrists, viewing heterosexual union as a sine qua non of mental health and happiness, have considered chronic bachelors and spinsters as self-centered, neurotic, and often sexually deviant individuals who live lonely, dispirited lives. Although some research studies have found lifelong singles to be lonelier than marrieds, most singles appear to be happy, socially adjusted individuals who are satisfied with their lifestyles and interact frequently with their families, friends, and coworkers (Cargan & Melko, 1982; Essex & Nam, 1987; Rubinstein, 1987). Many women who have remained single are professional careerists who value their personal freedom and economic and social independence more than the emotional, sexual, and financial security of marriage. Such women may be highly educated, but a substantial percentage of those who remain single have a less than average amount of formal education (U.S. Bureau of the Census, 1992).

Never-marrieds do not fit a particular personality stereotype. In a study of unmarried men, Rubinstein (1987) identified three personality types: (1) socially active men who were quite sophisticated and had many friends; (2) social isolates who spent much of their time alone but reached out for company when they wanted it; (3) outsiders who were truly isolated from other people.

Of course, not all singles live alone; many live with relatives or friends. In addition, most singles are not sexually frustrated creatures who have no outlet for their erotic impulses. Some are "swinging singles" who opt for temporary heterosexual unions, some are cohabitants, and some are homosexuals.

Cohabitation

An estimated 50% of all couples living together in heterosexual relationships today are nonmarried cohabitants. Most of these relationships are fairly short-term arrangements that end in either marriage or separation, whereas others may last for years (Macklin, 1988). In some instances, the cohabiting couple decides to forego a traditional marriage ceremony and become common-law partners by declaring themselves to be married. They combine their assets, file joint tax returns, and can only dissolve their common-law marriage by divorce or death. In states that recognize common-law marriages, the spouses can collect insurance, social security benefits, and community property after a stipulated time has expired. However, fraudulent claims resulting from common-law marriages have led many states to outlaw them (Marriage, 1993).

Cohabiting couples who eventually marry tend to hold traditional views concerning the roles of husband and wife, and in marriage they are quite similar to noncohabiting marital partners in terms of the degree of closeness, conflict, equality, and satisfaction experienced. Despite the belief that living together before marriage helps a couple to become better acquainted, premarital cohabitation does not necessarily make marriage better. In fact, there is some evidence to the contrary (Booth & Johnson, 1988). Because cohabitants tend to be less conventional, less religious, and of lower socioeconomic status than noncohabitants, they are more likely to become divorced (DeMaris & Rao, 1992).

Homosexual Relationships

The social environments of most large cities is conductive to cohabitation among homosexual males (gays) and females (lesbians). Marriages between homosexuals are not legally sanctioned in the United States, although legislation concerning such domestic partnerships has received support in certain cities (e.g., San Francisco, New York) and states (e.g., Hawaii).

Relatively little longitudinal research has been conducted on gay and lesbian relationships (Kimmel & Sang, 1995; Kurdek, 1991a, 1991b, 1995a, 1995b), but some facts are available. For example, informal marriages between homosexuals tend to be less stable than legal marriages between heterosexuals. Lesbians are more monogamous than gays, more likely to confide in one another, do things together more frequently, and remain together for longer periods of time (Blumstein & Schwartz, 1983).

Bell and Weinberg (1978) differentiate between *close-coupled*, or enduring monogamous relationships, and *open-coupled* relationships in which two homosexuals live together but have other lovers as well. Close-coupled, or "exclusive," relationships are generally happier than open-coupled ones and are more common among older than younger gays. Many of these partnerships are satisfying and enduring (Butler & Lewis, 1993). The fear of AIDS has also influenced the durability of homosexual relationships in recent years, resulting in a greater frequency of gay "marriages" that are close-coupled. Relationships between lesbian couples can also be described as close- or open-coupled, but significantly more of them are close-coupled than in the case of gays. Lesbian couples are generally warm, tender, and caring toward each other, but such relationships are also more likely to break up than heterosexual marriages (Nichols & Lieblum, 1983).

Bell and Weinberg (1978) characterize the social/sexual relationships of gay men who live alone as functional, dysfunctional, or asexual. They found that approximately 10% of these men were in *functional* relationships: They lived alone but had active sex lives, were self-reliant, and felt comfortable with their homosexuality. The homosexual community serves as a kind of extended family for such men (Francher & Henkin, 1973). Bell and Weinberg (1978) classified another 12% of the gay men whom they studied as *dysfunctionals*. These men also lived alone and sometimes had active sex lives, but they were unhappy and troubled about their status. The last and largest category of gays identified by Bell and Weinberg were the *asexuals*. This category consisted of the 16% of live-alone gays who were withdrawn, lived quiet lives, had little sexual contact, but appeared untroubled by their sexual orientation. Like gays, lesbians who live alone may have functional, dysfunctional, or asexual relationships, although a much smaller percentage of lesbians than gays fall into the last two categories.

Close-coupled homosexual relationships go through phases similar to those of heterosexual marriages (Kurdek & Schmitt, 1986). However, the pattern of roles and activities for the male and female members of heterosexual unions is found less often in homosexual partnerships. Role assignments are less fixed and more negotiable in gay and lesbian households, resulting in less of a power struggle than that observed in many heterosexual households.

The conception of aging homosexuals as lonely, depressed, and sexually frustrated is an overgeneralization. Living in a predominantly heterosexual society creates problems for older homosexuals, but there are also compensations. Among the problems are discrimination against homosexuals by society as a whole, disrespect from family members, inability to have their marriages sanctioned by law, and, in some cases, lack of visitation rights with their children by former marriages. One advantage of homosexuality, particularly in older adulthood and especially for lesbians, is the availability of partners (Raphael & Robinson, 1980).

MY LIFE 6–2

Marriage and Unmarriage

One often hears about "wedded bliss" or "matrimonial harmony," but these are obviously not descriptive of many conjugal relationships. It may be that marriages are made in heaven, though it is doubtful unless one is a bride of Christ or married to the church. Duration is certainly not a sure-fire indicator of marital happiness. Most people who get married probably intend to stay that way, but, as one young woman explained to me, "If it doesn't work out there are always divorce courts." Still, you can't equate marital stability with marital satisfaction. One 90-something-year-old couple celebrated their diamond wedding anniversary by untying the knot. They confessed that they had never really liked each other but decided to wait until the children had grown old and died before going their separate ways.

Perhaps place has something to do with connubial comfort. We tend to associate people with the places and circumstances in which we first met them and with what they were doing then. First impressions, whether positive or negative, also play an important role, and impressions are affected by circumstances. Remember the vaudeville joke about the dizzy couple who met in a revolving door and kept going around together? Well, my wife and I didn't meet in a door, but we did meet in a mental hospital (a nonrevolving door?). Occasionally, after a disagreement of some sort, one of us will suggest to the other that he or she should go back there for a long visit.

Time of day also seems to be a factor in affectionate regard for another person. Most people are more romantic in the evening, when the low illumination and the dreamy atmosphere make both genders more attrac-

---

Marriage

Marriage is a legal, religious, social, and personal affair. It is an institution, a sacrament, a promise, and a contract entered into with some thought of enduring until death, but with only a 50–50 chance of doing so. Although marriage may not last until death, there is some evidence that men who get married do not die as soon as those who remain single. Whether the greater longevity of married men is due to the fact that marriage selects rather than protects, that is, that healthy, long-living people are more likely to marry and stay married, it is also possible that the emotional ties and the sharing of labor and mutual responsibility of marriage encourage health and long life—at least in males. However, it seems that, in terms of longevity, women benefit less from marriage and suffer less than men from being single. At least, this was the finding in a study by Gove (1973). A subsequent investigation conducted by Kobrin and Hendershot (1977) on a national sample of people who died between the ages of 35 and 74 yielded complex findings concerning the

tive. Unfortunately, your nocturnal soulmate may not be recognizable by the cold, unforgiving light of day. If you enjoy kissing her (or him) in the morning, you'll enjoy it anytime. Or as one reluctant groom responded when urged by the preacher to kiss the bride, "I'll pass if you don't mind!"

I've always believed that it is a good idea to try marriage at least once, but some people carry it to ridiculous extremes. Two cases in point are Tommy Manville with his 25 wives and Elizabeth Taylor with her 8 husbands. Of course, Liz, like my own mother, married (and divorced) the same man twice. The couple apparently needed a second go-round before coming to the conclusion that they really couldn't stand each other after all.

Having more than one mate poses a problem of what to do with them. If you live in a polygamous society or can travel rapidly from place to place, it may not be necessary to get rid of them at all. Extinguishing an old flame by paying her (or him) off is another pos-sibility, but the method of figuratively ("Jane Eyre") or literally ("Bluebeard") burying your mistakes is definitely not recommended. Furthermore, even if you like your spouses a lot, you shouldn't follow the example of some ancient kings and try to take them with you when you die.

It is conceivable that the rate of spouse-disposal could be reduced by "heading it off at the pass." One might make a "Scenes from a Bad Marriage" videotape of all the things that can go wrong with a match and play it back several times for people who are contemplating coupling. It is doubtful, however, that even the most graphic depictions and predictions will deter two individuals who are blinded by love and intent on getting hitched. Love and marriage continue to go together like work and play, life and death, or a horse and carriage. The question is who will be the driver and who the driven, and how long will it be before the horse bolts or the driver jumps off the rig?

effects of marriage on longevity. In general, however, the results of this and other studies (e.g., Berkman & Syme, 1979) support the conclusion that close social ties and higher social status, which are more likely to be found in marriage than outside it, favor greater longevity. This relationship suggests that social interaction, such as is found in marriage, is as important as diet, alcohol consumption, smoking, or exercise in promoting a long life (see House, Robbins, & Metzner, 1982).

In 1995, 50% of males, 56% of females, 60% of non-Hispanic whites, 40% of blacks, and 55% of Hispanics in the United States over age 14 were married. Figure 6–3 shows that the median age of first marriages for both men and women during this century declined until the 1950s and then rose again. That many Americans do not get married until their late thirties, if ever, is indicated by the fact that in 1995, 33% (13.6 million) of those aged 25–34 had never been married. However, many unmarried couples in this group were living together (Saluter, 1996).

As shown in Figure 6–4, the percentage of married women increases

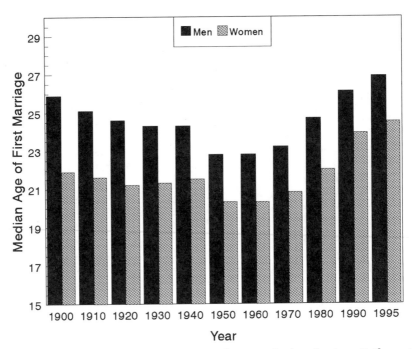

Figure 6-3 Median age for first marriage by year during the twentieth century.
(Based on data from Saluter, 1996.)

until the forties and then declines. However, the percentage of married men reaches a maximum approximately 10 years later and declines less rapidly than the percentage of married women. At all ages, the percentages of black men and women who are married are lower than those of Hispanic and non-Hispanic white men and women. Less than 75% of black women, compared with 90% of white women, eventually marry, and they tend to marry at a later age. Also note the steep drop in the percentage of married women produced by widowhood in later life (U.S. Bureau of the Census, 1992).

People get married for many different reasons other than love and romance: familial and peer expectations and pressures; to improve their economic and social positions; to raise a family; to cope with feelings of loneliness, inadequacy, and insecurity. Some women still get married because they are pregnant, but out-of-wedlock births have become fairly common and less likely to produce personal, social, and economic handicaps than they once were.

Although *traditional marriage*, in which the husband is the dominant partner and decision maker and the wife is the principal housekeeper and child rearer, has been declining in popularity, it is still the most common type. Other marital arrangements include companionate, colleague, open,

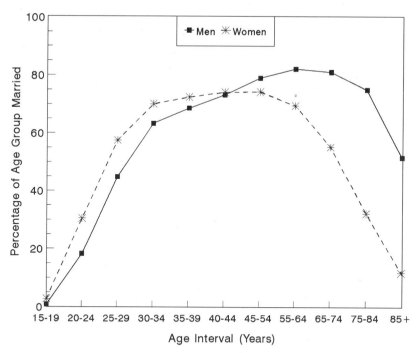

Figure 6–4 Percentage of married men and women as a function of age in 1995. (Based on data from Saluter, 1996.)

and group marriages. In *companionate marriage*, no distinction is made between male and female roles. Both husband and wife can assume any of the duties, rights, and obligations of the family unit. Different from companionate marriage in terms of role assignments, but also democratic, is *colleague marriage*. Here, specific duties and responsibilities are assumed by each partner and recognized as such by the other marital partner. Companionate and colleague marriages are especially popular among highly educated, middle- and upper-middle-class couples (Duberman, 1974).

At the more liberal end of the traditional–modern continuum of marital arrangements are open and group marriages. An *open marriage* is a legally sanctioned union, but both partners find it perfectly acceptable to have sexual relationships with other people. *Group marriage* is a communal arrangement in which a number of couples are legally married to one another but decide to share living quarters, duties, and sexual partners (Duberman, 1974).

A major task in marriages of various sorts is that of role differentiation and the associated process of power division. A research study conducted by Miller and Olson (1978) found evidence for nine different patterns of role and power differentiation between husband and wife: wife-led (disengaged, congenial, or confrontive), husband-led (disengaged, engaging, confrontive, conflictive, or cooperative), and shared leadership. A strong determinant of power in marriage, whether wife-led or husband-led, was money. Women who had high incomes tended to be equal to or higher in power than their husbands. In a further analysis of their data, Miller and Olson were able to describe most marriages in terms of dominance, conflict, and affect. The affect dimension included such behaviors as humor or laughter, disapproval of the spouse, and self-doubt on the part of the husband.

Other researchers who have analyzed changes in the ways that marital partners deal with problems of authority, control, and power over time have delineated various phases through which married couples pass in their relationships with each other. Kurdek and Schmitt (1986) differentiated between the blending phase of the first year, the nesting phase of the second and third years, and the maintaining phase of the fourth and subsequent years of marriage. The *blending phase* consists of learning to live together and to think of the marital partners as an interdependent pair. The *nesting phase* involves an exploration by the partners of limits on their compatibility and the time that they should spend on shared activities. Stress and disillusionment are frequently at a maximum during this phase of marriage. In the third and final phase, the *maintaining phase*, family traditions are established, the individuality of each partner is recognized, and the level of stress declines.

All marriages are obviously not successful or happy ventures. Unwillingness or inability to compromise, inflexibility, and a refusal to acknowledge one's own inadequacies and failures as well as those of one's spouse are characteristic of partners in unhappy marriages. Short marriages are typically unhappy ones, but endurance does not necessarily imply satisfaction. Many middle-aged couples, women in particular, who have been married for two decades are dissatisfied with their marriages. The good news for these individuals is that marital satisfaction generally increases in later life (Anderson, Russell, & Schumm, 1983; Lee, 1988). It is usually highest during the first years of marriage, declines until the children begin leaving home, and then rises again (Berry & Williams, 1987).

A number of factors are associated with enduring marriages. Included among them are the relative maturity of the partners when they are married, the degree of financial security, and a feeling that the relationship is an equal one (Diamond, 1986). Among other factors that can interfere with marital happiness and have an effect on the length of a marriage are pregnancy or delivery prior to the marriage ceremony, the physical appearance of one's spouse (Margolin & White, 1987), whether or not there are children in the home, and the personal and behavioral characteristics of the spouse (dependency; argumentativeness; addiction to alcohol, tobacco, and drugs). With older couples, the situation in which the husband is retired but the wife continues to work outside the home can become a source of conflict and dissatisfaction in marriage (Lee, 1988).

In general, married couples, as with any two people who live close to each other for years in an interdependent, symbiotic relationships, experience periods of cooperation and conflict, like and dislike. The longer two people live together, the greater their investment in the marriage and, hopefully, the greater their involvement and desire to make it work. The traditional virtues of tolerance, patience, consideration, respect, and affection are as important in marital happiness and longevity as they are in any effective human relationship and must be practiced by both partners.

Divorce

Nothing lasts forever; love dies, a spouse dies, and many marriages end in divorce. Marital discord occurs for a number of reasons, 11 of which are listed in Figure 6–5. Not all of these reasons necessarily lead to divorce, but they are now more likely to do so than in previous times. In the last century, marriages ended in death as often as in divorce, but divorce has become the principal cause of marital breakups in this century. Legal grounds for divorce in previous times—adultery, alcoholism, brutality, desertion, and nonsupport—are still acceptable reasons, but incompatibility is a more common reason, and "no-fault" divorces are also becoming fashionable. Unlike former times, when the marital roles of husband and wife were relatively fixed and men and

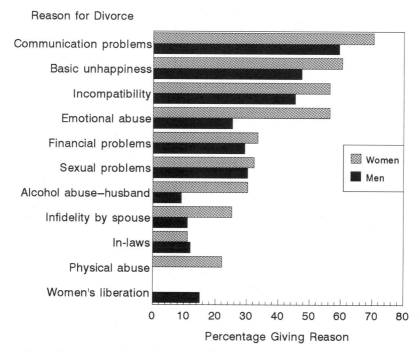

Figure 6–5   **Reasons given for divorcing.** (Based on data from Cleek & Pearson, 1985.)

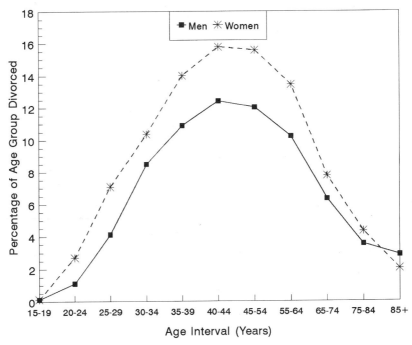

Figure 6–6   Percentage of divorced men and women as a function of chronological age in 1995. (Based on data from Saluter, 1996.)

women were not expected to understand the opposite sex but simply to fulfill their vows and duties, today's couples are less apt to endure marriages in which disagreements and conflicts are frequent.

As shown in Figure 6–6, divorce rates for both men and women are at a peak in the early forties. The average number of years of marriage before divorcing has been declining and is now slightly over 6 years. Approximately 40% of first marriages in the United States end in divorce, a figure that is among the highest in the world. The divorce rate is higher for blacks than for whites, and higher for whites than for Hispanics. Among Hispanics, Puerto Ricans have higher divorce rates than Mexican Americans and Cuban Americans (Bean & Tienda, 1987). The divorce rate is also higher for people who either failed to graduate from high school or had some college than for those who terminated their formal education with high school graduation (12 years) or college graduation (16 years) (U.S. Bureau of the Census, 1992).

As might be expected, divorce is now more common among young women who married when they were teenagers and were pregnant or had a child prior to marriage. Higher frequencies of divorce are also found in lower income groups and among those who attend religious services infrequently (Glenn & Supancic, 1984; U.S. Bureau of the Census, 1992).

The increased financial and social independence of women, the availability of welfare, and changes in public attitudes and mores have contributed to the increase in the divorce rate and the increased acceptability, if not respectability, of divorce as a means of solving marital problems and achieving personal fulfillment. Divorced people usually find that the change in their marital status has not solved all their problems; for example, they are often even more depressed than when they were married (Menaghan & Lieberman, 1986).

Although it is usually the wife who files for divorce, in the short run the husband usually suffers more from it (Bloom & Caldwell, 1981; Kelly, 1982). Not only does a divorced man experience feelings of rejection and failure, but fathers who do not have custody of their children tend to see them less often, are less involved in decisions regarding their lives, and frequently end up as bitter enemies of their ex-wives (Ahrons & Rodgers, 1987; Furstenberg & Nord, 1985; Seltzer, 1991). In the long run, however, the reduced financial status of the wife and, in most cases, the fact that she is awarded custody of any children from the marriage, create a greater hardship on her. Not only must she continue to perform the roles of homemaker and parent, but she is also responsible for taking care of all the practical and financial matters that were previously the husband's responsibilities. Furthermore, it is usually more difficult for a divorced woman than for a divorced man to find a new heterosexual partner. This is particularly true when the woman is no longer young and has children to take care of.

The effects of divorce on a child depend on the age, sex, and personality of the child and his or her relationships with the parents. Young children tend to be more emotionally vulnerable, to experience greater stress, and to suffer feelings of guilt, blame, and abandonment, whereas adolescents are more likely to react with confusion and anger (Cooney & Uhlenberg, 1990). In general, teenagers cope better than younger children, especially when they have a close relationship with the custodial parent. There is also some evidence that divorced parents express less affection for their children and that this may be accompanied by sexual promiscuity in girls and gender-role reversal in boys (Hetherington, Cox, & Cox, 1977; Kelly & Wallerstein, 1976).

Remarriage

Everyone deserves a second chance, and many people take it. Four out of 10 marriages in the United States are remarriages for at least one of the parties. Remarriages are more likely for men than for women, for young adults than for middle-aged and older adults, for whites than for blacks or Hispanics, and for less educated than for highly educated women (U.S. Bureau of the Census, 1992). Remarriage is more likely shortly after divorcing and declines in probability as the time since the divorce increases.

People remarry for many of the same reasons they married the first time—romance, affection, companionship, security, regard, and so on. Sex is an important reason for remarriage at all ages but less so with older adults. As people grow older, closeness and intimacy become more important than sexual relations.

Despite the popular song that love is more comfortable the second time around, remarriages tend to be even less stable than first marriages. As it was with the first divorce, the likelihood of redivorce after a second marriage is higher for younger than for older couples. Apparently, older couples are more likely to think twice before remarrying, to select more wisely, and to have learned from experience that compromise and consideration are necessary in order to make marriage work. Remarriage among older adults after the death of a spouse also has a greater chance of success than remarriage after a divorce (U.S. Bureau of the Census, 1992).

A successful remarriage requires not only the efforts of both partners but also those of the relatives and friends of the marital partners. The newlyweds usually need all the support, understanding, and acceptance they can get from those who are close to them. This is particularly true in the case of stepchildren. Adolescents, especially boys, and when the stepparent is a man, typically adjust better than younger children to a new stepparent (Hetherington, Cox, & Cox, 1982). In any case, it is natural for a child or an adolescent to be concerned about someone who demands much of the time, attention, and love of the natural mother or father. Conflicts between stepparents and stepchildren and their consequent inability to adjust to each other are a major reason for the failure of second marriages in which there are children from a previous marriage (White & Booth, 1985).

SUMMARY

The purpose of life is more than reproduction, but there is no question that sex and love make life more interesting and exciting. Sexual behavior is regulated to some extent by hormones secreted by the hypothalamus, the pituitary gland, and the gonads, but it is also affected by experience and practice. The sexual response cycle in adult human beings consists of four phases: excitation, plateau, orgasm, and resolution. A large percentage of males and females have had intercourse by the time they reach 20 years of age, but the frequency of intercourse declines after age 30. Be that as it may, many men, but fewer women, in their seventies and eighties continue to enjoy sexual intercourse.

Most older women who stop having sex do so because their husbands stop, or because they are widows who are unable or unwilling to find another partner. Vaginal changes produced by menopause cause pain and irritation during sexual intercourse, but hormone replacement therapy and other treatments can reduce the discomfort. Older men experience changes in the testes, the prostate gland, and in sexual functioning, but the notion of a "male menopause" similar to that of women is incorrect.

Sexual dysfunctions in both men and women may be temporary conditions produced by excessive consumption of food or alcohol, fatigue, boredom, stress, and conflict. Chronic conditions, such as impotence in males and frigidity in females, are associated with a variety of disorders and medications. Hysterectomy in women and prostate surgery in men can also affect sexual interest and activity, but typically not reversibly. A variety of chemical, surgical, and psychological procedures are used to treat sexual dysfunctions. The rapid, effective treatment of sexual inadequacy was pioneered by William Masters and Virginia Johnson.

Various classification systems have been proposed for describing different kinds of love. Among these are Elaine Hatfield's distinction between passionate or companionate love; Rollo May's differentiation between eros, philia, and agape; and Robert Sternberg's six types of love (infatuated, romantic, fatuous, empty, consummate, companionate), plus nonlove and liking. Sternberg's eight categories consist of various combinations of the component dimensions of passion, intimacy, and decision/commitment. The three components are dynamic, changing in particular ways in successful and unsuccessful relationships.

A number of research studies have been conducted on how people become attracted to one another and fall in love. Three important determinants of attraction are proximity, physical attractiveness, and similarity. Although opposites attract in certain cases, in general similarity in interests, abilities, and background has greater pulling power than complementarity.

Passion and sexual intimacy are typically of greater importance to younger than to older adults, but the rank orders of factors that are important to love are similar at different ages. One study found that emotional security, respect, communication, help and play behaviors, sexual intimacy, and loyalty were ranked in that order of importance for a mate by young, middle-aged, and older adults.

Women tend to emphasize interpersonal relationships more than men, and they also fall in love in different ways. Compared with men, women tend to be less romantic but more cautious, more pragmatic, and more determined to make a love relationship work. Courtship and marriage behaviors and practices vary not only with age and gender but also with social class and culture.

Approximately 90% of Americans marry at least once, the percentage being lower for blacks than for whites and Hispanics. Marriage is, however, not essential for happiness. Most single adults are quite active socially and appear to be fairly well satisfied with their lifestyles.

Half of all couples who live together are nonmarried cohabitants, and a sizable percentage of these couples eventually marry. Unfortunately, the experience of having lived together prior to marriage does not guarantee a happier or more enduring marriage.

Homosexual relationships may be either close-coupled or open-coupled, with more lesbians than gays having close-coupled relationships. The social/sexual relationships of gays have also been characterized as functional, dys-

functional, or asexual, in order of increasing frequency. These three categories are also descriptive of lesbian relationships, but the functional category
is the largest for lesbians.

The average age for first marriages increased by more than three-and-
a-half years between 1970 and 1995. Blacks tend to marry later, and at all ages
a smaller percentage are married, than whites and Hispanics. Traditional
marriage, in which the husband is the dominant partner and chief decision
maker, has declined in popularity, while companionate and colleague marriages have increased in recent decades. Other, less popular arrangements
include open and group marriages.

Role differentiation and power division between marital partners is a
major task of a marriage and can lead to various combinations of responsibilities assumed by the husband and wife. The relationship between marital
partners can also be characterized in terms of dominance, conflict, and affect.

Most marriages pass through a series of phases in which the partners
attempt to deal with the problems of authority, control, and power. One
descriptive system depicts marriages as progressing from an initial blending
phase in the first year to a nesting phase in the second and third years, and
finally to a maintaining phase in the third and ensuing years.

The level of satisfaction is usually highest during the first years of a
marriage, declining until the children begin leaving home, and then rising
again. Happiness in marriage is, however, not merely a function of time but
also of finances, health, social support, the personalities of the spouses, the
presence of children, and other factors.

Divorce is the principal cause of marital breakup and has become increasingly easy to obtain in this century. The number of years of marriage
before divorcing has also declined. The divorce rate is higher for blacks than
for whites and Hispanics, for lower than for higher income groups, and for
women who were pregnant or had given birth before marriage. Men usually
suffer more from divorce in the short run, but women suffer more in the long
run.

Four out of 10 marriages in the United States are remarriages. Remarriage
is more common for men than for women, for young than for middle-aged and
older adults, and for less educated than for highly educated women. Remarriages tend to be even less stable than first marriages, failing for many of the
same reasons as first marriages, in addition to the presence of stepchildren
in the home.

SUGGESTED READINGS

Aiken, L. R. (1995). *Aging: An introduction to gerontology* (Ch. 7). Newbury Park, CA: Sage
    Publications.
Blumstein, P., & Schwartz, P. (1983). *American couples*. New York: Morrow.
Bulcroft, K., & O'Connor-Roden, M. (1992). Never too late. In H. Cox (Ed.), *Aging* (8th ed., pp.
    66–68). Guilford, CT: Dushkin.

Butler, R. N., & Lewis, M. I. (1987). *Love and sex after forty: A guide to men and women for their mid and later years*. New York: BDD LT Group.

Butler, R. N., & Lewis, M. I. (1993). *Love and sex after sixty*. New York: Ballantine.

Masters, W. H., Johnson, V. E., & Kolodny, R. C. (1994). *Heterosexuality*. New York: HarperCollins.

Olivero, M. (1992). Playing the not-so-newlywed game. In H. Cox (Ed.), *Aging* (8th ed., pp. 46–47). Guilford, CT: Dushkin.

Sexuality and aging: What it means or be sixty or seventy or eighty in the '90s. In H. Cox (Ed.), *Aging* (11th ed., pp. 40–44). Guilford, CT: Dushkin.

Sheehy, G. (1993). *The silent passage: Menopause*. New York: Pocket Books.

CHAPTER 7

Families and Friends

Human beings are gregarious creatures. We live together, play together, learn together, work together, and attempt to solve our problems together. We are members of families, teams, classes, clubs, unions, and many other formal and informal groups. By obeying the norms and playing the roles assigned to us by these groups, we are able to satisfy our biological and psychological needs more effectively than most of us could ever hope to do by acting alone.

A person's first social experiences usually take place in a family setting. These early encounters with other people condition the individual to expect certain things and to behave in specific ways in preparation for entry into the larger society. As representatives of that society, parents, siblings, and other family members can instill a sense of personal confidence and capability in the individual on the one hand, or feelings of insecurity and anxiety on the other. These feelings, initiated in a family setting, generalize to other social situations and set the stage for the person's lifestyle in adulthood.

In their roles as socializers and educators of the young, most families provide not only care and support, but they also communicate social norms and values, and guide their members in the behaviors appropriate for the roles they must play. Many of these roles are age-stratified or age-graded, in that they change with the chronological age as well as gender, culture, and social status. Society holds different expectations for people of different ages and assigns different statuses and roles to different age groups. Traditionally, by the time people are in their twenties or thirties, they are supposed to assume adult roles and begin the process of transferring their culture from one generation to the next. Quite common as people age is a gradual disengagement from social activities and a reduction in the roles they are expected to play. Be that as it may, most older adults prefer to engage in personally and socially significant activities. Many of the social roles that give meaning to the lives of adults of all ages are those that involve relationships with family and friends, as well as those associated with being members of various organizations.

Although the population as a whole has increased dramatically during this century, the average family size has decreased. In contrast to a typical family of yesteryear, consisting of many members whose life spans were often quite short, today's families are more likely to consist of only four or five people residing under the same roof but with several generations of the same family still living. This *beanpole family* structure, as it has been labeled (Bengtson, Rosenthal, & Burton, 1990), has resulted in less time overall being spent in child rearing but with children having not only living grandparents but also great-grandparents and even great-great-grandparents.

In addition to being smaller, the families of today are different in other ways from what they used to be. Social changes have been accompanied by higher educational levels, higher divorce rates, a greater number of single-parent families, more mothers employed outside the home, earlier and more extensive retirement of older family members, and more leisure time and entertainment. Such developments have affected the attitudes, values, behaviors, and expectations of all family members, and particularly the younger ones. This chapter considers many of these structural and dynamic changes in the population and how they have affected the activities and ambitions of individual members of families.

PARENTS AND CHILDREN

Strictly speaking, a childless couple constitutes a family, but almost every adult knows what it means when a woman is alleged to be "in a family way." In fact, nearly half as many children today are born out of wedlock as are born in it (Rosenberg et al., 1996). One of the main purposes of getting married is to have children, but not all married people have them or even want to. Some married adults, so-called *early articulators*, have known since childhood or adolescence that they did not want children, and others (*postponers*) simply delay having children until it becomes obvious that they will never be parents (Veevers, 1980).

Birthrates

The National Center for Health Statistics, which compiles and publishes monthly and annual statistics on births, deaths, and marriages in the United States, distinguishes between the birthrate and the fertility rate in a population. The *birthrate* is the number of births per 1,000 total population during a specified time period (usually a year), whereas the *fertility rate* is the number of births per 1,000 women aged 15–44 years. The *crude birthrate* is the number of births per 1,000 population, and the *age-specific birthrate* is the crude birthrate computed on a designated chronological age group.

The overall birthrate in the United States has declined fairly steadily during this century. An exception to the trend was the decade from 1947–1957, known as the postwar baby-boom years. In 1995, the crude birthrate was 14.8 and the fertility rate was 65.6. Of course, birthrates vary with the age

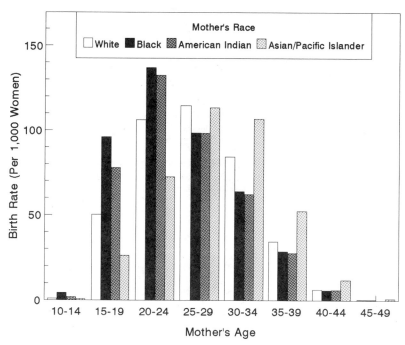

Figure 7–1 Birthrate by age and ethnicity of mother. (Based on data from Ventura, Martin, Curtin, & Matthews, 1997.)

group of women. Figure 7–1 shows that in 1995, the age-specific birthrate for all ethnic groups combined rose from 1.3 for women aged 10–14 years to 112.4 for women aged 25–29 years, and fell to .3 for women aged 45–49 years. Approximately 42% of these births were a first child, 32% were a second child, 16% were a third child, and 10% were a fourth child and over.

The birthrate varies not only with age, but also with ethnicity, nationality, and other demographic factors. Of the five ethnic groups represented in Figure 7–1, the maximum birthrate was higher and occurred at an earlier age for Hispanics, Native Americans[1], and Blacks than for Asian/Pacific Islanders and Whites (Rosenberg et al., 1996). International data indicate that the average number of children born to a woman in her lifetime varies with the continent and country, estimated in 1996 as ranging from a high of 5.7 for the African continent to a low of 1.5 for Europe (see Figure 7–2). Not surprisingly, the fertility rate is inversely related to the number of women using contraceptives.

Within the United States, the highest birthrate in 1995 was in Utah, and the lowest was in Maine. Over 13% of the mothers of newborn babies were

[1]Includes Aleuts and Eskimos.

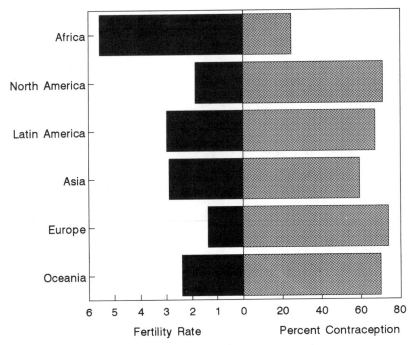

Figure 7–2 Fertility rate and percentage of women using contraception by continent. *Fertility rate* is the average number of children born to a woman in her lifetime at the current birthrate. *Percent contraception* is the total percentage of married women using contraception. (Based on data from Population Reference Bureau, 1997.)

teenagers, a figure that includes 11.5% of births to white mothers, 23.2% to black mothers, and 18% to Hispanic mothers. Overall, 32% of the mothers were unmarried (25.3% white, 69.5% black, 40.8% Hispanic), almost 20% had received no prenatal care during the first trimester of pregnancy, 21% had cesarean deliveries, and 7.3% had babies with low birth weights (under 2,500 grams) (Rosenberg et al., 1996).

Child Rearing

Whether planned or not, the birth of a child has a significant effect on the feelings and behaviors of the parents. Parents of newborns no longer have as much time or freedom to pursue their own interests or relationships with each other or outside the immediate family. Despite being forewarned, first-time parents are usually surprised and disconcerted to discover the amount of time (24 hours per day, 7 days per week) required and the change in lifestyle that having a child entails (Alpert & Richardson, 1980; Sapiro, 1990).

Because a child competes for their attention and often dominates their lives, the parents' personal happiness and satisfaction with their marriage frequently suffers (Wallace & Gotlib, 1990). Mothers in particular complain that they are tied down by children and that children limit their ability to work outside the home and achieve financial stability (Jacoby, 1982; Roper Organization, 1985). In a study by Thompson and Walker (1990), one-third of the mothers who were interviewed reported that they derived no meaning or enjoyment from motherhood, and another one-third had mixed feelings about it. These negative responses should, however, not be interpreted as meaning that parenthood is without rewards. A child brings love, joy, and meaningfulness to most mothers and fathers, and the process of bringing up a child can have a positive effect on the development of both the child and the parents. For example, Lowenthal, Thurnher, and Chiriboga (1975) found that the parents they interviewed evaluated the task of rearing a child as having been a source of growth and maturity for them personally. Be that as it may, full-time parenting is admittedly hard, time-consuming, and often frustrating work.

Like all behaviors, effective parenting is a combination of natural endowment and relevant experience. Some people seem to be "born parents," whereas others are clearly unsuited by temperament or ability to assume that role. At best, the latter do only a mediocre job of child rearing, whereas the former seem to know instinctively what to do in either calm or crisis. As much as it may seem to be innate, good parenting is a learned skill. Still, it cannot be learned exclusively from lectures and books. Effective parenting is, to a great extent, the result of growing up around people who know how to be parents—observing what they do, and applying those practices to the rearing of one's own children. It certainly helps if the child is attractive in physical appearance and behavior—good looking, healthy, and regular in eating and sleeping habits. Thank goodness, most babies are cute and appealing; otherwise, the task of rearing them would probably be even more difficult than it is.

Even under the best of circumstances, and with the best of intentions, child rearing is something of a juggling act. All parents make mistakes, but one should not despair. The resilience of children, coupled with the willingness of parents to learn from their mistakes, usually results in children who are fairly acceptable to the family and to society as a whole.

Parental Behaviors and the Personalities of Children

There are all kinds of children: Some are shy and passive, others are sociable and active; some are bright and quick, others are dull and slow. However, most children are somewhere in between, not "average," but not extreme either. Just as there are different kinds of children, there are different types of parents and different styles of parenting. For example, Baumrind (1971, 1972) classified parents as being of three types: authoritarian, permissive, and authoritative, each of which presumably leads to certain behaviors on the part of children. *Authoritarian parents* are restrictive, rule-emphasizing individuals who expect children to be obedient and who punish behavior that deviates from their rules. In contrast, *permissive parents* are nondemanding individuals who permit children to establish their own standards of conduct. Finally, *authoritative parents* set behavioral limits and standards and enforce them with a combination of power and reasoning. The children of authoritative parents are encouraged to conform to these limits, but they are also permitted to contribute their own reasoning concerning them. Baumrind found that the children of both authoritarian and permissive parents behaved similarly in many respects: The sons were more hostile than normal, and the daughters were more socially retiring individuals who gave up easily. The children of authoritative parents, whom Baumrind considers the most effective of all three parenting styles, were able to conform to group norms without sacrificing their own individuality.

Modifications of Baumrind's (1972) model were proposed by Schaefer (1959) and Becker (1964), and by Maccoby and Martin (1983). The two dimensions of parental behavior in the Becker–Schaefer model are *permissiveness/ restrictiveness* and *warmth/acceptingness*. Parents who are high on both the permissiveness/restrictiveness and warmth/acceptingness dimensions are reasonably controlling but accepting of their children. Children of these parents tend to be socially outgoing, independent, creative, and low in hostility. Parents who are high in permissiveness/restrictiveness but low in warmth/acceptingness are permissive but hostile and rejecting of their children. Children of these parents tend to be aggressive, noncompliant, and delinquent. Parents who are low in permissiveness/restrictiveness but high in warmth/acceptingness are restrictive and overcontrolling but warm and accepting of their children. Children of these parents tend to be submissive, nonaggressive, and dependent. Parents who are low on both the permissiveness/ restrictiveness and warmth/acceptingness dimensions are restrictive and overcontrolling as well as hostile and rejecting. Children of these parents tend to be quarrelsome, shy, and to have psychological problems.

The Maccoby–Martin model is similar to the Schaefer–Becker model in its definitions of two dimensions of parenting behavior—*demandingness* and *responsiveness* to the child. Combinations of these two dimensions result in four types of parents and the child personality characteristics associated with them.

Authoritarian parents in the Maccoby–Martin model assert their power without warmth, nurturance, or reciprocal communication between parents and child. Such parents value obedience, respect for authority, work, tradition, and the preservation of order, and they attempt to control and evaluate the child's behavior according to a set of absolute standards. Children of these parents are moderately competent and responsible, but they are socially withdrawn and lack spontaneity. The daughters tend to be dependent and lower in achievement motivation; the sons are higher in aggressiveness but lower in self-esteem than other boys their age (Coopersmith, 1967).

Indulgent parents in the Maccoby–Martin model make few demands on their children. Although the children of these parents are more positive in their moods and have greater vitality than the children of authoritarian parents, they tend to be immature, impulsive, and socially irresponsible. They are also low in self-reliance and have problems in handling aggression.

Neglecting parents in the Maccoby–Martin model ignore their children and are indifferent to or uninvolved with them. Neglecting parents do not necessarily abuse their children, but they are self-centered rather than child-centered in their behavior. They have little social interaction with their children and usually do not know where their children are or what they are doing. Children of such parents tend to be impulsive, moody, unable to concentrate, and low in frustration tolerance. Also characteristic of such children are problems in controlling aggression, lack of emotional attachments to other people, and truancy.

Authoritative parents are accepting, responsive, child-centered, and yet controlling; they expect their children to behave according to their abilities and ages but solicit the children's opinions and feelings in family decision making. Though these parents are warm and nurturing, they are not averse to imposing punitive and restrictive measures. However, they provide reasons and explanations to their children when they do so. According to Maccoby and Martin (1983), the children of authoritative parents tend to be independent, self-assertive, friendly, and cooperative.

Working and Single Mothers

It is popularly believed that the nuclear family, consisting of mother, father, and children, is the most psychologically healthy living arrangement for children. The basis for this belief is the assumption that children need both adult male and female figures from whom they can learn sex-appropriate behavior and after whom they can pattern their interests and activities. For this reason, it is maintained, single-parent families not only place an extra burden on the parent but also create identity problems for the child. It can be argued, however, that a home situation in which the parents do not get along has a greater potential for psychologically damaging the child than a one-parent home resulting from separation or divorce. Furthermore, in most instances the children of single parents are closer to that parent than children in two-parent households are to either of their parents.

Of all American children who were under age 18 in 1995, approximately 27% were living with only one parent and 69% were living with both parents. As illustrated in Figure 7–3, 78% of non-Hispanic white children, 63% of Hispanic children, and 33% of black children lived in two-parent households. However, in many of these households, both parents performed remunerative work outside the home. Of all households containing children under age 18, both parents were employed outside the home in 37% of the cases in

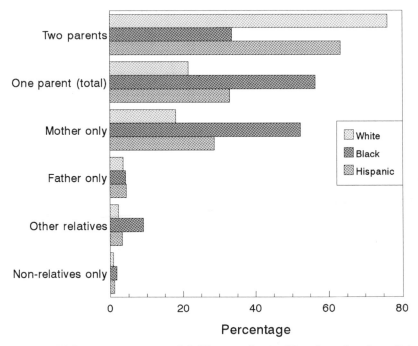

Figure 7–3   Living arrangements of children under 18. (Based on data from Saluter, 1996.)

which there were children under age 6, 42% of the cases in which there were children aged 6–11, and 46% of the cases in which there were children aged 12–17 (Saluter, 1996). Many of the couples with young children arranged to work split shifts, so one parent could be at home while the other was working. Furthermore, although mothers now spend less time with their children than ever before, fathers and day-care employees have assumed greater responsibility in meeting the needs of infants and young children.

The effects on young children of the mother's daily absence at work are certainly a matter of concern, but the overall research findings provide little evidence of developmental delays in the behaviors of such children. In addition, working mothers are happier, higher in self-esteem, lower in depression, and manifest fewer signs of stress than mothers who want to work but have to remain at home (Hoffman, 1986). Because the time that they spend with their children is more likely to be "quality time," working mothers are often better parents than mothers who stay at home but would rather be employed.

The situation for single mothers is not quite so favorable as it is for working mothers who are married. However, separation, divorce, and premarital childbearing has caused one-parent families to be much more common today than they were two or three decades ago. This is true for all races in combination as well as separately. For all races combined, approximately 23% of children under age 18 live with their mothers in one-parent households. Included in this figure are the 16% of non-Hispanic white children, 28% of Hispanic children, and 52% of black children living with their mothers alone (see Figure 7–3).

The U.S. Bureau of the Census has estimated than 60% of American children spend at least some time in a one-parent family (Kotre & Hall, 1990). The single parent may be a divorced or widowed spouse, but in an increasing number of cases, the parent, who is usually the mother, has never been married. Some of these unmarried mothers have either given birth by choice or adopted a child, but most are young women or teenagers who did not plan the births. They may attempt to rear their children by themselves, but, lacking adequate financial resources, many must turn to relatives or other sources for assistance.

Stepparents, Foster Parents, and Adoption

To those who are familiar with fairy tales, the words *wicked* and *stepmother* are closely associated. Cinderella, Snow White, and certain other fictional heroines suffered at the hands of their stepmothers. "Wicked stepfather" is not as fearful a combination, though admirers of Hamlet might think otherwise.

Demographic predictions indicate that roughly one-third of all children in the United States will spend part of their childhood with a stepparent. Approximately 11% of all American children are living with a stepparent at any one time, in most cases a stepfather. Because it is still unusual for fathers to retain custody of minor children after a divorce, less than 1% of children in married-coupled family households are living with a stepmother (Kantrowitz & Wingert, 1990; U.S. Bureau of the Census, 1992).

Hopefully, only a small fraction of stepparents turn out to be "wicked," but it would be overly optimistic to assume that the relationships between children and their stepparents are always congenial. The quality of these relationships varies with the ages and genders of both the child and the stepparent. Interactions between stepparents and stepchildren appear to be most positive if they are friendly but not intense and when the stepparent and stepchild are of the same sex. Because most stepparents are men, the implication is that conflict is more common between stepfathers and stepdaughters. This appears to be particularly true when the stepdaughter is an adolescent. Regardless of their age or sex, children who are temperamental and have greater difficulty coping with change are more apt to experience discordant relations with their stepparents (Allison & Furstenberg, 1989; Hetherington, Cox, & Cox, 1985; Vuchinich, Hetherington, Vuchinich, & Clingempeel, 1991).

The rise in the numbers of children being born out of wedlock has led to an increase in the number of foster homes and adoptive parents. In 1995,

258,000 American children under age 18 lived in foster homes. Forty-four percent of these children were boys, 56% were girls, 52% were black, 34% were white, and 13% were Hispanic (Saluter, 1996). Of particular concern are children who are shuffled in and out of foster homes and provided with little opportunity to establish roots and develop a stable, socially acceptable personal identity.

Adopted children presumably have a better chance than foster children, perhaps because adults who adopt children are more likely really to want them and are willing to make preparations and concessions for them. Adoptive parents usually come in couples, but it is possible for a single parent—typically a woman—to adopt a child. In addition, gay or lesbian couples may adopt and rear their own or someone else's natural children. The concern on the part of some critics that children reared in homosexual households experience sexual-identity problems does not appear to be supported by research evidence (Flaks, Ficher, Masterpasqua, & Joseph, 1995; Patterson, 1995). Furthermore, Flaks et al. (1995) found that lesbian mothers had greater awareness of parenting skills than heterosexual mothers.

Parents in Middle Age

By the time parents reach late middle age, they are well down the frequency curve of the number of children still living with them. Less than 10% of households headed by parents in their early fifties contain children under 18 years of age (see Figure 7–4). This is the so-called *empty nest* or *postparental phase* of the family life cycle. It is the time when the children have moved out and parents are left alone to be either depressed or rejuvenated, depending on one's point of view. It actually turns out that, although the departure of one's children is stressful for some parents, for most parents the empty-nest period is a time of even greater satisfaction than when the children were younger and living at home (Neugarten, 1970). The parents now have more time for avocational and vocational pursuits, for reestablishing their relationships with each other as well as with relatives and friends, and for contemplating what to do with the rest of their lives.

The postparental phase of the family life cycle occurs sooner in middle-class and white American families than in working-class and nonwhite families. Because working-class and nonwhite families have more children, they are present for a longer period of time than in middle-class and white families. Regardless of class or color, today's young adults do not always remain "out of the nest"; financial pressures and personal difficulties often result in their returning home for brief or even prolonged periods. Not only are parents often surprised when their adult children come home to stay, but many are downright unhappy about it (Barber, 1989). This is also true when children delay their departure from home as long as possible, forcing their parents to hint and hustle them on their way to independent living.

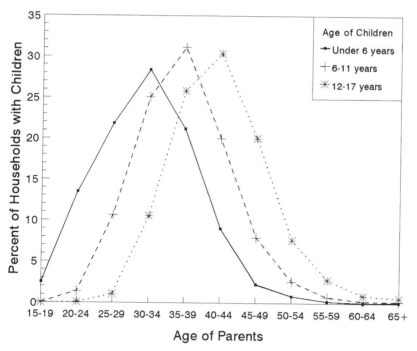

Figure 7–4   Percentage of households with children, by age of parents and children. (Based on data from Saluter, 1996.)

Middle-agers are also referred to as the *sandwich generation*, a term that reflects their position between the generation of their children and that of their own parents. Being "caught in the middle," as it were, is obviously not pleasant when pressure comes from one's children and one's own parents. In general, middle-aged adults spend a lot of time, energy, and money helping their children and their parents (Brody, 1990). The life-satisfaction and self-evaluations of most middle-agers who have children are greatly affected by how those children have turned out. Even though the children may no longer live with their parents, the interpersonal relationship between the two generations usually improves when the latter become young adults and set out on their own paths (Troll & Bengtson, 1982).

Older Parents and Adult Children

Unlike the situation of yesteryear, only a small percentage of older adults now live with their children. Still, they usually live close enough to call on them in medical emergencies or when other needs arise. Intergenerational contacts are fairly frequent, being motivated by mutually positive feelings for one another and a sense of duty (Harris & Associates, 1975). Most adult children have strong feelings of *filial responsibility* for their parents; that is, that they have an obligation to maintain relationships with their older parents and come to their aid when needed. To some extent, older parents feel the same way, that is, that they are responsible for and have a duty to take care of their adult children. However, most older parents do not believe that their children should feel as responsible for them as the children actually report feeling (Hamon & Blieszner, 1990). People of all ages like to feel independent and are generally more willing to give than to receive. This is particularly true of older adults, in whom the reception of aid from others can arouse feelings of dependency, helplessness, uselessness, and of having reached the end of life.

For the most part, adult children have fairly frequent contacts with their parents. Daughters see their parents more often than sons, and older widows see their children more often than older married couples (Frank, Avery, & Laman, 1988). As might be expected, the geographical distance between the residences of adult parents and children affects the amount of interpersonal contact (Moss, Moss, & Moles, 1985), but in most cases the relationships are close. The influence between generations flows in both directions. Many older parents, albeit sometimes too quickly, attempt to influence their children in areas such as health, work, finances, and legal matters. On the other hand, adult children offer advice to their older parents on health, living arrangements and conditions, money, dress, and household management (Moss et al., 1985). Adult children may also, sometimes successfully, attempt to influence their parents' views on politics, religion, and gender roles (Bengtson et al., 1990).

With respect to services performed, there is frequent interchange between older adults and their children on housekeeping, baby-sitting, meal preparation, transportation, and other chores. For example, many adult children help their parents with shopping, transporting them to doctors' offices, and in dealing with governmental and social agencies. Each generation may provide financial assistance to the other, but most often it is the older parents who give money to their children rather than vice versa. The kinds of services performed across generations also vary with socioeconomic status. The services performed for their parents by working- and lower-class adult children are more likely to involve hands-on activities such as home maintenance, whereas middle-class sons and daughters tend to assist their parents by providing emotional support and money (Chappell, 1990). Sons are more likely than daughters to give monetary assistance to their parents, but in most instances, affluent parents are on the giving rather than the receiving end of financial aid. Because the relationship between mother and daughter is usually closer than that between father and daughter, mother and son, or father and son, most intergenerational assistance takes place between mothers and daughters. Mothers and daughters provide a great deal of emotional support and hands-on care to each other.

Although there are exceptions, most families do their best to provide adequate care for their older members. Consequently, efforts by federal and state governments to enact and enforce *filial responsibility laws* requiring families to provide more financial support for elders are probably unnecessary and even counterproductive.

GRANDPARENTS

Usually less involved in child rearing than parents, but still important members of families, are grandparents. More children today have living grandparents than ever before (Peterson, 1989). Grandparents may live a long time after a grandchild is born, knowing him or her as an infant, a child, an adolescent, a young adult, and perhaps even a middle-aged parent. This is particularly true of grandmothers, who live an average of 6–7 years longer than grandfathers and hence occupy the grandparenting role for a greater period of time. Even great-grandparents and great-great-grandparents, who were once extremely rare, are becoming more common, and often it is these long-lived individuals rather than grandparents who fulfill the traditional grandparenting role.

Even though multigenerational households are less common today than a generation or so ago, thousands of American children live under the same roof as one or more of their grandparents. In 1995, for example, 4 million children under age 18 lived in the home of their grandparents, and in 37% of the cases neither parent was in the home. Forty-eight percent of children living in households headed by a grandparents were boys, 52% were girls, 44% were black, 13% were Hispanic, and 41% were non-Hispanic whites (Saluter, 1996). As shown in Figure 7–5, the number of children residing with their grandparents varies not only with race but also with the age of the child. Larger percentages of minorities and young children than white and older children live with their grandparents. When a child's parents must work or for other reasons are unable to take care of him or her, the grandparents may assume the role of surrogate parents, becoming the primary caregivers and doing everything for the child that parents normally would. "Skip-generation" parents, who take full responsibility for their great-grandchildren, are common in families where teenage pregnancy is customary. Because the "young" grandmother refuses to assume the role of surrogate parent for her teenage daughter's child, the responsibility for caring for the child falls on the shoulder's of the grandmother's mother. Though, strictly speaking, they are not surrogate parents, many other grandparents are highly involved with their grandchildren. They see them often, provide them with advice and suggestions, and help them with practical matters (Cherlin & Furstenberg, 1985).

Becoming a grandparent has multiple meanings for a person. The birth of a grandchild can give one a sense of biological renewal and perpetuation of the family. The role of grandparent can be even more gratifying than that of

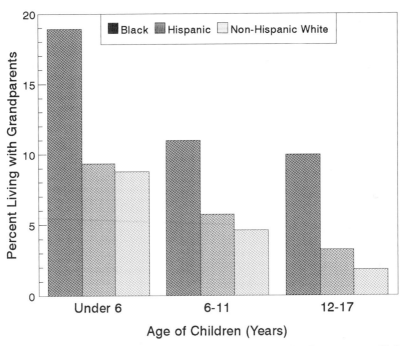

Figure 7–5 Percentages of children in different age and ethnic groups living in households headed by a grandparent. (Based on data from Saluter, 1996.)

parent. Because grandparents have no prescribed functions, they can usually relate to the child as they please. Becoming a grandparent provides new roles that are not as demanding as those required of parents. Grandparents can find enjoyment and satisfaction in teaching and guiding their grandchildren, and experience a feeling of pride or vicarious achievement in their accomplishments. Realization of the continuity of generations and the family can also lead grandparents to reexamine and reevaluate their own experiences and deeds. On the other hand, rather than feeling pleasure and excitement at a new personality that one helped create and an opportunity to begin again without the weight of past mistakes on one's shoulders, some grandparents experience only a sense of growing old and feelings of remoteness from both the past and the future.

Unfortunately, the wisdom and practical knowledge of older adults are less valued in today's technologically based society than they once were. Certain cultures, such as those of China, Japan, and other countries with a stronger tradition of respect for the elderly, and even certain subcultures in Western society itself, value grandparents more than others. For example, African-Americans, Asian-Americans, and Hispanic-Americans tend to value grandparents more and expect them to be closely involved in the lives of their

---

MY LIFE 7–1

My Grandparents

When I was a young boy, it seemed to me that people who were over 50 were not merely old but *ancient*. Like most children, I had two sets of grandparents. My paternal grandfather died when I was only 2, so I didn't get to know him. Sometimes it seems to me that I remember one rather embarrassing incident at which he was a spectator, featuring little me in a transparent dress accompanied by the guffaws of the observers. But I am no longer certain whether I truly recall the scene, recall the memory of it, or merely recall being told about it.

My other three grandparents are more memorable. All were hardworking people who had various aches and pains but still appreciated jokes, were kind to animals, and always took time to talk to and help us children. My paternal grandmother, whom we called "Grandma Aiken," was a seamstress who made slipcovers, cooked fried chicken, black-eyed peas, and hoecake, took B.C. powders with Coca-Cola, and paid me to run errands for her. My maternal grandmother, whom we called "Cork," was a practical nurse who worked all the time, baked lots of tasty pastry, put money under our pillows while we slept, and always got a big new spoon from me at Christmas.

My maternal grandfather, whom we called "Pop," was the patriarch of my mother's family. Pop was a rather stern-faced carpenter and cattleman who smoked mail-order tobacco in an old wooden pipe, traded for a new Hudson every year until they quit making them, and made me hoe grapefruit trees, chase stray cows, and fix fences. When he was thirsty, Pop let juice dribble down the front of his shirt as he drank, and when he was hungry he could eat a whole pint of ice cream. I remember thinking on Pop's sixtieth birthday (I was 5 at the time) that he couldn't last much longer because he was so old. However, he and both of my grandmothers fooled me and lived well into their ninth decade.

Today I am older than Pop was when I was 5, and I have three grandsons. They are not as old as I was when Pop was 60, so perhaps they don't view me in quite the same way as I did him then. They still seem willing enough to accept me as a playmate, to ride around on my shoulders, and to tell me what they are doing and thinking. I suspect that much of that will change as they grow older, but I hope not too much!

---

grandchildren (Bengtson, 1985). The overall picture, however, is one of decreasing interaction between grandparents and grandchildren (Rodeheaver & Thomas, 1986). Grandparent–grandchild relationships are becoming increasingly more detached rather than involved (Bengtson & Robertson, 1985; Kornhaber & Woodward, 1981; Rodeheaver & Thomas, 1986). Geographical mobility, independent households, employed grandmothers, and the rising divorce rate are all contributing to the separation between generations. The social and emotional separation between the old and the young that has come to characterize so much of our society has also been encouraged by our tendency to segregate people into different age groups. However, children and grandparents still need each other, and isolating them from each other does a disservice to both.

Some research has provided evidence for different "types" of grandparents (Cherlin & Furstenberg, 1986; Neugarten & Weinstein, 1968; Robertson, 1977; Wood & Robertson, 1976), but the role of grandparent tends to be too idiosyncratic to be described in terms of a typology (Bengtson & Robertson, 1985). First-time grandparents in the United States range in age from the late twenties to the seventies and even eighties. However, most are in their early fifties, the average age being greater for men than for women and for whites than for blacks and other minorities. To some extent, the way in which grandparents respond to their grandchildren is affected by the grandparents' age. Younger grandparents tend to adopt a more fun-seeking, companionate style, whereas older grandparents are more formal or distant in their behavior (Cherlin & Furstenberg, 1986; Neugarten & Weinstein, 1968). Grandparenting style also varies with the age of the child. Grandparents are more likely to play games and have fun with younger grandchildren, but either to discuss things with older grandchildren or simply leave them alone. In any event, children under age 10 generally have closer relationships with their grandparents than older children and teenagers do (Kahana & Kahana, 1970a).

The relationships between grandparents and other family members also vary to some extent with gender. Whereas grandfathers are more like "secretaries of state," grandmothers usually take the role of "kin keeping," maintaining contact with family members and keeping the family together (Cohler & Grunebaum, 1981; Troll, 1983). For the most part, grandmothers interact more with their grandchildren than grandfathers do. This is particularly true of the relationships between grandmothers and granddaughters and when the grandmother is the mother's mother. Grandmothers presumably possess more useful knowledge and skills to communicate to their granddaughters, and, of course, females of all ages are more sociable and talkative than males (Kennedy, 1990; Matthews & Sprey, 1985).

Grandchildren of all ages usually feel closer to their mother's parents than to their father's parents, and they tend to like the maternal grandmother best of all. When the 4- to 5-year-olds who were questioned in a study conducted by Kahana and Kahana (1970b) were asked what kinds of grandparents they liked, they said that they preferred grandparents who gave them food, love, and presents. The 8- and 9-year-olds indicated a preference for grandparents who did fun things with them, whereas the 11- and 12-year-olds said that they liked grandparents who let them do whatever they wanted to. By the time children reach adolescence, even those who have been close to their grandparents begin pulling away and may even feel alienated from them. This should not be surprising, because it is the fate of most parents as well. However, many adolescents and young adults remain close to both their parents and grandparents, visiting them often and valuing their advice and assistance.

SIBLINGS AND OTHER RELATIVES

Approximately 90% of all Americans have at least one brother or sister. The average number of siblings is slightly less than 1.5 for all ethnic groups combined; it is higher for Hispanics than for Blacks and higher for Blacks than for non-Hispanic Whites (Saluter, 1996).

Siblings usually have more in common with each other than with any other member of the immediate family. This is particularly true when siblings are of the same sex and close in age. In families in which parents express a great deal of dissatisfaction and hostility toward each other and/or the children, or when a parent has been lost by death, separation, or divorce, siblings are likely to turn to each other and develop their own little social world or subfamily. Brothers and sisters may be intensely loyal toward each other, a loyalty and closeness that deepens with age (Dunn, 1984; Mosatche, Brady, & Noberini, 1983). Long after they have left their parents' home and even after the parents have died, siblings who were close as children continue to provide emotional and material support to each other in times of crisis (Matthews, Werkner, & Delaney, 1990; Rosenthal, 1985). Anxiety and depression are lifted when a brother or sister shows concern and an eagerness to be of help.

Some of the most negative, as well as the most positive, feelings are directed toward siblings. Even as mature adults, some siblings have not gotten over the interpersonal rivalry that occurred in their childhood (Greer, 1992). In most cases these feelings become less intense with age, but even in later life siblings may have strong hostile feelings toward each other. Actually, feelings and relationships with one's siblings in later life run the gamut from highly positive to highly negative. Thus, Gold (1989, 1990) was able to classify sibling relationships in older adulthood into five categories: intimate, congenial, loyal, apathetic, and hostile. *Intimate siblings* were extremely close; they were best friends and confidants and totally accepted each other. Another group, *congenial siblings*, were also close but did not share the same degree of empathy as intimate siblings. Relationships between *loyal siblings* were based on family ties or belongingness rather than affection or interdependence. The fourth group, *apathetic siblings*, were indifferent to one another, whereas the relationships between siblings in the fifth group, *hostile siblings*, were characterized by anger, enmity, and resentment.

As siblings grow older, sisters, who have the strongest and most intimate feelings toward one another, tend to maintain more frequent contacts than brothers (Connidis, 1988; Lee, Mancini, & Maxwell, 1990). At all ages, sisters are closer to each other than they are to brothers or than brothers are to one another (Adams, 1968). However, black brothers are more likely than white

MY LIFE 7–2

My Sister

Even when she was a little girl, my sister planned to become a school-teacher. She would take her books, climb a tree, and study and practice on her woody perch for hours. On descending to earth, she immediately recruited me as her favorite pupil. She frequently tutored me on grammar, geography, and history, and even took me to her school classroom sometimes. As a romantically precocious kindergartner, I was thrilled on those occasions when I was doted on by her second-grade girlfriends. My sister was superior in every subject except arithmetic, so our roles as teacher and pupil were reversed when I gladly agreed to instruct her and the other girls in that arcane subject.

My sister also liked to sing, and she and I occasionally performed at local churches. She usually sang "God Put a Rainbow in the Sky," and I recited Bible verses that my mother had drilled me on the night before. My sister liked movie musicals in particular, and paid my way to the theater (sans popcorn) on many occasions. During high school, she became interested in opera, listened to the Metropolitan every Saturday afternoon on the radio, bought many opera records, and urged me to accompany her Mimi with my Rudolfo in the garret where we lived. I usually declined the invitation, but ended up learning something about opera in spite of myself. Later, I expanded my interest repertory to symphonies, but could never get her involved in them to the same degree as opera.

Some years later, my sister graduated from college and was issued a teaching certificate in Spanish and social studies. She found a job in New York, although some wag humorously remarked that teaching Spanish to New York immigrant children was rather like carrying coals to Newcastle. After working for a while in the Empire State, she left for a job teaching Southern history in Georgia. Because our mother was a New York yankee and our father a Georgia cracker, it seemed like an appropriate compromise for my sister to divide her time between the two states. An indication of her efforts to resolve the apparent conflict between subject specialties was when she taught history in Spanish or took a historical perspective in lecturing on the culture of southern Spain.

My sister no longer works in the schools, but she still seems like a teacher to me. Consequently, I know that when I visit her I must be prepared to listen attentively and take good notes. I never know when she may decide to give me a pop quiz on what she has just said! Incidentally, she still enjoys opera and sings arias when she thinks no one else is listening.

brothers to possess and retain positive relationships with each other (Gold, 1990). In any case, sisters and brothers tend to visit more in later life than they did in middle age.

Relatives outside the nuclear family do not interact with or assist family members as much as they once did. Aunts, uncles, cousins, and other members of the extended family can no longer be depended on to "rush into the breech" when the nieces, nephews, or other relatives need help. Among the reasons for this situation are the increased geographical separation of members of extended families, less time for interacting with relatives, and the fact that public agencies now assume much of the responsibility for family care that was once borne by the families themselves. In some ethnic and religious groups, however, extended families are eager and active in promoting family welfare. This is the case, in particular, for Mormons, blacks, and Hispanics. For blacks, the extended family provides economic, emotional, and physical support to family members of all ages. The role of older women as *kin keepers*, who assume the responsibility of keeping in touch with family members, providing for their needs and arranging family get-togethers, is well-defined in the black community. Both older women and older men are usually the givers rather than the receivers of assistance to black family members (Sussman, 1985; Wilson, 1989).

FRIENDSHIPS

Will Rogers's assertion that he never met a man he didn't like may seem a bit Pollyanaish, but almost everyone possesses some characteristics of which we approve. However, the great majority of these individuals remain at the acquaintance or associate level, and very few become close friends.

Next to relatives, and often before them, friends are our closest companions and confidants (Dickens & Perlman, 1981; Larson, Mannell, & Zuzanek, 1986). Viewing our friends as honest, kind, sympathetic, and understanding, and like ourselves in many ways, we enjoy being around them and intimate even to the point of disclosing things about ourselves that we might never reveal to a relative.

As with love, friendship is most apt to flourish when beliefs, values, and personalities are similar. Beliefs and values are, of course, related to age, sex, ethnicity, socioeconomic status, proximity, abilities, and interests. With respect to proximity, friendships are more apt to develop between people who live and work in the same area and among those who spend a great deal of time together. Physical appearance is also a factor in friendships. Though we may appreciate and even desire beautiful people, we tend not to pursue them but rather to choose as friends those who are similar to us in physical appearance, so our advances are less likely to be rebuffed (Cash & Derlega, 1978; Murstein & Christy, 1976).

With respect to the give and take involved in friendship, equitability is important in that both parties must feel that the costs and rewards of the friendship are approximately equal. Perhaps even more critical for enduring friendships are feelings of mutual trust. Trust that a friend will not knowingly betray a confidence or harm you and can be counted on to be there when you need him or her can be even more important than similarity of background,

MY LIFE 7–3

My Boyhood Friends

I had some funny friends when I was a boy. One might say they were superlative. Billy certainly was. At 5 he could ride a bicycle and a horse, throw a baseball over a two-story building, and "pee" across the road. Johnny was even more outstanding. He could stand on his head for hours, eat tobacco worms and light bulbs, and endure hard blows to the stomach without flinching. However, it was Stephen who accomplished the most dramatic feat of all. Like Sampson, Stephen had long hair which he seldom cut and from which he apparently derived great strength. Once, after a hurricane, Stephen lowered himself into the rushing waters of a drainage ditch on a dare, but was not able to extricate himself immediately. He held on to the side of the ditch for dear life, lest he be swept downstream and drown. After a half-hour or so of struggling and continually declaring that "nothing can defeat the Führer!," Stephen rose from the troubled waters none the worse for wear.

My two best friends in high school were the Brainy brothers. They had moved down from Connecticut and lived with their folks in a trailer by the river. Their father was a practical nurse and something of a local character. He spouted poetry at the trees, solved geometry problems by scratching on the ground with a stick, and frequently screamed "Damn the neighbors!" out the door. I don't believe he ever became rich and famous, but he and his wife eventually moved out of the trailer and into a house. The Brainy brothers represented my first encounter with intellectuals, defined as people who think they know more than I.

I moved away from our town after high school graduation, and I'm not really certain what happened to my boyhood friends. I was told that Billy was admitted to a mental hospital, Johnny shot himself when he mistakenly concluded that he could withstand a rifle bullet, and Stephen joined the Navy. The Brainy brothers were a bit more successful: They became university employees and were never heard from again.

Although my boyhood friends were all entertaining, they were never quite so available as my imaginary baseball team. Each member of the team was named after a variation of my own name: there was Little Lewis, Big Lewis, Little Roscoe, Big Roscoe, Little Junior, Big Junior, and three other players whose names I have forgotten. The opposing team consisted of fancied representations of people I didn't like. In any event, the nice thing about having my own imaginary team was that I won all the games. Unhappily, though, there were still occasional arguments concerning such matters as close plays and batting orders. Perhaps this is merely another example of fantasy being patterned after reality or art imitating life!

behavior, and interests. Feelings of trust encourage mutual self-disclosure, the sharing of private experiences and feelings that are a critical part of close friendships and love.

Effects of Friendships

By providing emotional and material support, entertainment, information, and serving as a sounding board for our ideas and feelings, friends make us feel good and increase our level of satisfaction with the world and our place in it. In fact, the extent to which people are satisfied with their lives in general can be predicted more accurately from friendships than from family relationships (Aizenberg & Treas, 1985). Complete honesty and self-disclosure between parents and children are often discouraged by the duties and obligations of the parent–child bond, whereas intimacy is crucial to the survival of close friendships. Furthermore, we choose our own friends, but we have no voice in the selection of our relatives.

In times of personal crises precipitated by the loss of a loved one, health problems, or other sources of emotional stress, friends can help cushion the shock and assist us in coping and rehabilitating ourselves. In contrast, a lack of friendships and other positive social relationships is associated with psychological problems and disorders, low academic achievement, and a lack of job success (Levinson, 1986; Sarason, Sarason, & Pierce, 1989). Friendships are related not only to psychological well-being but also to physical health (Crohan & Antonucci, 1989). For example, having more friends and social contacts has been found to be associated with lower mortality rates (Hirsch, 1981; House et al., 1982; McKinlay, 1981) and even reduced susceptibility to the common cold (Cohen et al., 1997).

Stages and Types of Friendships

Unlike "love at first sight," friendships tend to develop gradually over time. Newman (1982) describes the growth of friendships as occurring in three stages. The first stage is characterized by the *mutual awareness* of two persons. In most cases, social interaction goes no further than this. If it does, then a second stage, in which *surface contact* is made, ensues. The behavior of the two parties at this stage is governed by social norms, and little self-disclosure takes place. With the beginning of self-disclosure, the relationship moves into a third and final stage, *mutuality*, marking the transition to bona fide friendship. Then, sincerity, emotional support, and other behaviors and feelings that are associated with close friendships begin to emerge.

Newman's three-stage theory is a description of the development of *deep friendships*, which go beyond the more superficial *interest-related friendships* based on similarity of lifestyles or interests (Keith, Hill, Goudy, &

Powers, 1984). Deep friendships typically occur much less frequently than interest-related friendships.

The types of friendships preferred and cultivated vary from person to person. For example, Matthews (1986) describes three basic friendship styles that are dependent on individual personality. Adults who prefer an *independent* style of friendship, who constituted 20% of the sample, had neither best friends nor close friends. They were willing to share good times with other people, but they preferred to remain self-sufficient and maintain a certain psychological distance between themselves and others. A second, *discerning* style of friendship is cultivated by a second group of adults identified by Matthews. These individuals, who comprised 13% of the same, had a small number of friends to whom they were close and considered very important. The largest group (67%) of adults in the sample consisted of those who had developed an *acquisitive* or *gregarious* style of friendship. This style was characterized by close relationships with a fairly large number of people.

Age Differences in Friendships

As a college professor for 35 years, I often remarked on how devoted to their friends my students were. At times, it seemed to me almost as if they would die or kill for their friends, and I am certain that some students cheated for their friends. It was almost as if a different moral standard applied to their behavior when it concerned their friends than when other people were involved.

As a group, young adults have more friends and acquaintances than middle-aged and older adults (Antonucci, 1985). Newly married young adults have more friends than adolescents, middle-aged adults, or older adults. They often make friends with other married couples and form two-couple relationships. By the time they are middle-aged, most adults have some "old friends" whom they may or may not see often. Once friendships have been established, they can be maintained even if the friends see each other infrequently. It may be enough simply to know that someone out there cares about you even if you rarely see him or her (Hess, 1971).

To the extent that older adults have fewer friends than other age groups, it is probably due in large measure to the fact that older adults, who typically do not attend school or work outside the home, encounter fewer people every day than in earlier years. In addition, most older adults have voluntarily disengaged to some extent from social life and have developed a more contemplative, "interiorized" perspective on life. Serious health problems can also lead to a decrease in interactions with friends and other people. Whatever the cause may be, the results of a study by Bossé, Aldwin, Levenson, Spiro, and Mroczek (1993) indicate that retirement is not directly responsible for any decline in the number and quality of friendships. In fact, retirees who engage in volunteer or new occupational activities develop new friendships, whereas retirees who choose not to undertake new work roles tend to experience a decrease in friends (Mor-Barak, Scharlach, Birba, & Sokolov, 1992; Van Tilburg, 1992). Those friendships that remain after retirement, though perhaps fewer in number, may, however, become even closer.

According to Carstensen (1993, 1995), social contact is motivated by the goals of information seeking, self-concept expression, and emotional regulation. The first of these is the major goal of young adults; the third is the principal goal of older adults, and the three goals are roughly in balance in middle-aged adults. As a result of these age changes in goals, older adults are much more selective than young and middle-aged adults in their social contacts. Thus, most people who are over age 65, and even those over age 85, continue to maintain old friends but are less likely to make new friends when the old ones die or move away. Still, the stereotype of the friendless, lonely, older adult who longs for someone to visit him or her is inaccurate. Most older adults continue to receive psychological support from both friends and relatives.

Not surprisingly, the amount of contact that an older person has and the degree of closeness felt with friends and family members are related to the person's health. The direction of the relationship, however, may not be as one expects. A study by Field, Minkler, Falk, and Leino (1993) found that older adults who were in poor health had fewer contacts with friends and relatives than those who were in good health. Though it might seem as if family members and friends would visit a person more if he or she is in poor health, interpersonal interaction is actually hampered by a lack of health and vitality. However, other evidence indicates that an active network of family, friends, neighbors, and even coworkers can bolster one's resistance to disease, perhaps by activating the immune system. For example, in an experimental study conducted by Cohen et al. (1997), it was found that 62% of a group of people with three or fewer cohesive social relationships came down with colds, compared with only 35% of a group of people with six or more such relationships.

Sex Differences in Friendships

Not only do women of all ages have more friends than men, but the nature and functions of those friendships are different. Women are more likely to initiate social interactions both within and outside the family and to develop deeper and longer-lasting friendships than men (Dickens & Perlman, 1981; Wright, 1989). Compared with men, women are more socially interdependent and more likely to engage in self-disclosure (Gilligan, 1982). Their friendships are characterized by the sharing of feelings and concerns and the giving and receiving of emotional support and suggestions (Fox, Gibbs, & Auerbach, 1985; Reisman, 1981). They talk more often and more openly and intimately to their friends, using conversation to make connections and share experiences, and not just to provide information (Berndt, 1992; Dindia & Allen, 1992). The bonds and feelings of support stemming from the friendships of both married and unmarried women, in particular, help them to cope with loneliness, isolation, and emotional stress (Essex & Nam, 1987).

Unlike women, men base their friendships on shared interests and activities, such as going fishing, drinking and telling stories, and engaging in competitive sports and other "minicompetitions." Whereas women explore relationships in their conversational interactions, men are more likely to convey solutions to problems (Tannen, 1990). Men are less likely than women to confide their concerns and feelings to each other, presumably because doing so might be interpreted as a sign of weakness or provide another man with an advantage over them (Huyck, 1982). The social pressures on men to be strong and brave prompts them to be constantly competitive with other males, a reaction that women may have difficulty understanding. For their own part, men find it hard to understand why women always want to talk about their problems (Tannen, 1990).

Another difference between the sexes is the tendency of men who establish friendships with women to sexualize those relationships, behavior which is rare among women (Rawlins, 1992). Be that as it may, a greater percentage of males than females report having friendships with the opposite sex (Usui, 1984). As they grow older, however, women are more likely to have cross-sex, companionate relationships with men (O'Connor, 1993). It is interesting that both men and women describe their friendships with women as being more intimate, enjoyable, and nurturing that those with men (Rubin, 1985; Sapadin, 1988). Apparently, both men and women who need empathy and understanding are more likely to turn to women than to men.

Other Factors in Friendship

With respect to the number of friends that one has, people of higher socioeconomic status tend to have more friends than those of lower status. On the whole, the latter are more kin-oriented than friend-oriented and hence have much closer relationships with their relatives than with nonrelatives. Ethnicity is also associated with the number of friends, with whites having more contact with friends and neighbors than blacks or Hispanics (Dowd & Bengtson, 1978). Ethnicity is, of course, related to socioeconomic status, so these two variables are not independent in their relationships to friendship.

Marital status is also related to the number and nature of friendships. Young, married adults typically have a greater number of friends and see them more often than single or widowed adults (Aizenberg & Treas, 1985). The situation is different among retired older adults. Unmarried retirees spend twice as much time as married retirees with friends (Larson et al., 1986). Older widows and widowers also see their friends more often than older married couples (Field & Minkler, 1988).

Contacts and Friendships

It is generally maintained that frequent contacts between people are necessary in order to develop friendships, but social contacts do not necessarily have to be person-to-person or "in the flesh." Many people have pen pals, faraway friends, or long-distance lovers whom they have never met in person but for whom they nevertheless have strong positive feelings. In addition, once they are established, friendships can be maintained even though the parties rarely see each other. Rather than requiring frequent, close contact in order to survive, perhaps the perception of continuing friendship is enough to keep a person happy and satisfied (Tesch, Whitbourne, & Nehrke, 1981). Like almost everything else studied by social scientists, the need for social contact varies with the individual. Certainly, most people who have been socially isolated for much of their lives do not report being unusually dissatisfied with their lot. By expecting less in the form of social interaction, they apparently have learned to live with less.

As the saying goes, even the best of friends must part, but friendship is not usually terminated when they do. Friendship may fade with absence and the passage of time, but there are always new friends for those who are willing to make an effort to acquire them.

SUMMARY

Society has different expectations for individuals in different age groups and assigns different statuses and roles to them. Among the social roles that give meaning to a person's existence are those prescribed as family members, friends, and by memberships in various organizations.

A typical family of today has been characterized as shaped like a beanpole, in that there are several living generations, but each generation has only a few members.

Nearly one-third of all babies born in the United States are illegitimate, and a sizable percentage are born to teenage mothers. The birthrate varies with age and ethnicity. It is highest for women aged 25–29 years and for Hispanics and blacks than for Asian/Pacific Islanders and whites. Internationally, the fertility rate is highest in African countries and lowest in European countries.

Though rearing a child is a time-consuming and often frustrating task, the experience can be a maturing one for both parents and child. Good parenting results from a combination of genetic endowment (of parent *and* child) and experience. Some people never learn to be good parents, whereas others seem to be naturally gifted with parenting ability. It helps to have good parents oneself, parents from whom one has personally benefited and after whom one can model. Still, children are fairly resilient creatures, and a few parental mistakes do not usually produce little monsters.

In general, authoritative parents, who set behavioral limits and standards, and enforce them with a combination of power and reasoning, have more socially adaptable children than authoritarian, indulgent, or neglecting parents. Children of authoritative parents tend to be not only independent and self-assertive but also friendly and cooperative.

Over one-third of all mothers of young children are gainfully employed outside the home. One might think that this would be psychologically harmful to young children, but research evidence indicates that this is not necessarily so. Mothers also benefit—both economically and psychologically—from working. Not only working mothers but also single mothers have increased in numbers in recent years. Having only one parent undoubtedly has negative effects on the development of children unless the lack of a parent is compensated for by a surrogate or in some other way.

The harmoniousness of relationships between children and their stepparents varies with the ages and genders of both the children and the stepparents. The potential for conflict is greatest between a stepfather and a stepdaughter, especially when the latter is a teenager. Children with foster parents tend to have more problems than those with adoptive parents.

The departure of adolescent and young-adult children from the parental fold or "nest" does not typically cause the parents to become depressed, emotional wrecks. An empty nest can provide more time for interspousal transactions, vocational and avocational activities, and other sources of personal enjoyment and growth. Nevertheless, most middle-aged adults whose children have "fled the coop" continue to spend time and energy in helping both the children and their own parents. Most adult children have a strong sense of filial responsibility, and older parents also feel a sense of duty toward their adult children.

Most adult children see their parents fairly often. This is particularly true of older mothers and adult daughters. The closeness of the relationships between older parents and children depends on the geographical distance between their respective residences and the closeness of the relationships in earlier years. Material and personal assistance between generations flows in both directions, the nature of the assistance depending, among other things, on gender and socioeconomic status.

Several million American children live with their grandparents and great-grandparents. In many cases, the child's parents do not reside in the home, and the grandparents or great-grandparents ("skip-generation" parents) must take care of the child by themselves. Grandparents typically experience positive feelings at the birth of a grandchild, but sometimes it makes them feel old and remote from the present. Whatever the case may be, the overall picture in today's world is one of increasing separation between grandparents and grandchildren.

Grandparenthood has been described in terms of several different types: fun-seeking, companionate, firm, distant, and so forth. However, the nature of the social interaction between grandparents and grandchildren depends as much on the gender and ages of the parties as anything else. In general, grandmothers, and especially the mother's mother, are closer than grandfathers to their grandchildren.

Same-sex siblings who are approximately the same age are typically closer to each other than to other family members. The loyalty between brothers and sisters tends to increase with age. However, the relationships between adult siblings range from intimate to hostile. Sisters of all races tend to maintain closer contacts with each other than brothers, and black brothers are usually closer than white brothers.

Friends are often closer and valued more than family members. Friends tend to be similar in age, appearance, and socioeconomic status, as well as interests, abilities, and temperament. They provide us with companionships, entertainment, feelings of acceptance and importance, and help us cope with emotional stress caused by a loss, a disorder, or a defeat. Deep friendships develop through a series of stages, beginning with simple awareness of each other and culminating in shared confidences. More superficial friendships are based on similarities of lifestyles and interests but do not involve as much self-disclosure as deep friendships. Styles of friendship have also been characterized as independent, discerning, and acquisitive/gregarious.

Young adults tend to have more friends than middle-aged and older adults, and middle-aged adults have more friends than older adults. However, most older adults, especially older women, continue to have friends and to receive emotional and material support from them.

Women of all ages have more friends than men. Women are also more likely to talk about their problems, express their feelings, and otherwise share confidences with friends. Men are more likely to engage in activities, such as minicompetitions, with their friends. People of higher socioeconomic status have more friends than those of lower socioeconomic status, and whites have more friends than blacks. Young, married adults have more friends than single or widowed adults, but unmarried retirees spend more time with friends than married retires, and older widows and widowers see their friends more frequently than older married couples.

SUGGESTED READINGS

Antonucci, T. C. (1990). Social supports and social relationships. In R. H. Binstock & L. K. George (Eds.), *Handbook of aging and the social sciences* (3rd ed., pp. 205–226). New York: Academic Press.

Bedford, V. H. (1992). Memories of parental favoritism and the quality of parent–child ties in adulthood. *Journal of Gerontology: Social Sciences, 47,* S149–S155.

Blieszner, R., & Bedford, V. H. (Eds.). (1995). *Handbook of aging and the family.* Westport, CT: Greenwood Press.

Field, D., Minkler, M., Falk, R. F., & Leino, E. V. (1993). The influences of health and family contacts and family feelings in advanced old age: A longitudinal study. *Journal of Gerontology: Psychological Sciences, 48,* P18–P28.

Gatz, M., Bengtson, V. L., & Blum, M. J. (1990). Caregiving families. In J. E. Birren & K. W. Schaie (Eds.), *Handbook of the psychology of aging* (3rd ed., pp. 404–426). San Diego: Academic Press.

Larsen, D. (December 1990/January 1991). Unplanned parenthood. *Modern Maturity,* pp. 32–36.

Minkler, M., & Roe, K. M. (1993). *Grandmothers as caregivers.* Newbury Park, CA: Sage.

Neidhardt, E. R., & Allen, J. A. (1993). *Family therapy with the elderly.* Newbury Park, CA: Sage.

CHAPTER 8

Gender, Race, and Social Status

It is characteristic of all human societies and many animal species as well to classify their individual members into collectivities or groups. Often, those groupings are based on ostensible physical features such as sex, skin color, or size, whereas other groups are constituted with reference to qualities such as age, language, religion, origin, ancestry, monetary wealth, property ownership, political party membership, or sexual orientation. Associated with the various ways of classifying people are certain behaviors on the part of the members of a group and certain attitudes, beliefs, and prejudices concerning the group that are held by other members of the society as a whole. In addition, a social status, rank, or perceived value of the group is assigned, either implicitly or explicitly, to individuals belonging to various groups. Members of these groups are then treated by other people in accordance with that status. Finally, individuals, and entire nationalities or races outside a particular society itself are often viewed negatively or positively and accordingly valued or devalued for their general characteristics or traits. These characterizations are almost always overgeneralizations, which may or may not be manifested by individual members of the society. For example, according to one writer, the English are "men of action," the French "men of reason," and the Spanish, "men of passion" (Ortega y Gasset, 1957/1932). Other nationalities and ethnic groups that have been assigned a general or stereotypical character are Germans, Jews, Blacks, Hispanics, Japanese, and Chinese. Even scholars such as Ruth Benedict (1960/1946) have overgeneralized in typifying the behaviors and philosophy of entire populations. Americans, for example, are said to be proponents of the philosophy "Trust in God and keep your powder dry."

American society has become increasingly diverse during this century. In the past 150 years, there has been a multifold increase in emigration to the United States by people of other nationalities, races, religions, and backgrounds. To many of these immigrants, this nation held out a promise of personal status, affluence, and happiness they could not hope to achieve in their native countries. Unfortunately, the differences between these people and those who had already settled in the United States formed the basis for attitudes that favored the dominant, mostly white, Anglo–Saxon Protestant resident group over the newcomers. In many cases, these attitudes led to discrimination and prejudice.

This chapter is concerned with classification of people according to gender, race, social class, and age, and the behaviors and conditions associated with those classifications. These are four principal ways in which Anglo-American society, and many other societies as well, classify people and develop sets of attitudes and behavioral expectations corresponding to those classifications. Although these characterizations or stereotypes are rarely completely false, their overgeneralized nature does not allow for the many exceptions and changes occurring in particular groups. People tend to attend to and use information that is consistent with their stereotypical beliefs and to discount information that is inconsistent with those beliefs or to view it as an exception to the general rule (Stephan, 1989). In addition to nurturing distorted perceptions, stereotypes often lead to self-fulfilling prophecies in which prejudices and resulting behaviors create the very situation that one presumes to exist.

The study of differences in the characteristics and behavior of the sexes, races, social classes, and chronological age groups stems from the field of *differential psychology*, which was inaugurated by Sir Francis Galton in 1883. As conceived by Galton, differential psychology is concerned with differences in the abilities and personalities of a variety of demographic groups, not just sex, race, social class, and age. Galton and the psychometricians who followed him were interested primarily in the measurement of these group differences and their origins. This chapter focuses on describing these differences and some of their origins and consequences.

GENDER

In the United States, approximately 105 boys are born for every 100 girls.[1] Thus, in terms of mortality rate, if not in physical strength, males are the weaker sex. At every age, females have a lower probability of dying than males. As shown in Figure 8–1, in middle- and older adulthood the number of women exceeds the number of men, a ratio that increases in old age. Based on unpublished data from the U.S. Bureau of the Census, the ratio of men to women in this country in 1997 declined from 84:100 at ages 65–69 to 77:100 at ages 70–74, 70:100 at ages 75–79, 58:100 at ages 80–84, and 40:100 after age 84. It is predicted that the age-related drop in this ratio will decline even further in the next century as proportionally more women than men continue to live to a ripe old age.

---

[1]The ratio of male to female newborns is even higher in countries that practice abortion on female fetuses or infanticide on girl babies. China, for example, encourages the abortion of female fetuses, a policy that has resulted in a ratio of male newborns to female newborns of 128:100.

The average life spans of both sexes have lengthened considerably in the past few decades, but the average life span of American women has increased more rapidly that than of American men. Consequently, the life expectancy of an American female at birth is over 6 years longer than that of an American male. The magnitude of this difference varies with race, being 2–3 years greater for black than white Americans. Because of their greater longevity and relatively larger numbers, the problems of later life—health, economic, living conditions, security, and so on—are primarily problems experienced by women of both races.

The greater increase in longevity for women than for men has been observed in other developed countries during this century, but less so in underdeveloped nations (Population Reference Bureau, 1996). A major factor in the differential increase has been the decreased risk of dying during childbirth (*maternal mortality*), but improvements in sanitation, diet, housing, and health care have contributed to the declining mortality rate for both sexes throughout the world.

Sex Differences

In the United States, a *real* boy climbs trees, disdains girls, dirties his knees, plays with soldiers, and takes blue for his favorite color. A real girl dresses dolls, jumps rope, plays hopscotch, and takes pink for her favorite color. When they go to school, real girls like English and music and "auditorium"; real boys prefer manual training, gym, and arithmetic. In college the boys smoke pipes, drink beer, and major in engineering or physics; the girls chew Juicy Fruit gum, drink cherry Cokes, and major in fine arts. The real boy matures into a "man's man" who plays poker, goes hunting, drinks brandy, and dies in the war; the real girl becomes a "feminine" woman who loves children, embroiders handkerchiefs, drinks weak tea and "succumbs" to consumption (Brown, 1965, p. 141; emphasis in original)

This example is a somewhat whimsical and obviously stereotyped description of the sexes, even those of bygone days. Such caricatures ignore the wide range of differences, within as well as between the sexes, differences that vary with age, physical features, culture, and other biological and sociocultural variables. On the average, however, males differ significantly from females in many ways other than anatomically, and the opinion of many people is aptly expressed in the cliché, "Viva la difference!"

Physical Differences

To anyone who has observed a number of newborn babies, it is obvious that, in addition to being equipped with different sex organs than baby girls, baby boys are, on the average, longer and heavier. It may or may not be obvious to a patient observer, but it is a good bet that a randomly selected newborn will be a boy. The ratio of males to females in the United States is approximately 105 to 100. Due to the higher incidence of fatal diseases and traumas for boys than for girls, this ratio is close to 1:1 by the time they become adults. There are, of course, other biological differences between the sexes, but they are not so obvious at birth. For example, the average boy is stronger, has faster and more coordinated gross body movements, but poorer tactile sensitivity and finger dexterity than girls. He is more likely than the average girl to be color deficient and left-handed, and he has a greater likelihood of being able to wiggle his ears (Myers, 1995). In boys, there is also a fair chance that the right hemisphere of the brain is dominant, whereas in girls, it is rarely so.

On the average, girls reach puberty 2 years earlier than boys, and in junior high school some boys may feel like shrimps alongside their female classmates. By the time both sexes have completed adolescence, females have substantially more body fat (70% more) than males but are shorter (5 inches), less muscular (40% less), and have less facial hair (Myers, 1995). These differences persist and others develop in young adulthood. For example, pattern baldness often starts showing in adult males in their late teens or early twenties. And with respect to the biology of sexual behavior, young women are more likely to become sexually aroused soon after experiencing orgasm.

As they age into middle- and older adulthood, women are more likely than men to develop chronic illnesses and physical problems. Consequently, many older women require help with ADLs (activities of daily living) and especially instrumental activities of daily living (IADLs) (Barer, 1994). Compared with men, they pay more visits to physicians and therapists and take more drugs for physical and psychiatric disorders (Unger, 1979). On the other hand, adult males are more susceptible than adult females to life-threatening illness and have a higher death rate for the 10 most frequent causes of death in the United States (Singh, Kochanek, & MacDorman, 1996).

Cognitive Differences

In addition to affecting perceptual and psychomotor abilities, biological differences between the sexes influence cognitive abilities and personality. A somewhat dated, but still valuable, summary of such differences may be found in Maccoby and Jacklin (1974; also see Eagly & Carli, 1981). One of the most obvious areas of sex differences in cognitive abilities is verbal–linguistic ability. Girls learn to talk and read sooner and, to some extent, better than boys. The incidence of dyslexia (reading disorder) is greater among boys, a larger percentage of boys being in remedial reading classes (Finucci & Childs, 1981; Halpern, 1992). Girls appear to retain their superiority in verbal abilities in elementary school, performing better than boys on tests of spelling, punctuation, reading comprehension, and verbal analogies.

For many years, senior high girls scored higher than boys on the verbal portion of the Scholastic Aptitude Test (SAT). In recent years, however, the gender gap in scores on tests of verbal abilities administered in senior high school appears to have disappeared. In 1997, for example, the mean SAT-Verbal score for females (503) was 4 points lower than that for males (507). These are overall means and not necessarily representative of the results for a particular ethnic group. For example, black females score higher than black males on the SAT-Verbal. On the SAT-Mathematical, males continue to make higher mean scores than females. In 1997, the mean SAT-Mathematical score for males (530) was 36 points higher than that for females (494). Males also score slightly higher than females on the second most popular college admissions test—the American College Test (ACT) (data courtesy of College Entrance Examination Board and American College Testing Program).

Numerous explanations have been offered for gender differences in SAT scores. One hypothesis is that the socioeconomic status of girls who took the SAT in the 1980s was lower than that of boys. Another possibility is that teenage girls who took the test were more concerned about dating and possible pregnancy and less committed to schoolwork than boys (Cordes, 1986). But whatever the causes of the sex difference in mean SAT scores, it appears to be declining (Shea, 1994).

Among other cognitive abilities in which sex differences have been explored are clerical abilities and visuospatial abilities. Males tend to be more adept at business pursuits, but females have better clerical abilities (Minton & Schneider, 1980). One of the most consistent sex differences, however, is in visuospatial abilities. This ability to perceive objects in space consists of two components: analytic and nonanalytic. Tests of analytic spatial abilities include disembedding figures from backgrounds (see Figure 8–1) and constructing block designs; tests of nonanalytic spatial abilities include mental rotations and reproducing spatial relations. Adolescent and adult males tend to make higher average scores than females on both analytic and nonanalytic tests of visuospatial abilities (Petersen & Wittig, 1979). It has been suggested that these sex differences may help to explain why males score significantly higher than females on standardized mathematics tests, and particularly geometry (Burnett, 1986; Linn & Petersen, 1985).

Personality Characteristics

Which sex (male or female) is more anxious, compliant with adults, demanding, depressed, empathic, fearful, immature, interdependent, irritable, people-oriented, socially sensitive, submissive, subtly aggressive (gossiping, snubbing, etc.), and timid? And which sex is more active, aggressive, competent, competitive, dominant, exploratory, impulsive, independent, logical, mature, productive, self-confident, self-reliant, violent, and worldly? Even if you did not grow up in mainstream American culture and disagree

This is a test of your ability to tell which one of five simple figures can be found in a more complex pattern.

Indicate your answer by putting X through the letter of the figure which you find in the pattern.

NOTE: There is only one of these figures in each pattern, and this figure will always be right side up and exactly the same size as one of the five lettered figures.

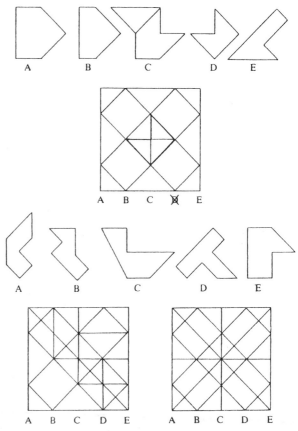

Figure 8–1 Sample Embedded Figures Test item. (Courtesy of the estate of the late Dr. Herman A. Witkin. Adaptations by Wm. C. Brown Co., Publishers.)

with some of the adjectives, you are not likely to experience much difficulty in answering these two questions. In one large study of college students from 30 countries across the world, the respondents consistently checked the following adjectives as descriptive of men: adventurous, strong, dominant, assertive, task-oriented, aggressive, enterprising, and independent. Women, on the other hand, were consistently described as sensitive, gentle, dependent, emotional, sentimental, weak, submissive, and people-oriented (Williams & Best, 1990). Other studies have found girls and women to be more empathic and sensitive to other people (Eisenberg & Lennon, 1983). They are also viewed as more dependent, fearful, irritable, and demanding, but less self-confident than males. Males, on the other hand, are characterized as more active, exploratory, and impulsive than females (Feshbach & Weiner, 1991). In short, as a group, women emphasize interdependence with other people, whereas men emphasize independence from others.

As discussed at length in Chapters 5 and 7 of this book, women are more relationship-oriented than men: They discover their identities through the responsibilities and attachments that characterize their relationships with other people. Whereas the self-esteem of a typical male is based on being successfully independent, the self-esteem of a typical female comes from achieving positive relationships with people (Josephs, Markus, & Tafarodi, 1992; Stake, 1992). Women are more willing than men to seek and accept help from others and to develop social networks that make this possible. In contrast, men are more apt to stress the importance of individual achievement, control, and management of their lives and those of their family and associates. As discussed in Chapter 5, however, sex differences in personality traits typically become less distinct with aging. Older women are somewhat more assertive, independent, and individualistic, whereas older men are more cooperative, submissive, and interdependent than they were in young and middle adulthood.

Mental Disorders

The fact that more women than men are treated in mental health clinics and psychiatric hospitals would lead one to believe that the rate of mental illness is higher among women than among men. This appears to be the case with respect to some, but certainly not all, mental disorders. Women tend to be more vulnerable to anxiety disorders, depression, and eating disorders, and they probably have a higher rate of *attempted* suicide than men. On the other hand, boys are more likely than girls to stutter, to be hyperactive, and to develop other conduct or behavioral disorders (Myers, 1995). As adults, they are more likely to become alcoholics and/or substance abusers and to develop antisocial personalities (Unger, 1979). Men also commit more crimes than women, and crimes of violence in particular (U.S. Department of Justice, 1996). Finally, substantially more men than women, and especially older white men, succeed in committing suicide (Singh et al., 1996).

Social and Economic Differences

The greater social sensitivity and empathy of females continues throughout their lifetimes, from childhood through old age. Placing more value on friendships and helping relationships in general, women develop more extensive social networks through which they give and receive assistance of a material and socioemotional nature. As discussed in Chapter 7, middle-aged and older adult women are more likely than men to maintain contact with their children and grandchildren and to provide assistance to and obtain it from them.

The social interests of women are not limited to family members and friendships but extend to the wider community and larger geographical units. Career-oriented women are more likely to enter helping professions such as child care, teaching, nursing, and social work than other fields (Eagly & Crowley, 1986). On a nonprofessional level, women are more likely than men to be called upon as caregivers. Many participate in community service, religious, and volunteer activities of various kinds. In the political sphere, their greater concern with the disadvantaged leads women to vote more often to support the Democratic platform and to vote for Democratic candidates in elections. This is particularly true when matters of great concern to them, such as abortion or child care, are at issue.

Even in old age, despite the fact that they are more likely than older men to be impoverished, the availability of a strong social network of other older women and family members assists women in confronting the problems of aging. Furthermore, unlike men, who are more likely to lose status in old age, most older women are able to maintain their position in the social hierarchy, An exception may occur, however, when all of a widow's friends and social contacts were made through her deceased husband or his friends and associates.

When serving as leaders, women's style tends to be participative and democratic rather than directive or authoritarian. Rather than dispassionately stating their opinions, asking questions, or presenting information, women are more likely than men to smile and gaze at others and to agree or express support. In contrast, men in leadership positions tend to be more directive and even autocratic. Men are less likely to become emotionally close to other people, preferring instead to maintain control by keeping the relationships fairly superficial and "letting the facts speak for themselves." Sometimes, however, men misinterpret eye contact or a smile from a woman as a promise, perceiving interpersonal warmth as a sexual come-on and friendliness as sexual interest (Abbey, 1987; Johnson, Stockdale, & Saal, 1991; Kowalski, 1993). In such cases, their responses to such false perceptions may leave men open to charges of sexual harassment.

Biological Correlates of Gender

Perhaps the most basic fact of human genetics is that females have two X chromosomes in the 23rd position but males have only one. There are, of course, exceptions to this rule, for examples, Turner's and Klinefelter's syndromes, but almost all women are endowed with two X chromosomes in each cell. The question is not whether males have an imbalance of X chromosomes, but rather to what extent certain disorders that are more common in males than females are attributable to the imbalance.

In addition to having more X chromosomes than males, females generally have a lower metabolic rate, a higher brain-to-body weight, and a lower level of testosterone. Could it be that such differences are responsible for behavioral and cognitive differences between the sexes? The possibility that female hormones have a protective effect and that male hormones promote certain disorders has been the subject of continuing research and controversy (Luria et al., 1982; Waldron, 1983). Sex hormones have also been found to be related to cognitive abilities. For example, Hier and Crowley (1982) obtained a positive correlation between spatial ability and secretions of male sex hormones during puberty. In addition, the results of several investigations suggest that testosterone, the most important male hormone, slows the development of the left hemisphere and enhances the development of the right hemisphere of the brain. Note that the right hemisphere is associated with the types of reasoning skills crucial for solving mathematical problems (Christiansen & Knussman, 1987).

Although the effects of testosterone on aggression in humans are not as clear as they are in other animals, a weak correlation between the two variables has been found. However, this finding does not necessarily mean that high testosterone levels cause aggressive behavior; the result can also be interpreted as indicating that repeated aggression increases the level of testosterone in the blood (Archer, 1991). With respect to the female hormone estrogen, Hampson (1990) and Kimura and Hampson (1993) reported that women perform better on tests of motor coordination and verbal facility but poorer on tests of spatial reasoning during times of the month when estrogen levels in the blood are highest.

Although genes, chromosomes, hormones, neural structure, and other biological factors contribute to the determination of sex differences before and after birth, environmental factors such as differential cultural reinforcement of sex-appropriate behavior, the imitation of gender-role models, and other psychosocial variables are at least as important (Wittig & Petersen, 1978). As with all human behavior, explanations of gender differences must take into account both the biology of the individual and the environment in which he or she has to function.

Gender Roles

An important concept regarding socially sanctioned, sex-appropriate behavior is that of *gender roles*—behavior patterns that are considered appropriate and specific to each gender. Included in the notion of gender role are the behavioral prescriptions and stereotypes that society associates with each sex. A person may not adhere to a particular stereotype concerning the role and behaviors assigned to a given sex, but it is at his or her own peril. Those who fail to comply must be prepared to pay the cost in terms of criticism, ostracism, and other social sanctions.

Two other important concepts concerning sex-role development are those of gender schema and gender identity. *Gender schemas* are beliefs about what men and women are and how they are supposed to act. *Gender identity*, defined as how the individual views him- or herself with respect to gender, is the introspective part of gender role. Cultures have differed in many ways throughout human history, but there has been a great deal of cross-cultural similarity in the roles assigned to men and women. An exception is the Tchambuli of New Guinea, among whom the usual roles of men and women are reversed (Mead, 1935). In most societies, women, who require sustenance, shelter, and safety in order to bear and bring up their children, acquire a more nurturing, caregiving role. The typical role of men, however, is that of provider and protector. As human beings became more civilized, the male role translated into that of home-builder (or purchaser), wage earner, and defender of the family and hearth. And as life became easier, the traditional childcaring and housekeeping roles of women became more diversified.

How are gender roles communicated, and how are they internalized? Starting at birth, male and female children are perceived and treated differently. For the most part, they are assigned sex-appropriate names, dressed in blue or pink, referred to as "pretty" or "handsome," and given what society views as sex-appropriate toys with which to play. In order to develop a set of expectations and behaviors with respect to a particular gender, a young child must be able to recognize representatives of that gender. This, however, does not usually pose a problem. Children as young as 9 months can distinguish between male and female faces (Leinbach & Fagot, 1993). By the time they are 3 years old, boys and girls can identify their own sex and that of other children, and by ages 5 to 7 they know what being a boy or girl means (Guardo & Bohan, 1971; Kohlberg, 1966). Young children are continually encouraged to engage in what adults consider "sex-appropriate" activities and interests (Lytton & Romney, 1991). Most first-grade children have a fair notion of what sex-appropriate behavior consists of and what happens to children who deviate from behaviors expected of members of their own sex (Stoddart & Turiel, 1985). By the fifth or sixth grade, children have a good knowledge of most sex-role stereotypes in the culture (Emmerich & Shepard, 1982).

Young girls are typically socialized differently from young boys. The emphasis on nurturance, responsibility, and emotional orientation in girls socializes them primarily for the expressive (emotion-oriented) behavior of companions and mothers, whereas the emphasis on achievement, self-reliance, and goal-directed orientation in boys socializes them principally for the instrumental behavior of breadwinners. The predominantly nurturing role of females and the achieving, environmental-manipulative role of males are further shaped in school by encouraging boys to take mathematics and science courses and girls to take language arts and social service courses. In keeping with these emphases, college women are more likely than men to major in humanities, the social sciences, and education, whereas more men

major in scientific fields and engineering. Women who elect to attend vocational schools rather than senior colleges are found in larger numbers in
health service, secretarial, and domestically oriented areas, while men are
concentrated in agricultural, technical, and trade/industrial programs (Wirtenberg, Klein, Richardson, & Thomas, 1981).

According to Eagly's (1987) theory of social roles, the actual differences
in the behaviors of men and women are amplified by inequalities in the social
roles they occupy. This is a context effect, in which people, chameleon-like,
take on the coloration of the roles they play. The actors in these dramas also
participate in the delusion by being victims of the self-fulfilling prophecy of
behaving according to how they are expected to and believing that they are
actually the roles they are playing. Thus, the roles assigned to men and
women in industrial societies lead them to develop attitudes and skills that
are congruent with those roles. However, the degree of gender bias or gender
discrimination can vary enormously from country to country. For example,
the percentages of management positions held by women ranges from 48% in
Switzerland, 28% in Austria, and 17% in the United States to only 3% in
Ghana and 2% in South Korea (Triandis, 1994).

As indicated by statistics such as these, specific gender roles appear to
be strongly entrenched in many, if not all, parts of the world. Despite the
feelings of certain social scientists that gender roles will probably never
completely disappear, some developmental psychologists maintain that children should be reared in a more androgynous, or non-sex-role, manner.
According to these authorities, young children should be taught the value of
both traditionally masculine and traditionally feminine activities and encouraged to participate in each kind. In any case, during the past three
decades, the emphasis on the civil rights of all social groups, exposure to a
wider range of customs and ideas, and the increasing influence of women in
the marketplace and the workplace have led to some erosion of traditional
sex-role stereotypes. The concept of men as independent, dominant, competitive, and self-confident individuals and women as dependent, submissive,
cooperative, and self-doubting has been changing. More and more, it is being
recognized that adults need the positive features of both the traditional male
and female roles in order to function successfully in contemporary society.

Sex Bias and Discrimination

If we consider all of the characteristics that serve as a basis for discrimination (sex, race, ethnicity, social class, age, etc.), the most significant in
terms of economic well-being is sex. From an economic standpoint, it is
certainly a disadvantage in our society to be black, poor, uneducated, and old,
but arguably, the greatest disadvantage of all is to be a woman.

Women have made progress in the workplace and public life in recent
years, but the great majority remain in traditional women's occupations doing

"women's work," including clerical and household occupations, food services, nursing, and school teaching. The large majority of higher-paying professional positions in business and industry, engineering, science, and technology are still occupied by men. Even in fields such as medicine and law, which have opened up for women to some degree in the past few decades, women tend to specialize in certain areas and men in others. Women doctors are more likely to specialize in pediatrics, psychiatry, and public health, while women lawyers tend to concentrate on domestic law and trusts rather than corporate or criminal law (Wass, 1993).

Despite some resistance from both officers and enlisted men (and sexual harassment scandals), more and more women are enlisting in the military services and being trained for all kinds of duties. So far, the concern that women are not physically or psychologically suited for combat, and that their presence interferes with male bonding and morale has restricted their assignment to noncombat positions. However, there is a great deal of political pressure to eliminate all sex distinctions in the treatment of women and men in all branches of the armed forces.

Sexism, the belief that the two sexes are fundamentally different in their abilities and that each is more suited for certain jobs or areas of concentration, is still quite prevalent in educational and employment contexts. Many people continue to feel that women's proper place is in the home and that they should not try to compete with men in the world of work. In many organizations, there appears to be a kind of *glass ceiling*, a subtle barrier to advancement by women—a level to which they can rise in a company but beyond which they cannot go. Certain authorities (e.g., Hymowitz & Schellhardt, 1986; Morrison & Von Glinow, 1990) maintain that a glass ceiling exists in the professions, private industry, and government. Women comprise 55% of the U.S. population aged 18 years and over and 46% of management, but only a small percentage are found on corporate boards of directors, in the U.S. Senate, or in state governors' chairs. Of course, this does not prove that the glass ceiling is the result of intentional discrimination against women. Perhaps women lack the abilities, personality characteristics, motivation, or stamina to succeed at higher levels of an organization. There is, however, no good evidence for the validity of this supposition. Rather, it would seem that the primary cause of the glass ceiling in most instances is quite purely and simply gender discrimination. It is practiced not only in the workplace but in the home, the school, the mass media, and the society at large. By being discriminated against, women find it difficult to attain the knowledge, skills, and social networks that come from interacting with other executives and staff professionals. Consequently, they are not given an adequate opportunity to demonstrate the incorrectness of the attitudes and biases toward them.

Another illustration of the problem of women not possessing the requisite skills for certain jobs occurs in the case of those who want or need to get back in the workforce but have little or no training and therefore have to settle for low-paying jobs with no chance for advancement and an inadequate retirement pension. Private pensions, in addition to Social Security, are made available to retired teachers and nurses, but in few other occupations that attract large numbers of women. Furthermore, for the most part, women's wages, and particularly the wages of minority women, are substantially lower that those for men. The median income of full-time working women in 1995 was $22,497, compared with $31,496 for men (U.S. Bureau of the Census, 1996). In recent years, legal attention has been given to the concept of *comparable worth*. According to this concept, pay should be made equal in those occupations that are determined to be equivalent in importance but in which the relative numbers of men and women employees are substantially different. However, because of the difficulty of evaluating the demands made by different jobs, thus far proposed systems for determining comparable worth have not proven very effective.

In addition to being denied equal status with men in the world of work, women are often sexually harassed and in other ways treated as sex objects rather than as individuals. Gender stereotypes abound in advertising and in other branches of the media. One illustration is *faceism*, the tendency to focus on men's faces but on women's bodies when photographing or filming them. As long as sex sells and the doctrine of free enterprise prevails, such practices will probably continue. However, men should be cautioned that women are more likely to find touching, staring, and related behaviors offensive than men are (Fitzgerald & Ormerod, 1991). The problem of mutual awareness and understanding between the sexes has led to the legal criterion of sexual harassment known as the *reasonable woman standard* (*Ellison v. Brady*, 1991). According to this standard, even if the male perpetrator of an action that allegedly involved sexual harassment did not consider it offensive, if it can be concluded that a "reasonable woman" would view it as offensive, then in law it is considered to be so.

RACE AND ETHNICITY

Since the 1960s, the traditional notion of America as a "melting pot" in which all nationalities and races would become intermingled has given way to the idea of multiculturalism. To a large extent, immigrants from European countries have become assimilated into the dominant Anglo-American culture that they found here, but those from Africa and Asia have remained more "ghettoized." Second- and subsequent-generation descendants of European immigrants were acculturated into mainstream America by adopting the behaviors and ways of thinking that were characteristic of the host group and by intermarrying with them. The culture and customs of the newer arrivals were also assimilated with those of the dominant group.

Although racially mixed children have also increased in number and efforts have been made to legislate equality among different racial and ethnic groups in this country, counterforces on both the left and the right have promoted separatism. Despite Thomas Jefferson's stated belief that "all men are created equal," after two centuries of discussion, conflict, and legislation, racial equality remains an aspiration rather than a fact. The quality of life in America, as indicated by economic, health, security, and other indicators, is not the same for people of all races. The problem of attaining equality has proven to be particularly difficult for Americans who possess visible and identifiable characteristics, such as different skin coloration. Those individuals are more likely to have met with prejudice and discrimination in all walks of life—in education, employment, housing, medical care, religion, and other social institutions. One consequence of discrimination in employment is the significant race-related difference in average annual income. Note in Figure 8–2 that median annual income, both household and per capita, is significantly higher for whites than for blacks and Hispanics.

Whereas *race* is a biological term designating a subdivision of the human species, an *ethnic group* consists of people who share the same language and culture. The major racial groups in this country are Caucasian (white), African-American (black), Asian/Pacific Islander, and Native American. Hispanics, who may be of any race but usually identify themselves as white, are an ethnic group. The estimated number of Americans, by age group, in

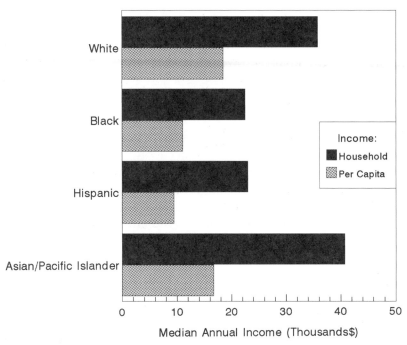

Figure 8–2 Median annual household and per capita income by race/ethnicity. (Constructed from data in U.S. Bureau of the Census, 1996.)

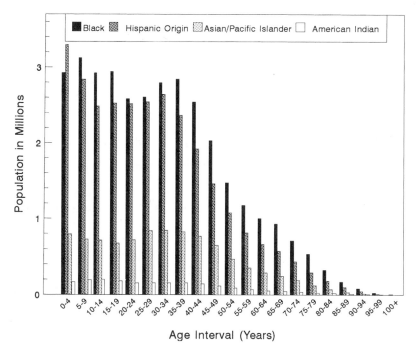

Age Interval (Years)

Figure 8–3   Estimated U.S. population by chronological age and ethnicity, January 1997. (Based on unpublished data from U.S. Bureau of the Census, 1997.)

each of four ethnic groups in 1997 is plotted in Figure 8–3. Not depicted in the figure is the projected increase in the percentage of minorities in the older American population during the next century. By 2050, it is anticipated that 32% of Americans over age 65 will be minorities, blacks, and Hispanics in particular, as compared with approximately 14% in 1990 (U.S. Senate Special Committee on Aging, 1991). Therefore, the problems of education, health, living conditions, and unemployment that are seen in today's minority elderly can be expected to multiply during the next century if no further progress is made toward solutions.

African-Americans

Statistics related to the quality of life for African-Americans are dismal indeed. Teenage pregnancy, out-of-wedlock births, and infant mortality are more common, life expectancy at birth is lower, and the rates of obesity, hypertension, and certain other diseases are higher than average. Significantly more blacks than whites die of HIV infection and homicide or other legal intervention. On the economic front, the rates of unemployment and poverty are higher, and incomes are lower than average. Affecting socioeconomic status is the fact that the percentage of blacks who graduate from high school is significantly lower than that for whites. Quality of life, as indicated by a greater rate of substandard housing, a larger percentage of single-parent families, a lower marriage rate, and a higher divorce rate, is poorer for blacks than for whites. Ladner (1971) attributes some of these problems to the long period of slavery and segregation to which blacks were subjected in the United States. Because black slaves were not permitted to marry, a family system that deemphasized legal marriage, tolerated premarital intercourse, and accepted illegitimate children developed. The contemporary African-American community, with its emphasis on the extended family, strong kinship bonds, and intrafamilial cooperation, also originated in the historical experiences of African-Americans —in Africa and, subsequently, in America.

Despite the seemingly bleak picture painted by the statistics summarized in the previous paragraph, African-Americans have made substantial progress in education, employment, and acceptance by the dominant American society during the past few decades. These statistics do not reveal the fact that a sizable percentage of African-Americans are middle-class professionals and business persons whose economic situation is on a par with that of middle-class American whites. The family structures of middle-class black Americans tend to resemble those of whites (Markides, Liang, & Jackson, 1990). The living conditions of older blacks have also improved in recent years, due in large measure to Social Security increases and Supplemental Security Income (SSI), and have helped to free them from the degrading stereotype of having to depend on welfare for survival. Being old in the black community also has the advantage of being associated with greater social respect and higher self-esteem than it typically is in the white community.

Hispanic-Americans

Hispanics, consisting primarily of a mixture of white, black, and Native American racial origins, are the second largest (and predicted to soon become the largest) ethnic minority in the United States. Of Hispanic-Americans, approximately 64% are Mexican, 11% are Puerto Rican, 5% are Cuban, and 13% are of Central or South American origin. Hispanic-Americans have the highest birthrate and the lowest divorce rate of all ethnic groups, but their per capita income is substantially lower than average (see Figure 8–3). In general, the incomes of Cuban-Americans are higher than those of Mexican-Americans, and the incomes of Mexican-Americans are higher than those of Puerto Rican-Americans (Torres-Gil, 1996). The percentage of Hispanics who have graduated from high school is also substantially lower, the unemployment rate is higher, and a greater percentage live below the poverty line than non-Hispanic-Americans ((U.S. Bureau of the Census, 1995).

The low income and low educational levels of Hispanics is due in large measure to the fact that many are recent immigrant laborers who were low on the socioeconomic scale in their country of origin. Another disadvantage, which they share with certain other immigrant groups, is a linguistic one. Those whose English is poor or nonexistent face a barrier, and consequent discrimination, against full participation in American society. This is particularly true of the thousands who enter the United States illegally.

Also, like many other ethnic minorities, the families of Hispanic-Americans are typically more close-knit than those of non-Hispanic whites. In the lives of most Mexican-Americans, in particular, the family is central and the group to which they owe their greatest allegiance. Mutual aid among family members, respect for age, and male leadership are dominant themes. The cooperative, group orientation of Mexican-Americans sometimes bodes well for the wider society, as in their patriotism and willingness to defend their country. However, it may also bode ill, as seen in violence among street gangs and the high crime rate among Hispanic youth.

Asian/Pacific Islander-Americans

The Americans in this group are immigrants or descendants of immigrants from China, Japan, Taiwan, the Philippines, Hong Kong, Indonesia, Korea, Thailand, Vietnam, and Pacific Oceania. The first Asian immigrants to the United States came as contract laborers in the nineteenth century, where they worked primarily on the railroad and in the mines. More recent Asian immigrants have been refugees and professionals, a large percentage of whom hold professional degrees. There is, however, a wide variation in the level of education and occupational status among Asian-Americans.

As a group, Asian-Americans are more highly educated and have higher incomes than African-Americans and Hispanic-Americans. But like the last two minorities, Asian-Americans tend to have close, supportive family relationships (Markides, et al., 1990). The principle of *filial piety*, that is, that one's parents and other older adults should not have to suffer from want or sorrow, is an important concept in Asian cultures. Adherence to this principle and other traditional beliefs and practices shared by immigrants from the Far East varies with the generation and the closeness of a person to that culture. Ties with traditional Japanese culture tend to be stronger for Issei (Japanese immigrants) than for Nisei (children of Japanese immigrants), and stronger for Nisei than for Sansei (grandchildren of Japanese immigrants). Second- and third-generation Japanese-Americans reportedly may not feel as obligated to support their elderly parents as their counterparts in Japan (Kim, 1983).

In addition to being more highly educated and affluent than other ethnic groups, Americans of Asian/Pacific Islander ancestry tend to be healthier as well. One explanation is that they are less likely to engage in high-risk behaviors such as smoking and drinking (Yu, Chang, Liu, & Kan, 1985).

U.S. immigration policies during the early twentieth century, which did not permit Asian and Pacific Island women to enter this country, combined with the detention of Japanese-Americans in concentration campus during World War II, left a reservoir of negative feelings in some members of the Asian-American community. Be that as it may, Asian-Americans are perhaps the best example of how the United States can still be a land of opportunity for immigrants who are skilled and motivated to work and save.

Native Americans

The three major subgroups of Native Americans, in order of population size, are American Indians, Eskimos, and Aleuts. Nearly one-half of them live west of the Mississippi River, and in Oklahoma, California, Arizona, and New Mexico, in particular. Like African-Americans and Hispanic-Americans, as a group they are below average for the U.S. population in educational attainment and income (U.S. Bureau of the Census, 1995).

In the eyes of the federal government, Native American have a different status than other minorities. They are viewed as a conquered people, poor unfortunates who must be protected, rather than independent citizens. They suffer from a variety of health problems, among which are high blood pressure, obesity, diabetes, lactose intolerance, alcoholism, cirrhosis of the liver, and tuberculosis. Although Native Americans have a lower than average risk for the three major killers of Americans—heart disease, cancer, and stroke—the high rate of other diseases and accidents during young and middle adulthood results in the shortest life span of all minority groups. Compared with a 70% rate for other Americans, only 42% of Native Americans reach age 65 (Singh et al., 1996).

Another problem confronting Native Americans is the multiplicity of languages (250 in all) spoken by the 400 tribal groups (Edwards, 1983). Moreover, the different lifestyles of the four major groups of Native Americans according to area of residence—reservation, rural, migrant, and urban—interact with tribal traditions and values.

On the whole, Native Americans are quite tolerant of what may seem to a white person as strange or idiosyncratic behavior. However, they are intolerant of greedy, selfish, or materialistic behavior of the sort in which they perceive most whites as engaging. The Native American conception of nature and humanity emphasizes their interdependence, and that human beings should be responsible for, rather than dominating, nature. Unlike the linear concept of time followed in technologically oriented cultures, Native Americans perceive events as being repetitious and circular. The seasons, for example, are continuous and alternating. Who is to tell which comes first: winter or spring? One follows the other, as in a circle. Even more than African-Americans, Native Americans have experienced great difficulty in adapting to Anglo-American culture, which is based on ideas and procedures that are so foreign to their traditional culture (Gonzalez, 1993).

Racial Discrimination

One of the thorniest problems throughout American history has been that of prejudice and discrimination against minorities. *Racism*, the belief that certain racial groups are inferior to others and should therefore be treated as such, is, of course, not indigenous to the United States. Subjugation, slavery, and other methods of discrimination by race are as old as human history and have occurred in many different countries and cultures.[2] But it is in the United States, where equality of opportunity and democracy have been eloquently preached but less often practiced, that racism has become more of a cause célèbre.

Put into effect after the Civil War as a compromise between Northern and Southern beliefs and interests, the doctrine of separate but equal facilities for whites and blacks was effective in maintaining a semblance of order and racial harmony for three generations. However, the illusion of "separate but equal" was shattered by the civil rights movement of the 1950s and 1960s and ensuing federal legislation. These laws and other efforts were designed to promote peaceful integration between the races, but discrimination and de facto segregation persist in many walks of life. African-American workers are still concentrated in less desirable blue-collar jobs and receive the lowest incomes. They live in the poorest neighborhoods, have the lowest percentage of home ownership, the lowest level of education, poorer health and sanitation, but a higher arrest rate than average. The middle-class values of education, hard work, and thrift, which are essential for getting ahead if one is not a gifted athlete, a star entertainer, or an adept criminal, are subscribed to by many minority families and taught to their children. Nevertheless, a large proportion of African-American families, in particular, remain at or below the poverty level in the central cities where they reside, inviting invidious comparisons between their own material circumstances and those of the "typical" white family living in a posh suburban home or as featured in many television programs. The lawlessness encouraged by a materialistic society polarized by "haves" and "have-nots" and the breakdown of the family structure have led to frequent confrontations and occasional riots in which African-Americans are pitted against the white establishment and its enforcers—the police.

Government programs, such as Aid to Families with Dependent Children (AFDC),[3] Social Security, SSI, and food stamps, have helped provide a minimal standard of living for many minorities, but the effects of these and other federal "giveaways" on the motivation and self-esteem of their recipients

---

[2]Even more extreme than slavery is *genocide*, the systematic extermination of a particular racial or ethnic group.

[3]It is maintained by some political conservatives that AFDC creates a class of poor people who see generating babies as a way of generating income as well. However, there is no evidence that high AFDC benefits operate as an incentive for fertility.

have been increasingly questioned. The situation for minorities is, however, demonstrably better than it was prior to the 1960s. As seen in the atmosphere surrounding the O. J. Simpson trials of 1996–1997, there are still differences in the ways in which blacks and whites view the world. For the most part, however, the two major ethnic groups appear to have established something of a *modus vivendi*—a mutual existence arrangement in which greater interracial tolerance is expressed in attitudes and behavior.

Education and employment, which are passports to greater influence and power in the wider society, have become less discriminatory but still have some distance to go. Racial stereotypes are less common, and interracial friendships, dating, and marriage have increased. Young adult members of minority groups of today certainly have more opportunities than they did prior to the civil rights era. At least, college-educated blacks no longer have to settle for jobs as porters on passenger trains, as they often did in the 1930s and 1940s.

Obviously, we have not reached a point in this society where we all love each other and can look upon all people as "brothers" and "sisters." But we seem to have adopted the recommendation made by Dr. Ralph Bunch some years ago: We are becoming more and more able to tolerate and even respect other races and ethnic groups on even terms. Better jobs, more political power, and greater material benefits should not only provide cohesion within but also less conflict between the races.

Equally encouraging is the fact that African-Americans have become less self-deprecating and are taking greater pride in their ethnicity. In the past, African-Americans have frequently viewed themselves as less competent, less responsible, and less valuable as human beings and citizens than whites (Ziajka, 1972). Furthermore, Mexican-American children born in the United States have stereotyped themselves as being more authoritarian, emotional, indifferent, lazy, proud, and less ambitious and scientific than those born in Mexico (Derbyshire, 1968). Such self-stereotypes need to change if people of all ethnic groups are to obtain some semblance of equality.

Despite cutbacks in federal programs targeted toward lower-income groups, efforts by both the public and private sectors to improve the living conditions of disadvantaged people will continue. Those who work with these groups will be more effective if they develop a greater awareness and understanding of the culture and traditions of the people whom they serve and learn the language or dialect in which they communicate. This is especially true when dealing with older adults who were not born in this country and are not proficient in the English language or knowledgeable about Anglo-American culture.

SOCIAL CLASS AND STATUS

Unlike the traditional culture of India, the United States has no system of social castes into which individuals are born and cannot escape. However, like other societies and even many animal species (e.g., DeVore, 1973), people in our society are evaluated and accorded status in terms of their appearance, skills, possessions, and group membership. *Social status* is related to a host of biological, cognitive, and affective variables, as well as demographic variables such as ethnicity and chronological age.

"Yankee City" Studies

It has been over 50 years since Warner and Lunt (1941) conducted their classic study of social class in a New England town fictitiously labeled "Yankee City." The researchers asked the citizens of Yankee City to rate the social status of their fellow citizens on the following variables: whether their incomes were salary, commission, or dividend; birth and family genealogy; memberships in social organizations; kind and location of residence; moral standing. An analysis of these ratings revealed three major social classes— upper, middle, and lower, each with an upper and a lower subdivision. People in the upper-upper, lower-upper, and upper-middle classes were perceived as being above the common people; those in the lower-middle and upper-lower classes were the level of the common people; those in the lower-lower class were below the level of the common people. The upper-uppers were old, established families whose wealth was inherited, whereas the wealth of the lower-uppers had been acquired more recently (the *nouveau riche*). The upper-middle class was made up of professionals and other financially solid, social-climbing citizens, and the lower-middle class was composed of small businessmen and some skilled workers. Semiskilled workers, small traders, and other steadily employed, poor-but-respectable people comprised the upper-lower class. And at the bottom, in the lower-lower class, were itinerants, migrants, and other "nonrespectable" people.

Four Social Classes

Although social researchers now generally classify people according to *socioeconomic status* rather than *social class*, those who employ the latter designation typically employ four categories—the upper, middle, working, and lower (poor) classes. The largest of these is the working class, followed by the middle class. Upper-class children attend private schools and the "best" private universities, where they are trained to be leaders in the nation's institutions. They tend to live privately, associating with people of their own class and engaging in activities that are more or less out of public view.

A large percentage of upper middle-class people tend to be college-educated professionals, managers, and other "paper-pushers" who maintain the records, make the computations, and control much of the nation's business. On the other hand, those in the lower-middle class tend to perform routine clerical, skilled blue-collar, and service work. Middle-class families

---

My Life 8–1

Social Status in Our Community

The South Florida community where I grew up had some small industry, but its economy was based primarily on farming and ranching. A handful of residents were fairly well to do, though most were working class or lower class. The children with whom I went to school were the sons and daughters of farmers, crate mill and canning-plant workers, and shopkeepers. Those were the days before the influx of migrant workers to the Sunshine State, and the vast majority of residents were fairly permanent.

Social class differences among the people in our community were not great. Most of the schoolchildren wore cotton clothes and assorted hand-me-downs to school. My mother made certain that my clothes were clean and not overalls or dungarees, which were a sure sign of lower class status. Although children went barefoot at home, everyone was required to don some sort of footwear at school. It would be three decades before denim and bare feet would become fashionable among middle-class students.

The children in our elementary school had an abundance of health problems, including such disorders as ringworm, tapeworm, pinworm, lice, and "ground itch." Every month or so we had to bring stools to school, and not the kind you sit on. However, the kids were tough little buggers, and very few of them died. Their physical prowess in fighting and general derring-do was also attested to by the multiple abrasions and contusions they proudly sported. On more than one occasion, I had a pugilistic appointment after school, once in response to a kid having flicked "cooties" at me during class.

The high failure rate at our school resulted in many teenage boys being stuck in the third or fourth grade for years. On one occasion, when I was challenged by a gang intent on revenge because I had answered too many questions in class, I enlisted the body-guarding services of one of these giants. My bodyguard, who had promoted himself as "140 pounds of walking hell" eventually dropped out of school before reaching junior high. I often wonder if he ever regretted having been denied the pleasure of studying algebra.

There were numerous indicators of social-class status among the residents of our community. In general, less affluent people drove and worked on old Fords and Chevrolets, chain-smoked Old Gold cigarettes or rolled their own with Bugler, hunted squirrels and rabbits, fished and harvested oys-

---

stress the necessity of planning, preparing, and "getting ahead," and are generally healthy and happy.

The semiskilled and unskilled blue-collar and service workers in the working class find life and labor fairly demanding and uncertain. Rather than aspiring for higher status, their emphasis is on not losing ground. Working-

ters in our polluted river, watched or participated in car races, and went to carnivals, circuses, and medicine shows. The "medicine" that was hawked at these shows was advertised as curing everything from arthritis to zoophobia, but usually cured nothing but sobriety.

On Saturday or Sunday, working-class people who could stand and walk attended the Pentecostal Holiness, Church of God, or Seventh-Day Adventist churches. Lower-middle class churchgoers typically went to the Baptist, Methodist, and Presbyterian churches. Although we were nominal Methodists, on occasion my grandfather decided to be a "Home Methodist" for that Sunday because he didn't have a dollar to put in the collection plate. On those Sunday mornings, I would either stand outside the African Methodist Episcopal Church and listen longingly to the music or attend the "Holy Roller" Church with a friend. I had a great time yelling out the hymns, speaking in tongues, flailing about, and running up and down and rolling in the aisles. Kids in our church did their best to pass the time during the service, kicking the seats and picking at each other, adding "under the bed" after all the hymn titles, snickering when the collection plate contained only a few cents, and fanning furiously to cope with the heat. Our minister became so incensed by all the fanning that he periodically stopped and ordered the congregation to desist. As an afterthought, he would add: "If you think it's hot here, just wait 'till you get to where most of you are going!" One young man of my acquaintance rose from his seat, shouted "What the hell am I doing here!," and never darkened the church door again.

Although the "F" word was not employed nearly as frequently as it is today, people used "ain't," double negatives, dangling participles, mixed metaphors, and lots of vernacularisms referring to the process of elimination. In addition, there was always much misinformed sex talk and a substantial amount of drinking among my lower-class acquaintances. Although my father was the manager of the local Postal Telegraph, and hence we would probably pass for middle class, my family was quite friendly and neighborly with our social inferiors. Their liking for us may have been due in part to the fact that my father was generous in loaning $5.00 on Monday to workers who were paid on Friday but had no money on Monday and needed a bottle to tide them over until the following Friday.

Having been spoiled by modern conveniences, I really have no desire to return to those "good old days." But they really weren't so bad. I cultivated a lot of friendships and learned something about sociocultural differences and tolerance. I also managed to obtain a fair education in classrooms, fields, and closets despite all the distractions and adventures.

class people tend to suffer more health problems than those in the middle and upper classes, and they are often forced to rely on SSI and other assistance to supplement their inadequate income and retirement benefits. Employed persons in the lowest social class, often referred to as "the poor, who are always with us," work at unskilled or semiskilled jobs such as custodian ("janitor"), dishwasher, household worker, and farm laborer. Lacking an adequate education and a proper upbringing for "getting ahead," their work is often irregular, and they must rely on public benefits in old age and even before in order to survive. The children of both working-class and poor people learn quite early that life and the fruits of one's labors are often unpredictable.

Social-Class Differences in Behavior

The higher a person's social class or socioeconomic status is seen as being, the greater his or her social prestige and expectation on the part of other people that the person is more knowledgeable and possesses habits and attitudes that are different from those of the common folk. Though there is a great deal of variability among the behaviors of individuals in a particular social class, there are significant between-class differences as well. Some social scientists have characterized persons of lower social status as behaving according to the "philosophy of immediate gratification," and those of higher social status as behaving according to the "philosophy of delayed gratification." Because the socioeconomic status of Asian- and Caucasian-Americans is generally higher than that of African- and Hispanic-Americans, ethnicity should be taken into account in interpreting the results of studies of behavioral differences between social classes. To the extent that attitudes, values, and expectations differentiate between people of upper and lower social status, they are most certainly shaped by differences in child-rearing practices. In any event, middle-class children are seen as striving primarily for the sake of succeeding and without the necessity of immediate material rewards, whereas the reverse is true of lower-class children. This is the reason, it is argued, that middle-class children are more likely that lower-class children to succeed in school, where rewards are less tangible and more delayed.

Differences also exist between the behaviors and attitudes of upper, middle, and lower-class adults. For example, greater percentages of people in the middle and upper social classes hold conservative viewpoints on political issues, and hence are more apt to vote Republican than those in the lower social classes (Lazarsfeld, Berelson, & Gaudet, 1944). Violence and mental illness are also more common in the working and lower classes than in the middle and upper classes. Personal health and happiness, however, are higher in members of higher social classes (Berger, Cohen, & Zelditch, 1973; Markides et al., 1990; Srole, Langer, Michael, Opler, & Rennie, 1962).

AGEISM

Old bag, bat, battle ax, biddy, bird, crow; dirty old buzzard, coot, codger, fogy, fossil, fuddy-duddy, geezer, goat; crock, turkey, dirt ball. These are just some of the terms that have been used to refer to elderly women and men.

Occasionally, positive terms such as *mature, mellow, distinguished*, and even *venerable* are applied to older adults, but all too seldom (Nuessel, 1982). The generalized application of such terms for elderly people is illustrative of *ageism*, which Robert Butler (1974, p. 11) defined as

> a process of systematic stereotyping of and discrimination against people because they are old—just as racism and sexism can accomplish this with skin color and gender. Old people are categorized as senile, rigid in thought and manner, old fashioned in morality and skills. Ageism allows the younger generation to see older people as different from themselves. Thus they subtly cease to identify with their elders as human beings.

Perhaps the most powerful agent that encourages ageism in the United States is television (Bell, 1992). Traditionally, elderly people have been stereotyped on television as comical, eccentric, foolish, and stubborn. More recently, portrayals of elderly people on television have become more positive—as affluent, free from health problems, mentally quick, socially sensitive, active, and independent. But even these positive depictions are inaccurate representations of elderly people in general. Such *positive ageism*, as it has been labeled by Palmore (1990), overlooks the problems of poverty, illness, and loneliness that occur among many older Americans.

Ageism is more common in youth-oriented cultures such as ours than in China, Japan, or other Asian countries that have a long tradition of respect for age and the aged. Even Shakespeare was not immune to describing old age in stereotyped, quasi-humorous poetry, but during the latter part of the nineteenth century, the labeling of older people with pejorative terms become more fashionable (Covey, 1988). In recent decades, negative stereotyping of older adults—in plays, films, and stories—has increased in frequency. Even the victims of these slurs and jokes sometimes joined in poking fun at their age-mates, exempting themselves, of course, from such stereotypes. Older people have been depicted as senile or as experiencing a second childhood, as rigid or inflexible, sexless, unattractive, chronically ill, and fit only to live in nursing homes.

Ageism is not limited to adults. Even young children, who, incidentally, may also make racist and sexist comments, complain about having to be around old people. In an interview study conducted by Serock, Seefeldt, Jantz, and Galper (1977), children between the ages of 2 and 11 described the elderly as "wrinkled, short, and gray-haired" people who "chew funny," "don't go out much," "sit around all day and watch TV in their rocking chairs," and "have heart attacks and die." When asked how they felt about growing old themselves, all but a few of the children stated that they simply did not want to do it.

Children, of course, learn these stereotypes from each other and from adults. Among the reasons for such stereotyping on the part of young adults are job competition between the young and the old, problems with one's own parents and other older relatives, association of old age with dying, a way of distancing themselves from the physical signs of aging and increased dependency, or any other reason that makes them feel threatened by older people (Hendricks & Leedham, 1980; Kite, Deaux, & Miele, 1991). Whatever the cause may be, ageism is based on inaccurate and overgeneralized information. On the whole, older people view themselves as less lonely, in better health, and more useful than they are perceived by other adults (Harris & Associates, 1981). Most older Americans are fairly optimistic about their lives and want to remain active and even gainfully employed.

If ageism were merely an attitude and not expressed in the treatment of older adults, it would be of less concern than it actually is. As with sexism and racism, however, ageism is manifested in the behavior of society toward older adults, and most particularly in employment contexts. Historically, older workers have been characterized as slower; less able to learn new skills; more prone to accidents; less able to get along with coworkers and customers; more resistant to supervision and change; more likely to miss work; slower in making judgments; lower in speed, strength, and endurance; less motivated; more stubborn and overcautious (Rhodes, 1983; Sparrow & Davies, 1988). When members of management believe these unproved assumptions, they are more likely to discriminate against older workers in making personnel decisions. Research involving managerial ratings of older workers has painted a more favorable picture (American Association of Retired Persons, 1989; Blocklyn, 1987), and other studies have shown that older workers generally do as well as younger workers (Salthouse, 1982). Older adults may have a lower work-output volume than younger adults, but their work is generally of higher quality and performed with less wasted effort and fewer mistakes (Hurlock, 1980). Older workers are also quite capable of learning new jobs, and their experience can compensate for age-related declines in the speed or strength of their performance (Rhodes, 1983; Stagner, 1985).

The civil rights atmosphere of the 1960s led not only to legislation requiring equal treatment of the races and sexes but also mandated equal treatment by age. For example, the federal Age Discrimination in Employment act of 1967 (ADEA) banned the use of age as a criterion in hiring, firing, promotion, training, retirement, working conditions, referral by employment agencies, job announcements, or any action taken against a person with regard to compensation, conditions, or privileges of employments. This act legally prohibits employers from hiring or discharging job applicants on the basis of age alone, or segregating or classifying them in any way that is detrimental to their performance or well-being. Exempt from the provisions of this act are the federal government, employers of less than 20 people, and jobs on which there is a *bona fide occupational qualification* (*BFOQ*). Examples of the latter are jobs requiring extraordinary degrees of speed, strength, agility, and alertness, such as firefighter or law enforcement officer. In addition, airline pilots over age 60 are prohibited from flying commercial airplanes. Even on these jobs, however, employers must demonstrate that age makes a critical difference in performance.

SUMMARY

This chapter is concerned with four demographic characteristics of social groups: gender, race/ethnicity, social class, and age. Stereotyping and discrimination based on these characteristics are fairly widespread and have been the subject of a substantial amount of research. The frequency of sexism, racism, and ageism, in particular, has also prompted legislation designed to ensure equal rights to individuals, regardless of their group membership. Such legislation has been directed at employment, education, living environments, and other activities, organizations, and privileges of American citizens.

There is a wide range of physical and mental differences between the sexes, but few, if any, of these differences can serve as a justification for sex discrimination, Furthermore, sex differences in cognition and personality traits are due in large measure to social stereotyping of sex-appropriate behavior and consequent differential reinforcement and modeling of children by their parents and other people. In general, women are socialized to be more interdependent, finding identity and self-esteem in positive relationships with other people. Men, on the other hand, are socialized to be independent, finding identity and self-esteem in individual achievement and from the control and management of their lives and those of others.

The women's movement and legal action against sex discrimination have led to a decline in sex discrimination in the workplace, but working women are still disadvantaged in comparison with working men. Sexism on the job has abated somewhat, though a *glass ceiling*, or barrier to advancement of women, continues to exist in many occupations. One result of legal attention to gender discrimination in the workplace has been the concept of *comparable worth*, in which pay is equalized in occupations judged to be equally important even though the relative numbers of men and women employees on those jobs are quite different. Another legal concept, the *reasonable woman standard*, has emerged from cases involving alleged sexual harassment at work.

For the most part, European immigrants to the United States were successfully acculturated and assimilated into Anglo-American society, but African-American and Asian immigrants had a more difficult time integrating with the mainstream. Social discrimination is more common among people who have different physical characteristics, such as skin color, from the dominant white majority. Differences in language and culture have also created barriers to full integration by minorities. These factors, combined with certain historical events, have led to discrimination against blacks, Hispanics, and Asians in this country. Asians were more successful in gaining a foothold in the United States and participating in its material wealth than blacks and Hispanics. The last two minorities, which are the largest in number, are below the national average in income, education, health, and many other contributors to the quality of life. The discrimination experienced by African-Americans and Hispanic-Americans may be viewed as either the cause or the effect of these conditions. One thing that is clear, however, is that affirmative action in the workplace and educational institutions has improved the lot of many members of these minority groups. Despite a number of important disadvantages, the close-knit family structure of minority groups is a definite plus for their members.

Native Americans have the lowest status of any minority in this country and have experienced more difficulty than other minorities in adapting to mainstream American life. In addition to having less income than other minorities, Native Americans suffer from a variety of health problems and the shortest life span of all ethnic groups. Although they are smaller in terms of population than any other minority group, the hundreds of Indian tribes and the many languages spoken by them, as well as variations in tribal cultures and lifestyles, have added to the problems experienced by Native Americans as a group.

The most glaring contradiction between American ideals and practices is racism, the belief that some races are naturally inferior to others. The civil rights movement exposed racism to public scrutiny and led to legal reforms in the treatment of minorities but did not abolish it. Racial prejudice and discrimination in this country have abated to some extent, but they continue to exist in more subtle forms. Many African-Americans, in particular, continue to have problems in coping with the predominantly white power structure and obtaining their portion of the American dream. Be that as it may, the economic condition and the social treatment of African-Americans and other ethnic groups is demonstrably better than it was prior to the 1960s.

There is no denying the existence of differences between the attitudes and lifestyles of the rich and famous and those of ordinary mortals. But the idea that there are distinct social classes in America, each with a unique pattern of behavior and little mobility between them, is not a viable one. Certainly, the moral behavior of the British royal family and our own political, economic, and social leaders reveals that, regardless of the magnitude of their wealth and popularity, people of all backgrounds and socioeconomic status share the same motivations and shortcomings.

Ageism, the stereotyping of and discrimination against people because of their age, has not prompted as much social and legal action as racism and sexism, but the economic and health problems of older Americans have led to increases in Social Security benefits and legislation designed to ensure adequate medical care and equal employment opportunities for older Americans. Today's older adults are healthier and more affluent than ever before, and most Americans would like to keep them that way.

SUGGESTED READINGS

Aiken, L. R. (1995). *Aging: An introduction to gerontology* (Ch. 8). Newbury Park, CA: Sage.

Barer, B. M. (1994). Men and women aging differently. *International Journal of Aging and Human Development, 38,* 29–40.

Gonzalez, M. C. (1993). Native American perspectives on the lifespan. In R. Kastenbaum (Ed.), *Encyclopedia of adult development* (pp. 360–364). Phoenix, AZ: Oryx Press.

Huyck, M. H. (1990). Gender differences in aging. In J. E. Birren & K. W. Schaie (Eds.), *Handbook of the psychology of aging* (3rd ed., pp. 124–132). San Diego: Academic Press.

Jackson, J. S., Antonucci, T. C., & Gibson, R. C. (1990). Cultural, racial, and ethnic minority influences on aging. In J. E. Birren & K. W. Schaie (Eds.), *Handbook of the psychology of aging* (3rd ed., pp. 103–123). San Diego: Academic Press.

Kastenbaum, R. (1993). Gender as a shaping force in adult development and aging, In R. Kastenbaum (Ed.), *Encyclopedia of adult development* (pp. 165–170). Phoenix, AZ: Oryx Press.

Leonard, F., & Loeb, L. (1992, January). Heading for hardship: The future of older women in America. *USA Today Magazine*, pp. 19–21.

Palmore, E. B. (1993). Japanese perspectives on adult development. In R. Kastenbaum (Ed.), *Encyclopedia of adult development* (pp. 258–261). Phoenix, AZ: Oryx Press.

Stevenson, M. R. (Ed.). (1994). *Gender roles through the life span.* Muncie, IN: Ball State University.

Taeuber, C. M. (1993, September). Women in our aging society: Golden years or increased dependency? *USA Today Magazine*, pp. 42–44.

Tavris, C. (1992). *The mismeasure of woman.* New York: Simon & Schuster.

Wass, H. (1993). Gender differences in the workplace. In R. Kastenbaum (Ed.), *Encyclopedia of adult development* (pp. 171–174). Phoenix, AZ: Oryx Press.

CHAPTER 9

Living Environments

We human beings are acquisitive creatures. We acquire knowledge, skills, friends, pets, spouses, children, and material things of all kinds. Many of us like to collect objects—large and small, or at least feel that we could have them if we wanted to. We may fill our lives with objects that we continually examine, admire, fondle, embellish, think about, and talk about. Our dearest possessions become a part of us—an extension of ourselves—and make us feel important, attractive, and perhaps even immortal.

Though many people are content to collect small things, such as rings, tools, or knickknacks, individuals of all ages also desire and cherish automobiles, houses, properties, and other large objects. By making us feel independent, safe, significant, and free, these possessions may literally "become" us and serve as the external manifestations of who and what we are.

Human beings are also territorial creatures. Territoriality, of course, is a part of acquisitiveness. The property in this case is the yard, farm, block, neighborhood, city, and perhaps even the state and country where we live. These places make up our life spaces, immediate and extended. As with our other possessions, we are fond of our territory, consider ourselves a part of it and it a part of us. Consequently, most of us would be prepared to defend it if the need arose.

This chapter is about the places in which people live, why they chose those places, and what they do in them. The major portion of the chapter is concerned with housing, whether it is owned, rented, or merely "borrowed." But a house is not necessarily a home, and how long we remain in a particular residence depends not only on whether we can survive and flourish there but also what the physical and social environments in which the residence is located mean to us.

LOCATION AND RELOCATION

Living environments consist not only of the dwellings in which people reside but also the neighborhoods or communities in which they live, work, and play. The places in which people settle and stay provide the wherewithal

---

My Life 9–1

Houses

It seems to me as if I have spent most of my life in houses. When I was a boy, we lived for a while in a yellow frame house across from a schoolhouse, which was convenient when I wanted to use the playground equipment. Later, we moved to a farmhouse with no electricity or plumbing. There were kerosene lamps to read and work by at night, but everyone still went to bed pretty early. We collected rainwater in a big tank and dug an artesian well, so we didn't die of thirst and stayed relatively clean. We washed our dirty clothes in a big black hotpot, hung them on a clothes line to dry, and then pressed them with a heated flatiron. We also built an outhouse about 30 yards from the main house, which was somewhat inconvenient when it rained or one of us was in a hurry. On experiencing a natural emergency, I would charge out the back door at full speed, throwing stones at the gobbler that chased me all the way to the outhouse. The following Thanksgiving, when we ate the turkey, everyone wondered why it was so bruised.

My family finally grew tired of the farmhouse and lived in a succession of apartment houses and single-story houses in towns and cities. One of these was next to a firehouse, which was great fun except when we wanted to sleep. After being awakened abruptly by the fire alarm late one night, we jumped out of bed and ran out into the street yelling "Fire!"

When I grew old enough to go away to college, I lived in a fraternity house supervised by a housemother who made us clean house frequently. After receiving my master's degree, I worked for a time in a mental hospital, known variously as a "bug house," "nut house," or "crazy house." Eventually, I decided to get married, and my wife and I set up housekeeping in a brick ranch house. We also bought a doghouse and housebroke the dog, but decided not to get a cat or bird house. Our house payments were fairly modest, less than $100 a month, so my salary as a criminal psychologist in the local jailhouse, where the residents were under fairly permanent house arrest and most assuredly not house proud, was adequate. My wife eventually became a housemother herself, but elected not to keep house all the time and went to work in a schoolhouse.

Realizing that a house is not necessarily a home, I now use the latter term to refer to the place where I live. Because I am no longer gainfully employed, I suppose that one might refer to it as my retirement home. It's probably better than a nursing home, but I'll have to wait and see before making a final judgment.

---

for satisfying their physical, social, and psychological needs. In these places, people can express their personal tastes and preferences and, to some degree, exercise control over their environment (Scheidt, 1993). The environments in which people live for a long period of time, and especially during their formative years, typically exert strong shaping and conforming influences on the behavior of the inhabitants and help guide their activities throughout childhood and adulthood. This is especially true of small towns, which exert a more intimate influence in encouraging place attachment.

In most cases, the living environment is sufficiently supportive of the needs of people to make them want to stay. The network consisting of family, friends, medical facilities, schools, jobs, stores, and other people and organizations should provide the necessary support systems for individual growth, productivity, and happiness. Sometimes, however, the environment or the individual changes in such a way that there is no longer a good match between what the individual requires or desires and what the physical or psychological environment of a community has to offer.

Throughout history, people have been continually on the move, seeing opportunity or safety over the next hill, the next mountain, or across the next plain or ocean. However, the great historical migrations rarely involved a majority of the population. Then, as now, most people preferred to "stay put," being less attracted by the adventure and opportunity of new places and things than frightened and repelled by the uncertainty and danger of the unknown.

Geographical Location

As illustrated in Figures 9–1 and 9–2, the geographical distribution of the adult population of the United States varies with chronological age. The most populated and fastest-growing region is the South, and the smallest population is found in the Northeast. Of course, the population of a given geographical area is related to its area, so the most populated place is not necessarily the most densely populated. Of the 50 states, California has the largest population, with Texas second, and New York third. California and Texas, along with Florida, are the most rapidly growing states in terms of population and are projected to retain their positions well into the next century. Due largely to the migration of older adults from New York, Canada, and other northern climes, Florida is fourth in the nation in overall population but second in the number of older adults. Florida gains 7 thousand new human residents every day, much larger than the number of new alligators! Arizona, California, and Texas also attract sizable numbers of retirees and other older adults. Migration to the Sunbelt has declined somewhat in recent years, but the number of people in the South and West is growing at a more rapid rate than in other areas of the country and is expected to continue doing so for the next 25 years or so (U.S. Bureau of the Census, 1995).

In 1995, the percentage of the population living in metropolitan areas[1] varied only slightly with chronological age, decreasing from a high of 82% of the 25–34 year age group to a low of 74% of the over-85 age group. Ninety-two

[1]A geographical region in the United States is defined as a *metropolitan statistical area* (*MSA*) if it includes a city of at least 50,000 population or a Census Bureau–defined urbanized area of at least 50,000, with a total metropolitan population of at least 100,000 (75,000 in New England) (Saluter, 1996).

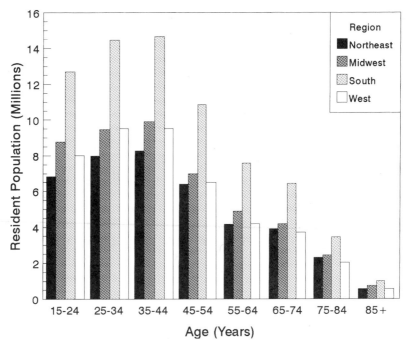

Figure 9–1   U.S. population by age and geographical region. (Prepared from published data in Saluter, 1996.)

percent of Hispanics, 86% of blacks, and 77% of non-Hispanic whites lived in metropolitan areas (Saluter, 1996). Among minority groups, larger percentages of blacks and Hispanics live in the South, whereas larger percentages of Asians, Pacific Islanders, Native Americans, Eskimos, and Aleuts live in the West. Of these, the Asian/Pacific Islander group is projected to be the fastest growing of all minority groups during the next quarter of a century. The American Indian, Eskimo, and Aleut populations will reportedly be second. The black population is growing at the most rapid rate in all regions of the United States except the West, where the Hispanic population is growing faster than any other minority. With respect to age, it is anticipated that the proportion of young adults in the population will decline and the proportion of older adults will increase in the next two or three decades (U.S. Bureau of the Census, 1995).

Relocation

Every year during the early 1990s, approximately one in six Americans changed residences. Two-thirds of these were local moves, from one resi-

Age (Years)

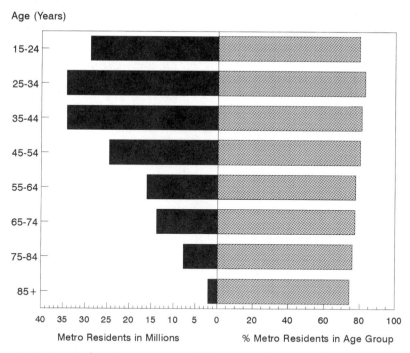

Figure 9–2   Number and percentage of U.S. metropolitan population by age group. (Prepared from published data in Saluter, 1996.)

dence to another in the same county. Of the remainder, approximately equal numbers were in-state and out-of-state. It is estimated that, during his or her lifetime, the average American moves about 12 times. Blacks and Hispanics move more often than whites, a statistic that is related to the lower median age of blacks and Hispanics than whites (Hansen, 1995). As might be expected, renters have much higher rates of moving than homeowners. This is true whether the person is living in a housing unit occupied by owners or renters (U.S. Bureau of the Census, 1995).

The highest mobility rates are found in adults in their twenties and early thirties, and their young children (U.S. Bureau of the Census, 1995). Adults in this age range move, on average, at least once every 2 years. This is the career entry and advancement, family-starting phase of life, a period when young adults seek opportunity and economic stability outside their home communities. A large percentage of these young adults migrate from small towns to large cities, where job advancement and business opportunities are greater. Unfortunately, the out-migration of young people from towns to larger cities, and the subsequent decline of the towns, has a debilitating economic effect on older residents in particular. Older people who have resided in towns for much of their lives may have appreciable economic and personal investment in their homes and communities, and the decline hits them especially hard (Norris-Baker & Scheidt, 1994).

Older adults are generally less mobile than young and middle-aged adults, spending most of their time in their home environment. Only about 10–15% want to move from their current homes, and most of those who do expect to be closer to their families. Those who are forced to move are typically tenants who cannot afford rising rents or otherwise have been displaced by redevelopment, eviction, or conversion of their places of residence to condominiums or apartments with rents too high for them (Kendig, 1990).

The rate of residential moves declines to about 5% for adults in their late seventies and early eighties. However, moves to retirement communities within- and out-of-state, in addition to nursing homes and other long-term-care institutions, cause a slight increase after then. Both the overall and local moving rates are higher for blacks and Hispanics than for whites, and higher for renters than for homeowners (Hansen, 1995).

The effects of relocation on the individual vary with age, personality, and a host of other factors. Understandably, involuntary or forced moves may be especially disruptive and upsetting. A home and neighborhood in which one has lived for a long time provides a feeling of security, structure, familiarity, and comfort. These are places that you know, with friendly people, good neighbors, and good memories (Sixsmith & Sixsmith, 1991).

Any move creates a certain amount of stress, depression, and even grief when the individual has lived there for an extended period of time, made friends, and become generally familiar with the community. Frequent moves punctuated by short stays can also have harmful effects on individuals and their families. On the other hand, a favorable new living environment can reduce the level of *relocation stress* fairly quickly. This is especially true when the move is voluntary, under the control of the mover, and familiar furnishings and mementos accompany the mover to the new place of residence (Scheidt, 1993).

Young adults and those with higher educational levels and social status are more likely to view moving to a new location as an opportunity and adjust to it better. In addition, people who have stronger social supports and a high proportion of same-age peers in the new community tend to cope with frequent moves more effectively than others. The physical characteristics of the new residence, including space, privacy, and convenience, are also quite important (Storandt, Wittels, & Botwinick, 1975).

As expected, local moves are less disturbing than long-distance out-migrations, but moves resulting in the loss of friends and surroundings to which one has become deeply attached can be quite disruptive. The degree to which family behavior patterns are disrupted, the personal loss at leaving one's former residence, and the distance involved in the move are all important factors in adjusting to it. The extent to which the move is under one's control and the reason or meaning of it also affect how it is perceived and reacted to. For example, moving an older adult from an accepting, supportive family environment to a nursing home is not generally viewed as a pleasant experience for anyone. These so-called *assistance migration* moves (Longino, 1990) occur when an older adult has no family to depend on for services or such severe disabilities that he or she can no longer be maintained in the family home.

Most older adults do not plan to move and reportedly do not want to move to another community or into the homes of relatives or friends (American Association of Retired Persons, 1996). They like where they live and prefer to stay there as long as possible. This is particularly true of older adults who own their own homes, but even those who rent may become attached to a neighborhood and feel that they belong there (American Association of Retired Persons, 1996). Unfortunately, many of the neighborhoods where older adults live are in central cities, replete with noise, traffic, litter, and high crime rates. Familiarity and habit, combined with lower than average incomes, keep older residents there.

For more affluent, and perhaps more flexible, older adults, a second type of migration, *amenity migration*, is available (Speare & Meyer, 1988). It occurs when an older adult changes residences in order to improve his or her lifestyle or to maintain a network of friends. This is the pattern followed by a small percentage of young-old mobile retirees who move either in- or out-of-state. The move may be temporary, as with the many New York-to-Florida winter *snowbirds* who fly or drive south in the winter and back north in the spring, or a relatively permanent transplantation to Florida, Texas, Arizona, or California. A third type of migration, *kinship migration*, is more prominent among some 65- to 74-year-olds and a larger percentage of over-75-year-olds who move every year to areas inhabited by their children or other close relatives (Longino, 1990). The number of older people who move in with or near their relatives increases significantly after the death of a spouse. This is particularly true of older widows, who are more likely to move in with a married daughter than a married son (Sussman, 1985). In addition, when an elderly parent needs day-to-day assistance, an unmarried adult child may move into the former's residence.

HOUSING

Americans have a wide array of housing arrangements. The majority reside in single-family dwellings, but many live in apartments, hotel rooms, mobile homes, and a few even live on boats. Finally, some Americans have no place at all they can call "home."

Homelessness

No one knows precisely how many homeless people there are in the United States, but estimates range from 250,000 to 2.5 million or more. Many people are homeless for a time—living in their cars, in tents, in the hills, on the beach, or in makeshift shelters—until they find more standard lodging. Others wander the streets, making their "rounds" by day, sleeping in alleyways, on buses and trains, on lawns, or even on the sidewalk at night. They may panhandle and sort through dumpsters and garbage cans for something to eat or otherwise use. Even those who migrate to warmer climes may seek temporary relief from the elements in a homeless shelter, especially when the weather is cold or wet, or when hunger and fear drive them there. Life on the streets can be quite stressful and very risky, so homeless people who wish to survive must remain ever-vigilant and canny.

A substantial percentage of homeless Americans, an estimated 25–30%, are over age 60 (Cohen, Teresi, Holmes, & Roth, 1988). Homelessness is, however, no respecter of age, and many teenagers and young adults live in the streets. Among the homeless are alcoholics, substance abusers, ex-mental patients, battered women, hustlers of all kinds, and other people who are down on their luck. In addition to both sexes (more men than women), all ethnic groups and educational levels are represented among the homeless population. Many have lost their jobs and cannot find employment or affordable housing, and many have simply stopped looking.

Federal, state, and local governments have programs for the homeless, but these programs are admittedly inadequate. Due to the scarcity of shelters in many cities, the homeless spend their lives in the streets, perhaps showing up for a free meal at Thanksgiving or Christmas but otherwise remaining fairly invisible to busy passersby. It is noteworthy that even those who are fortunate enough to find shelter and perhaps a semipermanent place to live confess to feeling a certain camaraderie with other street people. Thus, it may not be surprising to find that, like certain tribal or aboriginal groups who have been provided with more conventional shelter and sustenance, some homeless people who have "come in from the cold" sooner or later "go on walkabout" again.

Single-Room Occupants

A common living situation for poorer middle-aged and older adults in large cities is *single-room occupancy* (*SRO*) in residential hotels. These accommodations vary in quality depending on location, newness, and the clientele to which they cater. The most deteriorated type, the skid-row hotels located in the central city, house low-income, mostly male occupants. At the next level are the relatively clean, working-class hotels that provide housekeeping services and have primarily male occupants. At the highest level are the more comfortable and more expensive middle-class hotels, which have equal numbers of male and female occupants and provide some activities (Erickson & Ekert, 1977).

A typical single-room occupant of a skid-row hotel is a retiree, a welfare client, or an ex-mental patient. During the day, he or she may wander the streets, gathering with others of similar circumstances in large outdoor parks, bus terminals, or other sheltered public places, and hustling to provide some income. Most skid-row residents are fiercely independent, possess a high capacity for survival, and are proud of their hustling abilities. The facilities provided by the hotels to these occupants are barely adequate. Their meals tend to be sporadic, perhaps cooked on a makeshift hot plate fashioned from an electric iron wedged between two Bibles.

Age and Social Differences in Housing

As shown in Figure 9–3, the social context in which Americans live varies with chronological age. Over 70% of adult Americans live in family situations, with smaller percentages living alone or with nonrelatives. However, the percentage of adults who live with relatives declines and the percentage who live alone increases dramatically in old age. Living arrangements also vary with ethnic group, with larger percentages of Hispanics than blacks or whites living with relatives and smaller percentages living alone.

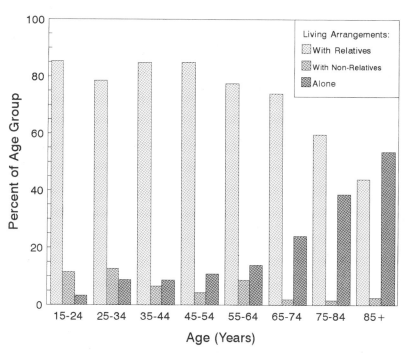

Figure 9–3   Percentages of three living arrangements in eight age groups. (Prepared from published data in Saluter, 1996.)

From 1970 to 1994, the percentage of family households declined by approximately 10%, while the percentage of nonfamily households increased by the same amount. The percentage of nonfamily households comprised of people who live alone also increased appreciably during this time period. The fact that large households are less common than in previous years is shown by the decline in the average household size from 3.14 in 1970 to 2.67 in 1994. Some of the decline in the average number of people per household can be attributed to the rise in single-parent families, the incidence of which is substantially higher among blacks than whites and higher for women than men (U.S. Bureau of the Census, 1995).

Establishing one's own home, whether it is a dormitory room, an apartment, a duplex, or a freestanding house, enhances a young adult's feelings of independence and freedom from parental control. These factors, in addition to privacy, comfort, accessibility, and attractiveness, may all contribute to the decision of when and were to set up housekeeping. However, for the majority of young adults, the critical factor is affordability.

Home Ownership

As represented in Figure 9–4, the percentage of adult Americans in particular age groups who own their own homes increases steadily from 10% in the 15- to 24-year-old age range to approximately 75% in the 75- to 84-year-old age group. The greatest rise in the number of householders occurs during the late forties to early fifties, when most American are well-established in their careers and families and are fairly secure financially.

A few decades ago, most young adults simply could not afford to move into their own homes. A large percentage of college students lived at home (30% still do), and single men and women who left home lived in rental quarters. However, the trend toward postponing marriage or deciding to remain single led many young adults to take the plunge into home purchasing. This decision was facilitated by adjustable-rate mortgages and balloon financing plans that made it possible to become a householder for a relatively low initial monthly payment. The payments increased over time, but by then, it was argued and expected, the young householder would be better able to afford them. Of course, it was usually necessary to make a sizable down payment as well, but relatives or commercial sources were willing to help out with that.

During the 1980s, the escalation of home costs and the shrinkage of the real-dollar incomes of adults in their late twenties and early thirties made it more and more difficult for them to establish independent households and duplicate the standard of living attained by their parents. Consequently, many young adults delayed their departure from the family stronghold or found themselves returning when they could no longer make financial ends meet.

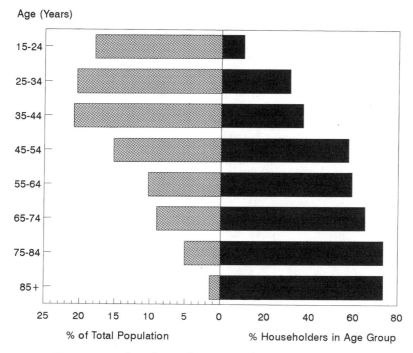

Age (Years)

% of Total Population   % Householders in Age Group

Figure 9–4 Percentage of total population and householders by age group. (Prepared from published data in Saluter, 1996.)

The sluggish housing market of the early 1990s caused many would-be homeowners to consider their purchases more carefully, but it did not stop them. People continued to buy even bigger and better homes. The acceleration of home ownership during middle adulthood (see Figure 9–4) was affected by the tendency to "trade up" to larger, more comfortable, and more convenient housing by mobile executives, professionals, and other traveling workers. Homeowners aged 55 or over, who had seen the value of their homes appreciate considerably, could sell them, with exemption from capital gains tax on the sale for up to $125,000.

Middle-aged adults, who want to live in places where they can rear their children and achieve greater occupational success and stability, are particularly interested in living accommodations that provide security, beauty, and a feeling of community. As they grow even older, convenience, ease of usage, safety, and security become even more important than they were in earlier years.

Home ownership varies not only with chronological age, but also with gender, ethnicity, place of residence, and other demographic variables. A greater percentage of whites than blacks, of blacks than Hispanics, and of males than females are home owners. This sex difference in home ownership is larger for whites than for any other ethnic group, but it is the reverse for blacks (Saluter, 1996). The rate of home ownership is lower inside than outside metropolitan areas, and higher in the suburbs than the central cities. It also varies with geographical region and state, being highest in Delaware and lowest in Hawaii (U.S. Bureau of the Census, 1994).

Housing of Older Adults

Compared with young and middle-aged adults, on the average older adults spend a smaller portion of their income on housing. The main reason is that a much larger percentage of older adults own their homes free and clear, though these homes are often of lower value than those of younger people. Furthermore, because their incomes are typically lower than those of homeowners, older adults who rent usually pay a higher percentage of their income for housing than other age groups. This is especially true of older residents in inner cities, who spend the largest portion of their monthly income on rent and utilities, followed by clothing, and only then by food.

Another characteristic of living arrangements of older adults is that a greater percentage of them live alone, many of whom are widows. Those who are physically and financially able to do so generally prefer this arrangement because it allows them to have more freedom and independence from their relatives or other housemates so they can do what the wish when they want to.

Whether they own or rent, and whether they live alone or with other people, older adults reside in a variety of dwellings—houses, apartments, hotels, modules, mobile homes, and so on—and facilities. Many of these dwellings are old, in disrepair, unclean, and unsafe. They tend to have fewer rooms and fewer amenities than the homes of younger and middle-aged adults. For the most part, the houses in which they live are in fairly sound condition, but the older ones tend to need repairs in plumbing, heating, electrical systems, and sewage disposal (Taeuber, 1993). Maintenance costs for leaking roofs, incomplete plumbing, kitchen facilities, and pest control tend to be high. Consequently, home repairs are not made as often as they should be, and remodeling is even less frequent. Some repairs and maintenance, such as roofing and plumbing, are *vital*, whereas others, such as kitchen and bathroom modernization, are *discretionary*. Discretionary remodeling of the home of an elderly person may include the installation of handrails in the hallways, grab bars in the bathroom areas, and adaptations to accommodate wheelchair access and sensory deficits that occur with aging.

Despite the expense of repair and remodeling, most elderly homeowners prefer not to move. This was one of the most salient findings of a recent telephone survey of Americans aged 50 and over (American Association of Retired Persons, 1996). In addition to indicating that they would like to stay in their homes and never move, a majority of the survey sample reported that they

1. Live in single-family, detached homes.
2. Own their own homes.
3. Live in households with one or more other people.
4. Are very satisfied with their housing and their neighborhoods.
5. Prefer to live in neighborhoods with people of all ages.
6. Prefer small-town and country life to living in cities or suburbs.
7. Have made very few modifications in their homes to deal with potential disabilities.
8. Would rather move to a care facility than move in with family members or friends if they were forced to move.
9. Have made few housing plans for the future.

According to Elias and Inui (1993), continuing to live in one's home reinforces the elderly person's feelings of "undiminished stature, sturdiness, functionality, permanence, and presence in the community" (p. 401). For this reason, it might seem as if cash-poor older homeowners would have opted for a *home equity conversion*. In this strategy, the value of the home, after subtracting any mortgage, is converted to cash to meet the person's living expenses. One type of home equity conversion is a *reverse annuity mortgage* (RAM), which lets a person who is 62 or older turn the equity in his or her home into cash without having to sell or move. The owner receives regular monthly payments for 3–10 years or as long as he or she lives in the home.[2] The loan is not repaid until the owner dies or sells the home, so he or she can remain there as long as long as desired and use the home as collateral for the loan. Another plan is a *sales leaseback*, in which the owner sells the home and leases it back from the purchaser for an indefinite time period. The owner now becomes a renter in what was previously his or her own home, and so is not responsible for taxes, repairs, maintenance, or property insurance. Although a high percentage of Americans aged 50 and over are apparently aware of RAMs and sales leasebacks, only about 3–6% have had any personal experience with home equity conversion or know anyone who has. A large majority indicate that they would not even consider such an arrangement (American Association of Retired Persons, 1996). The unpopularity of these mortgaging methods for defraying home expenses is undoubtedly due in some measure to the psychological factor of living in a home that one does not own. When zoning laws permit, other ways of meeting expenses, such as taking in boarders, are possibilities. However, they too are not popular with older adults.

The need for adequate housing of both older and younger adults of limited means has led to the development of programs designed to meet some of those needs. A number of programs are supervised by state and federal agencies such as the U.S. Department of Housing and Urban Development

---

[2]Information and assistance on obtaining government-backed reverse mortgages can be obtained free of charge from the U.S. Department of Housing and Urban Development.

(HUD) and the Department of Agriculture. The programs, most of which apply to Americans of all ages, are concerned with providing (1) financial incentives and assistance for refurbishing existing buildings and constructing new rental units; (2) subsidies for rental payments of lower income persons; (3) financial assistance in the form of block grants, low interest loans, and loan guarantees to cities, counties, and states to fund low-rent apartments; (4) tax incentives to investors in rental projects that allocate a certain percentage of the units to low-income families; and (5) assistance to homeless people who need emergency food and shelter (Golant, 1992).

Continuing-Care and Retirement Communities

A wide variety of arrangements for meeting the housing needs of older Americans have been devised. For the more socially oriented and physically capable, there is *shared housing* in which 5–15 unrelated people live together and share household expenses and chores. For those with a strong desire for privacy, an option is an *ECHO house*—a small, temporary living unit in the yard of another single-family dwelling. Another possibility that may work well as long as the resident continues to feel like a homeowner rather than a boarder or renter is an accessory apartment built by middle-aged adults in the home of an aging parent.

Depending on his or her physical condition and financial status, a older adult may decide to live in a congregate housing community, a continuing-care retirement community, or a retirement village. As a rule, the more active, less sociable orientation of men causes them to experience more difficulties in adjustment to relocation to age-segregated "retirement" or senior housing. Men often react with outright resistance, on the one hand, to resignation, on the other, when moving to a retirement home or long-term care facility (Barer, 1994).

Tenants in a *congregate housing community* have their own apartments but take their meals in a common dining room. This arrangement, which is appropriate for older adults with mild physical impairments, provides both housekeeping and security. Unfortunately, the increased dependency produced by having most of one's needs taken care of by someone else can lead to a more rapid deterioration and a decline in a person's competence level.

A greater range of services is provided by a *continuing-care retirement community* (CCRC) than offered by a congregate housing community. CCRC residents pay a sizable initial fee plus a monthly maintenance fee for food, rent, utilities, maid services, and nursing care. The residents, who are assured that their needs will be met as long as they live, are typically in their seventies, unmarried, childless, well-educated, and higher than average on the socioeconomic scale.

Although residents of congregate housing or CCRC communities may be characterized as "slow-go" (and some even "no-go"), most residents of retirement villages are definitely "go-go." Communities designed exclusively for adults developed initially after World War II and have blossomed in the southern and western regions of the United States in particular. Examples are Sun City near Phoenix, Leisure Worlds in California, Park West in Miami, and The Sequoias in San Francisco. Many retirement villages are quite luxurious, providing heated swimming pools, tennis courts, golf courses, bowling greens, restaurants, libraries, classrooms, medical clinics, closed-circuit television, and security guards, who patrol within the community walls around the clock. Of course, such luxury is not for everyone, even those who can afford it. Playing and relaxing, and no longer being a part of the business and bustle of the world, may become tedious and stultifying to capable, creative individuals. Furthermore, the perception of older people as flocking in large numbers to retirement communities is largely inaccurate. Only a small percentage of older people move to retirement communities. The great majority are interspersed among the general population consisting of all age groups.

Long-Term-Care Facilities

As people become very old, the incidence of both physical and mental disorders increases. This is particularly true for the 85-and-over segment of the population. About one-fourth of very old Americans require personal care and supervision in addition to room and board, but not continuing nursing care. For them, some form of group housing may meet their needs adequately, as seen in *residential care homes* or retirement homes.

Residents of residential care homes are not as ill as those in nursing homes and require less medical care. They are functionally independent people who need a clean, safe, and sheltered living environment that provides housekeeping, laundering, and meal services, as well as some medical care. Residential care homes usually have 25 beds or more, but some of the smaller ones often try to provide adequate care for residents who would be better off in an intermediate care facility or a nursing home. Similar in purpose, but somewhat closer to nursing homes in their functions, are *intermediate care facilities*. These facilities emphasize personal care service rather than intensive nursing care, catering to patients who need help with daily routines (eating, bathing, dressing, walking, etc.) but are not in severe distress. These facilities are often referred to as *assisted living residences*, which, depending on the resident, provide different amounts of living assistance and nursing care. In addition to nursing care, an assisted living residence through Marriott, Capson Living Quarters, and other organizations provides a private room, meals, housekeeping, and organized activities for an average cost of $2,160 per month. However, the cost may range up to $4,000 per month, a not inconsiderable sum. The financial burden is eased somewhat in states that allow Medicaid to cover part of the cost, and private health insurance may also pay a good portion. Additional information on assisted living residences can be obtained from the National Eldercare Locator (800-677-1116).

The provision of good care to patients who are in medical distress is the function of *nursing homes*. In 1995, there were 16,700 nursing homes in the United States, housing a total of 1,548,600 patients. Approximately 33% of the homes were in the Midwest, 33% in the South, and 17% each in the Northeast and West. Nearly 66% of the homes were proprietary, in that they were privately owned and expected to make a profit. Of the proprietary homes, 54.3% were run by chains and 45.5% by independents. One-fourth of the homes were voluntary, nonprofit institutions designed for patients with a specific religious, fraternal, or union affiliation. The remaining 8% or so were government nursing homes run by the federal government, individual states, or counties (Strahan, 1997).

The demographics of nursing home residents in 1995 are depicted in Figure 9–5. A large percentage of nursing home residents are older, white widows who are suffering from chronic physical illnesses and/or mental disorders. At one time in our history, it was the responsibility of the family to care for older relatives outside of institutions. But family members or friends who are willing and able to provide health support, supervision, and maintenance for their older relatives are not as common today as they once were.

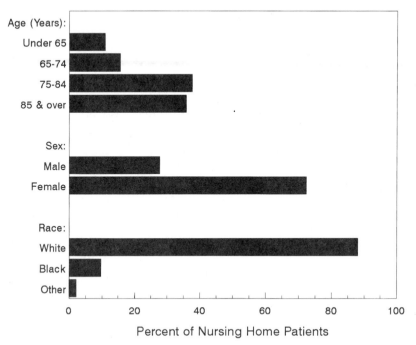

Figure 9–5   Demographics of nursing home patients in U.S. in 1995. (Prepared from published data in Strahan, 1997.)

Consequently, housing and care within institutions has become the most popular way of dealing with the problem of chronically ill and disabled older relatives.

The negative perception that society, and older adults in particular, have of nursing homes is due in part to the desire of older adults to remain with their families in familiar surroundings rather than being placed in an unfamiliar environment to be tended by strangers and await death. Accounts of unsanitary and unsafe conditions and inadequate treatment of patients by nursing home staff during the 1970s and 1980s prompted a number of investigations of the entire nursing home industry. One result of these investigations and the attendant publicity was passage of the Nursing Home Reform Act of 1987, containing a set of regulations that apply to all nursing home facilities. This legislation resulted in the gradual phasing out of the distinction between nursing homes and intermediate care facilities, and, more importantly, to a greater respect for patients' rights. Nursing home patients are now more likely to be treated as individuals who merit respect and should be permitted and encouraged to exert control over their environment. All too often in the past, nursing home patients have fallen into a psychological state of *institutionalism*, the symptoms of which are automatic behaviors, expressionless faces, general apathy, disinterest in personal appearance, and deteriorated morale. Interestingly enough, the survival rate among nursing home patients has been found to be related to a cluster of personality traits, including aggression, hostility, assertiveness, and narcissism (Tobin & Lieberman, 1976). These are the same traits that contribute to survival in a number of other stressful situations, such as living on the street or in prison.

Older adults who require daily nursing do not necessary reside in intermediate care facilities or nursing homes. *Adult day-care* (senior day-care) facilities are available in many communities to provide nutritional and nursing care, as well as medical monitoring for those who wish to continue living in their own homes. The expansion of *home health care agencies* during the past few years has also led to a decline in the number of older adults who are placed in residential care or nursing homes. The phenomenal growth of home health care agencies, which permit older adults to recover from illnesses at home rather than in a hospital or nursing home, has resulted from efforts to control health care costs, the introduction of medical technology that is more appropriate for home use, and governmental support for these services (Strahan, 1997).

TRANSPORTATION AND ASSISTANCE

Delivering and receiving the goods and services provided by society depend greatly on the availability of transportation and communication facilities. The style and quality of one's life and the ability to engage in the wide range of work and play activities depend on the ease with which one can communicate with responsible people and organizations and be transported to appropriate locations. Communication, of course, provides information, and information is power—personal, economic, social, and political. Likewise, the capacity to move people and materials quickly from place to place increases productivity and the general efficiency with which the physical and social environment can be dealt with. An adequate transportation system permits people to have access to their places of employment, residences, shopping facilities, health services, contacts with others, and many different activities.

Transportation in the Twentieth Century

For thousands of years, people walked or ran, rode or were pulled by horses or other animals and persons, or floated on slow-moving barges and boats to get from place to place. Very little progress in the speed of transportation was made until the middle of the nineteenth century, when the locomotive and the steamship made their debut. Then, toward the end of the nineteenth and beginning of the twentieth century, the automobile and airplane appeared on the scene in rapid succession and ushered in a revolution in transportation.

The invention of the internal combustion engine, which powers automobiles, trucks, and most other motor vehicles, has changed the nature of industrial production, business, work, and leisure during this century. In 1995, the 204.1 million registered motor vehicles in the United States were driven a total of 2,405 billion miles by the 177.4 million licensed drivers. Shortly before that time, the speed limit on the nation's highways had been 55 miles per hour, but only four states have preserved that limit. In fact, one state has no speed limit at all. Laws concerning driving while intoxicated (.08–.10 blood-alcohol concentration), use of seat belts, child safety seats, motorcycle helmets, breath alcohol ignition interlock devices, and so forth, are on the books of most states, but the majority of injuries and accidental deaths are still attributable to accidents involving motor vehicles (National Safety Council, 1996). Furthermore, in spite of share-a-ride programs and carpool lanes for motor vehicles carrying additional passengers, the modal number of riders is still one. People depend and dote on their cars, which are essential not only to their livelihood, health, and leisure, but are often psychological representations or expressions of their status, power, and self-concept.

Automobiles are, of course, not the only means of transportation that has increased in popularity during this century. Travel by rail increased for many decades, but, in spite of rapid transit programs in many cities, has become less common in recent years. Streetcars are gone except for the tourist attractions in San Francisco and New Orleans. People in cities and in some rural areas continue to rely on buses to carry them from one location to another. Furthermore, individuals who are in less of a hurry can still take a boat or a ship and perhaps enjoy the scenery when their seasickness subsides. In recent years, however, perhaps the greatest growth in methods of transportation has been in air travel. At one time, the expense and uncertainty of air travel limited its use to the relatively affluent and businessmen in a hurry, but nowadays almost everyone flies.

Transporting Older Americans

Like people of all ages, older adults have transportation and communication needs. The availability of telephones, which most older adults depend on and use a great deal, facilitates communication with and by them. Many older adults also own and depend on having their own cars and may be distressed by stricter licensing requirements. In a survey conducted by the American Association of Retired Persons (1996a), 86% of a large sample of Americans aged 50 and over indicated that they continue to drive themselves as their usual means of transportation. The remainder rely on family and friends (9%), use taxicabs, vans, or public transportation (3%), or walk (2%). Two-thirds of the respondents indicated that if they could no longer drive, they would rely on family or friends for rides. The highest percentage of older adults who do not drive are found in cities, where they are more likely to walk or take public transportation.

Elderly people who live in urban areas can usually catch buses, but those who live in rural or suburban areas with little public transportation may face real problems in getting around. The problems are particularly acute when food stores, doctors' offices, banks, and other places where older people have business are many blocks or even miles from their residences. Often, a relative is willing to serve as chauffeur and companion on trips to stores or offices if they are not too frequent, but constant demands to be taken somewhere can be a nuisance for even well-meaning relatives or friends. A scarcity of convenient, inexpensive transportation restricts the life space and lifestyle of older adults, frequently leading to isolation, loneliness, and virtual imprisonment in their own home.

Problems of traveling from place to place are especially difficult for older adults who are ill or disabled. Those who do not have their own automobiles may find that buses and trains are inconvenient and potentially dangerous modes of travel. Taxicabs would seem to be a better bet, but cab drivers often view older passengers as time-consuming, troublesome, and poor tippers, and hence are less likely to stop for them.

One solution to the transportation needs of older adults are Medicabs, Dial-a-Ride, Dial-a-Bus, and similar programs supported by federal funds that pay the driver's salary plus the cost of the vehicle. Through these programs, door-to-door transportation to doctors' offices, grocery stores, and other places where elderly people have business is provided. Taxicab companies may also have contracts with governmental agencies that permit older pas-

---

MY LIFE 9–2

Automobiles

Rather than bestowing the title of "The Great Emancipator" on Abe Lincoln, they should have reserved it for the automobile. The railroad may have opened up the West, and the airplane brought the continents together, but it was the automobile that blurred the boundaries between rural and urban America. In addition, it gave country boys like me something to tinker with, as long as we had plenty of bailing wire, rubber bands, and wrenches.

Like many other Southern boys, I had a love affair with the automobile. Automobiles are liberating, fun-to-run, mechanically intriguing, places of solace and contemplation, and things of beauty. They not only get you and the stuff you wish to transport from place to place in a hurry, but you can socialize in them, sleep in them, have love affairs in them, and even live in them if you aren't claustrophobic or mysophobic. As one perpetual car-resider confessed to me, "It beats the hell out of living in the street!"

When I was 14, my grandfather taught me to drive in an old '37 Nash, which I accidentally steered into one of the gas tanks at a local filling station. Despite this mishap, I was successful in getting a junior license, warned the world to "Back up and watch out!" and burned up the road between our farm and the nearest town. In the half-century that has passed since then, I have owned 15 or so automobiles of all makes, models, sizes, shapes, and colors. I have had sedans, coupes, station wagons, and hatchbacks, but (alas!) no convertibles or trucks. There have been black cars, blue cars, brown cars, green cars, and white cars, three of which were Fords and three Chevys.

My first automobile was a '38 Dodge coupe, which I bought for $450. I was so excited by my purchase that I accidentally left the emergency brake on, smelled something burning, and extinguished the fire with a wad of Spanish moss. Those were the days before Hugh Hefner's derogatory comments concerning owners of Dodge cars, so I was fairly successful in attracting the glances of a certain class of female when I drove slowly by our high school. My next automobile was a '39 Mercury, which I bought from a little old lady (no kidding!), and which was one of the first cars with the gear shift on the steering column. Eventually one of my uncles "totalled" it—causing $1,000 damage to a $750 car. My next automobile was a '48 Ford, an ex-taxicab with a truck clutch, which

---

sengers to purchase fare coupons at a reduced rate. Adults aged 62 and over can also obtain discount fares when traveling by bus, train, or airplane between cities. Mass transit and reduced fare programs for the elderly have also been supported by federal grants made by the U.S. Department of Transportation. Other grants concerned with the transportation needs of older Americans have been awarded by the Federal Highway Administration and by state and local governmental agencies (Golant, 1992).

accompanied me to college. It made a loud bass noise when changing gears, but no one seemed to know why or even cared. Some years later I bought a previously owned '63 Chrysler loaded with extras. In addition to roaring like thunder when the accelerator was pressed to the floor, it spewed black smoke from the exhaust pipe, enveloping anyone in its wake in a black cloud.

Perhaps the funniest of all the cars that I've owned was a '69 Gremlin. Some of my friends expressed doubts about my masculinity when I purchased that car, but it ran well enough for a time. However, it soon developed a few gremlins (oops!)—overheating, losing spark plugs, and dissolving the blacktop with a stream of gasoline that it frequently leaked. It also had an alternator meter that was permanently stuck on "discharge," a problem I ingeniously solved by disconnecting the meter from the battery. At one time or another, every member of our family owned "that Gremlin," and everyone of us drove it across the United States at least once. When it became senescent, I sold it to a non-English speaking teenager for $200. Some weeks later he begged me to take it back, but a sale is a sale.

Our favorite family car was a '68 Ambassador station wagon, which, unlike its Nash predecessor, was not equipped with a folding bed and consequently had no effect on the birth-rate. The Ambassador was blue and had only a single-barreled carburetor. However, I really wanted the white one with red upholstery and double barrels. My wife had the last word when she cautioned that highway patrolmen were more likely to stop red cars—exterior or interior—than those of any other color. We finally traded the Ambassador when the kids got bigger and our idea of the perfect automobile got smaller. Since then we have owned mostly Plymouths and Hondas, our contribution toward commercial accord (oops!) between Japan and the United States.

My wife and I always shop for new cars together. In typical feminine fashion, she goes for beauty and comfort, whereas I go for mechanical soundness and toughness. In the end, however, we always compromise by agreeing that cost should be the deciding factor. You might call us "cheap," but I prefer the term "economical." This may seem like a contradiction, because we both like lots of extra gadgets on our automobiles. Of course, the automobiles of yesteryear also had gadgets and features I liked. I'm speaking of running boards, flipper vents on windows, rumble seats, and throttles, to name a few. My '38 Dodge had three of these. I loved to start it, set the throttle, stand on the running board, and steer the car through the vent. They don't make 'em that way anymore!

Assistance in Daily Living

Transportation is, of course, not the only public service that is provided to older adults who have difficulties getting around and managing their affairs. Many older people who continue to live in their own homes need assistance in personal care *activities of daily living* (ADLs), such as bathing, dressing, eating, getting in and out of bed and chairs, walking, going outside, and using the toilet. Also required is assistance in *instrumental activities of daily living* (IADLs), such as preparing meals, shopping for personal items, managing money, using the telephone, and doing light or heavy housework (Dawson, Hendershot, & Fulton, 1987).

Among the government-sponsored programs that provide assistance to older Americans are Meals on Wheels, which delivers meals to the home at modest cost, and Aids to the Elderly, which provides help with personal care matters, in addition to light housework and cooking. Additional assistance is provided by Handyman and homemaker services, telephone reassurance service, and the Friendly Visitor Program. In most communities, police, public utility workers, and other concerned workers who make frequent visits to the residences of elderly people are taught to be alert to signs that help is needed and to report their observations and/or provide direct assistance.

SUMMARY

The most populated and fastest growing section of the United States is the South, which attracts migrants of all ages. More Americans, particularly minority groups, live in urban than in rural areas. The concentration of older adults in metropolitan areas is somewhat less than that of younger adults, but three-fourths or more of all age groups live in cities and towns. Greater percentages of minority groups also live in the South and West than in the Northeast and Midwest.

The rate of migration from one geographical location to another varies inversely with age, being greater for younger than older adults. But retirement and poor health lead to a slight increase in the frequency of relocation in late life. Residential moves produce a certain degree of relocation stress, but it is less for young adults, for those of higher educational and socioeconomic status, and for those who understand the reasons for moving and can control the process.

Three types of relocations or migrations by older adults were discussed in this chapter: assistance migration, amenity migration, and kinship migration. An example of assistance migration is moving into a nursing home. Amenity migration consists of moving in order to change one's lifestyle or to maintain a friendship network. Kinship migration is moving to an area inhabited by one's children or other close relatives.

Life for the 225,000 to 2.5 million homeless people in the United States is an uncertain, often dangerous experience. Shelters, free meals, and other amenities supported by governmental and charitable organizations are of some benefit to the homeless, but such programs do not solve the problem. The living situation for single-room occupants in large cities is better than that of the homeless, but, in many cases, not much more so.

Most Americans live in single-family dwellings and in family contexts.

The percentage of Americans who live alone is greater in older adulthood than in young or middle adulthood, and higher for women and whites than for men and minority groups.

The proportion of Americans who own their own homes increases with age, is greater for men than for women, and for whites than for minority groups. Home ownership is also more common among suburban residents than among those who live in the central cities, and higher in certain states than others. Many young adults were able to purchase homes in the 1960s and 1970s, but the increasing cost of housing and the decline in the real-dollar incomes of young adults during the 1980s and 1990s reversed this trend somewhat.

Older adults who own their own homes pay a smaller portion of their income than the average citizen on housing. On the other hand, older adults who rent spend a higher percentage of their income on housing than other age groups. Whether owned or rented, the dwellings of older adults are often old and in need of repair but in most instances in fairly sound condition. Most older adults prefer to remain in their own homes and are fairly well satisfied with their home and neighborhood. House-rich but cash-poor older adults may be aware of the availability of home equity conversion, a reverse annuity mortgage (RAM), or a sales leaseback, but a very small percentage actually use such strategies for solving their financial problems.

Among the wide range of plans for meeting the housing needs of older Americans are shared housing, ECHO houses, congregate housing, continuing-care retirement communities, and retirement villages. For older adults with mild physical impairments, a congregate housing community may be appropriate. In this arrangement, residents have their own apartments but eat in a common dining room and are provided with housekeeping and security. More services are offered by continuing-care retirement communities (CCRCs), but the cost is greater. For a minority of active and affluent older adults, a retirement village such as Leisure Worlds or Park West has proven to be a suitable living arrangement.

Long-term care is provided by residential care homes, intermediate care facilities, and nursing homes. The residents of residential care homes (retirement homes) are typically less ill than those in intermediate care facilities or nursing homes. Residents of intermediate care facilities are, in turn, typically less ill than those in nursing homes. The majority of nursing homes are privately owned and expected to make a profit, but some are voluntary, nonprofit institutions and others are government-run. The Nursing Home Reform Act of 1987 has led to improvements in the conditions and services of nursing homes in the United States. Many older adults who would formerly have been placed in nursing homes are now able to remain in their own homes, being cared for during the day in adult day-care centers and/or taken care of at home by home health care agencies.

The great majority of adult Americans—old and young—drive their own automobiles to get from place to place. The percentage who drive declines somewhat with age, but most of those who do not drive depend on family and friends for rides. Governmental agencies have sponsored less expensive and more convenient modes of transportation, such as Medicabs and Dial-a-Ride, for older Americans, but support for these programs has wavered. Assisting older Americans who have difficulties performing activities of daily living (ADLs) and instrumental activities of daily living (IADLs) is a function of other government programs (Meals on Wheels, Aids to the Elderly, and so forth).

SUGGESTED READINGS

Aiken, L. R. (1995). *Aging: An introduction to gerontology* (Ch. 11). Newbury Park, CA: Sage.

Blank, T. O. (1993). Housing as a factor in adult life. In R. Kastenbaum (Ed.), *Encyclopedia of adult development* (pp. 215–222). Phoenix, AZ: Oryx Press.

Charness, N., & Bosman, E. (1990). Human factors design for older adults. In J. E. Birren & K. W. Schaie (Eds.), *Handbook of the psycholoy of aging* (3rd ed., pp. 446–463). San Diego: Academic Press.

Golant, S. M. (1992). *Housing America's elderly: Many possibilities/few choices.* Newbury Park, CA: Sage Publications.

Kendig, H. L. (1990). Comparative perspective on housing, aging, and social structure. In R. H. Binstock & L. K. George (Eds.), *Handbook of aging and the soical sciences* (3rd ed., pp. 288–306). San Diego: Academic Press.

Parmalee, P. A., & Lawton, M. P. (1990). The design of special environments for the aged. In J. E. Birren & K. W. Schaie (Eds.), *Handbook of the psychology of aging* (3rd ed., pp. 464–488). San Diego: Academic Press.

Scheidt, R. J. (1993). Place and personality in adult development. In R. Kastenbaum (Ed.), *Encyclopedia of adult development* (pp. 370–376). Phoenix, AZ: Oryx Press.

CHAPTER 10

Income, Employment, and Retirement

From the very beginning of our existence, we need many different things in order to survive and grow. Some of these things, according to the old song the best things, are free, but others have a price. When we are children, our parents and other responsible people who care for us make certain that we receive at least the minimum amount of nourishment and attention required for our comfort and development. But as we mature, a quid pro quo situation, in which we are expected to give something in return for what we get, occurs. At first these "payments" are little things, such as cleaning our room, doing our homework, or helping mother or father with some chore. As we grow into adolescents and young adults, however, most of us are expected to prepare ourselves for a lifetime of work and actually begin our 40-year labors. In addition to providing feelings of accomplishment and self-satisfaction, working in an occupation or pursuing a career is rewarded with money, a medium that can be exchanged for what we absolutely require for survival as well as providing the means to indulge our interests in many other objects and experiences.

INCOME AND POVERTY

As indicated by its gross national product (GNP), the United States is the most affluent country in the world. However, when we divide the capital GNP by the size of the population, the resulting figure for the United States ($26,980 in 1996) is lower than that of Japan ($39,640) and Germany ($27,510), and only slightly higher than the average for all Western European countries ($26,760) (Population Reference Bureau, 1997). Still, when the cost of living in various countries is taken into account, the United States is not surpassed by any country in the standard of living enjoyed by its citizens.

Income Demographics

Real estate and other material possessions contribute to affluence, but a person's disposable income is the single, most important indicator of his or her economic status. As shown in Figure 10–1, the median income for both men and women rises sharply from young adulthood to middle age and then declines fairly abruptly in old age. The increase in income from young to middle adulthood is, of course, accounted for by the fact that most young people must become established in a job or profession, gaining experience and advancement before they begin to make high salaries.

Despite the fact that their average incomes are lower than those of young and middle-aged adults, older adults are much better off financially than they were only a few decades ago. Average income has increased for all demographic groups of older Americans—men and women, blacks, whites, and Hispanics, married and unmarried. Today's older Americans have much more discretionary income than formerly, a circumstance that has encouraged business to develop products and services specially for the over-age-55 consumer market. Increases in Social Security benefits, expansion of private pension funds, property tax relief, supplemental government programs, and senior discounts offered by many commercial organizations allow older

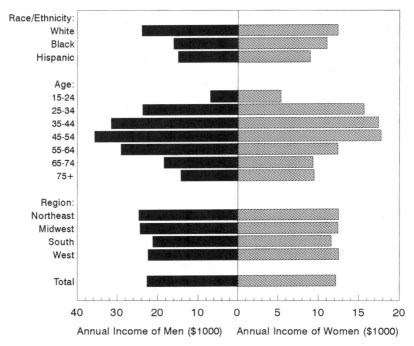

Figure 10–1   Median annual incomes of men and women in the United States in 1995 by race, age, and geographical region. (Based on data from U.S. Bureau of the Census, September 1996.)

adults to spread their money further than younger adults are able to do. Another factor, the high percentage of home owners in the 65+ age group of Americans, has led to the characterization of many older adults as being "house rich" but "cash poor." However, the financial burden of older adults with low incomes is moderated by Supplemental Security Income (SSI), Medicaid, food stamps, and other sources of *in-kind income*—goods and services that require no expenditures.

Income varies not only with age, but also with gender, ethnicity, geographical region, education, and other demographic variables. Average income is higher for men than women, higher for whites than blacks and Hispanics, higher in the Northeast and Midwest than in the South and West, and higher in the suburbs than in the central cities (Taeuber, 1993). As might be expected, median annual income for both full- and part-time workers varies directly with educational attainment. Even when education is equated, however, the annual median incomes of full-time female workers is less than 80% of that for full-time male workers (see Table 10–1). This is true for all ages and ethnic groups and for women in various circumstances. Older widows, for example, have less income than older widowers. Married women, who share in the wealth of their husbands, tend to have higher incomes than single women and widows. To some extent, the income differential between the sexes is due to the type of industry or other organization in which men and women work, as well as the specific job and level within the organization. For example, only a disproportionately small percentage of women have been able to break into the upper echelons of corporate management.

Sources of Income

The biggest source of income for the largest number of people is, of course, earnings, which vary not only with productivity and length of time

TABLE 10–1 Median 1995 Income
of Men and Women by Educational Attainment

	Men		Women	
Educational attainment	Total	Full-time	Total	Full-time
Less than 9th grade	11,723	18,354	7,096	13,577
9th–12th grade	15,791	22,185	8,057	15,825
High school graduate	23,365	29,510	12,046	20,463
Some college, no degree	28,004	33,883	15,552	23,997
Associate degree	31,027	35,201	19,450	27,311
Bachelor's degree	39,040	45,266	24,065	32,051
Master's degree	49,076	55,216	33,509	40,263
Professional degree	66,257	79,668	38,588	50,000
Doctorate degree	57,356	65,336	39,821	48,141

Source: Data from U.S. Bureau of the Census, September 1996.

on the job but also with the perceived value of the job to the hiring organization and society as a whole. Of the 188 million Americans over age 14 receiving incomes in 1995, approximately 75% (140 million) had earned incomes. However, anyone who has attempted to complete an income tax form knows that gainful employment is not the only source of income. Depending on their age and status, people may receive income from any of the sources listed in Figure 10–2. As shown in this figure, many people have interest, Social Security, dividend, and pension income. Smaller numbers of people receive substantial amounts of income from survivors' benefits, disability benefits, alimony, workers' compensation, and other sources ((U.S. Bureau of the Census, 1996).

Poverty

When compared with other industrialized nations, the United States is far from an impoverished country. Except for an occasional bag lady, street bum, or panhandler, poverty in the United States is not ordinarily very vis-

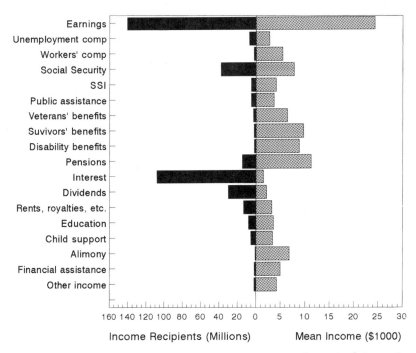

Figure 10–2   Number of recipients and mean incomes in the United States in 1995 by source. (Based on data from U.S. Bureau of the Census, September 1996.)

ible. This is in sharp contrast to the situation in the 1930s, when the streets and highways were full of people who were down on their luck and begging for a dime.

The official definition of *poverty* now employed by the U.S. Government includes a set of money income thresholds, varying with the size and composition of the family. The definition is based on money income alone and does not include capital gains, the value of noncash benefits such as health insurance, food stamps, Medicare, Medicaid, or public housing. Families or individuals whose income is below their appropriate poverty thresholds are designated as *poor* (Baugher & Lamison-White, 1996).

According to the official definition, 36.4 million people in the United States, or 13.8% of the total population, were classified as poor in 1995. As shown in Figure 10–3, the number of poor people in this country varies with ethnicity, age, geographical region, location of residence, and nativity. In 1995, the poverty rate was 8.5% for non-Hispanic whites, 14.6% for Asian/Pacific Islanders, 29.3% for blacks, and 30.3% for Hispanics. However, the largest percentage (45%) of all poor people were non-Hispanic whites.

The under-18 age group has both a larger number and a larger percentage

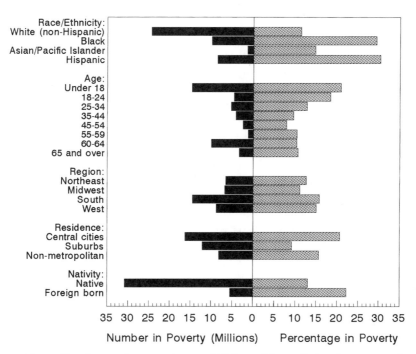

Figure 10–3 Number and percentages of U.S. residents living in poverty in the United States in 1995 by race, age, region, residence, and nativity. (Based on data from Baugher & Lamison-White, 1996.)

of poor people than any other age group. More than one American child in five is now classified as being below the official poverty level. The age group containing the second largest number of poor people is 60–64, but the percentage of poor is higher in the 18–24, 25–34, and 65 and over age groups. With regard to geographical region, both the largest number and the largest percentage of poor people live in the South, followed by the West. Central cities contain a greater number and a greater percentage of poor people than suburban and nonmetropolitan areas. The number of poor people is higher in the suburbs than in nonmetropolitan areas, but the converse is true for the percentage of poor people. Finally, although a large majority of poor people in the United States are native-born, the percentage who are poor is higher for foreign-born than native-born Americans (Baugher & Lamison-White, 1996).

Public Pension Programs

The major federal pension programs benefiting older Americans, their dependents, and survivors are Civil Service Retirement, the Railroad Retirement Program, the Veterans Pension Program, Old-Age and Survivors Insurance Program, and the Supplemental Security Income Program. Other public pension programs are managed by state and local governments.

The Civil Service Retirement program, managed by the U.S. Civil Service Commission, is the principal retirement system for federal civilian employees and is financed by employee contributions matched by the employing agency plus congressional appropriations. Under this program, monthly retirement benefits based on past earnings and length of service are paid to eligible retirees and their survivors. The Railroad Retirement Program, managed by the Railroad Retirement Board, is financed by a payroll tax on railroad employees and employers. Monthly benefits are paid to retired workers, their wives, and survivors. Only employees with 10 or more years of railroad service are eligible; otherwise, their claims are transferred to the Social Security Administration. The Veterans Pension Program, managed by the Veterans Administration, which is the modern-day descendent of the first federal pensions granted in 1792 to veterans of the American Revolution, provides monthly cash benefits to veterans with 90 days or more of military service, including at least one day of wartime service, who are 65 years and older and meet certain income limitation requirements. Benefits vary with the veteran's annual income and are also paid to a designated survivor.

The most extensive and expensive of all public pension programs is the Old-Age and Survivors Insurance Program (OASI) managed by the Social Security Administration. In 1995, 37.5 million Americans, including 92% of those aged 65 years and over, received an average of $7,656 under Social Security (U.S. Bureau of the Census, September 1996). The program is financed by a payroll tax on employees, employers, and self-employed persons. Employees are eligible to receive full monthly benefit payments at age

65 or reduced benefits beginning at age 62. The exact amount received in benefits is determined by applying a legislative formula to the number of quarters worked and the amount earned by the retired worker. Cash benefits are also paid to dependents and survivors of retired workers. The dollar value of benefits is tied to the consumer price index and involves annual cost-of-living adjustments. The premium for Part B (Supplemental Medical Insurance) of Medicare is also deducted from the recipients' monthly Social Security check.

Monthly Social Security checks have increased during recent years, but they are still insufficient for many poor and disabled Americans. For this reason, the SSI program, which guarantees a certain minimum monthly income to aged, blind, and disabled persons with no income and very limited resources of other kinds, was introduced. In 1995, 4.8 million Americans, including 4.2% of those age 65 and over, received an average of $4,066 under SSI (U.S. Bureau of the Census, September 1996). Under the provisions of SSI, the states may, and in some cases, must, supplement federal monthly benefits.

For many years the solvency of the Social Security system has been a source of concern for the federal government and the public at large. However, certain changes enacted in the system by the U.S. Congress have led to the expectation that it will remain solvent at least until the middle of the twenty-first century. Another matter of some concern that is related to Social Security and other government programs for older Americans involves the question of *generational equity*, that is, that older Americans should not receive a disproportionate share of public resources while so many American children are living in poverty (Neugarten & Neugarten, 1989).

Private Pension Programs

Sources of income for older couples and individuals in 1994 included Social Security (42%), followed by other public and private pensions (19%), earnings (18%), asset income (18%), and other sources (3%) (American Association of Retired Persons, 1996b). As indicated by these percentages, private pensions are not the major source of income for older Americans, but they are a substantial one: In 1995, 8.8 million Americans received an average of $8,378 under the provisions of company or union pensions. Annuity, IRA, Keogh, 401(k), and other private pension plans also made payments to nearly 1 million Americans (U.S. Bureau of the Census, September 1996).

Business and professional organizations in most industrialized countries provide private retirement programs for their employees. Under these programs, retirees are either given monthly payments or, in countries such as Australia and Japan, a single lump sum. In the United States, private pension plans can be divided into two types: defined-benefit and defined-contribution plans. The provisions of a *defined-benefit plan* promise the employee a specific monthly retirement income when he or she reaches a certain age and has worked in the organization for a certain number of years. The benefit amount is calculated from a prescribed formula, for example, a percentage of final salary times years of service. Approximately 80% of private pension plans are of the defined-benefit type, which are found mostly in large industries. An alternative is the *defined-contribution plan*, under which a certain percentage of the employee's earnings is deposited into a tax-sheltered account every pay period by both the employee and the company. The funds are invested and accumulate during the employee's tenure with the company, the total value of the account fluctuating with the financial markets and any amounts accrued from profit-sharing plans. For this reason, in contrast to the fixed retirement benefit of the defined-benefit plan, the retirement benefit under the defined-contribution plan is variable. Defined-contribution plans, which are more common in smaller, nonunion firms than in larger, unionized organizations, can also be combined with a defined-benefit plan, making a portion of retirement income predictable and a portion unpredictable.

Private pension plans cover only about one-third of retirees in the United States, usually those who have worked for large corporations. Women, whose work histories are often interrupted for family reasons, are less likely than men to qualify for private pensions, and those who do usually receive less than men. Furthermore, many people—women and men—fail to receive a private pension because they do not stay with the company long enough to be considered "vested." Making such plans "portable" from one company to another increases the retirement incomes of women, minorities, and unskilled workers who tend to remain on a particular job for a relatively short period of time. However, private pension plans can be expensive both to workers and organizations, so the cost of increasing the number of eligible employees and the size of benefits must ultimately be borne by consumers of the products or services provided by those organizations.

EMPLOYMENT

To love and to work—these are the two major activities of adulthood that Sigmund Freud viewed not only as outlets for one's energies and creativity but also as giving meaning to individual existence. One does not have to be a staunch advocate of the Protestant ethic to realize that our work defines our identity—what we are, organizes our time and our lives, and provides us with social stimulation and a sense of pride. Consequently, it is not surprising to hear many people confess that they would continue to work at something even if they were paid nothing for doing so or became so rich that they no longer needed to labor in order to support themselves and their families. The fact that the need to engage in productive work continues even when monetary rewards for doing so are no longer forthcoming is seen in the activities of retirees whose pensions and other assets are sufficient to let them do whatever they wish. Most retirees who are physically capable of doing so continue to pursue nonrecreational as well as recreational activities of various sorts, merely for the sake of personal enjoyment in doing and producing something.

Many of today's workers, and young adults in particular, do not subscribe to the Bismarckian notion that the purpose of life is to do one's dutiful work. They look upon work as a means to an end rather than an end in itself. Thus, they work to attain self-actualization and to provide them with the where-withal to pursue other, nonwork interests. Rather than adhering to the traditional ethic of company loyalty, today's workers place more emphasis on their own personal needs and those of their families, and on control over their own lives (Noble, 1993). According to management consultant Roger Herman, "Corporate loyalty is dead" (Bianco, 1997). A large percentage of young workers do not remain on a particular job very long, a tendency that is likely to increase in the future; they move to where they can get the best deal in terms of pay, benefits, and hours, which may be contract and temporary work. Furthermore, in order to meet household expenses, pay off debts, save money, or buy something special, nearly 7% of American workers are holding down more than one job (Bianco, 1997).

Occupations

The term *occupation* encompasses all kinds of work—short- and long-term, unskilled, skilled, and professional. At the bottom of the occupational status scale are *marginal* workers whose discontinuous work histories or unstable work patterns may be caused by various physical, behavioral, or cognitive disabilities. Somewhat higher up the status scale are the *blue-collar* workers in occupations demanding greater physical than intellectual skills, but who hold jobs ranging from simple, unskilled labor up through highly complex skills. Even higher up the occupational scale in terms of status, if not pay, are *white-collar* and *pink-collar* occupations held by people who work in offices rather than in factories or outdoors. The term *pink-collar* designates fairly low-paying jobs such as clerical work, bank teller, and receptionist that are usually held by women (Cavanaugh, 1997). At the top of the occupational status scale are executives and professionals, who are usually thought of as having *careers* rather than occupations. These more prestigious occupations generally require a substantial amount of education and experience. Career-oriented people tend to remain in a specific occupational field and, if they perform satisfactorily, advance over time to higher levels of responsibility, authority, and financial compensation.

The U.S. Department of Commerce groups occupations into a dozen or so categories, each containing a number of subcategories. As indicated in Figure 10–4, the greatest number of year-round, full-time workers are in the category designated as "Administrative support, including clerical." The greatest number of part-time and temporary workers, on the other hand, are in the "Service worker" category. Other categories containing large numbers of

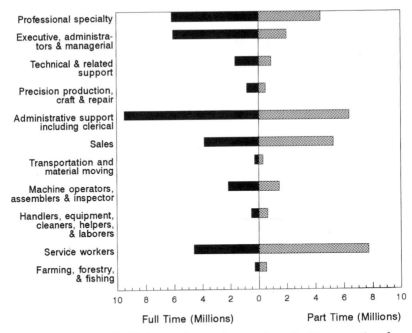

Figure 10–4   Number of full-time and part-time workers in 12 occupational groups.
(Based on data from U.S. Bureau of the Census, September 1996.)

workers are "Professional specialty," "Executive, administrator, and managerial," and "Sales."

The number of workers in a particular occupational category is not necessarily a good indicator of the level of education, training, or remuneration associated with the occupations contained in that category. However, education, training, and experience are positively related to financial compensation. For example, consider the 12 occupations associated with the highest median weekly earnings, as shown in Figure 10–5. It should not come as a great surprise that physicians, lawyers, engineers, and airplane pilots are among the highest-paid occupations. However, these occupations also require a great deal of education and training, and, in some cases, involve a certain amount of risk.

Although most occupations with high salaries also have high status or prestige in the eyes of the general public, the demand for individuals who are trained in specific professional and nonprofessional occupations is greatly influenced by conditions in the national and world markets. During the past two decades, in particular, the globalization of production has been accompanied by extensive changes in the number and kinds of jobs that are avail-

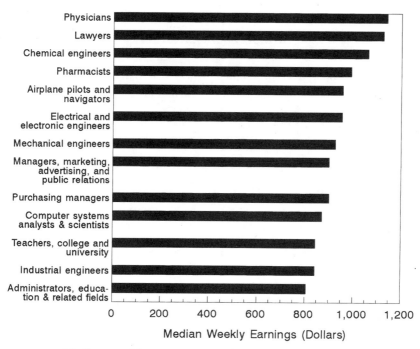

Figure 10–5   Median weekly earnings in dollars of the 12 occupations with the highest incomes. (Based on data from U.S. Bureau of the Census, September 1996.)

able to workers and in the skills associated with those jobs. In particular, individuals who are trained in computers and other technical skills have been increasingly in demand. Because the specific skills that are needed can change quickly, workers who wish to continue being in demand must be trained in a variety of skills and remain up-to-date in their knowledge of technology. Those workers, young and old alike, who are unable or unwilling to be retrained are faced with a not-so-bright future in the job market. As a rough estimate, a typical American man can expect to work slightly less than 40 years on the average and a typical American woman slightly less than 30 years, but these numbers can shift dramatically downward when workers' skills become outmoded.

In addition to the demand, the supply of workers and trainees in a particular profession or skilled occupation can change. For example, although physicians enjoy the top position on the occupational ladder—both in status and earnings, the supply of medical students has declined substantially in recent years. The reasons for the decline in medical school applications include overregulation, excessive overhead and malpractice insurance costs, and preset fee schedules (Reskin & Roos, 1990).

MY LIFE 10–1

My Occupational History

Once upon a time there was a television program called "What's My Line?" on which the panelists had to determine the guest's occupation by asking a series of questions to be answered "yes" or "no." It was interesting to watch them zero-in on a specific occupation by beginning with very general job categories and proceeding deductively to more specific ones. I sometimes think that the reasoning process employed by the panelists on this show had a lot in common with my occupational history.

I began my work experience, in a very global way, as a kind of jack of all trades and master of none. Even before my eighteenth birthday, I had been a newspaper boy, a grocery clerk, a delivery boy, a tobacco picker, a stock boy, a dishwasher, a waiter, a railroad-car unloader, a soda jerk, a cook, a floor sweeper, a lawn mower, and an occasional preacher! I took out an ad in the

local newspaper proclaiming my interest in making money by doing anything that was legal and moral. To my great surprise I received numerous responses involving a variety of jobs. As a result of my initiative, I ended up working at many vocations in many locations. I picked citrus fruit and rounded up cows in Florida, delivered papers and packages in Georgia, picked cotton and peaches in South Carolina, harvested and strung tobacco in Connecticut, waited on tables and washed dishes in Pennsylvania, and repaired houses and automobiles in New York. I never became an expert in any of those things, but I did save some money for my college expenses. Unfortunately, it wasn't enough, and when it ran out I enlisted in the Marine Corps. Under the tutelage of the marine drill instructors, I became fairly competent in performing many other tasks: I could duck-walk with buckets of sand,

---

Vocational Development and Choice

Not all children are created equal. Different children have different genetic potentials that cause them to be better at some things and worse at others than their peers. In addition, the human and nonhuman environments in which children grow up have a marked effect on their patterns of behavior and the choices they make. Vocational interests are no exception. Differential reinforcement by, and modeling of, parents and significant other people, in addition to other environmental factors and just plain luck, are important in shaping interests. However, research has also indicated that children are born with a hereditary predisposition to be interested in certain activities and things (Grotevant, Scarr, & Weinberg, 1977). It is commonly believed that parental behavior is more influential than heredity in shaping a child's interests, but parents may be much less influential than one might suspect. According to Grotevant et al., the role of parents should be one of providing children with a variety of experiences and models so that whatever interest

scream "Yes, Sir!" and "No, Sir!," sing the Marines hymn with someone banging on a pail placed over my head, stand nose-to-nose with another recruit while both of us laughed for an hour or two, climb over and under six dozen double-decker bunks, stand at attention for two hours, strip and reassemble a rifle in the dark, shave with a pair of tweezers, and let mosquitos bite me without slapping them. The marines also trained me as an aviation electronics technician, an occupation close to the furthest thing from my interests. However, the monotony was occasionally relieved by an electric shock when I accidentally touched the wrong wire while crawling around in an airplane belly. Even planes seemed to be conspiring against me in those days.

About the only part of my military career that I really enjoyed was attending technical classes, so after being discharged I decided to become a professional student. Fancying myself something of a renaissance man, when I wasn't pursuing girls I attended all kinds of college classes—biology, chemistry, physics, mathematics, English, philosophy, foreign languages, tennis, typing, music, art—you name it. I didn't take a lot of any of those subjects, just a lot of subjects. By the time I had earned over 100 semester hours credit, I discovered that I didn't have enough of anything for a major. An introductory psychology course failed to make me proficient in reading minds and curing mental disorders, but I did learn a little bit about a lot of things. This experience was the start of my occupational awakening and provided a focus for my adult life. Late one night, none the worse after a few beers, I made up my mind to specialize in general psychology! This may seem absurd to narrow technocrats and other drones of limited perspective, but it suited me fine. For four decades it has enabled me to survive, and even moderately prosper, while doing what I wanted to all along—a little bit of everything, but not too much of anything!

predispositions or inclinations they inherit will have a better opportunity to develop.

The choice of an occupation and progress in it are not always rational, planned affairs. Rather, the decision to enter a particular occupation is often an accidental or impulsive affair, made on the basis of incorrect information and unduly influenced by social pressure. However, the occupational histories of most people can be characterized in terms of a series of stages or periods. The most prominent theories are those of Ginzberg and Super. According to the findings of Ginzberg, Ginsburg, Axelrad, and Herma (1951), interests, values, and abilities are all important in the choice of an occupation. These researchers see the development of vocational interests as proceeding from a *fantasy stage* in early and middle childhood, when a child's interests are arbitrary and unrealistic, through a *tentative stage* from ages 11–18, when possible vocations are considered, to a *realistic stage* from ages 18–21, beginning with exploration and culminating in the crystallization of a vocational pattern.

According to Super (1969, 1985, 1990), individuals select those occupations that allow their self-concepts to be expressed. Super views occupational development in adolescence and adulthood as occurring in a series of eight stages. The first stage, *crystallization*, is one of exploration: The adolescent explores various fields and attempts to match them with his or her needs, interests, abilities, and values. Following the crystallization stage is a *specification stage*, a transitional period occupied by job training. At this stage, the individual learns more about specific careers and combines this knowledge with the reality of his or her own situation to make decisions concerning specific occupations. Among these "reality factors" are the individual's financial situation, the availability of education and/or job training, and supply-and-demand factors that determine the marketability of individuals who enter specific occupations.

Beginning at about age 21 or 22 is an *implementation stage*, when the individual tentatively commits him- or herself to an occupation and takes an entry-level position. It is during this time that the individual may be guided by a *mentor*—an experienced person who takes a personal interest in the young worker and smooths the way toward competence and advancement in his or her chosen vocation. Beginning workers generally fare better with mentors of their own gender, so sexual attraction and discrimination are less likely to enter the picture. Women, in particular, have been found to be significantly more productive when they have women mentors than when their mentors are men (Goldstein, 1979). Having a good mentor can help cushion the shock of discovering that a job is never quite the same as books and brochures make it out to be.

After the implementation stage comes the *establishment stage*, the beginning of an orderly career and a settling down into an occupation at about age 25. This stage is characterized by stability, production, and advancement in an occupation. The next stage, the *consolidation stage*, begins at around age 35 and is the time when the now-experienced worker is on the threshold of advancing as far as he or she will go. Some workers, the *fast-trackers*, advance rapidly, whereas others, the *dead-enders*, reach their threshold of advancement fairly soon. Another transitional period—the *maintenance stage*— begins at about age 45 and lasts to age 55. By this time, the person's goals have either been already met or are seemingly unattainable. This stage lasts until retirement looms and shifts into the *deceleration stage* of the mid-fifties. Preparation for retirement begins, and the individual begins to separate him- or herself from the job. Last, there is the *retirement stage*, when one becomes formally separated from the work role. Of course, not all people follow the same career time line or experience the same outcomes. In addition to drifting or reaching one's goals late, a person's career progress can be interrupted by personal setbacks such as accidents or illness and by external events such as recession, war, and sociopolitical events.

Betz (1992, 1994) extended Super's emphasis on the importance of the self-concept in occupational preferences. Adapting Bandura's (1977) perceived self-efficacy model to vocational counseling, Betz maintained that counseling to enhance self-efficacy should concentrate on four sources of information in Bandura's model: performance accomplishments, vicarious experience, verbal persuasion, and emotional arousal (see Bandura, 1977). Also of importance in vocational counseling is the realization that jobs possess many different features that change over time. Consequently, there is usually enough diversity in most jobs for people with different interests and abilities to adapt satisfactorily. However, it should be emphasized that interests are not necessarily indicative of abilities. Some people do not possess the abilities that are required for success on jobs in which they are interested, and other people are not interested in jobs for which their abilities are adequate. For this reason, scores on interest inventories, such as the Strong Interest Inventory, and on tests of cognitive abilities should be interpreted in the light of other information about the individual—school marks, awards, extracurricular activities, community service, experiences, and motivation.

Vocational Personalities

The relationships of vocational interests to other personality variables have been studied more generally by Roe (1956), Holland (1985), and other researchers (Darley & Hagenah, 1955; Osipow, 1983). The most extensive and influential of these conceptions is Holland's theory of vocational personalities and work environments. According to Holland, people seek and remain in environments that are congruent with their personalities, and they are happier and more productive in such environments. But if a particular environment proves incompatible with a person's personality, either the environment must change or the person must seek a more compatible environment. With respect to vocational choice in particular, the theory predicts that the congruence between an individual's personality and particular occupations is the principal factor in occupational selection, stability, and satisfaction.

The six vocational personalities, which are the same as the six work environments in Holland's model, are depicted in Figure 10–6; they are

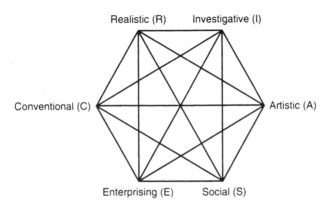

Figure 10–6   Holland's hexagonal model of vocational interests.

INVENTORY 10–1

Directions: This inventory relates your expressed interests and personality characteristics to possible careers for you. Read and follow the directions for each part carefully.

Part I. Mark the one statement (1, 2, 3, 4, 5, or 6) in this part that is most descriptive of you.

1. You like and are good at manipulating tools, machines, and other objects, and working outdoors with plants and animals.
2. You like and are good at observing, learning, investigating, analyzing, evaluating, and solving problems.
3. You like and do well in unstructured situations in which your creativity or imagination can be expressed.
4. You like and are good at working with people—developing, enlightening, informing, training, curing, and helping or supporting them in various ways.
5. You like and are good at influencing and persuading other people, and you would like to lead or manage an organization.
6. You like and are good at arithmetic and clerical activities such as filing, record keeping, and data processing.

According to your expressed interests, the following prediction concerning your vocational future can be made: (Refer to the statement in Part III having the same number as the statement you checked in Part I.)

Go to Part III

Part II. Check the one statement (1, 2, 3, 4, 5, or 6) in this part that is most descriptive of you.

1. You are a realistic, practical, conforming, and natural person.

(R)ealistic, (I)nvestigative, (A)rtistic, (I)ntegrative, (E)nterprising, and (C)onventional. These six types are idealizations, and a specific personality or environment is a composite of two or more ideal types. Five concepts that involve relationships among the various types are consistency, differentiation, identity, congruence, and calculus. The *consistency* of an interest pattern is the extent to which the person's high scores on the six types are close to each other on the model (see Figure 10–6). The greater the degree of *differentiation* of interests, the smaller the number of high scores. A person who has a small number of vocational goals in a few major categories is said to have a keen sense of *personal identity*; *environmental identity* exists when the goals, tasks, and rewards in a particular environment are stable over time. When there is a match between personality types and environmental types, a state of *congruence* exists. A fifth concept in the theory, that of *calculus*, refers to the

2. You are a rational, cautious, curious, independent, and introversive person.
3. You are an imaginative, introspective, complicated, emotional, expressive, impulsive, nonconforming, and disorderly person.
4. You are an cooperative, friendly, helpful, persuasive, tactful, and understanding person.
5. You are an aggressive, ambitious, energetic, domineering, pleasure-seeking, self-confident, sociable, and talkative person.
6. You are a conscientious, efficient, inflexible, obedient, orderly, persistent, and self-controlled person.

According to your description of your personality, the following prediction concerning your vocational future can be made: (Refer to the statement in Part III having the same number as the statement you checked in Part II.)

Go to Part III

Part III. Predictions

1. Jobs such as automobile mechanic, farmer, or electrician are more likely to appeal to you.
2. Jobs in fields such as chemistry, physics, biology, geology, and other sciences are more likely to appeal to you.
3. Jobs such as actor, musician, or writer are more likely to appeal to you.
4. Jobs in clinical or counseling psychology, speech therapy, teaching, and related fields are more likely to appeal to you.
5. Jobs such as manager, business executive, or salesperson are more likely to appeal to you.
6. Jobs such as banker, bookkeeper, and tax expert are more likely to appeal to you.

Go to Part II if you have not completed it.

extent to which the six types of personality and environment can be ordered according to a hexagonal model in which the distances are consistent with their theoretical relationships.

Work Satisfaction and Stress

As might be expected, the degree of satisfaction experienced on a job varies with the status, power, financial compensation, and other rewards indicative of successful performance. Chronological age is also significantly related to the level of job satisfaction. In general, both young and older workers express more job satisfaction than middle-aged workers (Warr, 1992). Despite a relatively high level of expressed job satisfaction, younger workers have more absenteeism, more disabling injuries, and higher accident rates,[1] and are less committed to the organization (Human Capital Initiative, 1993).

Various factors contribute to the lower level of job satisfaction and occupational well-being shown by middle-aged workers. Realizing that their careers and chances for advancement are limited, and experiencing boredom with the present circumstances and concerns for the future, middle-aged workers are more likely to experience dissatisfaction than either younger or older workers. It would seem that these same factors would cause older adults to be even more dissatisfied with their jobs, but such is not the case. Among the explanations that have been offered for the high job satisfaction of most older adults are the following:

1. Realizing that they do not have much time left and having lowered their expectations, older adults have settled for a job in which they are reasonably happy.
2. Because of the way in which they were brought up, older adults learned to value work of all types more than younger cohorts.
3. Older adults, who may have changed jobs frequently over the years, have ended up in more fulfilling jobs than younger adults.
4. Work is less of a factor in the lives of older adults, and because of lower work motivation, they require less to remain satisfied with their occupation (Bray & Howard, 1983).

Job dissatisfaction can, of course, occur at any age and on any type of work—unskilled, semiskilled, skilled, or professional. In interviews with a large sample of workers in many different occupations, Terkel (1974) found that a sizable majority were dissatisfied with their jobs. Many of the interviewees indicated that their jobs were merely temporary, stopgap measures until they were able to do what they really wanted to. To Terkel and other observers (e.g., Dawis, 1984; Roth, 1991), the dissatisfaction with work expressed by so many individuals is related less to wages and benefits than to a feeling that their work is dull and meaningless and that their efforts are unrecognized and unappreciated by their supervisors and coworkers.

Dull, uninteresting work can lead to *alienation*, a feeling of personal disconnectedness or self-removal from the job. This is particularly likely when workers feel that their efforts are meaningless and unappreciated, and they fail to see the connection between what they do and the final product. Because worker alienation is costly to an organization, management has been alerted to the need to prevent it and cope with it. Involving employees in the decision-making processes of an organization, making work schedules flex-

---

[1]However, younger workers recover more quickly from serious accidents and are less likely to become permanently disabled (Sterns, Barrett, & Alexander, 1985). Young workers also experience less difficulty than older workers in adjusting to night-shift work (Harma, Hakola, & Laitinen, 1992).

ible (*flextime*[2]), and instituting worker development and enhancement programs are procedures that employers have instituted to avoid alienation among workers (Roth, 1991).

Unlike the alienated worker, who perceives his or her job as boring and unrewarding, the burned out worker finds it too involving and demanding. *Burnout*, a condition precipitated by the stress of overwork, is characterized by a cluster of physical, psychological, and behavioral symptoms. These include emotional exhaustion, negative attitudes, headache, backache, reduced productivity, feelings of depersonalization, and social withdrawal. An employee suffering from burnout can no longer keep up with the pace and pressure—often self-imposed—of an occupation, and eventually his or her energy and motivation become severely depleted. Burnout is not limited to the job; it carries over into the family situation. In general, burnout and other signs of stress on the job are more likely to affect family life than stress in the family is to affect performance at work. In addition, burnout is more common in married, female workers, who are subject to a greater amount of both work and nonwork stress than their husbands. Working women are more likely to show *multiple-role strains*, in that stress arising from the demands of the role of worker interfere with the effective performance of the roles of wife and mother (Repetti, Matthews, & Waldron, 1989).

Some of the same techniques for dealing with alienation can be used with burnout: Workers should be made to feel that they are an important part of the organization by involving them in decisions; communication and helpfulness on the part of management should be improved, and a sense of camaraderie and teamwork should be promoted. Workers who suffer from burnout should also be encouraged to lower their expectations as to what they can realistically expect to accomplish and assisted in their efforts to deal with constraints on the job and elsewhere.

Although the direction of emotional stress is more apt to be from work to home that vice versa, emotional problems stemming from the stress of an unhappy home life can make workers more distractible, increasing the likelihood of work accidents. Of course, stress on the job can also increase the likelihood of accidents on the job itself. Whatever the cause may be, frustrated, worried, and angry workers tend to have more accidents than happy, contented workers. Part of the explanation appears to lie in personality. For example, Shaw and Sichel (1971) found that workers who had repeated accidents were less emotionally stable, more hostile toward authority, and higher in anxiety than nonrepeaters. More recently, Hansen (1989) reported that measures of social maladjustment and neurotic distractibility were significantly related to the rate of accidents on the job. The results of these and other studies (Arnett, 1990; Montag & Comrey, 1987; Perry, 1986) support the

---

[2]Employees who work on a *flextime* schedule can work whatever hours they wish, as long as they work the required number of hours and are at work during a specified "core period."

conclusion that personality variables are associated with accident frequency in various kinds of work situations.

Unemployment

Arguably, the most severe source of stress associated with employment is the loss of it. Layoffs can occur at all status levels of the occupational hierarchy. Not only semiskilled and skilled workers lose their jobs, but corporation executives and professional persons are also subject to termination. The overall unemployment rate in the United States for 1996 was 5.4%. Among Americans aged 16 years and older, the annual rate of unemployment was over twice as high for black men (11.1%) as for white men (4.7%) and over twice as high for black women (10%) as for white women (4.7%). The rate was higher for widowed, divorced, separated, and single persons than for married persons with spouse present (data provided by U.S. Employment Service, personal communication).

The loss of a job can lead to anxiety, depression, a feeling of emptiness, a decline in physical health, alcoholism, and even suicide (DeFrank & Ivancevich, 1986; Kelvin & Jarrett, 1985). The effects of unemployment are felt not only by laid-off workers but also by all members of their families (McLoyd, 1989). Relationships between husbands and wives, parents and children, and among children themselves may all suffer.

Job loss and unemployment can have serious repercussions for older and less-educated individuals, who may have great difficulty in finding another job (Kinicki, 1989). For many older workers, unemployment is the first step in early retirement (Robinson, Coberly, & Paul, 1985). On the other hand, the loss of a job is less disastrous for younger workers, who can expect to change jobs 5–10 times during their working years (Toffler, 1970). American workers can no longer count on lifetime employment with the same company. Younger workers who are laid off because of downturns in the economy, technological changes, corporate buyouts and mergers, competition, and downsizing are usually able to find new jobs if they are patient and continue searching. For example, most workers with marketable skills found new jobs after the massive downsizing of industries in the early 1990s.

The psychological effects of job loss are typically even greater for middle-aged adults than for younger and older adults. Young adults, who have their whole working lives ahead of them, are generally more optimistic and realistically hopeful of finding other jobs, and older adults can retire. But unemployed, middle-aged adults, particularly those who have reached a fairly high level in the corporate hierarchy, are faced with the prospect of being unable to find a position of comparable status and may not be ready to retire.

In order for business and industry to meet the challenge of international competition, workers must be willing to be retrained by the corporations themselves or by community and technical colleges. Workers who avoid accepting the necessity of such retraining in hopes that their old jobs will reappear are usually indulging in wishful thinking. Skilled workers and managers, and especially unskilled or semiskilled workers, must accept the fact that education and training for work will be a continuing process throughout their working years. Job counseling programs and self-help groups of unemployed workers, for example, groups of former business executives, are also helpful in encouraging unemployed persons to face the challenge of upgrading their skills and finding jobs.

As with the psychological reactions to any loss or threat to a person's competency and security, the effects of job loss and unemployment in general vary with the reasons for the loss and what it means to the individual. If it can be rationalized as not being one's fault and not a rejection of one's value as a breadwinner and a human being, it is likely to be taken in stride and dealt with effectively. This is more apt to occur when there is strong social support from the unemployed worker's family and peers and when he or she has effective skills for coping with frustration and personal setbacks (Mallinckrodt & Fretz, 1988).

Despite the loss of income, unemployment compensation and other sources of financial support help ensure that unemployed workers will not become destitute. Finally, chronically unemployed persons must be able to distance themselves from work and learn to accept the fact that there is more to life than labor (Kinicki & Latack, 1990). This does not mean that the approximately 5% of the nation's labor force who are unemployed at any one time should simply stop looking for a job, as many of them do, but time spent in searching should be balanced by attentiveness to other rewarding aspects of living.

RETIREMENT

An estimated 135,634,000 Americans were in the civilian labor force in February 1997, but 7,205,000 Americans were unemployed and looking for work. As shown in Figure 10–7, the percentage of people in the labor force declines with age, to approximately 17% men and 9% women in the age 65 and over group. These last figures show the effects of retirement. However, approximately 54% of these individuals (51% men and 63% women) were employed part time (American Association of Retired Persons, 1996b). Of course, not all people who are unemployed or not in the labor force consider themselves "retired." Many are still economically active, at least on a part-time basis, and others are continuing to look for work or plan to return to work at some future date if the opportunity presents itself.

Because of the increase in life expectancy and the fact that many more people are choosing to retire early, it is estimated that by the year 2000, at least 33 million Americans will be retired and will spend an average of 14–18 years in retirement. One effect on this situation will be a further in-

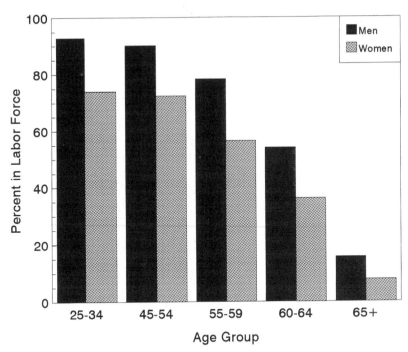

Figure 10–7 **Percentages of men and women of various ages in the work force in 1992.** (Based on data from Kinsella & Gist, 1995.)

crease in the *dependency ratio*—the ratio of persons aged 65 and over per 100 persons aged 20–64 in the population, which will be an estimated 1:3 in the year 2000.

The increasing popularity of retirement among older Americans during the past 60 years can be attributed to a combination of social, economic, and biological events. The shift from an agricultural to a manufacturing economy and the rise in productivity due to mechanization and technological advances led to a larger, more affluent population in which the demands for labor were substantially less than they were during the nation's predominantly agrarian past. In addition, the increase in life expectancy, the obsolescence of older workers' skills, and the unwillingness of assembly-line manufacturers and managers to make allowances for individual differences in work style and rate resulted in a large population of older Americans whose labor was no longer needed to keep the economy growing. This army of older workers was also viewed as contributing to unemployment among younger adults.

Although the United States was one of the last industrialized nations to institute an old-age pension system, with the passage of the Old-Age and Survivors Insurance Program ("Social Security") in the mid-1930s, it became possible for large numbers of older Americans to retire at age 65, or even earlier, if they were willing to accept partial benefits. The idea that people are born to labor and should do so until they become disabled or drop was the prevailing philosophy in most Western countries until the first half of this century. The social philosophy that government should bear a measure of responsibility for protecting and supporting its citizens was in part a cause and in part a consequence of social welfare legislation during the twentieth century. This philosophy, which was first championed by Eugene V. Debs and the Socialist Party early in the century, also came to be espoused by the Democratic Party and to some extent even by the Republican Party from the Roosevelt Era of the 1930s onward. Today, rather than being a privilege accorded to a select few, retirement pensions and other benefits that accompany it are viewed as rewards to older workers for contributing to the nation's growth and prosperity.

In addition to its humanitarian side, retirement has the practical effect of making more jobs available to younger adults. It also provides an incentive to workers to endure demanding or otherwise undesirable jobs and a way for management to get rid of ineffective workers. Social Security has become such a fixture of American life, for both the young and old, but particularly for the politically powerful older American population, that even more conservative politicians are reluctant to consider reducing or eliminating benefits under the plan. To a lesser extent, the same is true of another benefit of retirement—Medicare. However, even with Social Security and Medicare, the reduction in income experienced after retirement makes it difficult for many older Americans to enjoy the same kind of lifestyle as they did prior to retirement.

Deciding to Retire

People retire for many reasons, and some for no conscious reason at all other than acceptance of the notion that people are supposed to retire by a certain age if they can afford to. Disabilities such as heart disease, hypertension, injuries, and mental disorders force many older adults to retire, even before age 65. In addition to health problems and disabilities, job loss or dissatisfaction, financial security, retirement of a spouse, pressure from younger workers, opportunity to participate in leisure and volunteer activities, feelings that they are not as productive as the once were, and discouragement over their inability to find a job all affect the decision to retire (U.S. Senate Special Committee on Aging, 1991; Human Capital Initiative, 1993). For many older adults, their jobs become increasingly burdensome and they begin to engage in a *preretirement role-exit process* (Ekerdt & DeViney, 1993).

Most older adults elect to retire as soon as it becomes financially feasible. In certain occupations, such as the military and civil service, this can be done after 20–30 years of service. And in some industries, workers in their late fifties and early sixties may be "bought out" by management and save money

---

MY LIFE 10–2

The Many Meanings of *Retire*

English can be a confusing language, especially when you are very young and the words aren't familiar or heard clearly. Imagine what visions phrases interpreted as "gladly the cross-eyed bear," "The Not-See Party," and "I led the pigeons to the flag" conjure up for a child. Even for adults, the meanings of single words, such as *affect* and *effect*, *eminent* and *imminent*, and *emigrant* and *immigrant* are hard to keep straight. Take the word *retire*, for example. When I was growing up, *retire* meant to go to bed and sleep—even if you didn't want to.

No one I knew when I was a child used *retire* for stopping work forever. The only people who "retired" in that sense were not sitting in rocking chairs on porches and reminiscing about how things used to be; they were either in the nuthouse or the graveyard. Reportedly, these permanent retirees would occasionally come back to finish some task they had not lived long enough to complete—such as scaring the living daylights out of people they didn't like.

In school I learned that the meanings of words can sometimes be figured out by breaking them up into smaller words or syllables. Knowing that *re* meant "again," I interpreted "retire" as "to get tired all over again" or "to put a new tire on a car." Obviously I was on the wrong track.

When I became familiar with the game of baseball, "retire" meant that the batter or the side was no longer at bat. I started collecting cards containing pictures of famous players, and learned that an occasional superplayer's uniform number was "retired" after he had played his last game.

Some years later, when I joined the U.S. Marine Corps, I learned another meaning for *retire*—to retreat from a battle or any other source of danger. I was also told that you can "retire" your debts, "retire" from office, "retire" a ship, and "retire" from duty. Incidentally, I was quite anxious to do the last for most of the time that I was in the Corps.

Eventually, I consulted a dictionary and discovered that all activities designated by the word *retire* refer to some sort of withdrawal, leaving, removal, or retreat. And so it finally made sense that a person could "retire" from a job, a vocation, or a career. However, I also found out that most people who "retire" do so in a very limited way. They may terminate their involvement in one type of productive activity, only to go on to another and another until they can "retire" no more. The last time they retire, they presumably expire. Whether they end up playing a lyre or fighting fire is a matter of conjecture.

---

for organizations during a time of slow economic growth and retrenchment. Less popular than early retirement is partial retirement, in which an employee's workload and salary are gradually reduced each year until he or she has completely retired (Quinn & Burkhauser, 1990). More men that women elect to retire early, presumably because they can afford to or have worked longer. In any case, the increasing number of retirees—the majority of whom are men—is somewhat offset by the increasing number of older women in the workforce.

Retirement Planning

The changes in status occasioned by retirement would seem to require some degree of planning and preparation. In most cases, however, any planning is done in a fairly informal manner and does not anticipate all of the problems that may accompany the event and process of retirement. Ideally, planning for retirement should begin 5 to 10 years prior to the actual event, but this is not what usually happens. Furthermore, although a majority of retirees report having made some plans, most are inadequate. For example, among the 572 adults age 30 or over questioned in a national Gallup Poll in 1995, only 31% stated that they had written down a financial plan for their retirement. A majority of the sample said that they were not earning enough money now to save for retirement, and those who had children felt that their children's education had a higher priority than saving for retirement. Only 26% of the sample was designated by the pollsters as "happily prepared" for retirement; 18% were designated as "cautious optimists," 32% as "worriers" or "irresponsibles," and 24% as "woefully unprepared." As shown in Figure 10–8, the individuals who were questioned in this survey were depending much more on personal savings than Social Security or employer pensions for the retirement income, but their personal savings were generally quite low (Moore & Saad, 1995).

Most business and industrial organizations provide some sort of formal retirement-planning programs covering finances, attitudes, and other matters of concern to retirees, but relatively few retirees who are in poor health and/or have low incomes participate in such programs. Most of the participants are in good health, have moderate incomes, and have a higher than average occupational level (Campione, 1988).

The Employees Retirement Income Security Act (ERISA) and the Old-Age Discrimination in Employment Act, combined with employees' concerns over whether the high cost of living would permit them to retire, acted as stimuli for the development of retirement-planning programs in many companies. Most of these programs, however, are unsystematic and seldom go beyond a discussion of pension benefits and other financial matters. Certain companies have taken the more ambitious step of developing their own comprehensive retirement-planning programs or adopting those of the American Management Association, the American Association of Retired Persons, or the National Council on the Aging. These programs include not only financial matters and health-related concerns, but also legal issues, leisure activities, and new vocational pursuits. Sexual behavior, adjustment to changing morals and values, and more mundane matters such as meal prepa-

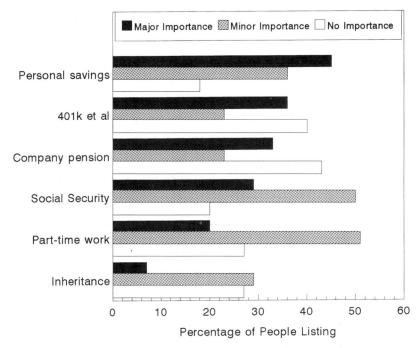

Figure 10–8   Percent of adults in a national survey anticipating each of six sources of retirement income as a major, minor, or no source. (Based on data from Moore & Saad, 1995.)

ration are also covered in some retirement-planning workshops. The workshops place greater emphasis on practical matters than on psychological concerns such as stresses within the family and feelings of self-worth, but the latter are also dealt with in some programs. Furthermore, because retirement affects not only the retiree but the whole family, retirees' spouses are also encouraged to participate in the program.

Adjusting to Retirement

For most older adults, retirement is an active, rewarding period of their lives. They now have time to pursue interests and complete tasks that they had to postpone or devote less time to during their working years. Not only do most people adjust well to retirement, but also their health and happiness may actually improve when they are no longer required to conform to the daily grind (Betancourt, 1991; Herzog & House, 1991; Quinn & Burkhauser, 1990). For these reasons, retirees are, on the whole, satisfied individuals who retain a sense of usefulness and pride in themselves and their accomplishments.

A 1995 Gallup Poll found that 51% of Americans aged 65 and older were "Very satisfied" with the way things were going in their personal lives, the highest of any age group. As might be expected, a much larger percentage (67%) of individuals whose annual incomes were over $75,000 than individuals whose incomes were in the $30,000–$49,999 bracket (53%), the $20,000–$29,999 bracket (43%), or the under $20,000 bracket (31%) indicated that they were "Very satisfied" with the way things were going in their personal lives (Moore & Newport, 1995).

Retirement is, of course, not a pleasant experience for everyone. Retirees with financial and health problems, whose identity was tied up with their jobs, who were forced to retire, and who have made few, if any, plans about what to do with the rest of their lives have difficulty adjusting. For these individuals, retirement is accompanied by feelings of diminished usefulness, insignificance, and dependence, and sometimes a sense that life is essentially over. The loss of meaningfulness and importance that occurs may, like any prolonged stress, accelerate the process of age-related decline. However, when anxiety and depression occur immediately after retirement, they are usually mild and short-lived (Palmore, Burchett, Fillenbaum, George, & Wallman, 1985). Certainly there is no evidence that postretirement depression increases the risk of suicide (Stenback, 1980).

Whether one is able to adjust satisfactorily to retirement depends to a large extent on attitudes and behavior patterns that developed during the working years. For highly work-oriented people who organized their lives around their jobs and have no substitute for them, retirement can be an unpleasant, extremely stressful experience. Blue-collar workers, who have lower incomes and are more likely to have neglected to develop hobbies and other leisure activities during their working years, usually want to keep on working and have a harder time adjusting to retirement (Riley & Foner, 1968). Because of the economic disadvantages that they have experienced during their working years, women seem to have even greater difficulty than men in adjusting to retirement (Perkins, 1992). But like men, healthier and more highly educated women tend to adjust better (Szinovacz & Washo, 1992).

In order for people to make a good adjustment to retirement, they must be willing to reorganize their lives and change their self-perceptions from worker to retiree. The change need not be one to total idleness; many retirees find part-time employment or become involved in volunteerism (Human Capital Initiative, 1993). In general, adjusting to retirement is easiest for those who are healthy, active, and well-educated, and have adequate incomes and a good social network of family members and friends, and who were satisfied and happy even before retirement (Palmore et al., 1985).

For the next 10 years or so, the percentage of the American population consisting of individuals in both the 25–64 and the 65 and over age brackets is expected to increase slightly. After 2010, however, the forecast is for the percentage of people in the 25–64 age bracket to decline, while the percentage of those in the 65-and-older bracket increases. By the year 2030, it is anticipated that the percentage of 25–64 year-olds will have declined from a

1995 figure of 51.6% to 47.4%, while the percentage of those 65 and over will have risen from a 1995 figure of 12.6% to 20.2%. Thus, by 2030 the greater numbers of the latter age group—the so-called "geezer boomers"—will be needed to compensate for the decline in the percentage of 25–64-year-olds (Silverstein, 1996). As larger numbers of older Americans remain in the work force, it is expected that the average retirement age will increase as the century wears on. Retirement may still be an attractive alternative to full-time employment, but it is likely to be postponed for greater numbers of people.

SUMMARY

The median income for both men and women increases from young adulthood to middle age and then declines in old age. Despite receiving lower incomes than younger and middle-aged adults, older Americans are financially better off than they were a few decades ago. Increases in Social Security and private pension benefits, coupled with tax breaks, senior discounts, and supplemental government programs for the elderly, have increased the discretionary income and overall standard of living of older Americans.

Average income is lower for women and minorities than for men and whites, lower for people with less education, lower in the South than in other parts of the nation, and lower in the central cities than in other metropolitan and nonmetropolitan areas. The biggest source of income for most people consists of earnings, but interest and divided income, Social Security, and other pension benefits make significant contributions to the incomes of many Americans.

Approximately 14% of the U.S. population was classified as poor in 1995. The poverty rate was highest for Hispanics and blacks than for Asian/Pacific Islanders and non-Hispanic whites, but more non-Hispanic whites than any other ethnic group were classified as poor. The poverty rate was higher for Americans under age 18 than for other age groups, and higher for foreign-born than for native-born Americans.

Many different pension program are managed by federal, state, and local governments, but the most extensive of all these programs is the OASI program managed by the Social Security Administration. In addition to OASI, the Supplemental Security Income Program (SSI) ensures that aged, blind, and disabled persons with no income and very limited resources of other kinds will have a minimum monthly income. However, the fiscal solvency of the Social Security program is a source of continuing economic and political concern.

Private pension plans supported by business and professional organizations in most industrialized countries are of two kinds—defined-benefit and defined-contribution. Most pension programs are of the defined-benefit kind, guaranteeing a specific monthly income to workers when they reach retirement age. Benefits are more variable under the defined-contribution plan, depending on fluctuations in the financial markets in which the pension funds have been invested. Because of their more irregular work histories, women are less likely than men to receive private pension benefits.

The largest number of full-time employees are clerical and other administrative support personnel, but service workers constitute the largest portion of temporary and part-time employees. Whatever the occupational category may be, the amount of financial compensation for work is related to training and experience. The highest paid of all individuals in the labor force are physicians, lawyers, engineers, and airplane pilots.

Donald Super's theory characterizes vocational interests and occupational choice as developing in a series of stages, beginning with the crystallization and specification stages of adolescence, progressing to the implementation and establishment stages of young adulthood, continuing into the consolidation and maintenance stages of middle adulthood, and declining in the deceleration and retirement stages of older adulthood. Betz extended Super's emphasis on the role of the self-concept in occupational choice to include Bandura's concept of self-efficacy development in the process of vocational counseling. Other theorists, such as Holland and Roe, have underscored the relationships between vocational interests and personality characteristics.

Job satisfaction varies not only with the status, power, financial and other rewards of the job, but also with the age and personality of the worker. Younger and older adults both express greater satisfaction than middle-aged adults with their jobs. Chronic dissatisfaction with one's job can lead to alienation, a feeling of dissociation or estrangement from the job. Flextime and worker development and enhancement programs can assist in countering alienation.

Burnout is precipitated by the stress of overwork and is characterized by a number of physical, psychological, and behavioral symptoms, including the inability to keep up with the pace and pressure of the job and a depletion of energy and motivation. Another source of work-related stress is multiple-role strain, which arises in working women who experience a conflict between the work role and the role of wife and mother. Chronic stress can also contribute to errors and accidents on the job.

Losing one's job is quite stressful, leading to psychological symptoms such as anxiety and depression as well as various physical and behavioral symptoms. The loss of a job is less serious for younger than for older adults, but it is typically viewed with greatest alarm by middle-aged adults. Middle-aged workers who are laid off are generally too young to retire, but they also experience the greatest difficulty in finding positions comparable in status and salary to their previous ones.

Larger numbers of Americans than ever before are retiring, retiring earlier, and living for a longer time after retirement. The decreased need for a large workforce of older adults and the increased attractiveness of financial incentives for retirement have expanded the population of retirees during the past few decades. The major reasons for early retirement are health and disability problems and the financial feasibility of doing so. In addition, many workers grow dissatisfied or discouraged with their jobs, and others retire simply because they and their families consider it time to do so.

Retirees typically have done little or no formal planning for retirement, but most companies provide sessions or workshops on financial, health-related, and other matters of concern to workers for whom retirement is imminent. Despite a minimum amount of planning in most instances, retirees on the whole adjust quite well to the event, status, and process of retirement. Those for whom adjustment to retirement is more of a problem tend to be individuals who have financial and/or health problems, who have difficulty envisioning a life without gainful employment, and who were forced to retire. Blue-collar workers and women usually experience greater difficulty than white-collar workers and men in adjusting to retirement; workers with less education also tend to have more problems than those with more education.

SUGGESTED READINGS

Aiken, L. R. (1995). *Aging: An introduction to gerontology* (Chs. 9 & 10). Newbury Park, CA: Sage.

Cascio, W. F. (1995). Whither industrial and organizational psychology in a changing world of work? *American Psychologist, 50*, 928–939.

Keita, G. P., & Hurrell, J. J., Jr. (Eds.). (1994). *Job stress in a changing workforce*. Washington, DC: American Psychological Association.

Leonard, F., & Loeb, L. (1992, January). Heading for hardship: The future of older women in America. *USA Today Magazine*, pp. 19–21.

Mergenbagen, P. (1994, June). Rethinking retirement. *American Demographics*, pp. 28–34.

Quinn, J. F., & Burkhauser, R. V. (1990). Work and retirement. In R. H. Binstock & L. K. George (Eds.), *Handbook of aging and the social sciences* (3rd ed., pp. 307–327). San Diego: Academic Press.

Smeeding, T. M. (1990). Economic status of the elderly. In R. H. Binstock & L. K. George (Eds.), *Handbook of aging and the social sciences* (3rd ed., pp. 362–381). San Diego: Academic Press.

Warr, P. (1992). Age and occupational well-being. *Psychology and Aging, 7*(1), 37–45.

CHAPTER 11

Spending, Leisure, and Other Nonemployment Activities

From conception until death, people are constantly engaged in activities of one sort or another. To be alive is to be doing something, whether it contributes to one's longevity, shortens it, or has no effect whatsoever on how long one lives. Some activities—essential or unessential—are performed regularly and repeatedly, whereas others occur only occasionally. One activity that takes place quite regularly is spending. Spending can be traumatic, but it can also be enjoyable and even therapeutic. A twist on the saying, "When the going gets tough, the tough get going," is the prescription that "When the going gets tough, the tough go shopping."

EXPENDITURES

It may be true that the best things in life are free, but most necessities and conveniences cost money. According to the Consumer Expenditure Survey conducted by the U.S. Department of Labor in 1995, approximately 95% of the average American's annual income after taxes was spent on a variety of essential and discretionary items. The amount of after-tax income that went for expenditures varied not only with the individual's total income but also with his or her chronological age (see Figure 11–1). Whereas the average person under age 25 spent 14% more than his or her income after taxes,[1] the percentage of after-tax expenditures declined to 97% for the 25- to 34-year-old age group, 93% for the 35- to 44-year-old age group, and 89% in the 45- to 54-year-old age group. It then rose to 93% in the 55- to 64-year-old age group and to 111% in the 65 and over age group (U.S. Department of Labor, 1996). Not surprisingly, individuals with larger incomes tend to spend more, but those with lower incomes tend to spend a greater percentage of it. The percentage of total income that goes for taxes is also greater for people be-

---

[1] Obviously, when a person spends more than his or her income, the difference must be made up of savings, gifts, or thefts.

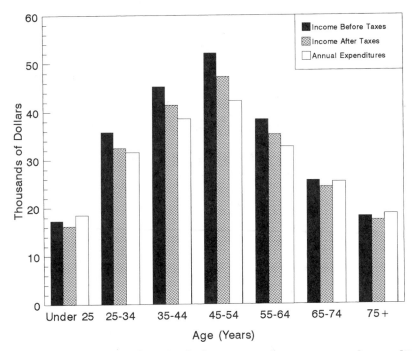

Figure 11–1   Average annual income before taxes and average annual expenditures by age group. (Based on unpublished data from U.S. Department of Labor, Bureau of Labor Statistics, November 25, 1996.)

tween the ages of 26 and 64—those whose incomes are higher—than for individuals under 25 or 65 and over.

Other Demographic Variables

Chronological age and income are, of course, not the only demographic variables that are related to annual expenditures. Because of their higher average incomes, professionals and executives spend more than people in occupations lower on the status scale. Some other variables that are associated with expenditures are race/ethnicity, education, geographical region of residence, urban versus rural location of residences, and whether the individual owns or rents his or her home. Illustrated in Figure 11–2 are the facts that, on the average, whites spend more than blacks, non-Hispanics spend more than Hispanics, college graduates spend more than noncollege graduates, homeowners spend more than renters, urban residents spend more than rural residents, and people who live in the West and Northeast spend more than people who live in the Midwest and South (unpublished data for 1995 provided

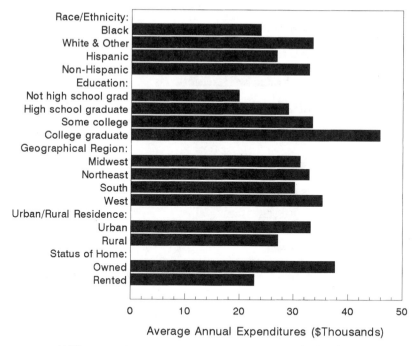

Figure 11–2   Differences in average annual expenditures by race/ethnicity, education, geographical region, and urban/rural residence. (Based on unpublished data from U.S. Department of Labor, Bureau of Labor Statistics, November 25, 1996.)

by U.S. Department of Labor). All of these demographic variables are, of course, interrelated and associated with the more general variable of socio-economic status.

Specific Categories and Items

The percentage of total income that is spent for particular categories of items also varies with chronological age and other demographic characteristics of purchasers. Note in Figure 11–3 that, in 1995, individuals in the 25- to 44-year-old age group and the 65 and over year group spent a greater percentage of their incomes on housing and food than those in the 45- to 64-year-old age group. Older adults also spent a higher percentage of their income on health care, utilities, and cash contributions than young and middle-aged adults. On the other hand, young and middle-aged adults spent higher percentages of their incomes than older adults on transportation, clothing, insurance, and pensions (U.S. Department of Labor, 1996).

The expense of specific items in the various expenditure categories in

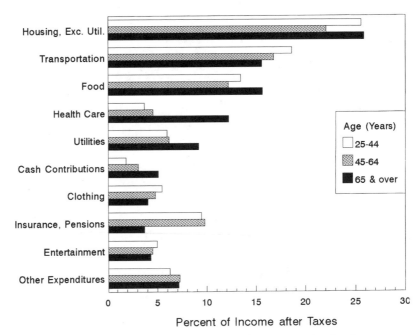

Figure 11–3 Percent of total income spent in various categories for three age groups. (Based on unpublished data from U.S. Department of Labor, Bureau of Labor Statistics, November 25, 1996.)

Figure 11–3 is also of interest. For example, in the "food" category, 62% was spent for food at home and 38% for food away from home; the most expensive food group was "meats, poultry, fish, and eggs." The most costly item in the "utilities" category was electricity, and in the "clothing" category, women's and girls' clothes cost more than boys' and men's clothes. The highest cost in the "transportation" category was for vehicle purchases, and the highest cost in the "health care" category was for health insurance.

Older Adult Consumers

In general, older Americans consume fewer goods and services than their younger contemporaries, but they spend a greater portion of their after-tax incomes on items that cost of living adjustments fail to weight properly (e.g., food, health care, utilities). The lower average expenditures of older adults are a reflection of the fact that their households have fewer members and the members have less expensive needs. In addition, more job-related items such as transportation, clothing, life insurance, pensions, and entertainment are less expensive for older than for young and middle-aged adults. Income taxes are also less for older Americans. Only about half of the age-65-and-over population pay any income tax at all, and the tax rate for those who do averages around 14%. However, above a certain income level, even Social Security benefits are taxed, and a certain portion of those benefits are withheld when the individual's earned income is above a specified maximum.

The growing size of the older American population and its increased purchasing power during recent decades has been accompanied by the realization that older adults represent a powerful economic force. In fact, the lagging economies of many nonmetropolitan communities in the Sunbelt and elsewhere have been shored up by the so-called *mailbox economy* stemming from Social Security checks and other sources of disposable income of older residents (Glasgow, 1991). Although older adults are not quite as avid consumers as teenagers, many marketers are now targeting the 50-and-over and the 65-and-over segments of the population.

Effective marketing requires an understanding of what motivates potential consumers and the ability to empathize with them (Wolfe, 1990). With respect to market segmentation based on chronological age, marketers must realize that the motivations of middle-aged and older consumers are different from those of teenagers and young adults. As a group, older consumers are motivated more than younger consumers by the desire for personal comfort, convenience, safety, security, independence, and even spirituality (Schewe, 1990). According to Wolfe (1990), older adults are influenced less by materialistic motives and more by the experience values of products and services. There are, however, significant differences in motivations among people of the same age. An 80-year-old driver in a red sports car may be unusual, but it can occur.

A market segmentation study conducted by Day, Davis, Dove, and French (1988) identified two groups of women consumers: self-sufficients and persuadables. Self-sufficients were high in internal locus of control,[2] independent, cosmopolitan, outgoing, and influential with other people. They read more books and magazines, and went shopping, attended concerts and sporting events, and ate in restaurants more often than persuadables. Persuadables, on the other hand, were high in external locus of control, had little confidence in their own opinions, were more easily persuaded by advertisements, preferred to stay at home rather than participating in outside activities, and watched more daytime television than self-sufficients. These differences between the two groups of consumers led the authors of the study to suggest that self-sufficients are more likely to be reached by print ads and persuadables by television commercials.

In addition to more traditional (and stereotypical) health products such as analgesics, dentures, hemorrhoid remedies, laxatives, moisturizers, ortho-

---

[2]*Locus of control* is J. B. Rotter's (1966) term for a cognitive–perceptual style characterized by the typical direction (internal or self vs. external or other) from which individuals perceive themselves as being controlled.

pedic shoes, and vitamins, older adults also spend money on art supplies, books, clothing, a wide variety of games (backgammon, mah-jongg, electronic and computer games), home furnishings, travel, and entertainment (Leventhal, 1991). For the sports-minded, there are lightweight rifles, special golf clubs, and other equipment adapted to age differences; for the more affluent, there are cruises and flights to everywhere, furs, jewelry, and luxury cars of all kinds; and for readers, there are magazines designed specifically for the mature market (e.g., *Active Aging, 50-Plus, Golden Years, Modern Maturity, Prime Time*). Older adults read newspapers and magazines more frequently than other age groups, and their preferred television viewing includes news and sports programs. Older shoppers also rely more on mass media and salespersons than younger shoppers.

Many businesses offer discounts ranging from 5% to 30% of the usual purchase price of goods and services to older consumers who are members of the American Association of Retired Persons. Lifetime passes to national historical sites, monuments, forests, and parks are also available to individuals aged 62 and over. Taking advantage of the many discounted products, permits, and fares that are offered can save older adults a great deal of money, contribute to their pleasure, and thus add life to years.

The extent to which consumer products add years to life and life to years depends, of course, on how safe those products are. Every year, nearly a million Americans over age 65 are treated in hospital emergency rooms for injuries associated with products they use every day. The death rate for older adults is approximately five times that of younger adults for unintentional injuries involving motor vehicles and other consumer products. Falls in bathrooms, on stairs, on stepstools, and on floors are particularly common. To reduce the frequency of such accidents, the U.S. Consumer Product Safety Commission (CPSC) recommends the use of grab-bars and nonslip mats by bathtubs, handrails on both sides of stairs, and slip-resistant carpets and rugs. CPSC also recommends that older adults have smoke detectors installed on every floor of their homes, that they use nightwear that resists flames, and that they turn the temperature of their water heaters down to 120 degrees to prevent scalding.[3]

Because children may be accidentally poisoned by medicines prescribed for adults, the packages are intentionally made to be "child-resistant." But many older adults have difficulty opening child-resistant packages, so the CPSC also recommends that pharmaceutical manufacturers develop innovative closures that appeal to the cognitive skills of older people rather than to their physical strength (U.S. Senate Special Committee on Aging, 1994).

---

[3]A free brochure, *Home Safety Checklist for Older Consumers*, describing the hazards in each room of the home and recommended ways of avoiding injury can be obtained by sending a postcard to Home Safety checklist, CPSC, Washington, DC 20207. Another brochure, *What Smart Shoppers Know about Nightwear Safety*, can be obtained from AARP, 610 E Street NW, Washington, DC 20049.

LEISURE ACTIVITIES

Merely because an activity is not absolutely necessary for survival does not mean that it is unimportant to one's sense of well-being. Time spent away from the demands of work or duty, or from the exercise of vital functions, is not always wasted or valueless. Leisure activities, pursued either inside or outside the home, may be just as essential to happiness as anything else that people do. Reading, listening to music, watching television, parlor games, and engaging in exercise and various hobbies frequently occur in the confines of one's living quarters. However, many leisure activities—jogging, field sports, attending the theater and restaurants—and other spectator or participant activities take place outside the home.

Leisure activities are desirable for a number of reasons. In addition to being a means of expressing one's personal interests and associating with people who have similar interests, leisure may help people to cope with stress, improve their physical and mental functioning, and generally contribute to positive feelings about themselves.

The degree to which play and leisure are pursued varies with personality, age, health, interest, ability, financial resources, transportation, and sociocultural factors, Because of their personality traits, energy level, concern with keeping fit and healthy, or simply searching for an interesting and meaningful lifestyle, some people spend as much time as they can in the pursuit of leisure activities.

In general, young adults participate in more leisure activities than middle-aged and older adults, and for longer periods of time. One indicator of the relationship of age to participation in leisure activities is seen in the decline in the percentage of income after taxes that is spent on entertainment, from about 6% by adults under age 25 to around 5% in middle age, and to under 4% in older adulthood (unpublished data, U.S. Department of Labor).

In middle age, the active-leisure orientation of young adults typically begins to give way to the more passive leisure style of old age. Rather than engaging in vigorous exercise and sports activities, middle-aged adults are more likely to become involved in clubs and other organizations and spend more time just "hanging out" with other people and enjoying social, cultural, travel, and organizational activities. These relatively passive pursuits become even more common in later life, and the rate of participation in active sports declines to an estimated 10% among people over age 65 (Bammell & Bammell, 1985). In some instances, it is the *portent of embarrassment* that causes older adults to avoid the playing field; they feel they will not be welcome and will fail in their attempts to do well.

Although most older adults restrict their leisure activities to fishing, shuffleboard, pool, golf, and gardening, some go in for strenuous sports such as tennis and skiing. Furthermore, the kinds of physical activities preferred by older adults are related to gender: Older men tend to participate more than women in outdoor recreational activities such as hunting, fishing, attendance

---

MY LIFE 11–1

Leisurely Work

I have always believed that the pursuit of leisure is one of the noblest ambitions of humanity. By "leisure," I don't mean to imply that one should play or rest all the time. Still, an occasional nap or frolic when things become tedious or tense certainly never hurt anyone.

Perhaps being able to relax completely is therapeutic, but I find it difficult to do. Even when I am supposed to be relaxing, I am usually thinking about something or other. Many of my best ideas and most reasonable solutions to problems have occurred when I was presumably resting or engaged in some other nonstrenuous pastime. However, I have found it wise to reexamine these cerebral outputs when I am in a more attentive and purposeful state of mind. What appears to be reasonable and ingenious when I am resting or playing often turns out to be fanciful and illogical when subjected to clearer scrutiny. This is particularly true when the thoughts are generated during deep sleep. I have been told that I occasionally lecture and even ask and answer questions in my sleep, but I sincerely doubt that these nocturnal mutterings make much sense.

When I was a boy and my sister and I went to a concert or some other public performance, she always took a book along with her. Then, if she found the performance uninteresting, she would open her book and begin reading. Although I was never quite as avid a reader as my sister, I never hesitated to drift off into constructive reverie under the same circumstances.

Now that I am an "older adult" who spends most of his time at home, I find that I am more productive than I ever was when gainfully employed. Part of the explanation may lie in the fact that I don't consider what I do now as work in the sense of labor. And when I become weary of what I am doing, I simply take a break and do something else. To me, work, like beauty, is a matter of perception. If I view what I am doing as work, it becomes an onerous chore. But if I think of it as a kind of game that I can stop playing at any time, I have a greater sense of enjoyment and usually accomplish more as well. When I am merely relaxing but still fairly attentive, or even doing something more active such as playing golf, walking the dog, driving the car, cooking, cleaning, or mowing the lawn, creative thoughts usually come more rapidly.

One thing I know for certain is that I can get too close to a problem or some other task and concentrate on it too hard. Then it is unenjoyable, more tension-provoking, or, in a word, more like work. The key for me seems to lie in not attempting to separate work and leisure. Therefore, I always try to work at a leisurely pace and to remain an interested participant in my leisure activities.

at spectator sport exhibitions, and traveling, whereas greater numbers of women prefer cultural and home-based activities (Lawton, Moss, & Fulcomer, 1986–1987). The extent to which people participate in outdoor activities and the kinds of activities in which they engage also vary with geographical area. There are more pleasant days in the Sunbelt than in the North, and adults of all ages take advantage of them. In fact, the enjoyment of outdoor leisure activities year-round is what attracts many people to the Sunbelt states. In addition, available coparticipants and areas and times set aside for leisure activities affect the degree of participation. It is noteworthy that older adults who live in retirement housing have higher levels of participation in leisure activities than those who live in dispersed housing (Moss & Lawton, 1982). It may also be the case that retirement communities are more appealing to people who enjoy participating in leisure activities.

Both health, which is more likely to decline in later life, and lack of money and transportation limit participation in action-oriented activities. For this reason, the most common physical activities engaged in by older men and women are walking, gardening, travel or camping, and outings. Many older adults also enjoy bingo and other games of chance, and gambling casinos throughout the United States count older adults, and women in particular, among their most loyal customers. Slot machines and video poker are especially popular not only among the elderly but also in all adult age groups. I have often observed an elderly woman playing two or three slot machines simultaneously for hours on end, defying anyone to interfere with her pleasure. However, most leisure activities engaged in by older Americans are solitary and are pursued in the home rather outside. As a group, older men and women also spend more time than young and middle-aged adults watching television (6 hours per week on average) and in reading, writing, and other solitary, sedentary, at-home activities.

It appears, however, that age differences in leisure activities are as much a reflection of cohort (generational) differences as they are of aging per se. Certainly the extent to which middle-aged and older adults participate in leisure activities is a lifelong habit pattern. People who were quite active and involved in sports or other nonwork pursuits during their youth tend to remain that way during the years of middle and older adulthood (McAuley, 1992; McAuley, Lox, & Duncan, 1993). Those who participated in a greater range of activities when they were younger usually have a greater number of role options in later life and hence a greater likelihood of making a successful adjustment to old age. Thus, although the leisure activities of older adults differ in some respects from those of younger adults, the differences are probably due as much to upbringing and cultural differences between generations as they are to chronological age. It is quite possible that, rather than spending their retirement years playing shuffleboard or checkers, or digging in the garden, the next generation of older adults will devote more time to swimming, jogging, playing musical instruments, and engaging in educational or other self-improvement pastimes of the sort that interest today's young and middle-aged adults. Many older adults indicate that they would like to have had more education and developed their mental abilities, but relatively few take advantage of opportunities for doing so in later life (De-Genova, 1992).

OTHER ACTIVITIES OF OLDER ADULTS

Spending money and engaging in leisurely pursuits are, of course, not the only nonemployment activities of older adults. Many older adults keep busy as members of various organizations, participate in religious activities of various kinds, serve as volunteers, become involved in politics, and even go back to school.

Volunteerism

As discussed in Chapter 7, most older adults spend some of their free time visiting friends and relatives. In addition, some volunteer their services to various public and private organizations. Several million American men and women aged 16 and over perform unpaid volunteer work each year. Volunteer activities provide them with opportunities to utilize and broaden their skills while extending their social contacts. The largest number of volunteers work in churches or other religious organizations, followed in order by schools or other educational institutions, civic or political organizations, hospitals or other health organizations, social or welfare organizations, and sport or recreational organizations (U.S. Department of Labor, 1990). Among the activities of these volunteers are visiting people who are home-bound and directing religious, cultural, and recreational programs for the young and old.

The Older American Volunteer Programs, sponsored by the federal AC-TION agency, enable older Americans to perform volunteer services in day-care centers, hospitals, schools, and other public service agencies. Included in these programs are the Retired Senior Volunteer Program (RSVP), the Foster Grandparent Program, and the Senior Companion Program (SCP).[4] Citizens aged 18 years and older can also serve in Volunteers in Service to America (VISTA), which sponsors community activities to reduce or elimi-nate poverty and poverty-related problems by assisting persons with disabil-ities, the homeless, the jobless, the hungry, and the illiterate or functionally illiterate. Other programs of interest to older volunteers include the National Council on the Aging's Family Friends, the Peace Corps, the Senior Commu-nity Service Employment Program, the Senior Environmental Employment

[4]For information, write to the appropriate program at ACTION, 806 Connecticut Avenue NW, Washington, DC 20525 (Phone: 202–634–9355).

Program, and the Service Corps of Retired Executives. Older adults who are concerned with social and political matters can also find an outlet for these concerns by serving on town councils and planning commissions. Those who become involved in community-service activities often make important contributions to traffic control, land-use regulation, establishing priorities for health and social services, and in other matters of concern to older adults and other age groups.

Memberships

As a group, older adults derive a great deal of personal satisfaction, information, and material support from being members of various professional, social, and religious organizations. In particular, membership in a professional or labor organization, or in a club or lodge, provides not only a sense of belongingness and camaraderie, but also feelings of security, well-being, and prestige. Organizations vary, of course, in their purposes and the age, gender, and socioeconomic groups to which they appeal. For example, business clubs, trade unions, and other occupational associations are particularly important to young and middle-aged adults who are active in the labor force. Although most retirees remain proud of their union membership, like all social interactions, being a member of an organization becomes less important in old age. This is especially true of older adults in the working class, who direct more of their social interests toward their own families. Older adults in the middle and upper social classes are more likely to remain active in social and religious organizations and to make new friends and find new pursuits and purposes from being affiliated with such groups.

Education

Another source of nonemployment activity throughout adulthood is formal education. The amount of formal education attained by American adults varies with a number of demographic characteristics. For example, more men than women have at least a bachelor's degree, whites have more formal education than blacks, and non-Hispanics have more formal education than Hispanics. Married persons with spouse present, never-married persons, and divorced persons have more education than married persons with spouse absent, separated persons, or widowed persons. People living in the Northeast, Midwest, or West have more formal education than those living in the South, and those living in metropolitan areas have more education than those living in nonmetropolitan areas (Day & Curry, 1995). These demographic differences in education are not independent of each other, and many are related to another demographic variable—chronological age. As shown in Figure 11–4, the average amount of formal education varies inversely with

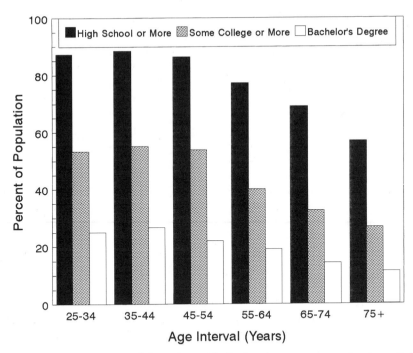

Figure 11–4   Percentages of American adults in six age groups having attained various levels of formal education in 1995. (Based on data from Day & Curry, 1995.)

chronological age. For example, 56.8% of those age 75 and above had completed high school, whereas 88.4% of those in the 35–44 age group had attained that level.

Of interest is the fact that the age distribution of the amount and percentage of annual income after taxes that was spent on education in 1996 had two modes—one mode of $667 (3.62%) in the under-25 age group and another mode of $1,028 (2.44%) in the 45–54 age group (unpublished data, U.S. Department of Labor). The first mode is self-explanatory, in that this is the time (under age 25) when students are attending college and obtaining other enlightening and preparatory educational experiences. Two factors are responsible for the second mode: Not only are many parents in that age group (45–54) contributing financially to their children's college education, but also a number of middle-aged parents, especially women, decide to seek further education when their children leave home. In fact, approximately 17% of adults between 35 and 54 and 6% of those over 54 enroll in college courses (U.S. Bureau of the Census, 1990a).

Adult education encompasses more than formal educational experiences in graded schools and colleges. Many community colleges and skills centers offer ungraded job-training programs and courses for adults of all ages. In addition, a large number of universities throughout the world have special programs and courses designed to attract older adults with varying interests. Many of these institutions are also a part of Elderhostel, an international network of educational and cultural institutions located in the United States, Canada, and 45 other countries. Low-cost travel and study opportunities are offered to participants aged 55 and over (and their companions aged 50 and over) in a wide range of liberal arts and science courses. The basic program consists of a stay of five or six nights, three academic courses meeting one-and-a-half hours each weekday, simple but comfortable dormitory accommodations, and some extracurricular activities. Prerequisite courses, homework, and examinations are not required, and no grades or credits are given for completing the courses (*Elderhostel United States and Canada Catalog*, February 1996). Courses are ungraded and special efforts are made to encourage students and strengthen their self-confidence. Most Elderhostel students have already had fairly extensive educational experiences, the great majority having graduated from high school and many from college.[5]

Many other organizations also provide continued learning experiences for older adults. Prominent among these are the Senior Center Humanities Program sponsored by the National Council on Aging, Interhostel, Northeastern Senior Seminars, University Vacations (UNIVAC), the federally-sponsored College Centers for Older Learners Program, and peer learning programs in which peers rather than paid faculty conduct classes. Another educational service for older Americans is Senior Net, in which older adults communicate by computer with a wide array of people and sources of information.

Despite the success of Elderhostel and other educational programs, the great majority of adult students are young. Even the select group of older adults who decide to return to the classrooms, laboratories, and libraries after absences of several decades may find that they must relearn how to learn. They must redevelop the required study habits and skills; control their anxieties concerning tests, term papers, and other required educational activities; learn to seek help from teachers, books, and fellow students; and stick to a schedule that is sometimes demanding. The self-efficacy of older students, and consequently their performance in college-level courses, may be enhanced by techniques such as arranging for early success, having them observe the success of other students of their age, verbal encouragement, and designing lessons and tests that take the students' abilities into account (e.g., testing for recognition rather than recall) (Rebok & Offermann, 1983).

The National Retired Teachers Association, the American Association of Retired Persons, and many other organizations recognize that older adults should not only be provided with opportunities to learn new skills and

---

[5]For more information on educational opportunities for older adults, write to Elderhostel, 75 Federal Street, Boston, MA 02110, and the Institute of Lifetime Learning, AARP, 610 E Street, NW, Washington, DC 20049.

further their education but also that the services of the old as teachers of the young should be utilized more extensively. Many retired professionals with time on their hands and an interest in working with people would make highly effective educational aides, tutors, and advisors for young students, Having the old teach and work with the young, rather than segregating themselves into communities populated only by their age-mates, can assist in breaking down the gap and alienation between generations.

Religious Activities

As indicated by the results of a telephone survey of over 3,000 American adults conducted by the Gallup Organization in 1995, the United States is a very religious nation. Ninety-five percent of the respondents in that survey stated that they believe in God or a universal spirit, 88% described religion as "very important" or "fairly important" in their lives, and 70% said they belonged to a specific church or synagogue. Eighty-four percent reported affiliation with a Christian denomination, 2% were Jewish, 6% claimed other religions, and 8% claimed no religious preference. However, only 43% (50% of women and 36% of men) of all respondents reported that they attend church or synagogue every week or almost every week. Attendance at religious services increases with age: Thirty-six percent of those aged 18–29, 42% of those aged 30–49, 44% of those aged 50–64, and 56% of those aged 65 and older reported attending their place of worship each week. Also of interest is that 38% of the respondents stated that they believe the influence of religion is increasing, whereas 57% said that they believe it is declining. Hardly surprising is the finding that Republicans and conservatives outnumbered Democrats and liberals among those saying that religion is very important and that they attend church every week. According to a combination of criteria, women are more religious than men and older adults are more religious than younger adults (Moore, 1995; Saad, 1996).

Americans are also strong in their beliefs in a life after death. Over 90% of all American adults indicate that they believe in God and that they pray (Koenig, Kvale, & Ferrel, 1988). The great majority also say that they believe in heaven and that they have a good chance of going there when they die (Woodward, 1989). Greater percentages of older than younger adults, of whites than blacks, of Southerners and Midwesterners than Easterners and Westerners, and of those who live in nonmetropolitan than metropolitan areas express beliefs in immortality and the hereafter (Bearon & Koenig, 1990; Gallup & Proctor, 1982).

As shown in Table 11–1, 94% of religiously affiliated persons in this country are Christians. The largest Christian family is Roman Catholic (36.6%), and the largest Protestant family is Baptist. Many of the Protestant families consist of several denominations. The largest non-Christian affiliation is Jewish, followed by Muslim.

Church attendance is higher for children and women than for adults and

TABLE 11-1 Religious Affiliations in the United States

Family/denomination	Total membership	Percent
Roman Catholic Church	59,858,042	36.6
Baptist churches	36,433,523	22.3
Methodist churches	14,285,851	8.7
Pentecostal churches	10,281,559	6.3
Lutheran churches	8,350,212	5.1
Latter-Day Saints churches	4,672,850	2.9
Presbyterian churches	4,273,721	2.6
Churches of Christ	3,679,736	2.2
Episcopal Church	2,504,682	1.5
Reformed churches	2,079,634	1.3
Orthodox (Eastern) churches	1,885,346	1.2
Jehovah's Witnesses	926,614	0.6
Adventist churches	794,859	0.5
Church of Christ, Scientist	700,000	0.4
Church of the Nazarene	591,134	0.4
International Council of Community Churches	500,000	0.3
Salvation Army	446,403	0.3
Christian and Missionary Alliance	302,414	0.2
Churches of God	267,676	0.1
Mennonite churches	249,798	0.1
Evangelical Free Church of America	226,391	0.1
Brethren churches	218,905	0.1
Christian Congregation	112,437	0.1
Friends (Quaker) churches	84,047	0.1
Other Christian churches (35 denominations)	753,550	0.5
Total Christian churches	154,470,621	94.4
Jews	5,981,000	3.7
Muslims	3,000,000	1.8
Buddhist Churches of America	19,441	<0.1
All religiously affiliated	163,471,391	100.0

Source: Wright (1997).

men; it is also higher among people with higher incomes and educational levels, and for longtime than short-time residents of a community. Of Roman Catholics, Protestants, and Jews, the frequency of attendance at religious services is highest for Roman Catholics, next highest for Protestants, and lowest for Jews (Harris & Associates, 1975).

Religious beliefs and practices also vary with age. According to a Harris Poll conducted some years ago (Harris & Associates, 1975), membership in churches and synagogues reaches a low point in early adulthood (ages 18–24), remains fairly constant from age 25 to 54, rises slightly from ages 54 to 80, and then declines somewhat. The decline in attendance during old age is caused to a large extent by problems of health and disability, lack of transportation, and financial difficulties. Despite the fact that they may no longer go to church as often as they did when younger, most people in their late seventies or over still listen to and watch religious programs on television and radio, as well as praying, reading the Bible, and meditating in the privacy of their own homes. For example, two-thirds or more of the older adults in Bearon and Koenig's (1992) study reported praying every day, As indicated by these findings, religious beliefs and commitment may actually increase rather than decrease during later life (Ainlay & Smith, 1984).

Worship is not the only reason why people participate in religious activities. Other reasons include fellowship or socialization, to establish and maintain a particular public image, and to cope with personal problems and stress. One study found, for example, that coping strategies associated with religion were employed by nearly 50% of the sample of adults who were surveyed (Koenig, George, & Siegler, 1988). African-Americans and older adults in particular are much more likely to consult a church minister than a mental health professional when they are under mental stress or are otherwise experiencing problems in their lives (Levin & Taylor, 1993; Veroff, Douvon, & Kulka, 1981).

As a group, African-Americans, and especially women, are intensely involved in religious activities (Levin & Taylor, 1993). Second only to the family in its influence on the personal, social, religious, and political lives of its African-American membership is the church. Throughout this century, with perhaps their finest hour during the Civil Rights Movement of the 1960s, African-American churches have served as centers for the advocacy of social justice in the black community (Roberts, 1980) and have helped cultivate many influential American leaders.

Religious observance does not always make people feel well adjusted and happy; both the threat of punishment and the promise of reward pervades religious teachings. However, reported life satisfaction is positively related to religious beliefs and practices. Correlation, of course, does not imply causation: It may be that people who are satisfied with their lives are also more religious, not because the practice of religion is satisfying, but because satisfaction leads to religion, or because both religion and satisfaction are products of a third variable. However, it is reasonable to suppose that attending religious services can provide people with feelings of social acceptance and community that contribute to their sense of well-being and life satisfaction (Markides, 1983; Ortega, Crutchfield, & Rushing, 1983). In contrast, feelings of self-worth are lowest of all for adults who have very little religious commitment (Krause, 1995). At the very least, religious beliefs and practices can reassure people that somebody else cares about them and is willing to be of assistance when they are in need. For most people, that is perhaps sufficient to enable them to weather and endure difficult times in their lives.

Religious Faith

Religious teachings typically begin with rituals and stories, progressing to faith and interpretation as the child's cognitive abilities develop. Compared with Islam, Christian teachings place more emphasis on the interpretation of religious writings. But despite the efforts of theologians and philosophers throughout history, no one has succeeded in devising a direct proof of the existence of God[6] or the correctness of any religious belief. Blaise Pascal's famous wager concerning the existence of God would probably be accepted as a good strategy by most people. The wager is that if you bet that God exists and He does not exist, you have lost nothing. On the other hand, if you bet that God does not exist and He does exist, you have lost everything. Therefore, given no choice but to bet, the better strategy is to bet that God exists and live your life accordingly.

Religion is ultimately based on faith: One either believes or does not. This does not necessarily imply that faith is irrational; faith can be the result of a very profound process of thinking.

According to James Fowler (1981, 1986), faith develops through a series of six stages, reminiscent of but not paralleling Lawrence Kohlberg's (1976) conception of six stages in the development of moral reasoning. By *faith*, Fowler does not mean religious faith exclusively, but rather anything that provides people with a reason for living and hope for happiness. Stage 1 in Fowler's theory—*intuitive–projective faith*—is a faith based on magic, imagination, and fantasy. At this stage, which is characteristic of children between the ages of 3 and 7, the power of God and the mysteries of life and death are interpreted magically, At Stage 2—*mythic–literal faith*—religious myths and stories are accepted as literally true and the power of symbols is believed in. This kind of faith, which is characteristic not only of middle childhood but also of some adults, involves the notion of reciprocity: God rewards or punishes those who obey or do not obey His laws.

Typical of Stage 3—*synthetic–conventional faith*—is the nonintellectual, tacit acceptance of religious values in an interpersonal context. This conformist type of faith is concerned with what makes sense or "feels right" in the individual's social world. Faith at Stage 4—*individual–reflective faith*—is characterized by detachment from cultural values and from the approval of other people. Perhaps stimulated by the college experience in the person's late teens or early twenties, simple acceptance of the usual order of things is replaced with an active commitment to a life goal and a lifestyle that may differ significantly from those of other people. Faith at Stage 5—*conjunctive faith*—incorporates seemingly contradictory conscious (rational) and unconscious (religious, spiritual) ideas. The magical understanding of symbols and myths that characterized Stage 2 is synthesized with the individual–reflective faith of Stage 4. People at Stage 5 can combine ideas

---

[6]One of the characters in Aldous Huxley's *Point Counter Point* (1928) provides the following mathematical "proof" of how God could have created the universe from nothing: Let ∞ = God, 0 = nothingness, and 1 = the universe. Since anything divided by 0 equals infinity, $1/0 = \infty$. Cross-multiplication yields $\infty \times 0 = 1$, proving that God (∞) could have created the universe (1) from nothing (0). Like Pascal's famous wager, there is a problem with this proof. Do you know what it is?

such as the worth of life compared with that of property to produce new truths.

Characteristic of Stage 6—*universalizing faith*—is a vision of universal compassion, justice, and love that compels the individual to live his or her life in a way that may seem saintly or foolish to other people. Those who reach this last stage in Fowler's developmental theory of faith are exceptional, examples being Moses, Gandhi, Martin Luther King, Jr., and Mother Theresa (Berger, 1994).

Despite the hierarchical nature of his theory, Fowler does not claim that one stage is necessarily better than another. The appropriateness of a given stage depends on what is right for the individual at that time in his or her life.

> Each stage has its proper time of ascendancy. For persons in a given stage at the right time *for their lives*, the task is the full realization and integration of the strengths and graces of that stage rather than rushing on to the next stage. Each stage has the potential for wholeness, grace and integrity, and for strengths sufficient for either life's blows or blessings. (Fowler, 1981, p. 274; emphasis in the original)

Politics

In the post-Watergate era of the 1980s and 1990s, many Americans became cynical about the motives and abilities of elected officials to do anything other than argue and beg for contributions to support their next campaign for public office. Politicians were seen as dishonest, corrupt, and self-promoting individuals, more concerned with their own egos and the exercise of power than with doing anything constructive to help the citizenry of this country.

Disinterest born of cynicism and lack of information about the functioning of government and its officials are found particularly among young adults, who vote in smaller numbers and are less familiar with political candidates and issues than middle-aged and older adults (Oreskes, 1990). The percentage of people who report voting in national elections increases dramatically from ages 25–34 to ages 35–44, then more slowly up to the 65- to 74-year-old bracket, after which it declines. The great majority of Americans over age 65 vote in presidential elections, constituting a larger voting bloc than any other age group (U.S. Senate Committee on Aging, 1991).

Regardless of the greater political interest shown by older adults, disenchantment with public officeholders and the activities of government has not been limited to the young. The growing alienation of the public at large is seen in the decreased voter turnout in all age groups.

Traditionally, older adults have devoted more attention than their younger contemporaries to political campaigns and have tended to demonstrate greater interest in political news (Jacobs, 1990). Older adults tend to spend more time listening to, reading about, and discussing politics than other age groups, perhaps because they have more free time in which to do so. Another factor affecting the greater political interest and activities of older adults is upbringing: Today's older adults grew up during a time of less personal wealth and greater concern about national survival—concerns about which the federal government, in particular, was expected to do something. Another reason why older adults are ostensibly more political is that they have reached a stage in life in which they are less apt to generate new wealth, and they must focus on ways to preserve and conserve what they have already acquired. Because of declining strength and abilities, older adults may also feel more vulnerable and insecure than they did in earlier years, and they expect government to help protect and support them when they are no longer able to do so by themselves.

The fact that older people tend to vote in larger numbers than younger ones is well known to most politicians, as indicated by the extreme caution exercised by Congress in tinkering with Social Security, Medicare, and other government programs for older Americans. Because of the wide range of individual differences within the 65-and-over age group, no politician has ever been able to deliver what has been called "the old-folks vote." Older adults are not a homogeneous group; they reflect the diversity of social and political interests of society as a whole. This very diversity and the fact that, unlike industrial workers or students, they do not meet as a group, act as barriers to unified political participation. Poor health and disabilities, in addition to the fact that there is no formal organization within the major political parties to represent the interests of older people, also limit their political participation as a group (Bond & Coleman, 1990).

The perception of younger adults as more politically liberal and of older adults as more politically conservative is true to some extent. In general, older adults have more conservative political views and are more likely than younger and middle-aged adults to support Republican candidates and issues. On the whole, they are more conservative on domestic economic and social issues and more "hawkish" on foreign policy. But when their own rights and living conditions are at stake, normally conservative older Americans typically adopt a more liberal position.

There is no evidence that people become more conservative as they grow older (Alwin, Cohen, & Newcomb, 1991; Jacobs, 1990). In fact, some polling data show that a greater percentage of older adults than younger adults identify themselves as Democrats (Stanley & Niemi, 1990). Many of today's young adults are far to the right, whereas many older adults are just as far to the left in a political sense. The relationship between political conservatism and chronological age appears to be largely a cohort or generational effect, in that there is a strong tendency for people to retain the same political orientation as they age.

Other demographic variables related to the frequency of voter turnout are gender, race/ethnicity, income, and location of residence. For example, greater percentages of men and whites than women and blacks report voting in national elections. But the gender gap is narrowing. Although older adult men are more likely to vote than older adult women, young adult women are more likely to vote than young adult men. In addition, people with higher incomes are more likely to vote than those with lower incomes, and residents of urban areas are more likely to vote than those who live in rural areas. Perhaps even more important than age, gender, and race in determining voter turnout is education: People in higher educational levels tend to vote in greater percentages than those in lower educational levels (U.S. Senate Special Committee on Aging, 1991; Wolfinger & Rosenstone, 1980). As in the case of age, however, the magnitudes of these differences are affected by the extent to which the candidates and the issues in a particular election are of interest and concern to the specific demographic group.

As indicated by voter turnout, race and gender are often more important than age in determining voter preference. For example, the most striking differences in Figure 11–5 are those between men and women and between blacks and whites in the percentage af the particular group voting for Bill Clinton in the 1996 presidential election. Among different age groups of men and women, there was a slight tendency for greater percentages of voters in the 18–29 year group than those in the other three age groups to favor Clinton,

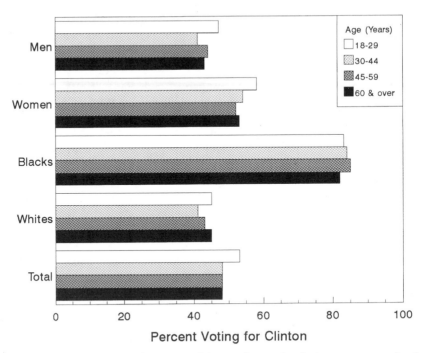

Figure 11–5 Percentages of votes within gender and ethnic groups received by Clinton in the 1996 presidential election. (Based on data published in the *New York Times*, November 10, 1996.)

the Democratic candidate. However, age differences were not nearly as great as gender (men vs. women) or race (black vs. white) differences. Over 80% of black voters in all age groups, compared with less than 45% of white voters, voted for Clinton. Similarly, over 50% of women voters in all age groups, compared with only slightly more than 40% of men voters, voted for Clinton.

Even more than most other professional occupations, politics is an art form that must be cultivated over many years. It is not an occupation that one can, with any great hope of success, enter late in life. There are, of course, many politicians in the 65-and-over bracket, and, in fact, a disproportionate number of older adults are found in certain public offices. For example, most governors and senators are well along in years (Hudson & Strate, 1985). However, the great majority of these individuals have been in politics most of their adult lives and have learned the art of influence by trial and error combined with personal charisma.

Though most older Americans are not political officeholders, they can and do support the efforts of such organizations as the American Association of Retired Persons, the American Society on Aging, the National Council on Aging, and other advocacy groups for the elderly. These organizations lobby for social services and programs for older adults, primarily adequate income, health care, housing, nutrition, and transportation. Political focus on the growing federal deficit in recent years has led to a reduction in federal support for such programs, and to a great extent the action has shifted to the state and local levels. In communities throughout the nation, public and private organizations (Golden Age, Live Long and Like It clubs, etc.) concerned with the needs and rights of older Americans have continued their activities.

SUMMARY

The average American under age 25 or over age 65 spends more than his or her annual after-tax income. Young and middle-aged adults spend around 90–95% of their disposable income, the remainder presumably going for savings and investments. Both younger and older adults spend more than middle-aged adults on housing and food. Older adults also spend more than other age groups on health care, utilities, and cash contributions, whereas young and middle-aged adults spend more on transportation, clothing, insurance, and pensions. Expenditures also vary with race/ethnicity, education, location of residence, and home ownership.

Growth in the numbers of older Americans and their discretionary income has led marketers to attend more closely to the needs and desires of the over-50 and the 65-and-over segments of the population. Manufacturers and advertisers have increased their efforts to design products and promotion materials that appeal to these age groups. Discounts, product adaptations, special sales, and other incentives are being used to attract older consumers.

The quality and quantity of leisure activities engaged in by adults vary with the age, personality, and circumstances of the individual. On the average, older adults are less active than younger ones, but participating in internal and external leisure activities is a lifelong habit pattern than need not decline greatly in later life. Furthermore, many of the differences between younger and older adults in the pursuit of leisure activities are probably attributable to generational or cultural factors rather than to age per se. In general, leisure activities have a beneficial effect on the health and sense of well-being of the participants.

Numerous opportunities for volunteer services are provided by government agencies, community organizations, and by religious, health, educational, and child-care centers. Many people also obtain social interaction and personal satisfaction from being members of social, religious, political, and other organizations. Some middle-aged and older adults elect to further their education and training by attending colleges and technical schools. Elderhostel, the Senior Center Humanities Program, and Interhostel are a few of the organizations that provide opportunities for continued educational experiences in middle- and late life.

The great majority of Americans believe in God and an afterlife, and most expect to go to heaven when they die. A majority are members of religious organizations, but less than half attend church services every week. The frequency of church attendance varies with age, sex, socioeconomic status, education, geographical region, and denomination. Church attendance declines in later life, but a large percentage of older adults still read the Bible and other religious literature, pray, meditate, and listen to and watch religious programs on the radio and television.

Religion is based on faith, which Fowler sees as developing through a series of six stages. Each successive state—from the intuitive–projective faith of young children to the universalizing faith of a few rare adults—is more complex than the stages that precede it.

A greater percentage of older adults than younger adults, of men than women, and of whites than blacks vote in national elections. Older adults also tend to be more conservative than younger adults, due in large measure to cohort rather than age differences. Thus, older adults can be quite liberal in their political views and practices when the issues pertain to the rights and benefits of the elderly. Despite some retrenchment during the 1990s in federal programs for older Americans, there is still a great deal of concern in the public and private spheres with health care, housing, income, nutrition, and transportation for this age group.

SUGGESTED READINGS

Alwin, D. F., Cohen, R. L., & Newcomb, T. M. (1991). *Political attitudes over the life span*, Madison: University of Wisconsin Press.

Chambré, S. M. (1993). Voluntarism by elders: Past trends and future prospects. *Gerontologist*, *33*, 221–228.

Cutler, S. J., & Hendricks, J. (1990). Leisure and time use across the life course. In R. H. Binstock & L. K. George (Eds.), *Handbook of aging and the social sciences* (3rd ed., pp. 169–185). San Diego: Academic Press.

Fischer, L. R., & Schaffer, K. B. (1993). *Older volunteers: A guide to research and practice.* Newbury Park, CA: Sage.

Jacobs, B. (1990). Aging and politics. In R. H. Binstock & L. K. George (Eds.), *Handbook of aging and the social sciences* (3rd ed., pp. 349–361). San Diego: Academic Press.

Krause, N. (1995). Religiosity and self-esteem among older adult. *Journal of Gerontology: Psychological Sciences*, *50B*, P236–P246.

CHAPTER 12

Crime, War, and Law

Both competition and cooperation play a role in the satisfaction of human needs, but these complementary processes are much more effective for society as a whole when they occur in an orderly fashion. Unbridled competition leads to conflict, the resolution of which is not always satisfactory to both parties in a dispute. Conflict, of course, does not always lead to violence, and not all violence is criminal. Violence may be justified in order to protect oneself or someone else, and it may even occur on a massive scale in war and yet be perfectly legal. Furthermore, even violent crimes are not always the result of dislike; robbery, rape, and even murder may represent an uncontrollable attraction for another person, or at least something the person possesses. Finally, violent crime is not the only type of illegal activity. Many misdemeanors and felonies do not involve violence. These property crimes, such as burglary, larceny–theft, and motor-vehicle theft, consist of efforts to acquire the possessions of other people by illegal, but nonviolent, methods.

This chapter is concerned with interpersonal conflict and with laws designed to cope with it. The first part of the chapter deals with criminal behavior and how it varies and changes as a function of age. The second part of the chapter considers the nature and causes of war, which is organized violence on a large scale. Finally, certain age-related legal problems and how they may be dealt with are described.

CRIME AND CRIMINAL BEHAVIOR

Criminal behavior is legally prohibited action or inaction that results in injury to person or property. Crimes need not be intentional; they may be the result of oversight or negligence. Intentional or willful criminal acts (*mens rea*) are usually considered more serious and typically lead to greater penalties than unintended acts. For example, first-degree murder, in which the act is the result of a premeditated intention by the murderer to kill, is considered a more serious offense than second-degree murder, in which the act is precipitated by malice but not premeditated. The law also views violent crimes more severely than property crimes, and felonies more severely than misde-

---

My Life 12–1

Crime in Our Town

There wasn't much crime in the South Florida town where I grew up, at least not much that I was aware of. People were arrested, of course, but mostly for being public nuisances, speeding over 25 mph, driving recklessly, or being drunk and disorderly. Like most towns our size, we had some petty theft, and merchants and customers tried to cheat each other on occasion. A few newspaper carriers admitted to collecting twice in the same week and making incorrect change. Boys also walked out of stores without paying or stole fruit from a neighbor's orchard, but when caught they were usually only lectured and then told to go and sin no more. On Halloween, the more reckless boys strung tin cans across the road to "catch" cars, threw "stink bombs" at girls, and soap-wrote on store windows.

Occasionally, a night burglar would break into a garage, a barn, or a store, but typically took little because there wasn't much to take. One thief with a conscience even left a note apologizing for his activities on the grounds of his inability to make an honest living.

Another man reported that someone had broken into his home at night when he wasn't there, jumped into bed, and had sex with his wife. The wife confessed that she thought the intruder was her husband until the latter came home and chased the former away. In a related case, a large gopher snake crawled through a hole in the floor and got into bed with a woman. She reached over and touched it but wasn't too surprised by the sensation because she considered her husband to be a "snake" anyway.

There was some vagrancy in our town, but we had a place for everyone and everyone knew his or her place.

---

meanors. Felonies, such as burglary or murder, are commonly punished in the United States by imprisonment for more than 1 year, whereas punishment for misdemeanors consists of fines, community service, short jail terms, and the like.

Uniform Crime Reports

Crime is considered one of the major problems in the United States and countries throughout the world by law enforcement authorities, political leaders, and the public at large. To provide detailed public information on the incidence of crimes of various kinds in the United States, and to serve as a basis for action in legislative action and law enforcement, each year the Federal Bureau of Investigation publishes a new edition of *Crime in the United States: Uniform Crime Reports.* This publication provides statistical data on offenses reported, offenses cleared, persons arrested, weapons used

We joked a lot about prostitutes and sex deviates, but most of us would have been scared to death to meet up with one. We also laughed at people who had too much to drink, and we smoked and drank a bit ourselves. Mostly, however, it was cheap wine and rabbit tobacco, or even coffee rolled in brown paper. We never got drunk, but we had fun pretending to be so.

We boys had normal libidos and a great curiosity about sex, and we were very interested in the carnival girlie shows that came to town every year. We were also aware that uncontrolled passion can cause trouble and even lead to violence. There were reports of men beating their wives (rarely vice versa), but murders were more likely to occur once every 10 years rather than 10 times a year. We knew from Warner Bros. movies that big cities were full of juvenile delinquents and gangsters, but thank goodness they weren't in our town. About our only acquaintance with capital punishment was an old tree in our neighborhood on which a horse thief had reportedly been hanged some 50 years earlier. The story (and the gory details) of that execution became embellished over time, and after a while most of us steered pretty clear of that tree!

In all likelihood, those times were not as safe and law-abiding as they seem in retrospect. There may well have been Lizzie Bordens waiting to make their mark and John Dillingers preparing to blast their way out of the quiet homes on the streets of our town. But few of us had any fear of going out at night—alone or otherwise—and if we did, it was the product of our imaginations and the thrill of spookiness rather than the threat of anything real that might have harmed us. Schoolwork, daily chores, and getting along with other people were difficult enough without making trouble for ourselves by worrying about or participating in criminal activities.

in violent crimes, and law enforcement personnel. Also designed to gauge fluctuations in the overall volume and rate of crime reported to law enforcement is a Crime Index. This index is composed of the violent crimes of murder and nonnegligent manslaughter, forcible rape, robbery, and aggravated assault, and the property crimes of burglary, larceny–theft, motor-vehicle theft, and arson. In 1995, the Crime Index total, 13.9 million offenses, or approximately 5,278 per 100,000 inhabitants, was lower than it had been since 1987. Still, the crime clock indicates that in 1995, on the average there was one murder every 24 minutes, one forcible rape every 5 minutes, one robbery every 54 seconds, one aggravated assault every 29 seconds, one burglary every 12 seconds, one larceny–theft every 4 seconds, and one motor-vehicle theft every 21 seconds (U.S. Department of Justice, 1996).

In addition to the *Uniform Crime Reports*, data on the incidence of crime in the nation as a whole are provided by the *National Criminal Victimization Survey*, an annual publication of the Bureau of Justice Statistics based on interviews of a sample of the U.S. population. Unfortunately, neither of these sources provides a completely accurate picture of crime in the United States. The statistics in the *Uniform Crime Reports* are based an offenses *reported* to law enforcement authorities, which are undoubtedly underestimates for most crimes. The corresponding difficulty with the *National Criminal Victimization Survey* is that the findings are obtained only from a sample of the total population, and an unrepresentative one at that. However, by using both of these sources in combination, a fair approximation to the actual state of crime in the United States can be obtained.

Crime is a function of several demographic variables, including race/ethnicity, sex (gender), chronological age, and socioeconomic status. The incidence of arrests for violent crimes, property crimes, and crimes as a whole varies with race/ethnicity, For example, the arrest rate for blacks is five times that for whites for violent crimes, four times that for whites for property crimes, and three times that of whites for all crimes in all age groups.

The number of arrests of both males and females increases up through the late teens and then gradually decreases into old age, but at all ages, the number of females arrested is substantially lower than of males (Figure 12–1). In 1995, young adults (ages 18–24), who comprised only 10% of the U.S. population, had an arrest rate of 26%. On the other hand, adults aged 55 and

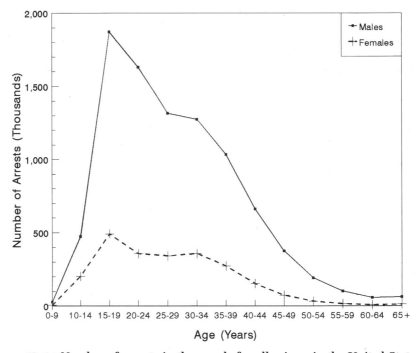

Figure 12–1   Number of arrests in thousands for all crimes in the United States in 1995. (Based on data from U.S. Department of Justice, 1996.)

over, who constituted nearly 21% of the U.S. population in 1995, had an arrest rate of only 2.3%. Regardless of the age group, the number of arrests is obviously not the same for all types of offenses. Alcohol-related offenses (driving under the influence, liquor law violations, and drunkenness) are more common among adults of all ages than other offenses. Property crime and drug abuse are second in frequency, followed by violent crime and disorderly conduct. The order of different offenses by frequency of arrests also varies with age. For example, individuals under age 18 are more likely than other age groups to be arrested for motor-vehicle theft, vandalism, and arson. But adults between the ages of 25 and 44 have a disproportionate number of arrests for fraud, prostitution, family violence, driving under the influence, and drunkenness. These crimes are reflective of the problems of earning a living and raising a family that are characteristic of the 25–44 year age group (U.S. Department of Justice, 1996; Mitchell, 1995).

Because the number of individuals in each age group varies with age, age-specific arrest rates for different crimes may be computed to determine how the incidence of specific crimes varies with age. Figure 12–2 is a plot of the age-specific arrest rates for violent and property crimes in 1995. The age-specific arrest rate for property crime is higher than that for violent crime in

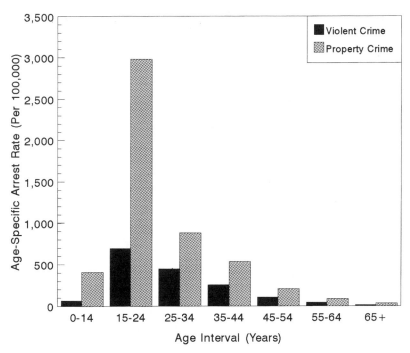

Figure 12–2 Relative percentages of arrests for all crimes, violent crimes, and property crimes in the United States in 1995. (Based on data from U.S. Department of Justice, 1996.)

all age groups. The arrest rates for both types of crime reach their highest levels in the 15–24 year age interval and decline to their lowest levels in the 65-and-over age group. Both rates decline markedly after early adulthood, but the decline is steeper for property crime than violent crime.

Attitudes toward Crime

Because the United States is the most violent industrialized democracy in the world.as well as one of the wealthiest, it is not surprising that concern and fear about crime are widespread in this country. In a recent national survey, for example, 31% of the respondents indicated that they were afraid to walk alone at night within a mile of their homes (Davis & Smith, 1994). However, fear is not necessarily the same as reality. For example, older adults, and women in particular, are reportedly more afraid than younger adults,[1] but younger adults are more likely than older adults to be victims of crime. In 1993, for example, 125.2 of every 1000 residents of the U.S. between the ages of 12 and 16, 120.5 of every 1000 residents between 16 and 19, and 97.7 of every 1000 residents between 20 and 24 were victims of personal crimes. However, only 7.8 of every 1000 residents aged 65 and over were victims of personal crimes in that year (Perkins, Klaus, Bastian, & Cohen, 1996). The crime victimization rate is lower for older persons than for any other age group (Ferraro & LaGrange, 1992; Perkins et al., 1996).[2] When crimes against the elderly occur, and especially violent crimes, they are much more likely than crimes against younger adults to take place in or near their homes (Church, Siegel, & Foster, 1988). When they are victimized, older adults are less likely to resist, and therefore less likely to be physically injured. Be that as it may, because of their lower financial status, the relative loss suffered by older crime victims is usually greater than that for younger victims. Older adults rarely have insurance or coverage through their place of employment, so the financial impact of crime can be quite severe. In addition, crime victimization can be emotionally devastating for older adults (Cook, Skogan, Cook, & Antunes, 1978; U.S. Senate Special Committee on Aging, 1994).

The incidence of a particular type of crime is also not always consistent with the public attention given to it. For example, there are more printed articles and television programs concerned with murder than aggravated assault, but the latter is more common than the former. More attention is also paid to burglary and larceny–theft than to motor-vehicle theft, but the latter crime is more common than the first two by a large margin (Wright, 1997).

---

[1]Employing a different methodology than previous investigations of fears of crime among the elderly, Ferraro and LaGrange (1992) found that younger adults (18–24 years old) were more fearful than older adults of most crimes. Among adults aged 75 years of age and older, the fear of property crime was lower than that for any other age group.

[2]Crime victimization rates are higher for males than for females, higher for blacks than for whites, and higher for Hispanics than for non-Hispanics (Perkins et al., 1996).

The extensive publicity given to crime by the media has undoubtedly contributed to the American public's fears and concerns about crime. Americans consider crime to be the nation's most serious problem. Thus, Gallup polls conducted in 1993 and 1994 found that 87% of both the white and black respondents believed that crime is on the rise, and 25% were deeply afraid of it (Gallup, 1996; McAneny, 1993). Furthermore, 80% of the persons in a representative sample polled by Moore (1994) indicated that they favored the death penalty for adults and 60% for juveniles who committed murder. Despite their fears concerning crime, the majority of residents of the United States who were questioned in McAneny's (1993) poll indicated that they took no special precautions to cope with it. Still, slightly over 40% of all people in this country report owning guns, a rate that is highest in the 18–20 age group (U.S. Department of Justice, 1994).

With respect to solutions to the problem of crime in the United States, older adults are more likely than younger adults to favor stricter gun-control laws, more police on the streets, restrictions on violence shown on television, and longer jail terms for criminals. However, older adults are less likely than younger adults to believe that job programs for inner cities would reduce the crime rate (Moore & Newport, 1994).

Murder

We live in a violent society, one in which people are conditioned to violence not only through a history of settling disputes by individual and collective fighting but by motion pictures, television dramas, and stories in the printed media that are replete with aggression, injury, and death. Prolonged exposure to violence and violent role models without compensating exposure to nonviolent situations and models causes people to become habituated to violence and makes it more natural and easier for them to commit violent acts.

The second and third least frequent of all violent crimes, but still the ones that receive the most attention in television news and dramas, are murder and rape. According to the *Uniform Crime Reports*, in 1995, an estimated 21,326 persons in the United States were victims of *murder and nonnegligent manslaughter*, "the willful (nonnegligent) killing of one human being by another" (U.S. Department of Justice, 1996, p. 13). As illustrated in Figure 12–3, both the number of murder victims and offenders peak in the late teens and early twenties. Offenders are, on the average, slightly younger than their victims, and nearly 10 times as likely to be male as female.

The murder rate also varies with race, socioeconomic status, time of year, and location. In most years, the murder rate is higher in August and December than in other months, on weekends and holidays, in the South than other areas of the country, in central cities than in suburbs or rural areas, and in the home (more women murdered in bedrooms, more men in kitchens). Murder

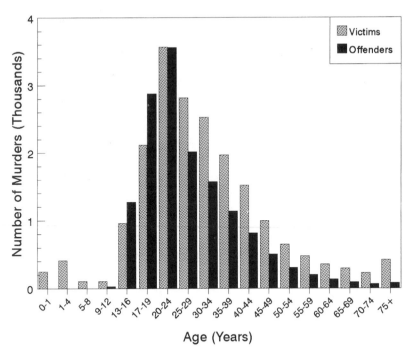

Figure 12–3   Number of murder victims and offenders by chronological age in the United States in 1995. (Based on data from U.S. Department of Justice, 1996.)

is also associated with alcohol consumption and economically prosperous times. The United States has one of the highest murder rates in the world, but it is surpassed by Colombia and Mexico (Humphreys, 1995; U.S. Department of Justice, 1996; Wright, 1997).

Sixty-eight percent of the murders in the United States in 1995 were committed with firearms, 12.7% with knives or other cutting instruments, and 5.9% with personal weapons (hands, fists, feet, etc.). Over 88% of the victims of male murderers were males, but only 9% of the victims of female murderers were females. Over 93% of the victims of black murderers were blacks. Of the murders committed in the United States in 1995, 83% occurred during robberies, narcotics law violations, or other felonies; 53% were committed during arguments or other nonfelonious acts; in the remaining 29%, the circumstances were not known (U.S. Department of Justice, 1996).

Forcible Rape

Forcible rape is defined as "the carnal knowledge of a female forcibly and against her will" (U.S. Department of Justice, 1996, p. 23). A total of 97,463

(37.1 per 100,000 inhabitants) cases of forcible rape was reported to law enforcement officers in this country in 1995. Rape was more common in the summer than at other times of the year. Seventy-five percent of the victims were under age 35, and only about 3% were over age 49. Unlike the traditional picture of the rapist as a stalking stranger, most victims know their attacker and over 40% are raped in or near their own home. However, the picture of rape as a nighttime crime is generally true. Furthermore, it is estimated that only about half of all rape victims report the attack to police (Wright, 1997). Shame, fear, and other emotions undoubtedly contribute to the decision not to report a rape or an attempted rape.

The two most frequent crimes in the violent offenses category used by the FBI in determining its annual crime index are robbery and aggravated assault. Whereas the murder rate in 1995 was 8.2 and the forcible rape rate was 37.1 per 100,000 inhabitants, the rates for robbery and aggravated assault were 230.9 and 418.3, respectively. *Robbery* is defined as "taking or attempting to take anything of value from the care, custody, or control of a person or persons by force or threat of force or violence and/or by putting the victim in fear" (U.S. Department of Justice, 1996, p. 26). *Aggravated assault* is defined as "an unlawful attack by one person upon another for the purpose of inflicting severe or aggravated bodily injury" (U.S. Department of Justice, 1996, p. 31). Whereas robberies are more frequent during the fall, the frequency of aggravated assaults is greater during the summer months. Also, unlike assaults, robberies are at least four times as likely to occur on a street or highway as in any other location. In 1995, robberies were more common in the Northeast and the West, whereas aggravated assaults were more common in the South and West than in other sections of the country. Metropolitan areas had higher rates of both robberies and assaults than nonmetropolitan areas. Firearms were the weapon of choice in robberies and other weapons (clubs, blunt objects, etc.) in aggravated assaults.

Property Crimes

The second class of crimes used by the FBI in computing its annual crime index are the *property crimes* of burglary, larceny–theft, motor-vehicle theft, and arson. Compared with a rate of 684.6 for violent crime, the rate of property crime in the United States in 1995 was 4,593 per 100,000 inhabitants. Of the four offenses in the latter category, the rate was highest for larceny–theft—"the unlawful taking, carrying, leading, or riding away of property from the possession or constructive possession of another" (U.S. Department of Justice, 1996, p. 43). Larceny–theft includes shoplifting, pickpocketing, purse snatching, thefts from motor vehicles, thefts of motor-vehicle parts and accessories, and bicycle thefts in which force, violence, or fraud is not involved. In contrast, *burglary*, the next most common category of property crime, is "the unlawful entry of a structure to commit a felony or theft" (U.S. Department of Justice, 1996, p. 38). Both burglary and larceny–

theft occur more frequently in July and August. *Motor-vehicle theft*—the stealing of automobiles, trucks, buses, motorcycles, motorscooters, snow-mobiles, and so on, has a lower rate than larceny–theft or burglary but represents more than half the value of all property that is stolen. The lowest rate among the four crimes in the property category is for arson—"any willful or malicious burning or attempt to burn, with or without intent to defraud, a dwelling house, public building, motor vehicle, or aircraft, personal property of another, etc." (U.S. Department of Justice, 1996, p. 53).

Causes of Criminal Behavior

As they say in crime dramas, a person is not a good suspect in a criminal case unless he or she had a motive and an opportunity to commit the crime. Opportunities for crime abound in the affluent society, and motives are plentiful among poor, frustrated, immoral, and just plain greedy persons. Motive and opportunity, however, must be accompanied by an ability to commit the crime and avoid detection and apprehension.

Like any other talent, criminal ability is partly learned and partly inborn. According to the *principle of differential association*,

> overt criminal behavior has as its necessary and sufficient conditions a set of criminal motivations, attitudes, and techniques, the learning of which takes place when there is exposure to criminal norms in excess of expo-sure to corresponding anticriminal norms during symbolic interaction in primary groups. (DeFleur & Quinney, 1966, p. 7)

Associating with criminal elements is usually not sufficient in itself to make a person into a career criminal; biological factors, perhaps hereditarily deter-mined, also appear to play a role in shaping criminal behavior (Yochelson & Samenow, 1976).

Criminal behavior is generally more common among teenagers and young adults, who have the strength and speed for crimes such as burglary, larceny, robbery, and, when they are frustrated, aggravated assault and even murder (see Figure 12–2). Older criminals, who are weaker but not neces-sarily wiser, are more likely to commit "white-collar" crimes such as em-ployee theft, embezzlement, and fraud.

Declines in speed and strength are not the only reasons why the fre-quency of violent crime decreases with age. Other factors include increased social status, economic self-sufficiency, and the discovery of different ways of prospering. Most people who have grown up in criminal subcultures find more subtle ways of getting ahead (Gove, 1985; Jolin & Gibbons, 1987).

As people grow older, their investment in the social order expands, and continuing to violate social norms and challenge society's institutions and mores becomes increasingly risky. The penalties for law-breaking become stiffer—at least up until old age—as the person ages into his or her twenties and thirties. For these and perhaps other reasons, to some extent people seem to grow out of crime as the get older. Even sociopaths appear to "burn out" after age 40, and young people who have grown up in a criminal subculture discover more subtle ways of getting ahead. Granted, there are so-called "career criminals," who begin by committing property crimes as teenagers and are somehow able to avoid being arrested when they become adults. They discover that society does not approve of but is less likely to punish "sharp operators" who use their brains rather than their fists and guns to get what they want, even though their activities are illegal.

Punishment

When a person is arrested and convicted of a crime, depending on the nature and seriousness of the offense, he or she may be fined, placed on probation, or incarcerated. Teenagers and older adults are much less likely than young and middle-aged adults to be incarcerated for the same crime. However, the conservative political and social climate of recent years has prompted less forgiveness on the part of the courts, not only for violent crimes but also for drug abuse violations and "victimless crimes."

Both the numbers of prisoners in federal and state prisons and county jails and the lengths of sentences have increased in recent decades. But due to the scarcity of prison space, convicted felons are often released earlier than they might otherwise have been. For those who are forced to remain in prison for extended periods of time, the experience is less likely to promote rehabilitation than it is to serve as a crime school. In addition, the youth-oriented culture of violence in most prisons, a culture characterized by impulsive action, physical courage, challenging rituals, and physical strength, provides little chance for older prisoners who might wish to reform (Sykes, 1958). The prison mentality is focused on conning, coolness, and conformity, and, in general, being able to do "hard time" without breaking.

Sociopolitical efforts to deal with crime in the United States have focused primarily on deterrent measures such as increasing the number of prisons and police rather than on retraining and rehabilitation of inmates or on crime-prevention measures. Still, the results of a recent *General Social Survey* (Davis & Smith, 1994) found that nearly 85% of the American public feel that the courts are too lenient in dealing with convicted criminals. Over one-third of the respondents in this survey also believed that too little is being spent to halt the rising crime rate and in law enforcement.

The question remains as to how long society will be willing to continue spending the billions of dollars required to keep more than 1.5 million Americans isolated, housed, clothed, fed, and otherwise occupied for years on end. This question becomes especially important when one realizes that it is the mainly white majority that is paying for the prisons that are protecting them from the increasing numbers of minority-group prisoners. For example, it is projected that, by the year 2050, one-fourth of the population of the United States will consist of Hispanics, who are also the fastest growing minority group in our prisons. Still, in the case of capital offenses, it costs less to keep the guilty parties in prison for the rest of their lives than to pay attorneys' and court fees required by the endless appeals involved in capital punishment sentences.

Elder Abuse

Because older adults, who have poorer physical strength and skill and frequently live alone, are more vulnerable to crime than their younger contemporaries, a number of public and private organizations have taken steps to combat the problem of crime against the elderly. Older residents of metropolitan areas, in particular, are often preyed upon by thieves and attackers, who want the monthly pension and benefit checks, cash, and other property of older adults. Aged widows and others who live alone are special targets of these young hoodlums, who lie in wait for them in the streets or invade their homes (see Aiken, 1995).

Strangers are not the only ones who abuse the elderly. Each year, an estimated 1 million older Americans are physically, psychologically, or financially abused by their relatives (Pillemer & Finkelhor, 1988). According to the National Aging Resource Center on Elder Abuse (NARCEA), *elder abuse* is one of the most underrecognized and underreported social problems of this country, and far less likely than child abuse to be reported (U.S. Senate Special Committee on Aging, 1994). Among the reasons for elder abuse are financial gain, revenge, hatred of the aged and of old age, and even displaced aggression.

Hickey and Douglass (1981) describe four types of elder abuse that may occur in the home: passive neglect, verbal or emotional abuse, active neglect, and physical abuse. *Passive neglect*, the most common and perhaps the least serious type of abuse, consists of leaving an older person alone, isolated, or forgotten. More common is *verbal or emotional abuse*, in which the victim is frightened, humiliated, insulted, threatened, or treated like a child. Even less common is *active neglect*—confining or isolating an elderly person, or withholding food or medication from him or her. The least common, and arguably the most serious, of all forms of elder abuse is *physical abuse*—hitting, slapping, restraining, or in other ways physically mistreating the victim. Older people may also be the victims of sexual abuse, nonconsensual sexual contact of any kind with an older person. The Special Committee on Aging of the U.S. Senate also provides a separate category of *financial or material exploitation*, defined as the unauthorized use of funds, property, or resources of an older person (U.S. Senate Special Committee on Aging, 1994).

In addition to the various types of *domestic abuse* described in the preceding paragraph are *institutional abuse* and *self-neglect* (*self-abuse*).

Institutional abuse may occur in institutional or residential facilities that provide board and care for older adults. Self-abuse is the neglectful or abusive conduct of an older person, directed at him- or herself, that threatens the person's safety. With respect to the criminal nature of various types of abuse, physical, sexual, financial/material abuses, and, in some instances, emotional abuse and neglect are crimes. However, no state views self-abuse by an elderly person as a crime (U.S. Senate Special Committee on Aging, 1994).

The popular conception of a son or daughter who is under extreme stress from having to take care of a physically impaired, dependent mother or father is not the typical scenario for elder abuse. Rather, in the majority of cases, the abuser is the spouse rather than the children of the victim, and the abuser is as dependent on the victim (for money, a place to stay, transportation, cooking, cleaning, etc.) as vice versa. Furthermore, older men are just as likely as older women to be the victims of abuse (Pillemer & Finkelhor, 1988; Wolf & Pillemer, 1989).[3]

Fraud

According to the *Uniform Crime Reports*, in 1995 there were 331,651 arrests for fraud and embezzlement in the United States. Only about 1% of these cases involved victims aged 65 and over, but there is no doubt that older consumers are often targeted by unscrupulous marketers. Because older people spend a good portion of their days at home, they are easier to contact by telephone, by mail, and door-to-door by con artists attempting to sell worthless goods. Such frauds pervade almost every aspect of an older person's life: from health care to housing, from investment programs to travel promotions.

> To the poor, they make "get rich quick" offers; to the rich, they offer investment properties; to the sick, they offer health gimmicks and new discoveries to cure ailments; to the healthy, they offer attractive vacation tours, and to those who are fearful of the future, they offer a confusing array of useless insurance plans. (U.S. Senate Special Committee on Aging, 1994, pp. 386–387)

Confidence rackets, such as the "Bank Examiner Swindle," the "Pigeon Drop Swindle" (see Report 12-1), home-repair scams, and medical swindles and quackery often seem to be directed exclusively at helpless (and perhaps a little bit greedy) older adults who are lured by the promise of a high percentage increase in their life savings or of obtaining a retirement home and other goods and services at rock-bottom prices. Another example of fraud is the "sweepstakes" or "free giveaways" scheme:

[3]Project Focus (Department P, FAS, Room 9438, 600 Hudson Street, New York, New York 10013) provides information on services available to older adults who need protection against abuse.

A consumer receives a postcard which announces that he or she is entitled to claim one or more prizes. The award notice is professionally designed to appear legitimate. The postcard bears a toll-free telephone number and the consumer is instructed that he or she must simply call to claim the prizes. Once the toll-free number is accessed, a recording instructs the consumer to touch numbers to the telephone which correspond with a "claim number" which appears on the postcard. Ultimately, the consumer receives no prize. What is received is a "telephone bill" which reflects a substantial charge for the call just as if a 900 number had been called. The entry of the sequence of numbers that matched the "claim number" engaged an automated information service for which the consumer is charged. (U.S. Senate Special Committee on Aging, 1994, p, 386)

Materials designed to assist older Americans in avoiding exploitation by con men and bunco artists are distributed by the American Association of Retired Persons Criminal Justice Service, the Food and Drug Administration, the Council of Better Business Bureaus, the United Seniors Health Cooperative, and many other agencies and organizations. Suggestions for ways of minimizing the financial losses and physical damage resulting from victimization are also available.[4]

WAR AND TERRORISM

To many people, war, the ultimate legitimization of violence, is a form of organized crime. Like violent crime, war involves aggression against other human beings, and like property crime, it may involve the expropriation of someone else's possessions. Although international law is often broken by warring countries, war is not necessarily illegal or even unethical in the same sense as criminal behavior. Thus, killing in peacetime is murder, but killing during wartime is often considered heroic. Countries may issue legal declarations of war and engage in armed conflict according to certain internationally agreed-upon conventions or articles of war. Still, not everyone who wages war adheres to such conventions, and when their side loses, violators may be branded and tried by a constituted court of law as war criminals.

Unlike political assassinations, genocide, and pogroms, war has usually been viewed as a legal, reasonable, and oftentimes heroic way of settling disputes between opposing groups. All able-bodied men are expected to serve in the military organizations of their country or group, doing their "duty" without question, risking and even sacrificing their lives for the honor and glory of their community or country. To the classical romanticist, the willing-

[4]Addresses are as follows: Criminal Justice Service, AARP, 601 E Street, NW, Washington, DC 20049; Food and Drug Administration, Center for Devices and Radiological Health, 5600 Fishers Lane, Rockville, MD 20857; Council of Better Business Bureaus, 4200 Wilson Boulevard, Suite 800, Arlington, VA 22203; United Seniors Health Cooperative, 1331 H Street, NW, Washington, DC 20005.

REPORT 12-1

Bank Examiner Swindle

A phony bank or savings-and-loan "investigator" calls you or comes to your home. He is very serious and may have brought along deposit slips from your bank or other official-looking papers. He tells you that the bank is checking up on a dishonest employee and explains how you can help. He says he wants to make a test to see what the suspected employee does when a customer draws money out of his account. He suggests that you go to your bank, draw out a specified amount of money, then let him use it for the test. Either he or a "bonded messenger" or some other official will pick up the money at some nearby point. You withdraw the money. Advised of the need for "absolute secrecy" and that the money must be in cash "in order to check the serial numbers," you ignore the bank teller's concern that you are drawing out such a large sum of cash. You give the money to the "examiner," who hands you a receipt, thanks you for your "cooperation," and may tell you how he plans to use it to trap the suspected employee. Once he is gone, you'll never see him or your money again. The bank, of course, has never heard of him.

Pigeon Drop Swindle

The victim is approached by one of the swindlers and engaged in a conversation on any sympathetic subject. Let's say the victim is an older man. When the swindler has gained his confidence, he or she mentions a large sum of money found by a second swindler who, at the moment, "happens" to pass by. The victim is led to believe that whoever lost the money probably came by it un-lawfully. The swindlers discuss with the victim what to do with the money. One of the swindlers says that he or she works in the vicinity and decides to contact his or her "employer" for advice. He or she returns in a few minutes and states that the boss has counted the money and verified the amount and agrees that because the money undoubtedly was stolen or belonged to a gambler (or some such variation on a theme), they should keep and divide the money three ways, but that each should show evidence of financial responsibility and good faith before collecting a share. The victim is then induced to draw his "good faith" money from his bank. After he has done this, either alone or in the company of one of the swindlers, the money is taken by the swindler to the "employer." Upon the swindler's return, the victim is given the name and address of the employer and told that the employer is waiting with his share of the money. The victim leaves and, of course, cannot find the employer or sometimes even the address. When he returns to where he left the swindlers, they, of course, are gone.

ness to join with one's countrymen in battle was one of the noblest attributes and highest values that a human being could possess. These sentiments are expressed in art and literature, for example, in Shakespeare's *King Henry the Fifth*:

> We few, we happy few, we band of brothers;
> For he to-day that sheds his blood with me
> Shall be my brother; be he ne'er so vile.
> This day shall gentle his condition;
> And gentlemen in England now a-bed
> Shall think themselves accursed they were not here.
> And hold their manhoods cheap whiles any speaks
> That fought with us upon Saint Crispin's day.

War may be *limited*, as when only the lives of members of the military are generally at risk, or *total*, when the lives of both the military and civilian populations are threatened. In total war, the entire country is considered a battleground, and hence all its resources—people, weapons, and other possessions—are subject to attack. War may also be either *external—between two different countries— or internal*—involving two or more groups of people within the same country. Internal wars in which rebel forces attempt to overthrow the existing government are referred to as rebellions, insurrections, revolutions, or civil wars.

Certain scholars have characterized the history of the world as a succession of wars separated by intervals of peace during which opposing forces made preparations for the resumption of armed conflict. This picture may be true of certain wars, such as the Hundred Years War, but certainly not all. Peace is not perceived by most political leaders as merely a respite before recommencing armed conflict. Most peacemakers envision peace itself as enduring, and in some cases, as in the nineteenth century, their efforts have contributed to a prolonged period with no significant wars.

A traditional way of ensuring peace is based on the idea that if a country maintains a sufficiently large stockpile of armaments, then would-be aggressors will be unlikely to start something. This was the reasoning in the policy of *mutual deterrence* practiced by the United States and the Soviet Union for over 40 years following World War II, a policy that led to a $17 trillion price tag for weapons. Although, in this instance deterrence would seem to have worked at least to some degree, from a historical viewpoint it has not been especially effective in preventing military conflict (Lebow & Stein, 1987). In fact, an analysis of the causes of military conflict over the past two millennia indicates that trying to prevent war by means of military buildup actually increased the likelihood that countries that did so would go to war (Kagan, 1995; Naroll, Bullough, & Naroll, 1974).

Historically, victory in war has been determined not only by the relative sizes of the opposing military forces but also, and often principally, by weaponry, leadership, and bravery. These and other factors, some natural and others man-made, influence the duration of wars. Wars may be fairly short-lived and not entail great loss of life or destruction of property. On the other hand, they can last for years and even decades, causing casualties to run into the millions and property damage in the billions of dollars (see Figure 12–4). During the twentieth century alone, something in excess of 100 million people have been killed in wars, approximately 25 million of them since World War II.

Causes of War

Wars have been fought since the beginning of history for a number of reasons: territory, wealth, security, power, religious beliefs, and as a defense against or retaliation for deprivation, injustice, and suffering. Historically, maintaining and defending territorial boundaries have been the principal causes of war, but religious wars have also been common. Unfortunately, the participants in wars fought in the name of religion were not always true to their religious principles. Thus, the Christian Crusaders of the Middle Ages slaughtered not only armed men but also hundreds of women and children as

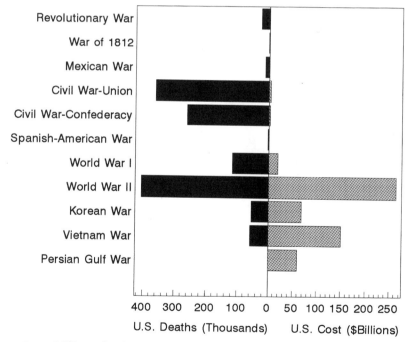

Figure 12–4   Military deaths and costs in wars fought by the United States. (Based on data from *World Book Encyclopedia* [Vol. 21], 1990, p. 25.)

they entered Jerusalem and other Moslem fortifications. Although most wars since the seventeenth century have been fought for materialistic rather than religious reasons, religious differences continue to be a source of armed conflict in certain parts of the world.

According to Sigmund Freud (1933), people possess an inborn "death instinct" (*Thanatos*) than conflicts with their life instinct (*Eros*). Freud maintained that *Thanatos* always wins in the end, but that it can be diverted into sports and creative activities. Rather than viewing the aggression expressed in warfare as caused solely by an inborn instinct or by simple frustration, most contemporary psychologists see it as the result of a complex interaction between biology and the physical and social environment. Human beings are equipped with the neural circuitry for aggressive, warlike behavior, but its expression depends on the presence of an appropriate instigating stimulus and the collective perception of how the interpersonal environment will react to an aggressive attack. Still, this formulation by itself does not adequately explain why nations decide to wage war.

Because it causes untold human suffering and seldom solves the problems that precipitated it, warfare would seem to be a highly irrational way of dealing with international arguments. However, certain military strategists have viewed war as a rational instrument of foreign policy. According to Berkowitz (1990), the decision made by a nation's leaders to declare war is almost always the result of a reasoning process, though not necessarily reasoning of a high order. The decision makers may misperceive or misinterpret statements made by political leaders on the opposing side and choose to ignore facts and events that might cause them to make a different decision (Tetlock, 1988). In addition, the leaders, and the public at large, may lack empathy with the opposing side and even characterize them as subhuman or diabolical and themselves as militarily and morally superior to their opponents (White, 1984).

Training and Combat

The task of turning civilians into combat soldiers is not an easy one; young men and women are not trained from childhood to risk their lives for an abstract cause that they may not understand, or that they perceive as having no effect on them personally. Discipline and obedience to orders, even when they are counter to one's natural impulses and upbringing, are, however, crucial in preparing people for battle. Propaganda, in which the enemy is depicted as barbaric and evil and one's own country as noble and virtuous, contributes to the conditioning of both members of the military and the civilian population for the sacrifices of war.

Although learning to do what one is told without question and entering into combat when ordered to do so often demands the suppression of one's natural and acquired survival tendencies, the need to be accepted by one's comrades and the reluctance to let them down helps soldiers to deal with their fears (Stouffer, Suchman, DeVinney, Star, & Williams, 1949). Furthermore, when war is still viewed as a winnable game, it can be exciting to young men of limited experience and a *joie de vivre*. Soldiers on the battlefield often experience a keen sense of excitement, of living on the edge. Time appears to collapse, and one lives only for the moment.

> I felt an overwhelming elation. It was not so much that one had left the firing line as that one had been in it.... Full of wretchedness and suspense as the last few days have been, I have enjoyed them. They have been intensely interesting. They have been wonderfully inspiring. (Holmes, 1985, p. 148)

However, witnessing the maiming and sudden deaths of other human beings, and being forced to endure miserable living conditions for days on end can be quite unnerving and depressing.

> I was looking straight at him as the bullet struck him and was profoundly affected by the remembrance of his face, though at the time I hardly thought of it. He was alive, and then he was dead, and there was nothing human left in him. He fell with a neat round hole in his forehead and the back of his head blown off. (Holmes, 1985, p. 176)

As a way of divorcing themselves from the reality of their situation, even combat-hardened veterans may come to exist in a kind of dreamy, unreal state, frozen in time, like robots going through their paces and intent only on eliminating, neutralizing, taking out, or wasting an impersonalized enemy (Holmes, 1985). Some soldiers become so caught up in the process that they take extreme chances, thereby sacrificing themselves for their comrades. In addition, in many military engagements, not only the enemy gets "whacked" or "zapped" but also soldiers on one's own side. As was true in both the Vietnam War and the Persian Gulf War, accidents and so-called "friendly fire" can kill and wound soldiers on both sides of a battle.

Meanwhile, on the home front, the civilian population may or may not provide moral and psychological support for the efforts of their armed forces. Due in some measure to the success of government propaganda and the greater clarity of the reasons for fighting during World War II, the civilian populations in countries on both sides were highly supportive of the efforts of their military forces. However, such was not the case with a large segment of the American population that was opposed to the Vietnam War. American soldiers who returned from Vietnam were not greeted by parades and glory. In fact, rather than being honored as heroes, they often found themselves vilified as "murderers" and "baby-killers." Incidents such as the napalm bombing of Vietnamese civilians and the My Lai Massacre increased the intensity of disapproval of the war and all who fought in it. In addition, during the Vietnam War, the murder rate in the United States increased by 42%, compared with an increase of only 11% in Canada—a noncombatant country. According to Archer and Gartner (1983, pp. 1639–1640), "What all wars have in common is the unmistakable moral lesson that homicide is an acceptable, or even praiseworthy, means of the attainment of certain ends." Thus, the legitimization of violence in war can lead to an increased tendency to resort to violence at home.

Captivity and Posttraumatic Stress Disorder

In reaction to the mistreatment of prisoners of war during the nineteenth century, beginning in 1864 a series of international meetings known as the Geneva Convention was held. The result was a set of rules regarding the humane treatment of prisoners of war, as well as the sick, the wounded, and those who died in battle. Despite some improvements as a result of the Geneva Convention and the rules for the treatment of prisoners of war that were defined at the Second Hague Conference of 1907, the conditions under which prisoners existed continued to be atrocious in many instances. During World War II, for example, American soldiers captured by the Japanese were subjected to inhuman treatment and forced to survive on a near-starvation diet. In many ways, however, American soldiers who were taken prisoner by the Viet Cong or North Vietnamese during the Vietnam War suffered an even worse fate. Reminiscent of the treatment of inmates in concentration camps during World War II, prisoners in Vietnam were malnourished, treated like animals, and made to perform unpatriotic or immoral acts. They suffered not only from physical disorders such as diarrhea, serious infections, and malnutrition but also from anxiety, depression, headaches, insomnia, irritability, nightmares, and other psychological disturbances.

> The camp's conditions beggar description. At any time there were about 11 men who lived in a bamboo hut, sleeping on one crowded bamboo bed about 16 feet across. The basic diet was three small cups of red, rotten, vermin-infested rice a day. Within the first year the average prisoner lost 40 to 50 percent of his body weight, and acquired running sores and atrophied muscles. There were two prominent killers: malnutrition and helplessness. (Seligman, 1992, p. 166)

The physical and psychological changes in one prisoner caused by the loss of any hope of release from captivity and his resulting feelings of helplessness were described by a survivor of a Viet Cong prison camp:

> Finally it dawned on him that he had been deceived—that he had already served his captors' purpose, and he wasn't going to be released. He stopped working and showed signs of severe depression: he refused food and lay on his bed in a fetal position, sucking his thumb. His fellow prisoners tried to bring him around. They hugged him, babied him, and when this didn't work, tried to bring him out of his stupor with their fists. He defecated and urinated in the bed. After a few weeks, it was apparent that [he] was moribund: although otherwise his gross physical shape was

still better than most of the others, he was dusky and cyanotic. In the early hours of a November morning he lay dying ... (Seligman, 1992, p. 168)

Depending on the length of imprisonment and the harshness of the treatment, prisoners of war who survive the experience of captivity generally manifest a variety of debilitating conditions: lowered resistance to disease and frustration, greater dependence on alcohol and drugs, and general emotional instability (Hunter, 1978; O'Connell, 1976; Wilbur, 1973). Even among Vietnam veterans who had not been imprisoned, the frequency of depression, marital problems, and divorce was more common than among individuals of the same age who did not go to war (Hunter, 1981). For months and even years after their return, many of these veterans continued to have anxiety attacks, nightmares, insomnia, relationship problems, substance-abuse problems, and "flashbacks" (reexperiencing a stressful event) related to their stressful experiences of combat and captivity. These symptoms, referred to collectively as *posttraumatic stress disorder* (PTSD) have also been observed in civilians who have suffered through earthquakes, airplane clashes, shipwrecks, and other highly stressful events.

Terrorism

Like war, *terrorism*, the use of violence and threats to intimidate or coerce, is a political act. The term dates back to the Reign of Terror (1793–1794) during the French Revolution, but hostage-taking and other acts of terrorism preceded that period. Among the most prominent terrorist groups in early times were the Jewish Zealots of Roman Judea, the Moslem Assassins of the Ottoman Empire, and the Indian Thugs.

Terrorists on the right and the left of the political spectrum have seldom been successful in their expressed aim of overthrowing the government. For example, despite the fact that they caused a popular uprising, the activities of the Jewish Zealots of the A.D. first century led to the mass suicide at Masada, the destruction of the Second Temple, and the *Diaspora*, or scattering of the Jews outside Palestine (Shurkin, 1988).

During the twentieth century, terrorism has been practiced by Russian revolutionaries, European anarchists, Irish nationalists, members of the Indian independence movement, Latin American revolutionaries, and the Palestine Liberation Organization. Bombings, kidnappings, hijackings, and other acts of random violence by terrorists have led to killings, but their primary aim has been to frighten, anger, and otherwise emotionally arouse citizens and government leaders.

Terrorism may be either international, in which case it crosses international borders, or domestic, when it is limited to a particular country. An example of the former was the midair bombing of an American commercial flight over Lockerbie, Scotland, in 1988. An example of the latter was the bombing of the Federal Building in Oklahoma City in 1995. Among other recent acts of terror affecting the United States were the taking of hostages in the American Embassy in Tehran, Iran, in 1979; the bombing of the U.S. Marine Barracks in Beirut, Lebanon, in 1983; the kidnapping of foreigners by pro-Iranian groups in Lebanon; and the bombing of the World Trade Center in New York. France, Great Britain, India, Israel, Japan, and Peru have also suffered from terrorist acts in recent years.

The reactions of governments to terrorist acts have included counterattacks, negotiations, and even total surrender to their demands. An example of counterattack was the retaliatory bombing raid on Libya conducted in 1986 by the United States in response to Libyan protection of terrorists who were reportedly involved in the airplane bombing over Lockerbie, Scotland.

The decision as to what to do when terrorism involves the taking of hostages is a difficult one. Every approach—direct force, protecting the lives of the hostages at all costs, refusing to deal with terrorists under any circumstances, negotiating under a total news blackout—has its downside, and there is no general agreement among experts as to which approach is most effective (Baron & Byrne, 1987; Jenkins, 1983; Merai, 1985; Pruitt & Rubin, 1986). The direct approach, which the Israelis used in freeing the hostages at Entebbe, worked fairly well in that instance, but in other instances it has resulted in a large loss of life. Some sort of negotiation would seem to be a more reasonable course, but it is seen as rewarding terrorists and may be viewed by the public at large as surrendering to their demands and encouraging other would-be terrorists. Even conducting negotiations between terrorists and authorities under a total news blackout, which denies terrorists the reinforcement and role-modeling resulting from open press coverage, has its drawbacks. Authorities, and public officials in particular, are faced with extreme pressures to do everything that they possible can to have hostages released, pressures that may prove to be irresistible when the hostages and their families make tearful, poignant pleas for their release in the media.

The official position of the United States Government has been that it does not negotiate with terrorists. However, as seen in the Iranian arms sales and other "arrangements" by representatives of the government, private agreements affecting terrorism and terrorists are sometimes made. Whether these arrangements represent violations of the letter of the law or only its spirit has been the subject of congressional debate and much discussion in the public press.

LAW AND THE ELDERLY

Crime and war are important matters covered by the laws of all nations, but there are many less conspicuous issues concerning property, contract, tort, and constitutional law. Despite our cherished freedoms and rights, our lives are governed and controlled by laws from the very moment of our birth. Certificates, licenses, permits, contracts, deeds, policies, and other legal documents pervade our day-to-day existence and regulate our behavior. As soon as we are born, our birth is registered on a birth certificate. As we mature and come of age, we may be issued a driver's license, a marriage license, an employment contract, a property deed; eventually, we make a will and finally have a death certificate issued with our name on it. Laws designed to protect us and society in general govern what we do in both our public and private lives. Attending school, taking a job, traveling abroad, paying duties and taxes, and other behaviors concerned with our education, employment, investments, and family lives require awareness of and some familiarity with the laws pertaining to those behaviors.

The Bill of Rights and other documents describe in detail what is permissible and what is not permissible under federal, state, and municipal laws, what we can and cannot do with impunity. Ignorance of these laws is seldom accepted as an excuse for breaking them. Violations of certain laws, such as minor traffic offenses, are forgiven to some extent on their first occurrence and by children, the mentally handicapped, and the elderly. However, repeated misdemeanors and even one-time felonies usually lead to some form of legal punishment, the exact nature of which depends on the particular state or municipality in which the crime occurred.

People of all ages are a concern of the law, but two groups have been the subjects of special attention—the very young and the very old. Although it has not always been so, today most children are seen as unable to take proper care of themselves and therefore requiring special protection and consideration under the law. This is particularly true of children with physical or mental problems and disabilities, so-called "special children." In addition, the high rate of juvenile delinquency and the increasing number of children committing "adult crimes" have led legal authorities to focus not only on teenagers but also on younger children as well. This is a book on adult development, so the topic of children and the law will not be considered further here. The reader is referred to the many texts on child development and legal psychology for more information (e.g., Wrightsman, 1994b).

Like children, the elderly have legal rights and needs that in the past have often gone unrecognized. Several matters concerned with the legal needs of the elderly were discussed earlier in this book, including benefits under Social Security, Medicare, and Medicaid; age discrimination in employment; elder abuse; consumer fraud; nursing home care, and living environments. Other legal matters affecting many older people are commitment, competency and guardianship, living trusts, wills, probate, and taxes. The remainder of this chapter is concerned with these matters.

Legal Assistance to the Elderly

State and county governmental agencies on aging are, under the provisions of the Older Americans Act of 1965, designated to serve as advocates for older people, coordinate activities on their behalf, and provide information to them regarding services and opportunities. Another governmental organization, the Legal Services Corporation, in cooperation with the National Senior Citizens Law Center, provides assistance and support to attorneys and paralegals throughout the nation. Several American universities have also established legal service centers to help older adults cope with governmental and private-sector bureaucracies. Professional organizations, such as the American Bar Association, the National Academy of Elder Law Attorneys, and the National Elder Law Foundation,[5] have contributed to the establishment of certification programs and procedures for attorneys specializing in the provision of legal assistance to older Americans. Many attorneys who specialize in such services focus on poor and middle-income older adults who require assistance in maintaining income, health, housing, and autonomy. More specifically, they deal with a host of legal problems ranging from faulty automobile repairs, bothersome door-to-door salesmen, writing a simple will, missing Social Security benefits, and evictions or home foreclosures.

Competency and Guardianship

The question of *competency* may arise in the case of a person who, because of physical or mental infirmity, has problems in taking care of his or her property and other affairs. If the person is found legally incompetent, the court will appoint a guardian to manage his or her property and situation. This process, referred to as *guardianship* or *conservatorship*, results in the person forfeiting his or her legal and personal autonomy. The guardian or conservator makes decisions concerning all aspects of the person's life—living arrangements, medical treatment, financial expenditures, and management of assets (Wilbur, 1991). A competency hearing should not be entered into lightly by a relative of the person at issue. Forcing an elderly person to become totally dependent on someone else can be personally debilitating and even expose him or her to exploitation and victimization.

The concept of *testamentary capacity* is a specific kind of competency—the competency to make a will. Establishing the testamentary capacity of a person requires a separate hearing to determine if the person knows (1) the nature of his or her property (bounty), (2) that he or she is making a will, and (3) who his or her natural beneficiaries are. Not only are the determination of competency and testamentary capacity separate legal matters, but they are also separate from the legal determination of insanity.

Wills and Probate

A substantial majority of Americans die *intestate*, that is, without ever having made a will, and some of those who do make out wills are quite

---

[5]Addresses are as follows: American Bar Association, 750 North Lake Shore Drive, Chicago, IL 60611; National Academic of Elder Law Attorneys, Inc. and National Elder Law Foundation, 1604 North Country Club Road, Tucson, AZ 85716.

creative. They may write a will an the back of a grocery bag, in rhyme, in a humorous fashion, or even in code. They may draft it in their own handwriting and not bother to have it witnessed (*holographic will*) or perhaps even tape-record it (*nuncupative will*). There are also *mutual wills* containing reciprocal provisions, as when a married couple leaves everything to each other without restrictions, and *conditional wills* containing provisions that take effect only when specific conditions described in the will have been met or certain events have taken place.

Holographic, nuncupative, and other nonstandard wills are not valid in all states, and in most cases, it is better for all concerned if an attorney is consulted and legal procedures are followed. In general, a will is legally binding if the *testator* (the person making the bequest) is at least 18 years of age and of sound mind, if the will is signed in the presence of witnesses (usually two) and contains certain required information. This includes the testator's name, address, and age, followed by a statement of his or her capacity to make a will and that the act is voluntary. Next is a list of the items in the estate and the names of the individuals to whom those items are being bequeathed. The name of the appointed executor of the will should also be provided, after which are the dated signature of the testator and the signatures and addresses of the witnesses. As long as the testator remains alive and in sound mind, he or she may alter or revoke the will.

Laws pertaining to inheritances and wills vary from state to state, but in most states, a will must be filed in a *probate court* or its nonexistence disclosed to the court within 10 days after the death. After the probate court has made a public announcement that the decedent's will is being probated, there is a specified time period during which claims against the estate must be settled and the property distributed by the executor according to the provisions in the will. In case of irregularities, such as no executor having been named or no will having been prepared by the decedent, the court appoints an administrator to handle the distribution of the decedent's property. If no legal heirs come forward, the estate becomes the property of the state.

Probate can be a lengthy and expensive process, involving a heavy tax burden on the estate. *Estate taxes* may be levied on the property left at death and must be paid from the estate before the remaining assets are distributed to the heirs. In addition, there may be *inheritance taxes*, which are levied on the heirs as a percentage of the value of the inherited property. Although some states have effectively abolished inheritance taxes, in most states estate and inheritance taxes range from 2% to 23% of the taxable property.

As a way of reducing the tax burden on his or her estate and heirs, one of the first things that a person with a sizable amount of property wants to know from an estates attorney is how to avoid probate. This may be done through annuitization (insurance, retirement plans, employee stock plans, annuities, etc.). which are exempt from probate. Furthermore, in many states, bank accounts that are held jointly may be treated like jointly held real estate and hence are not subject to probate. Another way to avoid probate is to transfer most of one's assets to other people while one is still alive or to transfer them in the form of co-ownership (joint tenancy). In addition, one can give $10,000 each to as many people as he or she wishes without the recipients having to pay taxes on the gifts. Stock can also be transferred to foundations or other charitable organizations with no tax liability.

Another popular way of avoiding probate is to set up a legal *trust* while the individual (*trustor*) is still alive. This method is commonly used by older adults who wish to continue providing support for their survivors after the trustor's own death. The trustor retains control of the property as long as he or she remains alive, but when the trustor dies, the property is distributed to his or her designated beneficiaries without being probated.

Because life insurance policies are also exempt from probate, many people use this method of making certain that their survivors are cared for. There are, however, many different kinds of life insurance, chief among which are term life insurance, universal life insurance, and variable life insurance, as well as group and individual life insurance policies. For this reason, and to make certain one is getting what he or she wants, it is important to study the terms and conditions of a life insurance policy before deciding to purchase it. Among the matters to be examined closely are the accidental death benefit, the double-indemnity clause, and provisions concerning payment in the case of homicide and suicide.

SUMMARY

Annual estimates of the incidence of crimes in the United States are provided by the FBI's *Uniform Crime Reports* and the Bureau of Justice Statistics' *Criminal Victimization in the United States*. The statistics included in the former publication are based on offenses reported to law enforcement authorities, whereas those included in the latter publication are based on the results of interviewing a large sample of the U.S. population. Neither of these sources gives a completely accurate picture of crime in the United States, but taken together they provide useful information on the occurrence of various crimes and the demographic variables and other conditions with which they are associated.

Both arrests and victimization rates are highest in young adulthood and decrease as one ages. The rates are also higher for property crimes than for violent crimes, for men than for women, for blacks than for whites, and for people of lower socioeconomic status. The media pay more attention, in news, drama, and other stories, to murder and other violent crimes than to more common crimes such as alcohol-related offenses.

Despite the fact that they are victimized less often than younger adults, due to their greater vulnerability and lesser recuperative powers, elderly people are more afraid of crime than middle-aged and younger adults are. Elderly people are most likely to be victimized at night, on check day, if unaccompanied, if they are women, and if they live in central cities.

The causes of criminal behavior are complex. Motive and opportunity are important, but differential association with individuals in criminal sub-cultures and even biological factors also play a role. In any event, risk-taking, which is related to the greater speed, strength, and other athletic abilities possessed a by teenagers and young adults and associated with criminal behavior, declines with age. With maturity, the individual finds other, more legal, or at least more subtly illegal, ways of prospering.

The most popular punishment for crime commission is incarceration, but it is not terribly effective. Imprisoned criminals are not usually rehabilitated and, in fact, may become more schooled in crime by associating with other imprisoned criminals. However, society, which for its protection demands that criminals be locked up for a substantial period of time, is less concerned with prevention and rehabilitation than with its immediate safety.

Child abuse has also been of concern to society for many years, but only recently has elder abuse come to the forefront of attention. Elder abuse includes passive neglect, verbal or emotional abuse, physical abuse, financial or material exploitation, as well as institutional abuse and self-neglect. In such cases, the abuser is typically a relative, most often the spouse, of the abused person. Older adults in a variety of circumstances are also susceptible to consumer fraud: get rich quick offers, health gimmicks and new cures, attractive vacation tours, and useless insurance plans. Among the most inventive schemes for bilking the elderly are the "Bank Examiner Swindle," the "Pigeon Drop Swindle," and the sweepstakes or free-giveaway scheme.

War represents a legitimization of violence that has occurred almost continuously throughout human history. War may be limited or total, and external or internal. The most common motive for war is to acquire the property of another group or nation, but religion, retribution, and other factors have also played significant roles in instigating wars. Freud and certain other students of human psychology have emphasized the importance of an inborn aggressive instinct as a cause of war. Contemporary psychologists admit that human beings possess the neural circuitry for aggressive behavior, but they emphasis that its expression depends on the occurrence of instigating stimuli and public perception of threat in the interpersonal or international environment. The decision to go to war is usually a reasonable one from the standpoint of the aggressor, but it is a deceptive rationality. War has been romanticized as glorious and heroic, but for most combat soldiers it is a frightening, debilitating experience. This is especially true of prisoners of war who are subjected to inhuman conditions, as in the Vietnam War. Armament buildup by both sides in a conflict may serve to deter outright war for a time, but in the long run is likely to encourage it.

Repeated random violence is not limited to war; it also occurs in genocide, terrorism, and serial murder. The ultimate aim of terrorists is not murder per se but rather to frighten or terrorize people to accomplish a political purpose. Various strategies for dealing with terrorism, and hostage-taking in particular, have been implemented, but each has its drawbacks. Legal matters of particular concern to older adults—income maintenance, health, housing, autonomy, and so on—are collectively known as elder law. Procedures for determining competency and testamentary capacity, the issue of guardianship or conservatorship, and wills, probate, and taxes were discussed briefly at the end of the chapter. Concern over the payment of taxes on a estate has given rise to a number of inventive procedures for avoiding probate. Among these are setting up a legal trust or living trust, investing in life insurance, or giving away a large portion of one's cash and property to other people or organizations.

SUGGESTED READINGS

Aiken, L. R. (1995). Crime and the law. *Aging: An introduction to gerontology* (pp. 337–365). Newbury Park, CA: Sage.

Ferraro, K. F., & LaGrange, R. L. (1992). Are older people most afraid of crime? Reconsidering age differences in fear of victimization. *Journal of Gerontology, 47*(5), S233–S244.

Friedman, M. (1992). Confidence swindles of older consumers. *Journal of Consumer Affairs, 6*(1), 20–46.

Haycock, J. (1993). Criminal behavior. In R. Kastenbaum (Ed.), *Encyclopedia of adult development* (pp. 98–105). Phoenix, AZ: Oryx Press.

Kagan, D. (1995). *On the origins of war.* New York: Bantam Doubleday Dell.

Muram, D., Miller, K., & Cutler, A. (1992). Sexual assault of the elderly victim. *Journal of Interpersonal Violence, 7*(1), 70–76.

Rapoport, A. (1995). *The origins of violence: Approaches to the study of conflict.* New Brunswick, NJ: Transaction.

Sellers, C. S., Forts, W. E., & Logan, K. M. (1992). Elder mistreatment: A multidimensional problem. *Journal of Elder Abuse and Neglect, 4*(4), 5–23.

Strean, H. S., & Freeman, L. (1991). *Our wish to kill: The murder in all our hearts.* New York: St. Martin's Press.

Wolf, S. S. (1995). Legal perspectives on planning for death. In H. Wass & R. A. Neimeyer (Eds.), *Dying: Facing the facts* (3rd ed., pp. 163–184). Washington, DC: Taylor & Francis.

CHAPTER 13

Death, Bereavement, and Widowhood

Man contains within himself a most profound contradiction. At the conscious, intellectual level he is absolutely convinced that he must die, this belief being reinforced and sustained by contacts with those around him who share it, as well as by the knowledge of the deaths of others. He can be more certain of his death than of his name. His unconscious is "immortal," however, denying the reality of his death and not allowing him to imagine himself dead. There is absolutely no way to eradicate the emotional feeling of immortality, so that the individual's emotions deny his death quite as steadfastly as his intellect affirms it.

DUMONT AND FOSS, 1972, pp. 104–105

Nothing lasts forever. Success and failure, pleasure and pain, joy and sorrow, even beauty and love—all have their day and disappear. Memories may survive longer, but in a changed, reconstructed form, resembling but not faithfully recording their origins. Personal identity is also transformed with time. As we grow older, our appearance and substance become altered and we eventually die. Then, all that is left to remind others that we once walked in this house, on this street, and in other familiar places and spoke in a voice that proclaimed our existence are a few faded pictures, a memento or two, a bit of property, and the good and bad thoughts that we left in the minds of those with whom we lived, worked, and played.

Despite the inevitability of death, some things can be done to postpone and deal with it. With respect to postponement, we obviously cannot optimize our heredity by choosing our own grandparents (although others may do it for us), but we can eat judiciously, exercise regularly, avoid dangerous substances and situations, and learn how to cope with stress. With respect to planning for death, we can prepare a will, make arrangements for our funeral, communicate our concerns to others, and do whatever we feel is necessary regarding our religious and philosophical beliefs. Actually, the wise person has been preparing for death all of his or her life—by engaging in constructive work, play, and other activities, by being of help and service to others, by

---

My Life 13–1

Quo Vadis?

I never thought much about death and an afterlife when I was growing up. Of course, there was some talk about dying, and an occasional funeral, but these events were of more interest in themselves than for what happened to the deceased afterward. Like many other children, I was told that if I was good I would go to heaven, but if I was bad I would go to hell. Because I had a greater fear of hell than an attraction to heaven, I was more concerned about not doing bad things than I was about doing good ones. Immortality was of little interest to me: Dracula and the Wolfman were presumably immortal, and look what happened to them: One got heartburn from a stake, and the other was shot by the Lone Ranger with a silver bullet! Furthermore, I realized my limitations and couldn't stand the thought of living with myself for more than two or three hundred

years at the most. Being a farm boy who was aware that dead animals rot, I also had difficulty seeing how a person who had been dead for centuries could be reconstructed into a recognizable sentient being on some distant day.

Like most kids, I was more involved with the present than either the past or the future, so where we came from when we are born, and where we are going when we die, were of little interest to me and my friends. Most of us were content with being little hypocrites: We professed beliefs consistent with those of our church, but underneath it all we had doubts or considered that what might or might not be was probably not worth worrying about when there were so many other interesting things in the present. When one of my friends told me that his pastor believed there was really nothing we

---

finding something enjoyable in every day, and otherwise making his or her life more vibrant and valuable. This may be the true meaning of the statement "In the midst of life, we are in death."

DEMOGRAPHICS AND CAUSES

Not surprisingly, death is much more common in old age than at other times of life. Over 75% of the estimated 2,312,180 persons who died in the United States in 1995 were at least 65 years old. Twenty-one percent were 35–64 years old, .4% were 15–34 years old, and only 2% were under age 15. As illustrated in Figure 13–1, specific death rate for both males and females rises gradually during early and middle adulthood and increases steeply in old age, but is higher for males than for females throughout the life span (Anderson, Kochanek, & Murphy, 1997).

Slightly less than 51% of those who died in this country in 1995 were

could do to influence what happens to us after death—that it was entirely a matter of God's grace rather than our own actions on this earth—I felt relieved and interpreted it as carte blanche to do whatever seemed okay to me and my conscience.

This didn't completely settle the matter in the long run, so for a college course project I decided to interview a sample of people and ask them where they thought they would go when they died. The following responses are representative:

"Dust to dust, ashes to ashes."
"To play harps and football with the angels."
"To become one with the cosmos."
"To sleep for eternity."
"Anywhere except New York City."
"To a distant planet, after an alien space ship picks me up."
"To Peaceful Valley cemetery, where my parents are buried."
"To the High Sierras or the Pacific Ocean, where my ashes will be scattered to the winds."
"To heaven to begin a new life."
"To my grave, where I shall await resurrection on Judgment Day."
"To hell if I don't change."
"To Atlanta. That's where I was born, and I have arranged for my remains to be sent there."

To a committed Christian, of course, Christ's answer to the "Quo Vadis?" question was that he was going to prepare a place for us. Whether that place has many mansions or is just a massive housing development and whether souls fly around on wings or in helicopters was of little concern to an eight-year-old girl to whom I posed the question of where she thought she would go when she died. Her delightfully refreshing answer, and probably one with which most people deep down would agree, was: "I don't know, but I hope it's a nice place."

Out of the mouths of babes.

males, and slightly more than 49% were females. Figure 13–1 shows that up until the 75–84 age range, the number of deaths and the age-specific death rate are higher for men than for women. The age-specific death rate for men remains higher than that for women in the 75–84 and 85+ age groups, but the number of deaths for women is greater than that for men in those age ranges. This reversal of the ratio of male to female deaths is due to the fact that because males die in greater numbers than females at all ages up to age 75, there are substantially fewer men than women left to die after that age.

Eighty-six percent of those who died in this country in 1995 were whites, 12% were blacks, .4% were American Indian, 1.2% were Asian or Pacific Islander, and 4% were Hispanic (Rosenberg et al., 1996).[1] Not only did the greatest numbers of deaths occur in the white and black populations, but the death rates were also higher in those groups than in other racial groups (see

[1]Hispanics may be of any race, but the great majority identify themselves as white.

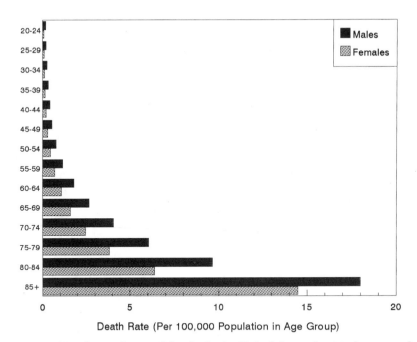

Figure 13–1   Number and rate of deaths in the United States in 1995 by age and sex. (Based on data from Anderson, Kochanek, and Murphy, 1997.)

Figure 13–2). The lower death rates for American Indians and Hispanics, however, are also influenced by the fact that they are younger populations than whites and blacks. Population age is also a factor in the higher death rates for European and North American countries than for Central and South American and Asian countries. However, the highest death rates in the world are found in African countries, which, though consisting of relatively young populations, also have poorer living conditions (poorer nutrition and sanitation, higher rates of infectious diseases, etc.) than most countries in other parts of the world (Population Reference Bureau, 1997). However, noncommunicable diseases such as cancer, heart diseases, and diabetes cause more deaths than infectious diseases in all areas of the world except India and sub-Saharan Africa. The major reason for the increasing importance of noncommunicable diseases as causes of death throughout the world is the graying of the global population. Another important factor associated with worldwide death rates is smoking, which contributes to heart disease, lung cancer, and other killer diseases (Maugh, 1996).

The 10 most common causes of death in the United States are listed in Figure 13–3. Although heart diseases and malignant neoplasms (cancers) are ranked in all age groups among the 10 causes of death having the highest frequency, the third most frequent cause for all ages combined—cerebrovascular

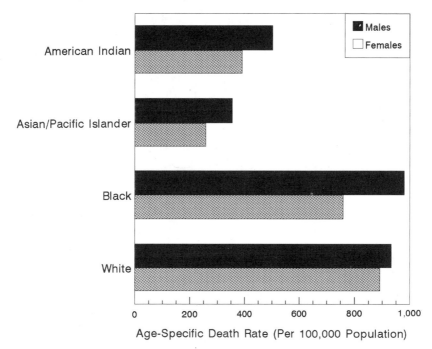

American Indian

Asian/Pacific Islander

Black

White

■ Males
□ Females

0   200   400   600   800   1,000

Age-Specific Death Rate (Per 100,000 Population)

Figure 13–2   Death rate in the United States in 1995 by sex and race/ethnicity. (Based on data from Anderson, Kochanek, and Murphy, 1997.)

diseases—does not appear among the top 10 until early adulthood. In addition, below age 25, the highest ranked cause of death is accidents and adverse effects; in the 25–44 age range, it is human immunodeficiency virus (HIV) infection; in the 45–64 age range, it is malignant neoplasms; and in the 65 years and over range, it is diseases of heart. The death rates for particular conditions also vary with sex and ethnicity. Men have a higher death rate than women for HIV infection, malignant neoplasms, pulmonary diseases, liver disease, accidents, suicide, and homicide; women have a higher death rate than men for diabetes mellitus, Alzheimer's disease, cerebrovascular diseases, pneumonia, and influenza. Whites have a higher death rate than blacks for malignant neoplasms, Alzheimer's disease, heart diseases, cerebrovascular diseases, pneumonia and influenza, and suicide; blacks have a higher death rate than whites for HIV infection, diabetes mellitus, accidents and adverse effects, and homicide (Singh et al., 1996). With respect to time of year, the death rate is higher during the winter months of January, February, and March than in other months. Of all areas of the United States, the District of Columbia has the highest death rate and Alaska the lowest (Rosenberg et al., 1996).

Although suicide, homicide, and accidents are not among the top 10

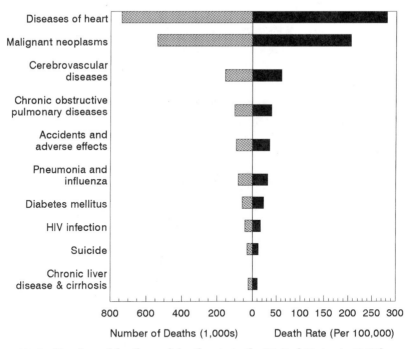

Figure 13–3   Number of deaths and death rate in the United States in 1995 by cause.
(Based on data from Anderson, Kochanek, and Murphy, 1997.)

causes of death for all age groups, they are of special interest because they are not diseases. As shown in Figure 13–4, the age-specific death rate for accidents and adverse effects declines from infancy to early adolescence and rises during adolescence and early adulthood. After then, it remains fairly constant until ages 65–74, after which it rises steeply. The high accidental death rate in later life is due primarily to accidents and adverse effects other than those caused by motor vehicles; falls, in particular, are a common cause of fatal accidents in many older people. The accidental death rate for men is substantially higher than for women and slightly higher for blacks than for whites. The age-specific death rate for homicide and legal intervention declines from infancy through early adolescence, reaches a peak during the late teens and early twenties, and then declines gradually for the remainder of the life span. Like the rate of deaths due to accidents, the homicide death rate is substantially higher for men than for women, and higher for blacks than for whites. The age-specific death rate for suicide is lower during childhood than at any other time of life. It increases during the late teens and early adulthood, declines slightly during middle age, and rises again after age 65. The suicide rate is higher for men than for women, and higher for whites than for blacks.

The rank order of the causes of death has also varied from year to year

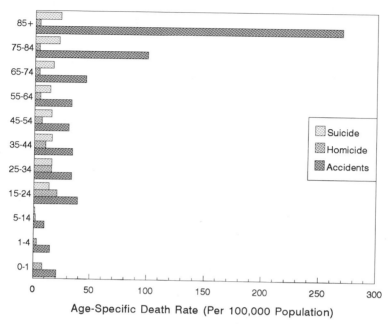

Figure 13–4   Age-specific death rates for accidents, homicide, and suicide in the United States in 1995. (Based on data from Anderson, Kochanek, and Murphy, 1997.)

during this century. One trend has been the replacement of acute illnesses with chronic illnesses as the major causes of death. From 1900 to 1920, influenza and pneumonia, tuberculosis, and gastroenteritis were close to the top of the list of causes of death in the United States. Medical breakthroughs in the prevention and treatment of these conditions have resulted in the near-disappearance of tuberculosis and a dramatic reduction in deaths caused by influenza and gastroenteritis. Pneumonia and influenza are still in the top 10, but they dropped from first place in 1900 to sixth place in 1995.

PERSPECTIVES AND EMOTIONS

Ideas and feelings about death have varied throughout human history. The preoccupation with wars, death, and disease during the late Middle Ages produced paintings and sculpture depicting the triumph of death, the dance of death (*danse macabre*), and *memento mori* urging people to "seize the day" (*carpe diem*) because their time was limited. Interest in the "maggotry" of death during the fourteenth and fifteenth centuries found expression in its physical aspects. Blood, decaying fish, worms, and other "realistic" images were prevalent, as well as illustrations in the *Ars Moriendi*[2] of deathbed scenes, grave diggers uprooting bones, and vicious black devils fighting with angels over a corpse or soul. Death was also symbolized in works of art and stories as an Angel, a Rider on a Pale Horse, the Grim Reaper, and the Twin Brother of Sleep. Death was represented more obviously by a skeleton, a mummy, a shrunken body, or an old man or woman, naked or dressed in a shroud, lying in a coffin, grinning or leering, and perhaps carrying a weapon (scythe, sword, dart, bow and arrows, etc.). Other death symbols were coffins, cemeteries, amputated limbs, skulls and crossbones, or more abstract symbols such as winter landscapes, ruins, leafless trees, dead birds, and vultures.

Death has been featured extensively in literature, the oldest known poem in which it figures being the *Epic of Gilgamesh*. In another famous literary work, the Indian poem *Mahabharata*, death is characterized as Mara, a beautiful dark-haired woman. In Islam, the god of time and the god of death are one—Zurvan, and in Hebrew literature, death is the angel Sammael. In more modern drama and literature, such as Ingmar Bergman's *The Seventh Seal*, death is depicted as a pale-faced man in a long, black cloak; and in Carlos Casteneda's *Journey to Ixtlan*, death is a hunter who stalks human beings.

Philosophical Ideas

For the most part philosophers have had little to say about death, being content to leave discussion of the topic to theologians and churchmen. Following Plato and St. Paul, most Christian teachers have emphasized the concept of death as a release of the soul from the body. Reminiscent of Eastern religious teaching is the philosopher Georg Hegel's definition of death as "the reconciliation of the spirit with itself, a reuniting of the individual with cosmic matter."[3]

The antitheological notion that death is personal extinction goes back at least as far as the Greek philosopher Epicurus, while Stoicism in the face of death was emphasized by Zeno of Cyprus. Another idea, that the only way to diminish the fear of death is to think about it constantly, was proposed by the Roman statesman Lucius Seneca. Seneca was apparently something of an early behavior modifier who attempted to apply the principle of response extinction to death anxiety. Unfortunately, he seems to have dwelled on it too much, because he committed suicide, albeit at the ripe old age of 90.

Benedict de Spinoza's statement that "a free man meditates on life rather than death," and Ludwig Feuerbach's statement that "life must be lived fully in spite of death" are counters to Seneca's preoccupation with it. Existential-

---

[2]The *Ars Moriendi* was a written treatise, apparently prepared by a group of German monks in the Middle Ages, which provides details on how to die in a dignified, holy manner.

[3]This definition of death and those following are paraphrased from Choron (1963) and Bardis (1981).

ists such as Martin Heidegger, who maintained that "a person's life becomes more purposeful or meaningful when he faces his own death" and Jean-Paul Sartre, who stated that "constant awareness of death intensifies the sense of life," emphasized the importance of death as a driver of life. According to the philosophy of existentialism, rather than death being the antithesis of life, only by accepting and confronting their mortality can people come to appreciate what it means to be alive and engage fully in creative efforts.

Cognitive Development and Perceptions of Death

Most children are too busy growing, playing, and exploring life to be much concerned about death, but their conceptions of it change as they get older. Some psychologists believe that children's conceptions of death begin forming in the first year of life, when the child becomes aware of absence, departure, and separation from people and things (Pattison, 1977). According to Wass and Stillion (1988), separation anxiety is closely related to death anxiety in young children and is the forerunner of fears of death in adulthood. Stimulated by Jean Piaget's conception of stages in cognitive development of children, Nagy (1948) observed and interviewed several hundred Hungarian children and then proposed a three-stage theory of the development of children's ideas about death. According to Nagy, children in the first stage (ages 3–5) do not distinguish between death and separation, and view death as a temporary departure or sleep. Children in the second stage (ages 5–9), which is parallel to Piaget's period of concrete operations, conceive of death as something that happens to old people, irreversible but avoidable. At this stage, death is personified as someone who mutilates people and carries them away. By the third stage (ages 9+), children have developed a more realistic, adultlike view of death and see it as inevitable, universal, and irreversible.

Some of Nagy's conclusions, for example, that appreciation of the finality and universality of death is related to chronological age, have been confirmed by later research, but nationality, cultural, and social-class differences also affect a child's conceptions of death. Bluebond-Langner's (1977, 1978) research with terminally ill children indicates that, rather than being restricted to a specific chronological age range, all views of death are present at every stage of development. In any event, the presence and support of people with whom they are familiar helps children cope with their fears of death.

Fears of Death

Adolescents, who need to maintain the illusion of invulnerability, usually reject thoughts of death (Kastenbaum, 1959). Like many adults, they tend to see death as something that happens to other people but not to them, or at least not until sometime in the distant future. However, the rapid changes in adolescents' physical structure and functioning may alarm those who have not been properly informed about what to expect and even make them feel as if they are about to die. Adolescents are also more likely to experience fears of death when they have other problems and difficulties. Psychologically healthy adolescents are able to cope with death more effectively than those who have emotional problems. In addition, fear of death tends to be greater among adolescents with lower cognitive abilities and poorer academic achievement than among those of higher abilities and achievement (Wass & Scott, 1978).

Expressed fear of death is more common and more intense in middle age than in either young adulthood or old age (Bengtson, Cuellar, & Ragan, 1977; Gesser, Wong, & Reker, 1987–1988; Kalish & Reynolds, 1981). Fear of death in middle age is precipitated in many cases by the individual's awareness of declining health and appearance, and the knowledge that his or her hopes and dreams have not been fulfilled. The death of one's parents, who previously had served as a kind of psychological barrier between oneself and eternity, can also prompt and intensify the fear of death in middle age. Furthermore, people who are living enjoyable, personally meaningful lives but are now seriously ill may become acutely aware of their own mortality. This awareness is exacerbated by the process of making an inventory of one's assets and liabilities and subjectively reckoning not how many years one has lived but how many one has left.

As people pass middle age, each passing year brings them closer and closer to the end of life. The personal past is seen as being relatively long and the personal future as fairly short. However, rather than showing great fear of death, when compared with the middle-aged, older adults are more apt to accept the fact that they have had their day and that dying in old age is only fair. Even terminally ill older adults tend to be less afraid than their younger contemporaries (Feifel & Jones, 1968). Consequently, older adults are, on the whole, better able to confront the reality of death and cope with their fears concerning it (Kalish, 1985). They spend more time in remembering and reflecting, and do not feel the necessity of planning as far ahead. They are more apt to fear isolation and loneliness rather than pain and sorrow at the prospect of leaving their families and friends. Still, like young and middle-aged adults, many older adults experience some regrets over lost opportunities and would welcome a chance to begin again.

The aforementioned picture is, of course, a general one, and fears of death may vary greatly from person to person in later life. For example, Butler and Lewis (1982) found that 55% of a sample of older adults whom they interviewed had resolved their fears of death in a realistic manner, 30% remained overtly afraid of it, and 15% coped with their fears by means of defensive denial. Older adults who are in poor physical or mental health, or who have a disabled spouse, dependent children, or important goals they expect to attain may be quite afraid of dying. For the most part, however, older adults fear the process of dying more than death itself. Their relatively greater serenity in the face of death is seen in the differences among the responses of groups of younger, middle-aged, and older adults who were asked how they would want to spend the time until they died if they had only 6 months to live. Significantly more old than young or middle-aged adults said that they would spend the time reading, contemplating, praying, or focusing on their inner lives (Kalish & Reynolds, 1981). According to Kalish (1985), the blurring of the boundaries of the ego or the diffusion of the sense of self in older adults provides them with a mechanism for transcending the fear of death and the pain of dying. The presence of family and social supports and having a sense of meaning or purpose in one's life also help in dealing with death.

Attitudes and Anxieties

Related to, but more diffuse or generalized than fears are attitudes and anxieties concerning death. Many factors contribute to death anxiety, including the physical suffering that death may entail, being reduced to a state of nothingness or nonbeing, punishment after death for our wrongdoings, and the loss of all that we hold near and dear in life. Table 13–1, which summarizes Aries's (1981) findings on changes in attitudes toward death throughout history, shows that these attitudes have varied significantly since the Middle

TABLE 13–1 Changes in Attitudes toward Death throughout History

Tame death (Middle Ages). Death is accepted and expected as a terrible but necessary human misfortune. The dead were thought to be merely sleeping until the Second Coming of Christ.

Death of the self (fourteenth and fifteenth centuries). Individuality was minimized. Without a last confession, at the moment of death, the immortal soul of the person was seized by a devil instead of an angel. Thus, dying in one's sleep or otherwise without confessing one's sins was to be avoided at all costs.

Remote death (seventeenth and eighteenth centuries). Death was a sorrowful but remote event. Human mortality was accepted, but thoughts of it still made people anxious. Romantic or macabre eroticism was intermingled with sex in art and literature.

Death of the other (early to middle-nineteenth century). The view of death as ugly and the belief in a literal hell began to diminish. Death was seen as a beautiful event leading to a happy reunion in paradise. The personal self survived death and roamed the earth with other disembodied spirits.

Denial of death (late-nineteenth century to present). Death became less visible. Dying people were hidden away in hospitals and children were spared the unpleasantness of viewing and knowing about death and dying. Public mourning was eliminated. Death was more likely to be seen as an accident or a medical failure, and the best way to die was in one's sleep.

Present time? Denial and externalization of death have diminished somewhat. Death is seen as a part of what it means to be human, and it is inhuman for people to die alone, connected to medical apparatus, and without having a chance to make their peace and say goodbye to others.

Source: Adapted from Aries, 1981.

Ages. Attitudes and anxieties concerning death and dying also vary with a number of demographic variables, including sex, culture, ethnicity, education, occupation, personal adjustment, and religion. Women make higher scores than men on questionnaires designed to measure death anxiety, but this may be caused by the fact that, rather than being more anxious, women are merely more open than men in expressing their attitudes and emotions (Lonetto, Mercer, Fleming, Bunting, & Clare, 1980; Pollack, 1979; Wass & Sisler, 1978). Women also appear to have different perceptions of death than men. Women are more likely to see death as a compassionate mother or an understanding doctor, whereas men tend to view it as an evil antagonist, a grinning butcher, or a hangman (Back, 1971).

Attitudes and beliefs concerning death vary extensively among different cultural and racial/ethnic groups. The findings of a study of Kalish and Reynolds (1981) of samples of white, African-, Japanese-, and Mexican-Americans to questions concerning death and dying are instructive. Significantly larger percentages of white and African-Americans than Japanese- and Mexican-Americans felt that patients should be told when they are dying. Compared with the other three groups, greater percentages of whites indicated that slow death is more tragic than sudden death, that death in childhood is most tragic of all, and that they had less contact with the dying and dead. Greater percentages of African- and Mexican-Americans considered the death of a woman as more tragic than the death of a man, indicated that they experienced the presence of someone who died, and said that they wanted to live past age 90. Mexican-Americans were also more likely than the other three ethnic groups to let people die if they wanted to; they also felt that people should be informed when they are mortally ill, and that people should try hard to control their emotions in public when someone close to them dies.

Similar to the findings with adolescents, more negative views and greater fears of death are expressed by less educated adults (Keith, 1979). Furthermore, people with less education are less likely to talk about death or to make plans for it (Riley & Foner, 1968). With regard to occupation, it would seem from these findings that people in lower status occupations would have greater fear of death than those in higher status occupations, but the data concerning this matter are inconsistent. However, there is some evidence that occupations in which there is a high level of exposure to death are associated with higher death anxiety (Neimeyer, Bagley, & Moore, 1986).

Also consistent with the findings on adolescents, adults who are emotionally and financially more stable and have attained most of their goals express greater acceptance of death than those who have been less successful (Hinton, 1972). For example, death anxiety tends to be higher in people with neurotic symptoms (Conte, Weiner, & Plutchik, 1982; Gilliland & Templer, 1985; Howells & Field, 1982). It is noteworthy that when patients with both depression and high death anxiety are treated for their depression, a reduction in death anxiety is observed when the depression is relieved (Templer, Ruff, & Simpson, 1974). Death anxiety also tends to be higher in defensive people who avoid threatening situations rather than confronting them (Kane & Hogan, 1985; Tobacyk & Eckstein, 1980).

A number of studies have found a negative relationship between death anxiety and religion: People who believe in some form of God and have integrated religion into their lives are more likely to face death without overwhelming fears than are those who feel uncertain about religion (Feifel & Nagy, 1981; Kübler-Ross, 1974a; Nelson & Nelson, 1973). Confirmed atheists also tend to face death with equanimity, but people who are inconsistent and uncertain about their religious beliefs appear to be most apprehensive of all about death (Aday, 1984–1985; McMordie, 1981). Thus, ambivalence or indecisiveness in one's religious beliefs is more apt than either strong religious beliefs or total disbelief to be associated with a fear of death.

Health Professions

Doctors and nurses who take care of terminally ill patients often feel frustrated, helpless, and embarrassed by death. Some handle their feelings by stereotyping and depersonalizing patients—treating them as diseases rather than people, and referring to them by room number rather than name. Trained more in saving lives rather than helping dying people, health professionals have a tendency to become detached specialists and spectators who protect themselves by objectifying and combating death rather than dealing with their personal feelings. Staff contacts with the patient decline markedly when an illness is diagnosed as terminal (Gordon & Klass, 1979). Nurses may be abrupt and tense with a terminally ill patient, whom they want to be "cooperative" and not die on their shift (Kübler-Ross, 1975; Mauksch, 1975).

On the other hand, many doctors and nurses are comfortable with dying patients; they may genuinely care for them and miss them when they are gone. These professionals have learned to view death as a natural event rather than a frightening consequence of a medical mistake. Such attitudes toward death and dying patients assist caretakers in their efforts to help terminally ill patients face the inevitability of death.

THE PROCESS OF DYING

The death of a person does not occur all at once. Different tissues, organs, and people die at different rates. Tissues and organs may be preserved and transplanted into living persons long after the donor has been declared medically dead. Furthermore, some people have a much slower *dying trajectory* than others, and linger on for years after others who became terminally ill at the same time have long since been dead.

The traditional signs of death—cessation of respiration, heart rate, and sensory and motor reflexes—are still important in establishing time of death, but the major medical criterion now applied in most states is the cessation of all electrical activity of the brain for a certain period of time. This diagnosis of *brain death* is usually made when the patient has a flat electroencephalogram (EEG) for at least 10 minutes. Determination of brain death and other designations of death listed under the Harvard criteria (Ad Hoc Committee of the Harvard Medical School, 1968) have become especially important in these times of frequent organ transplants. However, the heart and lungs of a person in a coma may continue to function even though neural activity in the higher brain centers has ceased.

Loss of functioning of the heart, lungs, and brain are signs of death but not its actual cause. Rather, death is due basically to a breakdown in the oxygen cycle due to failures of the circulatory and respiratory organs and the respiratory centers in the brain stem. When the oxygen source to the brain is cut off, the cells of the higher brain die first, within 5 to 10 minutes; then, the cells in the medulla of the lower brain stem, which regulate heartbeat, respiration, and other vital reflexes, die.

Time of Death

The rapidity with which terminally ill people die depends on the nature of the illness, the age and lifestyle of the patient, the manner in which the illness is treated medically, and certain psychological factors. A longer dying trajectory is usually less stressful for survivors and gives the patient a better chance to settle remaining financial and family matters. However, a shorter dying trajectory may be preferable when the patient is severely deteriorated and in great pain. Supporters of physician-assisted suicide argue that dying with dignity rather than remaining connected to tubes and machines while enduring suffering for weeks or even months is a fundamental right of a human being. When the dying trajectory is fairly long, the reactions expected by the patient vary with his or her age. Older, dying patients are expected to be more passive and less emotional, whereas younger people are expected to be more active and resistant in the face of death (Sudnow, 1967).

Though most people do not have the ability to determine the exact time of their death, psychological factors can hasten or delay death. Folklore is full of stories of people who felt that it was time for them to die and decided simply to give up and let it happen. Those who have difficulty coping with the pain, frustration, and expense of a prolonged, fatal illness may vacillate for a period of time between the desire to live and the desire to end it all, eventually deciding in favor of the latter. The results of uncontrolled observational and correlational studies also indicate that at least some people possess the ability to either hasten or delay death by means of their own thoughts, feelings, and motivations (Kastenbaum & Aisenberg, 1976; Phillips & Smith, 1990; Trelease, 1975). Indirect evidence of the role of psychological factors is also found in numerous anecdotes indicating that people can be scared to death (e.g., Barker, 1968; Kalat, 1984) or simply die because of feelings of helplessness and hopelessness (Engel, 1971; Seligman, 1975, 1992). Furthermore, data from more rigorous scientific investigations on nursing home patients indicate that death can be hastened when patients are made to feel totally dependent and permitted no voice or choice in what they can do or what is done for them (Langer & Rodin, 1976; Rodin & Langer, 1978). Whether or not they are able to control the time of death by their feelings and behavior, many individuals are reportedly aware that they are about to die (Kalish & Reynolds, 1981). In addition, people often show signs of impending death in their behavior. There is, for example, evidence for a *terminal drop*—a decline in cognitive and sensorimotor abilities and personality characteristics such as assertiveness—during the last few months in the lives of older adults (Lieberman & Coplan, 1969; Riegel & Riegel, 1972).

Stages in Dying

Persons who die suddenly from an accident or other trauma have, of course, the shortest of all dying trajectories and no choice in the matter. But persons who are suffering from terminal disorders, who have been informed that their condition is terminal and even approximately how much time they have left, experience many emotional ups and downs. Elisabeth Kübler-Ross (1969) maintained that in the interval between the time when they are informed that their illness is terminal and when they actually die, patients pass through a sequence of attitudinal or psychological stages. As shown in Figure 13–5, Kübler-Ross posits five stages in the dying process: denial, anger, bargaining, depression, and acceptance. Each stage features a different attitude or emotion on the part of the patient. At Stage 1, the patient denies the fact that the illness is terminal. Denial eventually gives way to a second stage—anger toward doctors, family, and even God. On coming to terms with the fact that anger cannot alter reality, the patient enters a third stage in which he or she attempts to strike a bargain with other people or even God if they will let him or her live. When this strategy does not work, the patient enters a stage of depression. Ideally, the depression eventually lifts and the patient becomes calm and accepts the reality of his or her imminent death.

Kübler-Ross's stage theory, which is frequently taught to doctors and nurses who work with terminally ill patients, has been criticized on a number of points. Certainly, not all patients go through the five stages in the order listed, and nurses who chide patients for their failure to do so are not practicing good medicine. Critics of Kübler-Ross's theory have proposed alternative approaches to understanding the dying process (e.g., Pattison, 1977; Shneidman, 1987; Weisman & Kastenbaum, 1968). Pattison (1977) proposed a descriptive model consisting of three stages in the *living–dying interval*—the interval between the initial death crisis and the actual time of death. First, there is an *acute phase*, during which fear and anxiety are at their peak, and

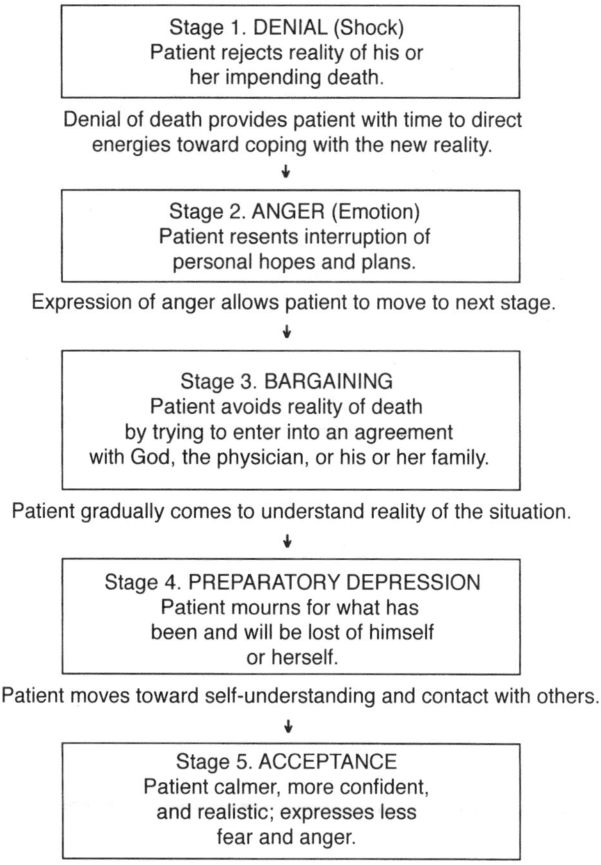

Stage 1. DENIAL (Shock) Patient rejects reality of his or her impending death.

Denial of death provides patient with time to direct
energies toward coping with the new reality.

↓

Stage 2. ANGER (Emotion) Patient resents interruption of personal hopes and plans.

Expression of anger allows patient to move to next stage.

↓

Stage 3. BARGAINING Patient avoids reality of death by trying to enter into an agreement with God, the physician, or his or her family.

Patient gradually comes to understand reality of the situation.

↓

Stage 4. PREPARATORY DEPRESSION Patient mourns for what has been and will be lost of himself or herself.

Patient moves toward self-understanding and contact with others.

↓

Stage 5. ACCEPTANCE Patient calmer, more confident, and realistic; expresses less fear and anger.

Figure 13–5 Psychological stages in the dying process. (Adapted from Kübler-Ross, 1975.)

which the patient usually copes with by means of defense mechanisms and other cognitive and affective resources. Next there is a *chronic living–dying phase*, in which anxiety is reduced and the patient asks questions about such things as the disposition of his or her body, what will happen to his or her "self," family, and friends while he or she is dying and dead, and what plans can be made. It is during this second phase that the patient begins to accept death gracefully, leading to a third and final stage—the *terminal phase*. During this last phase, the patient continues to want to live but accepts the fact that death will not go away. The patient's energy level is low, and, desiring mainly comfort and caring, he or she begins the final social and emotional withdrawal from life.

Some thanatologists are skeptical of all stage theories and emphasize that the way in which people die varies greatly from person to person. For example, Shneidman (1987) maintains that, as with any crisis, a person's reactions to and ways of dealing with the prospect of his or her own death vary with culture, personality, and experience.

Treatment of Dying Persons

People no longer die in large numbers at home. The majority of dying takes place in hospitals, nursing homes, and other long-term-care institutions. Extensive, even heroic, efforts are often made to keep patients alive as long as possible, but the outcome is inevitable—at least, in the long run. Although a certain number of patients sign living wills to the effect that they do not wish extraordinary medical procedures to be employed when death is imminent, most patients still want to live as long as possible.

Observations by Glaser and Strauss (1968) of dying patients and the way they were treated by medical personnel in six care facilities revealed that the appropriate treatment depended to a large extent on whether the patient had a *lingering* or a *quick-dying* trajectory. The treatment of patients with lingering trajectories consisted mostly of comfort, care, and custodial routine, with an emphasis on patience and inevitability. The treatment of patients with quick-dying trajectories, on the other hand, depended on whether a quick death was expected or unexpected. The latter tended to create a crisis atmosphere in the hospital or long-term-care institution, particularly in the rare case where death occurred on an obstetrical ward (Mauksch, 1975).

Nursing homes are usually better equipped than hospitals to deal with patients having lingering trajectories, because hospitals are oriented more toward recovery and cures than dying. Doctors and nurses in nursing homes are more likely to let terminally ill patients die without making extensive efforts to sustain or resuscitate them by mechanical, electrical, or chemical procedures.

The treatment of all dying patients emphasizes comfort and pain control. Hospice treatment has stressed the control of pain and discomfort by means of *Brompton's mix*, a mixture of morphine, cocaine, ethyl alcohol, and a sweetener, or even by morphine alone. Rather than being a specific place, a *hospice* is an organization that provides services to dying patients and their families. Hospice care may take place almost anywhere—in a hospital or other institution, or even in a private residence. In addition to controlling pain and discomfort, hospice care involves discussions of death and dying between patients and the medical staff, and the right to die with dignity and a sense of self-worth rather than feelings of isolation and aloneness (Saunders, 1980). Only patients who are dying from cancer or another terminal illness are accepted for hospice treatment. In addition, the prognosis of death must be in terms of months, not years, and the patient must live within a reasonable distance of the hospice. Finally, a primary caregiver must agree to assume continuing responsibility for the patient's care.

Wherever a person may die—in a hospital, in a nursing home, in a hospice, or at home, it is never a pleasant experience. Consequently, it is typically accompanied by evasiveness and often a so-called *conspiracy of silence* on the part of caregivers not to talk about death at all with the patient. Reassurance, denial, changing the subject, fatalism, and discussion are among the strategies used by medical personnel and others in responding to dying patients (Kastenbaum & Aisenberg, 1976). Most desirable and effective of all, however, is open communication with patients, many of whom are eager to share their thoughts and feelings with other people. Dying adults of all ages are usually grateful at being told the truth concerning their condition, and they welcome the opportunity to discuss it (Glaser & Strauss, 1965; Puner, 1974). Although dying people need to be aware of their impending death, they can deal with the information better when it is presented by a compassionate, companionate person. Then, the patient can feel free to express his or her fears, make whatever confessions need to be made, and obtain understanding, support, and forgiveness from a sympathetic, caring listener.

Psychological support to dying persons may be provided by family members, medical personnel, clergy, and even by professionals who specialize in counseling the dying. Professional counselors, who must be careful not to impose their own values on patients, may employ a variety of techniques. Among these are uncritical acceptance, attentive listening, reflection of feelings, life review, and group-oriented therapy (Kalish, 1977). The specific goals of such counseling depend on the patient and the situation, but the general aims are to help the patient overcome his or her feelings of sadness and despair, resolve remaining conflicts with family members and others, and acquire insight into the meaning and value of life.

THE AFTERMATH OF DEATH

Funeral Practices

Historically, funerals were designed to serve the purposes of honoring the dead, supplying them with the means for existence in the next world and gaining favor with the gods. Funerals still honor the dead, but the main function served by modern funeral practices is to allow survivors to work through their own feelings concerning the deceased. However, the sense of loss, sadness, and other feelings associated with the death of a loved one do not end with the funeral. A period of bereavement and mourning by the survivors, and the spouse of the deceased in particular, may continue for months and even years after the funeral.

Modern Funerals.   Modern funerals are often preceded by some sort of wake, in which the groomed and often embalmed corpse is on display in a funeral home or private residence. Relatives of the deceased are informed by telephone or telegram of the time and place of the wake, and a notice is placed in the obituary columns of local newspapers. Depending on the prominence of the deceased, not only family members and friends, but also many others may come to the wake to view the corpse and pay their respects. The casket is usually open but may be closed at both the wake and the funeral service when the corpse has been disfigured by disease or accident. The psychological significance of the open casket in providing a "memory picture" of the deceased is debatable, but certain religious and cultural groups place great store in its importance.

The nature and location of the funeral service also vary with the cultural and religious background of the survivors. For example, Roman Catholics, who are more likely than Protestants to hold funerals in a church rather than in a funeral home, are more favorably disposed toward elaborate funerals (Khleif, 1976). In both the United States and other countries, secular funerals have become more commonplace (Norbeck, 1995). Another modern trend has been toward simpler funerals or memorial services characterized by an emotional toning down of the service and a deritualization of mourning.

Following the funeral service, and usually on the same day, the corpse is buried, or, if cremated, may be disposed of in other ways. In the tradition of "dust-to-dust," Orthodox Jews and Muslims generally adhere to in-ground burial, whereas Hindus and Buddhists stress cremation. Either burial in the ground or entombment, and, to an increasing extent, cremation, is acceptable to most Christian denominations.

In the United States, only about one-fifth of all corpses are cremated, but the practice is more popular in Canada and in Asian countries. Public concern over the cost of funerals and the marketing methods of the funeral industry has led to greater regulation of the industry in the United States and the increased popularity of memorial services and cremation. Greater openness and fewer cultural constraints with respect to death and dying have also contributed to the growing popularity of simpler, more economical, but still dignified and meaningful, funeral practices.

Bereavement. Bereavement, the loss of a loved one by death, is almost always followed by the mental state of sorrow and distress known as *grief.* The culturally prescribed pattern of behavior by which the grief caused by bereavement is expressed is referred to as *mourning.* The duration of mourning and the specific conduct of mourners, such as wearing black and restricting one's social activities, and flying flags at half mast, have varied with the historical period and culture. In today's Western culture, the duration of mourning is typically fairly short, and many older customs associated with it have been abandoned. Numerous practical matters concerned with the funeral, the deceased's estate, and new domestic and other duties of the spouse or other immediate family members must be taken care of. In addition, the survivors must contend with various psychological and social concerns associated with the death. In short, the survivors must find ways to let go of the deceased and get on with the business of living.

During and immediately after the funeral, there is typically an outpouring of support for the survivors, but with time, the level of social contact and the emotional support associated with it diminish. Being alone to contemplate and express one's grief in private is not a bad thing if it does not last for a prolonged period of time and is not accompanied by bizarre behaviors. A period of quiet grief and contemplation is a healthier reaction to bereavement than denial or escapist pursuits such as immersing oneself into the social whirl.

Feelings of grief are not always expressed immediately after the loss of a loved one, but may be delayed for months or even years. On the other hand, so-called *anticipatory grief* may be expressed even before the death of a loved one. Typically, however, the grieving occurs after the death and consists of three phases (Gorer, 1965): initial, intermediate, and recovery. During the *initial phase*, which lasts from about 3−6 weeks, the bereaved person experiences shock and disbelief, and may feel cold, dazed, empty, numb, and confused. The initial phase is followed by an *intermediate phase* characterized by sorrow and loss punctuated by crying spells. In addition to deep sadness, it is fairly normal in the intermediate phase of grief to feel angry, anxious, and guilty. Anger may be expressed toward anyone whom the bereaved views as having contributed, either by commission or omission, to the death, or as having been unkind to the deceased while he or she was alive. Favorite targets of anger are medical personnel, family members, business associates of the deceased, and even oneself. When anger is expressed toward oneself for not having done more to prevent the death or in other ways serve the deceased, it often changes to guilt. Bereaved persons may also have feelings of hopelessness, depersonalization, disorientation, unreality, a loss of interest in things, and an inability to concentrate. They may cry, have difficulty sleeping, have little energy, and become dependent on sleeping medications, alcohol, and tranquilizers. They may have feelings of tightness in the throat, choking, shortness of breath, digestive upsets, and headaches. In an effort to find meaning in the death, the bereaved person may also continually engage in a mental review of his or her interactions with the deceased (Clayton, Halikes, & Maurice, 1971; Imara, 1995; Parkes, 1972).

The third phase of grief—*recovery*—normally begins approximately a year after the death, but, depending on how the person died and the bereaved's relationship with him or her, it may take much longer and perhaps never occur completely. Thompson, Gallagher-Thompson, Futterman, Gilewski, and Peterson (1991) found that, on the average, the experience of grief lasted for at least two-and-a-half years following the death of a spouse. In particular, if the death was sudden or unanticipated, as in an accident, murder, or suicide and/or the deceased was quite young, the third phase of grief may be delayed indefinitely.

Pathological reactions to bereavement can occur when the loss is a profound one. Regression, hallucinations, obsessional review, overidentification with the deceased, idealization of the deceased, and mummification of the deceased have all been observed. In *regression*, the bereaved person behaves in a childlike manner. *Hallucinations*, in which the bereaved hears the deceased moving about the house or otherwise senses him or her, and converses and consults with and dreams about the deceased every night, may also occur (Glick, Weiss, & Parkes, 1974). In *obsessional review*, the bereaved person repeatedly reviews the events that took place immediately before and after the death. In *overidentification with the deceased*, the bereaved person talks and otherwise acts like the deceased—wearing the same clothes, using the same objects, and attempting to think like the deceased. *Idealization* or *sanctification of the deceased* consists of remembering only good things about him or her, even when the deceased actually abused the bereaved person. *Mummification of the deceased* consists of keeping all of the deceased's possessions in order, as if he or she were still alive.

The process and progress of grieving are, of course, not the same for all people. At one extreme are those who remain calm and efficient throughout the wake, the funeral, and the postfuneral periods. They show few signs of grief and quickly adapt to the loss (Lieberman & Peskin, 1992). At the other extreme are those who experience intense emotional reactions that persist for years after the death. In a phenomenon referred to as the *anniversary reaction*, the bereaved person reexperiences feelings of grief on the anniversary of the death.

In general, emotional reactions to the loss of a spouse are less intense and the period of grief is shorter in older than in younger people (Ball, 1977). Grief also tends to be more intense when the death occurred unexpectedly as a result of an acute illness or injury. In such cases, the *bereavement overload* and consequent depression may be so great that the bereaved person attempts to commit suicide. Suicide as a result of *postbereavement depression* is a particularly serious risk for older men who have lost a spouse (Stroebe & Stroebe, 1987). A bereaved person may also die from natural causes, such as a heart attack precipitated by the loss. The results of several research studies (Clayton et al., 1971; Helsing, Szklo, & Comstock, 1981; Parkes, Benjamin, & Fitzgerald, 1969) indicate that the death rate for bereaved persons during a year or so after the loss is significantly higher than that for nonbereaved persons of comparable age. The death of a spouse, for example, is associated with lower activity of the immune system and an increased risk of various physical and psychological disorders (Bradsher, Longino, Jackson, & Zimmerman, 1992).

A proposed explanation for the higher mortality rate of bereaved persons is the *desolation effects hypothesis*. According to this hypothesis, the event of widowhood and the circumstances surrounding it have deleterious, debilitating effects on the bereaved person. These effects consist of grief, feelings of hopelessness, new worries and responsibilities, and changes in diet, work routine, and financial situation (Epstein, Weitz, Roback, & McKee, 1975). Other explanations for the higher mortality rate of bereaved persons have been proposed (see Epstein et al., 1975), but none is quite as convincing as the desolation effects hypothesis.

WIDOWHOOD

To a great extent, widowhood in the United States is a status of older women. There are sizable numbers of widowers and young widows, but in 1995, nearly two-thirds of all widowed persons in this country were women aged 65 and over. As shown in Figure 13–6, the number of widows increased dramatically after middle age but fell abruptly after age 75. Despite the decline in the number of widows caused by deaths after the eighth decade of life, the percentage of widows continues to increase in the eighth decade of life. The age-related pattern in the number and percentages of widowers is similar to that of widows, but both measures are substantially lower. In 1995, only 13.5% of men aged 65 and over, compared with 47.3% of women in that age group, were widowed (Saluter, 1996).

The number of widowed persons varies not only with gender and chronological age, but also with race, Hispanic origin, metropolitan residence, geographical region, and other demographic variables. Reflective of the younger status of the Hispanic population of this country is the fact that, compared with the percentages of widowed persons in the non-Hispanic white (6.9%) and black (7.1%) populations in 1995, only 3.9% of Hispanics were widowed (see Figure 13–7). In addition, black women tend to become widows at an

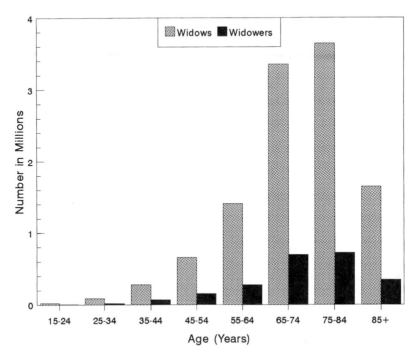

Figure 13–6   Number and percent of widowed persons in the United States aged 15 years and over, March 1995, by chronological age. (Based on data from Saluter, 1996.)

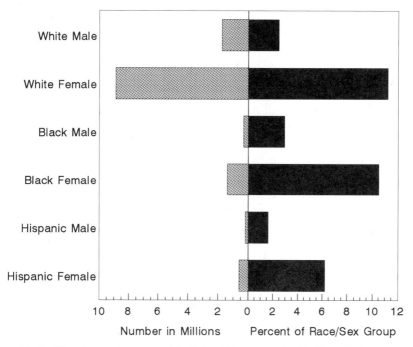

Figure 13–7   Number and percent of widowed persons in the United States aged 15 years and over, March 1995, by sex and race/ethnicity. (Based on data from Saluter, 1996.)

earlier age than whites or Hispanics, and nonwhite Hispanic widows tend to be slightly younger than white widows.

The fact that the percentage of widowed persons living in metropolitan areas of the United States (6.3%) was slightly less than the percentage of widows in the country as a whole (6.6%) in 1995 is probably caused by the larger percentage of Hispanics and other younger age groups of people who live in metropolitan than in nonmetropolitan areas. The age distribution of the population is also reflected in the percentages of widowed persons in the four major sections of the United States: Northeast (7.3%), Midwest (6.7%), South (6.7%), and West (5.6%) (Saluter, 1996). In general, residents of states in the Northeast tend to be older, and those in the West tend to be younger than residents of states in other parts of the country. The differences in age distributions of the populations of those states affect the percentages of widowed persons residing in them.

Family and Social Relationships

Interactions between recently widowed persons and their extended families tend to increase for a while, but they usually decline as time passes.

Young widows, who may experience great hardship when no close relatives are nearby, are likely to look to their parents for support. Unlike the awkward social status of young widows, widowhood in older women is considered more normal and socially acceptable. Social support from family members and community is usually greater for older widows, making the transition from wife to widow easier for them than for younger widows.

Social support for a widow of any age is more likely to come from her own family than from her husband's, even when she has had congenial relations with her in-laws. A young widow with children can take solace in them but may find that the physical and psychological effort required to rear children on her own can be insurmountable. Older widows and widowers with grown children tend to grow closer to them and may even move in with them. However, the potential for intergenerational conflict, particularly when the daughter or son has a family of her or his own, usually makes this solution to the problem of what to do with a widowed mom or dad undesirable. A widow who lives with her son's or daughter's family is expected to help around the house and take care of the grandchildren—chores that she may not relish. Rather than resigning herself to a subordinate position in another woman's home and becoming involved in the management and conflict of another household, most widows opt for "intimacy at a distance" (Lopata, 1973).

Widows who relied on their husbands' business and social contacts may find that their social activities are reduced for a time, but most are able to make new connections and establish new social relationships if they make an effort to do so. Because there are many individuals in like circumstances to choose from, finding companionship outside the home is rarely difficult for older widows. Churches, adult and senior centers, and volunteer organizations of various kinds provide ample opportunities to make new social contacts and friends.

Because of her changed status, a widow may find that her married friends treat her differently than before. Consequently, she may feel awkward and even perceive herself as something of a sexual threat to them (Field & Minkler, 1988). Not wanting to intrude, she may decline invitations and stay at home and be lonely. She may feel that she is not supposed to be interested in other men but is expected to devote herself to keeping the family together and preserving the memory of her late husband. This is particularly likely when her identity is principally that of wife and mother whose activities are limited to her immediate family. Now she finds that she has no cultivated interests or abilities, no knowledge of how to acquire them, and no motivation to do so.

Husbands and wives are frequently so interdependent that when one dies, the other feels lost and cannot function effectively. Loneliness and the need for companionship may be even more problematic for a widower whose only close friend was his wife, and who depended on her for social relationships outside the family. Widows usually have little difficulty obtaining sympathy and support from other widows, but widowers are usually not as close to other people and find it harder to make friends with other widowers

(Connidis, 1989; Connidis & Davies, 1990). In addition to being emotionally unprepared to live out their lives alone, widowers often find that they lack the information and skills needed to handle routine domestic chores such as cooking, shopping, and cleaning (Marshall, 1980). Loneliness and homemaking duties are two reasons why widowers become receptive to the overtures of widows who vie for their attentions. Having discovered that they cannot forego the companionship, sex, and support provided by a wife, many widowers remarry within a year or two after their wife's death. They usually marry women who are a few years younger than they and whom they have known for years (Bengtson et al., 1990). Remarriage is less of an option for older widows, who must compete with large numbers of women in similar circumstances. Although the opportunity to remarry is not as great for older women as it is for older men, research indicates that it is not as difficult as most older women think (Jacobs & Vinick, 1979).

Loneliness and Money

Widows and widowers are, on the whole, lonelier than married people, but their loneliness does not necessarily come from living alone. Loneliness is more of a problem for younger than for older widows and for working-class than for middle-class widows (Atchley, 1975). Loneliness also tends to be higher for widows residing in metropolitan areas than for those in medium-sized cities and small towns (Atchley, 1975; Kunkel, 1979; Lopata, 1973). The relationship of loneliness to age, social class, and location differences in loneliness depends on the number of social contacts the person has. Older widows tend to have more friends than younger widows, and middle-class widows have more time and a greater tendency than working-class widows to establish new friendships. A number of factors could account for the greater loneliness of widows who live in metropolitan areas, but the principal one is that the psychological climate, traveling distances, and safety conditions in large metropolitan areas are less favorable for social interactions than those of small- and medium-sized towns.

Loneliness is, of course, not limited to widows; widowers also get lonely. The results of certain studies seem to indicate that widows are somewhat lonelier than widowers, but this may be due to the fact that more widows than widowers live alone (Murphy & Florio, 1978; Troll, 1982). There is no consistent support for the notion than widowers are less able than widowers to live alone or that they are more likely to become lonely (Atchley, 1994). However, it is true that widows are more likely than widowers to maintain close relationships with family members and to have at least one confidant (Lopata, 1975). Widows are also more likely than widowers to maintain contact with their families (Powers, Keith, & Goudy, 19075). Finally, both widows and widowers may cope with feelings of loneliness by keeping pets that they can take care of, talk to, and love.

Another problem experienced by widows is financial hardship. Income from insurance policies, estate settlements, profit-sharing trusts, and the like result in some fortunate widows being even better off financially than when their husbands were alive. The majority of widows, however, must manage on small savings, a modest insurance or death benefit, and Social Security. And for most working-class women, widowhood pushes them financially over the line into poverty. Although widows of all ages have problems with money and its management, those problems are more acute for younger than for older widows (Wyly & Hulicka, 1975).

Not only does the decreased income of widows lead to a reduction in the pursuit of interests and activities that cost money, but the individual's self-concept may also be affected. Furthermore, a widow who depended on her husband to keep their possessions in good condition may feel inadequate, insecure, and hopeless when forced to do everything by herself. On the other hand, the need to rely on one's own resources rather than depending totally on someone else can be a growth experience for both widows and widowers. In general, it has been found that the great majority of men and women are able to cope with widowhood. Their morale and self-confidence tend to be high and their attitudes quite positive (Kunkel, 1979).

A New Beginning

The average American widow is not a poor, sad creature who has few friends and is in chronically poor health. Most widows are in good physical and mental health and are not racked by arthritis, osteoporosis, or the fear of cancer. To be sure, they may miss their husband's companionship, but they may also be pleased to discover that they have less housework, more time to visit and travel, and an opportunity to develop long-dormant interests and skills and cultivate new ones. Because of their greater social abilities and unfulfilled potential, older women usually cope with widowhood better than older men. In fact, surveys have found that the morale of older widows is even better than that of older married women (Morgan, 1976).

As we have seen, a woman who has lost her husband need not and usually does not become either a "social isolate" or a "merry widow." Many widows choose to make few changes in their lives, continuing the same levels of activities in similar roles and situations as before. Another group of widows, whom Lopata (1973) designated "self-initiating women," selects new roles and develops new friendships. The status of widowhood has provided these women with a long-awaited opportunity to control their own lives and to do things that they may always have wanted to but felt they could not do while their husbands were alive. Rather than retreating from reality or resigning themselves to a lonely existence, they look forward to a life filled with joy and anticipation. For them, as for all of us, life goes on and tomorrow is another day!

MY LIFE 13–2

The Death and Transfiguration of Our Town

In a way, my life ended the day I left Our Town. At least my childhood did. On that day, I stopped thinking of myself as a boy and set out on a path I could never reverse. I had left Our Town before, but only for short periods of time on trips that made me appreciate it even more.

The life of Our Town as I knew it also ended the day I left. The town continued to exist within and without me, but it wasn't the same. Not that I agree with the solipsistic notion that places and things have no independent existence outside one's own mind. I believe there is a real world outside myself that obeys its own laws and holds all of us in its grasp. No, I refer to the phenomenological notion that every person's perception of the world is unique and private. Other people may perceive a similar world, but it is not exactly the same.

When I say that Our Town died the day I left, I mean that the town that I had known ceased to exist. Actually, it wouldn't have mattered if it had remained physically the same, which, of course, it didn't. No, it changed in large measure because my conception of it changed and continues to change as I acquire new experiences and become mentally disabled with age. As I am altered, so that which I attempt to reconstruct in memory is altered, and the picture that I remember is different every time.

So now I know that I can't go home again, at least not to my childhood home. This simple fact has both advantages and disadvantages. One advantage is that it would be difficult if not impossible for anyone to prove that things were not or did not happen the way that I say. A possible disadvantage is that I can never truly relive the events of my childhood that were most enjoyable and meaningful to me. Considering my tendency to see the past through rose-colored glasses, perhaps it's just as well. Leveling of some experiences, sharpening of others, and assimilation of still others into a generalized background of my present attitudes and beliefs are just some of the processes that occur when I try to reconstruct the past. My successes loom ever larger in retrospect, and my failures are not as devastating. I am loved more and hated less, and I return the favor in kind. The friends that I had were the very best of friends, with whom I spent many pleasurable hours.

The past is always with me, and usually more inviting and interesting than the present. Down the long stretch of days and years, I can still feel my boyhood presence moving in and out of places, interacting with other people, doing many things for the first and the last time. Now, in the evening of my life, I call upon my past frequently. It never fails to respond, providing me with the reason and the will to continue the game until past, present, and future finally merge into one.

SUMMARY

Death is much more common in old age than at other times of life: Approximately three-fourths of all death in the United States occur in people aged 65 years and over. Reflective of the age distribution of different ethnic groups in the United States is the fact that the death rate is slightly lower for blacks than for whites, and even lower for American Indians, Hispanics, and Asians. Differences in the age distributions of populations are also a factor in the higher death rates in Europe and North America than in Asia and South America. Because of poor living conditions, the death rate is higher in Africa than in any other part of the world. The death rate in the United States is higher during the winter months than at other times of year, being highest in the District of Columbia, and lowest in Alaska.

The three most common causes of death in the United States are heart disease, cancer, and stroke. These and other chronic disorders have replaced the acute illnesses of yesteryear as the major causes of death among Americans. Deaths due to homicide are greater in frequency during the late teens and early twenties, whereas deaths due to accidents and suicide are more common in old age. The frequency of accidental deaths and homicide are higher for men than for women, and higher for blacks than for whites. Suicide is more common among older white men than any other age or ethnic group.

Death and its symbolism have been expressed in art and literature for hundreds of years. Philosophers have been less concerned with the subject of death, preferring to leave it to theologians and the clergy. An exception are the existentialists, who emphasized that the realization of death spurs a search for meaning in life.

Separation anxiety in children is the forerunner of the fear of death in adulthood. Fear of death is less common in young and older adults than in middle-aged adults. Fears of death vary not only with age but also with personality, health, socioeconomic status, and culture. Attitudes toward death depend on individual characteristics, culture, and race/ethnicity. Religious beliefs affect death attitudes and anxiety: People who are ambivalent or indecisive about religion tend to have greater fears of death than either confirmed believers or nonbelievers.

The main criterion of death in most states is the cessation of all electrical activity of the brain, though cessation of respiration, heart rate, and reflexes are also important signs. Death of the body does not occur all at once: Different tissues and organs die at different rates. It is common practice to remove a healthy kidney, heart, or other viable organ for transplant purposes after the donor is considered medically and legally dead. In addition, the speed or pace at which dying occurs (the "dying trajectory") varies with the patient, the disorder, and the treatments administered.

Some people manifest a "terminal drop" in cognitive and sensorimotor abilities and a change in personality during the last few months of life. Although no one can consciously control the exact moment of his or her death, it is apparently possible to hasten or delay death by means of one's thoughts, feelings, and motivations.

Kübler-Ross's five-stage model of the dying process—denial, anger, bargaining, depression, acceptance—is descriptive of the psychological changes that take place in some dying patients, but the model should not be interpreted as a invariant sequence of stages through which all dying patients pass. An alternative model proposed by Pattison consists of three stages in the living–dying interval: acute, chronic living–dying, and terminal phases.

Most people die in institutions, sometimes only after extraordinary measures have been applied to keep them alive. Hospice care is a less expensive, and often more humane, alternative to hospital or nursing home care of terminally ill persons. In addition to focusing on the control of pain and discomfort, hospice care consists of discussions of death and dying between patients and staff members, and an emphasis on dying with dignity and a sense of self-worth rather than feelings of isolation and aloneness.

Open communication is preferable to the conspiracy of silence that has often pervaded social interactions with dying patients. Information about death and dying can be dealt with more effectively by terminally ill patients when it is discussed with a compassionate, companionate person. In addition to the psychological assistance provided by family members, nurses, doctors, and the clergy, the services of professional counselors may also be made available to dying persons.

Modern funerary rituals include the wake, the funeral service, and the postfuneral period. The body of the deceased is usually placed in a casket, which may or may not be open during the wake and the funeral service. The location and nature of the service and the manner in which the body is disposed of vary with the culture, religion, and other preferences of the deceased and his or her family. Although funerals have traditionally been held in churches and the body buried afterward, secular services and cremation have become increasingly popular in recent years.

Three phases of grieving over the death of a loved one have been identified: a short initial phase characterized by shock, a longer intermediate phase involving a complex of physiological and psychological reactions to the stress of bereavement, and a recovering phase beginning about 1 year after the death.

Widowhood in the United States is primarily a status of older women. The percentage of widowed persons varies not only with age and sex, but also with race/ethnicity, metropolitan versus nonmetropolitan area of residence, and geographical region. Greater percentages of widows are white, and they are more likely to live in metropolitan areas and in the Northeast. Differences in the age distributions of different racial/ethnic groups and area of residence are related to differences in the number of widows in the groups.

Loneliness can be a serious problem for both widows and widowers, but widows usually have a network of other widows to help combat their feelings of loneliness. Widowers usually make friends less readily than widows, but the availability of unmarried women enables widowers to remarry fairly easily if they so desire.

Another problem experienced by many widows is financial hardship. Lack of training in money management adds to the financial woes of widows attempting to live on reduced income. Responsibility for keeping the car, the house, and other possessions in good order is another chore that must be undertaken by most widows. These new tasks may be difficult to bear for widows who depended totally on their husbands for maintaining their home and other possessions. However, the great majority of widows are able to "get their act together" and learn to do what they must. Developing new capabilities provide widows with a sense of pride and competence and may lead to a personal reawakening. Skills and interests that have long laid dormant may be resurrected in widows' determination to take hold of their lives and get on with the business of living.

SUGGESTED READINGS

Aiken, L. R. (1994). *Dying, death, and bereavement* (3rd ed.). Newton, MA: Allyn & Bacon.

Burnell, G. M. (1993). *Final choices: To live or die in an age of medical technology.* New York: Plenum Press.

Fulton, R. (1995). The contemporary funeral: Functional or dysfunctional? In H. Wass & R. A. Neimeyer (Eds.), *Dying: Facing the facts* (3rd ed., pp. 185–209). Washington, DC: Taylor & Francis.

Howarth, G., & Jupp, P. C. (Eds.). (1996). *Contemporary issues in the sociology of death, dying, and disposal.* New York: St. Martin's Press.

Irish, D. P., Lundquist, K. F., & Nelson, V. K. (1993). *Ethnic variations in dying, death, and grief: Diversity in universality.* Washington, DC: Taylor & Francis.

Lattanzi-Licht, M., & Connor, S. (1995). Care of the dying: The hospice approach. In H. Wass & R. A. Neimeyer (Eds.), *Dying: Facing the facts* (3rd ed., pp. 143–163). Washington, DC: Taylor & Francis.

Moller, D. W. (1996). *Confronting death: Values, institutions, and human mortality.* New York: Oxford University Press.

Nuland, S. B. (1994). *How we die: Reflections on life's final chapter.* New York: Knopf.

Rando, T. A. (1995). Grief and mourning: Accommodating to loss. In H. Wass & R. A. Neimeyer (Eds.), *Dying: Facing the facts* (3rd ed., pp. 211–241). Washington, DC: Taylor & Francis.

Samarel, N. (1995). The dying process. In H. Wass & R. A. Neimeyer (Eds.), *Dying: Facing the facts* (3rd ed., pp. 89–116). Washington, DC: Taylor & Francis.

Stillion, J. M. (1995). Death in the lives of adults: Responding to the tolling of the bell. In H. Wass & R. A. Neimeyer (Eds.), *Dying: Facing the facts* (3rd ed., pp. 303–322). Washington, DC: Taylor & Francis.

Glossary

Acceptance According to Elisabeth Kübler-Ross, the final stage in a person's reactions to impending death. This phase is characterized by "quiet expectation" and acceptance of the inevitability of death. The dying person wants to be alone with one or two loved ones and desires only freedom from pain.

Accommodation Automatic change in the shape of the lens of the eye so that an image can be brought into sharper focus on the retina.

Activities of daily living (ADLs) Activities such as bathing, getting in and out of bed or a chair, using the toilet, and dressing.

Activity theory The theory that active, productive people are happiest at any age.

Acute brain syndrome Reversible, but frequently severe, brain disorder resulting from disease, injury, malnutrition, alcoholism, and other conditions.

Acute phase (of dying) The first phase in Pattison's three-phase model of psychological reactions during the living–dying interval. The anxiety and anger, which are at a peak during this phase, are reduced by defense mechanisms and other affective and cognitive responses of the dying person.

Ageism Social stereotyping of and/or discrimination against older people.

Age norm The average or expected characteristics or behaviors of a person of a particular chronological age.

Age-specific birthrate The crude birthrate computed on a designated chronological age group.

Age-specific death rate Crude death rate computed on a designated chronological age group.

Age stratification Assignment of social roles to persons according to chronological age.

Aging The continuous process (biological, psychological, social), beginning with conception and ending with death, by which organisms mature and decline.

Alienation A feeling of personal disconnectedness or self-removal from the job that results when workers feel that their efforts are meaningless and unappreciated and they fail to see the connection between what they do and the final product.

Alzheimer's disease A chronic brain syndrome, usually occurring in older adulthood, characterized by gradual deterioration of memory, disorientation, and other features of dementia.

Anger According to Kübler-Ross, the second stage in a person's reactions to impending death. During this stage, the person partially accepts the knowledge that he or she is going to die but becomes angry at the unfairness of having to die while others go on living.

Angina pectoris Chest pain, with feelings of suffocation and impending death, due most often to insufficient oxygen supply to heart tissue and brought on by effort or excitement.

Angor anima A fear of impending death, often accompanying a heart attack.

Angry type Reichard's term for a maladjusted personality pattern persisting into old age. The person is bitter and blames other people for his or her failures.

Anniversary reaction A condition in which an emotional reaction in a survivor associated with the death of a loved one occurs on the anniversary of the death.

Annulment of marriage Setting aside, by judicial decree, of a purported marriages that was void at its inception. Grounds for annulment include mental incompetence, being under the age of consent, physical cause, duress, and fraud, such as bigamy, on the part of one of the parties.

Anticipatory grief Grieving or mourning that begins in the survivor before the death of a loved one.

Anxiety neurosis A type of neurotic disorder characterized by persistent anxiety.

Apoplexy *See* **cerebrovascular accident**.

Aptitude The ability to profit from training and experience in an occupation or skill.

Arcus senilis A cloudy ring that forms around the cornea of the eye in old age.

Armored–defended personality Reichard's term for a personality pattern, persisting into old age, in which the person defends him- or herself against anxiety by keeping busy.

Ars Moriendi A written treatise, apparently prepared by a group of German monks in the Middle Ages, which provides details on how to die in a dignified, holy manner.

Arteriosclerosis Abnormal hardening and thickening of the walls of the arteries in old age.

Arthritis Degeneration and/or inflammation of the joints.

Atherosclerosis A type of arteriosclerosis resulting from an accumulation of fatty deposits on the walls of arteries.

Attitude A tendency to respond positively or negatively to some object, person, situation, or event.

Audiometer A frequency generator for measuring a person's sensitivity to various frequencies in the audible range of human hearing; used to determine the degree of deafness.

Authoritative parents Accepting, responsive, child-centered and yet controlling parents.

Autoimmunity theory Theory that the immunological defenses of a person decline with age, causing the body to "turn on itself," and consequently increasing the likelihood of autoimmune diseases such as arthritis.

Autointoxication A state of being poisoned by toxic substances produced within the body.

Bargaining According to Kübler-Ross, the third stage in a person's reactions to impending death. This stage is characterized by attempts to buy time, and by bargaining with the doctors, God, or with anyone or anything that the patient believes can protect him or her from death.

Beanpole family Family structure in which there are several living generations but each generation is relatively small in number.

Behavior modification (behavior therapy) Psychotherapeutic procedures based on learning theory and research, designed to change inappropriate behavior to more personally and socially acceptable behavior. Examples of such procedures are reinforcement, systematic desensitization, counterconditioning, aversion, extinction, implosion (flooding), and modeling.

Bereavement Loss of a loved one by death.

Biological age The anatomical or physiological age of a person, as determined by changes in organismic structure and function; takes into account such features as posture, skin texture, hair color and thickness, strength, speed, and sensory acuity.

Bipolar disorder Mental disorder in which an individual's mood fluctuates between euphoric mania and depression.

Body mass index (BMI) A standard way of describing obesity; computed as 697.5 times the weight (in pounds) divided by the square of the height (in inches).

Brain death Irreversible cessation of all functions of the brain, including the brain stem.

Breakdown theories Theories according to which aging is the result of wear and tear, stress, or exhaustion of body organs and cells.

Burnout Syndrome characterized by emotional exhaustion, lessened productivity, and feelings of depersonalization; precipitated by the stress of overwork.

Capital punishment Punishment for a crime by the death penalty.

Cardiovascular diseases Diseases involving structural damage and malfunctioning of the heart and blood vessels.

Carpe diem Latin for "seize the day." Enjoy the present instead of placing all hope in the future.

Case advocacy Routine litigation in which lawyers contest on behalf of clients.

Cataracts   Ocular disorder, more characteristic of old age, in which opacity of the lens of the eye obstructs the passage of light to the retina.

Centenarian   A person who is at least 100 years old.

Cerebral arteriosclerosis   Chronic hardening and thickening of the arteries of the brain in old age.

Cerebrovascular accident (CVA)   A sudden rupture (hemorrhage) or blockage (thrombosis) of a large cerebral blood vessel, leading to impairment of brain functioning (stroke, apoplexy).

Cherry angiomas   Small red spots on the skin in the trunk area of the body.

Chronic brain syndrome   Mental disorder caused by long-standing injury to the brain; gradual, insidious changes in personality occur.

Chronic living–dying phase   Second phase in Pattison's three-phase descriptive model of the dying process. During this phase, anxiety is reduced and the patient asks questions about what will happen to him or her as well as family and friends after death.

Cirrhosis of the liver   Chronic disease of the liver, one of the major causes of death in the United States.

Class-action suit   Litigation on behalf of an entire group of people.

Client-centered therapy   A type of psychotherapy, pioneered by Carl Rogers, in which the client decides what to talk about and when, without direction, judgment, or interpretation on the part of the counselor. Unconditional positive regard, empathy, and congruence characterize the counselor's attitude in this type of therapy.

Climacteric   Change of life in women signaled by decline in the functioning of the ovaries and culminating in menopause.

Close-coupled relationship   An enduring monogamous relationship between homosexuals.

Cockayne's syndrome   A childhood form of progeria (premature aging).

Cognitive therapy   Psychotherapeutic process in which a person's faulty cognitions or beliefs are changed to more realistic ones.

Cohabitation   Arrangement in which a couple lives together without being legally married.

Cohort   A group of people of the same age, class membership, or culture (e.g., all people born in 1900).

Cohort differences   Physical and psychological differences between individuals born in different time periods and hence belonging to different generations.

Cohort-sequential design   Developmental research design in which successive cohorts are compared over the same age ranges. For example, changes in attitude or ability from age 60 to 70 in a group born in 1910 are compared with changes in attitude from age 60 to 70 in a group born in 1920.

Collagen   Fibrous protein material found in the connective tissue, bones, and skin of vertebrates; becomes gelatinous when heated.

Common-law marriage   Marriage without ceremony or formalities entered into by express mutual agreement of the parties for the purpose of establishing the relationship of husband and wife. Common-law marriage is legally recognized in some jurisdictions if it is followed by cohabitation and public recognition of marital duties and obligations.

Companionate marriage Marital partnership in which the couple share interests and a reciprocate love for each other.

Comparable worth The legal principle that pay should be made equal in those occupations that are determined to be equivalent in importance but in which the relative numbers of men and women employees are substantially different.

Competency Legal determination that a person has sound judgment and can manage his or her own property, enter into contracts, and so on.

Conduction deafness Deafness resulting from a failure of the mechanical vibrations corresponding to sound waves to be transmitted adequately through the three small bones in the middle ear into the cochlea of the inner ear.

Confidentiality Maintaining confidence in regard to the results of research or assessment of an individual.

Confounding Situation in which two measures or characteristics vary in such a way that the independent effect of each cannot be determined. Age and cohort differences are confounded in cross-sectional research, and age and time of measurement are confounded in longitudinal research.

Congregate housing Rental housing in which residents have their own living quarters but share meals in a common dining room and have a variety of other supporting services.

Conspiracy of silence Tacit agreement on the part of family, friends, and medical personnel not to talk with a dying person about death.

Contingency management Control of institutionalized persons by differentially reinforcing them for socially approved and socially disapproved behavior; makes certain kinds of pleasures or privileges contingent upon keeping neat and clean, eating properly, interacting with other patients, or engaging in other socially acceptable behaviors. Also known as *token economy* when the reinforcers are tokens that can be exchange for something that the patient desires.

Continuing-care retirement community (CCRC) Housing that provides various levels of care. Residents pay a monthly fee for food, rent, utilities, housekeeping, and nursing care.

Continuity theory Persistence of personality characteristics and typical behaviors throughout the individual's lifetime.

Coolidge effect Sexually stimulating effect of another partner.

Coronary A heart attack, resulting from obstruction of a coronary artery and usually destroying heart muscle.

Correlation The degree of relationship between two variables, signified by an index (a "correlation coefficient") ranging from −1.00 to +1.00.

Counseling A general term for giving advice and guidance to individuals who need assistance with vocational, academic, or personal problems.

Cross-linkage Inadvertent coupling of large intracellular and extracellular molecules, causing connective tissue to stiffen.

Cross-sectional study Comparisons of the physical and psychological characteristics of different age groups of people.

Cross-sequential design Developmental research design in which two or more successive cohorts are studied longitudinally. For example, the change in attitude or ability from 1970 to 1990 in groups of individuals born in 1920, 1940, and 1960 are compared.

Crude birthrate Number of births per 1,000 population during a particular period of time, usually a year.

Crystallized intelligence R. B. Cattell's term for mental ability (knowledge, skills) acquired through experience and education. Specific to certain fields, such as school learning, and applied in tasks where habits have become fixed (*see* **Fluid intelligence**).

CVA *See* **Cerebrovascular accident**.

Danse macabre ("dance of death") A symbolic dance in which Death, represented as a skeleton, leads people or skeletons to their graves; a common representation in art, especially during the Middle Ages.

Dark adaptation Adjustment of the eye to a dark environment.

Death rattle A rattling or gurgling sound produced by air passing through mucus in the lungs and air passages of a dying person.

Defense mechanisms In psychodynamic theory, psychological techniques that defend the ego against anxiety, guilt, and loss of self-esteem resulting from awareness of certain impulses or realities.

Defined-benefit pension plan A pension plan in which the employer agrees to pay a specified retirement benefit when employees reach a certain age and a specified length of service with the organization.

Defined-contribution plan A pension plan in which the employer and the employee contribute a specific amount to the employee's pension fund every pay period into a tax-sheltered annuity plan.

Delusion A false belief, characteristic of paranoid disorders. Delusions of grandeur, persecution, and reference are common in these psychotic conditions.

Dementia Severe mental disorder involving impairment of mental ability.

Demography The science of vital and social statistics (births, marriages, diseases, etc.) of populations.

Denial According to Kübler-Ross, the first stage in a person's reactions to impending death. During this stage, the person refuses to accept the fact of death and seeks reassurance from other (medical and nonmedical) people.

Dependency ratio Ratio of the number of dependent (retired) persons to the number of active wage earners in a population.

Dependent variable The variable in an experiment that changes as a function of changes in the independent variable. Variations in magnitude of the dependent variable, plotted on the Y axis of a graph, can be viewed as the experimental effect.

Depressant Any drug that slows down nervous system activity. Examples of depressants are alcohol, barbiturates, and opiates.

Depression (1) Mood disorder characterized by dejection, loss of interest in things, negative thoughts (including suicidal thoughts), and various physical symptoms (e.g., loss of appetite, insomnia, fatigue). (2) According to Kübler-Ross, the fourth stage in a person's reactions to impending death. The patient fully accepts the fact of death but becomes depressed by all that has been suffered and all that will have to be given up.

Desensitization Extinction of anxiety evoked by a stimulus or situation, resulting from repeated exposure of the individual to that situation under "safe" conditions.

Desolation effects hypothesis Hypothesis proposed by Epstein and his colleagues that both the event of widowhood and the circumstances stemming from it have deleterious effects in terms of grief, feelings of hopelessness, new worries and responsibilities, and changes in the diet, work routine, and financial situation of the bereaved.

Differential association (principle of) Theory that criminal and deviant behavior is learned through close and frequent association with behavior patterns, norms, and values manifested by criminals and other social deviants.

Disengagement theory Cumming's theory that aging brings about a change in self-perception, and adjustment occurs through withdrawal from responsibility and participation.

Dying trajectory The rate of decline in functioning from health to death; can be fast or slow, with many starts and stops, depending on the nature of the disorder, the patient's age and lifestyle, the kinds of medical treatment received, and various psychosocial factors.

Ego Loosely speaking, the "I" or "self" of personality. In psychoanalytic theory, the executive, reality-oriented aspect of personality, which acts as a mediator between the id and superego.

Elder abuse Physical or psychological abuse of older adults.

Elder advocacy Concern for and legal action on behalf of the elderly.

Elderhostel Organization that offers low-cost travel and study opportunities for individuals aged 55 and over and their spouses in a wide range of course work.

Electroconvulsive therapy (ECT) A form of treatment for severe depression and certain other mental disorders; electrical current is passed briefly through the head, producing unconsciousness and convulsions.

Embolism Obstruction of a blood vessel by an air bubble or other abnormal particular (thrombosis).

Empathic model Use of special devices (earplugs, special glasses, etc.) to simulate the sensorimotor disturbances of older people, and especially handicapped older people. The methods enable younger adults to experience the world from the perspective of an elderly person, and hence to understand the sensorimotor limitations of old age.

Emphysema   Disorder involving the destruction of millions of little air sacs (alveoli) in the lungs. The patient has great difficulty inhaling and may develop a barrel-chested appearance.

Empty nest   Situation in which all of a parent's children have moved out of the parental home.

Epic of Gilgamesh   A mythological tale from ancient Babylonian times, which deals with the adventures of a Sumerian king who is searching for the secret of eternal life.

Epidemiological studies   Prospective or retrospective investigations designed to determine the risk factors associated with a particular disease.

Epigenesis   The theory that an embryo develops from the successive differentiation of an originally undifferentiated structure.

Erectile dysfunction   Inability to have or maintain an erection.

Error accumulation theory   Theory that interprets aging as the accumulation of errors, perhaps errors in protein synthesis within the body cells.

Estate taxes   Taxes imposed on a decedent's property, assessed on the gross estate before distribution to the heirs.

Euthanasia   Either active or passive contribution to the death of a human being or animal suffering from a terminal illness or injury.

Excitement phase   First phase in the sexual response cycle. In the male, the penis becomes erect, the scrotal sac is flattened and elevated, and the testes are partially elevated; vaginal lubrication and enlargement, and vasocongestion of the clitoris occur in the female. Muscle tension, blood pressure, and heart rate increase in both sexes.

Extended care facility   As originally designated by Medicare legislation, a health facility that provides more extensive professional care than a nursing home.

Faceism   The tendency of photographers and other cameramen to focus on the faces of men and the bodies of women.

Family therapy (family counseling)   Treatment of psychological problems in a family setting; based on the doctrine that many, if not most, psychological problems originate in the interpersonal family situation and consequently can be treated more effectively in that context.

Felony   A serious crime punishable by death or incarceration in a state penitentiary. Felonies include murder, manslaughter, larceny, burglary, and arson. (*see* **Misdemeanor**)

Fertility rate   Average number of children per woman of childbearing age in a given population.

Filial piety   An important principle of traditional Asian culture that one's parents and other older adults should not have to suffer from want or sorrow.

Filial responsibility laws   Laws that specify the extent to which families are legally responsible for the support of needy older family members.

Five-factor model   A model of human personality, based on the results of factor analysis, that characterizes personality as a composite of five factors:

neuroticism, extroversion, openness, agreeableness, and conscientiousness.

Fixation Any stereotyped form of behavior resulting from frustration and resistance to change.

Fluid intelligence R. B. Cattell's term for inherent, genetically determined mental ability, as seen in problem-solving or novel responses.

Free radicals Highly reactive molecules or parts of molecules that may connect to and damage other molecules; thought to play a role in the process of aging.

Gender identity An individual's view of him- or herself with regard to gender; the introspective part of **Gender role**.

Gender role A culture-specific pattern of behavior that is considered appropriate to a particular gender; develops in childhood and persists until death.

Gender schema Internalized beliefs about what men and women are and how they are supposed to act.

Generational equity Issue concerned with whether older adults receive a disproportionately large share of public funds when increasing numbers of children are living in poverty.

Geriatrics A branch of medicine dealing with the prevention and treatment of health problems in older adulthood.

Gerontology A branch of knowledge (science) concerned with the characteristic and problems of the aged.

Glass ceiling A subtle barrier to advancement by women in an organization; a level to which they can rise in a company but beyond which they cannot go.

Glaucoma Visual disorder characterized by increasing pressure within the eye caused by concentration of fluid.

Group marriage A communal arrangement in which a number of legally married couples share living quarters, duties, and sexual partners.

Group therapy Type of psychotherapy in which several individuals share their feelings, experiences, and expectations with each other under the direction or guidance of a therapist or other group leader.

Hallucination Perception of an object or situation in the absence of an external stimulus.

Hayflick limit Limit in the ability of the cells of a species to divide; the limit in human fetal tissue is approximately 50.

Holographic will An unwitnessed will prepared in the testator's (legator's) own handwriting; recognized as valid in some states.

Hospice An organization that provides health services to dying persons and their families.

Hot flashes Sensations of extreme heat and a drenching sweat, particularly in the upper part of the body, experienced by many women following menopause.

Hyperoxygenation Breathing pure oxygen under high atmospheric pressure; a process that in certain investigations has improved learning and retention of information by the elderly.

Hypertension   High blood pressure.

Id   In the psychoanalytic, three-part theory of personality, the reservoir of instinctive impulses and strivings. The id, or "animal nature" of man, is concerned only with immediate gratification of impulses.

Idealization of the deceased   When survivors remember only good things about a deceased person. Also called *sanctification of the deceased.*

Identity   A person's gradually emerging, and continually changing, sense of self.

Incompetency   Legal decision that a person is suffering from a mental disorder, causing a defect of judgment such that the person is unable to manage his or her own property, enter into contracts, and take care of other affairs.

Independent variable   The variable whose effects (on the dependent variable) is attempting to be determined in an experiment.

Infant mortality   Death before the age of 1 year.

Informed consent   Consenting to participate in a research investigation after being told the nature of the investigation, how the results will be used, and that the participant is free to withdraw at any time.

Inheritance taxes   Taxes levied on an heir, the rate being a percentage of the value of the property inherited by the heir.

In-kind income   Goods and services that require no monetary expenditures.

Insanity   An imprecise legal term for severe mental disorders involving lack of responsibility for one's actions. According to the M'Naghten Rule, an insane person is one who cannot distinguish right from wrong. However, other precedents, such as the Durham decision, are applied in determining insanity in some states.

Institutionism   A psychological state associated with being institutionalized, the symptoms of which are automatic behaviors, expressionless faces, general apathy, disinterest in personal appearance, and deteriorated morale.

Instrumental activities of daily living (IADLs)   Activities such as doing light housework, preparing meals, doing laundry, and shopping.

Integrity versus despair   Crisis of old age in which acceptance of one's life leads to a sense of integrity, and feeling that it is too late to make up for missed opportunities leads to despair.

Intelligence   Many definitions of this term have been offered, such as the "ability to judge well, understand well, and reason well" (Binet) and the "capacity for abstract thinking" (Terman). In general, what is measured by conventional intelligence tests is the ability to succeed in schoolwork and similar academic tasks.

Intergenerational equity   Equitable distribution of the resources of a society across various age groups.

Interiority   A turning inward of the personality, or movement from active to passive mastery, observed in many people during old age.

Intestate To die without leaving a will.

Involuntary commitment Legal process by which a person is committed to a mental institution against his or her will.

Involutional period Decline in body energy during middle age or early old age, signaled by the menopause in women.

Involved grandparent Grandparent whose relationship with a grandchild is like that of a parent.

Kinesthetic sense Proprioceptive sense of the position of body members, such as the arms or legs, the receptors of which are found in the muscles, tendons, and joints of the body.

Korsakoff's syndrome Chronic brain disorder associated with alcoholism and caused by long-term deficiency of vitamin B.

Larceny Fraudulent and unauthorized taking of the personal property of another person, with the felonious intent of depriving or defrauding the owner.

Learned helplessness Acquired perception on the part of the individual of his or her lack of influence or control over external events; can lead to apathy and depression.

Levirate Custom of marriage between a man and his brother's widow, required during biblical times under certain circumstances.

Life-cycle group therapy Life-review therapy extended to a group of 8–10 members of different chronological ages.

Life expectancy The average life span of persons born in a certain year; probable length of life of an individual.

Life review Reminiscence, or a split-second review of one's life just prior to impending death.

Life-review therapy Form of psychotherapy in which patients reminisce about their personal experiences.

Life span Theoretical maximum number of years of life that is biologically possible for a given species.

Lifestyle Relatively permanent organization of activities, including work, leisure, and associated social activities, characterizing an individual.

Lingering trajectory Glaser and Strauss's term for dying over a long period of time, in which the patient seems to "drift out of the world, sometimes almost like an imperceptible melting snowflake."

Lipofuscin A pigmented granule containing lipis, carbohydrates, and protein. The number of these granules in various body cells increases with aging.

Living–dying interval In Pattison's three-stage theory of dying, the interval between the initial death crisis and the actual time of death.

Living will Formal document stating that the person wishes no artificial methods of prolonging his or her life to be employed.

Locus of control A cognitive–perceptual style characterized by the typical direction ("internal" or self vs. "external" or other) from which individuals perceive themselves to be controlled.

Longevity   Length of life, long duration of life.

Longitudinal investigation   Studying the development of the same individual(s) at different ages over a period of years.

Long-term memory (LTM, or secondary memory)   Memory that lasts at least 10–20 minutes, involving more permanent storage mechanisms of the brain.

Mahabharata   An ancient Hindu poem in which Mara (or Mrtya), a beautiful, dark-eyed woman, came from within Brahma, creator of the world, and was ordered by him to kill all the world's creatures. Only by the intercession of the god Shiva were the deaths not made permanent, the slain individuals being reincarnated as other forms of life.

Major stroke   Heart failure resulting from blockage of a large cerebral blood vessel (*see also* **Cerebrovascular accident**).

Manic–depressive psychosis   An affective disorder characterized by severe mood swings and excitability.

Manic disorder   Excessive agitation and excitability, which may or may not alternate with depression (*see also* **Manic–depressive psychosis**).

Manslaughter   Illegal killing of another person without intent to kill during the heat of passion (voluntary manslaughter), or illegal but nonwillful killing of another person without malice aforethought, as during a misdemeanor such as reckless driving (involuntary manslaughter). (*See* **Murder**.)

Maturation   Developmental changes due to genetic factors rather than learning, injury, illness, or other life experiences.

Mature type   According to Reichard, a personality pattern persisting into old age, in which the person is relatively free of neurotic conflicts and can accept him- or herself and grow old with few regrets.

Maximum breathing rate   Amount of air moved through the lungs in 15 seconds while breathing as rapidly as possible.

Medicaid   Comprehensive health care program, in which funds for emergency and long-term care are made available to the poor.

Medicare   National health insurance program, primarily for acute care, for persons 65 and over who are covered by Social Security.

Memento mori   ("Remember, you must die"). Any object, such as a human skull, that reminds one of mortality.

Menopause   Cessation of menstruation, usually occurring sometime between ages 45 and 50.

Mentor   A coworker who advises a new worker and teaches the rules of an organization to him or her.

Misdemeanor   A minor crime such as simple assault that is not a felony. Misdemeanors are punishable by imprisonment for 1 year or less, by fines, or other less serious measures than felonies (*see* **Felony**).

Mitochondria   The little "energy machines" within the cytoplasm of body cells that are composed of highly unsaturated fats, sugar, and protein molecules.

Morbidity   The percentage of deaths resulting from a specific disease.

Mortality Being subject to death.

Mourning Manifestation of sorrow or lamentation for the death of a person; usually indicated by wearing black clothes or a black armband, hanging flags at half mast, and other cultural rituals.

Multi-infarct dementia Mental disorder, formerly referred to as senile dementia, due to cerebrovascular disease and associated with hypertension and vascular damage.

Murder Illegal killing of another person with malice aforethought and (1) with deliberation, premeditation, or while committing another serious crime (first-degree murder, or murder one), or (2) with intent but without deliberation or premeditation (second-degree murder or murder two (*see* **Manslaughter**).

Mutual will A special type of will containing reciprocal provisions, as when a husband and wife decide to leave everything to each other without restrictions.

Myocardial infarction A heart attack caused by blockage in a coronary artery.

Nerve deafness A form of deafness caused by damage to the inner ear or auditory nerve; usually involves a loss of sensitivity to high-frequency sounds. Also called *presbycusis*.

Nesting phase Period during the second and third years of marriage, when the partners are exploring their compatibility.

Neurofibrillary tangles Bundles of helical filaments that occur in small numbers in normal brains and in large numbers in diseased brains.

Neurosis (psychoneurosis) Nonpsychotic mental disorder characterized by anxiety, obsessions, compulsions, phobias, and bodily complaints or dysfunctions having no demonstrable physical basis.

Norms Average scores of people in a given demographic (age, sex, race, geographical region, etc.) on a psychological test or other assessment device.

Nuncupative will A will made by an oral (unwritten) declaration of the testator; valid only under certain conditions.

Obsessional review Frequent, periodic review by the bereaved of the events leading up to and immediately following the death of the deceased.

Octogenarian A person who is 80–89 years old.

Older Americans Act Federal legislative act that provides for a national network of services and programs for older Americans, in addition to funds for research, training, and model projects concerned with the aged.

Ontogeny Developmental history of the individual organism.

Open marriage A legally sanctioned union in which the partners find it perfectly acceptable to have sexual relationships with other people.

Open-coupled relationship A relationship in which two homosexuals live together but have other lovers as well.

Organic brain damage Damage to brain tissue caused by disease or injury; may result in a mental disorder.

Organic psychosis Severe mental disorder caused by organic brain damage resulting from alcoholism, encephalitis, cerebral arteriosclerosis, and other diseases, drugs, and injuries.

Orgasmic dysfunction An inability to experience orgasm.

Orgasmic phase The third phase in the sexual response cycle. Breathing rate, blood pressure, and heart rate reach a maximum, resulting in a release of muscular tension and vasoconstriction built up during the first two phases. The orgasmic phase ends with ejaculation by the male and contractions of the orgasmic platform in the female.

Osteoarthritis Chronic, degenerative disease process creating changes in the bones of the joints associated with the wear and tear of aging.

Osteoporosis A gradual, long-term loss of bone mass in old age, especially in elderly women; the bones become less dense, more porous, and fracture more easily.

Overidentification with the deceased When a survivor identifies excessively with a deceased person, as, for example, when a widow begins to talk and act like her dead husband.

Paranoid disorder A general term for a broad class of mental disorders of varying severity characterized by suspiciousness, projection, excessive feelings of self-importance, and complex delusions of grandeur, persecution, or ideas of reference.

Parkinsonism A progressive brain disorder resulting from damage to the basal ganglia and occurring most often in older adulthood. The symptoms are muscular tremors; spastic, rigid movements; propulsive gait; and a mask-like, expressionless face. Also called *Parkinson's disease.*

Passive mastery Passive view of the self and increased focus on inner life more characteristic of 60-year-olds than 40-year olds.

Personality Sum total of all the qualities, traits, and behaviors that characterize a person's individuality and by which, together with his or her physical attributes, the person is recognized as unique.

Phenomenal field That part of a person's physical environment that is perceived by and has meaning for him or her.

Phylogeny Biological development of a species.

Placebo effect Change in behavior resulting from administration of a chemically inert substance to people who believe they are receiving an active drug.

Plaque Accumulation of fatty tissue and calcified material in the cerebral blood vessels of old people, resulting in clogged arteries and interference with blood circulation.

Plateau phase The second stage of the sexual response cycle; muscle tension, blood pressure, and heart-rate changes become intensified, terminating in the occurrence of an orgasmic platform in the female and rapid breathing in both sexes.

Postformal thought Dialectical thinking characterized by an understanding that different points of view have merit and can be integrated into a workable solution to a problem.

Posttraumatic stress disorder (PTSD)   A persisting anxiety reaction precipitated by a severely stressful experience, such as military combat; characterized by a reexperiencing of the stressful event and avoidance of stimuli associated with it. Other symptoms include feelings of estrangement, recurring dreams and nightmares, and a tendency to be easily startled.

Poverty   Having little or no money, goods, or means of support. The official definition of poverty now employed by the U.S. Government includes a set of money income thresholds, varying with the size and composition of the family.

Presbycusis   *See* **Nerve deafness**.

Presbyopia   Literally, "oldsightedness," a condition of farsightedness resulting from a loss of elasticity of the lens of the eye due to aging.

Primary aging   Refers to a genetically regulated set of biological processes that occur over time and result in gradual deterioration of the organism.

Primary memory   Short-term memory (STM) lasting up to half a minute, as in remembering a specific telephone number only until it has been dialed.

Probate   All matters pertaining to the administration, settlement, and distribution of a decedent's estate by a legal court.

Progeria   A very rare disorder that mimics premature aging. A progeric child typically begins to look old as early as age 4. Also known as *Hutchinson–Guilford syndrome*.

Progressive muscle relaxation   Alternately tensing and relaxing each one of the 16 muscle groups of the body while attending to the feelings of tension and relaxation. Progressive relaxation is a common therapeutic procedure for coping with stress and a part of systematic desensitization in the treatment of phobias.

Prospective study   Research investigation that follows up, over time, people having different characteristics or lifestyles to determine which ones develop a particular condition or disorder.

Psychosis   Severe mental disorder characterized by faulty perception of reality, deficits of language and memory, disturbances in the emotional sphere, and other bizarre symptoms.

Psychotherapy   Psychological methods of treating mental disorders, involving communications between patient(s) and therapist and other special techniques.

Quick-dying trajectory   Strauss and Glaser's term for the process of dying quickly, an event that may or may not have been expected by the medical staff.

Rape   Felonious sexual intercourse with a woman against her will. *Statutory rape* is sexual intercourse with a female under the age of consent, usually age 18.

"Reasonable woman" standard   A standard exercised in sexual harassment cases, to the effect that even if the male perpetrator of an action that allegedly involved sexual harassment did not consider it offensive, if a "reasonable woman" would presumably view it as offensive, then in law it is legally considered to be so.

Refractory period A period of time, after orgasm, during which sexual arousal cannot recur.

Regression Return or reinstatement of an early stage of development; a common response to frustration (e.g., thumbsucking in an older child or adult).

Reliability The extent to which a psychological test or other assessment instrument measures something consistently.

Remote grandparent Grandparent who maintains a reserved, formal relationship with a grandchild.

Resolution phase The final phase of the sexual response cycle; there is a gradual return to the physiological state that prevailed prior to the excitement phase.

Retirement Withdrawal from one's occupation or from active work.

Retirement village A group of houses or condominiums restricted to individuals aged 50 and above.

Retrospective study Comparisons of the incidence of a disorder or other condition in two or more groups of people having different backgrounds, behaviors, or other characteristics.

Reverse annuity mortgage (RAM) A loan based on the owner's equity in a home, permitting the owner to receive regular monthly payments for 3–10 years or as long as he or she lives in the home.

Rigidity Inflexibility or unwillingness to change one's way of thinking or behaving; allegedly a characteristic of older people.

Robbery Taking and carrying away, by force or threat of harm, money or other property belonging to or in the care of another person.

Rocking-chair type According to Reichard, a personality pattern in which the person views old age in terms of freedom from responsibility and as an opportunity to indulge passive needs.

Role A social behavior pattern that an individual is expected to display under certain conditions or in certain situations.

Role-exit theory Blau's sociological theory of old age as a time for abandoning certain roles and assuming other roles.

Sales leaseback Agreement in which the owner sells his or her home and leases it back from the purchaser for an indefinite time period.

Sandwich generation A term descriptive of the position of middle-aged adults between the generation of their children and that of their own parents.

Schizophrenia Psychotic disorder characterized by withdrawal from reality and disturbances of thinking, emotion, and behavior; a breakdown of integrated personality functioning.

Secondary aging Decrements in bodily structure and function produced by disease, trauma, and other environmental events that are not directly related to heredity.

Secondary memory As contrasted with primary memory and tertiary memory, memory that lasts from a few minutes to several hours.

Self That part of an individual's phenomenal field (or "awareness") that he or she perceives as his or her own personality.

Self-actualization Fulfillment of one's potentialities; to attain a state of congruence or harmony between one's real and ideal selves.

Self-concept Fairly consistent cluster of feelings, ideas, and attitudes toward oneself.

Self-hating type According to Reichard, a maladjusted personality pattern persisting into old age, in which the person is depressed and blames him- or herself for his or her disappointments and misfortunes.

Senescence The state of being old or the process of growing old.

Senile keratoses Brown spots dotting sun-exposed areas of the skin.

Senile plaque *See* **Plaque**.

Senile purpura Purplish skin spots caused by cutaneous bleeding.

Senility An imprecise term used to refer to deterioration of the brain and behavior observed in some elderly individuals; disability caused by illness or injury as a person ages.

Senium praecox Premature senility (*see also* **Progeria** and **Werner's syndrome**).

Septuagenarian A person who is 70–79 years old.

Sex roles An aggregation of traits and behaviors that males and females in a given culture are expected to display.

Sexagenarian A person who is 60–69 years old.

Sexism Belief that the two sexes are fundamentally different in abilities and other personal characteristics and should be treated as such on the job and in other social contexts.

Sexual response cycle As described by Masters and Johnson, the four phases of the sexual response cycle are excitation, plateau, orgasm, and resolution.

Short-term memory (STM) Retaining items of information in memory from 1 second to several minutes at most; also known as **Primary memory**.

Single-room occupancy (SRO) Living arrangement of many older people consisting of inexpensive single rooms in old residential hotels, usually in the center of the city.

Small stroke Blockage of a small blood vessel in the brain.

Social age Age of a person as determined by the social roles and activities in which he or she is expected to engage, or which are considered appropriate for an individual at a particular age or stage of maturity.

Social class Informal classification of people in a society according to a composite of economic, educational, occupational, and other status criteria.

Social gerontology Subfield of gerontology dealing with social factors in aging, elderly group behavior, and the causes and effects of growth in the elderly segment of the population.

Supplemental Security Income (SSI) Federal program of financial assistance to elderly poor people.

Stimulus persistence theory   Theory that aging causes a slowdown in recovery from the short-term effects of stimulation.

Superego   In psychoanalytic theory, the part of the personality that represents the internalization of parental prohibitions and sanctions—the moral aspect of personality, or conscience.

Synovial fluid   Lubricating fluid in the joints, a loss of which characterizes osteoarthritis.

Systematic desensitization   Behavior therapy technique in which a hierarchy of anxiety-provoking situations is imagined or directly experienced while the individual is in a deeply relaxed state. In this manner, the situations gradually come to be experienced without anxiety.

Terminal drop   Decline in intellectual functions (intelligence, memory, cognitive organization, sensorimotor abilities, personality) during the last few months of life; observed in many elderly people.

Tertiary memory   As contrasted with primary and secondary memory, memory that lasts from a few hours to may years.

Testamentary capacity   The legally determined competency of a person to make a will.

Testator   A person who makes out a will.

Thanatos   Ancient Greek personification of death; in psychoanalysis, the death instinct, as expressed in extreme aggression toward the self or other people.

Thrombosis   *See* **Embolism**.

Time-lag design   Developmental research procedure for examining several cohorts, each in a different time period.

Tinnitus   Persistent ringing, buzzing, or roaring in the ears.

Tranquilizer   Psychotherapeutic drug having antianxiety or antipsychotic effects.

Trust   A legal, fiduciary relationship in which one person (the trustee) holds the title to property (the trust estate or trust property) for the benefit of another person (the beneficiary).

Validity   The extent to which a psychological or educational assessment instrument measures what it was designed to measure.

Visual acuity   The ability to see detail and discriminate among different visual patterns.

Vital capacity   The amount of air that can be moved in and out of the lungs in a deep breath.

Vital signs   Pulse rate, body temperature, blood pressure, and respiration rate.

Vital statistics   Statistics concerning human life, the conditions affecting it, and the maintenance of the population (e.g., births, marriages, divorces, and deaths) during a specified time period.

Voluntary commitment   Unforced submission of oneself to a mental hospital for examination and treatment (*see* **Involuntary commitment**).

Wear-and-tear theories   Biological theories of aging that state that aging is caused by the fact that the body simply wears itself out from combating environmental stress.

Werner's syndrome A condition of arrested growth occurring between the ages of 15 and 20; thought to be a later-developing progeria.

Widower's syndrome Impotence in a man who has lost his spouse and has not had sexual intercourse for a long time.

Will A legal declaration of a person's desires concerning the disposition of his or her property after death; usually written and signed by the person (testator) and witnessed (attested to) by two or more witnesses.

References

Abbey, A. (1987). Misperceptions of friendly behavior as sexual interest: A survey of naturally occurring incidents. *Psychology of Women Quarterly, 11*, 173–194.

Adams, B. N. (1968). *Kinship in an urban setting*. Chicago: Markham.

Adams, B. N. (1979). Mate selection in the United States: A theoretical summarization. In W. Burr, R. Hill, I. Nye, & R. Reiss (Eds.), *Contemporary theories about the family. Vol 1: Research-based theories* (pp. 259–267). New York: Free Press.

Aday, R. H. (1984–1985). Belief in afterlife and death anxiety: Correlates and comparisons. *Omega, 15*, 67–75.

Adelson, J. (1985). Adolescence for clinicians. In G. Stricker & R. Keisner (Eds.), *From research to clinical practice* (pp. 313–326). New York: Plenum Press.

Ad Hoc Committee of the Harvard Medical School to Examine the Definition of Brain Death. (1968). A definition of irreversible coma. *Journal of the American Medical Association, 205*, 337–340.

Ahammer, L. M. (1973). Social-learning theory as a framework for the study of adult personality development. In P. B. Baltes & K. W. Schaie (Eds.), *Life-span developmental psychology: Personality and socialization* (pp. 253–294). New York: Academic Press.

Ahrons, C., & Rodgers, R. H. (1987). *Divorced families: A multidisciplinary view*. New York: Norton.

Aiken, L. R. (1995). *Aging: An introduction to gerontology*. Newbury Park, CA: Sage.

Aiken, L. R. (1997). *Psychological testing and assessment (9th ed.)*. Needham Heights, MA: Allyn & Bacon.

Ainlay, S. C., & Smith, D. R. (1984). Aging and religious participation. *Journal of Gerontology, 39*, 357–363.

Aizenberg, R., & Treas, J. (1985). The family in late life: Psychosocial and demographic considerations. In J. Birren & K. Schaie (Eds.), *Handbook of the psychology of aging* (2nd ed., pp. 169–189). New York: Van Nostrand Reinhold.

Allison, P., & Furstenberg, F. (1989). How marital dissolution affections children: Variations by age and sex. *Developmental Psychology, 25*, 540–549.

Alpert, J. L., & Richardson, M. S. (1980). Parenting. In L. W. Poon (Ed.), *Aging in the 1980s* (pp. 441–454). Washington, DC: American Psychological Association.

Alwin, D. F., Cohen, R. L., & Newcomb, T. M. (1991). *Political attitudes over the life span*. Madison: University of Wisconsin Press.

American Association of Retired Persons. (1989). *Business and older workers*. Washington, DC: Author.

American Association of Retired Persons. (1996a). *Understanding senior housing into the next century*. Washington, DC: Author.

American Association of Retired Persons. (1996b). *A profile of older Americans 1996*. Washington, DC: Author.

American Cancer Society. (1987). *Cancer facts and figures*. New York: Author.

American Heart Association. (1995). *1995 heart and stroke facts*. Dallas, TX: Author.

American Psychiatric Association. (1994). *Diagnostic and statistical manual of mental disorders* (4th ed.). Washington, DC: Author.

American Psychological Association. (1992). Ethical principles of psychologists and code of conduct. *American Psychologist, 47*, 1597–1611.

Americans discouraged by government's ineffective war on crime. (1993, December). *The Gallup Poll Monthly*, pp. 28–36.

Anderson, R. N., Kochanek, K. D., & Murphy, S. L. (1997). Report of final mortality statistics, 1995. *Monthly Vital Statistics Report, 45*(11), suppl. 2. Hyattsville, MD: National Center for Health Statistics.

Anderson, S. A., Russell, C. S., & Schumm, W. R. (1983). Perceived marital quality and family life-cycle categories: A further analysis. *Journal of Marriage and the Family, 45*, 127–139.

Angleitner, A., & Ostendorf, F. (1994). Temperament and the Big Five factors in personality. In C. F. Halverson, Jr., G. A. Kohnstamm, & R. P. Martin (Eds.), *The developing structure of temperament and personality from infancy to adulthood* (pp. 69–90). Hillsdale, NJ: Erlbaum.

Antonucci, T. C. (1985). Personal characteristics, social support, and social behavior. In R. Binstock & E. Shanas (Eds.), *Handbook of aging and the social sciences* (pp. 94–128). New York: Van Nostrand Reinhold.

Archer, D., & Gartner, R. (1983). War and violent crime. In S. H. Kadish (Ed.), *The encyclopedia of crime and justice* (pp. 1639–1652). New York: Free Press.

Archer, J. (1991). The influence of testosterone on human aggression. *British Journal of Psychology, 82*, 1–28.

Arenberg, D., & Robertson-Tchabo, E. (1977). Learning and aging. In J. E. Birren & K. W. Schaie (Eds.), *Handbook of the psychology of aging* (pp. 421–445). New York: Van Nostrand Reinhold.

Arenberg, D., & Robertson-Tchabo, E. (1980). Age differences and age changes in cognitive performance: New "old" perspectives. In R. L. Sprott (Ed.), *Age, learning ability, and intelligence* (pp. 147–159). New York: Van Nostrand Reinhold.

Aries, P. (1962). *Centuries of childhood*. New York: Knopf.

Aries, P. (1981). *The hour of our death*. (H. Weaver, Trans.). New York: Knopf.

Arnett, J. (1990). Drunk driving, sensation seeking, and egocentrism among adolescents. *Personality and Individual Differences, 11*, 541–546.

Atchley, R. C. (1975). Dimensions of widowhood in later life. *Gerontologist, 15*, 176–178.

Atchley, R. C. (1994). *Social forces and aging: An introduction to social gerontology* (7th ed.). Belmont, CA: Wadsworth.

Axelrod, S., & Cohen, L. D. (1961). Senescence and embedded-figure performance in vision and touch. *Perceptual and Motor Skills, 12*, 283–288.

Axelrod, S., Thompson, L. W., & Cohen, L. D. (1968). Effect of senescence on the temporal resolution of somesthetic stimuli presented to one hand or both. *Journal of Gerontology, 23*, 191–195.

Back, K. W. (1971). Metaphors as a test of personal philosophy of aging. *Sociological Forces, 5*, 1–8.

Ball, J. F. (1977). Widow's grief: The impact of age and mode of death. *Omega, 7*, 307–333.

Baller, W. R., Charles, D. C., & Miller, E. L. (1967). Mid-life attainment of the mentally retarded: A longitudinal study. *Genetic Psychology Monographs, 75*, 235–329.

Baltes, P. B. (1968). Longitudinal and cross-sectional sequences in the study of age and generation effects. *Human Development, 11*, 145–171.

Baltes, P. B., & Willis, S. L. (1982). Plasticity and enhancement of intellectual functioning in old age: Penn State's Adult Development and Enrichment Program (ADEPT). In F. I. M. Craik & S. E. Trehub (Eds.), *Aging and cognitive processes* (pp. 353–389). New York: Plenum Press.

Bammell, L. L. B., & Bammell, G. (1985). Leisure and recreation. In J. E. Birren & E. W. Schaie (Eds.), *Handbook of the psychology of aging* (pp. 848–863). New York: Van Nostrand Reinhold.

Bandura, A. (1977). *Social learning theory*. Englewood Cliffs, NJ: Prentice-Hall.

Barber, C. E. (1989). Transition to the empty nest. In S. J. Bahr & E. T. Peterson (Eds.), *Aging and the family* (pp. 15–32). Lexington, MA: Lexington.

Bardis, P. D. (1981). History of thanatology. Washington, DC: University Press of America.

Barer, B. M. (1994). Men and women age differently. *International Journal of Aging and Human Development, 38*, 29–40.

Barker, J. C. (1968). *Scared to death*. London: Frederick Muller.

Baron, R. A., & Byrne, D. (1987). *Social psychology: Understanding human interaction* (5th ed.). Boston: Allyn & Bacon.

Bartoshuk, L. M., & Weiffenbach, J. M. (1990). Chemical senses and aging. In E. L. Schneider & J. W. Rowe (Eds.), *Handbook of the biology of aging* (3rd ed., pp. 429–443). San Diego: Academic Press.

Baruch, G., Barnett, R., & Rivers, C. (1983). *Life prints: New patterns of love and work for today's women*. New York: McGraw-Hill.

Basseches, M. (1984). *Dialectical thinking and adult development*. Norwood, NJ: Ablex.

Baugher, E., & Lamison-White, L. (1996). U.S. Bureau of the Census, Current Population Reports, Series P60-194, *Poverty in the United States: 1995*. Washington, DC: U.S. Government Printing Office.

Baumrind, D. (1971). Current patterns of parental authority. *Developmental Psychology Monographs, 1*, 1–103.

Baumrind, D. (1972). Socialization and instrumental competence in young children. In W. W. Harrup (Ed.), *The young child: Reviews of research* (Vol. 2, pp. 202–224). Washington, DC: National Association for the Education of Young Children.

Bayley, N., & Oden, M. H. (1955). The maintenance of intellectual ability in gifted adults. *Journal of Gerontology, 10*, 91–107.

Bean, F., & Tienda, M. (1987). *The Hispanic population in the United States*. New York: Russell Sage Foundation.

Bearon, L. B., & Koenig, H. G. (1990). Religious cognitions and use of prayer in health and illness. *Gerontologist, 30*, 249–253.

Becker, W. C. (1964). Consequences of different kinds of parental discipline. In M. L. Hoffman & L. W. Hoffman (Eds.), *Review of child development research* (Vol. 1, pp. 169–208). New York: Russell Sage Foundation.

Bell, A. P., & Weinberg, M. S. (1978). *Homosexualities: A study of diversity among men and women*. New York: Simon & Schuster.

Bell, A., & Zubek, J. (1960). The effect of age on the intellectual performance of mental defectives. *Journal of Gerontology, 15*, 285–295.

Bell, J. (1992). In search of a discourse on aging: The elderly on television. *Gerontologist, 32*, 305–311.

Bellah, R. N., Madsen, R., Sullivan, W. L., Swidler, A., & Tipton, S. M. (1985). *Habits of the heart: Individualism and commitment in American life*. Berkeley: University of California Press.

Belmont, L., & Marolla, F. A. (1973). Birth order, family size, and intelligence. *Science, 182*, 1096–1101.

Benedict, R. F. (1960). *Patterns of culture*. New York: Mentor Books. (Originally published in 1946)

Bengtson, V. L. (1985). Diversity and symbolism in grandparental roles. In V. Bengtson & J. Robertson (Eds.), *Grandparenthood* (pp. 11–26). Beverly Hills: Sage.

Bengston, V. L., Cuellar, J. B., & Ragan, P. K. (1977). Stratum contrasts and similarities in attitudes toward death. *Journal of Gerontology, 32*(1), 76–88.

Bengtson, V. L., & Robertson, J. F. (Eds.). (1985). *Grandparenthood*. Beverly Hills, CA: Sage.

Bengtson, V. L., Rosenthal, C., & Burton, L. (1990). Families and aging: Diversity and heterogeneity. In R. H. Binstock & L. K. George (Eds.), *Handbook of aging and the social sciences* (3rd ed., pp. 263–287). San Diego: Academic Press.

Ben-Porath, Y. S., & Waller, N. G. (1992). Five big issues in clinical personality assessment: A rejoinder to Costa and McCrae. *Psychological Assessment, 4*, 28–25.

Berger, J., Cohen, B. P., & Zelditch, M., Jr. (1973). Status characteristics and social interaction. In

R. J. Ofshe (Ed.), *Interpersonal behavior in small groups* (pp. 194–216). Englewood Cliffs, NJ: Prentice-Hall.

Berger, K. A., & Zarit, S. H. (1978). Late life paranoid states: Assessment and treatment. *American Journal of Orthopsychiatry, 48,* 628–637.

Berger, K. S. (1994). *The developing person through the life span* (3rd ed.). New York: Worth.

Berkman, L. F., & Syme, S. L. (1979). Social networks, host resistance, and mortality: A nine-year follow-up study of Alameda County residents. *American Journal of Epidemiology, 109,* 186–204.

Berkowitz, L. (1990). Biological roots: Are humans inherently violent? In B. Glad (Ed.), *Psychological dimensions of war* (pp. 24–40). Newbury Park, CA: Sage.

Berndt, T. J. (1992). Friendship and friends' influence in adolescence. *Current Directions in Psychological Science, 1,* 156–159.

Berry, R. E., & Williams, F. L. (1987). Assessing the relationship between quality of life and marital and income satisfaction: A path analytic approach. *Journal of Marriage and the Family, 49,* 107–116.

Betancourt, R. L. (1991). *Retirement and men's physical and social health.* New York: Garland.

Betz, N. E. (1992). Counseling uses of career self-efficacy theory. *Career Development Quarterly, 41*(1), 22–26.

Betz, N. E. (1994). Self-concept theory in career development and counseling. *Career Development Quarterly, 43,* 32–42.

Bianco, E. (1997, February 18). More Americans hold down two jobs to keep cash flow up. *Los Angeles Times,* p. A5.

Blair, S. N., Kole, H. W., Paffenbarger, R. S., Clark, D. G., Cooper, K. H., & Gibbons, L. W. (1989). Physical fitness and all-cause mortality. *Journal of the American Medical Association, 262*(17), 2395–2401.

Blanchard-Fields, F., & Irion, J. C. (1988). The relation between locus of control and coping in two contexts: Age as a moderator variable. *Psychology and Aging, 3,* 197–203.

Blanchard-Fields, F., & Robinson, S. L. (1987). Age differences in the relation between controllability and coping. *Journal of Gerontology, 42,* 497–501.

Block, J. (1995). A contrarian view of the five-factor approach to personality description. *Psychological Bulletin, 117*(2), 187–215.

Blocklyn, P. L. (1987). The aging workforce. *Personnel, 65*(5), 63–65.

Bloom, B. L., & Caldwell, R. A. (1981). Sex differences in adjustment during the process of marital separation. *Journal of Marriage and the Family, 43,* 693–701.

Bluebond-Langner, M. (1977). Meanings of death to children. In H. Feifel (Ed.), *New meanings of death* (pp. 47–66). New York: McGraw-Hill.

Bluebond-Langner, M. (1978). *The private worlds of dying children.* Princeton, NJ: Princeton University Press.

Blumenthal, J. A., Emery, C. F., Madden, D. J., Schniebolk, S., Walsh-Riddle, M., George, L. K., McKee, D. C., Higgenbotham, Cobb, F. R., & Coleman, R. E. (1991). Long-term effects of exercise on psychological functioning in older men and women. *Journal of Gerontology: Psychological Science, 46,* P352–P361.

Blumstein, P., & Schwartz, P. (1983). *American couples: Money, work, and sex.* New York: Morrow.

Bond, J., & Coleman, P. (1990). Ageing into the twenty-first century. In J. Bond & P. Coleman (Eds.), *Aging in society: An introduction to social gerontology* (pp. 276–290). Newbury Park, CA: Sage.

Booth, A., & Johnson, E. (1988). Premarital cohabitation and marital success. *Journal of Family Issues, 9,* 387–394.

Bortner, R. W., & Hultsch, D. F. (1972). Personal time perspective in adulthood. *Developmental Psychology, 7,* 98–103.

Bossé, R., Aldwin, C. M., Levenson, M. R., Spiro, A., III, & Mroczek, D. K. (1993). Change in social support after retirement: Longitudinal findings from the Normative Aging Study. *Journal of Gerontology: Psychological Sciences, 48,* P210–P217.

Bouchard, T. J., Jr., Lykken, D. T., McGue, M., Segal, N. L., & Tellengen, A. (1990). Sources of human psychological differences: The Minnesota Study of Twins Reared Apart. *Science, 250*, 223–228.

Bouchard, T. J., Jr., & McGue, M. (1981). Familial studies of intelligence: A review. *Science, 212*, 1055–1059.

Bradsher, J. E., Longino, C. F., Jackson, D. J., & Zimmerman, R. S. (1992). Health and geographic mobility among the recently widowed. *Journal of Gerontology: Social Sciences, 47*, S261–S268.

Brannon, L., & Feist, J. (1992). *Health psychology: An introduction to behavior and health* (2nd ed.). Belmont, CA: Wadsworth.

Bray, D. W., & Howard, A. (1983). The AT&T longitudinal studies of managers. In K. W. Schaie (Ed.), *Longitudinal studies on adult psychological development* (pp. 266–312). New York: Guilford.

Brim, O. G., Jr., & Ryff, C. D. (1980). On the properties of life events. In P. B. Baltes & O. G. Brim, Jr. (Eds.), *Life-span development and behavior* (Vol. 3, pp. 368–387). New York: Academic Press.

Brody, E. M. (1990). *Women in the middle: Their parent-care years.* New York: Springer.

Brown, J. D., & McGill, K. L. (1989). The cost of good fortune: When positive life events produce negative health consequences. *Journal of Personality and Social Psychology, 57*, 1103–1110.

Brown, R. (1965). *Social psychology.* New York: Free Press.

Burke, K. C., Burke, J. D., Regier, D. A., & Rae, D. S. (1990). Age at onset of selected mental disorders in five community populations. *Archives of General Psychiatry, 47*, 511–518.

Burnett, S. A. (1986). Sex-related differences in spatial ability: Are they trivial? *American Psychologist, 41*, 1012–1014.

Burt, J. J., & Meeks, L. B. (1985). *Education for sexuality: Concepts and programs for teaching* (3rd ed.). Philadelphia: Saunders College.

Buss, D. M., et al. (1990). International preferences in selecting mates: A study of 37 cultures. *Journal of Cross-Cultural Psychology, 21*, 5–47.

Butcher, J. N., & Rouse, S. V. (1996). Personality: Individual differences in clinical assessment. In J. T. Spence, J. M. Darley, & D. J. Foss (Eds.), *Annual Review of Psychology, 47*, 87–111.

Butler, R. N. (1974). Successful aging. *Mental Health, 58*(3), 7–12.

Butler, R. N., & Lewis, M. I. (1982). *Aging and mental health* (3rd ed.). St. Louis: Mosby.

Butler, R. N., & Lewis, M. I. (1993). *Love and sex after sixty.* New York: Ballantine.

Byrne, D. (1961). The Repression–Sensitization Scale: Rationale, reliability, and validity. *Journal of Personality, 29*, 334–349.

Byrne, D. (1971). *The attraction paradigm.* New York: Academic Press.

Cahalan, D. (1991). *An ounce of prevention: Strategies for solving tobacco, alcohol, and drug problems.* San Francisco: Jossey-Bass.

Campbell, D. P. (1965). A cross-sectional and longitudinal study of scholastic abilities over twenty-five years. *Journal of Counseling Psychology, 12*, 55–61.

Campione, W. A. (1988). Predicting participation in retirement preparation programs. *Journal of Gerontology, 43*, 591–595.

Cargan, L., & Melko, M. (1982). *Singles: Myths and realities.* Beverly Hills, CA: Sage.

Carlson, R. (1981). Studies in script theory: I. Adult analogs of a childhood nuclear scene. *Journal of Personality and Social Psychology, 40*, 501–510.

Carson, R. C., & Butcher, J. N. (1992). *Abnormal psychology and modern life* (9th ed.). New York: HarperCollins.

Carstensen, I. L. (1993). Motivation for social contact across the life span: A theory of socioemotional selectivity. In J. E. Jacobs (Ed.), *Nebraska Symposium on Motivation: Vol. 40. Developmental perspectives on motivation* (pp. 209–254). Lincoln: University of Nebraska Press.

Carstensen, I. L. (1995). Evidence for a lifespan theory of socioemotional selectivity. *Current Directions in Psychological Science, 4*, 151–156.

Cash, T. F., & Derlega, V. J. (1978). The matching hypothesis: Physical attractiveness among same-sexed friends. *Personality and Social Psychology Bulletin, 4*, 240–243.

Cavanaugh, J. C. (1997). *Adult development and aging* (3rd ed.). Pacific Grove, CA: Brooks/Cole.

Centers for Disease Control. (1992, January 3). Sexual behavior among high school students—United States, 1990. *Morbidity and Mortality Weekly Report, 4,* 885–888.

Chappell, N. L. (1990). Aging and social care. In R. H. Binstock & L. K. George (Eds.), *Handbook of aging and the social sciences* (3rd ed., pp. 438–454). San Diego: Academic Press.

Charles, D. C., & James, S. T. (1964). Stability of average intelligence. *Journal of Genetic Psychology, 105,* 105–111.

Cherlin, A., & Furstenberg, F. F., Jr. (1986). *The new American grandparent: A place in the family, a life apart.* New York: Basic Books.

Choron, J. (1963) (J. Barea, trans.). *Death and western thought.* New York: Macmillan.

Christensen, H., Mackinnon, A., Jorm, A. F., Henderson, A. S., Scott, L. R., & Korten, S. E. (1994). Age differences and interindividual variation in cognition in community-dwelling elderly. *Psychology and Aging, 9,* 381–390.

Christiansen, K., & Knussman, R. (1987). Sex hormones and cognitive functioning in men. *Neuropsychobiology, 18,* 27–36.

Church, D. K., Siegel, M. A., & Foster, C. D. (1988). *Growing old in America.* Wylie, TX: Information Aids.

Clayton, P. J., Halikes, J. A., & Maurice, W. L. (1971). The bereavement of the widowed. *Diseases of the Nervous System, 32,* 597–604.

Cleek, M. B., & Pearson, T. A. (1985). Perceived causes of divorce: An analysis of interrelationships. *Journal of Marriage and the Family, 47,* 179–191.

Cohen, C., Teresi, J., Holmes, D., & Roth, E. (1988). Survival strategies of older homeless men. *Gerontologist, 28,* 58–65.

Cohen, G. D. (1990). Psychopathology and mental health in the mature and elderly adult. In J. E. Birren & E. W. Schaie (Eds.), *Handbook of the psychology of aging* (3rd ed., pp. 359–374). San Diego: Academic Press.

Cohen, S., Doyle, W. J., Skorer, D. P., Rabin, B. S., & Gwaltney, J. M. (1997). Social ties and susceptibility to the common cold. *Journal of the American Medical Association, 277*(24), 1940–1944.

Cohler, B. J., & Grunebaum, H. V. (1981). *Mothers, grandmothers, and daughters: Personality and child-care in three-generation families.* New York: Wiley.

Cole, S. (1979). Aging and scientific performance. *American Journal of Sociology, 84,* 958–977.

Coleman, P. D. (1986, August). *Regulation of dendritic extent: Human aging brain and Alzheimer's disease.* Paper presented at the 94th Annual Meeting of the American Psychological Association, Washington, DC.

Comfort, A. (1964). *Aging: The biology of senescence.* New York: Holt, Rinehart & Winston.

Commons, M. L., Richards, F. A., & Kuhn, D. (1982). Systematic, metasystematic, and cross paradigmatic reasoning: A case for stages of reasoning beyond Piaget's stage of formal operations. *Child Development, 53,* 1058–1068.

Connidis, I. A. (1988, November). *Sibling ties and aging.* Paper presented at the Gerontological Society of America, San Francisco.

Connidis, I. A. (1989). The subjective experience of aging: Correlates of divergent views. *Canadian Journal of Aging, 8,* 7–18.

Connidis, I. A., & Davies, L. (1990). Confidants and companions in later life: The place of friends and family. *Journal of Gerontology: Social Sciences, 45,* S141–S149.

Conte, H. A., Weiner, M. B., & Plutchik, R. (1982). Measuring death anxiety: Conceptual, psychometric, and psychoanalytic aspects. *Journal of Personality and Social Psychology, 43,* 775–785.

Cook, F. L., Skogan, W. G., Cook, T. D., & Antunes, G. E. (1978). Criminal victimization of the elderly: The physical and economic consequences. *Gerontologist, 18,* 338–349.

Cooney, T. M., Schaie, K. W., & Willis, S. L. (1988). The relationship between prior functioning on cognitive and personality dimensions and subject attrition in longitudinal research. *Journal of Gerontology, 43,* 12–17.

Cooney, T. M., & Uhlenberg, P. (1990). The role of divorce in men's relations with their adult children after mid-life. *Journal of Marriage and the Family, 53,* 677–688.

Cooper, K., & Gutman, D. (1987). Gender identity and ego mastery style in middle-aged, pre- and post-empty nest women. *Gerontologist, 27,* 347–352.

Coopersmith, H. S. (1967). *The antecedents of self-esteem.* San Francisco: Freeman.

Corby, N., & Solnick, R. L. (1980). Psychosocial and physiological influences on sexuality in the older adult. In J. E. Birren & R. B. Sloane (Eds.), *Handbook of mental health and aging* (pp. 893–921). Englewood Cliffs, NJ: Prentice-Hall.

Corby, N., & Zarit, J. M. (1983). Old and alone: The unmarried in later life. In R. B. Weg (Ed.), *Sexuality in the later years* (pp. 131–145). New York: Academic Press.

Cordes, C. (1986, June). Test tilt: Boys outscore girls on both parts of the SAT. *APA Monitor,* pp. 30–31.

Corso, J. F. (1977). Auditory perception and communication. In J. E. Birren & K. Schaie (Eds.), *Handbook of the psychology of aging* (2nd ed., pp. 535–553). New York: Van Nostrand Reinhold.

Costa, P. T., Jr., & McCrae, R. R. (1980). Still stable after all these years: Personality as a key to some issues in adulthood and old age. In P. Baltes & O. G. Brim, Jr. (Eds.), *Life span development and behavior* (Vol. 3, pp. 65–102). New York: Academic Press.

Costa, P. T., Jr., & McCrae, R. R. (1986). Personality stability and its implications for clinical psychology. *Clinical Psychology Review, 6,* 407–423.

Covey, H. C. (1988). Historical terminology used to represent older people. *Gerontologist, 28,* 291–297.

Cowan, C. P., & Cowan, P. A. (1992). *When partners become parents.* New York: Basic Books.

Cowley, M. (1980). *The view from 80.* New York: Viking.

Craik, F. I. M., & McDowd, J. M. (1987). Age differences in recall and recognition. *Journal of Experimental Psychology: Learning, Memory, and Cognition, 13*(3), 474–479.

Crohan, S. E., & Antonucci, T. C. (1989). Friends as a source of social support in old age. In R. Adams & R. Blieszner (Eds.), *Older adult friendship: Structure and process* (pp. 129–146). Beverly Hills, CA: Sage Publications.

Cronbach, L. J., & Drenth, P. J. D. (Eds.). (1972). *Mental tests and cultural adaptation.* The Hague: Mouton.

Cronin, J., Daniels, N., Hurley, A., Kroch, A., & Webber, R. (1975). Race, class, and intelligence: A critical look at the IQ controversy. *International Journal of Mental Health, 3*(4), 46–132.

Crooks, R., & Bauer, K. (1980). *Our sexuality.* Reading, MA: Benjamin/Cummings.

Cutler, S. J., & Grams, A. E. (1988). Correlates of self-reported everyday memory problems. *Journal of Gerontology: Social Sciences, 433,* S82–S90.

Darley, J. B., & Hagenah, T. (1955). *Vocational interest measurement.* Minneapolis: University of Minnesota Press.

Darwin, C. (1859). *On the origin of species by means of natural selection.* London: Murray.

Das, J. P., Naglieri, J. A., & Kirby, J. P. (1994). *Assessment of cognitive processes: The PASS theory of intelligence.* Boston: Allyn & Bacon.

Davis, J. A., & Smith, T. W. (1994). *General Social Surveys, 1972–1994.* Chicago: National Opinion Research Center.

Dawis, R. V. (1984). Job satisfaction: Worker aspirations, attitudes and behavior. In N. C. Gysbers (Ed.), *Designing careers* (pp. 275–301). San Francisco: Jossey-Bass.

Dawson, D., Hendershot, G., & Fulton, J. (1987, June 10). *Aging in the eighties: Functional limitations of individuals 65 and over.* (Advance Data, No. 144). Washington, DC: National Center for Health Statistics.

Day E., Davis, B., Dove, R., & French, W. (1988). Reaching the senior citizen market(s). *Journal of Advertising Research, 28,* 23–30.

Day, J., & Curry, A. (1995). Educational attainment in the United States: March 1995. *Current Population Reports,* P20-489. Washington, DC: U.S. Department of Commerce.

de Beauvoir, S. (1972). *The coming of age* (P. O'Brien, Trans.). New York: Putnam.

DeFleur, M. L., & Quinney, R. (1966). A reformulation of Sutherland's differential association theory and a strategy for empirical verification. *Journal of Research in Crime and Delinquency, 3,* 1–22.

DeFrank, R., & Ivancevich, J. M. (1986). Job loss: An individual level review and model. *Journal of Vocational Behavior, 19*, 1–20.

DeGenova, M. K. (1992). If you had your life to live over again: What would you do differently? *International Journal of Aging and Human Development, 34*, 135–143.

DeLongis, A., Coynce, J. C., Dakof, S., Folkman, S., & Lazarus, R. S. (1982). Relationship of daily hassles, uplifts, and major life events to health status. *Health Psychology, 1*, 119–136.

DeMaris, A., & Rao, K. V. (1992). Premarital cohabitation and subsequent marital stability in the United States: A reassessment. *Journal of Marriage and the Family, 54*, 178–190.

Denckla, W. D. (1974). Role of the pituitary and thyroid glands in the decline of minimal O_2 consumption with age. *Journal of Clinical Investigation, 51*, 572–581.

Dennis, W. (1940). The effect of cradling practices upon the onset of walking in Hopi children. *Journal of Genetic Psychology, 56*, 77–86.

Dennis, W. (1960). Causes of retardation among institutionalized children: Iran. *Journal of Genetic Psychology, 96*, 47–59.

Dennis, W. (1966). Creative productivity between the ages of twenty and eighty years. *Journal of Gerontology, 21*, 1–8.

Derbyshire, R. L. (1968). Adolescent identity crisis in urban Mexican-Americans in East Los Angeles. In E. B. Brody (Ed.), *Minority-group adolescents in the United States* (pp. 73–110). Baltimore: Williams & Wilkins.

Derlega, V. J., Winstead, B. A., Wong, P. T. P., & Hunter, S. (1985). Gender effects in an initial encounter: A case where men exceed women in disclosure. *Journal of Social and Personal Relations, 2*, 25–44.

Dermer, M., & Pyszczynski, T. A. (1978). Effects of erotica upon men's loving and liking responses for women they love. *Journal of Personality and Social Psychology, 36*, 1302–1309.

DeVore, I. (1973). Primate behavior. In M. Argyle (Ed.), *Social encounters: Readings in social interaction*. Chicago: Aldine.

Dey, A. N. (1996). Characteristics of elderly home health care users: Data from the 1995 National Home and Hospice Care Survey. *Advance Data from Vital and Health Statistics*, No. 279. Hyattsville, MD: National Center for Health Statistics.

Diamond, J. (1986). I want a girl just like the girl … *Discover, 7*(11), 65–68.

Dickens, W. J., & Perlman, D. (1981). Friendship over the life cycle. In S. W. Duck & R. Gilmour (Eds.), *Personal relationships: 2. Developing personal relationships* (pp. 91–122). New York: Academic Press.

Dindia, K., & Allen, M. (1992). Sex differences in self-disclosure: A meta-analysis. *Psychological Bulletin, 112*, 106–124.

Dohrenwend, B. S., Krasnoff, L., Askensay, A., & Dohrenwend, B. P. (1978). Exemplification of a method of scaling life events: The PERI Life-Events Scale. *Journal of Health and Social Behavior, 19*, 205–229.

Doty, R. L., Deems, D. A., & Stellar, S. (1988). Olfactory dysfunction in parkinsonism: A general deficit unrelated to neurologic signs, disease stage, or disease duration. *Neurology, 38*, 1237–1244.

Dowd, J. J., & Bengtson, V. L. (1978). Aging in minority populations: An examination of the double jeopardy hypothesis. *Journal of Gerontology, 33*, 427–434.

Duberman, L. (1974). *Marriage and its alternatives*, New York: Praeger.

Dumont, R. G., & Foss, D. C. (1972). *The American view of death: Acceptance or denial?* Cambridge, MA: Schenkman.

Dunn, J. (1984). Sibling studies and the developmental impact of critical incidents. In P. B. Baltes & O. G. Brim, Jr. (Eds.), *Life-span development and behavior* (Vol. 6). New York: Academic Press.

Dutton, D., & Aron, A. (1974). Some evidence for heightened sexual attraction under conditions of high anxiety. *Journal of Personality and Social Psychology, 30*, 510–517.

Eagly, A. H. (1987). *Sex differences in social behavior: A social role interpretation*. Hillsdale, NH: Erlbaum.

Eagly, A. H., & Carli, L. L. (1981). Sex of researchers and sex-typed communications as determinants of sex differences in influenceability: A meta-analysis of social influence studies. *Psychological Bulletin, 90*, 1–20.

Eagly, A. H., & Crowley, M. (1986). Gender and helping behavior: A meta-analytic review of the social psychological literature. *Psychological Bulletin, 100*, 283–308.

Edwards, E. D. (1983). Native American elders: Current social issues and social policy implications. In R. L. McNeely & J. L. Cohen (Eds.), *Aging in minority groups* (pp. 74–82). Beverly Hills, CA: Sage Publications.

Eichorn, D. H., Hunt, J. V., & Honzik, M. P. (1981). Experience, personality, and IQ: Adolescence to middle age. In D. H. Eichorn, J. A. Clausen, N. Haan, M. P. Honzik, & P. H. Mussen (Eds.), *Present and past in middle life* (pp. 89–116). New York: Academic Press.

Eisdorfer, C. (1963). The WAIS performance of the aged: A retest evaluation. *Journal of Gerontology, 18*, 169–172.

Eisenberg, N., & Lennon, R. (1983). Sex differences in empathy and related capacities. *Psychological Bulletin, 94*, 100–131.

Eisenhandler, S. (1989). More than counting: Social aspects of time and the identity of elders. In L. Thomas (Ed.), *Research on adulthood and aging* (pp. 163–181). Albany, NY: State University of New York Press.

Ekerdt, D. J., & DeViney, S. (1993). Evidence for a preretirement process among older male workers. *Journal of Gerontology: Social Sciences, 48*, S535–S543.

Elias, C. J., & Inui, T. S. (1993). When a house is not a home: Exploring the meaning of shelter among chronically homeless elderly men. *Gerontologist, 33*, 396–402.

Ellison v. Brady, 924 F.2d 872 (1991).

Emmerich, W., & Shepard, K. (1982). Development of sex-differentiated preferences during late childhood and adolescence. *Developmental Psychology, 18*, 406–417.

Encyclopedia of Associations (28th ed.). (1994). Washington, DC: Gale Research, Inc.

Engel, G. L. (1971). Sudden and rapid death during psychological stress. *Annals of Internal Medicine, 74*, 771–782.

Engen, T. (1977). Taste and smell. In J. E. Birren & K. W. Schaie (Eds.), *Handbook of the psychology of aging* (pp. 554–561). New York: Van Nostrand Reinhold.

Epstein, G. L., Weitz, L. Roback, H., & McKee, E. (1975). Research on bereavement: A selective and critical review. *Comprehensive Psychiatry, 16*, 537–546.

Epstein, S. (1997). This I have learned from over 40 years of personality research. *Journal of Personality, 65*, 4–32.

Erickson, R., & Ekert, K. (1977). The elderly poor in downtown San Diego hotels. *Gerontologist, 17*, 440–446.

Erikson, E. H. (1963). *Childhood and society* (2nd ed.). New York: Norton.

Essex, M. J., & Nam, S. (1987). Marital status and loneliness among older women. *Journal of Marriage and the Family, 49*, 93–106.

Evans, D., Funkenstein, H., Albert, M., Scherr, P., Cook, N., Chown, M., Hebert, L., Hennckens, C., & Taylor, D. (1989). Prevalence of Alzheimer's disease in a community population of older people. *Journal of the American Medical Association, 262*, 2551–2556.

Feifel, H., & Jones, R. (1968). Perception of death as related to nearness of death. *Proceedings of the 76th Annual Convention of the American Psychological Association, 3*, 545–546.

Feifel, H., & Nagy, V. T. (1981). Another look at fear of death. *Journal of Consulting and Clinical Psychology, 49*, 278–286.

Felton, B. J., & Revenson, T. A. (1987). Age differences in coping with chronic illness. *Psychology and Aging, 2*, 164–170.

Ferraro, K. F., & LaGrange, R. L. (1992). Are older people afraid of crime? Reconsidering age differences in fear of victimization. *Journal of Gerontology: Social Sciences, 47*, S233–S244.

Feshbach, S., & Weiner, B. (1991). *Personality* (3rd ed.). Lexington, MA: D. C. Heath.

Field, D., & Millsap, R. E. (1991). Personality in advanced old age: Continuity or change. *Journal of Gerontology: Psychological Sciences, 46*, P271–P274.

Field, D., & Minkler, M. (1988). Continuity and change in social support between young-old and old-old or very-old age. *Journal of Gerontology: Psychological Sciences, 43*, P100–P106.

Field, D., Minkler, M., Falk, R. F., & Leino, E. V. (1993). The influences of health and family contacts and family feelings in advanced old age: A longitudinal study. *Journal of Gerontology: Psychological Sciences, 48*, P18–P28.

Finucci, J. M., & Childs, B. (1981). Are there really more dyslexic boys than girls? In A. Ansara, N. Geschwind, A. Galaburda, M. Albert, & N. Gartrell (Eds.), *Sex differences in dyslexia* (pp. 1–9). Towson, MD: Orton Dyslexia Society.

Fitzgerald, L. F., & Ormerod, A. J. (1991). Perceptions of sexual harassment: The influence of gender and academic context. *Psychology of Women Quarterly, 15*, 281–294.

Flaks, D. K., Ficher, I., Masterpasqua, F., & Joseph, G. (1995). Lesbians choosing motherhood: A comparative study of lesbian and heterosexual parents and their children. *Developmental Psychology, 31*, 105–114.

Folkman, S. L., & Lazarus, R. S. (1980). An analysis of coping in a middle-aged community sample. *Journal of Health and Social Behavior, 21*, 219–239.

Folkman, S. L., Lazarus, R. S., Dunkel-Schetter, C., DeLongis, A., & Gruen, R. J. (1986). The dynamics of a stressful encounter: Cognitive appraisal, coping, and encounter outcomes. *Journal of Personality and Social Psychology, 5*, 992–1003.

Folkman, S. L., Lazarus, R. S., Gruen, R., & DeLongis, A. (1986). Appraisal, coping, health status and psychological symptoms. *Journal of Personality and Social Psychology, 50*, 571–579.

Folkman, S., Lazarus, R., Pimley, S., & Novacek, J. (1987). Age differences in stress and coping processes. *Psychology and Aging, 2*, 171–184.

Fowler, J. W. (1981). *Stages of faith: The psychology of human development and the quest for meaning.* New York: Harper & Row.

Fowler, J. W. (1986). Faith and the structuring of meaning. In C. Dykstra & S. Parks (Eds.), *Faith development and Fowler.* (pp. 15–42). Birmingham, AL: Religious Education Press.

Fox, M., Gibbs, M., & Auerbach, D. (1985). Age and gender dimensions of friendship. *Psychology of Women Quarterly, 9*, 489–502.

Fozard, J. L., Vercruyssen, M., Reynolds, S. L., Hancock, P. A., & Quilter, R. E. (1994). Age changes and changes in reaction time: The Baltimore Longitudinal Study of Aging. *Journal of Gerontology, 49*(4), P179–P189.

Francher, J. S., & Henkin, J. (1973). The menopausal queen: Adjustment to aging and the male homosexual. *American Journal of Orthopsychiatry, 43*, 670–674.

Frank, S., Avery, C., & Laman, M. (1988). Young adults' perceptions of their relationships with their parents: Individual differences in connectedness, competence, and emotional autonomy. *Developmental Psychology, 24*, 729–737.

Freud, S. (1933, reprinted 1950). Why war? In *Collected works* (Vol. 16). London: Imago.

Friedman, H. S. (Ed.). (1990). *Personality and disease.* New York: Wiley.

Friedman, H. S., & Booth-Kewley, S. (1987). Personality, Type A behavior, and coronary heart disease: The role of emotional expression. *Journal of Personality and Social Psychology, 53*, 783–792.

Fulton, M., Thomson, G., Hunter, R., Raab, G., Laxen, D., & Hepburn, W. (1987). Influence of blood lead on the ability and attainment of children in Edinburgh. *Lancet, 1*, 1221–1226.

Furstenberg, F. F., Jr., & Nord, C. W. (1985). Parenting apart: Patterns of childbearing after marital disruption. *Journal of Marriage and the Family, 47*, 893–912.

Gallup, G., Jr. (1996). *The Gallup poll: Public opinion 1995.* Wilmington, DE: Scholarly Resources.

Gallup, G., & Proctor, W. (1982). *Adventures in immortality.* New York: McGraw-Hill.

Gatz, M., Popkin, S. J., Pino, C. D., & VandenBos, G. R. (1985). Psychological interventions with older adults. In J. E. Birren & K. Schaie (Eds.), *Handbook of the psychology of aging* (2nd ed., pp. 237–263). New York: Van Nostrand Reinhold.

Geer, J. T., O'Donohue, W. T., & Schorman, R. H. (1986). Sexuality. In M. G. H. Coles, F. Donchin, & S. Porges (Eds.), *Psychophysiology: Systems, processes, applications.* New York: Guilford.

Gesser, G., Wong, P. T. P., & Reker, G. T. (1987–1988). Death attitudes across the lifespan: The development and validation of the Death Attitude Profile (DAP). *Omega: Journal of Death and Dying, 18*(2), 113–128.

Giambra, L. M., & Arenberg, D. (1980). Problem-solving, concept learning, and aging. In L. W. Poon (Ed.), *Aging in the 1980s* (pp. 253–259). Washington, DC: American Psychological Association.

Gilligan, C. (1982). *In a different voice: Psychology theory and women's development.* Cambridge, MA: Harvard University Press.

Gilliland, J. C., & Templer, D. I. (1985). Relationship of death anxiety scale factors to subjective states. *Omega, 16,* 155–167.

Ginzberg, E., Ginsburg, S. W., Axelrad, S., & Herma, J. L. (1951). *Occupational choice: An approach to a general theory.* New York: Columbia University Press.

Glaser, B. G., & Strauss, A. L. (1965). *Awareness of dying.* Chicago: Aldine.

Glaser, B. G., & Strauss, A. L. (1968). *Time for dying.* Chicago: Aldine.

Glasgow, N. (1991, March). A place in the country. *American Demographics,* 24–30.

Glenn, N. D., & Supancic, M. (1984). The social and demographic correlates of divorce and separation in the United States: An update and reconsideration. *Journal of Marriage and the Family, 46,* 563–575.

Glick, I. O., Weiss, R. S., & Parkes, C. M. (1974). *The first year of bereavement.* New York: Wiley.

Golant, S. M. (1992). *Housing America's elderly: Many possibilities/few choices.* Newbury Park, CA: Sage.

Gold, D. T. (1989). Sibling relationships in old age: A typology. *International Journal of Aging and Human Development, 28,* 37–54.

Gold, D. T. (1990). Late-life sibling relationships: Does race affect typological distribution? *Gerontologist, 30*(6), 741–748.

Goldberg, L. R. (1980, April). *Some ruminations about the structure of individual differences: Developing a common lexicon for the major characteristics of human personality.* Paper presented at the annual meeting of the Western Psychological Association, Honolulu, HI.

Goldberg, L. R. (1994). Basic research on personality structure: Implications of the emerging consensus for applications to selection and classification. In M. G. Rumsey, C. B. Walker, & J. H. Harris (Eds.), *Personnel selection and classification* (pp. 247–259). Hillsdale, NJ: Erlbaum.

Goldstein, E. (1979). Effect of same-sex and cross-sex role models on the subsequent academic productivity of scholars. *American Psychologist, 34,* 407–410.

Gonzalez, M. C. (1993). Native American perspectives on the lifespan. In R. Kastenbaum (Ed.), *Encyclopedia of adult development* (pp. 360–364). Phoenix, AZ: Oryx Press.

Gordon, A. K., & Klass, D. (1979). *The need to know: How to teach children about death.* Englewood Cliffs, NJ: Prentice-Hall.

Gordon, L. (1996, November 11). A boom in high-rise burials. *Los Angeles Times,* pp. A1, A16.

Gorer, G. (1965). *Death, grief and mourning.* New York: Doubleday Anchor Books.

Gove, W. (1973). Sex, marital status, and mortality. *American Journal of Sociology, 79*(1), 45–67.

Gove, W. R. (1985). The effects of age and gender on deviant behavior: A biopsychosocial perspective. In A. S. Rossi (Ed.), *Gender and the life course* (pp. 115–144). Chicago: Aldine.

Granick, S., & Patterson, R. D. (1972). *Human aging II: An eleven year follow-up biomedical and behavioral study.* Washington, DC: U.S. Government Printing Office.

Graves, E. J., & Gillum, B. S. (1996). *1994 Summary: National Hospital Discharge Survey, Advance data from vital and health statistics; no. 278.* Hyattsville, MD: National Center for Health Statistics.

Greer, J. (1992). *Adult sibling rivalries.* New York: Crown.

Grotevant, H. D., Scarr, S., & Weinberg, R. A. (1977). Are career interests inherited? *Psychology Today, 11,* 88–90.

Guardo, C. J., & Bohan, J. B. (1971). Development of a sense of self-identity in children. *Child Development, 42,* 1909–1921.

Guilford, J. P. (1967). *The nature of human intelligence.* New York: McGraw-Hill.

Gutmann, D. L. (1974). Alternatives to disengagement: The old men of the highland Druze. In R. A. LeVine (Ed.), *Culture and personality: Contemporary readings* (pp. 232–245). Chicago: Aldine.

Gutmann, D. L. (1977). The cross-cultural perspective: Notes toward a comparative psychology of aging. In J. E. Birren & K. W. Schaie (Eds.), *Handbook of the psychology of aging* (pp. 302–326). New York: Van Nostrand Reinhold.

Halpern, D. F. (1992). *Sex differences in cognitive abilities*. Hillsdale, NJ: Erlbaum.

Hamon, R. R., & Blieszner, R. (1990). Filial responsibility expectations among adult-child older parent pairs. *Journal of Gerontology: Psychological Sciences, 45*, P110–P112.

Hampson, E. (1990). Variations in sex-related cognitive abilities across the menstrual cycle. *Brain and Cognition, 14*, 26–43.

Hansen, C. (1989). A causal model of the relationship among accidents, biodata, personality, and cognitive factors. *Journal of Applied Psychology, 74*, 81–90.

Hansen, K. R. (1995). *Geographical mobility: March 1993 to March 1994*. U.S. Bureau of the Census, Current Population Reports, P20-485. Washington, DC: U.S. Government Printing Office.

Harkins, S. W., Price, D. D., & Martinelli, M. (1986). Effects of age on pain perception. *Journal of Gerontology, 41*, 58–63.

Harma, M. I., Hakola, T., & Laitinen, J. (1992). Relation of age of circadian adjustment to night work. Fifth US-Finnish Joint Symposium on Occupational Safety and Health: Occupational epidemics on the 1990s. *Scandinavian Journal of Work, Environment and Health, 18*(Suppl. 2), 116–118.

Harman, D. (1987). The free radical theory of aging. In H. R. Warner, R. N. Butler, R. L. Sprott, & E. L. Schneider (Eds.), *Modern biological theories of aging* (pp. 81–87). New York: Raven Press.

Harman, S. M., & Talbert, G. B. (1985). Reproductive aging. In C. E. Finch & E. L. Schneider (Eds.), *Handbook of the biology of aging* (2nd ed., pp. 457–510). New York: Van Nostrand Reinhold.

Harris, L., & Associates. (1975). *The myth and reality of aging in America*. Washington, DC: National Council on the Aging.

Harris, L., & Associates. (1981). *Aging in the '80s: America in transition*. Washington, DC: National Council on Aging.

Hatfield, E., & Walster, G. W. (1981). *A new look at love*. Reading, MA: Addison-Wesley.

Havighurst, R. J. (1953). *Human development and education*. New York: Longman.

Haycock, J. (1993). Criminal behavior. In R. Kastenbaum (Ed.), *Encyclopedia of adult development* (pp. 95–105). Phoenix, AZ: Oryx Press.

Hayflick, L. (1977). The cellular basis for biological aging. In C. E. Finch & L. Hayflick (Eds.), *Handbook of the biology of aging* (pp. 159–186). New York: Van Nostrand Reinhold.

Hayflick, L. (1980). The cell biology of human aging. *Scientific American, 242*, 58–66.

Helsing, K. J., Szklo, M., & Comstock, G. W. (1981). Factors associated with mortality after widowhood. *American Journal of Public Health, 71*, 802–809.

Hendricks, J., & Leedham, C. A. (1980). Creating psychological and societal perspectives in old age. In P. S. Fry (Ed.), *Psychological perspectives on helplessness and control in the elderly* (pp. 369–394). Amsterdam: Elsevier North Holland.

Hertzog, C., Schaie, K. W., & Gribbin, K. (1978). Cardiovascular disease and changes in intellectual functioning from middle to old age. *Journal of Gerontology, 33*, 872–883.

Herzog, A. R., & House, J. S. (1991, Winter). Productive activities and aging well: Meaningful but flexible opportunities are needed. *Generations*, pp. 49–55.

Hess, B. (1971). *Amicability*. Unpublished doctoral dissertation, Rutgers University, New Brunswick, NJ.

Hetherington, B. M., Cox, M., & Cox, R. (1977). The aftermath of divorce. In J. H. Stevens, Jr., & M. Mathews (Eds.), *Mother–child, father–child relations* (pp. 149–176). Washington, DC: National Association for the Education of Young Children.

Hetherington, B. M., Cox, M., & Cox, R. (1982). Effects of divorce on parents and children. In M. E. Lamb (Ed.), *Nontraditional families: Parenting and child development* (pp. 233–288). Hillsdale, NJ: Erlbaum.

Hetherington, E. M., Cox, M., & Cox, R. (1985). Long-term effects of divorce and remarriage on the adjustment of children. *Journal of the American Academic of Child Psychiatry, 24*, 518–530.

Hickey, T., & Douglass, R. S. (1981). Neglect and abuse of older family members: Professionals' perspectives and case experiences. *Gerontologist, 21*, 171–176.

Hier, D. B., & Crowley, W. F., Jr. (1982). Spatial ability in androgen-deficient men. *New England Journal of Medicine, 306*, 1202–1205.

Hill, C. T., Rubin, Z., & Peplau, A. (1976). Breakups before marriage: The end of 103 affairs. *Journal of Social Issues, 32*, 147–167.

Hill, R. D., Storandt, M., & Malley, M. (1993). The impact of long-term exercise training on psychological function in older adults. *Journal of Gerontology: Psychological Sciences, 48*, P12–P17.

Hinton, J. (1972). *Dying* (2nd ed.). Baltimore: Penguin.

Hirsch, B. J. (1981). Social networks and the coping process: Creating personal communities. In B. H. Gottleib (Ed.), *Social networks and social support* (pp. 149–170). Beverly Hills, CA: Sage Publications.

Hoffman, L. W. (1986). Work, family, and the child. In M. S. Pallak & R. O. Perloff (Eds.), *Psychology and work: Productivity, change, and unemployment* (pp. 173–220). Washington, DC: American Psychological Association.

Holland, J. L. (1985). *Making vocational choices: A theory of careers: A theory of vocational personalities and work environments.* (2nd ed.). Englewood Cliffs, NJ: Prentice-Hall.

Holmes, R. (1985). *Acts of war.* New York: Free Press.

Horn, J. L. (1985). Remodeling old models of intelligence. In B. B. Wolman (Ed.), *Handbook of intelligence: Theories, measurements, and applications* (pp. 267–300). New York: Wiley.

Horn, J. L., & Donaldson, G. (1980). Cognitive development in adulthood. In O. G. Brim, Jr., & J. Kagan (Eds.), *Constancy and change in human development* (pp. 445–529). Cambridge, MA: Harvard University Press.

Horn, J. L., & Donaldson, G. (1976). On the myth of intellectual decline in adulthood. *American Psychologist, 31*, 701–719.

Horn, J. L., & Hofer, S. M. (1992). Major abilities and development in the adult period. In R. J. Sternberg & C. A. Berg (Eds.), *Intellectual development* (pp. 44–99). Cambridge, UK: Cambridge University Press.

House, J. S., Robbins, C., & Metzner, H. L. (1982). The association of social relationships and activities with mortality: Prospective evidence from the Tecumseh Community Health Study. *American Journal of Epidemiology, 116*, 123–140.

Howells, K., & Field, D. (1982). Fear of death and dying among medical students. *Social Science and Medicine, 16*, 1421–1424.

Hoyer, W. J., & Plude, D. J. (1980). Attentional and perceptual processes in the study of cognitive aging. In L. Poon (Ed.), *Aging in the 1980s* (pp. 227–238). Washington, DC: American Psychological Association.

Hudson, R. B., & Strate, J. (1985). Aging and political systems. In R. H. Binstock & E. Shanas (Eds.), *Handbook of aging and the social sciences* (2nd ed., pp. 554–585). New York: Van Nostrand Reinhold.

Hultsch, D. F., & Dixon, R. A. (1990). Learning and memory in aging. In J. E. Birren & E. W. Schaie (Eds.), *Handbook of the psychology of aging* (3rd ed., pp. 258–274). San Diego: Academic Press.

Hultsch, D. F., & Plemons, J. K. (1979). Life events and life-span development. In P. B. Baltes & O. G. Brim, Jr. (Eds.), *Life-span development and behavior* (Vol. 2, pp. 1–36). New York: Academic Press.

Human Capital Initiative. (1993). *Vitality for life: Psychological research for productive aging.* Washington, DC: American Psychological Association.

Humphreys, R. A. L. (1995). Crime and criminology. *Encyclopedia Americana* (Vol. 8, pp. 193–201). Danbury, CT: Grolier.

Hunter, E. J. (1978). The Vietnam POW veteran: Immediate and long-term effects. In C. R. Figley (Ed.), *Stress disorders among Vietnam veterans* (pp. 188–206). New York: Brunner/Mazel.

Hunter, E. J. (1981). *Wartime stress: Family adjustment to loss* (USIU Report No. TR-USIU-81-07). San Diego: United States International University.

Hurlock, E. B. (1980). *Developmental psychology: A lifespan approach* (5th ed.). New York: McGraw-Hill.

Huxley, A. (1991). *Point counter point* (Reprint edition). Cutchogue, NY: Buccaneer Books. Originally published in 1928.

Huyck, M. H. (1982). From gregariousness to intimacy: Marriage and friendship over the adult years. In T. M. Field, A. Huston, H. C. Quay, L. Troll, & G. E. Finley (Eds.), *Review of human development* (pp. 471–484). New York: Wiley.

Hyde, J. S. (1986). *Understanding human sexuality* (3rd ed.). New York: McGraw-Hill.

Imara, M. (1995). Death: Psychological aspects of death. *Encyclopedia Americana* (Vol. 8, pp. 565–567). Danbury, CT: Grolier.

Inglis, J., Ankus, M. N., & Sykes, D. H. (1968). Age-related differences in learning and short-term memory from childhood to the senium. *Human Development, 11,* 42–52.

Jacobs, B. (1990). Aging and politics. In R. H. Binstock & L. K. George (Eds.), *Handbook of aging and the social sciences* (3rd ed., pp. 350–361). New York: Academic Press.

Jacobs, R. H., & Vinick, B. H. (1979). *Reengagement in later life: Re-employment and remarriage.* Stamford, CT: Greylock Publishers.

Jacoby, S. (1982, June). The truth about two-job marriages. *McCall's,* pp. 127–128.

Jahoda, M. (1958). *Current concepts of positive mental health.* New York: Basic Books.

Jamison, R. N., Burish, T. G., & Wallston, K. A. (1987). Hyperbaric oxygen: Temporary and for senile minds. *Journal of the American Medical Association, 209,* 1435–1438.

Jarvik, L. F., & Bank, L. (1983). Aging twins: Longitudinal aging data. In K. W. Schaie (Ed.), *Longitudinal studies of adult psychological development* (pp. 40–63). New York: Guilford.

Jenkins, B. M. (1983). *Some reflections on recent trends in terrorism.* Santa Monica, CA: Rand Corporation.

Jensen, A. R. (1980). *Bias in mental testing.* New York: Free Press.

Johnson, C. B., Stockdale, M. S., & Saal, F. E. (1991). Persistence of men's misperceptions of friendly cues across a variety of interpersonal encounters. *Psychology of Women Quarterly, 15,* 463–475.

Johnson, M. P., & Leslie, L. (1982). Couple involvement and network structure: A test of the dyadic withdrawal hypothesis. *Social Psychology Quarterly, 4,* 34–43.

Jolin, A., & Gibbons, D. C. (1987). Age patterns in criminal involvement. *International Journal of Offender Therapy and Comparative Criminology, 31,* 237–260.

Jones, H. E., & Conrad, H. S. (1933). The growth and decline of intelligence: A study of a homogeneous group. *Genetic Psychology Monographs, 13,* 223–298.

Josephs, R. A., Markus, H. R., & Tafarodi, R. W. (1992). Gender and self-esteem. *Journal of Personality and Social Psychology, 63,* 391–402.

Jourard, S. M. (1971). *Self-disclosure: An experimental analysis of the transparent self.* New York: Wiley.

Kagan, D. (1995). *On the origins of war and the preservation of peace.* New York: Doubleday.

Kahana, B., & Kahana, E. (1970a). Changes in mental status of elderly patients in age-integrated and age-segregated hospital milieus. *Journal of Abnormal Psychology, 75,* 177–181.

Kahana, B., & Kahana, E. (1970b). Grandparenthood from the perspective of the developing grandchild. *Developmental Psychology, 3,* 98–105.

Kalat, J. W. (1984). *Biological psychology* (2nd ed.). Belmont, CA: Wadsworth.

Kalish, R. A. (1977). Dying and preparing for death: A view of families. In H. Feifel (Ed.), *New meanings of death* (pp. 215–232). New York: McGraw-Hill.

Kalish, R. A. (1985). *Death, grief, and caring relationships* (2nd ed.). Belmont, CA: Brooks/Cole.

Kalish, R. A., & Reynolds, D. K. (1981). *Death and ethnicity: A psychocultural study.* Farmingdale, NY: Baywood.

Kane, A. C., & Hogan, J. D. (1985). Death anxiety in physicians: Defensive style, medical specialty and exposure to death. *Omega, 16,* 11–22.

Kantrowitz, B., & Wingert, P. (1990). Step by step. *Newsweek: Special Edition—The 21st century family,* pp. 24–34.

Kastenbaum, R. (1959). Time and death in adolescence. In H. Feifel (Ed.), *The meaning of death* (pp. 99–113). New York: McGraw-Hill.

Kastenbaum, R. (1966). On the meaning of time in later life. *Journal of Genetic Psychology, 109,* 9–25.

Kastenbaum, R. J., & Aisenberg, R. (1976). *The psychology of death.* New York: Springer.

Kaufman, S. R. (1986). *The ageless self.* Madison: University of Wisconsin Press.

Kausler, D. H. (1985). Episodic memory: Memorizing performance. In N. Charness (Ed.), *Aging and human performance* (pp. 101–141). Chichester, UK: Wiley.

Keith, J. (1990). Age in social and cultural context: Anthropological perspectives. In R. H. Binstock & L. K. George (Eds.), *Handbook of aging and the social sciences* (3rd ed., pp. 91–111). San Diego, CA: Academic Press.

Keith, P. M. (1979). Life changes and perceptions of life and death among older men and women. *Journal of Gerontology, 34,* 870–878.

Keith, P. M., Hill, K., Goudy, W. J., & Powers, E. A. (1984). Confidants and well-being: A note on male friendships in old age. *Gerontologist, 24,* 318–320.

Kellaghan, T., & MacNamara, J. (1972). Family correlates of verbal reasoning ability. *Developmental Psychology, 7,* 49–53.

Kelly, J. B. (1982). Divorce: The adult perspective. In B. B. Wolman (Ed.), *Handbook of developmental psychology* (pp. 734–750). Englewood Cliffs, NJ: Prentice-Hall.

Kelly, J. B., & Wallerstein, J. S. (1976). The effects of parental divorce: Experiences of child in early latency. *American Journal of Orthopsychiatry, 45,* 20–32.

Kelvin, P., & Jarrett, J. A. (1985). *Unemployment: Its social and psychological effects.* Cambridge, UK: Cambridge University Press.

Kendig, H. L. (1990). Comparative perspectives on housing, aging, and social structure. In R. H. Binstock & L. K. George (Eds.), *Handbook of aging and the social sciences* (3rd ed., pp. 288–306). San Diego: Academic Press.

Keniston, K. (1970). Youth: A "new" stage of life. *American Scholar, 39,* 631–654.

Kennedy, G. F. (1990). College students' expectations of grandparent and grandchild role behaviors. *Gerontologist, 30,* 43–48.

Kenshalo, D. R. (1977). Age changes in touch, vibration, temperature, kinesthesis, and pain sensitivity. In J. E. Birren & K. W. Schaie (Eds.), *Handbook of the psychology of aging* (pp. 562–579). New York: Van Nostrand Reinhold.

Kermis, M. D. (1986). The epidemiology of mental disorder in the elderly: A response to the Senate/AARP report. *Gerontologist, 26,* 482–487.

Khleif, B. (1976). The sociology of the mortuary: Religion, sex, age and kinship variables. In V. R. Pine, A. H. Kutscher, D. Peretz, R. J. Slater, R. DeBellis, & D. J. Cherico (Eds.), *Acute grief and the funeral* (pp. 55–91). Springfield, IL: Thomas.

Kilbride, H. W., Johnson, D. L., & Streissguth, A. P. (1977). Social class, birth order, and newborn experience. *Child Development, 48,* 1686–1688.

Kim, P. K. H. (1983). Demography of the Asian-Pacific elderly. In R. L. McNeely & J. L. Cohen (Eds.), *Aging in minority groups* (pp. 29–41). Beverly Hills, CA: Sage.

Kimmel, D. C., & Sang, B. E. (1995). Lesbians and gay men in midlife. In A. R. D'Augeli & C. J. Patterson (Eds.), *Lesbian, gay, and bisexual identities over the lifespan* (pp. 190–214). New York: Oxford University Press.

Kimura, D., & Hampson, E. (1993). Neural and hormonal mechanisms mediating sex differences in cognition. In P. A. Vernon (Ed.), *Biological approaches to the study of human intelligence* (pp. 375–297). Norwood, NJ: Ablex.

King, A. C., Taylor, G. B., Haskell, W. L., & DeBusk, R. F. (1989). Influence of regular aerobic exercise on psychological health: A randomized, controlled trial of healthy, middle-aged adults. *Health Psychology, 8,* 305–324.

King, P. M., Kitchener, K. S., Wood, P. K., & Davison, M. L. (1989). Relationships across developmental domains: A longitudinal study of intellectual, moral, and ego development. In M. L. Commons, J. D. Sinnott, F. A. Richards, & C. Armon (Eds.), *Adult development: Vol. I. Comparisons and applications of adolescent and adult developmental models* (pp. 57–72). New York: Praeger.

Kinicki, A. J. (1989). Predicting occupational role choices after involuntary job loss. *Journal of Vocational Behavior, 35,* 204–218.

Kinicki, A. J., & Latack, J. C. (1990). Explication of the construct of coping with involuntary job loss. *Journal of Vocational Behavior, 35*, 204–218.

Kinsella, K., & Gist, Y. J. (1995). *Older workers, retirement, and pensions: A comparative international chartbook*. Washington, DC: U.S. Bureau of the Census.

Kite, M. E., Deaux, K., & Miele, M. (1991). Stereotypes of young and old: Does age outweigh gender? *Psychology and Aging, 6*, 19–27.

Klein, R. (1972). Age, sex, and task difficulty as predictors of social conformity. *Journal of Gerontology, 27*, 229–235.

Kobasa, S. C. (1979). Stressful life events, personality, and health: An inquiry into hardiness. *Journal of Personality and Social Psychology, 37*, 1–11.

Kobasa, S. C., Maddi, S., & Kahn, S. (1982). Hardiness and health: A prospective study. *Journal of Personality and Social Psychology, 42*, 168–177.

Kobrin, F., & Hendershot, G. (1977). Do family ties reduce morality? Evidence from the United States, 1966–68. *Journal of Marriage and the Family, 39*, 737–745.

Koenig, H. G., George, L. K., & Siegler, I. C. (1988). The use of religion and other emotion-regulating coping strategies among older adults. *Gerontologist, 28*, 303–310.

Koenig, H. G., Kvale, J. N., & Ferrel, C. (1988). Religion and well-being in later life. *Gerontologist, 28*, 18–28.

Kohlberg, L. (1966). A cognitive-development analysis of children's sex-role concepts and attitudes. In E. Maccoby (Ed.), *The development of sex differences* (pp. 48–64). Stanford, CA: Stanford University Press.

Kohlberg, L. (1969). *Stages in the development of moral thought and action*. New York: Holt.

Kohlberg, L. (1976). Moral stages and moralization: The cognitive-developmental approach. In T. Lickona (Ed.), *Moral development and behavior: Theory, research and social issues* (pp. 31–53). New York: Holt, Rinehart & Winston.

Kolodny, R. C., Masters, W. H., & Johnson, V. E. (1979). *Textbook of sexual medicine*. Boston: Little, Brown.

Kornhaber, A., & Woodward, K. L. (1981). *Grandparent/grandchildren: The vital connection*. Garden City, NJ: Doubleday.

Koss, E., Weiffenbach, J. M., Haxby, J. V., & Friedland, R. P. (1988). Olfactory detection and identification performance are dissociated in early Alzheimer's disease. *Neurology, 38*, 1228–1232.

Kotre, J., & Hall, E. (1990). *Seasons of life*. Boston: Little, Brown.

Kowalski, R. M. (1993). Inferring sexual interest from behavioral cues: Effects of gender and sexually relevant attitudes. *Sex Roles, 29*, 13–36.

Krakoff, I. H. (1993). Cancer. *Encyclopedia Americana* (Vol. 5, pp. 528–532). Danbury, CT: Grolier.

Krause, N. (1995). Religiosity and self-esteem among older adults. *Journal of Gerontology: Psychological Sciences, 50B*, P236–P246.

Kübler-Ross, E. (1969). *On death and dying*. New York: Macmillan.

Kübler-Ross, E. (1974). *Questions and answers on death and dying*. New York: Macmillan.

Kübler-Ross, E. (1975). *Death: The final stage of growth*. Englewood Cliffs, NJ: Prentice-Hall.

Kunkel, S. R. (1979). *Sex differences in adjustment to widowhood*. Unpublished master's thesis, Miami University, Oxford, OH.

Kurdek, L. A. (1991a). Predictors of increases in marital distress in newlywed couples: A 3-year prospective longitudinal study. *Developmental Psychology, 27*, 627–636.

Kurdek, L. A. (1991b). The relations between reported well-being and divorce history, availability of a proximate adult, and gender. *Journal of Marriage and the Family, 53*, 71–78.

Kurdek, L. A. (1995a). Developmental changes in relationship quality in gay male and lesbian cohabiting couples. *Developmental Psychology, 31*, 86–94.

Kurdek, L. A. (1995b). Lesbian and gay couples. In A. R. D'Augelli & C. J. Patterson (Eds.), *Lesbian, gay, and bisexual identities over the lifespan* (pp. 243–261). New York: Oxford University Press.

Kurdek, L. A., & Schmitt, J. P. (1986). Early development of relationship quality in heterosexual married, heterosexual cohabiting, gay, and lesbian couples. *Developmental Psychology, 22,* 305–309.

Labouvie-Vief, G. V. (1985). Intelligence and cognition. In J. E. Birren & K. W. Schaie (Eds.), *Handbook of the psychology of aging* (2nd ed., pp. 500–543). New York: Van Nostrand Reinhold.

Labouvie-Vief, G. V., Hakim-Larson, J., & Hobart, C. J. (1987). Age, ego level, and the life-span development of coping and defense processes. *Psychology and Aging, 2,* 286–293.

Ladner, J. L. (1971). *Tomorrow's tomorrow: The black woman.* New York: Doubleday.

Langer, E., & Rodin, J. (1976). The effects of choice and enhanced personal responsibility for the aged: A field experiment in an institutionalized setting. *Journal of Personality and Social Psychology, 34,* 191–198.

Larson, R., Mannell, R., & Zuzanek, J. (1986). Daily well-being of older adults with friends and family. *Psychology and Aging, 1,* 117–126.

LaRue, A., Dessonville, C., & Jarvik, L. F. (1985). Aging and mental disorders. In J. E. Birren & K. W. Schaie (Eds.), *Handbook of the psychology of aging* (2nd ed., pp. 664–702). New York: Van Nostrand Reinhold.

Lawton, M. P., Moss, M., & Fulcomer, M. (1986–1987). Objective and subjective uses of time by older people. *International Journal of Aging and Human Development, 24,* 171–188.

Lazarsfeld, P. F., Berelson, B., & Gaudet, H. (1944). *The people's choice.* New York: Duell.

Lazarus, R. S., & Folkman, S. (1984). *Stress, appraisal, and coping.* New York: Springer.

Lebow, R. N., & Stein, J. G. (1987). Beyond deterrence. *Journal of Social Issues, 43,* 5–71.

Lee, G. R. (1988). Marital satisfaction in later life: The effects of nonmarital roles. *Journal of Marriage and the Family, 50,* 775–783.

Lee, J. A. (1977). *The colors of love.* New York: Bantam.

Lee, T. R., Mancini, J. A., & Maxwell, J. W. (1990). Sibling relationships in adulthood: Contact patterns and motivation. *Journal of Marriage and the Family, 52,* 431–440.

Lehman, H. C. (1953). *Age and achievement.* Princeton, NJ: Princeton University Press.

Leinbach, M. D., & Fagot, B. I. (1993). Categorical habituation to male and female faces: Gender schematic processes in infancy. *Infant Behavior and Development, 16,* 317–332.

Lentzer, H. R., Pamuk, E. R., Rhodenhiser, E. P., Rothberg, R., & Powell-Griner, E. (1992). The quality of life in the year before death. *American Journal of Public Health, 82,* 1093–1098.

Lerner, R. M., & Busch-Rossnagel, N. (Eds.). (1981). *Individuals as producers of their own development.* New York: Academic Press.

Leventhal, R. C. (1991). The aging consumer: What's all the fuss about anyway? *Journal of Consumer Marketing, 8*(1), 29–34.

Levin, J. S., & Taylor, R. J. (1993). Gender and age differences in religiosity among black Americans. *Gerontologist, 33,* 16–23.

Levinger, G. (1978, August). *Models of close relationships: Some new directions.* Invited address presented at the annual meeting of the American Psychological Association, Toronto.

Levinson, D. J. (1978). *The seasons of a man's life.* New York: Knopf.

Levinson, D. J. (1986). A conception of adult development. *American Psychologist, 41,* 3–13.

Levinson, D. J., & Levinson, J. D. (1996). *Seasons of a woman's life.* New York: Knopf.

Lewine, R. R. J. (1981). Sex differences in schizophrenia: Timing or subtype? *Psychological Bulletin, 90,* 432–444.

Lieberman, M. A. (1965). Psychological correlates of impending death: Some preliminary observations. *Journal of Gerontology, 20,* 71–84.

Lieberman, M. A., & Coplan, A. S. (1969). Distance from death as a variable in the study of aging. *Developmental Psychology, 2,* 71–84.

Lieberman, M. A., & Peskin, H. (1992). Adult life crises. In J. E. Birren, R. B. Sloane, & G. D. Cohen (Eds.), *Handbook of mental health and aging* (2nd ed., pp. 119–143). San Diego: Academic Press.

Lindenberger, U., & Baltes, P. B. (1994). Sensory functioning and intelligence in old age: A strong connection. *Psychology and Aging, 9,* 339–355.

Lindenberger, U., Mayr, U., & Kliegl, R. (1993). Speed and intelligence in old age. *Psychology and aging, 8,* 207–220.

Linn, M. C., & Petersen, A. C. (1985). Emergence and characterization of sex difference sin spatial ability: A meta-analysis. *Child Development, 56,* 1479–1498.

Loevinger, J. (1976). *Ego development.* San Francisco: Jossey-Bass.

Lonetto, R., Mercer, G. W., Fleming, S., Bunting, B., & Clare, M. (1980). Death anxiety among university students in Northern Ireland and Canada. *Journal of Psychology, 104,* 75–82.

Longino, C. F., Jr. (1990). Geographical distribution and migration. In R. H. Binstock & L. K. George (Eds.), *Handbook of aging and the social sciences* (3rd ed., pp. 45–63). San Diego: Academic Press.

Lopata, H. Z. (1973). *Widowhood in an American city.* Cambridge, MA: Schenckman.

Lopata, H. Z. (1975). On widowhood: Grief, work, and identity reconstruction. *Journal of Geriatric Psychiatry, 8,* 41–55.

Lowenthal, M., Thurnher, M., & Chiriboga, D. (1975). *Four stages of life.* San Francisco: Jossey-Bass.

Luria, M. H., Johnson, M. W., Pego, R., Seve, C. A., Manubens, S. J., Wieland, M. R., & Wieland, R. G. (1982). Relationship between sex hormones, myocardial infarction, and occlusive coronary disease. *Archives of Internal Medicine, 142,* 42–44.

Lynch, J. J. (1977). *The broken heart: The medical consequences of loneliness.* New York: Basic Books.

Lynn, R. (1982). IQ in Japan and the United States shows a growing disparity. *Science, 297,* 222–223.

Lynn, R. (1987). The intelligence of the mongoloids: A psychometric, evolutionary and neurological theory. *Personality and Individual Differences, 8,* 813–844.

Lytton, H., & Romney, D. M. (1991). Parents' differential socialization of boys and girls: A meta-analysis. *Psychological Bulletin, 109,* 267–296.

Maccoby, E. E., & Jacklin, C. (1974). *The psychology of sex differences.* Stanford, CA: Stanford University Press.

Maccoby, E. E., & Martin, J. A. (1983). Socialization in the context of the family: Parent–child interaction. In P. H. Mussen (Ed.), *Handbook of child psychology: Vol. 4. Socialization, personality, and social development* (pp. 1–101). New York: Wiley.

Macklin, E. D. (1988). Heterosexual couples who cohabit nonmaritally: Some common problems and issues. In C. S. Chilman, E. W. Nunnally, & F. M. Cox (Eds.), *Variant family forms,* (pp. 56–72). Beverly Hills: Sage.

MacPhee, D., Ramey, C. T., & Yeates, K. O. (1984). Home environment and early cognitive development: Implications for intervention. In A. W. Gottfried (Ed.), *Home environment and early cognitive development: Longitudinal research,* (pp. 343–369). Orlando, FL: Academic Press.

Mallinckrodt, B., & Fretz, B. R. (1988). Social support and the impact of job loss on older professionals. *Journal of Counseling Psychology, 35,* 281–286.

Manton, K. G., Corder, L. S., & Stallard, E. (1993). Estimates of change in chronic disability and institutional incidence and prevalence rates in the U.S. elderly population from the 1982, 1984, and 1980 National Long-Term Care Survey. *Journal of Gerontology: Social Sciences, 48,* S153–S166.

Margolin, L., & White, J. (1987). The continuing role of physical attractiveness in marriage. *Journal of Marriage and the Family, 49,* 21–27.

Markides, K. S. (1983). Age, religiosity, and adjustment: A longitudinal analysis. *Journal of Gerontology, 38,* 621–625.

Markides, K. S., Liang, J., & Jackson, J. S. (1990). Race, ethnicity and aging: Conceptual and methodological issues. In R. H. Binstock & L. K. George (Eds.), *Handbook of aging and the social sciences* (3rd ed., pp. 112–129). San Diego: Academic Press.

Marriage. (1993). *Encyclopedia Americana* (Vol. 18, pp. 345–353). Danbury, CT: Grolier.

Marshall, V. W. (1980). *Last chapters: A sociology of aging and dying.* Monterey, CA: Brooks/Cole.

Maslow, A. H. (1970). *Motivation and personality* (2nd ed.). New York: Harper & Row.

Masters, W. H., & Johnson, V. E. (1970). *Human sexual inadequacy.* Boston: Little, Brown.

Masters, W. H., Johnson, V. E., & Kolodny, R. C. (1991). *Human sexuality* (3rd ed.). Boston: Little, Brown.

Masters, W. H., Johnson, V. E., & Kolodny, R. C. (1994). *Heterosexuality.* New York: HarperCollins.

Matthews, S. H. (1986). *Friendships through the life course.* Beverly Hills, CA: Sage.

Matthews, S. H., & Sprey, J. (1985). Adolescents' relationships with grandparents. *Journal of Gerontology, 40,* 621–626.

Matthews, S. H., Werkner, J. E., & Delaney, P. J. (1990). Relative contributions of help by employed and nonemployed sisters to their elderly parents. *Journal of Gerontology: Social Sciences, 49,* S36–S44.

Maugh, T. H. (1996, September 16). Worldwide study finds big shift in causes of death. *Los Angeles Times,* pp. A1, A14.

Mauksch, H. O. (1975). The organizational context of dying. In E. Kübler-Ross (Ed.), *Death: The final stage of growth* (pp. 7–24). Englewood Cliffs, NJ: Prentice-Hall.

May, R. (1969). *Love and will.* New York: Norton.

McAdams, D. P. (1993). *The stories we live by: Personal myths and the making of the self.* New York: Morrow.

McAdams, D. P. (1994). Can personality change? Levels of stability and growth in personality across the life span. In T. F. Heatherton & J. L. Weinberger (Eds,), *Can personality change?* (pp. 299–313). Washington, DC: American Psychological Association.

McAneny, L. (1993, December). Most Americans again see crime on the rise. *Gallup Poll Monthly,* pp. 18–27.

McAuley, E. (1992). Understanding exercise behavior: A self-efficacy perspective. In G. C. Roberts (Ed.), *Understanding motivation in exercise and sport* (pp. 107–128). Champaign, IL: Human Kinetics.

McAuley, E., Lox, L., & Duncan, T. E. (1993). Long-term maintenance of exercise, self-efficacy, and physiological change in older adults. *Journal of Gerontology: Psychological Sciences, 48,* P218–P224.

McClearn, G. E., Johansson, B., Berg, St., Pedersen, N. L., Ahern, F., Petrill, S. A., & Plomin, R. (1997). Substantial genetic influence on cognitive abilities in twins 80 or more years old. *Science, 276,* 1560–1563.

McCrae, R. R., Arenberg, D., & Costa, P. T., Jr. (1987). Declines in divergent thinking with age: Cross-sectional, longitudinal, and cross-sequential analyses. *Psychology and Aging, 2,* 130–137.

McCrae, R. R., & Costa, P. T. (1987). Validation of the five-factor model of personality across instruments and observers. *Journal of Personality and Social Psychology, 52,* 81–90.

McCrae, R. R., & Costa, P. T. (1990). *Personality in adulthood.* New York: Guilford.

McKinlay, J. B. (1981). Social network influences on morbid episodes and the career of help seeking. In L. Eisenberg & A. Kleinman (Eds.), *The relevance of social science for medicine* (pp. 000–000). Dordrecht, Holland: D. Reidel.

McLoyd, V. C. (1989). Socialization and development in a changing economy: The effects of paternal job and income loss on children. *American Psychologist, 44*(2), 293–302.

McMichael, A. J., Baghurst, P. A., Wigg, N. R., Vimpani, G. V., Robertson, E. F., & Roberts, R. J. (1988). Port Pirie cohort study: Environmental exposure to lead and children's abilities at the age of four years. *New England Journal of Medicine, 319,* 468–475.

McMordie, W. R. (1981). Religiosity and fear of death: Strength of belief system. *Psychological Reports, 49,* 921–922.

McNeil, J. K., LeBlanc, E. M., & Joyner, M. (1991). The effects of exercise on depressive symptoms in the moderately depressed elderly. *Psychology and Aging, 6,* 487–488.

McNemar, Q. (1942). *The revision of the Stanford-Binet scale.* Boston: Houghton Mifflin.

McNemar, Q. (1964). Lost: Our intelligence? Why? *American Psychologist, 10,* 871–882.

Mead, M. (1935). *Sex and temperament in three primitive societies.* New York: Morrow.

Menaghan, E. G., & Lieberman, M. A. (1986). Changes in depression following divorce: A panel study. *Journal of Marriage and the Family, 48,* 319–328.

Merai, A. (Ed.). (1985). *On terrorism and combating terrorism.* College Park, MD: University Publications of America.

Miller, B. D., & Olsen, D. (1978). *Typology of marital interaction and contextual characteristics: Cluster analysis of the I.M.C.*. Unpublished paper available from D. Olsen, Minnesota Family Study Center, University of Minnesota, Minneapolis.

Miller, E. M. (1994). Intelligence and brain myelination: A hypothesis. *Personality and Individual Differences, 17*, 803–832.

Miller, I. J., Jr. (1988). Human taste bud density across adult age groups. *Journal of Gerontology: Biological Sciences, 43*, B26–B30.

Minton, H. L., & Schneider, F. W. (1980). *Differential psychology*. Monterey, CA: Brooks/Cole.

Mirowsky, J., & Ross, C. E. (1992). Age and depression. *Journal of Health and Social Behavior, 33*, 187–205.

Mitchell, S. (1995). *The official guide to the generations*. Ithaca, NY: New Strategist Publications.

Moehringer, J. R. (1997, July 11). Most married but little missed. *Los Angeles Times* pp. A1, A17.

Montag, I., & Comrey, A. (1987). Internality and externality as correlates of involvement in fatal driving accidents. *Journal of Applied Psychology, 72*, 339–343.

Moore, D. W. (1994, September). Majority advocate death penalty for teenage killers. *Gallup Poll Monthly*, pp. 2–6.

Moore, D. W. (1995, February). Most Americans say religion is important to them. *Gallup Poll Monthly*, pp. 16–21.

Moore, D. W., and Newport, F. (1994, January). Public strongly factors stricter gun control laws. *Gallup Poll Monthly*, pp. 18–24.

Moore, D. W., & Newport, F. (1995, June). People throughout the world largely satisfied with their personal lives. *Gallup Poll Monthly*, pp. 2–7.

Moore, D. W., & Saad, L. (1995, May). Most Americans worried about retirement. *Gallup Poll Monthly*, pp. 17–21.

Moore, M. M. (1995). Courtship signaling and adolescents: "Girls just wanna have fun." *Journal of Sex Research, 32*(4), 319–328.

Mor-Barak, M. E., Scharlach, A. E., Birba, L., & Sokolov, J. (1992). Employment, social networks, and health in the retirement years. *International Journal of Aging and Human Development, 35*, 145–159.

Morgan, L. A. (1976). A re-examination of widowhood and morale. *Journal of Gerontology, 31*, 687–695.

Morrison, A. M., & Von Glinow, M. A. (1990). Women and minorities in management. *American Psychologist, 45*, 200–208.

Mosatche, H. S., Brady, E. M., & Noberini, M. R. (1983). A retrospective life-span study of the closest sibling relationship. *Journal of Psychology, 113*, 237–243.

Moss, M. S., & Lawton, M. P. (1982). Time budgets of older people: A window on four lifestyles. *Journal of Gerontology, 37*, 115–123.

Moss, M. S., Moss, S. Z., & Moles, E. L. (1985). The quality of relationships between elderly parents and their out-of-town children. *Gerontologist, 30*, 143–140.

Murdock, S. H. (1995). *An America challenged: Population change and the future of the United States*. Boulder, CO: Westview Press.

Murphy, C. (1986). Taste and smell in the elderly. In H. L. Meiselman & R. S. Rivlin (Eds.), *Clinical measurement of taste and smell* (pp. 343–371). New York: Macmillan.

Murphy, J., & Florio, C. (1978). Older Americans: Facts and potential. In R. Gross, B. Gross, & S. Seidman (Eds.), *The new old: Struggling for decent aging* (pp. 50–57). Garden City, NY: Doubleday Anchor.

Murstein, B. I. (1985). *Paths to marriage*. Beverly Hills, CA: Sage.

Murstein, B. I., & Christy, P. (1976). Physical attractiveness and marriage adjustment in middle-aged couples. *Journal of Personality and Social Psychology, 34*, 537–542.

Myers, D. G. (1995). *Psychology* (4th ed.). New York: Worth.

Nagy, M. H. (1948). The child's theories concerning death. *Journal of Genetic Psychology, 73*, 3–27.

Naroll, R., Bullough, V. L., & Naroll, F. (1974). *Military deterrence in history: A pilot cross-historical survey*. Albany: State University of New York Press.

National Center for Health Statistics. (1990). *Health, United States, 1989*. Washington, DC: Department of Health and Human Services.

National Center for Health Statistics. (1991). Current estimates from the National Health Interview Survey, 1990. *Vital and Health Statistics*, Series 10, No. 181. Washington, DC: U.S. Government Printing Office.

National Center for Health Statistics. (1992). *Monthly Vital Statistics Report*, 40(13). Hyattsville, MD: U.S. Department of Health and Human Services.

National Center for Health Statistics. (1993). *Monthly Vital Statistics Report*, 42(2). Hyattsville, MD: U.S. Department of Health and Human Services.

National Center for Health Statistics. (1995). *Health, United States, 1994*. Hyattsville, MD: Public Health Service.

National Safety Council. (1996). *Accident facts, 1992 edition*. Itasca, IL: Author.

Needleman, H. L., Schell, A., Bellinger, D., Leviton, A., & Allred, E. N. (1990). The long-term effects of exposure to low doses of lead in childhood. *New England Journal of Medicine*, 322(2), 83–88.

Neimeyer, R. A., Bagley, K. J., & Moore, M. K. (1986). Cognitive structure and death anxiety. *Death Studies*, 10, 273–288.

Nelson, B. (1982, July 7). Venereal, liver disease deaths higher in state. *Los Angeles Times*, p. I-15.

Nelson, L. P., & Nelson, V. (1973). *Religion and death anxiety*. Presentation to the annual joint meeting of the Society for the Scientific Study of Religion and Religious Research Association. San Francisco.

Nettelbeck, T., & Rabbitt, P. M. (1992). Aging, cognitive performance, and mental speed. *Intelligence*, 16, 189–205.

Neubeck, G. (1972). The myriad motives for sex. *Sexual Behavior*, 2, 50–56.

Neugarten, B. L. (1964). *Personality in middle and late life*. New York: Atherton Press.

Neugarten, B. L. (1970). Adaptation and the life cycle. *Journal of Geriatric Psychiatry*, 4, 71–87.

Neugarten, B. L. (1973). Personality changes in late life: A developmental perspective. In C. Eisdorfer & M. P. Lawton (Eds.), *The psychology of adult development and aging* (pp. 311–338). Washington, DC: American Psychological Association.

Neugarten, B. L. (1977). Personality and aging. In J. E. Birren & K. W. Schaie (Eds.), *Handbook of the psychology of aging* (pp. 626–649). New York: Van Nostrand Reinhold.

Neugarten, B. L., Havighurst, R. J., & Tobin, S. S. (1968). Personality and patterns of aging. In B. L. Neugarten (Ed.), *Middle age and aging* (pp. 173–174). Chicago: University of Chicago Press.

Neugarten, B. L., & Neugarten, D. A. (1989). Policy issues in an aging society. In M. Storandt & G. R. VandenBos (Eds,), *The adult years: Continuity and change* (pp. 147–167). Washington, DC: American Psychological Association.

Neugarten, B. L., & Weinstein, K. K. (1968). The changing American grandparent. In B. L. Neugarten (Ed.), *Middle age and aging: A reader in social psychology* (pp. 280–285). Chicago: University of Chicago Press.

Newman, B. M. (1982). Mid-life development. In B. Wolman (Ed.), *Handbook of developmental psychology* (pp. 617–635). Englewood Cliffs, NJ: Prentice-Hall.

Nichols, M., & Lieblum, S. R. (1983). *Lesbianism as personal identity and social role: Conceptual and clinical issues*. Unpublished paper, Rutgers University, New Brunswick, NJ.

Niemcryk, S. J., Jenkins, C. D., Rose, R. M., & Hurst, M. W. (1987). The prospective impact of psychosocial variables on rates of illness and injury in professional employees. *Journal of Occupational Medicine*, 29(8), 645–652.

Nisbet, J. D. (1957). Intelligence and age: Retesting after twenty-four years interval. *British Journal of Educational Psychology*, 27, 190–198.

Noble, B. P. (1993, September 19). Dissecting the '90s workplace. *New York Times*, p. F21.

Norbeck, E. (1995). Funeral. *Encyclopedia Americana* (Vol. 12, p. 168). Danbury, CT: Grolier.

Norris-Baker, C., & Scheidt, R. J. (1994). From "Our Town" to "Ghost Town"? The changing context of home for rural elders. *International Journal of Aging and Human Development*, 38, 181–202.

Nuessel, F. H. (1982). The language of ageism. *Gerontologist*, 22, 273–275.

Ochs, A., Newberry, J., Lenhardt, M. L., & Harkins, S. W. (1985). Neural and vestibular aging associated with falls. In J. E. Birren & K. W. Schaie (Eds,), *Handbook of the psychology of aging* (2nd ed., pp. 278–299). New York: Van Nostrand Reinhold.

O'Connell, P. (1976, November). Trends in psychological adjustment: Observations made during successive psychiatric follow-up interviews of returned Navy–Marine Corps POWs. In R. Spaulding (Ed.), *Proceedings of the 3rd Annual Joint Meeting Concerning POW/MIA matters* (pp. 16–22). San Diego, CA.

O'Connor, P. (1993). Sam gender and cross-gender friendships among the frail elderly. *Gerontologist, 33,* 24–30.

Oreskes, M. (June 28, 1990). Profile of today's youth: They couldn't care less. *New York Times,* pp. A1, D21.

Ortega, S. T., Crutchfield, R. D., & Rushing, W. A. (1983). Race differences in elderly personal well-being: Friendship, family and church. *Research on Aging, 5*(1), 101–118.

Ortega y Gasset, J. (1957). *The revolt of the masses.* New York: Norton. (Original published in 1932)

Osborn, A. F. (1953). *Applied imagination.* New York: Scribner.

Osipow, S. H. (1983). *Theories of career development* (3rd ed.). Englewood Cliffs, NJ: Prentice-Hall.

Overweight people now a majority, U.S. says. (1996, October 16). *Los Angeles Times,* p. A21.

Owens, W. A., Jr. (1953). Age and mental abilities: A longitudinal study. *Genetic Psychology Monographs, 48,* 3–54.

Owens, W. A., Jr. (1966). Age and mental abilities: A second adult follow-up. *Journal of Educational Psychology, 57,* 311–325.

Paffenbarger, R. S., Jr., Hyde, R. T., Wing, A. L., & Hsieh, C. (1986). Physical activity, all-cause mortality, and longevity of college alumni. *New England Journal of Medicine, 314,* 605–613.

Palmore, E. (1982). Predictors of the longevity difference: A 25-year follow-up. *Gerontologist, 225,* 513–518.

Palmore, E. (1990). *Ageism: Negative and positive.* New York: Springer.

Palmore, E., Burchett, B., Fillenbaum, G. G., George, L. K., & Wallman, L. M. (1985). *Retirement: Causes and consequences.* New York: Springer.

Palmore, E., & Cleveland, W. (1976). Aging, terminal decline, and terminal drop. *Journal of Gerontology, 31*(1), 76–86.

Parkes, C. M. (1972). *Bereavement: Studies of grief in adult life.* New York: International University Press.

Parkes, C. M., Benjamin, B., & Fitzgerald, R. G. (1969). Broken heart: A statistical study of increased mortality among widowers. *British Medical Journal, 1,* 740–743.

Pascual-Leon, J. (1983). Growing into human maturity: Toward a metasubjective theory of adult stages. In P. B. Baltes & O. G. Brim, Jr. (Eds.), *Life-span development and behavior* (Vol. 5, pp. 118–156). New York: Academic Press.

Patterson, C. J. (1995). Lesbian mothers, gay fathers, and their children. In A. R. D'Augelli & C. J. Patterson (Eds,), *Lesbian, gay, and bisexual identities over the lifespan* (pp. 262–290). New York: Oxford University Press.

Pattison, E. M. (1977). Death throughout the life cycle. In E. M. Pattison (Ed.), *The experience of dying* (pp. 18–27). Englewood Cliffs, NJ: Prentice-Hall.

Peck, R. C. (1968). Psychological developments in the second half of life. In B. L. Neugarten (Ed.), *Middle age and aging: A reader in social psychology* (pp. 88–92). Chicago: University of Chicago Press.

Peplau, L., & Gordon, S. L. (1985). Women and men in love: Sex differences in close heterosexual relationships. In V. O'Leary, R. K. Unger, & B. S. Wallston (Eds.), *Women, gender, and social psychology* (pp. 257–292). Hillsdale, NJ: Erlbaum.

Perkins, C. A., Klaus, P. A., Bastian, L. D., & Cohen, R. L. (1996). *Criminal victimization in the United States, 1993.* Washington, DC: Bureau of Justice Statistics.

Perkins, K. (1992). Psychosocial implications of women and retirement. *Social Work, 37,* 526–532.

Perlmutter, M., Adams, C., Barry, J., Kaplan, M., Person, D., & Verdonik, F. (1987). Aging and memory. In K. W. Schaie & K. Eisdorfer (Eds.), *Annual review of gerontology and geriatrics* (Vol. 7, pp. 57–92). New York: Springer.

Perlmutter, M., & Hall, E. (1992). *Adult development and aging* (2nd ed.). New York: Wiley.

Perlmutter, M., & Mitchell, D. (1982). The appearance and disappearance of age differences in adult memory. In F. I. M. Craik & S. Trehub (Eds.), *Aging and cognitive processes* (pp. 127–144). New York: Plenum Press.

Perlmutter, M., & Nyquist, L. (1990). Relationships between self-reported physical and mental health and intelligence performance across adulthood. *Journals of Gerontology, 45*, P145–P155.

Perry, A. (1986). Type A behavior pattern and motor vehicle drivers' behavior. *Perceptual and Motor Skills, 63*, 875–878.

Petersen, A. C., & Wittig, M. A. (1979). Sex-related differences in cognitive functioning: An overview. In M. A. Wittig & A. C. Petersen (Eds,), *Sex-related differences in cognitive functioning: Developmental issues* (pp. 1–17). New York: Academic Press.

Peterson, E. T. (1989). Grandparenting. In S. J. Bahr & E. T. Peterson (Eds.), *Aging and the family* (pp. 157–174). Lexington, MA: Lexington.

Petruzello, S. J., Landers, D. M., Hatfield, B. D., Kubitz, K. A., & Salazar, W. (1991). A meta-analysis on the anxiety-reducing effects of acute and chronic exercise. *Sports Medicine, 11*, 143–182.

Pfeiffer, H., Verwoerdt, A., & Davis, G. C. (1974). Sexual behavior in middle life. In E. Palmore (Ed.), *Normal aging II: Reports from the Duke longitudinal studies, 1970–1973* (pp. 243–251). Durham, NC: Duke University Press.

Phifer, J., & Murrell, S. (1986). Etiological factors in the onset of depressive symptoms in older adults. *Journal of Abnormal Psychology, 95*, 282–291.

Phillips, D. P., & Smith, D. G. (1990). Postponement of death until symbolically meaningful occasions. *Journal of the American Medical Association, 263*(14), 1947–1951.

Pillemer, K., & Finkelhor, D. (1988). The prevalence of elderly abuse: A random survey. *Gerontologist, 28*(1), 51–57.

Plomin, R. (1988). The nature and nurture of cognitive abilities. In R. J. Sternberg (Ed.), *Advances in the psychology of human intelligence* (Vol. 4, pp. 1–33). Hillsdale, NJ: Erlbaum.

Plomin, R. (1980). Environment and genes: Determinants of behavior. *American Psychologist, 44*, 105–111.

Pollack, J. M. (1979) Correlates of death anxiety: A review of empirical studies. *Omega, 1*, 97–121.

Poon, L. W. (1985). Differences in human memory with aging: Nature, causes and clinical implications. In J. E. Birren & K. W. Schaie (Eds.), *Handbook of the psychology of aging* (2nd ed., pp. 427–462). New York: Academic Press.

Poon, L. W., & Siegler, I. C. (1991). Psychological aspects of normal aging. In J. Sadavoy, L. W. Lazarus, & L. F. Jarvik (Eds,), *Comprehensive Review of Geriatric Psychiatry*. Washington, DC: American Psychiatry Press.

Population Reference Bureau. (1997). *1997 World population data sheet*. Washington, DC: Author.

Powers, E. A., Keith, P., & Goudy, W. H. (1975). Family relationships and friendships. In R. C. Atchley (Ed.). *Environments and the rural aged* (pp. 67–90). Washington, DC: Gerontological Society.

Pruitt, D. G., & Rubin, J. Z. (1986). *Social conflict: Escalation, stalemate, and settlement*. New York: Random House.

Puner, M. (1974). *The good long life: What we know about growing old*. New York: Universe Books.

Quinn, J. F., & Burkhauser, R. V. (1990). Work and retirement. In R. H. Binstock & L. K. George (Eds,), *Handbook of aging and the social sciences* (3rd. ed., pp. 308–327). New York: Van Nostrand Reinhold.

Rabbitt, P. (1977). Changes in problem-solving ability in old age. In J. E. Birren & K. W. Schaie (Eds.), *Handbook of the psychology of aging* (pp. 605–625). New York: Van Nostrand Reinhold.

Racial overtones evident in Americans' attitudes about crime. *Gallup Poll Monthly*, pp. 37–42.

Raphael, S., & Robinson, M. (1980). The older lesbian: Love relationships and friendship patterns. *Alternative Lifestyles, 3*, 207–229.

Raskind, M. A., & Peskind, E. R. (1992). Alzheimer's disease and other dementing disorders. In J. E. Birren, R. B. Sloane, & G. D. Cohen (Eds.), *Handbook of mental health and aging* (2nd ed., pp. 477–513). San Diego: Academic Press.

Rawlins, W. K. (1992). *Friendship matters.* Hawthorne, NY: Aldine de Bruyter.

Rebok, G. W., & Offermann, L. R. (1983). Behavioral competencies of older college students: A self-efficacy approach. *Journal of Gerontologist, 23*, 428–432.

Reedy, M. N. (1983). Personalty and aging. In S. Woodruff & J. E. Birren (Eds.), *Aging: Scientific perspectives and social issues* (2nd ed., pp. 112–136). Monterey, CA: Brooks/Cole.

Reedy, M. N., Birren, J. E., & Schaie, K. W. (1981). Age and sex differences in satisfying love relationships across the adult life span. *Human Development, 24*, 52–66.

Reese, H. W., & Rodeheaver, D. (1985). Problem solving and complex decision making. In J. E. Birren & J. W. Schaie (Eds.), *Handbook of the psychology of aging* (2nd ed., pp. 474–499). New York: Van Nostrand Reinhold.

Regier, D. A., & Burke, J. D. (1989). Epidemiology. In H. I. Kaplan & B. J. Sadock (Eds.), *Comprehensive textbook of psychiatry* (5th ed., pp. 308–332). Baltimore: Williams & Wilkins.

Reichard, S., Livson, F., & Petersen, P. G. (1962). *Aging and personality.* New York: Wiley.

Reimanis, G., & Green, R. F. (1971). Imminence of death and intellectual decrement in aging. *Developmental Psychology, 5*, 270–272.

Reinke, B. J., Holmes, D. S., & Harris, R. L. (1985). The timing of psychosocial changes in women's lives: The years 25 to 45. *Journal of Personality and Social Psychology, 48*, 1353–1364.

Reisman, J. M. (1981). Adult friendships. In S. W. Duck & R. Gilmour (Eds.), *Personal relationships: 2. Developing personal relationships* (pp. 205–230). New York: Academic Press.

Repetti, R. L., Matthews, K. A., & Waldron, I. (1989). Employment and women's health: Effects of paid employment on women's mental and physical health. *American Psychologist, 44*, 1394–1401.

Reskin, B. F., & Roos, P. A. (1990). *Job queue, gender queues: Explaining women's inroads into male occupations.* Philadelphia: Temple University Press.

Reynolds, C. R., Chastain, R. L., Kaufman, A. S., & McLean, J. E. (1987). Demographic characteristics and IQ among adults: Analysis of the WAIS-R standardization sample as a function of the stratification variables. *Journal of School Psychology, 25*, 323–342.

Rhodes, S. R. (1983). Age-related differences in work attitudes and behavior: A review and conceptual analysis. *Psychological Bulletin, 93*, 328–367.

Richardson, J. L., Zarnegar, Z., Bisno, B., & Levine, A. (1990). Psychosocial status at initiation of cancer treatment and survival. *Journal of Psychosomatic Research, 34*, 189–201.

Riegel, K. F. (1973). Dialectical operations: The final period of cognitive development. *Human Development, 16*, 346–370.

Riegel, K. F. (1976). The dialectics of human development. *American Psychologist, 31*, 689–701.

Riegel, K. F., & Riegel, R. M. (1972). Development, drop, and death. *Developmental Psychology, 6*, 306–319.

Riley, M. W., & Foner, A. (Eds.). (1968). *Aging and society* New York: Russell Sage Foundation.

Rinn, W. E. (1988). Mental decline in normal aging A review. *Journal of Geriatric Psychiatry and Neurology, 1*, 144–158.

Roberts, J. D. (1980). *Roots of a black future: Family and church.* Philadelphia: Westminster.

Roberts, L. (1988, July 8). Vietnam's psychological toll. *Science, 241*, 159–161.

Roberts, P., & Newton, P. M. (1987). Levinsonian studies of women's adult development. *Psychology and Aging, 2*, 154–163.

Robertson, J. F. (1977). Grandmotherhood: A study of role concepts. *Journal of Marriage and the Family, 39*, 165–174.

Robinson, P. K., Coberly, S., & Paul, C. E. (1985). Work and retirement. In R. H. Binstock & E. Shanas (Eds.), *Handbook of aging and the social sciences* (2nd ed., pp. 503–527). New York: Van Nostrand Reinhold.

Rodeheaver, D., & Thomas, J. L. (1986). Family and community networks in Appalachia. In N. Datan, A. L. Greene, & H. W. Reese (Eds.), *Life-span developmental psychology: Intergenerational relations* (pp. 77–98). Hillsdale, NJ: Erlbaum.

Rodin, J., & Langer, E. (1977). Long-term effects of a control-relevant intervention with institutionalized aged. *Journal of Personality and Social Psychology, 35,* 897–902.

Roe, A. (1956). *The psychology of occupations.* New York: Basic Books.

Roper Organization. (1985). *The Virginia Slims American women's opinion poll.* New York: Roper.

Rosen, R. C., & Hall, E. (1984). *Sexuality.* New York: Random House.

Rosenberg, H. M., Ventura, S. J., Maurer, J. D., Heuser, R. L., & Freedman, M. A. (1996). Births and deaths: United States, 1995. *Monthly Vital Statistics Report, 45*(3, Supplement 2)., Hyattsville, MD: National Center for Health Statistics.

Rosenthal, L. (1985). Kin-keeping in the familial division of labor. *Journal of Marriage and the Family, 45,* 509–521.

Roth, W. F. (1991). *Work and rewards: Redefining our work-life reality.* New York: Praeger.

Rotter, J. B. (1966). Generalized expectancies for internal versus external control of reinforcement. *Psychological Monographs, 81*(1, Whole No. 609).

Rubin, L. B. (1985). *Just friends: The role of friendship in our lives.* New York: Harper & Row.

Rubin, Z. (1973). *Liking and loving: An invitation to social psychology.* New York: Holt, Rinehart & Winston.

Rubin, Z., Hill, C. T., Peplau, L. A., & Dunkel-Schetter, C. (1980). Self-disclosure in dating couples: Sex roles and the ethic of openness. *Journal of Marriage and the Family, 42,* 30.

Rubinstein, R. L. (1987). Never-married elderly as a social type: Reevaluating some images. *Gerontologist, 27,* 108–113.

Rybash, J. M., Hoyer, W. J., & Roodin, P. A. (1986). *Adult cognition and aging: Developmental changes in processing, knowing, and thinking.* New York: Pergamon.

Saad, L. (1996, January). Americans' religious commitment affirmed. *Gallup Poll Monthly,* pp. 21–23.

Salthouse, T. A. (1982). *Adult cognition: An experimental psychology of human aging.* New York: Springer Verlag.

Saluter, A. F. (1996). *Marital status and living arrangements: March 1995. PPL-52.* Washington, DC: U.S. Bureau of the Census, Fertility & Family Statistics Branch, Population Division.

Sands, L. P., & Meredith, W. (1992). Blood pressure and intellectual functioning in late midlife. *Journal of Gerontology, 47,* P81–P84.

Santos, J., Hubbard, R., & McIntosh, J. (1983). Mental health and the minority elderly. In L. Breslau & M. Haug (Eds.), *Depression and aging: Causes, care, and consequences* (pp. 51–70). New York: Springer.

Sapadin, L. A. (1988). Friendship and gender: Perspectives of professional men and women. *Journal of Social and Personal Relationships, 5,* 387–403.

Sapiro, V. (1990). *Women in American society* (2nd ed.). Palo Alto, CA: Mayfield.

Sarason, I. G., Sarason, B. R., & Pierce, G. R. (1989). *Social support: An interactional view.* New York: Wiley.

Saunders, C. (1980). St. Christopher's Hospice. In E. S. Shneidman (Ed.), *Death: Current perspectives* (2nd ed., pp. 356–361). Palo Alto, CA: Mayfield.

Schaefer, E. S. (1959). A circumplex model for maternal behavior. *Journal of Abnormal and Social Psychology, 59,* 226–235.

Schaie, K. W. (1967). Age changes and age differences. *Gerontologist, 7,* 128–132.

Schaie, K. W. (1977). Quasi-experimental research designs in the psychology of aging. In J. E. Birren & K. W. Schaie (Eds.), *Handbook of the psychology of aging* (pp. 39–59). New York: Van Nostrand Reinhold.

Schaie, K. W. (1977–1978). Toward a stage theory of adult cognitive development. *Aging and Human Development, 8,* 129–138.

Schaie, K. W. (1979). The Primary Mental Abilities in adulthood: An exploration in the development of psychometric intelligence. In P. B. Baltes & O. G. Brim, Jr. (Eds.), *Life-span development and behavior* (Vol. 2, pp. 68–115). New York: Academic Press.

Schaie, K. W. (1983). The Seattle Longitudinal Study: A twenty-one year exploration of psychometric intelligence in adulthood. In K. W. Schaie (Ed.), *Longitudinal studies of adult psychological development* (pp. 64–135). New York: Guilford.

Schaie, K. W. (1990). Intellectual development in adulthood. In J. E. Birren & K. W. Schaie (Eds.), *Handbook of the psychology of aging* (3rd ed., pp. 291–309). San Diego: Academic Press.

Schaie, K. W. (1990). The optimization of cognitive functioning in old age: Prediction based on cohort-sequential and longitudinal data. In P. B. Baltes & M. Baltes (Eds.), *Longitudinal research and the study of successful (optimal) aging* (pp. 94–117). Cambridge, UK: Cambridge University Press.

Schaie, K. W. (1994). The course of adult intellectual development. *American Psychologist, 49*(4), 304–313.

Schaie, K. W., & Parham, I. A. (1976). Stability of adult personality: Fact or fable? *Journal of Personality and Social Psychology, 10,* 305–320.

Schaie, K. W., & Willis, S. L. (1986). Can decline in adult cognitive functioning be reversed? *Developmental Psychology, 22,* 223–232.

Scheidt, R. J. (1993). Place and personality in adult development. In R. Kastenbaum (Ed.), *Encyclopedia of adult development* (pp. 370–376). Phoenix, AZ: Oryx Press.

Schewe, C. D. (1990, June). Get in position for the older market. *American Demographics,* pp. 38–41, 61–63.

Schieber, F. (1992). Aging and the senses. In J. E. Birren, R. B. Sloane, & G. D. Cohen (Eds.), *Handbook of mental health and aging* (2nd ed., pp. 252–306). San Diego: Academic Press.

Schonfield, D., & Robertson, B. A. (1966). Memory storage and aging. *Canadian Journal of Psychology, 20,* 228–236.

Schover, L. R. (1986). Sexual problems. In L. Teri & P. M. Lewinsohn (Eds.), *Geropsychological assessment and treatment: Selected topics* (pp. 145–187). New York: Springer.

Scribner, S., & Cole, M. (1973). Cognitive consequences of formal and informal schooling. *Science, 182,* 553–559.

Seligman, M. E. P. (1975). *Helplessness: On depression, development and death.* San Francisco: Freeman.

Seligman, M. E. P. (1992). *Helplessness* (Rev. ed.). San Francisco: Freeman.

Seltzer, J. A. (1991). Relationships between fathers and children who live apart: The father's role after separation. *Journal of Marriage and the Family, 53,* 79–102.

Serock, E., Seefeldt, C., Jantz, R. K., & Galper, A. (1977). As children see old folks. *Today's Education, 66*(2), 70–73.

Sexuality and aging: What it means or be sixty or seventy or eighty in the '90s. (1997). In H. Cox (Ed.), *Aging* (11th ed., pp. 40–44). Guilford, CT: Dushkin.

Shaw, L., & Sichel, H. S. (1971). *Accident proneness: Research in the occurrence, causation, and prevention of road accidents.* New York: Pergamon.

Shea, C. (1994, September 7). "Gender gap" on examinations shrank again this year. *Chronicle of Higher Education,* p. A54.

Sheehy, G. (1976). *Passages: The predictable crises of adult life.* New York: Dutton.

Sheehy, G. (1981). *Pathfinders.* New York: Dutton.

Sheehy, G. (1993). *The silent passage: Menopause.* New York: Pocket Books.

Shneidman, E. S. (1987, March). At the point of no return. *Psychology Today,* pp. 54–58.

Shock, N. W., Greulick, R. C., Andres, R., Arenberg, D., Costa, P. T., Lakatta, E. G., & Tobin, J. D. (1984). *Normal human aging: The Baltimore Longitudinal Study of Aging* (NIH Publication No. 84-2450). Washington, DC: U.S. Government Printing Office.

Shurkin, J. (February 1988). Modern terrorists are "anemic." *New Republic,* p. 6.

Siegel, A., & White, S. H. (1982). The child study movement: Early growth and development of the symbolized child. In H. W. Reese (Ed.), *Advances in child development and behavior* (Vol. 17, pp. 234–285). New York: Academic Press.

Siegler, I. C. (1983). Psychological aspects of the Duke Longitudinal Studies. In K. W. Schaie (Ed.), *Longitudinal studies of adult psychological development* (pp. 136–190). New York: Guilford.

Siegler, I. C., McCarty, S. M., & Logue, P. E. (1982). Wechsler Memory Scale scores, selective attribution, and distance from death. *Journal of Gerontology, 37*, 176–181.

Silverstein, S. (1996, April 26). Job prospects look hot for "geezer boomers" in 2020. *Los Angeles Times*, pp. D-1, 2.

Singh, G. K., Kochanek, K. D., & MacDorman, M. F. (1996). Advance report of final mortality statistics, 1994. *Monthly Vital Statistics Report, 453*(3), suppl. Hyattsville, MD: National Center for Health Statistics.

Sixsmith, A. J., & Sixsmith, J. A. (1991). Transitions in home experience in later life. *Journal of Architectural Planning and Research, 8*, 181–191.

Skolnick, A. (1981). Married lives: Longitudinal perspectives on marriage. In D. Eichorn (Ed.), *Present and past in middle age*, (pp. 269–298). New York: Academic Press.

Smith, T. W. (1990, February). *Adult sexual behavior in 1989: Number of partners, frequency, and risk*. Paper presented to the American Association for the Advancement of Science, New Orleans.

Sparrow, P. R., & Davies, D. R. (1988). Effects of age, tenure, training, and job complexity on technical performance. *Psychology and Aging, 3*, 307–314.

Speare, A. Jr., & Meyer, J. W. (1988). Types of elderly residential mobility and their determinants. *Journal of Gerontology, 43*, S74–S81.

Spence, A. P. (1989). *Biology of human aging*. Englewood Cliffs, NJ: Prentice-Hall.

Spitzer, M. E. (1988). Taste acuity in institutionalized and noninstitutionalized elderly men. *Journal of Gerontology, 43*, P71–P74.

Srole, L., Langer, T. S., Michael, S. T., Opler, M. K., & Rennie, T. A. C. (1962). *Mental health in the metropolis: The Midtown Manhattan Study*. New York: McGraw-Hill.

Stagner, R. (1985). Aging in industry. In J. E. Birren & K. W. Schaie (Eds.), *Handbook of the psychology of aging* (2nd ed., pp. 789–817). New York: Van Nostrand Reinhold.

Stake, J. E. (1992). Gender differences and similarities in self-concept within everyday life contexts. *Psychology of Women Quarterly, 16*, 349–363.

Stanley, H. W., & Niemi, R. G. (1990). *Vital statistics on American politics* (2nd ed.). Washington, DC: CQ Press.

Starr, B. D. (1993). Sex in the later years. In R. Kastenbaum (Ed.), *Encyclopedia of adult development* (pp. 429–432). Phoenix, AZ: Oryx Press.

Stenback, A. (1980). Depression and suicidal behavior in old age. In J. E. Birren & R. B. Sloane (Eds.), *Handbook of mental health and aging* (pp. 616–652). Englewood Cliffs, NJ: Prentice-Hall.

Stephan, W. G. (1989). A cognitive approach to stereotyping. In D. Bar-Tal, C. F. Graumann, A. W. Kruglanski, & W. Stroebe (Eds.), *Stereotyping and prejudice: Changing conceptions* (pp. 37–57). New York: Springer Verlag.

Sternberg, R. J. (1986). A triangular theory of love. *Psychological Review, 93*, 119–135.

Sternberg, R. J., & Lubart, T. I. (1991). An investment theory of creativity and its development. *Human Development*, 1–31.

Sternberg, R. J., & Lubart, T. I. (1992). Buy low and sell high: An investment approach to creativity. *Psychological Science, 1*, 1–5.

Sterns, H. L., Barrett, G. J., & Alexander, R. A. (1985). Accidents and the aging individual. In J. E. Birren & K. W. Schaie (Eds.), *Handbook of the psychology of aging* (2nd ed., pp. 703–721). New York: Van Nostrand Reinhold.

Stevens, J. C., & Cain, W. S. (1985). Age-related deficiency in the perceived strength of six odorants. *Chemical Senses, 10*, 517–529.

Stevens, J. C., & Cain, W. S. (1986). Smelling via the mouth: Effects of aging. *Perception and Psychophysics, 40*, 142–146.

Stevens, J. C., & Cain, W. S. (1987). Old-age deficits in the sense of smell as gauged by thresholds, magnitude matching, and odor identification. *Psychology and Aging, 2*, 36–42.

Stoch, M. B., & Smythe, P. M. (1963). Does undernutrition during infancy inhibit brain growth and subsequent intellectual development? *Archives of Disorders of Childhood, 38*, 546–552.

Stoddart, T., & Turiel, E. (1985). Children's conception of cross-gender activities. *Child Development, 56,* 861–865.

Storandt, M., Wittels, I., & Botwinick, J. (1975). Predictors of a dimension of well-being in relocated healthy aged. *Journal of Gerontology, 30,* 97–102.

Stouffer, S. A., Suchman, E. A., DeVinney, L. C., Star, S. A., & Williams, R. J., Jr. (1949). *The American soldier: Adjusting during army life.* Princeton, NJ: Princeton University Press.

Strahan, G. W. (1997). An overview of nursing homes and their current residents: Data from the 1995 National Nursing Home Survey. Advance data from *Vital and Health Statistics,* No. 280. Hyattsville, MD: National Center for Health Statistics.

Strayer, H. L., Wickens, C. D., & Braune, R. (1987). Adult age differences in the speed of capacity of information processing: 2. An electrophysiological approach. *Psychology and Aging, 2,* 99–110.

Stroebe, W., & Stroebe, M. (1987). *Bereavement and health: The psychological and physical consequences of partner loss.* New York: Cambridge University Press.

Sudnow, D. (1967). *Passing on: The social organization of dying.* Englewood Cliffs, NJ: Prentice-Hall.

Super, D. E. (1969). Vocational developmental theory: Persons, positions, and processes. *Counseling Psychologist, 1,* 2–8.

Super, D. E. (1985). Coming of age in Middletown: Careers in the making. *American Psychologist, 40,* 405–414.

Super, D. E. (1990). A life-span space approach to career development. In D. Brown & L. Brooks & Associates (Eds.), *Career choice and development* (2nd ed., pp. 197–261). Hillsdale, NJ: Erlbaum.

Sussman, M. B. (1985). The family life of old people. In R. H. Binstock & E. Shanas (Eds.), *Handbook of aging and the social sciences* (2nd ed., pp. 415–449). New York: Van Nostrand Reinhold.

Sykes, G. M. (1958). *The society of captives: A study of maximum security prison.* Princeton, NJ: Princeton University Press.

Szinovacz, M., & Washo, C. (1992). Gender differences in exposure to life events and adaptation to retirement. *Journals of Gerontology, 47,* S191–S196.

Taeuber, C. M. (1993). *Sixty-five plus in America.* (U.S. Bureau of the Census, Current Population Reports, Special Studies P23-178RV). Washington, DC: U.S. Government Printing Office.

Tannen, D. (1990). *You just don't understand.* New York: Morrow.

Templer, D. I., Ruff, C. F., & Simpson, K. (1974). Alleviation of high death anxiety with symptomatic treatment of depression. *Psychological Reports, 54,* 216.

Terkel, S. (1974). *Working.* New York: Pantheon.

Tesch, S., Whitbourne, S. K., & Nehrke, M. F. (1981). Friendship, social interaction, and subjective well-being of older men in an institutional setting. *International Journal of Aging and Human Development, 13,* 317–327.

Tetlock, P. E. (1988). Monitoring the integrative complexity of American and Soviet policy rhetoric: What can be learned? *Journal of Social Issues, 44,* 101–131.

Thomas, G. E., Alexander, K. L., & Eckland, B. K. (1979). Access to higher education: The importance of race, sex, social class, and academic credentials. *School Review, 87,* 133–156.

Thompson, L., & Walker, A. (1990). Gender in families: Women and men in marriage, work, and parenthood. *Journal of Marriage and the Family, 51,* 845–869.

Thompson, L. W., Gallagher-Thompson, D., Futterman, A., Gilewski, M. J., & Peterson, J. (1991). The effects of late-life spousal bereavement over a 30-month interval. *Psychology and Aging, 6,* 434–441.

Thorndike, R. L., Hagen, E. P., & Sattler, J. P. (1986). *The Stanford–Binet Intelligence Scale: Fourth Edition, Technical manual.* Chicago: Riverside Publishing.

Tobacyk, J., & Eckstein, D. (1980). Death threat and death concerns in the college student. *Omega, 11,* 139–155.

Tobin, S. S., & Lieberman, M. A. (1976). *Last home for the aged.* San Francisco: Jossey-Bass.

Toffler, A. (1970). *Future shock.* New York: Random House.

Torres-Gil, F. (1986). Hispanics in an aging society. *Daedalus, 115,* 325–348.

Traupmann, J., Eckels, E., & Hatfield, E. (1982). Intimacy in older women's lives. *Gerontologist*, *22*, 493–498.

Trelease, M. L. (1975). Dying among Alaskan Indians: A matter of choice. In E. Kübler-Ross (Ed.), *Death: The final stage of growth* (pp. 27–37). Englewood Cliffs, NJ: Prentice-Hall.

Triandis, H. C. (1994). *Culture and social behavior*. New York: McGraw-Hill.

Troll, L. E. (1982). *Continuations: Adult development and aging*. Monterey, CA: Brooks/Cole.

Troll, L. E. (1983). Grandparents: The family watchdogs. In T. H. Brubaker (Ed.), *Family relationships in later life* (pp. 63–74). Beverly Hills, CA: Sage.

Troll, L. E., & Bengtson, V. (1982). Intergenerational relations throughout the life span. In B. B. Wolman (Ed.), *Handbook of developmental psychology* (pp. 890–911). Englewood Cliffs, NJ: Prentice-Hall.

Tuddenham, R. D., Blumenkrantz, J., & Wilkin, W. R. (1968). Age changes in AGCT: A longitudinal study of average adults. *Journal of Counseling and Clinical Psychology*, *32*, 659–663.

Ullmann, C. A. (1976). Preretirement planning: Does it prevent postretirement shock? *Personnel and Guidance Journal*, *55*, 115–118.

Unger, R. K. (1979). Toward a redefinition of sex and gender. *American Psychologist*, *34*, 1085–1094.

U.S. Bureau of the Census. (1990a). *Statistical abstract of the United States* (110th ed.). Washington, DC: U.S. Government Printing Office.

U.S. Bureau of the Census. (1990b). *The need for personal assistance with everyday activities: Recipients and caregivers* (Current Population Reports, Series P-780, No. 19). Washington, DC: U.S. Government Printing Office.

U.S. Bureau of the Census. (1992). *Marriage, divorce, and remarriage in the 1990's*, (Current Population Reports, Series P23-180). Washington, DC: U.S. Government Printing Office.

U.S. Bureau of the Census. (1994, December). *How we're changing: Demographic state of the nation* (Current Population Reports, Series P23-188). Washington, DC: U.S. Government Printing Office.

U.S. Bureau of the Census. (1995). *Population profile of the United States: 1995* (Current Population Reports, Series P23-180). Washington, DC: U.S. Government Printing Office.

U.S. Bureau of the Census. (1996, February). *How we're changing: Demographic state of the nation: 1996* (Current Population Reports Special Studies, Series P23-191). Washington, DC: U.S. Department of Commerce.

U.S. Bureau of the Census. (1996, September). Money income in the United States: 1995 (Current Population Reports, Consumer Income, P60-193). Washington, DC: U.S. Department of Commerce.

U.S. Department of Justice, Bureau of Justice Statistics. (1994). *Sourcebook of criminal justice statistics*. Washington, DC: Author.

U.S. Department of Justice, Federal Bureau of Investigation (1996). *Crime in the United States, 1995. Uniform Crime Reports*. Washington, DC: Author.

U.S. Department of Labor, Bureau of Labor Statistics. (March 29, 1990). *Thirty-eight million persons do volunteer work*. Press Release USDL 90-154. Washington, DC: Author.

U.S. Department of Labor, Bureau of Labor Statistics. (February 1996). *Consumer expenditures in 1994. Report 902*. Washington, DC: Author.

U.S. Senate Special Committee on Aging. (1991). *Aging America: Trends and projections*. Washington, DC: Author.

U.S. Senate Special Committee on Aging. (1994). *Developments in aging: 1933*. Washington, DC: U.S. Government Printing Office.

Usui, W. N. (1984). Homogeneity of friendship networks of elderly blacks and whites. *Journal of Gerontology*, *39*, 350–356.

Valliant, G. E. (1977). *Adaptation to life*. Boston: Little, Brown.

Valliant, G. E. (1979). Natural history of male psychologic health: Effects of mental health on physical health. *New England Journal of Medicine*, *301*, 1249–1254.

Van Tilburg, T. (1992). Support networks before and after retirement [Special issue: Social networks]. *Journal of Social and Personal Relationships*, *9*, 433–445.

Veevers, J. E. (1980). *Children by choice*. Toronto: Butterworth.

Ventura, S. J., Martin, J. A., Curtin, S. C., & Mathews, T. Q. (1997). Report of final natality statistics, 1995. *Monthly Vital Statistics Report* (vol. 45, no. 11, suppl. 2). Hyattsville, MD: National Center for Health Statistics.

Veroff, J., Douvon, E., & Kulka, R. A. (1981). *Mental health in America: Patterns of help-seeking from 1957 to 1976*. New York: Basic Books.

Verrillo, R. (1980). Age-related changes in sensitivity to vibration, *Journal of Gerontology, 35*, 185–193.

Verrillo, T. T., & Verrillo, V. (1985). Sensory and perceptual performance. In N. Charness (Ed.), *Aging and human performance* (pp. 1–46). New York: Wiley.

Vuchinich, S., Hetherington, E. M., Vuchinich, R. A., & Clingempeel, W. G. (1991). Parent–child interaction and general differences in early adolescents' adaptation to stepfamilies. *Developmental Psychology, 27*, 618–626.

Waldron, I. (1983). Sex differences in human mortality: The role of genetic factors. *Social Science and Medicine, 17*, 321–333.

Wallace, P. M., & Gotlib, I. H. (1990). Marital adjustment during the transition to parenthood: Stability and predictors of change. *Journal of Marriage and the Family, 51*, 21–29.

Wallas, G. (1926). *The art of thought*. New York: Harcourt.

Walster, E., & Walster, G. W. (1978). *Love*. Reading, MA: Addison-Wesley.

Walters, J. (1987). Lasting intimacy. *Longevity, 1*(5), 37–38.

Warner, W. L., & Lunt, P. S. (1941). *The social life of a modern community*. New Haven, CT: Yale University Press.

Warr, P. (1992). Age and occupational well-being. *Psychology and Aging, 7*(1), 37–45.

Wass, H. (1993). Gender differences in the workplace. In R. Kastenbaum (Ed.), *Encyclopedia of adult development* (pp. 171–174). Phoenix, AZ: Oryx Press.

Wass, H., & Scott, M. (1978). Middle school students' death concepts and concern. *Middle School Journal, 9*(1), 10–12.

Wass, H., & Sisler, H. (1978, January). *Death concern and views on various aspects of dying among elderly person*. Paper presented at the International Symposium on the Dying Human, Tel Aviv, Israel.

Wass, H., & Stillion, J. M. (1988). Death in the lives of children and adolescents. In H. Wass, F. M. Berardo, & R. A. Neimeyer (Eds.), *Dying: Facing the facts* (2nd ed., pp. 201–228). Washington, DC: Hemisphere.

Wechsler, D. (1958). *The measurement and appraisal of adult intelligence* (4th ed.). Baltimore: Williams & Wilkins.

Weindruch, R., & Walford, R. L. (1988). *The retardation of aging and disease by dietary restriction*. Springfield, IL: Thomas.

Weiner, M. B. (1992). Treating the older adult: A diverse population [Special issue: Psychoanalysis of the mid-life and older patient]. *Psychoanalysis and Psychotherapy, 10*, 66–76.

Weisman, A. D., & Kastenbaum, R. (1968). The psychological autopsy: A study of the terminal phase of life. *Community Mental Health Journal*, Monograph No. 4.

Wellman, F. E., & McCormack, J. (1984). Counseling with older persons: A review of outcome research. *Counseling Psychologist, 12*, 81–96.

Whitbourne, S. (1985). *The aging body: Physiological changes and psychological consequences*. New York: Springer Verlag.

Whitbourne, S. K., Culgin, S., & Cassidy, E. (1995). Evaluation of infantilizing intonation and content of speech directed at the aged., *International Journal of Aging, 41*, 109–116.

White, L. K., & Booth, A. (1985). The quality and stability of remarriages: The role of stepchildren. *American Sociological Review, 50*, 689–698.

White N., & Cunningham, W. R. (1988). Is terminal drop pervasive or specific? *Journal of Gerontology: Psychological Sciences, 43*, P141–P144.

White, R. (1984). *Fearful warriors: A psychological profile of U.S.–Soviet relations*. New York: Free Press.

Weiffenbach, J. M., Cowart, B. J., & Baum, B. J. (1986). Taste sensitivity and aging. *Journal of Gerontology, 41,* 400–468.

Wilbur, K. H. (1991). Alternatives to conservatorship: The role of daily money management services. *Gerontologist, 31,* 150–155.

Wilbur, R. S. (1973, June 2). POWS found to be much sicker than they looked upon release, *Los Angeles Times,* p. I-4.

Williams, J. E., & Best, D. L. (1990). *Measuring sex stereotypes: a multi-nation study.* Newbury Park, CA: Sage.

Willis, S. L. (1985). Toward an educational psychology of the older adult learner: Intellectual and cognitive bases. In J. Birren & W. Schaie (Eds.), *Handbook of the psychology of aging* (2nd ed., pp. 818–847). New York: Van Nostrand Reinhold.

Willis, S. L. (1990). Introduction to the special section on cognitive training in later adulthood. *Developmental Psychology, 26,* 875–878.

Willis, S. L., & Nesselroade, C. (1990). Long-term effects of fluid ability training in old-old age. *Developmental Psychology, 26,* 905–910.

Willman, M., & Colker, D. (1996, October 17). Confusion reduced on obesity remark. *Los Angeles Times,* p. A35.

Wilson, M. N. (1989). Child development in the context of the black extended family. *American Psychologist, 44,* 380–385.

Wirtenberg, J., Klein, S., Richardson, B., & Thomas, V. (1981, January). Sex equity in American education. *Educational Leadership,* pp. 311–319.

Wittig, M. A., & Petersen, A. C. (Eds,). (1979). *Sex-related differences in cognitive functioning.* New York: Academic Press.

Wolf, R. S., & Pillemer, K. A. (1989). *Helping elderly victims: The reality of elder abuse.* New York: Columbia University Press.

Wolfe, D. B. (1990). *Serving the ageless market: Strategies for selling to the fifty-plus market.* New York: McGraw-Hill.

Wolfinger, R. E., & Rosenstone, S. J. (1980). *Who votes?* New Haven, CT: Yale University Press.

Wood, V., & Robertson, J. F. (1976). The significance of grandparenthood. In J. F. Gubrium (Ed.), *Time, roles, and self in old age* (pp. 278–304). New York: Human Sciences Press.

Woodward, K. L. (1989, March 27). Heaven. *Newsweek.* pp. 52–55.

Wright, P. (1989). Gender differences in adults' same- and cross-gender friendships. In R. S. Adams & R. Bleiszner (Eds.), *Older adult friendship* (pp. 197–221). Newbury Park, CA: Sage Publications.

Wright, J. W. (Ed.). (1997). *The universal almanac, 1997.* Kansas City: Andrews & McMeel.

Wrightsman, L. S. (1994a). *Adult personality development: Vol. 2: Applications.* Thousand Oaks, CA: Sage Publications.

Wrightsman, L. S. (1994b). *Psychology and the legal system* (3rd ed.). Pacific Grove, CA: Brooks/Cole.

Wyly, M., & Hulicka, I. (1975, August). *Problems and compensations of widowhood: A comparison of age groups.* Paper presented at the meeting of the American Psychological Association, Chicago.

Yeasavage, J. A., & Rose, T. (1984). The effects of a face–name mnemonic in young, middle-aged, and elderly adults. *Experimental Aging Research, 10,* 55–57.

Yerkes, P. M. (Ed.). (1921). Psychological examining in the United States Army. *Memoirs of the National Academy of Sciences, 15.*

Yochelson, S., & Samenow, S. E. (1976). *The criminal personality* (Vol. 1). New York: Aronson.

Yu. E. S. H., Chang, C., Liu, W. T., & Kan, S. H. (1985). Asian–white mortality differences: Are there excess deaths? In Department of Health and Human Services (Ed.), *Black and minority health: Vol. III. Cross-cutting issues in minority health.* Washington, DC: Department of Health and Human Services.

Zajonc, R. B. (1976). Family configuration and intelligence. *Science, 192,* 227–236.

Zatz, M. M., & Goldstein, A. L. (1985). Thymosins, lymphokines, and the immunology of aging. *Gerontology, 31,* 263–277.

Zeskind, P. S., & Ramey, C. T. (1981). Preventing intellectual and interactional sequelae of fetal malnutrition: A longitudinal transaction, and synergistic approach to development. *Child Development, 52,* 213–218.

Ziajka, A. (1972). The black youth's self-concept. In W. Looft (Ed.), *Developmental psychology: A book of readings* (pp. 249–268). Hillsdale, IL: Dryden Press.

Author Index

Subject Index

Information concerning many of the topics considered in the book may also be found in the Glossary.